The City and the Grassroots

Pour Alain Touraine, qui m'apprit le métier
et
A Françoise Sabbah, qui m'apprit la vie

California Series in Urban Development
Edited by Peter Hall and Peter Marris

Great Planning Disasters
Peter Hall

The City and the Grassroots: A Cross-Cultural Theory of Urban Social Movements
Manuel Castells

The City and the Grassroots

A Cross-Cultural Theory of Urban Social Movements

Manuel Castells
Professor of City and Regional Planning
University of California, Berkeley

University of California Press
Berkeley and Los Angeles

University of California Press
Berkeley and Los Angeles, California

Printed in the United States of America
  2 3 4 5 6 7 8 9

Library of Congress Cataloging in Publication Data

Castells, Manuel.
  The city and the grassroots.
  1. Sociology, Urban—Cross-cultural studies.
2. Cities and towns—History—Cross-cultural studies.
3. Social movements—History—Cross-cultural studies.
4. Urbanization—History—Cross-cultural studies.
5. Social change—History—Cross-cultural studies.
I. Title.
HT119.C29 1983   307.7′6   82-40099
ISBN 0-520-04756-7 (U.S.)
ISBN 0-520-05617-5 (ppbk)

Text set in 11/12 pt Plantin Compugraphic

Contents

Preface   ix

Acknowledgements   xi

Introduction   xv

Part 1 Cities and People in a Historical Perspective   **1**

1   Introduction   3

2   Cities and Freedom: The Comunidades de Castilla, 1520–22   4

3   Cities and Revolution: The Commune of Paris, 1871   15

4   The Industrial City and the Working Class:
The Glasgow Rent Strike of 1915   27

5   The Dependent City and Revolutionary Populism:
The Movimiento Inquilinario in Veracruz, Mexico, 1922   37

6   The Post-Industrial City and the Community Revolution:
The Revolts of American Inner Cities in the 1960s   49

7   Conclusion: The Historical Production of Urban Meaning   67

**Part 2 Housing Policy and Urban Trade Unionism:
The Grands Ensembles of Paris**   **73**

8   Introduction: The Rise and Fall of the Grands Ensembles   75

9   The Emergence of Urban Trade Unionism: Sarcelles   78

10   The Social Limits of Urban Design: Val d'Yerres   86

11   Conclusion: From Urban Trade Unionism to Urban Movements   94

Part 3 City and Culture: The San Francisco Experience   **97**

12   Introduction: San Francisco – The Social Basis of Urban Quality   99

13   Urban Poverty, Ethnic Minorities and Community Organization: The Experience of Neighbourhood Mobilization in San Francisco's Mission District   106

14   Cultural Identity, Sexual Liberation and Urban Structure: The Gay Community in San Francisco   138

15   Conclusion: The Richness of Diversity, the Poverty of Pluralism   170

Part 4 The Social Basis of Urban Populism: Squatters and the State in Latin America   **173**

16   Introduction: Squatter Communities and the New Dynamics of the World System   175

17   The Social Dimensions of Marginality   179

18   The Structural Causes of Urban Marginality   185

19   Squatters and the State: The Dialectics between Social Integration and Social Change (Case Studies in Lima, Mexico, and Santiago de Chile)   190

20   Conclusion: The Social Making of the Dependent City   209

Part 5 The Making of an Urban Social Movement: The Citizen Movement in Madrid towards the end of the Franquist Era   **213**

21   Introduction   215

22   The Crisis of a Political Model of Urban Development   217

23   A Social Profile of Madrid's Citizen Movement   224

24   Inside the Neighbourhoods: Selected Case Studies   242

25   The Transformation of City, Culture and Politics by the Citizen Movement   258

26   City, Class, Power and Social Movements   264

27 City, Community and Power:
    An Analytical Model to Evaluate the Citizen Movement in Madrid as
    an Urban Social Movement   276

Part 6 A Cross-Cultural Theory of Urban Social Change   **289**

28 Introduction: In Search of a Theory   291

29 The Process of Urban Social Change   301

30 The Process of Historical Change   305

31 The New Historical Relationship between Space and Society   311

32 The Alternative City:
    The Structure and Meaning of Contemporary Urban Social
    Movements   318

33 The Social Significance of Contemporary Urban Movements   327

34 History in the City   331

35 Conclusion: The Theory of the Good City and A Good Theory of the
    City   335

The Methodological Appendices   337

Endnotes   396

Bibliography   424

Index   443

Preface

The research presented in this book represents over twelve years work in a variety of countries. No individual could have undertaken such an effort without the full support and collaboration of literally hundreds of people, including the social actors themselves. Also several institutions have been decisive in helping this research come to life. My gratitude to all of them is something more than rhetoric: it is the public recognition of the collective character of the work presented here under my own individual responsibility.

The names of many of the most important contributors to this book will not be cited here: I have to respect their privacy, as well as to recognize the necessary distance between their social commitments and political values, and my own interpretation as presented in this book.

Yet there are numerous other persons who must be cited as key sources for the information I obtained, as well as for many of the ideas I have developed.

Both Alain Touraine and Chris Pickvance convinced me of the importance of approaching the problem from a historical perspective. John Foster provided some crucial insights on the subject, and Joseph Melling generously contributed most of the material and ideas for my analysis of Glasgow. Alejandra Moreno-Toscano first put me on the track of the movement in Veracruz. And John Mollenkopf, Mike Miller, Janice Perlman, and Roger Friedland usefully guided me to the right sources on the American community movements.

The chapter on Paris is based on the collaborative research I conducted for years with my research team at the Centre d'Etude des Mouvements Sociaux (CEMS, Paris): they are Eddy Cherki, Francis Godard, and Dominique Mehl.

The chapter on San Francisco could never have been written without the, again, generous collaboration of John Mollenkopf. Mike Miller, Jim Shoch, Steve Barton, Luisa Ezquerro, Harry Britt, and Eric Craven introduced me to the secrets of San Francisco's local politics. My research on the gay community in San Francisco was jointly conducted with Karen Murphy. Allan Jacobs taught me most of what I finally learned about the urban problems of San Francisco.

The chapter on Latin America mainly relies on the research programme I directed in Chile, in 1970–72, in collaboration with Jaime Rojas, Rosemond Cheetham, Franz Vanderschueren, Francois Pingeot, Christine Meunier, Joaquin Duque, Ernesto Pastrana, and several other researchers still living under Pinochet. I also used information from my studies in Mexico, with the support of Oscar Nunez, Diana Villarreal, and Martha Schteingart. Additional data were provided by Etienne Henry in Lima, and by Magaly Sanchez in Caracas.

The study on Madrid was fully supported by the Citizen Movement. Several of its leaders were my main sources of ideas and information. Among them were Ignacio Quintana, Felix Lopez-Rey, Miguel Angel Pascual, Isabel Vilallonga, Javier Angulo y Marian Alvarez-Bullia. Additional help and information came from Eduardo Leira, Ramon Tamames, Javier Garcia-Fernandez, Fernando de Teran, Nuria Pascual, and Alfonso Alvarez-Mora.

Several colleagues took the time to comment on earlier versions of the manuscript, or on parts of it, and were certainly influential in its final form. Among them were: Chris Pickvance, Alain Touraine, Susan Fainstein, Allen Scott, Allan Jacobs, John Friedmann, John Mollenkopf, Peter Hall, Vicente Navarro, Joseph Melling, Claude Fischer, Alejandro Portes,

Ruth Cardoso, Frances Piven, Michael Teitz, Janice Perlman, Kevin Lynch, Richard Meier, and David Collier. Finally, the ideas, hypotheses and theoretical construction presented in this book are largely the result of the continuous intellectual dialogue with a small circle of friends who remain my intellectual point of reference. They are Nicos Poulantzas (my brother who will always live in my memory); Alain Touraine and Jacques Attali in Paris; Jordi Borja in Barcelona; Emilio de Ipola, now in Mexico; Fernando Henrique Cardoso in Sao Paulo; and Martin Carnoy in San Francisco.

The production of the book was made possible by the professionalism and personal support of Virginia Rogers, of the Department of Sociology, University of Wisconsin, Madison, and of Kathy Crum, of the Institute of Urban and Regional Development (IURD), University of California at Berkeley. In Berkeley, Nene Ojeda, Candy Wynne, and Dorothy Heydt did excellent work on the completion of the manuscript. Hélène Lydenberg (CNRS, Paris) has helped me throughout with the organization of my research work.

This book has greatly benefited from the combined editorial effort of Richard Ingersoll, a Ph. D. candidate in Architectural History at Berkeley who did a superb job in helping me to revise the first draft; Karen Reeds, of the University of California Press, who guided me during the revision of the manuscript and generously provided her always discerning comments; and my publishers, Edward Arnold, who have contributed so much to the publication of this book. I am convinced that my gratitude to all three will be shared by the readers.

The Centre d'Etudes des Mouvements Sociaux of the Centre National de la Recherche Scientifique (Paris) and the Institute of Urban and Regional Development of the University of California at Berkeley were my main support-bases during all these years. I am grateful to their directors, Alain Touraine, Mel Webber, and Peter Hall. Additional institutional support came from the University of Wisconsin-Madison, from the Ecole des Hautes Etudes en Sciences Sociales (Paris), from the Centro Interdisciplinario de Desarrollo Urbano (Universidad Catolica de Chile), from Desarrollo e Iniciativa Ciudadana (DEINCISA), Madrid, and from Urbanismo, Ingenieria, Arquitectura (UIA), Madrid, who took care of the art work for the Madrid study.

Several persons generously provided some of the photographs for this book: Manuel Perló and Alejandra Moreno-Toscano for Veracruz; Joseph Melling for Glasgow; Magaly Sanchez for Caracas; Christine Meunier for Santiago de Chile; Françoise Sabbah for San Francisco; and Elena Cachafeiros and Marian Alvarez-Bullia for Madrid. I publicly thank all of them.

Finally, the intellectual environment provided by the Department of City and Regional Planning of the University of California at Berkeley, since my arrival here in 1979, was a crucial element in allowing my research work to come together in the present form. Thus, to some extent, this book and my intellectual life are inextricably intertwined, for better or for worse. The final judgment is up to the reader.

Manuel Castells
Berkeley, California, June 1982

Acknowledgements

The author and publishers would like to thank the following for the use in this book of their material:

Tables

Jacques Rougerie and Gallimard-Archives for Tables 3–1 and 3–2; Macmillan Accounts and Administration Ltd., London and Basingstoke, for Table 6–1 from Roger Friedland: *Crisis, Power and the Central City* and also Schocken Books Inc., reprinted by permission from Roger Friedland: *Power and Crisis in the City* (American title) © by Roger Owen Friedland; John Mollenkopf and Department of Government, Harvard University for Tables 6–2, 6–3, 6–6 and 6–7; Princeton University Press for Tables 6–8 from John Hall Fish: *Black Power/White Control: The Struggle of the Woodlawn Organization of Chicago.* Copyright © 1973 by Princeton University Press. Table 4, p. 309 reprinted by permission; SCIC, Paris for Table 9–1; INSEE, Paris for Tables 9–2, 9–3 and 9–4; US Census for Tables 14–1, and A–3 to A–10; Stanford University Community Development Study for Tables 13–1 and 13–2; Johns Hopkins University Press for Table 16–1 from Grimes: *Housing for Low-Income Urban Families* excerpts from Table A1 copyright © 1976 by the International Bank for Reconstruction and Development; DESAL, Santiago de Chile for Tables 17–1 and 17–2; Ricardo Infante and Magaly Sanchez for Tables 17–3 and 17–4; Secretaria de Industria y Commercio, Mexico DF for Table 18–2; Hugh Evans and the Department of Architecture, University of Cambridge for Table 18–3; David Collier and Instituto de Estudios Peruanos, Lima for Table 19–1; The FLACSO Survey on Chilean Squatters, 1972 for Table 19–2; J. Duque, E. Pastrana and Facultad Latinoamericana de Ciencias Sociales, Santiago de Chile for Table 19–3; The Coro Foundation for Table A–11
Richard DeLeon, Courtney Brown and Department of Political Science, San Francisco State University for Table A–13; Harry Britt and his staff for information on legislation introduced and measures provided by gay representatives on San Francisco board of supervisors; CIDU, Santiago de Chile for Table A–15.

Maps and figures

Schema directeur de la région Parisienne for Map 8–1; Sage Publications, Inc. for permission to reproduce some of the maps on San Francisco which appeared in our article in Norman Fainstein and Susan Fainstein, eds., *Urban Policy Under Capitalism* (California: Sage, 1982.); Siglo XX1 Editores for permission to reproduce some of the maps of Madrid; Computronics Research, 1977 for Figure 14–1;
Information in the 1977 Voter registration tape/computer program prepared by Doug De Young in Map 14–2 Harvey; Milk Campaign Office for information in Map 14–3;
Information recorded in Bob Damron's address book and mapping by Michael Kennedy in

Map 14–4; Golden Gate Business Association Buyers' Directory for information on which Map 14–5 is based;
Key Informants Mapping for Map 14–7 and particularly Richard Schlachman.

Plates

Bibliothèque Nationale, Paris for Plate 3–1; Joseph Melling, the Mitchell Library and the Glasgow Herald for Plate 4–1; Alejandra Moreno-Toscano, The Director of Archives, Archivo General de la Nacion, Estados Unidos Mexicanos, Ciudad de Mexico for Plates 5–1 and 5–2, photographs by Mr Waite; Joaquin Segarra for Plate 5–3; Popperfoto and UPI for Plate 6–1; Françoise Sabbah for Plates 13–1 and 14–1; F. Molina for Plate 19–1; C. Meunier for Plate 19–2; E. Cachafeiros for Plate 24–1; and M. Alvarez-Bullia for Plate 24–2.

The City and the Grassroots

'Houses make a town, but citizens make a city.'

Jean-Jacques Rousseau,
cited by Lewis Mumford.[1]

Introduction

Cities are living systems, made, transformed and experienced by people. Urban forms and functions are produced and managed by the interaction between space and society, that is by the historical relationship between human consciousness, matter, energy and information.

While the structure of all urban dynamics can ultimately be described in such terms, the decisive input of purposive social action in the shaping of space and material conditions of everyday life has been highlighted by recent historical experience at two different levels.

On the one hand, the new international and inter-regional spatial division of labour, the growing importance of collective consumption through urban services, and the fact that public goods are most necessary while still being unprofitable for private capital, have led to systematic intervention by the state in the urban realm. Urban issues are thus at the forefront of contemporary political conflicts, and politics have become the core of the urban process.

On the other hand, the search for spatial meaningfulness and cultural identity, the demands for social goods and services, and the drift toward local autonomy, have triggered in the last decade a series of urban protest movements that, in very different contexts, called for urban reform and envisioned an alternative city. The squatter communities in Germany, Holland, and Denmark; the youth movement in Zurich; the neighbourhood associations in Spain; the massive uprisings over public services in Italy; the tenants struggles in Frances; the revolt of inner cities in England; the growing urban mobilization in the metropolises of newly industrialized countries, such as Caracas, Rio de Janeiro, Sao Paulo, and Mexico; the self-reliant squatter settlements of the Third World, from Lima to Manila; the widespread new neighbourhood movement arising in American cities from the ashes of urban revolts of the 1960s, across a much broader social spectrum; the environmentalist movement throughout the world. In spite of their obvious diversity, all these movements have proposed a new relationship between space and society. And they all have challenged prevailing cultural values and political institutions, by refusing some spatial forms, by asking for public services, and by exploring new social meanings for cities. While the historical significance of these urban movements is still unclear, they have already had a major impact on public policies and spatial structures. Yet, we know very little about the direction and the extent of such an impact, and we are equally ignorant about the intertwined network of relationships between the state, space, and society.

In fact, there is an increasing gap between urban research and urban problems. In the last 30 years, we have achieved substantial progress in the fields of spatial economy, land use planning, quantitative geography, regional development, environmental symbolism, and urban design. Such an impressive record has greatly contributed to our capacity to understand the built environment. Yet, we are still helpless when we wish to act on cities and regions, because we ignore the sources of their social change and fail to identify with sufficient accuracy the political processes underlying urban management.

Nevertheless, under the pressing demands of current events and government commissions, urban experts have done their homework in recent years. We now have a number of thorough studies of the urban crisis, as well as a series of monographs on urban protest. Yet, most existing research on community organization and social movements (including those of this author) combine romantic descriptions with populist ideology, leaving us with no reliable explanation of the hows and whys of these movements.

Furthermore, the interpretations of the urban crisis tend to be couched strictly in economistic terms, identifying the source of our problems in a single factor that varies (according to the author's ideological taste) from the inherent logic of monopoly capital to the inevitable incompetence of public bureaucracy. Thus, despite serious efforts at gathering data and elaborating theory in the aftermath of urban crises and protests, we still have a long way to go before we understand the fundamental processes at work in the production of the material basis of most of our experience: the city.

The reasons for such an intellectual failure lie deep in the theoretical foundations of most social research. We believe that the difficulty arises precisely from the separation between the analysis of the crisis and the analysis of social change. Or in other words, the distinction between the urban system on the one hand, and social movements on the other. Collective action is usually seen as a reaction to a crisis created by an economically determined structural logic. Alternatively, random individual decisions are supposed to affect public policies according to some abstract rationality aimed at optimizing profit or power. Either way, people and the state, economy and society, cities and citizens, are considered as separate entities: one may dominate the other, or both may behave independently, but the logic of the analysis never allows them to interact in a meaningful structure. As a result, we are left with urban systems separated from personal experiences; with structures without actors, and actors without structures; with cities without citizens, and citizens without cities.

This book, on the contrary, assumes that only by analysing the relationship between people and urbanization will we be able to understand cities and citizens at the same time. Such a relationship is most evident when people mobilize to change the city in order to change society. For methodological reasons, thus, we will focus on the study of urban social movements: collective actions consciously aimed at the transformation of the social interests and values embedded in the forms and functions of a historically given city. Yet, if the process of production of cities by societies is most evident in the case of social revolt and spatial innovation, it is not limited to such exceptional events. Every day in every context, people acting individually or collectively, produce or reproduce the rules of their society, and translate them into their spatial expression and their institutional management. Because society is structured around conflicting positions which define alternative values and interests, so the production of space and cities will be, too. Urban structures will always be the expression of some institutionalized domination, and urban crises will be the result of a challenge coming from new actors in history and society.

Accordingly, if urban research is to respond to the questions of our time – the urban crisis, the role of the state, the challenge of urban protest – we need to integrate our analyses of structure and processes, of crisis and change. Our purpose is to cautiously construct a new theory of urban change that can light the path to a new city.

This book intends to contribute to the development of such a theory by focusing on the study of urban social movements as the heart of a broader theory of urban social change. Relying on a series of case studies in different socio-cultural contexts we will try to understand how urban movements interact with urban forms and functions; how the movements develop; why they have different social and spatial effects; and what elements account for their internal structure and historical evolution. But while we will present several detailed empirical studies, we are not simply gathering evidence. Rather, we want to work out a theory of urban social movements – even if such a theory must necessarily be limited by our current state of knowledge. Nevertheless, this theoretical purpose is informed by a methodological perspective that is distrustful of former experiences involving the useless construction of abstract grand theories. Therefore, we are determined to ground this attempt at theory-building on reliable research, and to avoid any hasty formalization of the proposed conceptual framework.

By this cautious strategy, we seek to rectify the excesses of theoretical formalism that have flawed social sciences in general and some of our earlier work in particular. In recent years, theorists in social science – as a healthy reaction against the short-sighted empiricism that forbade thinking about any phenomenon that could not be measured by very rudimentary statistical tools – have tried to construct systems of categories and propositions that would enable us to recode observations in a meaningful, cumulative form. Yet, their theoretical models (from functionalism to structuralism, or from symbolic interactionism to Marxism) have turned out to be as useless as they are sophisticated. In the practice of research, these conceptual frameworks required an arduous recoding of experience without adding any new knowledge. On contemplating these failures (the result, we believe, of unnecessary and ill-considered attempts to ape the natural sciences) it seemed to us that our best hope of understanding society (and therefore cities) lay in a much more patient approach to gathering information and building theories. We have followed the lead of the most fruitful studies in the social sciences, whatever their theoretical assumptions and technical tools, and we have moved freely back and forth among historical experience, our own research on contemporary urban movements, and a variety of methodologies and intellectual traditions, in a deliberate attempt to find new kinds of questions to ask about urban social change, and new, satisfying ways to answer them. Consequently, the methodological problem – how to construct a theory – has been as much a part of our research endeavour as studying the phenomenon of urban social movements itself. As we expected from the start, the particular circumstances of each case study modified the profile of our tentative theory and led us to tighten the argument.

Thus, our strategy of theory-building has relied on an articulated sequence of research operations. We started by asking some fundamental research questions, themselves generated by the social issues arising from historical experience. How do structurally defined actors produce and reproduce cities through their conflicts, domination, alliances, and compromises? How do spatial forms, economic functions, political institutions, and cultural meaning combine themselves in a process of urbanization that we view as the outcome of social struggles and social bargaining? How do class, sex, race, ethnic origins, cultural tradition, and geographical location, contribute to the formation of the social actors that intervene in the urban scene? How does such a pattern of relationships vary in different historical contexts? What is the role of urban movements within urban social change? How far are the fates of cities and societies linked in the process of historical development? How and why contemporary urban crises express some of our deepest social contradictions? How do contemporary urban movements contribute to the formation of new historical actors, and, therefore, to the general process of social change?

We asked the questions at a very general, tentative level, borrowing concepts and approaches from different intellectual traditions. (In Part 6 we explicitly describe the variety of sources to which we have gone.) Yet, because no existing body of theory addresses these questions, we had to elaborate a provisional, theoretical framework that, without being a general theory of society, would be comprehensive enough to stimulate our thinking, suggest specific cases of urban movements to study, and provide the ground for interpreting our observations.

We have preferred to present such a tentative theoretical framework in the last Part of the book, after modifying its profile and tightening the argument on the basis of the historical and empirical research carried on under its inspiration. The reasons for this method of presentation is that our theory is produced and not simply tested by the interpretation of our case studies. Therefore, the analysis of each urban movement under observation will provide the occasion for the in-depth elaboration of particular elements of our theory, with the result that the bringing together of all the elements in the final Part will be better understood on the basis of the preceeding discussions. So the reader will be asked to have the patience of watching our theoretical framework grow, with different emphases corresponding to the successive social processes under observation. We hope that the result will be to increase the clarity of our analysis and to link it more explicitly to our empirical research.

Nevertheless, since the selection of the cases of urban mobilization was itself largely determined by our research approach, it is important to make explicit the major hypotheses underlying our entire investigation. In a very schematic way, our argument can be summarized as follows:

1 The city is a social product resulting from conflicting social interests and values.
2 Because socially dominant interests have been institutionalized and resist change, major innovations in the city's role, meaning, and structure tend to be the outcome of grassroots mobilization and demands; when these mobilizations result in the transformation of the urban structure, we call them urban social movements.
3 Yet the process of urban social change cannot be reduced to the effects produced on the city by successful social movements. Thus a theory of urban change must account for the transformation resulting both from the action of the dominant interests and from the grassroots resistance and challenge to such a domination.
4 Finally, although class relationships and class struggle are fundamental in understanding the process of urban conflict, they are by no means the only or even the primary source of urban social change. Our theory must recognize other sources of urban social change: the autonomous role of the state, gender relationships, ethnic and national movements, and movements that specifically define themselves as citizen movements.

We have linked these general hypotheses with major themes currently posed by contemporary urban crises and urban protests in a variety of social contexts. Our study will derive its force from the interaction between these general theoretical concerns and the historical trends we have observed.

Urban protest movements, in our societies and in our epoch, seem to develop around three major themes:

1 Demands focused on *collective consumption*, that is, goods and services directly or indirectly provided by the state.
2 Defense of *cultural identity* associated with and organized around a specific *territory*.
3 *Political mobilization* in relationship to the state, particularly emphasizing the role of *local government*.

Finally, we must keep in mind throughout a crucial fact: a movement develops not only in relationship to its own society, but also in relationship to a world-wide social system. In this book we have had to exclude analyses of the 'state-planned societies' because of the absence of reliable data on urban movements in such a context. But we can and must study the differential process of urban mobilization in *dominant* and *dependent* societies within the capitalist system.

Thus, we aim first at understanding the interaction between cities and social change, but this research is designed to be a part of a broader investigation that will consider:

1 The new relationship between production and consumption through the growing role of the state in both processes.

2 The role of territoriality in the definition of cultural identity and symbolic meaning.
3 The forces at work in the re-definition of the relationship between the state and civil society by people's demands for self-management and local autonomy.

We have organized our process of theory-building around four empirical studies which maximize the chance to observe the social logic underlying the three major themes of our research – collective consumption, cultural identity, and political power – in relation to spatial forms and urban movements.

In particular we will study:

— The relationship between urban movements and *collective comsumption* as revealed by the emergence of urban trade-unionism in suburban public housing in the *Paris Metropolitan Area*.
— The development of urban movements around the issue of *cultural identity*, as expressed in two different versions, by the Latino community and the gay community in *San Francisco*.
— The subordination of urban movements to the *political system* according to the experience of urban populism in the *squatter settlements of Latin America*, with particular emphasis on the *pobladores movement in Santiago de Chile*. This study will also introduce the characteristics of the *dependent city*.
— The *interaction of collective consumption, culture, and politics through the urban movements*, as observed by the analysis of the movement that, during the 1970s, most clearly attempted to articulate these three dimensions in its struggle: the *Citizen Movement in Madrid*.

In addition to the analysis of contemporary urban protest movements, we tried to incorporate in the book another element that is crucial for our theory. Although urban social movements have been among the sources of urban forms and structures throughout history (as will be argued in the final Part of this book), the historical conditions peculiar to our societies make their impact much more evident than ever before. Therefore we will open our analysis by a historical overview that, while limited to recent modes of production of Western societies, will try to uncover the variation of urban meaning throughout different historical contexts. We have selected five historical cases to follow a very tight sequence of social evolution: the transition from feudalism to the absolutist state is examined through the revolution of the *Comunidades de Castilla* in the sixteenth century; the transition from the *Ancien Regime* to capitalism is exemplified by the *Commune de Paris* in 1871; the coming of the industrial capitalist city underlies our analysis of the Glasgow Rent Strike of 1915; the peculiar conditions of the capitalist-dependent city are shown by the study of the *Inquilinarios* of Veracruz, Mexico, in 1922; and the new urban issues of the post-industrial capitalist city are revealed by the revolt of American inner cities in the 1960s. It should be emphasized that, while analyses of contemporary urban movements rely on original fieldwork carried out by the author, the historical accounts presented in the first part of the book are dependent upon the work of other investigators. They should be merely considered as a fruitful way to introduce the subject matter of our theses on the relationship between cities and social movements.

Yet how accurate can be a demonstration based upon a limited number of case studies? In fact it is because our purpose is to further the process of theory-building that the case-study approach appears to be the best. Case studies have always been praised because they permit in-depth analysis, but blamed because of their singularity, disallowing any extrapolation of the findings. Nevertheless, we should remember that, from a historical point of view, *all* social situations are unique, and so are the findings of empirical research. A representative sample of the residents of Madison, Wisconsin, in 1977, or even of the manual workers of the United States of America in 1980, is as singular a universe as the neighbourhood organizations of the

Mission District in San Francisco in 1971. The general value of *any* observation depends on the purpose of its use. If we want to predict the outcome of a political election, an opinion poll of potential voters, on the basis of a representative sample, is an adequate research instrument (at least, sometimes). If we want to understand the new cultural patterns introduced by immigrants, we need to establish a typology of ethnic communities and weigh their differential evolution in relationship to mainstream society, on the basis of an anthropological observation. And if we want to elaborate a theory of urban social movements on the basis of historical experience, we must observe unique situations in which a particular phenomenon, considered by our theory to be crucial, is amplified. This has been the rationale that has informed our research design. It is only when and if we obtain a grounded theory of urban social movements and an understanding of how fully they relate to the evolution of cities, that we can compare mobilized and passive neighbourhoods *vis-à-vis* their differential effect on urban functions and forms. Thus, while case studies cannot provide a systematic verification of established propositions, they are invaluable in the pathbreaking efforts of generating new theories.

The complexity of the methodological operations involved in this research, as well as the diversity of the empirical sources, could submerge the main lines of the argument under a flood of data, description of techniques, and epistemological reasoning. We have therefore placed all epistemological and technical elements that are not necessary for the understanding of the social contexts and of substantive theory in a detailed Methodological Appendix. Interested readers are referred to it for a discussion of the logic of the demonstration and specific information about the empirical research underlying each case study.

But it is important to point out here that, from the outset, we have rejected the construction of a formal theory of urban social change. By a formal theory we understand a theory whose main concerns are trans-historical comprehensiveness and logical consistency. For the social sciences – whose historical and experimental character is quite unlike formal sciences, such as mathematics – the crucial test of a theory is its *adequacy*, rather than its coherence. By adequacy we mean the capacity of a series of intellectual tools to generate new knowledge about a given phenomenon. Following the teaching of Gaston Bachelard, we believe that the most useful concepts are those flexible enough to be deformed and rectified in the process of using them as instruments of knowledge. It is this capacity of enabling us to understand social processes and situations, and not the endless exercise of re-coding experience in a comprehensive paradigm, that is the actual test of the fruitfulness of a theory.

What we need now are not trans-historical theories of society but rather theorized histories of social phenomena.

This is not, and should not be, a general epistemological position. Someday perhaps we will reach a cumulative and comprehensive theoretical paradigm of history and societies, but not now and not soon. In the meantime, we need humble but effective strategies of theory-building that can lead us away from short-sighted empiricism without becoming lost in the artificial paradises of the grand theory. This book is an attempt to walk cautiously, yet relentlessly, that path.

Thus, the book opens with an investigation of the historical evolution of the process through which social actors produce cities and urban meaning. It continues with the analysis of urban demands as elements of collective consumption in suburban Paris. It poses the question of the relationship between culture and space on the basis of the San Francisco experience. It examines the effects of the subordination of urban movements to the political system by summarizing evidence, including ours, on squatter communities in Latin America. And it studies the relationship between consumption, culture, and politics by focusing on the Citizen

Movement in Madrid. On the basis of a series of *ad hoc* analytical models, supported by our empirical observations for each case study, all findings are integrated in a final Part that proposes a cross-cultural theory of urban social change.

The purpose of this research effort goes beyond our scholarly endeavour. For, only if we are able to understand how people create cities might we be able to create cities for people.

Part 1

Cities and People in a Historical Perspective

1

Introduction

Urban history is a well-established discipline. Historians have been able to reconstruct the city form and urban life of our past, sometimes relying only on the traces of archaeological discoveries but often with more accuracy than urban sociologists have been able to describe contemporary cities.[1]

Yet there is a great unknown in the historical record: citizens. We have, of course, descriptions of people's lives, analysis of their culture, studies of their participation in the political conflicts that have characterized a particular city.[2] But we know very little about people's efforts to alter the course of urban evolution. There is some implicit assumption that technology, nature, economy, culture, and power come together to form the city which is then imposed on its dwellers as given.[3] To be sure, this has been the general case. But while most historical time in peasants' lives has been spent in submissive labouring, historians have not neglected to identify peasants' revolts and their decisive impact on agrarian social structure.[4] It is our view that a similar process has occurred in cities, that citizens have created cities: directly when they won or indirectly through the impact of their defeat on the social forms still dominated by the established powers of each epoch. The scope of this book cannot undertake such an investigation. Our aim, instead, is limited to observing throughout recent historical evolution the continuous interaction between social change and urban form, identifying the themes, the actors, and the values of those urban social movements, whose historical trace is likely to be found in our contemporary research. We want, furthermore, to establish some distance from our world, so that the specific trends of our context can be identified in relationship to the more general theoretical framework we are trying to construct in order to understand urban change.

To place our analytical effort in a historical perspective we have selected five cases concerning major social movements consciously oriented toward the transformation of the city in very different historical contexts. The *Comunidades* of Castilla were one of the major revolutionary attempts in Europe to challenge the absolutist monarchy in the construction of the nation state. The Commune of Paris was a municipal revolution that marked forever the labour movement. The Glasgow Rent Strike of 1915 was a working class struggle that underlies the origin of the public housing policy of the capitalist state. The strike of the *inquilinarios* of Veracruz, Mexico in 1922, although less universally known was probably the most important social struggle triggered by urban issues to take place in Latin America before World War 2. The revolt of the American inner cities in the 1960s challenged the emerging 'post-industrial' society, with the old historical demands of community control and racial equality. Our analysis will rely on existing research, presented in each one of the historical case studies.

Unlike the outlook in the following chapters we will be more concerned here with asking the right questions rather than providing definitive answers. Those questions will primarily relate to the interplay between social classes, urban forms, gender positions, and political institutions in the simultaneous production of cities and societies. It may be useful to state from the outset that our analytical model does not presuppose the preeminence of one set of factors over the others, but rather it examines their interaction and their differential social outcome according to specific historical contexts. If there is an underlying theme to the analysis presented in Part 1 of this book, it is precisely our conviction that class analysis is an insufficient approach to the understanding of urban change throughout history. While preserving the important contribution of a class analysis perspective, its particular focus must be integrated into a more comprehensive model of social causality, able to account for the diversity of human experience.

Finally, the conclusions arising from the analyses presented in Part 1 can only be tentative because the information that supports them, while reliable and considerable, has not been produced to meet our specific research interests. Yet by examining the interaction between cities and people in a historical perspective, we should be able to detect some basic mechanisms underlying the social production of urban life and forms.

2

Cities and Freedom: The Comunidades of Castilla, 1520–22

Introduction

The Castilian cities that revolted in 1520–22 against the royal authority of Carlos V gave life to one of the most significant urban social movements in history. It was at the same time a citizen movement for local autonomy, a social movement challenging the feudal order and a political movement in search of a modern constitutional state.

Our analysis does not pretend to contribute to the existing historical research on this major event or to provide a systematic account of the movement. Instead we have relied upon Joseph Perez's major synthesis, *La Revolution des Comunidades de Castille (1520-1521)*[5] Another exceptionally fine analysis, Jose Antonio Maravall's *Las Comunidades de Castilla*[6] has nurtured our thought with some key hypotheses. Our aim is to place the findings of historians within the framework of a general theory of urban social movements. We do not want to illustrate our theory but to construct it on the basis of historical experience in order to avoid the ethnocentric bias implicit in most urban research.

Our main interest in analysing the experience of the Castilian *comuneros* is to identify the values, goals, and the social characteristics of the movement, and to understand their attempt to propose a new form of city and a new form of state, and thus a new society. We are less interested in considering what would probably be the main concern for the historian or the political analyst, namely the reasons for their defeat and the consequences of such a defeat for the evolution of the Spanish state. It is true that the triumph of absolutist monarchy, supported by the feudal nobility, frustrated the promise of democracy represented by the *comuneros* and marked forever Spanish society. Yet our purpose is not to mourn lost democracies, but to understand the historical process of the formation of social movements, the ultimate sources of democratic life.

Cities, Classes and the State in Sixteenth Century Castilla

The revolution of the *Comunidades* started in Toledo in May 1520 and extended to the majority of the cities that had the privilege of sending representatives to the Spanish parliament (the *Cortes*) which, under the authority of the king, had the power to supervise the taxes imposed by the crown on the cities. It started as a fiscal revolt and a protest over the undemocratic form of representation in the *Cortes*. The movement's goals were immediately defined in very political terms around two major objectives:

1 The support of the programme of the federated government of cities established in Tordesillas, the *Junta de Tordesillas* which clearly set up the basis for a modern constitutional state by requiring the king to accept the powers of a parliament elected by the cities.
2 The democratization of municipal power, establishing the principle of election for local officials and their obligation to report to popular committees organized at the ward level.

Since they were able to organize a powerful army, the *comuneros* seemed to be close to a military and political victory by the end of 1520. Yet its privileges threatened the Spanish nobility who at first was somewhat distant from the young king (he was born and grew up in Gand and so was considered a foreigner by many), brought all its power to the struggle in exchange for some major concessions from the crown. On 23 April 1521, the combined forces of Spanish lords and the royal army defeated the popular militia in Villalar. The cities were then reduced one after another. Toledo resisted until February 1522. The repression was particularly severe and the leaders of the revolution, Bravo, Maldonado, and Padilla, were executed. The Castilian cities lost most of their freedom. The Spanish monarchy, relying on the Catholic Church and now supported by the nobility, felt strong enough to undertake the building of a world-wide empire, in a storm of bloody conquest, religious fanaticism, and economic ineptitude.

The immediate causes of the revolution have been clearly established by historical research. They were related to the crisis of the state during the difficult transition between the Catholic kings and Carlos V. He had been absent from the country during his childhood until 1517 and was more concerned with the conquest of Europe than with the government of Spain.[7] The weakening of the state's authority aggravated the legitimacy crisis induced by unlimited royal absolutism. Taxes were raised too often; the preference of the king for the Flemish was too openly expressed in his high ranking appointments, including Cardinal Adriano as his representative in Spain; the monarchy treated the *Cortes* with excessive arrogance, convening the cities' delegates only to vote for taxes reflecting the royal will. The crisis of legitimacy developed into a crisis of political control because of the ambiguous attitude of the Spanish nobility, who were quite happy to take advantage of the uncertain situation to remind the young king of how much he was in need of their support, and particularly of the active commitment of the *Grandes de España*, feudal lords controlling armies, men, land, villages, and cities. Until the revolution of the *Comunidades* began to threaten the entire political order, the nobles withheld their full support from the monarchy, only to make their decisive role more evident in curbing the challenge from emerging urban social groups.

Furthermore, the political crisis developed in a context of acute economic crisis in the Castilian cities: local artisans, urban merchants and the first textile industrialists were being ruined by a converging movement involving the privileges of those associated in the powerful *Mesta* (organization of Castilian sheep-raisers and dealers), and the competition from the Flemish textile industry and its allies, the big Castilian merchants specializing in the import-export business.

However, apparent these sources of discontent were, the movement of the *Comunidades* expressed much deeper social contradictions, and its own dynamics opened up a perspective on the transformation of society and on the revolution of the state. We need to explain how the progress from a crisis to revolutionary consciousness was achieved. Was there a process of class struggle? If so, which were the classes that participated in it, and how did they express their interests?

In terms of its social basis the *Comunidades* were primarily a movement of the urban middle classes (clerks, artisans, merchants) in the free cities. They were joined by a sector of the religious orders and by some isolated elements of the low-level nobility (the *caballeros*).[8]

The immediate enemy of the movement was precisely the segment of the nobility living in the cities, the *caballeros*. But they were not opposed because they were nobles, but because they were the ones that, according to the royal laws, held the power in the municipal institutions. The *comuneros* did not originally fight against the feudal lords. They only reluctantly confronted them in a second stage of the revolution when the nobles threw their armies against the cities, fearful of the effects of the political agitation upon the social order of the countryside and upon the democratic character of the future state. At its birth, the *Comunidades* were not a class movement; they were, on the contrary, a multi-class, popular movement that did not recognize itself as a 'class,' but as a community (*comunidad*). As Perez says, 'They had no identity as producers, but a solidarity as consumers.'[9] They respected their internal social diversity, and they proposed representation to the *Cortes* according to three equal parts: one third for the urban nobility; one third for the priests; one third for the 'commons,' that is for people without any special privilege, and therefore compelled to pay taxes.

The most distinctive feature of the movement was its project to reform the local political institutions around the concept of the *Comunidad*. The key element of the new institution was the municipal assembly. 'In the assembly were seated not only members of the privileged groups, that had up until then held the monopoly of municipal power, but also the delegates of the ward committees, the actual holders of popular power because of their capacity to call ward meetings and mobilize the residents'.[10] The assembly designated a municipal council that appointed different commissions for specific tasks.

Thus the very core of the project of the *Comunidades* concerned the structure of state institutions. At the level of the central state, they called for representative democratic institutions. At the local level, they called for first, local autonomy (free cities); second, elected representative municipal assemblies; and third, decentralization of municipal power at the ward level. In fact, the *Comunidades* were a movement aimed at what we would call today the articulation between representative democracy and grassroots democracy.[11]

The *comuneros* gathered all urban social classes around the municipal institutions. Thus the *Comunidades* were not a class movement. Such an important statement needs some further elaboration. First, we should note that all classes and social groups that participated in the movement were strictly urban. They represented a great diversity of social situations that we will call 'low popular strata', including out-of-work artisans, masterless domestic servants, low-level bureaucrats, street merchants, and errant peasants arriving in the city to escape serfdom. When we refer to the 'urban social groups' we must keep in mind the specificity of the social context of the Castilian cities in the sixteenth century, and, more generally, the human world of the European city at the origins of the modern age.[12]

This diverse social universe provided the actors of the '*comunero*' movement: they included social classes in the process of formation and decomposition, social groups in crisis, old and new social elites struggling for power, classless individuals losing their social identity while maintaining their social myths; and there were also among them people learning to be free through their autonomy in the process of work. The *comuneros* were all of these at the same time, and, from this point of view, the *Comunidades* are at the opposite side of the historical category of social class.

Although the *Comunidades* did not act as a class and did not so define themselves, they did oppose a class designated by the *comuneros* as the exploiters and the oppressors: the great nobility. Nevertheless, as we pointed out on the basis of available evidence, such opposition is neither the historical origin nor the social foundation of the movement. The *Comunidades* did not arise as an anti-feudal movement. They were forced to fight the nobles when the latter began to support the crown to destroy the project of a democratic state. If it is true that a constitutional state could have been a deadly threat to the feudal order, we must not, analytically, confuse the social effects of a movement with the social definition of its opponent around which the movement was actually formed. In this particular sense, the *comuneros* apparently fought for the political freedom of the cities and for the defense of the 'commons' (the popular urban state), but they did not directly mobilize against the social domination of the nobility in the countryside. In fact, in the first phase of the movement, they looked for alliances with the nobles against the king, and they did obtain some very important supporters like the Count of Salvatierra, whose army was a major military factor in the campaigns of Northern Castilla. We should stop here short of rejoining the thesis maintained by some liberal Spanish historians like Maranon, for whom the *Comunidades* were actually a demagogic populist movement manipulated by the feudal nobles to resist the modernizing effort represented by the absolutist monarchy.[13] Such an interpretation has been empirically rejected by the findings of historians.[14] But neither can we consider it as an anti-feudal movement. The confrontation with the nobility resulted from the internal dynamics of a movement whose growing radicalism came to threaten all established social institutions.

To summarize: the *comuneros* designated their opponents in terms of their monopoly over the political institutions and not on the basis of their social privileges. Although they were an anti-feudal movement at the political level, the *Comunidades* did not represent a class struggle at the level of the social organization, if we make an exception for some of the episodes such as the campaign of the radical Bishop Acuna against the nobles' domains in the Tierra-de-Campos. The major argument in support of our thesis is that those areas, such as Andalucia, where the cities were under the tight social control of the landed aristocracy often living in those cities, were precisely the least influenced by the *comuneros*. The revolution did not develop where the feudal order was most oppressive, but rather in those regions where the emerging urban society had reached the highest level of autonomy.

Our analysis of the *Comunidades* as a non-class urban movement seems to contradict the view of the leading historian Jose Antonio Maravall, for whom the *Comunidades* were a political movement of the emerging Castilian bourgeoisie. Are we, in fact, in the presence of the birth of a class, the bourgeoisie, growing up in the protected space of the free cities, to challenge the hegemony of the feudal nobility? Given the importance of the question, let us examine more carefully who the actors in the movement were.

We have already established the multi-class composition of the movement, that included a heterogeneous, across-the-board representation of all medieval urban *plebs*. Yet the leadership of the movement was somewhat different, dominated as it was by the 'middle classes' – a rather vague notion under which Maravall includes the urban bureaucracy (municipal employees, clerks, legal officers), some Church and university dignataries, and above all, the artisan guilds in the cities. With the development and radicalization of the movement, the dominance shifted from the bureaucrats and legal officers to the artisans. Towards the end of the movement, in the revolutionary ward committees of Valladolid (the '*Cuadrillas*'), and in the parishes of Toledo, in 1521, the movement represented the '*Oficios*' (the artisan guilds), relying on the support of the urban *plebs*.

In fact the commercial bourgeoisie, the rich merchants, opposed the revolution. The most clear expression of such an attitude was the behaviour of the city of Burgos, which was largely dominated by great merchants involved in European trade. Burgos offered some mild support to the initial demands by the cities, but quickly changed its alliances by establishing solid ties with the *Condestable de Castilla*, the leader of the feudal nobility. In a symmetrical reaction, the *Comunidades* in Burgos recruited exclusively among the urban poor, and became a very radical movement that attacked all social privileges, isolating themselves from the middle strata and suffering complete defeat and fierce repression at the beginning of the revolution.

So it seems rather difficult to consider the *Comunidades* as a 'bourgeois' movement, even in the Sombartian meaning that Maravall gives to the concept of bourgeoisie[15]. The exercise of the leadership by the literate urban middle classes seems to be another confirmation of the general observation about social movements, by which their leaders tend to originate from groups of a relatively high social status once those groups are seen be identify with a movement formed mainly by the popular masses. So, available historical evidence seems to point instead to the artisan guilds as the backbone of the *Comunidades*. Because of their level of organization, social influence, and political consciousness, the artisans seem to have been the elite leading the urban popular masses mobilized around the programme of the *Comunidades*. When the debate between 'moderates' and 'radicals' developed within the movement, the artisans were often those who voiced the popular concerns *vis-à-vis* the literate bureaucracy that had occupied the new municipal institutions.

The artisans' role in the movement, however, did not apparently have much to do with their support for an alternative economic order. Although severely affected by the economic crisis provoked by the arrival of European manufactured products, their economic programme never went beyond the request of some protective tariffs or the claim for fiscal autonomy of the cities to avoid the overwhelming royal taxes. The healthy reaction of some of the best historians against the idealism of traditional historiography has led to an excessive economism that has tried to find in all occasions the 'true' economic interests as the driving force behind the scenes of social movements and political conflicts. Such an interpretation is often inaccurate. And it seems certainly inappropriate in the case of the *Comunidades*, in which the commercial bourgeoisie did not participate in the revolution, and in which the presence of the artisan guilds as the leading element of a massive urban popular movement, is not enough an argument by itself to assimilate the *Comunidades* to the rising of an incipient industrial capitalism: such a project never existed either in the programme or in the consciousness of the *comuneros*. It seems better to consider the *Comunidades* as a *proto-national movement*, using Maravall's own terms, that is, a movement aimed at the constitution of the modern nation state. We would also add, as will be argued below, its definition and orientation as a citizen movement. We are not dealing with the rising or decline of a social class following the rules of a changing economy, but examining the meaning of a political revolution that arises within the medieval urban world and transforms it into a city as a new cultural category and a new political reality. Let us explore the precise meaning of this fundamental hypothesis.

The Comunidades: A Political Revolution

As a way to understand the social content of the *Comunidades*, Maravall has investigated the historical and semantic meaning of the word in the sixteenth century Castilla. Three meanings appear to be simultaneously attached to the term *Comunidad*:

1 The *comun* (common) refers to the ensemble of non-privileged citizens, that is the residents of a city that must pay taxes.

2 The *comuna* (commune) is an association of free citizens bound by oath to the military defense of the city's self government. It is the Spanish version of the Italian Medieval free 'commune' organized around the legal-political institution of the *conjuratio*.

3 The *comunidad* (community) is the term used to name a revolutionary action based on the democratic principles of free election.

Such a plurality of meanings is certainly not an accident, but the cultural recognition in the language of a historical process: the process through which a new constitutional order struggles to emerge from the decomposition of the feudal institutions. Yet it would be a mistake to consider what seems to be a political conflict in relationship to the construction of the new state as a struggle between old and new social classes. To be sure this is not a question of denying the obvious relationship between class struggle and the political system, but it is important to reject the pure assimilation between the two levels of the analysis to avoid treating them as a single dimension in which each political form must correspond to the interests of a particular social class. Let us consider the issue in early sixteenth century Spain.

The Catholic kings, in order to build a strong central state that would be an agent of modernization of Spanish society, relied on the growing economic and demographic power of the Castilian cities to curb the privileges of the nobility and to establish the authority of the state above the particular interests of each feudal lord. Such an ambitious project had two limits. On the one hand, the nobility still dominated the political institutions and used its position to oppose some royal reforms, particularly on decisive matters such as the creation of a permanent modern royal army, independent of the contingents provided by each lord in case of emergency. When in 1516 the Cardinal Cisneros, Regent of Castilla, tried to recruit such an army among the citizens of the free communes eligible for military service (*gente de ordenanza*), the fierce opposition from the nobles frustrated the attempt. Interestingly enough, many of the military cadres of this aborted royal army became the leaders of the militia organized by the *Comunidades*.

On the other hand, the alliance proposed by the crown to the cities did not guarantee them an effective participation in the power system. In fact a municipal administration dominated by the *corregidores*, royal bureaucrats directly appointed by the king, substituted for the customary institution of the 'open council' through which the cities had been exercising their self-government. The *corregidores* were aided by *magistrados*, likewise nominated by the king. The municipal government also included a deliberative body, the *regimiento*, formed by life-tenured councilmen recruited among the low-level urban nobility: the *regidores*. Only a fourth category of municipal officials, the *jurados*, were directly elected by the citizens through parish based electoral districts. The municipal corporation as a whole (*ayuntamiento*) was chaired by the *corregidor*, and ruled by an assembly formed by the *magistrados*, the *regidores* and the *jurados*. The last, who were the only elected members of the corporation, did not have the right to vote. Thus the political power of the cities was seriously limited at least in three ways, in spite of their alliance with the monarchy:

1 The cities' delegates to the national parliament (the *procuradores*) were not truly representative of the citizens, and the parliamentary powers themselves were overshadowed by the royal decisions, at least since 1480.

2 The municipalities had little local autonomy, since they had to submit to the authority of the *corregidores* appointed by the king.

3 The municipal corporations were not an expression of the citizens democratic will, since their only elected representatives had little impact on the decision making process.

In fact the strategy of the monarchy was perfectly expressed in this complex municipal machinery. The implicit agenda was to rally the urban middle classes to countervail the nobles' power, in exchange for granting them the economic control of their cities under the surveillance of the royal officials. But it was well understood that such a relative autonomy of the local elites should not threaten the king's authority at the level of the state or be extended to the popular strata in city government. Such a delicate equilibrium was dramatically altered by the crisis of the state in the early years of the sixteenth century when the favours of the crown towards the Flemish appointees disturbed the complex balance of agreements between the monarchy, the nobility, and the dominant urban elites. The last tried to broaden their popular support by reforming the municipal institutions to make them more representative. So the guilds and the popular sectors could be incorporated into a common struggle to win some power for the cities. The urban elites were particularly keen to strengthen their influence in the parliament when faced with a monarchy that had increased their tax burden, failed to protect the guilds against foreign competition, and had upset the power relationship with the cities through the actions of an ever more interventionist royal bureaucracy.

The participation of the urban *plebs* in the municipal government of the increasingly auto-nomous cities considerably enlarged the political perspective of the popular strata. Thus, the *comuneros* superseded the limits of the corporatist view that characterized most urban revolts in the late middle ages. For instance, the famous revolt of the *ciompi* in Florence in 1378 was the expression of the artisans who had been excluded from the group of 14 guilds that kept control of the city's government until that date. Yet their project never went beyond the demand to participate in the established political institutions as they were. On the contrary, the matters in the discussions held in the *cuadrillas* of the *Comunidad* of Valladolid, probably the radical wing of the movement, primarily concerned the principles for a new political organization of the kingdom, along with the revival of religious fundamentalism. It seems certain that in the movement of the *Comunidades*, the *popolo grasso* (the rich merchants and urban nobility) were often overwhelmed by the *popolo minuto* (the urban *plebs*).[16] From this point of view, it does not seem unreasonable to accept the parallel that some historians have proposed between the *comuneros* and the *sans culotte* of the French Revolution. The implicit historical sequence could have then been the passage from the feudal order to a proto-demo-cratic state without going through the *ancien régime* and the absolutist monarchy. Yet we should stop short of adopting hastefully-made historical assimilations that take advantage of formal resemblances to jump over the centuries without considering the specificity of each historical epoch. What can be retained from this discussion is that the project of a political revolution seems actually to have been the dominant aspect of the multiple social meanings of the *Comunidades*. It was a Utopian movement at the economic level: it proposed the total suppression of taxes. It was nostalgic and reactionary at the ideological level, with a pre-dominance of religious traditionalism and cultural nationalism. Yet the political programme of the *Comunidades* was extremely precise and astonishingly modern. They asked for a constitutional monarchy in which the king should obey the parliament. They called for democratic representation in the parliament, whose power and autonomy should be guaranteed. They required autonomy and democratization of municipal governments. They proposed the decentralization of local government at the ward level with a procedure of citizen participation in the public affairs. And, finally, they proclaimed the equality of rights among all free citizens and demanded legal and judicial protection against the arbitrary decisions of the lords and monarchy.

It is our hypothesis that it was precisely this strong stand of the *comuneros* as political revolu-tionaries that caused their defeat. Given the radicalism of the institutional changes advocated by the *Junta de Tordesillas*, however moderately they were phrased, it precipitated an antagonistic coalition including the king, the nobility, the Church and the commercial bourgeoisie. But the defeat of the *Comunidades* was not caused by the 'betrayal' of the bourgeoisie (as if the bourgeoisie should always be democratic) or by the 'historical immaturity of the objective conditions for a democratic state' (as if history were a train running to schedule). The *comuneros* were defeated not because they were unable to create a new state, but because they tried too hard; not so much because of their excessive emphasis on local autonomy, but because their attempt from their municipal trenches was the creation of a modern centralized state, founded on democratic representation.

In fact, as the fundamental ensemble of studies on the formation of European states edited by Charles Tilly seems to indicate,[17] the logic of the construction of the nation-state in Europe carried an implicit centralized structure, as a consequence of their reliance upon a land-based army and a state-appointed bureaucracy. The internal contradiction of the *comuneros*' movement came from the fact that, on the one hand, as Maravall says, 'Their position derivated from the fifteenth century urban culture, in which the city, as a political form, represented a very advanced step toward the modern State'.[18] But, on the other hand, the attempt of the *Junta de Tordesillas* was to establish a new centralized Spanish state on the basis of a democratic parliament, although restricting the representation to the 18 cities already entitled to send delegates to the *Cortes*. Was the only choice to challenge a centralized absolutist state with a centralized democratic one? Other possibilities existed: for instance, a constellation of free cities as shown by the Flemish and Italian experiences. In the particular conditions of sixteenth century Castilla, to look for the military and administrative tools of a national state while still attempting to construct it on the principle of democratic representation was to prove a Utopian project. In line with the Catholic kings, Carlos V needed the instruments to fulfil his imperial ambitions, but he would never fully obtain them because of his necessary reliance on the nobility, a trend that was to decisively handicap the Spanish monarch in Europe. But the failure of the absolutist path towards modernity in Spain does not imply the likelihood of the success of a liberal democratic process of modernization and state-building, in which the *Comunidades* would have been the historical vector. The free cities, in spite of the defeats suffered by the Italian *Communes* in their struggle against the autocratic lords at the end of the sixteenth century, were not just a step towards the nation state. They were an alternative political form, another social project towards modernity, not necessarily inferior in terms of technology, political effectiveness, or even military power (for instance, the first European military artillery was that of the *Commune* of Florence). Indeed the shortcomings of the *comuneros*, and the fatal adversaries they provoked, arose precisely from their attempt to move forward to build a nation-state on the basis of municipal freedom as if that were a historical rule they had to follow. But, in fact, the city-state and the nation-state do not constitute an inevitable historical sequence: they are deeply antagonistic political forms in which the relationship between the state and civil society differ profoundly.

The Comunidades: A Citizen Movement

In the context of our research, the main interest of the *Comunidades* of Castilla lies in the fact that they formed an extraordinarily innovative citizen movement from whose experience some fundamental lessons can be learned about the interaction between urban evolution and social change.

We have shown that the movement's dominant aspect appears to be its meaning as a political revolution. Yet it was more specifically a citizenly political revolution. What do we imply by such a term? Certainly the movement's scene and setting were the Castilian cities, particularly the largest ones: Toledo, Valladolid, Segovia, Salamanca. Its participants were exclusively drawn from urban social groups. But is it enough to consider the *Comunidades* as an urban movement? Does the term 'urban' include everything that happens in the city, understanding 'city' to mean a large and dense human settlement concentrated in a given space? Surely not. For many years, our whole analysis of the urban phenomenon has relied on the thesis that 'urbanism' is a cultural category socially produced.[19] Therefore the meaning and problem of 'urban issues' depended upon explicit social relationships, characteristic of each mode of production and of each historical period. Our position actually follows the classical approach by Max Weber for whom the city is a specific spatial form of socio-political organization.[20] Maravall also places his analysis of the *Comunidades* in the same theoretical tradition when he writes, 'the *Comunidad* is never an urban ensemble, physically defined, or the formless agglomeration of a collection of dwellers. It is the moral and political body constituted by the members of the *Comunidad*.'[21] All through history, urban form and meaning have been determined by patterns of social organization and not the other way around, as has been demonstrated in the classical works of Lewis Mumford[22], Gideon Sjoberg[23], Jorge Hardoy,[24] and in a more precise way, by the research of Robert MacAdams on the comparative evolution of Babylon and Tenochtitlan.[25] From this intellectual perspective, how precisely are the *Comunidades* an urban movement? And how does this particular urban meaning influence their context and projects as a social movement?

To answer these questions – the most important ones for our research interests – we can rely on the well-known sociological analysis of Max Weber on the occidental city.[26] Although the historical research on which he relied, particularly the work by Fustel de Coulanges, has been challenged by the French school of the historical journal *Annales*[27], the general theoretical framework still throws some decisive light on the relationship between the medieval city and the social transition to the modern age, an issue which underlines our specific analysis of the *Comunidades* de Castilla.

For Max Weber, '. . . The city of the Medieval Occident was economically a seat of trade and commerce, politically and economically a fortress and garrison, administratively a court district, and socially an oath-bound confederation.'[28] Out of all these elements, the last is the decisive one, 'Contrary to current belief the cities did not originate in the guild corporation but the guild emerged in the context provided in the proto-city.'[29] That is, the city as a social organization and as an autonomous political organization and institution was the precondition for the generation of a new economy and of a more productive division of labour. The medieval city, as with all historical urban forms, was much more than a specific spatial arrangement. It was a political culture, defined by its institutional autonomy and by its commitment to some form of representative democracy. The category of 'urban' in such a historical moment is defined as the spatial setting of freedom and refers to the specific process of defending the collective and individual rights of the citizens against the feudal order and the absolutism of the monarchy. The city becomes a community only when and where its spatial entity becomes the territory in which are recognized and enforced laws and institutions corresponding to the new democratic rules of a state constructed around the rational-legal principle of legitimacy. Furthermore, for Weber, when the cities were not free or autonomous, or when they ceased being free, they were no longer cities in the strict sociological sense, but became physical concentrations of population and activities subjected to a religious-political apparatus and/or to the uncontrolled rules of the economic market.

Precisely this project of spatio-cultural community underlies the new political order that emerged in the European medieval towns and actually constituted them as cities. This phenomenon has very often been assimilated to the rise of the commercial bourgeoisie, seen as the social vector of this new political project. Such is probably the case in Venice or Genoa, in the German cities of the Hansa, and in the Flemish cities of the fourteenth century, particularly after their victory in Courtrai. But the proposition cannot be sustained as a general rule or an expression of a uniform pattern of historical development. The Parisian bourgeoisie rapidly deserted Etienne Marcel's revolt in 1358 against the royal power in spite of his position as the *Prevost des Marchands*. He actually died in an armed confrontation with elements of the bourgeois opposition. The subsequent Parisian revolts (the *Maillotins* in 1382, the *Cabochiens* in 1413) were even more clearly dominated by the *plebs* and by the guilds. For the Italian cities, Alessandro Pizzorno has shown[30] the cultural and political inter-penetration between the urban bourgeoisie and the nobility. The noble patricians generally lived in the cities and were closely connected to the commercial and financial operations of the bourgeoisie. Reciprocally, most bourgeois families strongly internalized the cultural values of the nobility and were in search of an accommodation within the existing political system that would allow them to share the power.

The reconstruction of the complex web of relationships between classes, cities, and monarchies at the end of the Middle Ages is certainly beyond the scope of our current analysis. But we can reasonably argue, as a general tendency, that what characterizes all cities is their attempt to affirm their cultural identity and their political autonomy. The only exceptions are those cities which are primarily the setting for the power of the noble aristocracy: in Spain's case, the city of Sevilla. Otherwise the tendency towards an urban culture fundamentally defined by the right to municipal self-government actually transcends the class composition of individual cities. On the contrary, the political values of the bourgeoisie are quite variable.

The big merchants, the main subjects of the primitive accumulation of capital, were very often absent from the cities' revolts, and even helped the monarchies to repress the citizens on several occasions. Therefore it seems empirically incorrect to identify the citizen movements during the Renaissance with the struggle of the bourgeoisie to create the political institutions of capitalism. What is true is that the potential for social autonomy resulting from such a project of citizen's self-government was certainly a stimulant for production and exchange, and could therefore undermine the feudal order and prepare the conditions for the development of capitalism. Furthermore, merchants' activities and artisans' ingenuity were factors that economically and culturally supported the demands for the autonomy of the cities. Thus the link is evident between the class dimension and the citizen dimension in the historical process. What is unacceptable is the merger of the two dimensions and the related hypothesis that interprets this historical process as the search by the merchant bourgeoisie to impose more favourable institutional rules for the fulfilment of its economic interests.

In this sense, the Weberian thesis on the medieval city as a specific socio-political form seems to us fully convincing. A much more questionable approach is his attempt, later theorized by Toynbee and by the Chicago School of urban sociology, of extrapolating from a historical situation the general definition of urban, to the extent of denying the use of the term of 'city' for other urban forms in other historical contexts. The symmetrically opposed position could be argued on the same grounds. We could also say, with Pierre Clastres,[31] that the city, as in the case of the first historically known city, Ur in Chaldea, is the primary organizational form of the state, and therefore of domination through violence and territorial conquest of the surrounding territory.

Such a debate could be endless, but we reject it. We reject the normative opposition between the city as a form of freedom and the city as a form of domination, to argue in favour of the historical differentiation of the social meaning of spatial forms.

What is missing in the Weberian analysis, prisoner of its own historical relativism, is an explanation of why the medieval city was a source of autonomy and freedom, unlike other large human settlements in history. Thus the search for a historical agent of the affirmation of the medieval city as a political institution is an entirely relevant question. What is unconvincing, in regard to the empirical record, is the usual answer that tries to identify the interests of the commercial bourgeoisie and of the artisan guilds as the sources of the struggle for municipal autonomy. Such a hypothesis is dependent upon an economistic view of history. But the sixteenth century was not a time that saw the formation of industrial capitalism: the economy did not yet dominate society, and the bourgeoisie was not yet the crucial historical actor. We are witness, however, to a very different, though fundamental battle: the struggle over the definition of the relationship between the state and civil society.

The project of medieval cities represented a new form of state, much more closely dependent upon the dynamics of civil society than the type of state that finally triumphed throughout most of Europe with absolutism and its quasi-royal lords. There was certainly a system of relationships between such a political struggle and the process of formation of new social classes in an emerging capitalist world. We leave to the historians the task of determining the nature of those relationships and the precise role played by old and new social classes in the combat between the free cities and the emerging national states. But we retain for the purpose of our own research the basic conclusion of the specifically political character of the citizen revolt across a variety of social formations and class interests.

This statement is particularly important for us because we maintain not only that space is socially determined, but also that the social meaning of each spatial form is produced in a process of struggle and institutionalization whose main goal is precisely to assess a cultural meaning from a spatial form – to institutionalize such a meaning so that it becomes 'spontaneously' internalized in the social behaviour of all social groups. Our thesis is that the medieval cities were constituted as socio-political communities by the historical action of the citizen movements, which transformed a given spatial form into an urban culture and a political institution.

In this sense the *Comunidades* of Castilla were a citizen movement, not so much because they were based in cities but because they attempted to impose the city as the basic cell of a new socio-political organization, both in the cities themselves (the commune) and in the overall state (the parliament) as a representation of free cities. The programme of the *Comunidades* primarily emphasized political democracy, fiscal autonomy, and local self-government. They were certainly not an urban movement in the sense given to this term in the 1980s because the demands over housing and urban services could only become crucial where the dissociation between the elements of the community had already taken place: the separation between production and consumption, and the contradiction between exchange value and use value.

The project of the *Comunidades* was, instead, to establish the city as an autonomous form of production, consumption, exchange, social relations, and political government. It was aimed at affirming the fundamental identity of the citizen's interests against the threat of their common domination by *supra* municipal powers, and above the internal divisions between social classes and social groups within the city. This kind of political vision cannot be considered as a Utopia: it was partly fulfiled by the cities of Northern Europe, particularly in Flanders. Those cities, marching along this alternative historical road, had a much more direct access to modernity, and their success is still present in their superior level of cultural pluralism, political democracy, and economic efficiency. To be sure, had the *Comunidades* been able to impose that political model, the institutionalization of urban autonomy would have given birth (as it did in Northern Europe) to new municipal oligarchies around a colonialist merchant plutocracy. But such is the fate of all social movements: they break the old order and inspire a new one that begins to age as soon as it has taken shape. The *comuneros* never reached such a stage of maturity. Their history, as for all defeated revolutionaries, was obscured by the brightness of their myth. Yet, on the basis of available historical research, the most innovative and perhaps most lasting aspect of their project was the affirmation of the free city as a superior form of life and government. As a political revolution, the *Comunidades* of Castilla failed. As a citizen movement they brought together forever in the collective memory of the Spanish people the idea of freedom, the right of municipal self-government, and the hope for a better life.

3

Cities and Revolution: The Commune of Paris, 1871

Introduction

The *Commune* of Paris has generally been considered, particularly in the Marxist tradition, as the first major proletarian political insurrection.[32] For Lenin, the experience of the *Commune* demonstrated at the same time the possibility of a politically orientated working class movement and the necessity of the destruction of the bourgeois state, to be replaced, if the revolution was to last, by a proletarian state.[33] There is in fact a classical debate between the Leninist view and the libertarian interpretation of the *Commune*, or in more French terms, between the *Jacobins* and the *Proudhoniens*.[34] Was the *Commune* a process of radicalization of republican ideals when confronted with the military defeat of the nation and the collapse of the Second Empire? Was it instead a political revolution furthering the demand for political freedom into a new institutional organization relying upon the project of a voluntary federation of free communes? Or should we maintain the Marxist belief in the potentials of the *Commune* as a socialist revolution, largely frustrated because of the inability of the Utopian liberals to perceive their historical role in the same correct political terms as the active minority of the 'internationalist' socialists?

In fact, our research concerns are somewhat different. Without being able in this text either to reconstruct or to assess such a fundamental debate, we want to call attention to other possible historical meanings of the *Commune*, some of which are full of significance for our understanding of the urban problem. We are particularly interested in exploring the hypothesis, posed by the great Marxist philosopher, Henri Lefebvre, on the *Commune* as an urban revolution.[35] If such an interpretation is correct, the extraordinary impact of the *Commune* on the politics and ideology of the labour movement would be an indication of the historical relationship established between the urban problem and the social movement that holds the central role in the process of capitalist industrialization. Instead of being a retarded continuation of the French Revolution[36] or the announcement of the coming socialist revolution,[37] the

Commune, in this perspective, could be considered as the point of contact between the urban contradictions and the emerging labour movement, both in its most archaic aspects (the revolt of the *Sans Culottes* against the abuses of the powerful) and in its anticipatory themes (the self-management of society).

This fundamental dimension of the *Commune*, which Lefebvre has championed, has been largely neglected because of the politicization of the debate between Marxists and Libertarians in relation to its historical meaning. Yet, the careful consideration of the study of this dimension, and the historical evidence for it, might prove to be extremely helpful for our enterprise of exploring the changing relationships between city, society, and the state. We will rely for such an analysis on two essential historical sources for the reconstruction of the events of the *Commune*: the classic history by Lissagaray, himself a *communard*,[38] and the extraordinary research on the trials of the *communards* by Jacques Rougerie, whose preliminary findings were published in 1978.[39] Other works consulted are cited in the endnotes.

The Communards

Who were the *communards*? What was the social composition of the *Commune*? At first glance, it appears to have been, on the basis of Table 3–1 constructed by Rougerie, a workers' insurrection unlike the insurgency of 1848 or the resistance to the *Coup d'Etat* of 1851. Furthermore, after his examination of the files of the trial against the *Commune*, Rougerie affirms that in almost every case the *communard* was a salaried person. And if clerks still were present among the 1871 revolutionaries, the liberal professions, renters, merchants, and clerks altogether account for only 16 per cent of people arrested in relationship with the

Table 3.1 Occupational activity of Parisians arrested or deported after the *Commune* of 1871 and after the Coup d'Etat of 1851.
(Absolute figures and Proportion over the Basis of 1,000)

| | 1871 | | 1871 | | 1851 | |
Occupation	Arrested	Per Thousand	Deported	Per Thousand	Arrested	Per Thousand
Agriculture	398	11	41	13	32	10
Wood industry	2,791	80	234	77	251	86
Textile & garment	1,348	39	103	34	224	76
Shoes	1,496	43	157	51	164	56
Leather	381	11	48	15	27	9
'Travail d'art, article de Paris' (Parisian craft)	2,413	69	221	73	198	67
Printing	925	27	84	27	71	24
Metallurgy	4,135	119	349	115	196	67
Construction	5,458	157	494	163	180	61
Labourers (*Journaliers*)	5,198	149	549	181	149	50
Clerks	2,790	80	295	97	188	64
Domestic servants and janitors	1,699	49	52	17	93	31
Small merchants	1,516	43	104	34	237	81
Liberal professions and businessmen	1,169	33	76	25	380	129
TOTAL	34,722	1,000	3,023	1,000	2,924	1,000

Source: Jacques Rougerie, *Proces des Communards* (Paris: Gallimard-Archives, 1978).

Table 3.2 Comparison between the occupational activity of the Parisian population, of the people who insurged during the *Commune*, and of the people deported after the Paris *Commune*, 1871. (Percentages over the Total Figure of each Category)

Occupational Activity	Population of Paris (%)	People Insurged (%)	People Deported (%)
Metallurgy	8	12	12
Construction	10	17	18
Labourers (*Journaliers*)	20	14	15
Textile and garment and shoes industry	8	9	9
Artisans and printers	10	10	9

Source: Jacques Rougerie, *Proces des Communards.*

Commune, while they were 27 per cent in 1851. Thus, most *communards* were manual workers. But what kind of workers? According to Rougerie, they were salaried workers of the new industrial activities, and especially of the metallurgy. But if we have a closer look at Rougerie's own data presented in Table 3-2, the picture is somewhat more complex.

Among the insurgents the most important group, and most over-represented in relationship to the active Parisian population as a whole, was that of the construction workers. They were not representative of the modern industry. In fact they expressed the fantastic urban development and urban renewal activities in Paris during the Second Empire, under the rule of one of the most ambitious city planners in history, Haussmann. If we consider that unskilled labourers (*journaliers*) accounted for 14 per cent of the *communards* (though under-represented in relationship to the population), and that many of them were also probably employed in miscellaneous urban services including public works, it appears that Rougerie's conclusion is inadequate since it proceeds from the arbitrary assimilation of metallurgy, construction, and labourers. Only the first activity is related directly to the expansion of the modern industry. The same preponderance of construction workers appears if we consider people deported after the *Commune*, who were likely to have been the most active. The traditional artisan activities account for 18 per cent of them, the new industry (metallurgy) for 12 per cent; and activities related to the process of urbanization for 25 per cent to 33 per cent, depending upon the estimate of the population of *journaliers* involved in public works and urban services. Therefore, if it is true that the great majority of *communards* were workers, most of them were not industrial proletarians, but traditional artisans and construction workers related to the process of urban growth. Rougerie using a different argument also comes to a similar conclusion after considering the very archaic character of the process of work accomplished by the metallurgical industry. In sum, Rougerie writes, '. . . there are no true artisans, nor true proletarians. We observe an intermediate working class, although somewhat closer to its past.'[40]

Thus the use of the term 'worker' is misleading when we really want to determine if the *Commune* was in fact a major episode in the class struggle between the bourgeoisie and the proletariat over the control of industrialization. What Rougerie's data (the most complete available) show is the very popular social base of the *Commune*, formed by a mixture between the artisan worker and the urban labourers, with a very small ingredient of the new industrial proletariat.

To complete the social profile of the *communards*, we must add two essential remarks. First, if the petty bourgeoisie represents a clear minority among the insurgents, it clearly holds the majority among the elected officials of the *Commune*: there were only 25 workers among the

90 delegates elected in the revolutionary municipal elections of 26 March 1871. The great majority of the assembly (*La Commune*), according to Lissagaray, was formed by 'petty bourgeois': clerks, accountants, doctors, teachers, lawyers, and journalists.[41] Even more important, the majority of officers and cadres of the military force of the *Commune*, the *Garde Nationale*, was composed of clerks, printers, and small merchants.[42]

Thus, to summarize, the actors of the *Commune* were only a very marginal fraction of the industrial proletariat. The empirical analysis of the social profile of the *Communards* reveals a petty bourgeois elite, allied to some artisan workers, leading an army controlled by other petty bourgeois of a lower level and supported by a mass of salaried manual workers, most of whom were related not to the process of industrialization but to urban growth and real estate speculation. And if we give some credit to the estimate, proposed by Lissagaray, of 300,000 Parisians out of work at the moment of the *Commune*,[43] we can conclude that its characterization as a proletarian insurrection is, at least, doubtful. It appears, instead, as a popular revolution, far more popular than any other Parisian revolution. It is particularly noticeable that there was absolutely no participation by the liberal bourgeoisie. Yet the *communards* were not the *Canuts de Lyon*, proto-martyrs of the industrial class struggle. They were the people of a great city in the process of mutation, and the citizens of a Republic in quest of its institutions.

Last, but not least, the *Commune* was decisively an action by the women. Lissagaray, an eye-witness, writes, 'Women started first, as they did during the revolution. Those of 18 March, hardened by the war in which they had a double share of misery, did not wait for their men.'[44]

Plate 3.1 The barricade of Chaussée Ménilmontant, 18 March 1871. (By kind permission of the Bibliothèque Nationale, Paris.)

It seems that their role during the *Commune* was crucial, and not just because of a few legendary figures such as Louise Michel, one of the few leaders to stand up in front of the military judges during the trials,' and Elisabeth Dmitrieva, president of the Women's Unions and probably the connection between Karl Marx and the Commune. Women were the most active element in the mobilizations by the people, in the combat with the army, in the neighbourhood meetings, and in the street demonstrations. The great majority of these women were of 'common' origin. Their family situations were generally 'irregular', – according to the bourgeois morality – most of them living unmarried with men, and many being separated from ther husbands. The press and the legal system were extremely harsh to these women, dubbed the *petroleuses*, because of the derogatory rumour according to which they carried bottles of petrol to start fires in the houses of bourgeois families. Many of the women that went on trial as *communards* had a criminal record – a fact that reveals the conditions in the nineteenth century cities where common women were often used as a source of pleasure by rich men and a source of profit by poor men. The world of lower class women was always on the edge of urban deviance.

Women's active participation in the *Commune* emphasises the popular and urban character of a social uprising in which the barricades were built more to mark spatially a social community in each neighbourhood than to be effective defenses against an army whose mobility was greatly facilitated by the military vision that Haussmann had applied in his city planning: large straight avenues to open the way for the charges of cavalry and the bullets of guns.

The Programme of the Commune

How did the *communards* define themselves – more as people of Paris, or more as workers of the capital? At the level of the official proclamations of the *Commune*, there is no doubt as citizens (*citoyens*). Such was the term employed in the 'Declaration to the French People' of 19 April (1871), in the Electoral Manifesto of 26 March, and in most interventions in the debates of the Commune, of the Central Committee of the *Garde Nationale*, and in the *Comite-des-Vingt-Arrondissements*. Yet history has generally recalled another image, portrayed by a single but notorious declaration, published in the *Officiel* (the journal of the *Commune*) on 21 March, which spoke on behalf of the *proletaires*. This was the text cited and used in length by Marx, described as an anonymous statement by Rougerie, but by Lissagaray as a manifesto written by Moreau, Rogeard and Longuet. It seems to have been directly inspired by the *Commune's* socialist minority, linked to the *Internationale*, that relentlessly argued for the *Republique Sociale* and the right of workers to self-emancipation.

In fact such a two-fold expression would seem an accurate self-portrait for the *Commune*, for most of the leaders, and probably most of the *communards*, considered themselves citizens, fighting for the Republic and for Paris. For the socialist minority, either *blanquiste* or *internationalist*, they were citizens because they were proletarians, since only the working class was able to defend at that historical moment freedom and the country, given the betrayal of the bourgeoisie in collusion with the Prussians and the supporters of the *ancien régime*: the *Republique* would be *Republique Sociale* or would not be at all. But whether majority or minority, they were agreed that they were Parisians. The 'Declaration to the French People' speaks of the '. . . aspirations and wishes of the Paris population . . .' and makes clear that, 'Once again, Paris works and suffers for the rest of France.' On the other hand, the famous article of 21 March, cited by Marx, describes the movement as being the action of '. . . the proletarians of the capital city.'[45] This self-definition as Parisian was a major theme of the *Commune*. It was as representative of Paris that the *Commune* opposed the national parliament controlled by a rural majority that chose to locate itself in Versailles, the spatial symbol of the absolutist monarchy. Furthermore, parliament retaliated by threatening to relinquish Paris of its role as the nation's capital. As a matter of fact, most *communards* were as convinced of this as Lissagaray that '. . . the rural people, weak, unorganized, bounded by a thousand ties, could only be freed by the cities and the cities were dependent upon Paris.'[46] The *Commune* cannot be understood without this self-affirmation of the Parisian people and of the revolutionary role they intended to assume as the social and political vanguard of a rural France and of a monarchist Europe. It was a local society self-proclaimed as the universal revolutionary embryo. Louis XIV had declared, 'The state is me'. The people of Paris were replying, 'Society is us'. To the centralism of the French state, the *Commune* of Paris matched the centralism of a local civil society. This Parisian messianism imprinted itself forever on French culture and politics, and their relationship to the rest of the world.

This is why the first demand of the *Commune*, and the trigger of the movement, was the re-establishment of municipal freedom and its first political act was the organization of the first municipal elections of nineteenth century Paris. Furthermore the *communards* made it clear that they were asking for '. . . serious municipal liberties.'[47] These were to be the suppression of the *Prefecture* controlling the city's authority; the right for the 'National Guard' to name its chiefs and modify its organization; the proclamation of the Republic as the legal form of government; and the prohibition to the army to enter the territory of the municipality of Paris; – in effect, an institutional framework where the municipal liberties could be used to establish the self-government of the local civil society. And for the rest of France.' The absolute autonomy of the *Commune* extended to all localities in France, ensuring each one (of the localities) the integrity of their rights.' Also, it was intended '. . . to find in the great central administration, delegation of federated communes, the practical fulfilment of the same principles . . .' that Paris had decided to put at work in its own institutions (Declaration of 19 April 1871) What were these principles?

The Right for Each Commune to Decide:

'The vote of the communal budget; the establishment and distribution of taxes; the direction of local services; the organization of the judiciary, of the police, and the education; the administration of communal property.'

'The power of the municipality in the designation, by election or appointment, with full responsibility and permanent right of control and revocation of all judges and communal officers of all kinds.'

'The absolute guarantee of individual freedom, of freedom of conscience and freedom of work.'

'The permanent intervention of citizens in the communal affairs, by the free expression of their ideas and the free defense of their interests.'

'The organization of the Urban Defense, and of the National Guard, that elects its chiefs, and has full responsibility to keep order in their city.'

Declaration to the French People, 19 April 1871

Thus, the *Commune* was primarily a municipal revolution, with the qualification that such an orientation does not imply any parochial view; on the contrary, the transformation of the state as a whole was at stake, with the municipal institution as the keystone of a new political construction. Such a perspective was not only the result of the Proudhonian inspiration identifiable in the authors of the Declaration of 19 April, but was a constant theme found in all the actions and discourses of the *communards* in Paris, and was likewise present in the attempts to extend the *Commune* to the provinces of Lyon, Marseille, Toulouse, Le Creusot, and the Limousin. In Saint Etienne, a predominantly working class industrial city, the *Communards* killed the *prefet*[48] who was an industrial capitalist. In spite of the violent confrontation involving workers, the *communards* did not express any kind of anti-capitalist feelings, and their main claim was concerned again with the request for municipal liberties.

To be understood in its precise meaning, the dominance of the municipal theme among the *communards* needs to be placed within the framework of the division between Paris and the provinces, the city and the countryside. The great city as the nest of the freedom was the decisive element needed to escape the control of the central state, which would still likely to be dominated by the conservative majority. Because the conquest of local autonomy could allow the local civil societies of the cities to fully express their revolutionary inclination, municipal freedom was understood as a fundamental political asset for the forces struggling for social change. We are far away from the limited horizon of Jeffersonian localism. The municipal leanings of the *Commune* were not the expression of a particular taste for one version of political philosophy. It was a social programme that only makes sense when replaced in the specific historical context of the political relationship between cities and countryside in late nineteenth century France. With this hypothesis in mind, the *Commune's* strange mixture of revolutionary Jacobinism and Proudhonian federalism, observed to the great astonishment of many historians, seems less incomprehensible.

Along with this fundamental goal of municipal liberties, the *Commune* also put forward some basic socio-economic demands, the first of which was the cancellation of all housing rents that were due, together with a fair legislation on the payment of commercial leases and financial loans. The spark that triggered the *Commune* (along with the attempt to disarm the National Guard on 18 March) was, in fact, the approval on 13 March of a decree requiring the forceful payment of all due rents and commercial debts. According to Lissagaray, 'Three hundred thousand workers, shopkeepers, artisans, small businessmen and merchants who had spent their savings during the seige [by the Prussians] and did not yet have any earnings were thrown into bankruptcy, depending on the will of the landlord. Between 13 and 17 March there were 50,000 legal demands for seizure.'[49] That is why once the insurrection was victorious, on 21 March, the Central Committee of the National Guard banned the sale of personal objects deposited in the *Mont-de-Piete*[50] to guarantee the loans. The same decision extended for a month the term to pay commercial debts, and explicitly forbade any tenants' eviction at the request of the landlords. So, the first series of social measures taken by the *Commune* did not concern the control over the means of production or over the working conditions. They were aimed, instead, at protecting people against speculation and at stopping the process of massive tenant eviction that was under way due to the dramatic increase in housing rents caused by urban growth and war calamities.

Even the measures taken later by the *Commune's* Delegation of Work and Exchange, controlled by the internationalist socialist Leo Frankel, were directed against the injustice of the bosses rather than towards the establishment of workers' control. They were: suppression of night work for the bakers; proposal of suppressing the pawnshops; and a ban on the arbitrary retention of a part of the workers' wages by management as a means of enforcing labour discipline. There was, in fact, a major initiative with a socialist orientation: the Decree of 16 April that opened the possibility of transforming all factories and shops abandoned by their owners into workers' co-operatives. But it must be noted that such a collectivization of the means of production concerned only the bourgeois on the run (actually quite a few), and still foresaw the voluntary reselling of the property of the workers if the owner should return. In fact, only 10 shops in all were requisitioned and reorganized under workers' self-management. Once again we can perceive the active presence of a socialist minority that was unable to direct the movement as a whole. The relationships with the capitalists were less troubled than one might imagine in the midst of a social revolution. If the Mechanical Workers' Union was considering taking control of the Usine Barriquand, one of the biggest industrial factories, some other companies not only continued to work, but two of the most important, Godillot and Cail, equipped the insurgent National Guard with shoes and machine guns. The *Commune* respectfully asked for loans from the Bank of France, whose gold and treasury bills could have been confiscated without any problem, and did not attack the banks or any other capitalist institution. The social goals of the *communards* were aimed at fighting speculation more than abolishing exploitation.

Municipal freedom and the well-being of the people were the main concerns in the programme of the *Commune*. It also fought for *La Republique* and for *La France*, but in a much more tenuous manner. To be sure, the revolution of the *Commune* was sparked by the defense both of Paris against the Prussians and of the Republic against the monarchists. But of the two, republicanism was less important to the *Commune*; with the exception of Delescluze, all republican representatives, including those with leftist feelings, chose to join the parliament in Versailles and remained there throughout the entire process of confrontation and repression of the *Commune*. The leader of the left, Gambetta, openly opposed the *Commune*. The *communards* did not need the guns of the National Guard to preserve the Republic in 1871. The conservative majority of the parliament was a better political formula for the preservation of social order than the shaken remnants of the defeated Second Empire. The *communards* were republicans, but the *Commune* was not an act of republicanism.

What about the patriotic theme? According to Rougerie, this was one of the great motivations of the *Commune*, the popular indignation against the military defeat and the betrayal of the nation by incompetent and selfish politicians. These feelings were clearly very strong during the siege of Paris and in the months preceeding the *Commune*. But it does not seem that the patriotic motive was a real driving force in the popular movement. One of the important achievements of the leaders of the *Commune*, before 18 March, was to convince the National Guard to abandon its project of a desperate armed resistance against the Prussian army when the latter decided to occupy some strategic military positions in Paris. Also, during the *Commune*, an implicit status quo was observed between the *communards* and the occupying troops. Lissagaray, an exalted patriot and an advocate of all-out resistance against the Prussians, actually recognized the reality of negotiations between the *Commune* and the Prussian Army, which did nothing to stop the *communard* militia when it occupied the Fort of Vincennes, theoretically under Prussian jurisdiction. Rougerie's arguments refer more to the National Guard than to the *Commune* as a whole. And, if the Guard was the crucial element of the insurrection during the two month process of the Commune, the main enemy was clearly identified as Versailles whose army was the real threat to the *communards*. On this particular point, Rougerie's view is probably biased by his source – the proceedings of the trials. Most *communards* used their republican and patriotic motivations as an argument to justify their action, playing down social and political principles in the hope of alleviating their punishment. In fact, the *Commune* co-existed with the Prussians. Yet this reality does not mean that the *communards* were the accomplices of the invader; as the reactionary press tried to make believe. In fact, Bismarck consciously facilitated the repression of the *Commune* by repatriating 60,000 war prisoners to make possible the reconstruction of the Versailles army. Once the

Commune was defeated, during the *Semaine Sanglante*, the Prussians stopped hundreds of escaping *communards*, sending them back to their killers. So there was no complicity between the *Commune* and the Prussian army but a common convenience to wait and see. The Parisian people hated the Prussians, but did not resist the foreign occupation: they used their situation to denounce the government of Versailles which was more willing to mobilize an army against Paris than against Berlin.

The *Commune* was born in a context of patriotic exaltation and republican ideals, but the *communards* died for the freedom of their city and the welfare of their people.

The Adversary of the Commune

The general line of our argument on the historical significance of the *Commune* appears to be strongly reinforced by the *communards'* own definition of their social adversary. Let us begin by stating the adversary was neither the bourgeoisie, nor the capitalists. And such a lack of direct opposition was reciprocated by the capitalists. On the contrary, during the massive arrests after the *Commune*, industrial entrepreneurs often went to the police to give personal letters and favourable statements to guarantee the 'good morality' of their workers, frequently obtaining their freedom. It is obvious that such a 'generosity' was influenced by the shortage in skilled workers in a city ready to go back to the serious business of capitalist development. Yet the bourgeoisie's attitude was a clear sign that this was not a direct confrontation between capital and the industrial proletariat, since each time such a confrontation occurred, the entrepreneurs were the first to ask for exemption from punishment of labour militants.

In fact, those apparently possessed by hatred against the *communards* during the savage repression that followed their defeat were the urban landlords and their janitors (the universally hated Parisian *concierges*). The unpaid rents of the Commune period were brutally punished with tenants categorically denounced as '*communards*' and exposed to possible imprisonment, deportation, or, in the early days, execution. The *Commune* of Paris holds the dubious title of being the most repressed rent strike in history.

For the *communards*, the enemy was also the speculator, the stockpiling merchant, the smuggler, the lender, the merchant who betted on the misery of the families to seize their scarce property, or the lender who charged abusive interest, exploiting dramatic needs. In sum, the enemy was the manipulator of the rules of exchange, not the one who appropriated the means of production. The *communards* opposed the ugly merchant, not the exploitative capitalist.

But the main enemies, as the violence of the *Commune* clearly emphasized, were the priests and the police – that is, the personal expressions of the *ancien régime*, the controllers of everyday life, the accountants of the old morality. They were the ones who were taken hostage and were the ones who were shot when the despair of defeat joined the desire for revenge against the coming massacre. Here we are still in the midst of the French Revolution – the obsession with the reactionary Church that had survived the rise of liberty and with a bureaucratic state that was rebounding with even greater repressive powers. To overcome the backwardness of rural France, it was necessary to curb the Church's cultural hegemony. To supersede a centralized state, it was essential to crush its police. For the *Commune* of Paris surplus value was a historical abstraction, but the *curé* and the *gendarme* were the daily nightmares and obvious targets.

This was not then a proletarian and socialist revolution unaware of its own historical meaning, but a popular citizen revolution, fighting for municipal freedom and for social justice and to defend the Republic against the *ancien régime*. Was it, at the same time, an 'urban revolution' and if so, in what sense? And what do we add to the historical knowledge by proposing such an interpretation?

An Urban Revolution

The *Commune* of Paris was an urban revolution at three different levels. First of all, it was a movement in opposition to the entire rural society, that is not only to the dominating classes but to the totality of classes and groups that formed the social world of the French countryside in the nineteenth century. Not only was it an urban based movement, but a mobilization self-defined as Parisian, in spite of the fact that three-quarters of the *communards* arrested were born in the provinces. Such a 'Parisianism' was not a form of primitive localism, but the affirmation of a local society whose economic and social development required a large auto-nomy in relationship to a political order based on an elected parliament, in which the interests of local societies far behind the level of social development and political consciousness reached by Paris still predominated. In fact, the established tradition of French centralism has always created a gap between Paris and the provinces, so that the problem of the centre and of the periphery have never been placed in the same historical problematic. In the *Commune* of Paris there was little intra-industrial opposition (bourgeoisie versus proletariat) nor a confrontation between the industrial and agricultural worlds. There was, instead, a political opposition between the city and the countryside, even if the Parisian bourgeoisie scared by the process of social radicalization of the *Commune*, finally rallied the dominant rural classes.

There was a second urban dimension of the *Commune*, closer to our contemporary concerns, and its most popular demand: the cancellation of rents, and through this measure, the claim to curb the speculation associated with the housing crisis. It was, as we have said, the first official measure approved by the *Commune*. To understand the significance of the matter, we should remember the conditions which were present in Paris at the end of the Second Empire.[51] The situation was characterized by an accelerated process of urban growth that brought to the city hundreds of thousands of poor provincial immigrants with no place to live. Many of these Parisians were those same construction workers and labourers that formed the main con-tingent of the *communards*. They were particularly sensitive to the housing issues, since they were the producers of an essential good to which they hardly had access. Furthermore, the housing crisis was not only caused by the massive immigration from the provinces but was also the consequence of massive displacement resulting from Haussmann's gigantic restructuring of Paris.[52] He opened up the city by tracing the grand boulevards, undertook public works so that the urban area could be expanded, and provided public services so that real estate busi-nesses could build, buy, sell, and make fantastic profits. Land speculation became the most important field of investment for financial capital, and was for many years counted *the* sub-stantial 'game to play'. With such a grandiose scheme and such immediate incentives, the city was rapidly transformed. Popular neighbourhoods disappeared or were gentrified. The new bourgeoisie in Paris expanded towards the West, on the ruins of the old *faubourgs*. The intra-urban exodus of displaced tenants rejoined the flow of immigrants to overcrowd the remaining popular wards, particularly at Belleville in the East, Montmartre in the North, and around the Butte-aux-Cailles, in the South-east: they all became the key points of the *Commune*.

The landlords took advantage of the acuteness of the housing crisis. They packed the tenants into dilapidated, tiny apartments; they charged very high rents; they policed the buildings with their *concierges*; and they proceeded to evict immediately those who delayed payments, since a very tight market guaranteed them full occupancy.

Given this background, the indignation of the Parisians is easily understood, when on 13 March 1871, the Parliament of Versailles passed a law authorizing eviction of tenants who had not paid their rent during the siege of Paris. Not only did they foresee a tidal wave of forceful evictions (that actually took place after the *Commune*), but such a law underlined the corruption of a government actively committed to the speculators. The real estate businesses remaking Paris for their profit and the landlords disciplining their tenants were much more immediate sources of concern for the people of Paris than the industrial shadow of capitalist exploitation.

Nevertheless if we are entitled to consider the *Commune* of Paris as an urban social movement, this is because it was primarily a municipal revolution, as we have tried to argue. By municipal revolution we mean a popular mobilization aimed at radically transforming the political institutions that represented the local society, both in their internal organization and in their relationship to the central state. *Vis-à-vis* the state, the *Commune* claimed the right to local autonomy and the extension of local governments' administration over all spheres of social life. *Vis-à-vis* the people, the *Commune* asked for the democratization of political institutions, advocating the permanent participation of citizens in the municipal government by means of a decentralization of power towards the ward committees.

At the third (and more general) level, the reconstruction of the state on the basis of the communal model was at stake. For the *Commune* of Paris, the city was essentially a particular political culture, a form of popular democracy, articulating grassroots democracy and representative democracy to reorganize the nation by the connection between successive levels of political delegation. Some observers and political personalities have blamed the lack of effectiveness of the *Commune* on the absence of a coherent revolutionary leadership.[53] In fact, the *Commune* elected a *Comite de Salut Public* with full powers: power that was never able to be exercised, since each ward and each administration acted autonomously and co-operated on the basis of reciprocal exchanges. When the *polytechnicien* Roussel, the Defense Delegate, tried to organize a unified and disciplined army, he was disobeyed, and finally arrested, by a National Guard that was used to electing its own chiefs. We can criticize the incapacity of the *communards* to seize state power and to keep it, but we cannot ignore their coherence in relationship to their own goals, namely the construction of new political institutions based upon the notions of federalism, municipalism, and popular participation. This coherence, and their stubborn refusal to rebuild a centralized state, made their defeat inevitable once the *Commune* was confined to Paris.

Thus, if by urban we understand,[54] at once, the reference to a specific spatial form (opposed to the rural form), the growing importance of a particular category of means of consumption (housing and urban services), and the autonomous political expression of a local and civil society (struggling to survive the pressures of the central state), we must accept that the *Commune* of Paris was an urban revolution, on the basis of historical discussion.

This seems to be the social meaning of the *Commune* in spite of the fact that the insurrection was triggered by a series of specific political events: the defeat in the war with Prussia; the breakdown of the Second Empire; and the hardships of the republican transition.

The *Commune* left a very important trace on the city, as well as on the politics and ideology of the twentieth century. Ideologically, the myth of the *Commune* simultaneously inspired the Marxist-Leninist theory of the state and that of self-managerial federalism – an unlikely combination. Politically, the fierce repression that followed the defeat of the *communards*[55] made the French labour movement and French socialism more revolutionary and more centralist: more revolutionary because the blood of the martyrs reminded them for many years of the difficulty of introducing an alternative social logic into a democratic state still dominated by a ruling class ready to kill to preserve its interests; more centralist because the municipal perspective had proved to be a failure – to succeed it was still necessary to climb to the summit of the political system. Such an understandable characterization, which resembled Tsarist Russia more than republican France, deeply influenced the political vision of the French left for decades. Municipal politics were considered as a mere step towards 'real' power, given the conception of the state as a crude instrument of power. The underestimation of the importance of processes of local civil societies and indeed the tendency to ignore issues of everyday life was characteristic of those plotting the avenues to state power. The consequences were very grave for the chances of developing a new cultural hegemony and a new political legitimacy for the socialist project in France.

The defeat of the *Commune* also had a dramatic lasting effect on the city of Paris. The government tightened its control, appointing the *Prefet de Police* to govern the city, and, in effect, the Parisians lost all political autonomy, something they only regained in 1977. And yet before giving back political freedom, the ruling elites took good care to favour the *embourgeoisement* of Paris through social segregation and urban renewal.[56] The absence of any power in the Parisian municipal institutions left the city without any defense against real estate speculation and, later on against the functional arrangements required to fulfil the needs of industrial and financial capital. As a result, Paris enjoys the most permanent housing crisis of all Western capitals. Thus the *Versaillais* finally conquered Paris. In April 1977, the first mayor of Paris with real power in almost 200 years was democratically elected. He was Jacques Chirac, the conservative leader of the neo-Gaullist right wing. Yet in 1977 only 1·5 million people were living in the city of Paris, as opposed to the total 9·4 million of the Paris Metropolitan Area. The remaining millions were living in the suburbs, most of them governed by socialist-communist municipal councils. They are the real heirs of the *Commune*.

The *Commune* is still alive fulfilling the wish cried by the *communards* at the time of their execution. It lives on as a message that the city exists against the state. It says as well that if most social movements are not class struggles (the Commune itself was not), they often challenge those institutions which are used both to control peoples' everyday life and to organize the power of the ruling classes. Because of this we can understand how an urban revolution became such a source of inspiration for the labour movement. The experience of the *Commune* nourished working class consciousness when it came to confronting the major obstacle to be met beyond the gates of the factory: the state. The labour movement, relying on its historical role as the class of producers and strengthened by the experience of industrial discipline, would eventually be able to successfully fight the capitalist state, penetrating it in parts and destroying it in others. Yet, by the same historical process, the working class movement was itself penetrated or absorbed by the state in many countries and at different levels. The *Commune*, at once an archaic urban revolt and an anticipatory communal Utopia, sank in a sea of blood. But its themes of grassroots participation and municipal democracy are today more appealing to us than the anthem of proletarian dictatorship, whose only lasting sounds are those of the chains forged on its behalf. Yet the labour movement could not accomplish the municipal revolution and nor could the *Commune*, an urban social movement, undertake the socialist revolution.

4

The Industrial City and the Working-Class: The Glasgow Rent Strike of 1915

Few historical events offer such a direct link between social struggle and urban policy as the one observed between the Glasgow Rent Strike of 1915 and the intervention of the British state in the housing field. Under the pressures of war, the social tensions accumulated in the second largest city of the British empire[57] and exploded in 1915, taking the form, among other conflicts, of one of the most important rent strikes in urban history. Starting in April 1915, it involved, at its peak in November, some 20,000 households, primarily concentrated in the working-class communities of the Clydeside area. It was organized by tenants' committees and women's associations, with the full support of the trade unions and left wing parties.

On 25 December 1915, a Rents and Mortgage Interest Restriction Act was approved, establishing rent control for low-cost housing. Under even more pressing claims, with particularly militant mobilization in the industrial areas throughout the country, Parliament passed a Housing and Town Planning Act in 1919, mandating local governments to build housing for the workers and providing the necessary funds. For the first time in history, housing was considered a right for the people, and the state was held responsible for it. Public housing was born.

To be sure, the Glasgow Rent Strike by itself could not produce such a dramatic shift in the urban policy of the British state. Municipal housing had been a demand of the Labour Movement for many years,[58] and C.G. Pickvance rightly reminds us of the convergence of different social interests and historical circumstances in the formation of a reform oriented housing policy: first, the convenience for industrial capital to deal with a housing shortage that was putting pressure on wages and provoking workers' unrest; second, the general high level of working class militancy; and third, the effort of national unity and steady production required by the war, something that had created a favourable attitude in the government towards urban renters' demands aimed at correcting speculation.[59] Yet the process of working class mobilization in Glasgow, and its powerful expression in the Rent Strike, seems to have been the immediate historical factor imposing a new housing policy against financial and real estate interests.

In spite of the fact that the housing crisis was a source of problems for the industrialists, any attempt by the state to interfere with the market forces had been successfully opposed until 1915. It was only when a social challenge appeared at the grassroots level that the power relationships were altered and the state was forced to intervene in the provision of housing.[60] How responsive this intervention was to the fundamental issues raised by the strikers was another matter – that we will discuss in a further step of the analysis.[61] We need first to recall some of the basic trends of the Rent Strike in order to consider the manner in which a conscious working class movement, in the very core of the process of capitalist industrialization, dealt with the city under the new conditions of urban industrial growth.

Such an analysis is apparently an easy task, at least from the point of view of the sources, since the Glasgow Rent Strike is a classic subject in the scholarly tradition of British social history. Yet only recently, historical research has attempted to deal with the questions that are relevant to an exploration of the relationships between social movements and the evolution of cities – the role of the working class, the connection with the women's movement, the influence of socialist parties, the interaction between the struggles in production and those in consumption, the role of the state *vis-à-vis* different factions of the propertied classes, and so on. We are now able to answer many of these questions on the basis of reliable evidence thanks to the invaluable research carried out by Joseph Melling, of the University of Glasgow, whose findings have been partially reported in a series of papers, some of them still unpublished.[62] A synthesis of existing research on the rent strike by Sean Damer[63] offers an interesting alternative view to Melling's interpretation while still converging toward the same empirical description of the phenomenon. It is on the basis of this very rich historical material that we will attempt some reflections on the interaction between class struggle and urban movements under the conditions of early industrial capitalism.

The Rent Strike

Around the turn of the century, the boom in shipbuilding and naval engineering production required by imperial expansion, dramatically accelerated industrial and demographic growth in the Clydeside region. Housing construction did not follow at the same pace. Furthermore, in 1911, in the midst of the urban crisis, 11 per cent of Glasgow's housing stock remained vacant for reasons of speculation. As a result, housing conditions rapidly deteriorated in Glasgow. Workers lived in overcrowded flats which were built on speculation over a very short period in the nineteenth century. In this sense, the housing crisis in Glasgow was particularly acute. Local landlords and rentiers obtained more benefit by overcrowding existing habitations with the masses of uprooted Highlanders and Irish people coming to the city in search of jobs, than by building new housing with longer and uncertain rates of return. For instance, between 1912 and 1915, while the population increased by 65,000 persons, only 1,500 housing units were built.[64] Since 70 per cent of the population was already living in overcrowded one or two room houses which were becoming increasingly dilapidated, the landlords found themselves in a situation of virtual monopoly. The rents rose to such a degree that even stable and well-to-do communities, including artisans and engineers, came under pressure and joined the slum areas in their anger over residential conditions. Their move highlighted an issue to which the British working class had been very sensitive for several decades,[65] particularly in Glasgow.[66] As early as 1885, at the time when the Royal Commission on Housing of the Working Class was discovering the gravity of the problem, socialist militants in Glasgow were demanding legislation and subsidies to build municipal housing. Supported by the Glasgow Trades Council, the Scottish Housing Council was organized in 1900, in connection with the Workmen's National Council founded in England in 1898 by three members of the Marxist Social Democratic Federation.[67]

Under pressure from the trade unions, a House Letting and Rating Act was approved in 1911. It gave some legal protection to the tenants and allowed monthly lets for low-income dwellings. Letting by month was a long-standing demand from tenants, who were previously forced to commit themselves to a year's rent payment while unable to foresee the stability of their jobs. Yet landlords immediately took advantage of the new law to increase rents more often. Housing protests mounted. In 1911 a City Labour Party was organized with housing reform as the main point in its programme. In 1913, John Wheatley, a Labour Party Town Councillor, published a leaflet, *£8 Cottages for Glasgow Citizens*, which proposed subsidized housing for workers on the basis of revenues obtained by the city from the municipalization of tramways. More radical were the measures requested by John McLean, Glasgow's Marxist leader, whose party, the Social Democratic Federation (SDF), organized in 1913 the Scottish Federation of Tenants' Associations to fight against rent increases and to ask for state provision of housing. Yet the major pre-war organizational effort came in 1914 when the Independent Labour Party (ILP) Housing Committee and the Women's Labour League formed the Glasgow Women's Housing Association, which became the driving force of the Rent Strike under the leadership of women such as Mary Barbour, Mary Laird, Mrs. Ferguson, and Helen Crawfurd.

The war sharpened the angles of industrial and urban contradictions in the city. The location in Clydeside of the munitions industry brought 16,000 new workers into Glasgow and 4,000 others into the suburbs. The landlords again took advantage of the new housing shortage to increase their rents by 23 per cent in the industrial areas of Govan and Partick surrounding the shipyards, where the impact of rent increases was particularly severe.

As labour unrest increased in the factories in defense of the workers' union rights threatened by the government's new war-time disciplinary measures,[68] the abuses practised by the landlords appeared to be an intolerable provocation. The ILP took the initiative of the protest, and in January 1915, under the leadership of Andrew McBride, organized a Housing Conference attended by 450 delegates who supported the Wheatley proposal for subsidized housing and opposed rent increases. To implement the demands, a Glasgow Labour Party Housing Committee was founded, with the full support of the Glasgow Trades Council. Yet the transition from this central initiative to the Rent Strike was operated by a series of grassroots organizations that was created in working class communities, generally as a result of initiatives taken by women. According to Melling, '. . . the vital links between the local housewives such as Mary Barbour and the Labour Party were the network of committees which emerged at this time. The Ward Committees were already functioning in the late nineteenth century, and Labour Representation Committees were being established, but to these were added the committees of the Women's Housing Association and the Tenants' Defense Committees.'[69] The same fact is confirmed by Sean Damer and Iain McLean. On the basis of this grassroots support, the Rent Strike started in May 1915 in the heavily industrial area of Govan, where many skilled workers lived. From its beginning the Strike comprised the refusal to pay the increase in rents, mass protection against evictions of strikers, if necessary through violent confrontation, and street demonstrations in support of the Labour proposals for a new housing policy. A contemporary witness, Gallagher, cited by Damer, reports the intensity of popular mobilization: 'All day long in the streets, in the halls, in the houses, meetings were held. Kitchen meetings, street meetings, mass meetings, meetings of every kind. No halt, no rest for anyone, all in preparation for the sitting of the court when the test case came on. As in the streets, so in the factories, will we allow the factors to attack our wages?'[70]

This powerful mobilization took place in a very peculiar context – the initial stages of the First World War, whose effects were keenly felt in a city that claimed some of the key military production sites. In fact the impact of this context on the movement proved a contradictory one.

The war created certain constraints on social protest by making it difficult to strike in the factories under the quasi-military regulations and the potential charges of sabotaging the nations' effort.[71] On the other hand, the rent strikers could legitimately argue against the rapacity of landlords who were taking unfair advantage of the housing scarcity stimulated by the war, while putting unbearable pressures on families often deprived of their young men who were serving in the armed forces. In fact, the first violent protest in the Govan district took place in April, to resist the eviction of a soldier's family. Evictions, repeatedly attempted by the landlords with the support of the police force, were the events that built the solidarity of the residents. Women engaged in attacks against the factors and sheriffs' men who came to evict tenants, pelting them with rubbish, flour and anything else they could lay their hands on from the home. In Govan, for instance, the sheriff's men attempted the eviction of a widow and son at Merryland Street on 18 October, when Mary Barbour, of the Glasgow Womens Housing Association was addressing a meeting nearby, 'The officers were assaulted with peasemeal, flour, and whiting, and after a confrontation between Mrs. Barbour and the officers, the latter visited the house and then withdrew.'[72]

In early summer, mass demonstrations expressed the strength of the movement that in August had reached, according to Ann and Vincent Flynn, a wide variety of communities.[73] Besides Govan and Partick, strongholds of engineers and skilled workers, tenants on strike were reported in Parkhead, Pollokshaws, Pollok, Cowcaddens, Kelvingrove, Ibrox, Govanhill, St. Rollox, Townhead, Springburn, Maryhill, Fairfield, Blackfriars, and Woodside. As Damer points out, 'What is interesting to note about these areas of the city is that they are markedly different: heavily industrial areas, more respectable artisanal areas, and slum areas.'[74]

In October 15,000 people were on rent strike. On 7 October a massive demonstration converged on St. Enoch's Square, under women's leadership. The Municipal Corporation alerted the government of the seriousness of the situation. An official committee was appointed to report on the rent issue in the Clydeside, under the chairmanship of a judge, Lord Hunter, the former liberal representative from the Govan district. The landlords, realizing the need to negotiate, moved against the rent strikes and pressed for new legal evictions in order to arrive at the bargaining table in a favourable position. In fact they inadvertently stiffened the movement and broadened its popular support. In November 1915 the number of rent strikers reached 20,000, and the massive resistance against legal repression almost assumed insurgent proportions. On 17 November a group of 49 strikers were legally compelled to appear before the sheriff, among them William Reid, Secretary of the Tenants' Defense Committee. They were accompanied by a crowd of 10,000 people who marched around George Square and massed in front of the City Chambers to listen to several speakers, including John McLean, the Marxist leader of the SDF. The situation became increasingly explosive because the trade unions were threatening to respond with strikes in the factory if the police attempted massive repression, disregarding the war-time regulations established for the munitions industry. William Reid, both a shop steward and a tenants' leader had already notified the corporations with a clear warning in relationship to the industrial workers' attitude, 'The temper of the men was such that, in the event of wholesale evictions taking place . . . they would not hesitate not only to prevent evictions, but to influence Parliament by every other means in their power. There could be no greater calamity at the present time than any stoppage of labour by men engaged in the engineering and shipbuilding industries, but as a last resort, . . . the men would rather take that risk than see the wives and children of soldiers being put into the street by the rapacity of the housewives in Glasgow.'[75]

As Melling correctly observes, 'Here lay the strength of the workers and the secret of the Rent Strike's success. Not only was there a common identity between many shipbuilding, engineering, and munition workers (often working for the same firm), but also between the point of production and the communities where the workers lived.'[76]

At the end of the 17 November demonstration, all legal actions against striking tenants were dropped. The State Secretary for Scotland, McKinnon Wood, asked the cabinet to freeze all rents at the pre-war level. On 25 November, a Rents and Mortgage Interest Restriction Bill was introduced in the British parliament. It received the Royal Assent on 25 December 1915. The 1919 Act, reacting to the contained working class protest over housing, extended the scope of state intervention, introducing the programme of council housing through which municipal governments were going to shelter the majority of manual workers in the following decades.[77] Furthermore, when in 1917, new housing for munition workers had to be built in Gretna, 100 miles south of Glasgow, it was carefully planned as an innovative garden city for working class people, apparently in response to the unrest in the Glasgow factories.

Beyond the obvious significance of this historic social struggle, and also beyond the romantic myth that surrounds it, we should characterize its components and dynamics and absorb some of the lessons it provides for our understanding of urban change.

A Working Class Struggle for the Reproduction of its Labour Power

As with all major social movements, the significance of the Glasgow Rent Strike has many facets.[78] Yet the most salient feature is its character as a movement of the industrial working class defending its living conditions in the sphere of consumption. This is not the case for many urban conflicts, even in the period of early capitalist industrialization. As John Foster usefully reminds us, London could hardly be considered primarily an industrial city at the turn of the century, and its urban problem was more dominated by the accumulation and management of capital than by the reproduction of labour power.[79] Glasgow, on the contrary, closely resembles the model of the capitalist city as formulated by some Marxist theory.[80] This is one of the most interesting aspects of the study of the Glasgow Strike on a more general, theoretical level.

The rent strikers were industrial workers, men and women, and their families were residents of workers' communities directly linked to local labour markets dominated by the shipyards, engineering factories, and munitions industries, most of them huge units of production. These plants were heavily unionized, and by the time of the Rent Strike had become the stronghold of the shop stewards' movement. Furthermore, the backbone of the movement was formed by areas such as Govan and Partick which had a majority of artisans, engineers, and craftsmen, namely the labour aristocracy.[81]

This observation is crucial when related to a major trend taking place at the same time in the factories. Because of the war, the government, in agreement with the industrialists, was breaking down the old privileges of the craft unions, simultaneously provoking a determined resistance from the traditional skilled workers and the homogenization of the working class. In so doing the government also, unwittingly, laid the ground for the new form of labour organization around elected shop stewards.[82] Since the craft unions were organized on the basis of the community, and since artisans and skilled workers were the main support of the ILP[83], we could easily sustain the hypothesis that the Rent Strike was a form of manifestation of old labour unionism in a sphere where the confrontation was less dramatic than in the factories under war-time government discipline. As a matter of fact, the industrial revolt that developed in the same period, under the leadership of the radical Workers' Committee, was severely repressed in 1916 and some of its leaders were imprisoned or exiled.[84] We are not contrasting here, as some authors have done, a radical shop stewards' movement centred on production issues with a reformist, craftsmen-inspired protest focused upon consumption.[85] In fact some of the tenants' leaders were also active shop stewards in the factories. What we are saying, instead, is that the Rent Strike provided a broad common ground for the unity of the different segments of the working class at the community level, and at the very moment when workers were weakened within the factories both by the recomposition of the work process and by the dramatic altering of the procedures for unionization and labour representation. Yet the success of the Rent Strike was due largely to the clear support of the trade unions and to the potential threat of industrial strikes. As a demonstration of this crucial point, when some years later, in 1922, about 20,000 tenants went on a rent strike again in Clydebank, they suffered a severe defeat because the local trade unions did not provide their support to this struggle.[86]

Thus the 1915 Rent Strike was overtly a working class mobilization, but in dealing with the harsh social conditions that had been imposed on workers for decades, was mainly directed towards consumption issues. Besides suffering overcrowding, dilapidation, and poor sanitary conditions, workers were subjected to continuous rent increases each time a new wave of industrial growth tightened the housing market. Non-payment of rents was severely punished by eviction and confiscation of the renter's property by the landlord under the hated 'Law of Urban Hypothec', leading to practices that even hardline landlords considered to be '. . . really barbarous and absolutely unproductive.'[87] Furthermore, the housing struggles had been connected from the beginning of the century with the opposition to increasingly high payments of municipal rates for public services such as gas, water and the police.[88]

Thus the struggle for decent, affordable housing and convenient public services, as a citizen's right enforced and satisfied by the state, clearly addressed the basic issues that recent research has characterized as the key elements of the process of collective consumption.[89] An organized and militant working class fighting for the reproduction of its labour power, and appealing to the state for the provision of its collective welfare, represents the first major social trend underlying the Glasgow Rent Strike.

A Women's Movement

All observers and historians agree – the Glasgow Rent Strike was organized, led, and enacted by women. Between the creation of the Glasgow Women's Housing Association in 1914 and the end of 1915, they had recruited over 3,000 members. Women were on the offensive regarding the housing issue. They were the ones leading the demonstrations carrying the banners of the great march on St. Enoch's Square on 7 October 1915 which read, 'Our husbands, sons and brothers are fighting the Prussians of Germany. We are fighting the Prussians of Partick. Only Alternative: Municipal Housing.'[90] They were also the women who launched the violent attacks against House factors trying to evict families.[91] The women were also the ones who called for the support of factory workers when it was necessary, 'Mrs. Barbour *got the men* from the shipyards in Govan to come to the street where the House Factor's offices was located, and they met with the woman and demanded a return of the money. On the Factor being shown the thousands of black faced workers crowding the street, he handed it over.'[92]

Who were these women? Many of them were housewives, or wives of skilled workers such as Mary Barbour. Others were widows of soldiers, left to sustain a family. A large number of them were factory workers themselves, called to work in industrial jobs to replace the men who had gone to war. Some were suffragettes, such as Helen Crawfurd, who had been in jail three times for her militant actions before the war.

Yet no feminist demands have been recorded as having been expressed by the movement. Women were the actors, not the subjects, of the protest. They claimed the right to live for their families and they were the agents of a consumption orientated protest, as a continuation of their role as consumption agents within the family, even when they were workers at the same time. They did not address the issue of sexually-based inequality in their demands. To be sure, the process itself probably transformed women's perception about themselves as well as their

Plate 4.1 Rent strikers at St. Enoch's Square, Glasgow, October 1915. (Originally printed in the Glasgow Bulletin. Photography supplied by the Mitchell Library and the Glasgow Herald.)

role in the community. Nevertheless if a social movement needs a conscious self-definition as such, we can describe the Glasgow strike as a women's movement that fell short of being a feminist movement.

But the fact that the movement was women-based was decisive to the unification of work and residence, factories and housing, and created the conditions for a successful social struggle. Women understood the social character of the consumption process, going beyond the short-comings of a wage-directed demand at the point of production. And they organized and mobilized politically, mainly through the Labour Party, for municipal housing. Such vision and tactics – linking the factory, the community and the state with a combination of direct action and institutional politics – is a rare occurrence in the early stages of working class mobilization, and our hypothesis is that they were related to the women's perception and consciousness of social experience.

Why did women have such a powerful and ultimately decisive role in the Glasgow Rent Strike? Some of the conditions seem to be ideological and political, with early feminism and socialism developing among the younger generations. But, at the level of the thousands of women who participated in the movement, the basic factor seems to have been the massive entry of women into the work force to replace men at war. Not only did existing privileges have to be forgotten, but women were in a stronger position because they were the breadwinners of many families. Furthermore, with the men far away, the social world of single women was suddenly enlarged, which made it possible not only to become aware of the social problems but to have the individual autonomy to deal with them. In fact the end of the war represented a serious setback both for the women's movement and for their contribution to social struggles; as Melling writes, in a very perceptive passage, '[After the war] if authority relations were to be restored at work and in local settlements, then the imagery of tranquil domesticity and the sexual division of labour was one step towards 'normalcy'. The renewal of rent strikes and violent direct action involving women after 1918 again demonstrated the deficiencies in this cultural offensive, but the mass unemployment of females pressed them back into customary defensive positions. There could be no return to the practices of pre-1914, as widespread aversion to domestic service in the twenties showed, but women undoubtedly lost much of their bargaining freedom with the declaration of peace and the resurgence of the sectionalism in industry and unions.'[93]

The Glasgow Rent Strike showed the possibility and the potential of combining production-based struggles and consumption-orientated issues in a comprehensive social movement. It also showed that women were the strategic agents of this type of social mobilization. But their continuing role as such seems to require the explicit assumption of women's specific goals by their movement, something that did not happen in Glasgow.

A Left Wing Political Movement

A very popular movement with its base in the working class, the Glasgow Rent Strike was not a spontaneous uprising. It was prepared and organized by left wing political parties that had agitated about housing issues for many years. The most predominant force was the ILP, whose growing influence between 1906 and 1915 was clearly related to its housing campaigns, particularly after Andrew McBride founded the Labour Party Housing Committee in 1913. In 1914, Mary Laird, of the Women's Labour League, became one of the founders of the Glasgow Women's Housing Association. And, as we wrote, the launching of the housing campaign that led to the Rent Strike took place in the Labour Party Housing Conference in January 1915. It was largely on the housing issue that the ILP built up a basis of municipal power that, along with the support of the trade unions, brought it to national government in 1923 and 1929.

Along with the ILP other socialist groups actively participated in the movement, particularly the Marxist SDF whose leader, John McLean, one of the most popular speakers during the Rent Strike, became the first consul of the Soviet Union in Glasgow, before being forced into exile.[94]

Furthermore, beyond partisan membership, a political vanguard seems to have been present within the Rent Strike movement, as Sean Damer has argued.[95] They formed a group, that became the recognizable and well-respected leadership of the strike and of the working class and women-based mobilization surrounding it. For some, the coming social revolution was the target. For others it was the reinforcement of the Labour Party and the winning of local elections that became the immediate task. Altogether their impact largely determined the majority obtained by Labour and Communist councillors in the 1930s in the town councils of Clydeside. Their vision of the political scene, their capacity to connect local struggles and national politics, and their relationships to a variety of constituencies, were key factors in the success of the Strike. But even more important for the analyst is the observation of a creative articulation between a highly political leadership and a grassroots movement able to set up its own democratic mechanisms of mobilization and decision. Political leadership and grassroots democracy do not seem to be incompatible but actually reinforce each other – at least in the crucial historical experience of Glasgow in 1915.

Capital, Rents and the Working Class

A working class movement, mobilizing women and politically aimed at imposing a dramatic change in state policies on behalf of people's needs – all these trends seem to point towards a major social movement, both in terms of its characteristics and its social effects. Yet its relationship to the process of class struggle is much more complex. The great paradox of the Glasgow Strike is that, although unquestionably a working class struggle, it can hardly be considered a struggle against capital, in that it did not oppose the capitalists. The point, overwhelmingly demonstrated by Melling, and empirically unchallenged by Damer in spite of his radically different interpretation, is that the industrial employers of Clydeside actually supported the rent control demands and the programme for state subsidized housing.[96] In fact they had been concerned for a long time that the housing crisis made it more difficult to attract skilled workers and created additional pressure on wages. They were engaged themselves in the construction of housing for their workers and did not follow local landlords in raising rents beyond the limits of the workers' means. Although during the strike they were concerned by the potential growth of social unrest and the political consequences of the process, they actually supported the proposal for housing reform explicitly as a means of ensuring social peace and creating channels for the integration of a militant working class. They recognized the incapacity of a free market to successfully provide and they encouraged the state's initiatives in the field of unprofitable but necessary consumption of goods and services.

The enemies of rent strikers were not the capitalists but the landlords, and individual speculators who were actually the extension of small rentiers. Two-thirds of Glasgow housing was built by individual owners borrowing money from small bondholders who were charging increasingly high interest. This explains both the inadequacy of the housing production and the harshness of the landlords who had to collect their rents in order to pay their interest. As well as this class of wealthy urban rentiers, the strikers also had to face the building industry, a very small business sector operating on an *ad hoc* basis under the control of the landlords. As Melling says, 'Although the Rents and Housing Legislations have to be seen in one sense as working class victories against the forces of property, they were not defeats for the employers as such. The bondholders and petty investors of Glasgow were probably the real losers rather than the great industrialists who won large contracts, acquired state aid for house building and avoided major stoppages. The legislation represented concessions to workers, but they were concessions that employers could well afford.'[97]

Pickvance has summarized the existing evidence on the attitudes of different groups towards the Rent Control Act in Parliament. Industrial capital clearly supported it.[98] Banks opposed it as a matter of principle against the interference of the state in the financial markets at any level. In fact they obtained some major legal corrections to protect the money lenders. The individual landlords and the building industry were most seriously hurt, and in the following years this led to an even deeper crisis in the private housing market, thereby reinforcing the need for municipal housing. In this sense the Rent Strike actually produced a rationalization of the circuits of capitalist production, in line with the strategy of most entrepreneurial capitalists whose aim was to extract surplus value from workers instead of just squeezing earnings from the families.

Yet we would be mistaken to consider the Glasgow struggle only from this angle. The level of social consciousness and organization reached by the working class through the struggle, the capacity of the labour movement to impose its own conditions on the process of consumption, and the definition of new social rights to which the state should respond were all major achievements for the working class as a class. Thus, from this point of view, the Glasgow Rent Strike contributed to a general weakening of the capitalist class *vis-à-vis* the labour movement in the overall set of power relationships. Also the rent strikers often presented themselves as workers fighting against capital.[99] So both from the point of view of the movement and from the point of view of its political effects, the Rent Strike appears as an episode of the class struggle. Yet the absence of any direct confrontation with the dominant factions of the capital, the deviation of the demands towards the request for state intervention, and the actual support of the capitalists for the new housing policies, clearly challenge any interpretation of the Glasgow Rent Strike as an anti-capitalist movement. The housing crisis being a secondary contradiction under the conditions of early capitalism[99bis] the emphasis on urban issues led to reformist orientations to which enlightened capital and empowered labour could agree, when and if both were still able to expand. Curiously enough the radical wing of the rent strikers probably pushed the housing struggle forward on the assumption of the correctness of Engels' analysis of the impossibility for capitalism to solve the housing crisis.[100] The Glasgow experience actually showed that, under conditions of working class pressure, the capitalist state could substantially improve the housing conditions but without being able to eliminate the urban crisis as a whole, particularly because of the continuing historical redefinition of social needs.

The consequence of the movement was therefore to give birth to some of the earliest manifestations of the Welfare State. A production-based movement, focused on consumption issues, instigated social reform within capitalism. The movement which counterposed the state against the speculators actually furthered the integration of the political representatives of labour within the historical framework of liberal democracy. The priority of urban goals under the conditions of industrial capitalism seem to have fostered social compromise and political participation more than class struggle and political revolution.

Conclusion: The Urban View of a Working Class Movement

The Glasgow Rent Strike shows clearly the intimate connection between industrialization and urbanization under the conditions of capitalist development. The housing crisis was caused by compulsory urban industrial concentration and urban rentier's speculation and triggered powerful working class struggles around the provision of shelter and public services. These urban struggles were based on the organization of labour both in the factories and in the workers' residential communities. Some of these communities had a very strong cultural identity, particularly those where artisans and craftsmen had built a pattern of social interaction around their productive skills.

Yet neither the Glasgow Rent Strikes nor the housing struggles that spread all over industrial Britain can be seen as reactions of community defense or projects for local political autonomy. The city had become dominated by the logic of industrial capital. The working class was challenging such a logic less in terms of their cultural forms than in relationship to the conditions of the appropriation of the product of its work. The rent strikers strove for control of speculators, decent and affordable public housing, convenient free urban services, and state intervention in the organization of people's consumption. The community as a cultural form, the city as a major political setting, were never at the centre of the Glasgow movement, but labour was calling to the state against the undesirable consequences of the capitalist market. For the movement's radical wing the Strike was also the launching platform for an anti-capitalist struggle. From the point of view of labour, the city had become a matter of collective consumption, and/or a step in the process of seizing state power. Reduced to the role of labour power sellers, the workers responded by broadening the scope and raising the level of their social wage. The city was for most of them little more than the spatial setting of their exploitation. Their communities were often refuges of solidarity and places for autonomous organization. But their goals and values shifted decisively to the production process and to the political struggle over the control of the central state.

The trade union movement became concerned with municipal administration in order to deliver better services to the workers. The city disappeared as a cultural entity, to be dissolved in the general process of class struggle between capital and labour. By generalizing the process of urbanization, and by submitting it to the logic of the productive forces, capitalist industrialization dramatically altered the social role of the city in history. Industrial workers, abruptly uprooted from a recent rural past, dreamed of village-like cottages while fighting to better reproduce their labour power, both in the factories and in their tenements.

While still being at the forefront of people's daily life, the urban problem became a somewhat marginal issue for the new historical dynamics of class struggle. The urban view of the working class was clearly dominated by the struggle over consumption and by the appeal to the state. For the first time in history, a major urban struggle could be won by the popular masses and still reinforce the rationality of the system without fundamentally challenging the interests of the dominant class. Urban issues had become a secondary contradiction in the structure of society and in the politics of the state.

5

The Dependent City and Revolutionary Populism: The Movimiento Inquilinario in Veracruz, Mexico, 1922

Between January and July of 1922, the majority of residents of the city of Veracruz, the first port of Mexico, took part in a massive urban protest organized by the tenants to pay lower rents and to obtain adequate repairs and maintenance of the buildings. Facing strong resistance from speculative landlords most of whom were foreigners (particularly Spaniards), the *inquilinarios* (tenants) set up grassroots committees, organized a tenants' union and closely allied their struggle to the emergent working class movement, and to anarchist and communist ideologies. Using the contradiction between the central government and the socialist populist governor of the state of Veracruz, they were able to organize most of the city's dwellers around their programme. When they were on the point of obtaining a major victory in the form of a rent control law, the government decided that the *inquilinarios* set a dangerous example in a volatile political situation and sent the army to violently repress the movement and jail its leaders.

However, in spite of its brief existence, the revolt of the *inquilinarios* was one of the richest urban struggles of twentienth century Latin America. Its study will make it possible to incorporate into our exploration of history the perspective of urban protest under the conditions of dependency,[101] by which we understand those cities whose dominant social dynamics basically rely on socio-political forces that are largely external to the institutional framework of their nation-state. By observing the process of social mobilization around the housing crisis of 1922 in Veracruz, we will be able to elaborate on the connection between the specific conditions of urban growth in Third World cities[102] and the emergence of populist movements as a major factor of the relationship between state and society in a post-colonial situation, thus significantly broadening the historical perspective of our research. Unfortunately there is very little scholarly work on the Veracruz experience and our analysis must be considered more an opportunity to include the questions posed by the *inquilinarios* in the general framework of our study, than as a contribution to Latin American urban history. Yet we have enough information to explore some hypotheses, particularly through the interesting historical monograph published by Octavio Garcia Mundo[103] and the data gathered by Moises Gonzales Navarro,[104] along with the thorough general analysis by Manuel Perlo on the relationship between housing and politics in Mexico between 1910 and 1950.[105] Additional precious information was obtained from two books written by witnesses of the movement, Rafael Ortega[106] and Arturo Bolio Trejo,[107] along with some historical sources cited in the Bibliography.

The Movement

'Estoy en Huelga y no pago renta esta es la ley de Heron Proal; y al que la pague le doy caballo para que no la vuelva a pagar . . .'	'I am on strike and I do not pay rent This is the law of Heron Proal; Whoever does pay rent I will beat up So that he will not pay it again . . .'
(Afro-Cuban rhythm sung by the rent strikers, Veracruz, 1922)	(Literal translation)

The rent strike in Veracruz was organized by a Revolutionary Tenant's Union, founded, led and profoundly influenced by Heron Proal, the so-called 'Mexican Lenin'.[108] Proal, in his mid-thirties at the time of the strike, and a tailor for the Veracruz seamen, had been a sailor. Although his ideology was roughly that of an anarchist, he considered himself a communist, participated in the congress of the recently founded Mexican Communist Party.[109] (The SRI – *Sindicato Revolucionario de Inquilinos* – declared itself under the sponsorship of the local section of the Communist Party.) Nevertheless, it would be a mistake to consider the SRI as a typical communist organization since, as we shall see, the movement exploded on the confrontation between Heron Proal and the local communist cadres. Furthermore, in spite of the organizational role of the SRI in the movement, the rent strike started spontaneously in January 1922, before the foundation of the SRI in February.

The first strike was launched in the *Patio San Salvador*, a tenement in the ward of *la Huaca*, the 'red light zone' (*zona de fuego*) where the numerous prostitutes of this port city lived.[109bis] In fact the prostitutes were the ones who really started the movement in a violent reaction against the rocketing rents they were paying for their miserable slums at a time of acute housing

Plate 5.1 The docks and slums of Veracruz, Mexico, 1908. (By kind permission of Professor A. Moreno-Toscano, Director of Archives, Archivo General de la Nacion, Estados Unidos Mexicanos, Ciudad de Mexico. Photograph: Mr Waite.)

shortages due to rapid urban growth. The slum lords had taken unfair advantage, as in the case of Glasgow, to increase the rents, refuse to make repairs, and evict the tenants as soon as they were unable to meet their payments. In the first weeks of 1922, when the police made a series of forceful evictions, popular discontent grew rapidly, particularly among the women. The mayor of Veracruz, Rafael Garcia, a labour leader, tried to respond to the demands by calling a meeting to organize the tenants and to set up an orderly protest. The meeting took place on 22 January at the 'People's Library' under the leadership of Dr. Reyes Barreiro, a friend of the mayor, and a moderate social reformer. The meeting was interrupted by several communist militants (Olmos, Sosa, Salinas) who called for a more radical form of protest. When the crowd ejected them from the room, they went looking for Heron Proal, whose prestige among the population was very high, and asked him to return with them to the meeting. Proal did so and addressed the audience:

'All property is a robbery! The house where we live is ours! We have already paid them in excess!'[110]

Plate 5.2 The market of Veracruz, Mexico, 1908. (By kind permission of the Director of Archives, Archivo General de la Nacion, Mexico. Photograph: Mr Waite.)

Many attendants left the room with Proal, who agreed to meet with them the following day in the Parque Juarez. Five hundred families turned out and the SRI was founded a few days later. It called on the population to stop paying their rent until the landlords agreed to negotiate a new system of rents contracted with the tenants' union. By March 1922, 55 per cent of the population of the city were supporting the rent strike. The tenants' group formed by the mayor dissolved itself to join Proal's effort. The movement obtained the neutrality and implicit support of the governor of the State of Veracruz, Colonel Adalberto Tejeda, a socialist-populist, whose position was rapidly heading towards conflict with the federal government and the moderate stand of President Alvaro Obregon.[110bis]

If the movement had been orginally restricted to demands on housing, the stubbornness of the landlords and the hostility of the local elite, loudly voiced in the local newspaper, *El Dictamen*, favoured a very rapid ideological radicalization of the *inquilinarios*, actively stimulated by the leader, Heron Proal. Housing demands were joined by a self-proclaimed class struggle for communism. At a more concrete level, the SRI's grassroots committees also extended their targets to the entire urban scene: they initiated a boycott against the tramway company to obtain a reduction in the cost of public transportation fares; squatted vacant housing; and organized 'price watching' committees to control the merchants, particularly in the

Plate 5.3 Heron Proal, leader of the Inquilinarios of Veracruz, aged 36, four years after the movement. (Photograph: J. Segarra.)

popular shops. At the same time, the movement repeatedly clashed with the police each time a rent striker was evicted. Furthermore the *inquilinarios* considered their struggle as a part of the working class struggle. In June 1922, when the local labour unions called for a general strike, the *inquilinarios* actively supported the strike, calling on the masses to generalize the struggle and to politicize its content by putting it into a revolutionary perspective.

Given the strength of the movement, in May 1922 some landlords began to give up, and entered into negotiation with the tenants' union and accepted its demands. At the end of June, a collective agreement was very close to being signed between the *inquilinarios* and an important sector of the slumlords. In a parallel move, Governor Tejeda, responding to the movement's demands, sent to the federal assembly Bill of Tenants, which was very favourable to the people. Under the pressures of real estate and business, including a good number the Mexican political leaders[111], the congress limited considerably the scope of the housing reform. Yet when the federal law came into official existence, in May 1923, it represented a considerable improvement in the living conditions of Veracruz's tenants.[111bis]

Nevertheless, if the housing demands of the *inquilinarios* could be relatively-well assimilated by the state, their ideological radicalism made the movement potentially dangerous in the midst of a highly unstable political situation. The peasant rebellion, inspired by Zapata, was still being crushed in Morelos; the workers of the Yucatan, Tamaulipas, and Veracruz were becoming increasingly militant; and the 'Red Battalion', that had supported Carranza to establish republican institutions, was being dismantled by a government convinced that the time had come to contain the revolution within the compatible interests of the new ruling elite and of the powerful neighbour to the North. Responding to the appeal of the local bourgeoisie, and to the complaints of the Spanish and American Consulates, the federal government organized the repression of the movement. Using as a pretext the violent confrontation within the tenants' union between the followers of Proal and the communist supporters of Olmos, on the night of 5 July 1922, federal troops arrested the leaders in the *Sindicato's* headquarters. When street demonstrations tried to oppose the army, the soldiers opened fire, killing some 70 people and injuring hundreds more. More than 100 active members of the movement were tried and convicted, although sentences were relatively light. Heron Proal, was freed several months later, only to be arrested again in 1924 by a special order of President Calles, who decided to stop the tenants' agitation that had reached other cities, including Merida and the Distrito Federal. Although the rent strike lasted for 38 months and the SRI maintained its organization throughout the decade, it ceased to exist as a social movement in Veracruz after the July 1922 repression. Many of its cadres quit the city to join peasants' agitation in the surrounding countryside where they helped to organize the *Liga de Comunidades Agrarias*. Yet the struggle of the *inquilinarios* in Veracruz deeply marked Mexican urban political history, both in its demands and the impression it left on the people's memory.

The Historical Context of the Movement: the Economic Crisis and the Consolidation of Revolutionary Institutions

A social movement is never a direct consequence of its historical context. Its orientations, evolution, and impact on society originates from the interaction between its components and the social forces confronting the movement. Nevertheless it is impossible to understand the meaning of a movement without some reference to the historical conditions in which the movement appears. It is important not just to place the movement within a framework, but to identify some of its characteristics, goals, and social dynamics.

Veracruz grew tremendously in the first quarter of the century, jumping from 29,166 inhabitants in 1900, to 48,633 in 1910, and then to 54,225 in 1921,[112] as a result of the dramatic increase in the import-export activities through its port, a sign of the rapid incorporation of Mexico into the commercial networks of the world economy. The revolution somewhat disturbed economic life but indirectly benefited Veracruz when in 1915, Carranza, threatened by the armies of Villa, retreated to Veracruz and transformed it into the nation's provisional capital, adding military and bureaucratic resources to the commercial activity of the city and to the incipient process of industrialization. Stimulated by the First World War, Veracruz's economy boomed, relying on the first Mexican oil exports and the high price of the Mexican silver in the international market. But in a dependent economy the sources of prosperity often become the causes of decay. At the end of the First World War, the export markets shrank, the American trade tariffs rocketed to protect her economy, and gold was recognized as the international means of payment, dramatically lowering the price of silver. The Mexican economy, relying on the flow of international trade, suffered a recession. And the down turn was particularly severe in Veracruz, whose import-export activities decreased considerably. As unemployment rose in the city, the intensification of the civil war in the surrounding rural areas forced thousands of peasants to leave their homes for Veracruz.

In these circumstances, capital investment tended to favour speculation as against production, so confirming the general rule that crisis situations stimulate the parasitical behaviour of
investors: capital's return was obtained more from monopoly rent or over-pricing than from
surplus value. As in many other non-industrialized cities, the housing needs generated by the
urban explosion of Veracruz became the best source of gain for the urban landlords and for the
capital holders who tended to switch their assets into real estate. Because of the low-level of
solvency of the incoming immigrants, rented housing was the only kind they could afford. To
minimize the risk, real estate investors built little and bought much. They obtained
substantial benefits by overcrowding people into the existing housing stock without spending
for maintenance or repair. With the expansion of housing demand, they did build some extensions onto the miserable dwellings causing even more precarious conditions (the so-called
accessorias rooms). Sanitary conditions rapidly deteriorated, though data on these matters are
insufficient. The pressures on the tenants were enormous. Some sources estimate a 500 per
cent increase in the rents between 1900 and 1910.[113] We do not have an estimate for the
amount of increases between 1910 and 1922 but it is likely that is was very high, since one of
the demands from the *inquilinarios* was to stabilize the rents at their 1910 level. The
acceleration of the rent increases and the generalized practice of eviction became particularly
intense in the period of 1920–22, as a result of the suppression of some of the legal protection
that the tenants had obtained. In 1916, President Carranza, in trying to obtain popular
support to overcome his delicate military situation, approved a rent control law, including a
clause making it very difficult for unjustified eviction of tenants. Although the law was
modified in September 1916 to authorize higher rent increases, the tenants still had some
effective legal protection. Everything changed after the advent of the new government in
1920. Under President Obregon, the new dominant class consolidated its power in Mexico,
establishing a solid alliance between economic power and the revolutionary political elite.

As Manuel Perlo says, '. . . there was a major change within the bloc of urban landlords with
the entry of a new fraction formed in the revolution, tied to the new ruling group which
included all the top leaders of the revolution. Such a change will have an enormous influence
on the social and economic character of real estate property, since it will be excluded from the
entire programme of social transformation undertaken by the government (agrarian reform,
nationalizations etc.) and will consolidate urban land property as one of the most solid and
important supports of capitalist accumulation in Mexico.'[114] The immediate effect on
Veracruz of such a dramatic reversal of the social policy at the general level was a new law
proposed by the then Governor Antonio Nova, which would abolish all the legal protections
previously granted to the tenants.

Thus the situation of Veracruz in 1921–22 was characterized by an economic crisis which
was dramatically lowering employment and income, an accelerated process of urban growth,
and a massive transfer from commercial capital to real estate investment to take advantage of
the predisposition of the newly established political power towards private capital's initiative.

But who owned this private capital? First, the commercial bourgeoisie, related to the
import-export business; second, an incipient industrial bourgeoisie, mainly investing in food
production and printing; third, the rural *latifundistas*, residents of the city, whose economic
power had survived the revolution; and fourth, medium and large merchants. If we add some
liberal professionals and government bureaucrats, we end up with the 2,063 persons (3.80 per
cent of the population) that in 1921 owned all the real estate property and, henceforth, were
the landlords of the remaining 96.2 per cent of the Veracruz residents.[115]

Another basic characteristic of the *Jarochan*[116] social structure, in 1921, was the presence in the city of 9,406 foreigners (17.3 per cent of the population), including 4,173 Spaniards and 978 Americans.[117] Although we do not have precise data of who the landlords were, given the predominance of Spaniards and Americans in the commercial activities and their impressive number, we may safely assume that the overwhelming majority of real estate owners were foreigners, and the great majority of them were Spaniards, a fact confirmed by Gonzalez Navarro.[118]

This is a crucial factor for characterizing the movement of *inquilinarios* in relationship to a situation of dependency. Veracruz was not only a dependent economy, oscillating according to the variations of international trade, it was also a dependent city in which the local social elite was largely formed by foreigners who maintained a colonial pattern of behaviour, and took financial advantage of the urban misery. This dependency was not only an individualized social relationship, it was also expressed through the direct political influence of the dominant countries, as shown during the rent strike by the repeated intervention of the Spanish and American consuls on behalf of the landlords. Such action was particularly influential given that the government of President Obregon was trying to obtain American recognition of the Mexican revolution as an institutional fact, fully compatible with the domination of the hemisphere by the USA as an emerging world power. Therefore it was crucial for Obregon to demonstrate that the embryos of social revolution would not proliferate, so that a co-existence could be arranged between Mexico and the country that was at the same time its potential client, its most powerful neighbour, and a pending military threat. So when the American magazine *Star* printed a very hostile article on the *inquilinarios* of Veracruz, and wrote that, 'It is a protest against foreign exploiters that still dominate Mexico commercially'[119] it was inadvertently pointing out one of the crucial dimensions of the movement. The *inquilinarios* presented their struggle as a revolt against the speculation on Mexican misery by foreigners, taking advantage of the difficulties of a people that had been fighting for their leaders to accomplish national political liberation.

Yet the new political contradictions which appeared within the Mexican revolution enabled the movement to expand for a long time without being repressed, a confrontation between the 'liberal bourgeois' project of institutional stability attempted by Obregon and the populist resistance from the socialist group formed by leaders such as Felipe Carrillo, governor of Yucatan, Portes Gil in Tamaulipas, Garrido Carrabal in Tabasco, and Adalberto Tejeda in Veracruz.[119bis] Without such a conflict between the federal government and the state governors (a conflict between the tendencies towards institutionalization and populist tendencies), the movement of *inquilinarios* could not have succeeded in keeping control over the city for almost six months. The political context of the movement was characterized by a crisis of the revolutionary state in a period when new institutions were too weak to systematically enforce the capitalist order, but were strong enough to repress popular upsurges if they threatened the newly established equilibrium of dominant social interests.

Finally, the *inquilinarios*' revolt exploded just as the political organization of the Mexican working class movement was emerging. The movement was already split between the predominant populist socialism, the new born Communist Party, and anarchist currents whose influence was growing rapidly among the most radical union militants. Heron Proal was a part of this anarchist trend (he was a member of the group *Antocha Libertaria*), yet he participated in the first ordinary congress of the Mexican Congress party, in January 1922. The communists maintained a strong presence within the *inquilinarios* but their unity with the anarchists was more a question of tactics. In fact the debate between the three different ideologies led the *inquilinarios* to their separation from the mainstream of the labour movement and later to their own internal split.

The strength of the *Movimiento Inquilinario* was its ability to set aside its internal ideological divisions. These splits, however, defined some of the limits that the political context imposed on the movement, and decisively contributed to its defeat and repression.

The Inquilinarios and the Working Class

The *inquilinarios* considered their *Sindicato* as a militant wing of the working class movement. They saw themselves as exploited proletarians and oppressed workers in a struggle for revolution and in search of communism. The greatest demonstration took place on 1 May 1922, when they joined the international celebration of Workers' Day. Rafael Ortega, an eyewitness described the demonstration, 'First, there were children of both sexes, all dressed in red; the women with red flags and banners with the movement's demands carrying portraits of Lenin, Trotsky, Marx and Bakunin; then came the men with horns, whistles, metal boxes, etc. marching to the sound of the 'International' . . .'[120] Their sympathy for the working class was soon to be proved. In June 1922 the movement mobilized in support of the workers' strike, in solidarity with the unions of the Yucatan.

And yet, in spite of their ideological sympathies, the relationship between the *inquilinarios* and the labour unions of Veracruz was actually quite difficult. In 1920 the anarcho-syndicalists of the *Confederacion General del Trabajadores* created the *Federacion de Trabajadores del Puerto de Veracruz*, one of whose leaders was Heron Proal. But the majority of the Veracruz workers, and particularly those in the port, were affiliated to the reformist CROM (*Confederacion Revolucionaria de Obreros Mexicanos*). The CROM attempted in February 1922 to form a tenants' union excluding Proal and his followers. Weeks later, as we pointed out, once the strike was a success under the leadership of Proal, the dissidents joined the SRI to support the tenants' demands. But from the beginning there was a clear hostility of the labour aristocracy to the radicalism of the anarchists and communists represented by Proal. The crisis between the unions and the *inquilinarios* exploded during the workers' strike of 1922. The strike was called jointly but when the confrontation with the government became inevitable, the CROM withdrew, leaving the *inquilinarios* and the anarchist CGT (*Confederacion General de Trabajadores*), alone in a very weak position.

Finally the unity between communists and anarchists in the *inquilinarios* movement was also revealed to be fictitious. The communists' aim was to transform the SRI into a demand orientated tenants' union, capable of becoming a nation-wide, popular organization, led by the party's militants in alliance with Heron Proal. Yet the growing radicalism of the movement was a matter of serious concern for the communists who feared catastrophic repression just when their demands seemed within reach. The tensions between the anarchists and communists came to a head at the end of June 1922, when the communist minority created a separate organization under the leadership of Olmos. And paradoxically enough the police provocation leading to the military repression of 5 July came as a consequence of an incident in which a group of demonstrators, supporters of Proal, tried to lynch Olmos after recognizing him in the street. Thus we may conclude that the contacts of the *inquilinarios* with the labour movement were restricted to their political connections, particularly through the CGT (anarchists), and that their self-definition as a working class movement was an act of political subjectivism.

Can the *inquilinario* movement be considered a working class movement on the grounds of its social basis? The answer must be, 'No'. Of course most of the Veracruz workers probably participated in the rent strike. But given the small proportion of industrial and port workers as against the total population, they only accounted for a minority of the strikers. Furthermore the trend for unionized workers to join the rent strike rather than tenants being incorporated into the labour movement is demonstrated by the failure of the CROM to organize its own tenants' union.

We know little about the social composition of the *Movimiento Inquilinario*. But it is safe to imagine that it represented mainly the low, popular strata of the city: the poor immigrants recently arrived from the countryside; the overseas immigrants coming into Mexico through Veracruz; sailors waiting in the city for occasional hiring; artisans and small merchants; some manual workers, particularly from the food factories; and the prostitutes. The last element is a most distinctive feature of the movement because it represents the synthesis between two highly significant dimensions: a massive struggle by the 'urban lumpenproletariat' and a struggle fundamentally based on the women's initiative (first, by the prostitutes, then by most common women). The first element expresses the reaction of the 'marginals' in a dependent city against the social decomposition generated by a largely speculative urban growth. The second element has provided the *inquilinarios*' movement with a title of glory that was intended as a pejorative label: a women's rebellion[121].

A Women's Rebellion

All accounts of the *inquilinarios*' movement converge on a precise point: the role of the women. It was women who spontaneously started the rent strike; women who organized the committees of *patios* (tenements); women who resisted the eviction by clashing with the police; women who organized themselves in a network of groups that would come in support on hearing the signal of a whistle; women who were the ones most often arrested; and women who took to the streets against the army when the moment came in July 1922.

Of even greater significance is that, when in 1923, Heron Proal from his prison tried to mobilize the population of Veracruz to protest the repression of the movement, he wrote a letter calling to the women to convince their men to go on strike by threatening them with their own strike on domestic work![122] This can be taken as an unequivocal sign both of Proal's conviction that women were the militant wing of the movement and of his paternalistic attitude towards them.

We also know that several activist women came from Mexico City to join the movement. Yet, as in other historical situations, we find no trace of explicit feminist themes in a movement whose leadership, unlike its militants, was entirely male. The fundamental truth remains that this was predominantly a women's movement.

Thus the *inquilinarios* formed a movement more focused on residence than on work; loosely linked with the labour movement more through ideology and political acquaintances than by its social basis; a movement of the urban *plebs* against the speculators, more than of workers against capital; and a movement of women in a revolt rooted in their role as agents of organization of all spheres of everyday life, from family consumption to illicit sexual pleasure. The *inquilinarios* of Veracruz did not constitute a class movement, but they were nonetheless a social movement that erupted from the depth of urban misery to struggle for life.

The Spiralling Dynamics of the Movement's Goals

The revolt of the *inquilinarios* developed against a revolutionary ideological background that was to prove a constant feature of the movement. But its demands evolved and expanded in a highly significant manner. In the first phase of the strike, the demands were very precise and strictly linked to the housing problem: rent control; establishment of a procedure to fix the amount of the rents on the basis of the declared value of the property; repair and maintenance of the buildings; provision of basic urban services; and measures for public hygiene. In their manifesto (which often provided the chance to list demands), the tenants typically added the slogan, 'Revolution, Pro-Communism'. Yet the ideological reminder did not exclude the very concrete character of their housing demands and the real desire for negotiation with the landlords. Furthermore, a decisive element for understanding the *inquilinarios'* perspective is that they always addressed themselves to the landlords, to the exclusion of any call to state intervention for the regulation of rents. What they wanted was a procedure for collective bargaining in which both contenders could try to enforce their demands by their own means. The 'Tenants' Law' approved in May 1923 was an initiative of Governor Tejeda that never counted on the support of the *inquilinarios*, at least not of the majority led by Proal.

Such an attitude does not imply that the *inquilinarios* did not have a broader vision beyond the immediate needs. In fact Proal was in the process of elaborating a general housing policy, as is shown by a letter written by him in prison during the movement, a letter that, because of its great significance, is worth reproducing in full:

' . . . The forces of the *Sindicato Revolucionario de Inquilinos*, without hesitation, are ready to launch the final assault, by requisitioning the habitations FOR REASON OF PUBLIC UTILITY, compensating the current landlords with the rents they perceived; and forcing them to pay back the tenants with the surplus from the excessive rents they obtained. We are also going to proceed with the equipment of water and lighting in the tenements. We also will nominate administrators, who will take care to pay the local taxes, deducting them from the rents, as well as to pay, under the same circumstances, all indispensable repairs; such as roofs, floors, kitchens, bathrooms, water closets, etc.

The Municipal Treasury may well perceive the rents for the houses on the basis of 2 per cent yearly of the declared property value, retaining from the rents the taxes and management expenses, and returning the surplus to the landlords (when they ask for) property. Taxes should not be reduced. On the contrary, they should be somewhat increased to subsidize hospitals and retirement houses (. . .) I will continue treating the subject another day. Enough for today.'

Municipal Prison, Veracruz, 31 March 1922   Revolucion. Pro-Comunismo. Heron Proal.[123]

Proal proposed the municipalization of housing as an instrument of an effective management of the housing stock. Yet he was certainly not referring to the same municipality whose prison he was occupying! Neither was he thinking of another political party holding office in the same municipal institution. He was referring to an alternative municipality, beyond the existing state, beyond the established political institutions. In fact, one of the most salient trends of the *inquilinarios* was their consistent rejection of legal institutions as well as of political elections as a way to reach their goals. The most clear expression of such an attitude came in the state elections celebrated on 2 July 1922, three days before the final repression of the movement. In the city of Veracruz, the *inquilinarios* called for the boycott of the elections, and the turn out proved negligible.

Were they Utopians? We would do better to describe them as revolutionaries pursuing a rational argument. For the *inquilinarios*, the solution to their housing problem could not be found in the city of Veracruz and in Mexican society. They kept negotiating until the end and tried to win demands and obtain concessions from the landlords. But such a struggle was a mere step in their overall scheme. What actually mattered to them was, on the one hand, the revolution, and on the other hand, as a possible basis for retreat, the construction of a communist colony in the vicinity of Veracruz. As usual in most Phalansterian experiences, the *inquilinarios* tried to fulfil their project in an extremely detailed way. They obtained permission from the governor to settle in the area of *Pocitos y Rivera*, on the periphery of the city, and on 1 May 1922, at the end of their demonstration of solidarity with the world's revolutionary movement, they set up the first symbolic stone of the colony, '. . . after a long walk under the burning sun rays'.[124] The *inquilinarios* started to 'expropriate' construction material for future use in the building of the colony. They also prepared a project for self-sufficiency based on cultivating rice and beans and rules for distribution. Each one would receive '. . . according to his/her needs . . .,' but '. . . the lazy ones would be expelled from the colony'. The mayor of Veracruz, arguing that the land was private property, opposed the construction of the colony and sent the police to keep the *inquilinarios* out. Fully committed to the success of their rent strike, the *inquilinarios* adjourned their project until the end of their urban struggle. But the colony represented their most cherished ambition and best reflected their attitude towards the city. Such a taste for the role of 'urban pioneers' is a recurrent theme that however deformed, manipulated, or enhanced, was going to be present in the squatter settlements that would characterize the process of urbanization in Latin America in the decades following the Veracruz rent strike.

Thus, the *inquilinarios* moved from a defensive rent strike to the proposal of a complex system of municipal management of the housing stock, and from there to the construction of the anti-city. In a few months their movement was galvanized into an attempt to build their own urban system and their own social institutions by the cries issuing from the depth of dirty slums against the walls of urban speculation.

Conclusion: The City of the Inquilinarios

For the *inquilinarios*, Veracruz was a damned city, synonymous with corruption and oppression. In his discourse on the future communist colony, fully representative of the *inquilinarios* view of urban life, Heron Proal said that, 'We must leave this badly smelling port, where the bourgeois exploit the people. And they are welcome to stay and to keep for them the so-called heroic port, with its cocaine, its heroin, its marijuana, and have a good digestion.'[125]

So the urban movement of Veracruz was anti-urban. For the *inquilinarios,* the city could neither be reformed or lived in. Only the revolution would be able to redeem it. In the meantime, they had to retreat, leave the city and settle in an alternative colony that would be uncontaminated by speculation or bourgeois politics. The 'urban marginals' dreamed of redefining centrality and abandoning the ruins of a civilization doomed to barbarism.

The dependent city, marked by economic parasitism and speculative investment, generated at the same time a labour movement that was incorporated into the new context through the defense of working conditions, and an urban movement that violently opposed the roots of its condition. In such a movement we find a mixture that has by now become familiar to the urban analyst of the Third World: dramatic survival demands; a populist leadership; and Utopian tendencies to reconstruct an alternative society in the space conquered by the struggle. The *inquilinarios* of Veracruz anticipated the most advanced experiences of urban squatters in Latin America.

6

The Post-Industrial City and the Community Revolution: The Revolts of American Inner Cities in the 1960s

Throughout the second half of the 1960s, the inner cities of most large American metropolises literally exploded. The massive riots in the black ghettos were the most spectacular and perhaps the most influential form of social protest of the time. Yet, numerous other grassroots mobilizations, ranging from rent strikes to welfare rights demands, fighting urban renewal or stopping highway construction, turned the American urban scene into a battlefield. What Daniel Bell and Virginia Held named, '. . . the community revolution . . .'[126] or what, years later, Harry Boyte highlighted as a crucial episode of the '. . . backyard revolution . . .'[127] called into question the pattern of urban development that had reshaped the American landscape for almost half a century.[128] To be sure, the movement took place in the context of a general upheaval of civil society in the USA which included the civil rights movement, the rise of women's liberation, the anti-war movement, the student protest, together with more militant labour demands and the challenge of alternative cultures which were destroying the myth of a conflict-free, post-industrial society, and shaking the basic mechanisms of social control.[129]

But the inner cities' revolt had its own specificity, as did the other movements, in relation to its structural causes, social behaviour, and organizational expressions. Beyond its internal diversity, the revolt came from a common matrix of contradictions underlying the fabric of the inner cities, defined as the spatial manifestation of ethnic segregation, urban poverty, economic discrimination, and political alienation.[130] It was triggered by the disruptive efforts of urban renewal,[131] by the process of legitimation opened by the programmes of social reform known as the 'War on Poverty',[132] and by the more favourable power situation in which the blacks and the poor found themselves in the aftermath of the Civil Rights Movement, begun in the South almost a decade before.[133] Nevertheless a social movement is never reducible to a reaction against some structural trend or to the imitation of some accidental protest by other people. The generality of the urban protest in all large metropolitan areas, the high level of militancy, the diversity of the forms of mobilization and the organization, the lasting effects on the metropolitan structure, on urban policies, and on social consciousness, are all indications pointing towards the existence of a major social movement that shook the foundations of the American city.

Yet many observers have proceeded to assimilate the very different elements of such a movement into a single category, 'The Poor' fighting back at 'The Establishment'. In fact the process of social change is far more complex, and we must follow the detours of such historical complexity to be able to assess the sources of a new urban culture as well as its plurality. Thus we will examine in a separate manner what seems to be, at least in appearance, two different forms of urban protest, developing at the same time and in the same places: the ghetto riots and community-based struggles. Then we will turn to consider in some detail what is being proposed as the conscious self-expression of an organized social movement emerging from the experience of urban protest: the Alinsky model of community organization.[134] On the basis of the results obtained at these three different levels of analysis of a complex historical experience, we will try to formulate some hypotheses on the relationship between city and society as established by the 1960s revolts in the urban core of advanced capitalism.

The Riots of Black Ghettos

Between 1964 and 1968 there were at least 329 important riots, involving hundreds of thousands of black people, which took place in 257 American cities leading to 52,000 arrests, 8,000 injured and at least 220 killed.[135] In 1969, some 500 'civil disorders' were recorded.[136] And beyond the media's attention, in 1970–71, the FBI still estimated 269 'race-related disturbances' in American cities.[137] Some were explosions apparently related to minor incidents, usually involving police action in the ghetto. Others actually expressed a conscious political protest, as with the popular rising that followed the assassination of Martin Luther King in 1968. In the month following that slaying there were 202 violent incidents in 172 cities with 27,000 arrests, 3,500 injured and 43 deaths.[138] The wave of riots in the black ghettos started in Harlem and Bedford-Stuyvesant, New York, in 1964, and represented the most direct challenge ever posed to the American social order, an order historically based upon racial discrimination and ethnic fragmentation among the lower classes.[139]

Typically a riot started as an incident with law enforcement officers of one kind or other: 'This final precipitating incident produced the gathering of a crowd that engaged in a form of political discussion regarding appropriate collective response to the incident. The next stage of the riot process normally was marked by excitement and destructiveness, in which residents of riot areas demonstrated that certain established limitations of conduct would no longer apply. The targets of ghetto violence were not selected at random; most had significance within the content of the unequal distribution of power in urban areas. The excitement phase was followed in the case of serious rioting by the appearance of a representative group of ghetto residents and by extensive looting. As the crowd on the street began to recognize the collapse of pre-existing restraints, they developed their own rules of conduct, some condoning activities previously regarded as criminal, some protecting favoured individuals or agencies from attack. In the final stage of the riot process, attained during the most serious riots, a state of siege emerged, in which all communications broke down, citizens could no longer move freely, and rioters battled with the large-scale paramilitary forces directed by authorities at rioters.'[140]

What is the social meaning of such a major historical phenomenon? To what extent can it be labelled an 'urban movement'? How does it relate to the city? What are its structural sources? What is the profile of the underlying social process?

The answers to these basic questions lie scattered around literally hundreds of documents, accounts, and analytical texts. Yet a partial examination of available evidence may open the way for a reliable and substantive hypothesis. We are fortunate in having five major synthetic sources on the experience of ghetto riots that agree as to the basic trends of the process despite the diversity of urban and social situations:

1   The series of research reports established by the National Advisory Commission on Civil Disorders[141] with the limit represented by the date of their completion, early 1968.
2   The collection of research essays on the riots prepared by Rossi, Beck, and Eidson.[141b]
3   The rigorous analysis by Spilerman on 'The Causes of Racial Disturbances',[142] one of the few examples of a fruitful use of quantitative sociology for the understanding of social movements.

Plate 6.1 Cicero, Illinois, 6 September 1966: Helmeted policemen intermingle with civil rights demonstrators as they march through Cicero, in support of open housing in this all white suburb of Chicago. (By kind permission of Popperfoto. Photograph: UPI.)

4   The expansion and deepening of the analysis of Spilerman's data by Roger Friedland in his important book on American central cities.[143]
5   The major synthetic effort on the subject by Joe Feagin and Harlan Hahn, whose book *Ghetto Revolts* carefully summarizes and considers all important empirical research existing on the 1960s riots.[144]

On the basis of this information the riots emerge not as irrational outbursts, but as insurrections, however limited in scale and in spite of there being no hope of seizing power. In fact, most insurrections in history have not so much aimed at overrunning the existing institutions as providing means of political protest, resorted to when the channels of official institutions were either non-existent or useless. But who protested and to express what?

The National Commission on Civil Disorders concluded that major grievances by riot area residents were aimed at issues concerning police brutality, unemployment and housing. At a lower level of concern, representatives of the rioters asked for better education, recreational facilities, and reform in the local government, protesting the living conditions in the ghetto and trying to improve them, along with obtaining a more responsive local political system, bypassing the 'porkbarrels'.

As a matter of fact blacks obtained more jobs, more services, easier access to welfare entitlement and some educational improvement, to a large extent through the pressure caused by the riots on the local authorities.[145] As a clear conscious expression of such a process, a national survey found that 40 per cent of the blacks in 1969 considered riots to be 'helpful', against 20 per cent in 1966, before the experience of the riots.[146] Yet it does not follow that deprivation and poverty were the principal causes of the rioting, nor that the search for economic gain was the driving force behind the movement. Misery and discrimination had been the experience of black Americans throughout their history, and the 1960s was actually a period when some improvements appeared feasible for the first time through the 'War on Poverty' programme. Furthermore, data on the characteristics of cities where riots were more frequent and intense show that riots happened more often in the cities where non-white income was higher,[147] where resident populations were more stable, and where housing was of better quality.[148] The riot torn cities were cities with declining populations, yet increased density, and with increasing non-white population.[149] Thus, although poverty was a general underlying condition for all black ghettos, poverty was not the immediate cause of black revolt. Nor can the reverse argument, that the blacks with relatively high status were influencing the lower strata to push for further upward mobility, be seen as the cause. The careful multivariate causal analysis carried on by Spilerman[150] established that all statistical relationships between urban characteristics and riots disappeared when controlled by the only two major explanatory variables: the size of the black population; and the location of this population in the Northern region of America. In other words, riots were primarily the product of large black ghettos formed in the inner cities of the oldest industrial metropolitan areas. Such findings are confirmed by other statistical analyses by Jibou[151] and by Downes.

Furthermore, Roger Friedland, in a very perceptive analysis, reorganized Spilerman's data for the 1967 and 1968 riots. His findings, summarized in Table 6–1, expand the field of explanation. Riots were basically associated with the size of the black population, particularly within a context of police harrassment and undemocratic local government. The severity of the riots was stimulated by additional variables linked to the housing crisis and to the federal urban policies such as the aggression of urban renewal and the legitimizing of opportunities offered by the 'War on Poverty' to organize the communities.

Table 6.1 The local origins of the black urban riots, 1967–1968.

Independent Variables Socio-Economic Conditions	Riot frequency 1967–1968			Aggregate Riot Severity 1967–1968		
	b	beta	t	b	beta	t
Non-white population growth	−0·00002	0·03	0·33	0·00004	0·04	0·54
Non-white population	0·42	0·45	5·3***	0·59	0·44	5·6***
Low rent housing demand	0·10	0·05	0·69	0 62	0·21	3·2***
Political Conditions						
War on Poverty funding	0·00016	0·10	1·18	0·00035	0·15	1·95***
Urban Renewal activity	0·0024	0·11	0·18	0·0045	0·13	1·88**
Police activity	0·07	0·27	2·85**	0·085	0·24	2·8***
Non-reformed	0·62	0·22	2·95***	0·74	0·18	2·7**
Region (1-South)	−0·39	−0·09	1·2	−0·81	−0·13	1·9**
n = 118						
r² = 0·47		r² = 0·47			r² = 0·57	

*significant at 0·10 level (one-tail)
**significant at 0·05 level (one-tail)
***significant at 0·01 level (one-tail)
Source: Roger Friedland, *Crisis, Power and the Central City* (London: Macmillan, 1983).

While such conclusions may appear to be a mere tautology (black riots happen when there are large concentrations of blacks and where urban policies provoke or facilitate these revolts), the interpretation of these findings does lead to a fundamental observation: the black ghetto provided the basis for a black revolt once blacks mobilized all over the country. This certainly does not explain the why and how of the black revolt but it does express the organizational basis of the revolt, analogous with the concentration of industrial workers in the large factories being indispensible to the formation of a labour movement. The fact that ghettos were the physical basis of the black revolt leads to the hypothesis that they were also their social basis: the black community emerged as a collective actor on the basis of the 'space of freedom' provided by the ghetto.[152]

The impact of large scale investment in and mechanization of agriculture, which was effectively a compulsory process, uprooted blacks from their small towns initiating a massive migration from the rural South. But this time it had also freed them from the social institutions of their direct masters. Housing segregation and landlord abuse in the Northern cities pushed blacks into the ghettos, where they suffered from urban decay, overcrowding and lack of services. It was in this harsh urban land left behind by the happy new suburbanites, where black people congregated in their churches and where autonomous social institutions were invented. Unemployment and underemployment crippled the reserve army of the newly urbanized blacks. Yet they learned the necessary survival skills, finding the loopholes of the system and escaping the workplace discipline that had broken the rebellious ethnic working class that had preceeded them in the urban fabric of the industrial factories. The ghetto became a city within the city, where alternative rules of an alternative society were to emerge.[152bis] The systematic targets of rioters during the upsurges were the white merchants of the ghetto and the police – the daily representatives of business and government, a foreign world for the community. All other demands by the movement were by-products of the spontaneous mobilization to defend the community's growing autonomy against the invaders, particularly the police, who were trying to curb some of the ghetto's economic activities, officially labelled as 'crime' by the rulers of the same society that had pulled their ancestors from Africa and their fathers from the Southern towns.

'Black power' was not just a slogan.[153] It was the practice of an excluded community that transformed the walls of its prison into the boundaries of its free city. On the basis of this self-reliance, of the newly conquered autonomy, it imposed demands, improved its conditions, and negotiated its entry into the institutional system. In this sense, the riots were not a continuation of the Civil Rights Movement, although they were largely stimulated by its battles and its victories.[154] As Frances Piven and Richard Cloward have shown, the Civil Rights Movement was fundamentally aimed at breaking the chains of terror in the South, and reaching political franchise for blacks. On the basis of their political organization they were then able to trade their support to the Democratic Party for some positions in the system, widespread legal reform, and some social programmes.

The ghetto revolts were at the same time more limited and more far reaching. Their specific demands concerned basic survival elements, public jobs, and welfare eligibility, more than urban services. The deeper significance of their demands addressed the basic issues of reform of the local political system, protection from police attacks, and building of an autonomous organizational network. Black power was actually fulfilled in the ghettos during the hours that rioters controlled them. Black power was enforced daily in the ghettos where the only white-dominated institution that still dared to penetrate were the heavily reinforced police patrols. The effectiveness of black power found some expression in the phenomenon of black mayors elected in Detroit, Gary, Buffalo, Cleveland, Newark, Washington, D.C., Atlanta, Los Angeles, Oakland, and many other cities. Some of these American cities were ruled directly by elected black officials, in spite of all the limits imposed by their alliances with big business. Yet, when 'black power' was transformed into a national goal through insurgent tactics, such as that of the Black Panthers, the bloody repression they met proved that the ghettos were not 'liberated zones'. Also, when 'black power' became a code word for enlarging the share of blacks within a system that remained substantially unchanged, deep splits were created within the black community, between the leadership trying to accomplish the impossible role of intermediary between legal equality and socio-economic exploitation, and the large mass of urban blacks still subject to discrimination, exposed to underemployment and suffering from poverty. Class issues started to emerge from behind the walls of the new black city. That the new black city was there at all was due to the community building that had its roots in the ghetto revolts triggered by urban segregation, and it allowed the expression and debate of a new range of problems.

The Social Anatomy of Community Mobilization

The challenge posed to the dominant social order by inner city residents had its most striking manifestation in the riots, but it took a diversity of forms whose mainstream was represented by the day-to-day militant work of community based organizations. The Community Action Program, funded by the Federal Office for Economic Opportunity, played a great role in providing the institutional support and the political legitimacy for grassroots organizing around the pressing social demands of poor neighbourhoods.[155] Taking advantage of such a favourable situation, thousands of popular organizations arose in the central cities of large metropolitan areas, laying the groundwork for the emergence of what some observers call the new neighbourhood movement in America.[156]

To assess the characteristics, effects, and meaning of community mobilization in America during the 1960s seems an impossible task in front of a highly diverse experience, of a multitude of scattered sources, and of the difficulty of using comparable criteria for the numerous case studies existing in every unique situation of urban protest. Yet the analysis of inner city revolts must consider the basic social trend underlying the community struggles, since they actually represented the most lasting connection between the new urban contradictions and the new forms of social movements. Fortunately, we can rely on a masterpiece of research carried out by John Mollenkopf on the basis of a representative sample of 229 community organizations in 100 cities over 50,000 population during 1970–71, to evaluate the work accomplished by OEO in the poor neighbourhoods.[157] Let us consider, step-by-step, the different elements of the process as a whole before trying to interpret the observed patterns of collective behaviour.

Table 6.2 Classification of community organization by type and ethnic dominance.

Organization Type (N = 229)		
Model cities or CAA group	23	(10%)
Neighbourhood associations	78	(35%)
Welfare rights organizations	17	(8%)
Tenants unions	19	(8%)
Black groups (civil rights, etc.)	37	(16%)
Spanish groups	10	(5%)
Civic associations	22	(10%)
Political groups	8	(4%)
Other	15	(7%)
Dominant Ethnic Group		
Black	156	(71%)
White	45	(21%)
Spanish	14	(6%)
Other or mixed	4	(2%)

Source: John Mollenkopf, *Community Organization and City Politics* (Cambridge, Mass.: Department of Government, Harvard University, Unpublished Ph.D. Thesis, 1973).

Table 6–2 provides a first overview of the different types of community organizations usually included under the same movement's label as well as an evaluation of the ethnic composition of community organizations in the poor neighbourhoods of inner cities. Two major findings are immediately apparent:

1 The internal diversity of the movement, calling for a more precise distinction of its components according to their differential behaviour and organization.
2 The very large predominance of blacks among the community organizations, requiring a specific analysis of the relations between the black movement and urban protests. Yet an important minority of the movement was not based on the black community, and we should pay attention to its differences in orientation to appreciate the diversity of experience.

Such a diversity is clearly expressed by the analysis of the goals of community organizations as presented in Table 6–3. Mollenkopf (to make the interpretation of these data easier) constructed a factor analysis that resulted in three separate clusters:

1 Focus on job counselling, child education, and teen counselling. It is what we might call the educational goals – trying to solve the social problems through individual advancement.

2 Focus on housing, public services, and participation – what we might call fostering participation through collective consumption.
3 Focus on political power and jobs – what we might call a political economic orientation.

It is important to notice that racial issues are not mentioned and that individual consumer goods are the least important concern for the organization as a whole.

Table 6.3 Community organizations' goals by organizational type, American inner cities, 1969. (Percentages represent fraction of groups which have the goal in question. All figures are expressed in percentages.)

	Political power	Job pressure	Housing	Participation	Job counselling	Teen training	Compensatory education	Improved public Svcs.	Improved consumer goods
Model cities/CAA	43	48	87	91	61	65	65	78	39
Neighbourhood assn	74	59	81	90	61	47	63	90	40
Welfare rights	70	62	88	95	59	53	61	79	58
Tenant union	56	41	84	79	53	47	47	88	28
Black group	78	78	71	81	69	69	71	71	34
Civic association	33	38	57	52	55	52	45	61	35
Other	64	42	75	75	63	50	54	61	7
Column Av. per cent	66**	56*	79	82**	61	54	60	78**	35**

*Chi-square statistic significant at 0·05
**Chi-square statistic significant at 0·01

Source: John Mollenkopf, *Community Organization.*

By studying the relationship between the type of organization and the importance of goals fostered by them, we have constructed a typology (Table 6–4) of community organizations on the basis of their two-fold relationship to the political system and to the status of their economic demands. We have indicated for each type what seems to be the predominant ethnic composition of each type of community organization:

Table 6.4 A typology of community organizations on the basis of their two-fold relationship to the political system and to the status of their economic demands.

Type	Description	Predominant Ethnic Membership
1	Defensive apolitical organizations (Civic associations, homeowners)	WASP
2	Urban defensive organizations (Tenants)	White *ethnic* groups
3	Participatory welfare rights Organizations	Blacks
4	Participatory collective consumption organizations (Neighbourhood associations, Community action groups)	WASP Ethnic white
5	Power orientated collective consumption organizations (Neighbourhood associations)	Blacks
6	Power orientated, Work orientated organizations (Black groups)	Blacks

Thus the so-called Community Organization Movement (COM) was actually composed of a contradictory array of collective mobilizations, ranging from the defense of the urban services, to the politics of production and going through welfare rights demands and collective consumption trade unionism. Yet whatever conflicts exist between these contradictory elements, they all came from the basic crisis of the inner city as a social form of consumption, human interaction, and political control.

On the basis of his case studies of community mobilization[158], Mollenkopf, supported in this point by an abundant literature[159] emphasizes the major roles played by the characteristics of the leadership on the orientation of the leadership by type of organization. Tables 6–5 and 6–6 give valuable information on the actual characteristics of the leadership by the type of organization. Besides confirming the importance of black leadership (78 per cent of all surveyed organizations), we can also observe the importance of three generally ignored social categories as major agents of urban mobilization:

1   Teachers and government employees, a public service orientated class of petty bureaucrats that tended to be the educated vanguard of the defined ethnic minorities.
2   The role played by religious ministers (leaders of 10 per cent of the organizations!) confirms the decisive influence of local churches as elements of genuine organization and mobilization among the American poor.
3   In 16 per cent of the cases the leadership was provided by housewives, emphasizing the role of women in urban movements.

Table 6.5   Community organization's leader occupation by organization type, American inner cities, 1969. (Per cent of groups having leaders of given type.)

	Unskilled labourer	Skilled Labourer	Housewife	Clerical	Small business	Teachers & Govt. employees	Ministers	Professionals
Model cities/Caa	7·1%	0·0%	7·1%	14·3%	*28·4%*	*35·7%*	7·1%	0·0%
Neighbourhood Assn.	16·9	*8·5*	16·9	10·2	8·5	22·0	5·1	11·9
Welfare rights	*26·7*	0·0	*23·3*	6·7	0·0	0·0	0·0	13·3
Tenant union	*23·1*	0·0	15·4	*15·4*	7·7	*30·8*	7·7	0·0
Black group	8·7	*8·7*	4·3	8·7	4·3	*30·4*	*13·0*	*21·7*
Civic association	14·3	*7·1*	7·1	14·3	*21·4*	28·6	0·0	7·1
Other	16·7	0·0	11·1	22·2	5·6	27·8	11·1	5·6
N =	25	8	25	19	15	38	10	16
Column per cent	16%	5%	16%	12%	10%	24%	6%	10%

(Disproportionate representation of a given occupation in italics.)
Source: John Mollenkopf, *Community Organization.*

A synthesis of Mollenkopf's data, relating the characteristics of the leadership to the form of community organization, maybe presented as the following typology:

1   Ministers and advocate professionals, led black groups, generally the most militant.
2   Housewives led welfare rights protests.
3   Government employees and teachers, led 'Community Action' groups.

Table 6.6 Community organization's leader characteristics by organization type, American inner cities 1969. (Per cent of groups whose leaders have given characteristic.)

	Median ed. (Years)	Board ties (Many)	Negative eval. (High)	Black	WASP	Ethnic	Spanish
Model cities/CAA	12	20%	29%	71%	7%	7%	*14%*
Neighbourhood assn.	13	28%	35%	71	*14*	8	8
Welfare rights	10	25%	40%	*85*	8	0	8
Tenant union	11	17%	36%	83	0	*17*	0
Black group	14	40%	61%	*100*	0	0	0
Civic no.	12	10%	53%	62	23	*15*	0
Other	13	35%	50%	87	13	0	0
Column per cent	12	27%	46%*	78%	10%	7%	5%

*Chi-square Sic. at 0·05.
(Disproportionate representation in italics.)
Source: John Mollenkopf, *Community Organization*.

4 Small business led civic and homeowners associations.
5 Skilled workers led neighbourhood associations.
6 Clerical and unskilled workers led tenants' unions.

A very significant trend is the connection of different types of leadership to specific forms of organization. Thus small business, clerks, and skilled workers shared the leadership of Civic Associations while ministers and professionals attracted some skilled workers in the direction of black militant groups, and the 'Community Action', federally funded organizations, included a variety of social groups under the supervision of government employees. Between the two emerging blocs of black militants and white citizens, the institutions of social reform tried to provide a common ground across the board, on the basis of neighbourhood issues.

The potential social divisions within the COM are clearly revealed through a cluster analysis performed by Mollenkopf of the relationship between the type of organization, the predominant goals, the characteristics of the leadership, the allies of the movement, and the tactics being used. Two distinct groups of community organization emerge as statistically separate clusters, with strong internal connections among the components of each cluster:

Group 1 is predominantly formed by the largely black neighbourhood associations. Leaders tended to be well educated professionals, ministers, and bureaucrats. They relied on a wide network of allies, particularly among government agencies and churches. They tended to use militant tactics and engaged in extensive protest activities. Their goals were very broad and tended to cover the whole spectrum of economic, social and political demands.
Group 2 brings together neighbourhood associations, tenants unions, welfare rights organizations, and civic associations. They were basically led by white businessmen with small concerns, clerks and skilled workers. They had few allies and did not easily mobilize in militant actions. They focused their concerns on the betterment of housing and public services, and tended to emphasize participation in the institutions instead of claiming political power.

We are, in fact, in the presence of two forms of social mobilization resulting from the crisis of the inner cities: a black-led, overall social protest, and a white, moderate income people's defense against urban decay.

What is the relationship between this two-fold process and the evolution of the urban services and policies? Mollenkopf's findings are absolutely clear in establishing the connection between the level and intensity of grassroots mobilization and the extent and direction of social change, all other variables being statistically unrelated or merely producing random effects. But what determines the determinant? In other words, what are the social sources of community mobilization?

Table 6.7 Sources of mobilization of community organization in 100 American inner cities, 1969.

Independent Variables	Sources of Mobilization (Standardized regression coefficients, N = 100 cities)					
				Dependent Variables		
	Alliances		No. of Groups			Militance
	EQ1	EQ2	EQ3	EQ4	EQ5	EQ6
Leadership						
Av. no. names/leader		11*		0·04		0·22**
Issues						
Rent Ch.		−0·02	−0·10		−0·10	
UR exp.		0·11	·09		0·01	
SMSA highway exp.		−0·10	−0·11		−0·05	
Black influx		0·30*	0·11		0·63***	
Networks						
CAA budget	0·14	0·04	0·01	−0·09	−0·10	−0·36**
Pct co hrs	0·22*	0·23**	0·05	0·09	−0·18	−0·09
CAA emphasis on co	0·09	0·10*	0·09	0·09	0·27**	0·30***
MC Funds		0·12		0·08		−0·11
Av. no. names 1st ldr		0·14*		0·27**		0·17*
City						
Decentralization		0·09		0·09		0·03
Unem Ch.	0·37**	0·40**	0·27**	0·29**	0·23**	0·09
Population	−0·01	−0·16	0·00	0·01	0·19	−0·06
% Black		0·02		0·02		0·14*
Black neighbourhood	0·07	−0·02	0·27**	0·16*	0·13	0·02
% Foreign Stock	0·19		0·23*		0·10	
South		−0·04		−0·07		−0·05
Pct Owner Occupancy		−0·21***		−0·27***		0·04
Multiple R² =	0·262***	0·376***	0·227**	0·336***	0·193**	0·245***

* = Sig. at 0·05. ** = Sig. at 0·01 *** = Sig. at 0·001.
Source: John Mollenkopf, *Community Organization.*

Table 6–7 provides some basic findings. The most important variable was the increase in the black population, followed by the increase in the proportion of residents from foreign stock. On the other hand, the proportion of homeowners, the proportion of white collar residents, and the high level of education are negatively associated with the level of urban mobilization. We are in the presence of a movement of poor people and oppressed ethnic minorities. This movement was triggered, according to Mollenkopf's statistical analysis, by three series of factors in the process of urban evolution:

1 The disruptive effects produced in the inner cities by urban renewal programmes, black

immigration, tight housing markets, and changing patterns of the job structure.
2   The development of social networks among poor and ethnic minorities around voluntary associations, churches, and government sponsored neighbourhood centres.
3   The influence of a strong leadership generally formed by the educated segment of the oppressed ethnic minority or economically deprived group.

Thus the observation of a national sample of OEO-sponsored community organizations clearly shows the connection between the urban crisis and the black movement as the back-bone of social change undergone by the American cities. Yet a significant sector of popular neighbourhoods trapped in their jobs and residences tried to protect themselves against the general process of urban decay in the old industrial cities. In spite of some latent racial tension between the two wings of community mobilization, the commonality of the problems suffered by most residents nourished the hope for reconstructing people's unity on the basis of multi-ethnic and multi-issue orientated community organizations. Such was the underlying motto of the Alinsky experience: a conscious effort to transform the diverse expressions of the inner cities' revolt into a network of unified urban social movements.

The Resurgence of Urban Populism: The Alinsky Model of Community Organization

Consciousness and self-definition are a major component of any social movement. The popular revolts that took place in American inner cities throughout the 1960s rarely identified themselves as 'urban movements' nor spoke on behalf of 'community organization'. They tended to see themselves as expressions of black power, of welfare rights, of tenants' interest, or of the needs of the poor. Although such a lack of consciousness actually reflects the hetero-geneity of the COM and the difficulty of reducing it to a common historical process, it is also true that the failure of urban protest to affirm itself on the basis of some common goals became one of the major causes for the failure of social struggles to fully achieve change.

There is, however, a major exception to this tendency: the so-called Alinsky model of community organization which actually tried to inspire and organize urban protest, and to draw lessons from different experiences in order to provide a fulfilling model of popular organization, able to improve the living conditions of the poor, empower the grassroots, and obtain more democracy and greater social justice. In spite of the defeats and shortcomings of most Alinsky initiatives, the experience and its ideology have become a major point of refer-ence for the American tradition of urban mobilization (and we will have cause to refer again to his work in our study of San Francisco). To some extent the Alinsky Model actually represents the major cultural heritage from the neighbourhood-based protests of 1960s, and its analysis is a key element for our understanding of the relationship between the conditions of social protest and the awareness of the process by the COM itself.

It is obviously impossible to refer in detail to the variety of experiences of organization and mobilization inspired by Alinsky, either directly, as an organizer or indirectly through his writings.[160] We are therefore fortunate to have two important works: one by Michael P. Connally[161] and the other by Joan Lancourt.[162] These research monographs examine in detail the history and ideology of Alinsky, as well as the practice of the main community organizations he inspired in the 1960s and 1970s. Both sources largely converge, and tend to be confirmed by our own observation of the organizational behaviour of community leaders influenced by Alinsky in several American cities.[163]

Saul Alinsky was a University of Chicago trained sociologist, greatly influenced by Park and Burgess, who started his career as a neighbourhood organizer in Chicago in 1936. During the troubled thirties, funded by the Catholic Church, he tried to organize the meat-packing workers in their residential communities, both to improve their living conditions and to challenge the growing influence among them of labour unions, led, for the most part, by communists and Trotskyite militants. After collaborating very closely with the miners workers' union leader, John L. Lewis, and having successfully contributed to organizing the Mexican-American labour movement in California, he went back to Chicago in the mid-fifties to start a private institute of his own, called the Industrial Areas Foundation (IAF). Until his death, in 1972, he relentlessly used IAF as an organizational tool to test his analysis and tactics all over America, mostly operating on the basis of funding and institutional support provided by different churches.

The basic approach of Alinsky's model was to provide poor and powerless people with the only real resource they might have had – their standing and organizational capacity, leading to mobilization, confrontation and negotiation, in order to increase their share in the distribution of wealth, and to strengthen their voice in the process of decision making. His thinking explicitly related itself to the themes developed by Jefferson and the American 'founding fathers'. He thought that local self-reliance and community-based organization was the only antidote against the rising spectre of Fascism (right or left) that Alinsky attributed to the trend of increasing political centralization. Pluralism, government accountability, local autonomy, and widespread citizen participation, were key elements in the Alinskyite view of urban politics. He called himself a 'radical' because he wanted to go back to the roots of America. Under the changing conditions of urbanization, he proposed the new populism of community organization to follow the tradition of nineteenth century rural populism. In other words there was nothing basically wrong with the system except its main problem: the insensitivity of the political institutions to the people, who were excluded because of bureaucratization, central-ization, corruption, and manipulation of information. Community organization in the Alinsky view was, first of all, a political tool and a new form of government, complementary to the representative institutions of liberal democracy.

Yet Alinsky saw himself not as an ideologue, but as a pragmatic organizer. He favoured action and wanted to see the model work. He thought that people could not be organized unless they mobilized, and that they could not mobilize around models but could around the defense of their immediate interests. Thus he proposed his famous tactics, the hard core of the Alinsky tradition: to organize people a sensible issue must be picked, a clear opponent identi-fied, and the people mobilized against the opponent on the basis of such an issue. Victory for the issue has to be attainable because only when people win do they feel that the effort has been worthwhile. On the basis of the victory, the organization has been established, new issues selected that, if solved for the benefit of the community, will have broadened the audience of the organization in a self-spiralling process. In a sense, the main outcome of the organization has been the organization itself, its influence, its representativeness, its internal democracy, and its growing status on the voice of a territorally defined community. The attainment of demands is important because peoples' lives are improved, but the basic goals of the struggle have been to provide people with the basic resource they seek: power. Once grassroots empowerment has been achieved and the unity of people preserved, the democratic institu-tions start working in their favour and the economic interests come under control.

The basic element in the Alinsky model, as the trigger of the process, is 'the organizer'. He is an outsider, a professional, devoted to the community but external to its interests and cleavages, sharing the principles of community participation but cool and distant enough to rely solely on his skills, training, and experience. Alinsky, a fervent anti-communist, would probably be outraged by the close resemblance of his organizer's profile with the one of the professional revolutionary depicted by Lenin in *What is to be Done?*[164] Yet there are some crucial differences: the Alinskyite organizer has to be called upon by the community, and has to leave the community as soon as the organization is solidly established and led by its own elected leaders. So, on one level, the organizer will not be accountable nor will he ever become part of the movement. He will go errant through the urban communities, to serve the people, when they need it, and when they have the money for it. This last point defines another crucial aspect of the Alinskyite organizer: he must be paid (not much) by the community itself, through funds raised by the community.

In practice Alinsky always required two main conditions before providing the services of his Foundation, first that it be requested by a representative segment of the community, and second, that the community should have raised the money for funding the initial budget covering the Foundation's costs and initial community organizing expenses. It would be improper to consider such a condition as a profit-making operation: the financial prerequisite in Alinsky's scheme fulfils the same function as the patient's payment to the psychoanalyst – in a capitalist society, a collective group has only really decided to undertake a long-term organizing effort when it is willing and able to raise the money.

The question raised by such a model is the potential dependency of the community organization process on the funding sources. Alinsky argued that the potential diversity of sources prevented any single source from excessive control. In fact most of the experiences were initiated by a single category of institution: Churches of all denominations, generally acting in unison. In this sense Alinsky was clearly an 'agent' of the churches, in spite of his Jewish origin. Yet the main reason for such a stand seems to have come from his populist approach. Churches have been the 'natural' form of popular organization in American history, and they represent, today, the grassroots expression of voluntary organizations within the systems' established patterns of behaviour. Since the main preconception in the Alinsky approach, as in all populist movements, is to organize and mobilize people 'as they are', without any conscious ideology, the Churches became the basic ally for mobilizing people to increase their share within the system, without challenging the structurally dominant interests or the institutionalized values. For Alinsky, such a stand did not imply renouncing social change but he insisted that the goals, direction, and focus of such a change had to come from the people themselves, and be discovered and expressed by the communities on the basis of their daily practice. Of course, we can easily demonstrate the ideological bias of such a 'non-ideological' model of social behaviour, as well as the naïveté of the belief in some sort of social vacuum, as if people were not influenced in their choice and representation by prevailing cultural values.

Nevertheless, it is not our purpose to enter the passionate debate surrounding the Alinsky model, which will doubtless involve the American community movement in an even noisier confrontation as distance allows the emergence of a myth. For his followers, Alinsky was the genial forerunner of the new citizen movement of our time. For his conservative detractors, he was a demagogue, subverting the democratic procedures of responsible community participation. For his left wing critics, he was a professional agent hired by the Churches to channel people's protest into the quiet waters of the neighbourhood walls, blurring racial lines, diluting class struggle, and confusing political consciousness. For us, his ideology is the myth that emerged as the most coherent form of self-representation from the community struggles of the 1960s and became a driving force of neighbourhood mobilization in the 1970s. And since there must be some connection between historical practice and the production of myths, we should consider what the actual experience of Alinsky inspired community organizations was, in order to formulate some tentative hypotheses on the overall social phenomenon.

Joan Lancourt has systematically surveyed the main experiences of community organizations initiated by Alinsky himself. According to her findings, the Chelsea Community Council, organized in 1957 in Manhattan's lower Eastside, collapsed in 1960 because of ethnic intolerance coming from a predominantly white community against Puerto Ricans, as well as of the disagreements over how to deal with tension between on the one hand the non-religious 'Hudson Guild', and on the other, the Jewish community, and Protestant and Catholic Churches.

The Northwest Community Organization created in 1961 in Chicago, under the sponsorship of the Catholic Church, to support a working class neighbourhood in preserving its physical shape, improving its services and attacking corruption of local officials, ended up as an alliance to preserve the area against the growing Hispanic minority influence, that by the early-1970s had come to represent 50 per cent of the neighbourhood.

In strong contrast with these two early cases, FIGHT organized in the mid-1960s in Rochester, New York, with the support of the Council of Churches, the black community against employment discrimination and successfully established itself as the major spokesman for black people. BUILD was a similar and successful, multi-issue, all-black organization in Buffalo, New York, in 1965, under the leadership of the First Presbyterian Church.

On the contrary, CATC (a training centre organized with OEO in Syracuse, New York, in 1966 in collaboration with the University) and CUA (a Church-sponsored organization in the black ghetto of Kansas City in 1965) collapsed under the attack of radical black students fostering the Black Power ideology. After trying to evaluate the overall performance of Alinsky-inspired organizations, and examining 504 active mobilizations by such organizations, Lancourt concludes that, concerning issues addressing housing, schools, business, employment, welfare, city services, police, and fire service programmes, 'In none of the categories indicated did (the community organizations) achieve anything even approximating a halting or reversing of the trend toward deterioration.' Community control was not achieved, yet, subjectively, 'Some hope was raised . . .'.[165]

Furthermore, concerning the factors affecting differential outcomes, '. . . the major explanation for differential outcomes among the organizations lay in external factors rather than internal factors. The dilemma between the short-term need to win and going beyond the available 'slack' in order to achieve terminal goals has not been resolved by any of the organizations.'[166]

A parallel conclusion can be drawn from an excellent research monograph by John Hall Fish[167] that provides a first-hand account of the most famous Alinsky-inspired community effort, the Woodlawn Organization (TWO) in the Southside ghetto of Chicago. Fish, a sympathetic Alinsky-style militant, who was an active participant in TWO for seven years, gives us what is to-date the best account of an Alinsky organizational effort. TWO started typically in 1961 to resist the urban renewal efforts by the University of Chicago to 'protect' its campus from the proximity of the ghetto. On the basis of a defensive reaction, and in the atmosphere of the emerging black movement of the mid-1960s, the community, advised by Alinsky and supported by several grants from the churches, became a partner in the planned renovation of the area. Yet when the new housing was built, under the management of a community-based agency, 'Woodlawn Gardens (did) not provide substantial housing for the poor . . .' and actually '. . . provided space for higher income residents.'[168] An attempt to control the merchants' abuses was abandoned by the organization itself when it became too divisive an issue within the community. Grants that TWO had solicited to relieve poverty were deviated to the mayor's office which kept political control over the use of funds. The attempt to influence the education system was blocked by the school district. The Model Cities

Programme that residents had asked for remained firmly under control of city hall, outside the reach of the community. Even more serious was TWO's attempt to address the political issue of youth gangs by integrating the Blackstone Rangers into the administration of a one million dollar job-training programme. The Rangers were instrumental in controlling black insurgency in the area, culminating in the absence of rioting in Woodlawn in 1968 when the Westside was in flames to protest Martin Luther King's assassination. Yet the city police systematically tracked the Rangers, in spite of TWO's opposition, and even used their participation in the programme against them to sentence the Ranger's leaders to several years in jail for mismanagement of public funds. By the early 1970s, TWO, with a multi-million dollar budget, had become a community development corporation, the responsible partner of the black community, with power and resources, but without militancy or active membership: a social service agency had substituted for a community organization. Table 6–8 constructed by Fish clearly depicts the evolution of the organization and its transformation.

Table 6.8   Major characteristics in development of TWO.

Year	Stance towards Outside Agencies	Major Task of Organization	Leadership Needs	Basis of Constituent Support
1962	Militant resistance	Build organization	Agitator-spokesman	Channeled hostilities
1965	Bargaining	Reallocation of resources	Spokesman	Politicized interests
1968	Community control	Redistribution of authority	Spokesman-manager	Community consciousness
1971	Coexistence	Community development programs	Manager-technician	Organized consent

Source: John Hall Fish, *Black Power, White Control: The struggle of the Woodlawn Organization in Chicago* (Princeton: Princeton University Press, 1973, p 309).

Most empirical evidence on the actual experience of Alinsky-inspired community organizations points toward the same basic conclusions:

1   The organizations generally could not be multi-ethnic. When they were, their ethnic components fought each other. The only real successes appear to have been linked to the capacity of an organization to become an authoritative representative of a mobilized black community.
2   The organizations generally failed in their material demands and were totally incapable of altering the logic of delivery of services. Yet they survived, sometimes, through their integration as subordinate parts of the institutional system.
3   The organizations did not achieve community control but were instead co-opted and absorbed into the management of the programmes they were supposed to control. They ran the programmes as their new sources of power and legitimacy, contributing to greater disaffection and lesser militancy among the membership.
4   On the other hand, the organizations were formed on a territorial basis and were able to represent the diversity of the neighbourhood's interests. These were the only two characteristics which corresponded to the 'Alinsky Model'. All the others suffered from the confrontation between the abstract definition of a 'common interest for the people' and the political patronage of city halls. And they crumbled when the ideology of community control was used

to quieten grassroots protest through *ad hoc* distribution of social programmes along the lines of co-optation, a scheme that was complemented by selective repression.

The urban revolts of the 1960s were marked by the signs of black liberation and inadvertedly favoured by a federally-based effort of social reform and community action. A model such as the one postulated by Alinsky – insisting on racial integration and fearful of black power – was focused on local governments and aimed at achieving, through conflict, a social consensus between contradictory interests. It could not fit into such a framework of social struggles and, finally, did not.

The reasons for the popularity of the Alinsky ideology and tactics come not from their adequacy in the 1960s revolts but from the correspondence of their characteristics with the new citizen movement that emerged during the 1970s. The most successful Alinskyite experiences – Citizens Actions Program in Chicago, Citizens Action League in California, Fair Share in Massachusetts – developed during the 1970s according to a very different type of action in a very different context. These were truly multi-ethnic, generally city-wide or even state-wide, and were based upon a broad range of issues on economic policy, from taxes to nuclear power, from health services to electricity rates. These issues were of concern more to a new middle class, struck by the economic crisis and affected by the rapid decay of the quality of life. As with many other myths, Alinsky became popular when his ideas actually corresponded to the needs of the new emerging practice. When he organized workers in the 1930s, the actual response, the New Deal, took paths of social reform diametrically opposed to his Jeffersonian principles. When he wrote in the late 1940s, the economic boom and suburbanization process of the 1950s substituted neighbours' tea parties for his praised demand-orientated block clubs. And when he appealed to poor people's unity in the 1960s, the Black Power Movement was actually the driving force behind the urban revolt. Only in the 1970s did the new citizen movement, based upon collective consumption issues and neighbourhood interaction, and focused on the local government level, discover the interest of the populist model of community organizing. Although ideas might be general, their practice is always historically circumscribed.

The Alinsky model was not the consciousness of the 1960s urban revolt in America. While it has been proposed as such, it was, in reality, a reconstructed myth, rediscovered by a collective practice, that corresponded to a new stage of urban mobilization throughout the 1970s. The uprising of American inner cities had very different roots and followed a very different logic, whose profile and social causes we will try now to summarize on the basis of the research findings we have presented.

The Meaning of American Urban Revolts

The 1960s inner cities protest in America appears to have combined three distinct forms of social mobilization:

1 A defensive reaction of popular neighbourhoods against the process of urban decay and the attack of urban renewal.
2 A widespread demand for housing, urban services and welfare rights, coming from a poverty stricken, resident population, stimulated by Federal promises of social reform.
3 An expression of the Black Power Movement, that used the semi-autonomous large urban ghettos as a form of social organization and institution-building for the new militant

community. Although the riots were the most open declaration of the state of insurgency against racist institutions, most of the daily work of the community organizations in the inner cities was also part of a black-related mobilization against the living conditions imposed by racial discrimination and economic over-exploitation of the ethnic minorities that were concentrated into those areas by urban segregation.

While the black revolt actually dominated the tone of urban struggles, and accounted for the most active and influential mobilizations, the three types of movement never actually merged. When such a merger was tried in a single organization on the basis of the ideology of people's unity, as in the case of the 'Alinsky Model', the attempt failed.

Yet all three trends were closely related to the specific characteristics of the American process of urban development, both in their causes and in their consequences.[169] Metropolitan concentration and massive rural-urban migration led millions of black and poor into the large cities. The process of suburbanization, deliberately stimulated by Federal policies on housing and transportation, led to the segregation of minorities, poor, and unemployed in the inner cities, where speculative landlords took advantage of their defenseless situation to overcrowd housing, stop repairs, and collect higher rents per unit. The mechanism of institutional fragmentation between local governments within the metropolitan areas extended inequality to the delivery of public services. When some key dominant functions in the central city were endangered, when urban renewal undertook the preservation of the cities' Central Business District (CBD) by displacing millions of persons without providing for their relocation, then residents resisted the demolition, asked for better housing and services, and tried to establish their own political autonomy when facing unresponsive local government. The black movement of the 1960s, developing the Black Power theme beyond the integrationist liberal tradition, emphasized the autonomy of the ghetto as a basis of social and political organization for blacks, whose demands for jobs and services were actually only the most immediate expression of the black community's aspirations.

Under the pressure of grassroots mobilization, particularly active in the ghetto areas, social programmes were provided by the Federal government, welfare rights extended, public jobs created, and urban services delivered by local governments that came under the growing influence of blacks and poor in the central cities of the metropolitan areas. Nevertheless such a series of major achievements met with serious shortcomings. The basic mechanisms of the economy were not altered; the efforts of social reform were limited to the places and times where the waves of the popular storm had superseded the established patterns of social control; the national political scene actually became more conservative, when Middle America had its usual 'Law-and-Order' reflex. As a consequence inner cities became ungovernable[170] under the conflicting pressures from the grassroots, from the dominant economic interests, and from the public sector workers. The central cities' local governments were challenged from the inside by changing popular constituencies and came increasingly under attack. The urban fiscal crisis was the most apparent expression of such a process.[171] The general economic and demographic decay of the central cities, particularly in the old industrial Northeastern and Northcentral areas, was the most acute symptom of a reversal of the model of urban organization, the contradictions of which inspired the social struggles in question.

The social mobilization of American inner cities in the 1960s expressed the new conditions of collective consumption in advanced capitalism.[172] The socialization of the consumption process through urban services was accompanied by the socialization of the struggles over those services. This mobilization also emphasized the conditions of social conflict in the informal economy of the black ghetto and along the divisions forced by racial discrimination.[173]

At the same time, the inner cities' revolts sang again an old chant of the urban condition: the transformation of the space of exclusion into the space of freedom. The ghetto territory became a significant space for the black community as the material basis of social organization, cultural identity, and political power.

The old cry of freedom rejoined the new demands for economic survival aimed at a system of service provision unable to deliver anything but additional bureaucracy. The depth of the revolt explains its intensity. It also accounts for the limitations of its positive lasting impact. Yet the community movement fundamentally altered the basic structure of American inner cities: unable to absorb all the pressures and still function, the old metropolitan model collapsed, with business and people fleeing to the suburbs, to the South, to the West, while preserving some essential functions within the retrenched encampment of the CBD. They left behind, trapped in the ghettos, communities conscious enough to resist manipulation although not powerful enough to alter the mechanisms governing their deprived condition. Unable to bring about social change, the inner cities' revolts drifted towards inter-personal violence.

7

Conclusion: The Historical Production of Urban Meaning

Our historical overview has shown the crucial importance of social movements in the evolution of cities in a variety of cultural and political contexts. It has also emphasized the role played by urban issues in the formation of processes of collective mobilization that has shaped the course of history. A close relationship between cities and people has been evident, since people have been and still are the makers of cities and cities are an essential raw material in the production of human experience.

The intellectual journey we have undertaken through several centuries has provided some insights into the relationship between social change and urban forms. We must however resist the temptation of a general theorization, accounting for the social process we have already uncovered. A systematic synthesis of such a wide range of historical observations can only provide the first step towards a general interpretative framework – something we are trying to construct in a series of research operations in which this historical perspective is only the first step. So we must wait until Part 6 before returning to our historical perspective armed with theoretical tools accurate enough to understand the full meaning of the social movements we have analysed.

Nevertheless there are several observations that are clear enough and significant enough for the development of our research to deserve some concluding remarks on the changing patterns of relationships between social protest and urban evolution.

First of all, there is, at the same time, a close connection and a clear distinction between the dynamics of social classes and the formation and outcome of urban social movements. If the observation about their connection is a classical one, the remark on their sharp distinction is clearly an uncommon conclusion. Of the five major movements studied, only the Glasgow

Rent Strike appears as the expression of a working class-based social movement. In all other situations the urban mobilization either brought together a variety of social classes around a city vision, or expressed a cultural subset of people, organized around classless lines and mobilized around issues that only indirectly relate to class power. So neither the assimilation of urban conflicts to class struggle nor the entire independence of both processes of social change can be sustained. On the contrary, only by focusing on the interaction between the social dynamics of class struggle and the urban dynamics whose content must be redefined in each historical situation, are we able to understand social change in a comprehensive manner. Furthermore the hierarchy of determination between classes and cities varies according to each historical formation. In Glasgow, as in the process of capitalist industrialization, the relationship between labour and capital directly determined the evolution of the city. This was not the case in Castilla, where the cities acted as they did in response to the formation of the absolutist state; nor in the American inner cities, where the segregated ghettos were primary sources of social influence on the patterns of class relationships. The first lesson of our historical journey is the need to analyse separately cities and classes in order to understand the connection between the two, and to identify the variations in the order and forms of their reciprocal influence.

The second major observation concerns the decisive role of women in several of the urban movements we have studied. Only the *Comunidades* of Castilla, separated by centuries from the other experiences, seemed to have been predominantly sustained by men (although the last leader of the last *Comunidad*, Toledo, was a woman, Dona Maria Pacheco. . .). In the American inner cities, women were as present as men, and in the other movements they actually played a leading role. It is our hypothesis that there is some connection between the social character of urban issues and the role of women in these movements, and we explore this hypothesis in detail throughout our analysis. For the moment we will only make explicit the theoretical assumption on which it relies. Throughout history male domination has resulted in a concentration and hierarchy of social tasks: production, war, and political and religious power – the backbone of social organization – have been reserved for men. All the rest, that is, the immense variety of human experience, from the bringing-up of children and domestic work to sensual pleasure and human communication, have been the women's domain. Men took on the state and left the care of civil society to women. Most urban struggles, particularly in capitalist societies, have many facets, involving issues over and above those of the production process and broader than the battle to seize the apparatuses of power. The role of women as organizing agents of social life is extended to the struggle for a better, or even an alternative, form of life. Their concern for a variety of issues, which is sometimes remote from immediate political instrumentalism, creates a predisposition among men to accept women's leading role in these struggles, and, more importantly, makes participation appealing for women in the defense or transformation of a world whose meaning is closely connected to their daily lives. If the urban experience follows the hidden detours of civil society more naturally than the large avenues towards the state, then, at some fundamental level, there is an intimate connection between women and the city, between urban movements and women's liberation. Our historical survey has revealed the women-based character of some major urban movements. Our study must investigate the question of the difficulty of the transition from these movements to movements orientated towards the transformation of the women's condition.

A third recurrent theme of our historical analysis is the connection between urban social movements and the political exercise of grassroots democracy, either as complementary or alternative organizations to state institutions. The movements that were primarily political, such as the communes of Castilla and of Paris, organized themselves on the basis of ward committees directly linked to a municipal assembly and fought for a political model in which the permanent and active participation of citizens could be ensured. The organization of tenants in Glasgow also emphasized the role of grassroots committees, and America in the 1960s fostered a multiplicity of forms of militant neighbourhood associations calling for participation in the decision making process of local government institutions. Although the *inquilinarios* of Veracruz had little esteem for democratic elections (it is true, in a very unreliable institutional context) all other movements examined here insisted on their demands for a democratic state, while pressuring for the decentralization of power and for enhanced local autonomy. The political dimension of the urban movements appears to be in open confrontation with a centralized state, with authoritorian tendencies, and with insulated bureaucracies. The penetration of the state by the demands of civil society, implicit in the social horizon of citizen movements, seems thus to be closely linked with the articulation between grassroots democracy and representative democracy posed by urban social movements as a superior form of participatory government.

Fourthly, the movements we have identified were not only urban-based but urban-orientated. What this means is that in all situations with the exception of sixteenth century Castilla, the movements were partially triggered by the crisis of housing and urban services. So what we have generally considered to be the 'urban problems' of each historical context were not merely pretexts for the triggering of urban conflicts. Movements reacted against housing conditions, the displacement by urban renewal, the harsh life imposed by real estate speculators. But we know that social mobilizations are not mechanical reactions to historical stimulii. For people to react against high rents or the destruction of their neighbourhoods, they had to be already in a situation in which the urban environment was their social frame and affordable housing rents the precondition to organizing their life. In all cases we are in a situation of rapid urbanization where an uprooted population was forced into the city and then threatened by continuous displacement according to the variations of the real estate market. The reaction against rent increases expressed the resistance to the commodification of the material basis of everyday life. The struggle to preserve the popular neighbourhoods against either the plans of Haussmann or the bulldozers of the American government was the resistance to the despotism of the state over social existence in the city.

At both levels, people were reacting not only against their economic exploitation but against the denial by the system to allow them to stabilize and build new social communities. Thus the process of urbanization led to a socialization of conditions of consumption that were met by collective action against the profit orientated organization of the production and distribution of urban services. The uprooting of most urban newcomers was confronted by residents wishing to start new lives against the market rule of spatial mobility according to the variations of profit. And the enforcement of the new urban system by a state transformed into a city planner was faced by increasing resistance from residents in defense of their neighbourhoods. While the forefront of the process of industrialization was occupied by the struggle between capital and labour to share the product and to shape the state, the backyards of the growing cities were the scene of a stubborn, often ignored resistance by residents to keep autonomy in their homes and meaning in their communities.

The fifth element that results from our historical investigation is the importance of space as a material basis for all forms of social organization. The medieval city became an autonomous political entity behind the protection of its walls, whose military function was in fact second only to the symbolic expression of the will to be free. The *Commune* of Paris wanted its territory forbidden to the army so that its values of social progress and political democracy could flourish in a fertile urban ground and become strong enough to take on the world. The *inquilinarios* of Veracruz rejected the dependent city and therefore hoped to settle in another space, as if the physical separation of their colony was the only definitive way to leave the bourgeois society they hated so much. The revolt of the black ghettos took advantage of urban segregation to transform the space of exclusion into the space of freedom, in which autonomous institutions could be built and from which a new power relationship could be established. Even the workers of Glasgow, who were more concerned with the defense of their own living conditions than with the construction of the city, relied on the protective setting of the working class communities of Govan and Partick to set up their tenant committees, to organize their struggle, and to debate their goals.

If it has long been accepted that space is the expression of a given social organization, the role of the territory in the production of social forms has been less seriously considered by researchers. The cause is an understandable reaction, that we fully share, against the primitive, physically-orientated approach of some human ecologists, treating social behaviour in terms of density, friction and distance, as if people and rats were interchangeable experimental subjects. Yet the emphasis upon the social and cultural determination of space must be combined with the recognition of the fundamental role played by territoriality in the configuration of social processes. Furthermore urban space is meaningful in historical terms. Its close association with social movements, as revealed by our research, expresses the fact that people always need a material basis on which to organize their autonomy against the surveillance of the political apparatuses controlling the spheres of production and institutional power. Only in the secrecy of their homes, in the complicity of neighbourhoods, in the communication of taverns, in the joy of street gatherings may they find values, ideas, projects and, finally, demands that do not conform to the dominant social interests. The control over space is a major battle in the historic war between people and the state.

Our remarks have emphasized the regularities to be found between urban social movements which occurred in very different historical contexts. While these similarities should stimulate some hypotheses with respect to a general theory of the relationships between city and society, they should not be interpreted as signs of a trans-historical social process, in which an external 'urban social movement' deployed its inherent logic throughout centuries and across cultures. Our conception, and findings, in fact support the opposite view of history, because the most important lesson that can be drawn from the research presented in these chapters is the historical diversity of the social meaning of urbanism.

The medieval city, was above all, a political culture and the project of a new political institution. But the urban debate present in the Glasgow Rent Strike had little to do with political autonomy and much to contribute to workers' consumption demands. The Parisian *communards* tried to generalize their urban culture as a superior form of social progress, while the dependent city was for the *inquilinarios* the material expression of foreign domination and moral corruption. The social content of the city as a spatial form, and therefore of the urban issues underlying the 'crises' and the struggles, are all historically determined and, therefore, vary in different modes of production, in different cultures, and in different stages of historical development. The meaning of the city in the European Middle Ages, in ancient Mesopotamia, or in the American ghetto, was a fundamentally different social reality, not only because the problems were different, but the role of spatial concentration of population and functions was specific to each historical context. What in Toledo was the spatial organization of political democracy might in Babylon have been the material organization of religious despotism. Thus the socio-cultural meaning of urbanism is a product of history.

But what are the origins of this product? How is a particular meaning, and therefore the definition of the issues, problems, crises and struggles provided to cities in each historical context? And who provides it? We have answered empirically this question in the five contexts studied. We will try a theoretical answer at a general level in the final part of the book when proposing a broader theory of urban social change.

Yet we can introduce here the beginnings of this theory in light of the analyses presented in this chapter. The historical definition of urban meaning is a conflictive one, as a result of the struggle between historical actors over the control of power, resources, space, and cultural categories, in exactly the same way that only those things considered 'productive' by the dominant class of a mode of production are valued, while 'socially useful' but structurally rewardless activities are counted insignificant. The definition of the city for each society is what historical actors struggling in such a society try to make it. This process is obviously not a purely subjective matter in terms of values, desires and wishes, but is determined by the productive forces, the relationship with nature, the institutional heritage, and the social relationships of production. But at the level of the historical production of the city's role in society, things come down to a particular social project, or sets of alternative conflicting projects, acted by social subjects. And here lies the most important role of urban social movements, their very *raison d'être* as a distinctive actor: they are the collective actions consciously aimed at fundamentally modifying the city's role in society, or redefining the historical meaning of 'urban'. It is in this sense that all the movements that we have studied are major urban social movements.

The Castilian *comuneros* tried to make the city the alternative political form of construction of the modern state *vis-à-vis* the nation-building absolutist monarchy. The Parisian *communards* tried to combine the defense of the people, the freedom of the Republic and the progress of humankind through a municipal revolution that would transform the city into an autonomous centre to inspire the federation of liberated communes. The Glasgow workers successfully forced the state to institutionally provide the means of consumption that the capitalist market could not produce at a level the workers could afford, and under conditions they could accept. Housing became a public affair. The Veracruz *inquilinarios* tried to survive in the dependent city while fundamentally rejecting it, and then they proposed the anti-city in a peripheral colony where they could reconstruct their own social world. And the American blacks consolidated their ghettos against the threat of urban renewal to preserve their social autonomy in a racist society, and to use their free space as a basis for a political challenge to win concessions from the institutional system.

Yet the social production of urban meaning is not a process involving a single actor. Thus the urban projects of the movements we have analysed met contradictory projects from their social antagonists: the city as a bureaucratic locus in the case of the Spanish monarchy; in Paris the city as a capital for the state, a service-provider for capital, and a source of speculation for money; in Glasgow the city as a place of industrial production and reproduction of labour power; in Veracruz the city as a foreign dependent trade centre, and as a speculative housing market; in America the city as a directional centre and a socially controlled reservation for ethnic minorities. The actual urban product, both in terms of material spatial structure and the cultural category assigned to the urban realm, resulted from the historical process of confrontation between these antagonistic projects along the lines we have described for each case. To be sure, our summary description here is far too schematic, and it would be impossible to reconstruct the entire mechanism connecting the variety of intervening social forces to the actual urban forms resulting in the five historical contexts. Our purpose, at this point of our analysis, is merely to underline a research perspective.

It is also to show the specific role of social movements in the production of urban forms and urban meaning, and to remind ourselves that their role is not limited to their great victories, which, alone, would be exceptional, but to the impact they had, even in defeat. Their lasting effects are present in the breaches produced in the dominant logic, in the compromises reached within the institutions, in the changing cultural forms of the city, in the collective memory of the neighbourhoods, and, ultimately, in the continuing social debate about what the city should be.

Such is the theoretical challenge we have discovered in our historical journey: how to understand the production of cities and urban meaning as a conflictive and permanently open process between historical social actors. If this mechanism is real, if it actually represents the underlying source of social change and social reproduction of urban systems, we should also be able to discover a similar logic in a variety of social contexts whose historical proximity to the observer will make it possible for a more systematic analysis of the process through which people produce cities as they make history.

Part 2

Housing Policy and Urban Trade Unionism: The Grands Ensembles of Paris

8

Introduction: The Rise and Fall of the Grands Ensembles

Paris is not Paris anymore. Less than 16 per cent of the 9,400,000 Parisians live within the administrative limits of the city. For the others, their home is the *banlieue*, the ring of suburbs built around the historic city during the accelerated metropolitan growth of the post-1945 period.[1] The suburban landscape is dominated by the *Grands Ensembles*, an image that since the 1960s has become as characteristic of Paris as the Eiffel Tower.

The *Grand Ensemble* is the ultimate expression of socialized housing production under state initiative.[2] It is a large, very dense, high-rise housing estate, generally built in the middle of nowhere (that is, on cheap agricultural land), connected to Paris by train and road, so that its 20,000 to 60,000 dwellers can commute every day either to Paris or to some industrial location in the surrounding periphery. The physical shape and the management system of the *Grands Ensembles* seem to fit almost too well into the theoretical model that sees housing as a means of reproduction of labour power.[3] The French government, under a variety of procedures which we will examine, provided public housing at the lowest possible cost, for a population struck by a housing crisis beyond the limits that the Fourth Republic, influenced by powerful left wing parties, could bear.[4] In 1954, almost 9 per cent of residents of the Paris metropolitan area did not have a regular home (in French statistical terms they lived in *logements de fortune*). In the category of blue collar workers, 14 per cent lived this way. Further statistics show that some 17 per cent of the total population were forced to share a flat with another family; 15 per cent of the housing units were overcrowded; 18 per cent did not have a kitchen; and 55 per cent did not have a water closet inside the flat.[5] Paris continued to be the most advantageous location for industrial firms in search of skilled workers and as a result, people from all over France emigrated to Paris, looking for a job.[6]

The housing demand, however, was not met by housing supply.[7] In the city of Paris, the 1948 Rent Control Law discouraged investment and sharply reduced the rotation of occupancy.[8] In the metropolitan area, the income levels of the workers could not meet the level of rents or prices required for new housing by the construction industry operating under conditions governed by a tight and speculative land market.[9] Industrialists foresaw the problem and feared the impact upon wage demands.[10] The labour unions and the Communist Party pushed for low-rent public housing. A Christian movement was organized around *L' Abbé Pierre* to defend the most desperate cases. Popular mobilizations developed and some squatting took place.[11] The government responded in 1953 with a major reform in housing policy: the *Plan Courant*.[12] Three measures were apparently at the core of a new orientation towards housing: all private businesses were required to contribute 1 per cent of the wages they were paying to a special public housing fund; a series of legal regulations gave the government, and the municipalities, extensive powers of eminent domain over development land; and a new major para-public developer, the Societé Centrale Immobilière de la Caisse des Depots (SCIC),[13] was empowered to build public housing, mainly on the basis of the savings deposited in the government-run 'Post Office's Savings', the first collector of people's savings in France.

The need for housing was so evident, the pressure for it so compelling, that the SCIC began work immediately, trying to build as quickly as possible and as much as possible. Thus cheap land was acquired, land for which lack of amenities, isolation, and distance from Paris made it unattractive to the private developer. Density for the projects was very high, so that the impact of land rent on the total cost of housing would be reduced,[14] and the quality of construction was set at the lowest level, minimizing the cost, maximizing the number of units, and reminding everyone of the welfare nature of the construction. From the outset therefore the project was an insult to the prospective inhabitants, and one that was accentuated by the 'aesthetics' of the *Grands Ensembles*, particularly the first generation ones (1955–1963). Using the rationale of standardization of construction in order to mechanize the building sector, uniform high-rise buildings in parallel rows were planted in a grid pattern open to the North wind and overwhelmed by the grey skies of the Parisian plain. Furthermore, if a city is something more than an agglomeration of housing units, then the *Grands Ensembles* did not become a city until many years later: they did not have, at their start, basic urban equipment such as health services, day-care centres, enough schools, cultural facilities, shops, or sufficient public transportation.[15] The French invented the expression of the 'right to the city',[16] and it is likely that such an imaginative statement was stimulated by the contrast between one of the richest urban cultures in the world – along the banks of the Seine – and the experience of reducing urban settlement to a state-provided concrete dormitory.

The impact on public opinion of the deteriorated way of life symbolized by the *Grands Ensembles* became considerably greater than had been anticipated. Films, songs, books, and jokes satirized the effort. A major reason for this reaction was probably that, in spite of the left wing ideological representation prevailing in France, the *Grands Ensembles* were not a working class settlement. The classical demographic study by Paul Clerc[17] on the social structure of the *Grands Ensembles* discovered that the profile of their residents was very similar to the one for the corresponding metropolitan area: manual workers, clerks, and low-level professionals shared the same residential space. The only substantial differences in relationship to the central city was the higher proportion of young couples with infants, and the over-representation of middle-level technicians among the residents of the *Grands Ensembles*. So while the new urban areas were seen by the left, and probably by the government, as the new strongholds of the working class, they were in fact the spatial setting of the new generation of Parisians, largely dominated by a new and expanding middle class largely employed in the service economy.[18]

In spite of all the criticisms, the *Grands Ensembles* mushroomed on the Parisian landscape for almost twenty years. They were the state's response to housing demands. They overwhelmed the horizon, submerging the romantic images of Paris, and forging a new, tough generation of metropolitan dwellers. Then, one day in the Spring of 1973, like the dinosaurs, they suddenly disappeared. Their trace, to be precise, still remains on the Parisian soil: the buildings are there, the people are there, and the housing bureaucracy is there. But these are remnants. From Spring 1973 on, not a single *Grand Ensemble* was to be built. Nor were they to be replaced as they decayed. The concept disappeared. And, as with the dinosaurs, it was a sudden extinction that, at first sight, remains a mystery. To be sure, French historians, armed with Cartesianism, will have a definite explanation: the 'Circulaire Guichard' of April 1973. As usual, French history will be considered as having been changed by decree, according to a government's initiative. It is true the decision of M. Guichard, Minister of Equipment, that forbade the construction of any residential ensemble larger than 2,000 units, signalled the death of the urban formula that had characterized the French metropolitan suburbs for many years.

Yet such a dramatic shift in housing policy was itself the expression of deeper and more meaningful social contradictions. The political setbacks of the Gaullist coalition in the March 1973 elections (particularly serious in the *Grands Ensembles*) as well as a generally hostile public opinion, led to a major rectification in public policy that modified the French metropolitan forms.[19] It is our hypothesis that this social process, and the resulting policy, was largely determined by the urban protest movements that took place in the Parisian *Grands Ensembles* during the 1960s and early 1970s. To test such a hypothesis on the reciprocal relationship between housing policy and urban movements, we carefully studied the first and the last *Grands Ensembles*. The first, Sarcelles, built between 1957 and 1974, was the source of all kinds of images, analyses, and myths, to the point that a word was invented in French to mean the psychological illness associated with urban alienation – '*sarcellitis*'. The last, the Val d' Yerres, built between 1966 and 1974, was a desperate attempt by the public developer (the SCIC) to respond to social criticism with a new form of large housing estate displaying the virtues of environmental quality and intense human interaction. Map 8–1 shows the situation of Sarcelles and Val d' Yerres in relation to the Paris region.

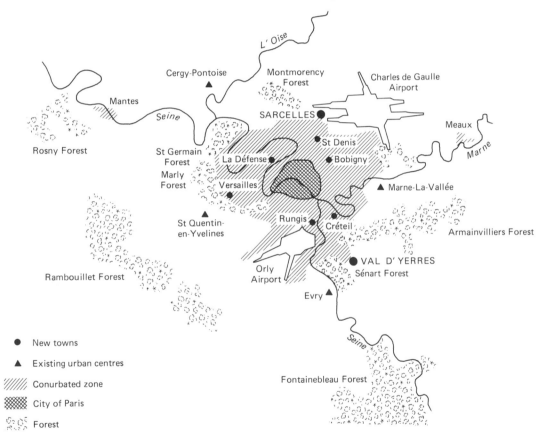

Map 8.1 Schematic map showing location of Sarcelles and of Val d'Yerres in relation to the Paris region. (*Source*: Schema directeur de la région Parisienne.)

In both cases, a very active tenants' and residents' movement developed, challenging housing policies and life styles. In both cases we investigated the revolt in detail, through two years of field work research by a team of four full-time researchers, according to procedures described and justified in the Methodological Appendix (see pp. 343–45). The result is an attempt to understand how the socialization of the city led to urban struggles aimed at the state – the manager of the urban process. And the research question we will try to answer is how a new housing policy could have given birth to a new form of urban trade unionism, that in turn, undermined the policy itself.

9

The Emergence of Urban Trade Unionism: Sarcelles

Sarcelles was the first *Grand Ensemble* built in the Paris metropolitan area and still remains in the collective memory of Parisians as the symbol of this particular urban form. It was also the first community to experience the development of a large resident mobilization to improve housing and living conditions, the observation of which provided the occasion to analyse the sources, limits, and outcomes of what, at first sight, appeared to be the mainstream of urban demand movements in Western Europe, that is, tenant unions in public housing.[20] It was also in Sarcelles that, for the first time, the discontent of dwellers concentrated in these newly built suburban dormitories resulted in a vote for a communist-dominated local government which has persisted since the municipal elections of 1965. Thus our analysis will pay special attention to the complex interplay between urban movements and local politics, whose dynamics account for the evolution of urban policies in the *Grands Ensembles*.

The construction of the *Grand Ensemble* started in 1954, in the territory of a small rural village, Sarcelles, 15 kilometres north of Paris, with a population of around 1,500.[21] Originally intended to receive 1,000 housing units, at its completion in 1974 Sarcelles contained over 13,000 units with a population of around 60,000 people. The long time span of its construction was due to the fact that it was not planned as a unit, but expanded when necessary as a response to the growing housing crisis. Table 9–1 clearly shows that the first residents of

Table 9.1   Reason for Leaving Former Residence for a Representative Sample of Dwellers of the *Grand Ensemble* of Sarcelles in 1962. (N = 4,002.)

Reason	Percentage of Total Sample
Overcrowded or dilapidated housing	43·0
Living in furnished hotels	14·0
Living with other families	12·5
Eviction	8·7
Refugee from Northern Africa	4·2
Being closer (in Sarcelles) to work place	4·3
Rent paid was too high	0·6
Provisional barracks	0·5
Other motives (including job transfer from another city)	12·1

Source: Paris: SCIC, Etude Statistique de l'Ensemble de Sarcelles, October 1962.

Sarcelles moved there to escape the unbearable housing conditions in Paris, with the exception of a few former French residents of Algeria, fleeing the country after its independence (about 4 per cent of the residents in 1962).

Built, developed, and administered by the same para-public institution, the SCIC, Sarcelles comprised three different types of housing, in accordance with the evolution of French housing policy in three different periods. From 1954 to 1960, five neighbourhoods were built and named with immutable bureaucratic logic: Sarcelles 1, 2, 3, 4 and 5. They were all low-rent public housing units of the HLM type (*Habitation Loyer Modère*: French public housing low income units), and although a broad social spectrum was aimed at, it attracted a predominance of blue-collar and clerical workers. Between 1960 and 1966, the improvement of economic conditions in France, as well as the political hegemony of the conservative Gaullist party, allowed the SCIC enough room to try and make some profitable housing investments, raising the level of rents and improving the quality of the habitations. At this time they built Sarcelles 6 and 7. The result was an upgrading of Sarcelles' social status, with fewer blue collar workers and an increasing proportion of middle managers and technicians. Later, in the 1966–74 period, the attempt to attract a more sophisticated type of resident to Sarcelles led to a policy of low-interest loans for home ownership. The last neighbourhoods built in the *Grand Ensemble*, Sarcelles 8 and 9, were predominantly condominiums for middle class families. In 1974 almost one-third of the residents were home owners: Table 9–2 the evolution of the social structure of the population for each area, as a consequence of the three subsequent housing policies underlying the construction of Sarcelles:

1 The basic aim of responding to the housing crisis that was present, though with a changing emphasis, throughout the twenty year period.
2 The effort to introduce private profitable investment in the public housing sector.
3 The attempt to break through the image of public rental housing by using public resources and authority to open a new home ownership market for the middle class.

Table 9.2 Evolution of Social Composition of Sarcelles for Each Neighbourhood, 1962 to 1968. (Percentage of the Total Population Living in Each Neighbourhood, Selected Categories.)

Occupational Category	Year	Sarcelles 1	Sarcelles 2	Sarcelles 3	Sarcelles 4	Sarcelles 5	Sarcelles 6 and 7	Sarcelles 8
Professionals	1962	7·0	6·7	5·6	6·4	5·0	—	—
and managers	1968	5·7	4·3	5·0	5·0	7·8	2·0	20·7
Middle management	1962	15·0	19·3	15·4	18·1	20·4	—	—
and technicians	1968	14·9	15·3	17·1	16·7	19·0	27·5	29·5
Clerks	1962	28·0	30·1	26·4	24·6	37·0	—	—
	1968	28·2	33·6	30·9	31·8	36·4	36·5	25·4
Manual workers	1962	41·7	31·5	41·0	40·4	29·1	—	—
	1968	42·0	34·4	35·7	33·6	26·4	16·5	16·0

Note: Percentages do not add to 100% because of rounding.
Source: Paris: INSEE Census, 1962, 1968.

The development of residents' mobilization over housing demands went along in a parallel way with the construction of Sarcelles. It took different forms and reached different levels of intensity – more active and less institutionalized in the first period, more political and somewhat more effective in terms of its urban impact in the late stages of the city's expansion. This emergence of an urban movement, and its contradictory relationship with the political system, are the focus of our analysis in this case study.

Two major factors seem to have been at the origin of the urban mobilization. On the one hand, the highly collective character of the production and management of the city: the SCIC was the developer, landlord, and manager for every building in the entire city, as well as the responsible institution for the production and delivery of all essential urban equipment. While people in Paris could hardly react collectively against their bad housing conditions, faced with a fragmented constellation of small landlords, everyone in Sarcelles confronted the same condition and had to deal with the same bureaucratic partner. The socialization of urban environment created the conditions for the discovery of common interests. Yet a second important element must be taken into consideration: the harshness of the living conditions for the first pioneers of Sarcelles. Though their housing situation dramatically improved in relation to what they had experienced in Paris, they were forced to live in the midst of a construction site, with no amenities, poor transportation, and a total absence of urban life. The studies on the social relationships in Sarcelles during the late 1950s and early 1960s show a dramatic decrease in the extension and richness of social networks and human interaction in comparison with the residents' former experience.[22] The isolation was especially acute for women, many of whom had to give up their jobs in Paris in order to take care of the children, while also losing their contacts with friends, family, and neighbours which they had enjoyed in their overcrowded but intense human environment.

Plate 9.1 Housing estates, the *Grand Ensemble* of Sarcelles. (Photograph: M. Castells.)

Almost at the time of the construction of the first buildings, in the Autumn of 1957, a residents' association, the *Association.Sarcelloise* (AS), was founded in reaction to both urban problems and social isolation, and initiated by political militants (left wing socialists of the *Parti Socialiste Unifie* [PSU] and communists of the *Parti Communiste Francais* [PCF]). It nonetheless clearly represented a broad range of public opinion, as demonstrated by its first president who was apolitical and moderate. By 1962, the AS had 800 members, and its bulletin, *Sarcelles*, had a regular circulation of 5,000 copies. The AS was organized by neighbourhood committees and building delegates, though its bureau was elected every year by a general assembly of its membership. The first task was to group people, not only on the basis of urban demands, but also according to a variety of social and cultural activities lacking in Sarcelles: a library, a civic club, a legal counselling service, a local newspaper, and so on. By the early 1960s, about 100 voluntary associations existed in Sarcelles due to the initiative and example of the AS militants.

In the general atmosphere of political deception in France in the 1960s, however, the merger between acute urban problems and a voluntary association's militancy needed some dramatic circumstances powerful enough to trigger spontaneous grassroots mobilization. The first such event came in 1963, when the heating system of a building exploded because of faulty construction. Three people were killed. Meetings of protest were organized, demanding the reorganization of the heating system, separating the central heaters from the building. The SCIC refused: it would be too costly and the public developer wanted to reduce expenses as far as possible, so that a maximum of those who suffered from the housing crisis could be absorbed into the *Grands Ensembles'* programmes. Then, a few weeks later, on a cold Sunday afternoon when most families were together at home, the heating system broke down again, leaving most flats freezing cold. 1,500 people took to the streets of Sarcelles. On their behalf the AS negotiated with the SCIC and obtained the ·revision of the entire installation, the removal of heaters from the buildings, and their location in buried sites, thus respecting the safety regulations. For the first time a mass mobilization had forced the builder to recognize that the *Grands Ensembles'* residents were not ready to indiscriminately accept conditions out of pure gratitude for cheap rental housing.

Safety subsequently became one of the main themes of urban demands in Sarcelles. For instance, in 1967, the stairs of Building 57 collapsed, killing one person. Under the pressure of the AS a commission found that most stairs were in an unstable condition (an occupational hazard of using one building model conceived by the same architect and constructed by the same company). The SCIC was forced to reconstruct the stairs in the entire city to meet safety standards. To some extent the struggle over safety expressed the confrontation between two logics. Sarcelles, for the residents, had to provide housing of good quality to compensate for distance, isolation, and lack of urban environment. The first stage of Sarcelles, for the SCIC, was some sort of urban welfare, so that costs had to be kept down, even if construction was so poor as to become dangerous. The first urban struggles forced widespread repairs and maintenance, while dissuading the developer from continuing to build housing at low standards. The SCIC consequently decide that if housing had to be of higher quality, the residents should pay for it. The succeeding programmes were thus designed for higher income people and the units already in existence had their rents raised. This move threatened the fragile family budget of most residents and led to one of the most important and significant struggles in Sarcelles: the rent strike of 1965.

In the Autumn of 1965, the SCIC launched its new policy of making public housing investments somewhat more profitable. Sarcelles was the largest *Grand Ensemble* and had a symbolic value, so rents were increased there first. The average rent increased by 25 per cent. The AS decided to resist the increase. A meeting of 400 residents voted to continue paying the rent at its former level while refusing to pay the increase. A demonstration by 1,700 tenants supported the decision. The SCIC reacted by threatening eviction, sending notices to all rent strikers. The AS collected over 500 of these notices and sent them back to the SCIC, categorically refusing to pay and denouncing SCIC's attempt to individualize the conflict since they wanted to establish the right to collective bargaining when dealing with their landlord (whereas SCIC was trying to deal with the tenants on an individual basis, the traditional landlord-tenant relationship). To nullify the rent increase in Sarcelles meant abandoning the new rent policy in all the *Grands Ensembles* under SCIC's management, since its public service role required the same policy to be followed nationally.

So, in spite of the residents' mobilization, SCIC rejected any negotiation and put increasing pressure on tenants, including the use of personal intimidation by the buildings' janitors. At the same time, the fact that the municipality played such an active role as the centre of social mobilization led to open conflict as autonomous urban movements developed in Sarcelles. To avoid being abandoned by its constituency, the AS withdrew in good order, declaring the end of the rent strike by January 1966. Yet the defeat was only an apparent one. As a result of the representativeness and determination shown by the AS, a long negotiation took place that resulted, in 1968, in the signing of an agreement between the SCIC and all the residents' associations on a lease for all rental housing in Sarcelles. The major improvement was the indexing of rent according to the cost of construction. The SCIC won the possibility of a steady increase every three years. The tenants won protection against arbitrary and sudden increases. Furthermore, the principle was established that the lease was to be the subject of collective bargaining so ending the traditional relationship between landlord and tenant. As a consequence of the socialization of housing production and management, collective bargaining entered the process of consumption.

In fact, the SCIC was well aware of this evolution. It knew that tensions were increasing in Sarcelles and that Sarcelles could well be the vanguard of a similar movement in all the *Grands Ensembles*. In 1965, M. Bloch-Lainé, chairman of the board of directors of the Caisse des Dépôts, the financial institution behind the SCIC, and an innovative Gaullist technocrat, asked the University of Paris' Institute of Political Science to study the situation. The Sérieyx Report concluded that '. . . the individual relationship that, according to the law, is the only link between the landlord and the tenant, is no longer a suitable framework for the new administrative and human reality of the *Grands Ensembles*.' As a result, the report recommended the creation of elected Residents' Councils in each *Grand Ensembles*, and the SCIC accepted. To implement the decision the SCIC opened negotiations with national tenant unions of all tendencies, to determine the content and functioning of these Residents' Councils. Significantly enough, the Confederation Nationale du Logement (CNL), Union Nationale des Associations Familiales (UNAF), Association Populaire des Familles (APF), and Confederation Syndicale des Familles (CSF), all of them national organizations, participated in the negotiation with the SCIC, along with the AS: a major indication of the strategic role played by the mobilization in Sarcelles in influencing the new participation policy of the public housing sector. On 26 June 1965 a national covenant was signed between the SCIC and all participating organizations that established the existence of a Residents' Council in each *Grand Ensemble*, elected on the basis of one vote per housing unit between the candidacies presented by voluntary associations existing in each *Grand Ensemble*. Grassroots movements saw their presence institutionally recognized for the first time. Under this new arrangement each Residents' Council was to be informed by the developer of all matters concerning rents and payments. It also had some rights of consultation on planning issues and once took responsibility for the management of cultural and collective facilities. Yet its powers were largely undefined and their extent was a function of the actual local power relationships, leading to endless conflicts. In Sarcelles, the Council was elected in February 1966. The 'AS' won the election, with eight seats out of eighteen, followed by the moderate *Association des Familles* (ADF) with six seats, and the Home Owners Association with three seats. Under the instigation of the AS, the Council, instead of being an instrument of participation, became a platform for urban struggle. Among other demands it obtained from the SCIC the decentralization of management of the *Grands Ensembles* from SCIC's national office to local cooperatives that took care of the problems of each residential unit. In most *Grands Ensembles*, however, the new Co-operative of Housing Management was simply a decentralized, more flexible, form of administration under the SCIC's total control. In Sarcelles, under pressure from the Residents' Council, the SCIC conceded something else: the residents' representation would share the management of the *Grand Ensemble*, including the budget. It was the beginning of a joint urban management strategy that the AS had included in its programme as a new approach to societal issues on the basis of urban mobilization. In that sense the agreement reached on 14 December 1967, opened the way for a far-reaching urban movement. Yet what appeared to be the most important victory of the AS became the source of its destruction. In settling on an explicit political strategy (the shared management of the urban system on the basis of grassroots organizations), the AS released the forces of an internal conflict that had been brewing for years, a conflict that became particularly acute after the municipal elections of 1965.

In 1965, on the basis of widespread urban unrest and grassroots organization, the left wing parties challenged the conservative coalition controlling the municipality. The challenge was not an easy task. The sector of population that had come from Algeria was a solid stronghold of the extreme right. While the suburban working class in Paris tended to vote more communist and socialist than any other sector of the population, Sarcelles did not have a working class majority. But on the basis of the urban mobilization of the middle class, the left obtained enough votes among this sector to win the election by a narrow margin (6,204 votes against 5,797). A city council was elected with 19 communists (including the mayor), six socialists, and six left wing socialists (PSU). Since then, in the 1971 and 1977 municipal elections, the left majority has been re-elected with the communist mayor increasing his vote and becoming in 1977 the representative of the Sarcelles district in the French parliament. Such a political success for the left dramatically reversed the situation in Sarcelles. The SCIC had to face a municipality ready to fight to obtain urban amenities, social services, and jobs for the city residents. Sarcelles increasingly became a major centre of demand and negotiation whose action was often decisive in improving the urban facilities. For instance, the city council participated very actively between 1971–74 in public mobilizations to obtain more schools from the Ministry of Education to meet the needs of the growing population of children in Sarcelles. At the same time, the fact that the municipality was acting as the centre of social mobilization led to open conflict with the development of autonomous urban movements in Sarcelles.

The confrontation centred on the role of the Residents' Council. For the communists, and for the majority of the city council, the Residents' Council was a useless trap designed to enable the developer to bypass the politically representative body of the population. For the AS, whose leadership was mainly in the hands of PSU, the Residents' Council had a different function from that of the municipality. The Council was supposed to represent the residents as tenants and urban consumers, while the municipality was to be the political representation of citizens within the limits of the state institutions. The distinction was too subtle for the communists of Sarcelles. Unable to control the AS and fearful of its influence in the Residents' Council, they split it. The AS communist militants withdrew to form the local branch of the CNL, the national tenant union close to the Communist Party. They challenged the AS in the next elections of the Residents' Council in 1968. The new Council gave six seats to the CNL, five to the AS, four to the moderate ADF, and three to the Home Owners Association. As a result of the split between the CNL and the AS, a home owner was elected president and the Council was paralysed forever. The AS did not survive the crisis and became reduced to a skeleton, a platform controlled by PSU militants, something totally different from the broad popular basis that was at its origin. The CNL never replaced it. Composed of Communist Party militants in 50 per cent of its members, it concentrated on following the national campaigns organized by the CNL and the local initiatives proposed by the municipality. The urban movement in Sarcelles has been dead since 1968 at least in the form of a voluntary grass-roots organization.

The crisis between the AS and the PCF was not a simple sectarian feud, but reflected deep differences in the conception of the relationship between urban demands and the political system. In Sarcelles as elsewhere, urban movements laid the foundation for the PCF, and its allies, to be elected at the local level. Municipalities were not seen mainly as elements of urban government but as instruments of demand, putting pressure on the central government to obtain the improvement of material conditions for the residents, so that they could identify such improvement with support for the Communist Party, thus opening the way for the election of a national government with strong communist participation. In this sense, the contradiction between the AS and the PCF was not a contradiction between movement and party, but between two conceptions of urban trade unionism. Since the municipality was considered a legitimate element of the democratic state, the AS felt that residents should organize on non-political grounds and take responsibility for their conditions, while expressing their political will at the municipal level. In contrast, the PCF argued that within the bourgeois state, municipalities, not urban movements, were the equivalent of labour trade unionism in the work place, and in the knowledge that they could not handle the urban crisis within the capitalist system, the PCF proceeded, by steps, from grassroots agitation to the control of local governments as a launching platform against the capitalist-controlled national government. This has been the reason for its implacable fight against the belief in urban self-management by the AS. To accept the existence of an autonomous urban movement would be to deprive the party of its only real weapon: its marshalling of the rebellious popular masses.

Yet the popular origins of Sarcelles' municipal trade unionism left their trace on the institutions of local government. The city of Sarcelles was one of the first in France to establish neighbourhood committees in which residents of each neighbourhood were (and still are) regularly informed by a city council member of matters of immediate concern, and given the chance to express their opinion.

Furthermore, the popular pressure exercised throughout the 1960s by the AS produced two major effects on the city:

1 It actually changed the political leanings of the population, particularly among the middle class. Table 9–3 indicates the extent to which the middle class and the clerical workers engaged themselves in Sarcelles against the interests of the SCIC, and as an indirect consequence, against the government's housing policy. The experience of collective mobilization on the basis of housing issues seems to account for the change of political attitude of a middle and lower-middle class marked until then by its separation from the working class, as an expression of the social distance between the two groups in the work place. It was on the basis of such a transformation of attitude that the left (led by the Communists) was able for the first time to conquer a suburban local government in a non-working class city.

2 Under the combined pressure of the AS between 1957–68 and the communist municipality since 1965, Sarcelles became a relatively well-equipped suburban commune, with extensive cultural and commercial facilities, social services, and good schools. From the simple repro-

Table 9.3 Comparison of the social composition of the leadership of the *Association Sarcelloise*, and of the *Association des Familles* in relation to the residents of Sarcelles and to the residents of the Paris metropolitan area, 1968. (Percentage total of each residential category, selected categories for Associations' Militants.)

	Paris Metropolitan Area	Sarcelles	'Association Sarcelloise'	Association des Familles
Manual workers	0·35	0·30	0·09	0·08
Clerks	0·22	0·31	0·37	0·16
Technicians and middle level management	0·14	0·19	0·37	0·59
Professionals and managers	0·09	0·07	0·09	0·24
Small business	0·08	0·02	—	—
Personal service workers	0·08	0·05	—	—
Farmers	0·006	—	—	—
Agricultural workers	0·006	—	—	—
Others	0·03	0·06	0·08	—

Sources: 1 Paris and Sarcelles: INSEE Census 1968.
2 Associations' militants: estimation on the basis of lists of candidacy to Residents Council elections and composition of the Associations' Boards.

duction of labour power, it shifted to the status of an advanced middle level city. This evolution was partly due to the SCIC's policy of increasing the proportion of condominiums and housing of high-quality in the city. But this policy was itself the result of pressures from the residents to obtain a quality of housing and urban services that the SCIC had tried to meet by raising prices and upgrading the social status of the housing. The municipality also tried to change the status of the suburban dormitory by attracting businesses and jobs, by building a giant shopping centre, and by helping the SCIC to construct extensive office space. Such attempts largely failed, but they were significant in terms of the magnitude of the effort undertaken by municipally-based, collective consumption trade unionism to challenge the urban status assigned to each locality by the spatial division of labour.

The debate remains open between the two styles of urban trade unionism, a debate that is perhaps best expressed in the favourite anecdote of Sarcelle's urban militants: the municipal library of 'M. Grassot.' He was a founding member of the AS and his passion was books. There was no public library in Sarcelles by 1959, so he undertook to create one. There were some books in the rural village's town hall; and 'M. Grassot' added a few of his own and of his friends, and ended up with a list of available books that he gave to the janitors of each building. Residents would check the list and ask for a book. Every month 'M. Grassot' would pick up the list of requests and ride his bicycle to the flat of each potential reader, to bring him or her the solicited book. Readership dramatically increased in Sarcelles. So when the left wing parties were elected to Sarcelles' city government, priority was given to building a municipal library. This was done, and the result was a modern, spacious building, with silent, carpeted reading rooms. It was open every day from nine in the morning to five in the afternoon, precisely the time that people were at work and most women occupied in child care and domestic work. 'M. Grassot', in recognition of his civic service, was appointed as municipal librarian. He felt, however, that his task no longer made sense. One day he sold everything, bought a van and a pile of books and left Sarcelles to go to Lozère, a beautiful rural province in Central France, where he still goes around the villages, lending books every month on the basis of requests from residents of communities without libraries who want to read at home.

'M. Grassot' was, of course, a romantic, but it was this same romanticism that equipped Sarcelles, laid the ground for the middle class to vote left, created the Residents' Councils, imposed collective bargaining on public housing rents, and ultimately, led the SCIC to alter the urban form it was producing by proposing a new model of *Grand Ensemble* whose prototype was to be the Val d' Yerres.

10

The Social Limits of Urban Design: Val d' Yerres

In 1965, the year the residents of Sarcelles elected a communist mayor for the first time, the SCIC launched the development of a new type of *Grand Ensemble* in response to the challenge posed by mounting public criticism to the results of its housing policy. The design of the Val d' Yerres for 6,000 housing units and about 30,000 people was aimed at overcoming the evils that Parisian residents and opinion makers had come to associate with the *Grands Ensembles*. In short the public developer wanted to prove that nothing was wrong with the concept of the *Grand Ensemble* and that the pitfalls of the early stages of such a housing policy were due mainly to the acuteness of the crisis, forcing a quick response to the dramatic needs of a rapidly growing population. By the mid-1960s France was relying on a sustained, high rate of economic growth.[23] A very active public housing policy in the Paris metropolitan area between 1953 and 1963 had eased to some extent the worst manifestations of the problem.[24] People could afford to pay more for housing, so private capital could be attracted to a joint venture strategy in exchange for state support in land policy and provision of urban services.[25] Profitability could be linked to public interest on the basis of an expanding, solvent market. On such solid ground, a new emphasis on the quality of housing could be substituted for the former priorities of quantity and affordability.[26] So much so that under pressure from urban protest, the SCIC would argue for urban design. The Val d' Yerres would be a new type of *Grand Ensemble*, and even more, a new urban form.[27]

To start with, the new form would overcome the separation between city and countryside by placing the city in the countryside: a garden city on a large scale. Thus it was essential to locate the city in rural surroundings, 25 kilometres south-east of Paris, on the territory of three communes, Epinay-Sous-Sénart, Boussy, and Quincy, where the SCIC could acquire a large piece of land (312 hectares) at a very low price (two and half francs per square metre). Besides the price, the criterion for the choice of site was its natural beauty: a wooded, hilly and green area crossed by a clear, small river, and boasting a charming centrally-placed old farm. The construction carefully preserved all these elements, including the farm, which was restored and transformed into the socio-cultural centre of the new *Grand Ensemble*. The result was a quite remarkable natural landscape that became one of the main advertising supports of the sales office, whose headquarters was naturally situated in *La Ferme*, as the restored, old farm was known.

Plate 10.1 *La Ferme,* the cultural centre of the *Grand Ensemble* of Val d' Yerres. (Photograph: M. Castellas.)

Furthermore, the quality of the environment was enhanced by a deliberate move towards architectural diversity. Instead of reproducing the gigantic high-rise buildings in parallel rows, typical of most *Grands Ensembles*, the Val d' Yerres took shape as a series of differently designed urban units scattered throughout a natural open space. The SCIC even tried some experiments of Nordic architecture, some of the neighbourhoods being built in the Finnish and Danish styles. And, for the first time in French public housing, single-family dwellings were built in a *Grand Ensemble*, mixed with high-rise buildings of moderate height and construction of unusually good quality.

The diversity of housing did not only stretch to its outward form, but, more significantly included a variety of housing standards and legal status, with 48 per cent of the units in home ownership, and 19 per cent of the total being single-family dwellings. The result was, as Table 10–1 shows, a very mixed urban profile that tried to combine the formation of a new environmental policy by the SCIC with its long-standing responsibility as an essential source of public housing policy, and so expected to fulfil its goals in the public interest. In fact, the Val d' Yerres was more open than Sarcelles to low-income groups, in spite of the higher level of rents. The reason for this paradox is that access to public rental housing in France was basically dependent upon the institutional channel selected to entitle future tenants. In the case of Sarcelles, industrial companies and public administrations, having contributed to the public housing fund, were given priority to house their employees. In the case of the Val d' Yerres, the *prefecture*[28] received 27 per cent of the HLM units, which were largely reserved for the most dramatic housing needs, particularly the families displaced in the city of Paris by the urban renewal programme. This is the means through which a substantial number of immigrant workers (around 10 per cent of the residents) managed to locate in the Val d' Yerres.

So the social composition of the population was extended towards the two ends of the social spectrum, to include a significant proportion of managers and professionals, as well as manual

Table 10.1   Distribution of housing units in the *Grand Ensemble* of Val d' Yerres, according to the commune of their location and to their characteristics. (Percentage of total of each commune, 1973.)

Communes	Housing Characteristics								
	Rental		Ownership		Buildings		Single family dwellings		Total
	N	%	N	%	N	%	N	%	N
Epinay	2,347	59·7	1,582	40·3	3,380	86·0	549	14·0	3,929
Boussy	297	22·5	1,027	77·5	887	67·0	43·7	33·0	1,324
Quincy	488	58·4	347	1·6	664	79·5	171	20·5	835
TOTAL	3,132	51·4	2,956	48·6	4,931	81·0	1,157	19·0	6,088

Source: Our calculation on the basis of SCIC documents.

workers, as is shown in Table 10–2. This social diversity was qualified, however, by a tendency towards residential segregation between these different social classes within the *Grands Ensembles*: the middle classes were concentrated in the municipality of Boussy, while Epinay-Sous-Sênart had a much higher proportion of manual workers, with Quincy occupying an intermediate position. Yet the main social division, as we might expect, was between rental housing and owner-occupied housing. And though Boussy concentrated the large majority of high standing, owner-occupied programmes, there was a significant amount of overlapping in the two other communes: the highest standing of single-family dwellings, the

Table 10.2   Social Composition of Val d' Yerres Residents, by Community and Housing Status, 1968 and 1971. (Percentage of Total of each Spatial Unit.)

	Boussy-1968 (The Entire Commune)	Quincy-1971 Home Owners	Epinay-1971 Home Owners	Quincy-1971 Rental Housing	Epinay-1971 Rental Housing
Professionals and managers	15·40	15·60	1·81	0·39	0·30
Technicians and middle-level management	24·30	31·60	26·40	11·33	7·76
Clerks	22·40	25·30	42·13	34·00	38·00
Manual workers	23·50*	10·00	15·90	36·33	41·10
Personal service workers	6·00	0·80	1·09	0·78	3·25
Small business and businessmen		4·00	12·10	3·80	0·78
Others	3·40	4·60	8·86	16·40	8·57

Source: 1   1968:   French government census (INSEE)
2   1971:   Survey by social workers of the communes,
members of SCIC's local staff

*These are mostly previous residents of Boussy, not included in the Val d' Yerres.

neighbourhood known as *Le Gué Mandres* (86 units) happened to be at Epinay-Sous-Sênart, surrounded by high-rise rental public housing.

Thus the project of the SCIC was clearly to reduce social segregation while maintaining social diversity, in spite of the trend toward spatial segregation between social groups according to the location of housing with different levels of quality and price. There was an explicit communal ideology aimed at reconstructing a shared social world within the *Grand Ensemble* to foster life in the neighbourhoods, in sharp contrast to the anonymity of the previous *Grands Ensembles* and great metropolis beyond. The Val d' Yerres was supposed not only to provide the joys of nature but to reconstruct the moral order of society. The major instrument for this ambitious project was a sophisticated institutional network of *animation sociale,* [29] that is, a combination of social work with cultural activities and community organizing, initiated and paid for by the SCIC itself. The common purpose of all these activities was to stimulate the residents to develop an active life in the neighbourhood, so that the *Grand Ensemble* would no longer be the space of social anonymity and cultural alienation that this urban form had come to symbolize. Nevertheless, the implementation of the community programme was differentiated according to social divides. *La Ferme* became the centre of a series of 'high class' activities, such as ballet lessons, music and theatre performances, public lectures, pottery and craft courses, as well as political meetings. On the other hand, in the public housing rental units, social workers were hired to help organize residents around their hobbies and their housing demands. The SCIC had learned their lesson by then: socialized housing was likely to lead to collective action, and it appeared more fruitful to accept the fact and to try and channel this energy from the beginning. The working class teenagers at Epinay-Sous-Sênart also had their *ad hoc* institution, the *Jardin de l' Aventure*. Behind this suggestive name there was an open space, dotted with trees, for their own use and a qualified social worker with training in athletics to provide sports coaching. The idea was for a free space where teenagers could be together after school under some general guidance. The goal was to prevent the formation of deviant youth-groups. A number of other activities, such as sport competitions, 'mother clubs', and social gatherings for the elderly, completed the organizations through which the SCIC hoped to overcome any lack of human contact and to improve social life in these communities which were designed to become the new generation of *Grands Ensembles*.

Yet this appealing urban vision started to fade from the moment of its inception. The communal networks never came to life except as a result of neighbourhood mobilizations, which we will come to. Most residents reacted with hostility to the attempt to create an integrated social space. The home owners of Epinay-Sous-Sênart petitioned to have their open space enclosed and separated, so that the children of the public housing units could not play with theirs. Immigrant families faced open racism, expressed through complaints against their smokey cooking and their noisy chatting. Youths were blamed for every possible mishap, and by 1972–73 many residents were asking for permits to own handguns as well as an increased police presence. In fact, our examination of the records in the local police district showed no evidence of significant increase in crime. The general feeling of insecurity seemed to come, to some extent, from the uneasiness of experiencing a propinquity to social groups that were formerly considered as strangers. By bringing together profitable housing and public service, the SCIC had broken the rules of segregation, while still trying to sell social status to the middle class. This was done in total disregard of the fact that distance is an essential component of symbolic distinction in a mass society where cultural differences are less apparent between individuals. [30]

The social segregation extended to community activities had been organized according to class divides: no workers, for instance, would visit *La Ferme*, let alone attend the cultural events there. Segregation increased the chances of each 'community' social programme reaching the critical mass that would foster spontaneous social interaction. Social workers spent most of their time helping people to handle their economic and urban problems. For Val d' Yerres' residents, daily commuting to Paris and the immediate periphery (two and half hours per day on average) consumed most of their energy, given the lack of public transportation from the *Grand Ensemble* to the suburban station, and the poor service offered by the railway system. Besides, while housing quality and the natural environment received special attention, most basic social amenities were missing for several years depending as they did on other government agencies. In 1974, nine years after the beginning of the *Grand Ensemble*, there was still no medical emergency service available for the 30,000 residents. The schools, required by law, were so slow to be approved that the SCIC had to advance the necessary funds to pay for the building of the schools. Facing the difficulties of daily life without places or occasions to meet or co-operate beyond the scheduled cultural activities, residents experienced an increasingly impoverished social neighbourhood. In short, community life did not take off as foreseen in the SCIC's scenario.

Yet, on one particular level, the strategy of social integration seemed to work: in spite of the large gaps in urban facilities, people did not stage collective protest for several years, in open contrast to what had happened in most Parisian *Grands Ensembles*. There were problems, but their solution generally followed a similar pattern. A typical example was the situation we discovered when we tried to understand the lack of demand for day care centres, in spite of the fact that many women were working full-time and desperately needed some provision of child care. We observed that most women started to work after they had settled in the Val d' Yerres because it was the only way for the family to pay the rent required for housing of such high quality (between 50 per cent and 100 per cent higher than an equivalent public housing unit in Sarcelles, while 90 per cent of tenants' families in the Val d' Yerres were earning less than 2,000 francs a month in 1973). The next question to ask was how families with only one salary were able to balance their budget. The answer was by taking care of the children of the working women. So each woman's salary was being shared (roughly in a 60–40 proportion) with another woman, so that children could be taken care of in the neighbourhood and that both women could contribute to the improvement of the family's standard of living by giving away their time at an incredibly low, hourly rate.[31] Under these conditions, any demand for public child care would threaten the delicate equilibrium established spontaneously by women as a way out of the problems of low-paid jobs and unsupported family responsibilities. This demand was therefore never expressed.

Nevertheless, by the time of our observation (1972–74) urban protest movements had begun to develop in the Val d' Yerres, calling into question the completion of the *Grand Ensemble* and seriously detracting from its image as a successful example of a more humane housing policy. The movements rose up on account of two very different issues, representing the major contradictions underlying the Val d' Yerres' experiment: on the one hand, there was the contradiction between its role as a public housing agency and the high cost of the housing units as a consequence of the improvement in the standards of quality; and on the other, the contradiction between the preservation of the natural environment and the high density of housing and urban functions that the SCIC had to achieve in order to maintain the level of profitability required by the private capital it had attracted.

The cost of the newly acquired housing quality appeared to be very high for the working class families of the rental housing sector. Yet it was difficult, as in Sarcelles, to oppose the level of rents because they were fixed at the national level by the public housing authority (the

HLM) for a given size and quality that put the Val d' Yerres into the very top residential category. Thus tenants were often unable to pay the rents and legal evictions for overdue payment were frequent, without any reaction from a resident population that knew the local public housing authority could do nothing to change the national rent policy.

Nevertheless, the rigidity of the public rent system also caused serious problems to the SCIC's management of the Val d' Yerres, since the maintenance costs were much higher than in any other *Grand Ensemble*. Unable to raise the rents, the SCIC acted on the elements of the budget over which it had some discretionary power: the charges for miscellaneous facilities (water, janitors, gardening, heating, cleaning, etc.). The dramatic rise of these charges in 1973 triggered the revolt in the Gerbeaux public housing unit at Epinay-sur-Sênart: 100 families refused to pay the increase and resisted the threats of eviction by the management. They successfully argued against the malfunctioning of water metres, the artificial differences in the price of heating between similar buildings, and the unfairness of the procedure that forced tenants to pay for maintenance of the natural environment, the main marketing device used in the first place by the SCIC to convince people to live in the isolation of the Val d' Yerres. After weeks of rent strikes, demonstrations and negotiations, the tenants won. The SCIC accepted that there had been miscalculations over the charges, lowered them, and paid back excess payments to the residents of the Gerbeaux (about 750 families) in the three years preceeding the struggle (about 170,000 francs were refunded to the tenants). Encouraged by this victory, the tenants created a local section of the CNL that quickly spread to other public housing rental units in all the neighbourhoods of the Val d' Yerres. Throughout the following year similar struggles took place on issues such as the water supply charges, the repair of the heating system, the replacement of public benches, and the strict regulation of automobile traffic within the residential units. Triggered by the high cost of housing, an urban trade unionism, similar to the one born in Sarcelles, gradually grew up in the very *Grand Ensemble* that was supposed to give birth to a modern communal Utopia.

Nevertheless, the decisive blow to the new urban scenario came from the rebellion of the well-to-do, single-family home owners of Boussy. Highly educated (45 per cent college graduates and including a majority of technicians and professionals among their numbers), they revolted when the SCIC tried to sacrifice some elements of the highly publicized environmental quality to enhance the programme's profitability. Once the image of the Val d' Yerres was established as a low-density, good quality, environmentally agreeable urban unit, the SCIC started to densify the *Grand Ensemble* by building several fifteen-storey buildings, as well as a shopping centre, in the middle of the most beautiful area at Boussy. To do so, they decided to bulldoze a small wood. The local residents opposed the move and appropriated the wood, planting flowers, installing playgrounds, and using it for picnics and promenades. They also attacked the SCIC's initiative as an unfair move that would damage the environmental quality of the Val d' Yerres after the programme had been sold on account of its beauty. Their mobilization altered the project: the wood was preserved, and the density of the new buildings was somewhat reduced.

In the process, a local residents' association consolidated its existence and became more militant. The Groupe d' Etude et de Recherche Buxacien (GERB) was initially formed by a group of young, middle class couples, echoing at their local level the themes of cultural innovation sparked by the May 1968 movement. The GERB's defense of the environment allowed it to shift from the movement's intellectual criticism, often expressed in the events at *La Ferme*, to an expression, at grassroot levels, of the residents' concerns. The favourite theme was a political one: information. Arguing that the cause for the potential destruction of environment was the secrecy of the negotiations between the SCIC and the municipal government about the future of the *Grand Ensemble*, the GERB demanded the institutionalization of extra-municipal committees where all residents could ask questions of the elected city council members and insist that they respect their public commitments. Denouncing the cynicism of the SCIC's selling of the Val d' Yerres, they undertook publicity campaigns against the SCIC. For instance, when, on a bright Sunday, the SCIC organized the Val d' Yerres' Olympic Games, and advertised them by radio to attract a crowd of potential home buyers, the GERB members disturbed the competition by parading in the streets of the *Grand Ensemble* with music, jokes, and painted banners. The GERB was opposed to the tightly controlled, cultural activities at *La Ferme*, and one of the organization's main goals was to make the streets a space where protest could be expressed and where social contact could take place. Yet it was at *La Ferme* that the group usually met, and the cultural activities found there provided the organizational basis for the creation of a socio-political network through which the public criticisms of several residents of one event or another could be addressed. What was intended to be an apparatus of social integration became the medium of cultural critique. Through the action of the GERB, the new suburban middle class discovered its own style of urban protest, focused on the defense of alternative life styles, however hazily perceived, rather than on strictly economic issues.

Thus, to some extent, the Val d' Yerres, instead of subduing the urban movement emerging in the *Grands Ensembles*, actually triggered it in two different ways. In addition to the Sarcelles-like collective consumption trade unionism, we observed in the Val d' Yerres the rise of an alternative urban culture, highly sensitive to the themes that would later become associated with the ecologists in America or the 'green parties' in Western Europe. The two forms of movement seem to correspond to two different social and urban situations, as Table 10–3 suggests.

Table 10.3   Estimated Social Profile of Membership in the local Tenants Union (CNL) and in the Ecologist-Type Neighbourhood Group (GERB). (Percentage of Total Membership.)

	GERB	CNL
Professionals and managers	22	3
Technicians and middle-management	35	10
Clerks	19	37
Manual workers	9	42
Others	15	8

Source: Our estimation on the basis of the Association's files.

On the one hand, we had a movement of working class tenants defending the price and level of their living conditions, and on the other, a new type of urban movement, formed by home owners, technicians, and professionals, orientated towards the defense of the environment, the improvement of neighbourhood life, and the enrichment of local democracy.

This kind of link between the characteristics of the urban situation, those of the movement's social make-up, and those of the movement's orientation seems to be a well-established pattern of urban mobilization. A clear confirmation of this hypothesis lies in the influence that the CNL tried to exert on the tenants' movements in the middle class dominated community of Quincy, or the organizational effort that middle class residents made (grouped in the

Carrefour de Recherche et d'Information [CRI]) in the predominantly working class Epinay-sur-Sênart, following the model of the GERB at Boussy. Both instances failed because of a lack of interest in these neighbourhoods in the kind of themes developed by local organizations working in an alien social context. Though we cannot (yet) draw conclusions about the difficulty presented by class alliances within the same urban movement, the very existence of the difficulty clearly indicates a likelihood that urban movements develop on different lines (and even fragment) according to the social classes within their membership.

Nevertheless, in the case of the Val d' Yerres, both forms of grassroots mobilization converged on the political crisis that shook the basis of the *Grand Ensemble*, precipitating crisis in the housing policy it symbolized. The CNL won the Residents' Council elections and transformed the Council into a platform to support its demands, instead of being an instrument of social integration. The GERB decided to enter municipal politics on its own, challenging parties from both the right and the left, and in the first municipal elections, in 1971, it came in second to the right wing list, with 24 per cent of the vote at Boussy. By 1971 the Val d' Yerres was still being formed and the traditional local notables were still able to control the municipal elections in the three communes. The expression of the urban protest in a strong electoral showing by left wing parties had to wait until the next election, in 1977, sometime after our field work had been concluded. Yet the crisis of urban policy came well before that year, under the combined impact of the grassroots protest and the new orientations in national housing policy, themselves partly influenced by that protest. The precipitative event towards the crisis of the Val d' Yerres was what the residents called 'The Battle of the ZAC' (Zone d' Aménagement Concerté)[32].

The ZAC ('zone of concerted planning') is a legal procedure, introduced in French urban law in 1967, that allows a developer, for reasons of public utility, to waive the restrictions imposed by the Master Plan[33], particularly in terms of the density of the urbanized area. By 1972, the SCIC realized that in order to reach its two goals of housing of good quality and financial profitability, it had to increase the density of housing at *Grand Ensemble*, even sacrificing some of the natural environment, to expand the programme from 6,000 housing units to 9,000. To do so, several fifteen-story buildings and a regional shopping centre were projected. As discussed above, residents mobilized to save a small wood that was labelled for clearance. The local governments, although they basically accepted the SCIC's plan, used the pretext of restless public opinion to bargain hard to obtain a substantial subsidy per unit to pay for the addition of newly required urban equipment. They also obtained the transfer of responsibility to the local governments for some of the basic social facilities, including *La Ferme*, the pride and joy of the developer. The negotiations took almost two years. When they were successfully concluded, in March 1974, and when the SCIC was finally ready to launch the new ZAC, to complete the Val d' Yerres, the final explosion happened.

The *prefet*, representing central government, denied permission for this new programme. There had been too much noise, too many bureaucratic battles, too much delay for the urban infrastructure, and, above all, the suburban residents were too sensitive to the renewed failure of a *Grand Ensemble* to enable the delivery of the urban promises the SCIC had publicized so prominently. In April 1973, the *Circulaire Guichard* called a symbolic halt to the *Grands Ensembles* policy. The SCIC did not really take it seriously: there was too much at stake, particularly as it was the biggest developer in France. Yet the residents of the Val d' Yerres reminded the government that their *Grand Ensemble* was getting bigger and bigger. The *prefet* stopped the new development. The GERB organized a joyful 'Burial of the ZAC' in the streets of a community brought to life by its struggles. Their victory celebration was the funeral of the *Grands Ensembles*.

The SCIC had stubbornly tried to overcome the residents' resistance by presenting a new urban product that anticipated all the demands in Sarcelles and in the large housing estates built in the early 1960s. Yet the search for more profitable construction led to higher density and called into question the well-preserved, natural landscape. The standards of quality achieved in rental public housing came hand-in-hand with increased housing costs that most working class tenants could not afford. Proximity of different social classes increased social hostility, reducing the chances of friendly local contacts. The mechanisms of social integration and cultural innovation became platforms of urban protest and expressions of alternative values. Political control over the *Grand Ensemble* was coming to an end, in spite of well-planned institutional fragmentation.

Designed as the new urban profile and to overcome the challenge of society to the first *Grands Ensembles*, the Val d' Yerres became instead the extreme expression of the contradictions in this public housing policy. By promising a good environment to the middle class, cheap rental housing to workers, and profitable investment to capital, the SCIC tried to demonstrate how urban contradictions could be superseded by urban design. Val d' Yerres was to be the first garden city of post-industrial France, but finished as the last *Grand Ensemble* of suburban Paris.

11

Conclusion: From Urban Trade Unionism to Urban Movements

The social process underlying the rise and fall of the Parisian *Grands Ensembles* offers a striking illustration of the interplay between grassroots protest and housing policy. To respond to popular demands and needs for affordable housing, the French state set up a comprehensive system of production and distribution of housing which took shape as the *Grands Ensembles*. Housing was partially socialized, that is, treated as a public service and integrated into a new type of urban unit that provided relatively uniform living conditions for a large cross-section of the population, under the centralized management of a government-supported agency. Operating within the constraints of a capitalist economy, such an agency still had to keep costs down and to lay the foundation for profitable private investment in the housing market. The production of as much housing as possible, as quickly as possible, and at the lowest possible cost, led to the type of urban units symbolized by Sarcelles.

Since the relative homogeneity of living conditions made it easier for residents to realize the commonality of the urban problems from which they were suffering, the socialization of housing led to the socialization of protest, overcoming the individual relationship between landlord and tenant. It is in this sense that we can think of the formation of a new type of movement: a collective consumption-oriented trade unionism that paralleled at the residence place what capitalist concentration of production and management has triggered in the form of labour unions at the work place.

The tenant unions organized in the *Grands Ensembles*, and the miscellaneous urban protests that took place in many suburbs throughout the 1960s,[34] drew the new service workers and professionals into collective action, action that contributed greatly to the public's view of the *Grands Ensembles*, although still reinforcing the social demand for housing as a public service. The political impact of these movements was considerable since, through their experience of collective protest, a significant faction of the new suburban middle class shifted its vote to left wing political parties, enabling the election of socialist and communist local governments between 1965 and 1977 in practically all the municipalities governing the *Grand Esembles* in the Paris metropolitan area.[35] The state in general, and the SCIC in particular, reacted to these trends by opening up the housing market to more affluent classes, by involving private capital in the ventures, and by producing a different type of urban product, emphasizing environmental quality and life in the neighbourhood. Our observation of the Val d' Yerres experience, the showroom of the new housing policy, suggests that the social contradictions that were supposedly being smoothed out by the new policy, were in reality made much deeper. The involvement of the well-to-do middle class in the battle over citizen participation and environmental conservation coincidenced with a new wave of tenant unionism. Everyone concerned was in search of an alternative life style, and increasingly critical of state bureaucratic management and the part played by capitalist investment in the production of urban forms.[36]

The *Circulaire Guichard* of April 1973 was an initial reaction to the political setbacks suffered by the Gaullists in the parliamentary elections of March 1973 over the Parisian *Grands Ensembles*.[37] But more important than the *Circulaire* itself was the confirmation in the following months and years that a new urban mood was predominant among the Parisian suburbanites, and that the large state-managed urban units were unprofitable in economic terms and unpopular in political terms. They were unprofitable because the bargaining power won by the Residents' Associations was forcing the management to deliver a quality of housing and a level of urban services that could no longer be financed as public housing without undertaking a major economic redistribution of urban goods and services. The *Grands Ensembles* were unpopular because the resident's tide of rebellion against their living conditions focused the attention of the media and of public opinion on the 'inhuman urban forms' of this type.

During the 1974 presidential campaign, Giscard D' Estaing, politically sensitive to the new ecological themes, put a clear distance between his approach to environmental issues and the heritage of Gaullist housing policy. Once he had won the election, he made a series of decisions: to stop the Paris Left Bank express way; to reconsider the Les Halles project; to halt extensive urban renewal; and to implement a total reversal of the policy over the *Grands Ensembles*.

Instead of discouraging the emergence of new urban movements, this new urban policy actually stimulated them, by legitimizing the arguments that had been urged for years against technochratic state housing.[38] The movements that flourished at the local level in all major French cities, however, and particularly those in suburban Paris, were much closer to the ones represented by the middle class in the Val d' Yerres than to those triggered in Sarcelles. Environmental concerns and grassroots democracy appeared more important for the new generation of neighbourhood militants than the level of housing rents or the repair of the elevators.[39] The collective consumption trade unionism that emerged with strong popular support during the 1960s faded away or stagnated. Two major factors seem to have been responsible for this surprising and significant evolution:

1 Their success led to an improvement in the existing public housing estates, and to a reversal of the housing policy that favoured individual loans and subsidies through the private market, and so revived the individual relationship in the housing field. It is crucial to note that this

individualization was only possible because of the strictly economistic nature of the tenant unions' demands. By focusing on rents, repairs, and maintenance – and by not dealing *in toto* with urban problems – the tenant unions tended to narrow their chances of success and to reduce the size of their audience. In this sense, it is significant to observe that while the traditional national organization of tenants (the CNL) lost ground during the 1970s, the second nation-wide organization, the Confédération Syndicale du Cadre de Vie (CSCV), received new life when it extended the realm of its initiatives from housing demands to all issues concerning the urban environment.[40]

2 Nevertheless, what is most important for analytical purposes is to understand why the urban trade unionists, in general, did not expand their sphere of action beyond very specific urban-related economic demands. The answer seems to be that they delegated all policy-orientated responsibilities to the left wing municipal governments. Urban movements, under left wing political leadership, were considered as the instruments for laying the foundations to enable the political parties (communists and socialists) to win local and national elections in order to implement the policies of urban reform.[41]

Thus the parallel between labour unions and collective consumption unions becomes apparent in its full meaning. They have been considered as two demand-orientated movements whose social impact could only be fully accomplished by the political parties in the state arena. Recent historical experience, however, in Paris as elsewhere, throws doubt on such a hypothesis, discrediting the elegant, although incorrect, theoretical model that came to regard both movements as flowing from the sources of production and consumption towards the state, under guidance from the party.

The French experience suggests that urban movements do not survive if they only seek economic demands on collective consumption: they must represent something more or they fade. These wider themes are partially suggested by the shadow cast by the *Grands Ensembles*, but what an urban movement may be and do must await another story.

Part 3

City and Culture: The San Francisco Experience

12

Introduction: San Francisco – The Social Basis of Urban Quality

The Background

Beautiful San Francisco is a headquarters city. It is the second largest banking centre in America, and the high-rise shape of its new downtown skyline tells the story. Between 1960 and 1980 the total amount of office space in San Francisco doubled, from 35·6 million to 71 million square feet. 29 high-rise projects of ten stories or more were built between 1970 and 1979. In 1981 20 additional buildings totalling 7·7 million square feet of office space were under construction, and the Planning Commission had already approved 16 more buildings that will add another 5·1 million square feet of office space.[1] By contrast, Los Angeles with a population five times that of San Francisco added only 0·5 million square feet of office space in 1980, and had just 1·8 million more in the planning stage. In the three square mile financial district of San Francisco there was a concentration, in 1980, of 53 million square feet of office space and 200,000 employees. The ten largest corporations based in San Francisco had, in 1979, 42·4 billion dollars in global sales, 37·6 billion dollars in assets, and 276,000 employees.[2] Among them Standard Oil of California, Utah International, Transamerica, Crown Zellerbach, Southern Pacific, Levi-Strauss, Bechtel Corporation, and the biggest bank in the world, the Bank of America.

The types of jobs available in San Francisco depend on the dominant corporations. Between 1960 and 1970, employment increased by 28·4 per cent in services; by 31·9 per cent in finance, insurance, and real estate; and by 26·4 per cent in government; while decreasing by 15·7 per cent in manufacturing.[3] Numbers of professionals climbed from 36,000 in 1950 to 56,000 in 1970, while operatives went down during the same period from 44,000 to 23,000.[4] Although data from the 1980 Census on the occupational structure were not available at the moment of the writing of these pages (October 1981), it seems very likely that the trend in the employment structure has accelerated the shift away from manufacturing to services and government. According to some estimates by the San Francisco Department of City Planning between 1970 and 1980, the city lost about 22,000 jobs in construction, manufacturing, transportation, utilities, and wholesale trade, while 65,000 jobs were created in retail trade, finance, insurance real estate and services.

At the same time the city's total population steadily decreased between 1950 (775,357) and 1975 (672,700), and has since stabilized at about the last figure (1980 Census estimate: 678,974).[5] Yet the number of households in the city has increased by 18,316 between 1970 and 1980, reflecting a major change in life styles that has had, and will continue to have, a significant effect on the use of housing and urban services in San Francisco.

Thus, not unlike the Gold Rush of 1849 which created a trade centre that became San Francisco,[6] the expansion of multinational capital and California's economic boom of the post-1940s gave new impetus to the city.[7] The entire downtown area had been subjected to development projects. Large sections of the city, particularly the predominantly black Western Addition, adjacent to the CBD, were demolished by urban renewal projects, displacing almost 8,000 families, most of them the poor, elderly, and the minorities.[8] With the

Embarcadero Centre nearing completion in 1981 and the construction of the Yerba Buena Centre about to begin (now called George Moscone Centre), the role of the city as a service and financial centre will be further enhanced.[9] In order to transport people to their downtown jobs, a regional mass transport system (BART) was built between 1962 and 1974 at a cost of 1·6 billion dollars.[10] As a result of it and the highway network built during the 1950s, San Francisco established itself as the core of a large metropolitan region, the Bay Area, in which 5,284,822 people live (in 1980).[10bis] This urban development closely followed the pattern characteristic of the rise of the post-industrial city,[11] with the additional assets of natural beauty and a sound international economic base.[12] But this is only one side of the story: during the time that San Francisco emerged as an international city and a sophisticated urban centre, it also became a residential area in which ethnic minorities accounted for about half of its residents.[13]

Black labourers who came to work in the shipyards during the Second World War located in the Fillmore and Western Addition areas which had been evacuated by the massive deportation of its previous Japanese residents. San Francisco's black population jumped from 4,900 in 1940 to 96,000 in 1970, then decreased to 86,400 (12·7 per cent of the city residents) in 1980. But in the last two decades San Francisco became the point of arrival for an increasing flow of ethnic minorities from all over the world. The city's status as a cosmopolitan centre has not only made it attractive to multinational banks and corporations, but also to the masses of foreign nationals forced out of their country of origin by conditions of misery, hunger, war, or political terror. By 1980, Asians and Pacific Islanders accounted for 21·7 per cent of the total population of San Francisco. Latinos, mainly from Central America make up at least 12·3 per cent, American Indians and Eskimos represented 0·5 per cent, and Other Races about 2 per cent. This is a very conservative estimate and, in all likelihood, if we could include Hispanics not recorded by the Census Bureau, and illegal immigrants of all origins, the proportion of ethnic minorities in San Francisco would be about 50 per cent of the city's population.[14] This picture closely resembles the model characteristic of central cities in 'post-industrial' America[15] – managers and minorities, skyscrapers and ghettos, 'the gold coast and the slum.'[16]

And yet these demographic data and land use patterns are misleading in relationship to San Francisco's urban dynamics because, unlike most American central cities, there is no sign of urban decay. On the contrary, there is a steady improvement in the quality and maintenance of the housing. The vacancy rate remains at a low 2 per cent of the housing market, two-thirds of which is rental property. It is one of the most active real estate markets in America, with an ever increasing demand from middle income and low income groups.[17] As one would expect given such a tight market, there is a process of displacement and gentrification under way. Such a process affects primarily the elderly renters and minorities.[18]

A major cause of the housing shortages in the San Francisco is that while the population has decreased, the number of households has increased regularly, with the average size of the households becoming gradually smaller (2·70 in 1950; 2·44 in 1960; 2·34 in 1970; 2·08 in 1980).[19] Divorce and separation seem to be a major cause for the formation of new households (more than 4,000 per year). An increasing proportion of single adults profoundly changed the social profile of the city.[20] New demands for middle class housing led to the displacement of minority residents from some parts of the city, notably through urban renewal projects like the Western Addition. But in the city as a whole, those moving out have been replaced by those coming in from other countries. San Francisco's airport officials report that between 1977 and 1980 5,000 immigrants arrived from Indo-China and 12,000 from Central America.[21] Thus, in spite of the efforts towards urban renewal and gentrification, the population has maintained a high proportion of minorities whose residence can neither be associated with a dilapidation of the housing stock nor any dramatic crisis in the urban services. On the contrary, housing rehabilitation and remodelling is practised on a large scale, most of it by private individuals. Although renovation generally goes along with gentrification by new middle class dwellers settling in an area, it is also a fact that many minority and working class residents are trying to preserve the neighbourhoods from the threat of compulsory urban renewal. Accordingly, housing maintenance is probably better than in any other large American city,[22] and the abandonment of buildings is unknown.

At the same time, the city has one of the best public health systems in the country, operates a large, efficient municipal transportation system, enjoys large areas of open space, and provides some of the most well-kept public facilities of any large metropolitan area in America. Furthermore neighbourhood life and urban culture have not been destroyed by the rapid transformation of the city into a world metropolis. New cultures have revitalized street life and public gatherings, and urban life has become richer.

So San Francisco presents something of an urban enigma. While transforming itself into one of the centres of the world's corporate establishment, it nevertheless houses expanding communities boasting alternative cultures, from the 1960s hippies to the 1970s gays. While the downtown area becomes more concentrated and more skyscrapers are built, old Victorian houses are renovated and street life is fostered. While the residential neighbourhoods are gentrified its minority population is maintained. While keeping its function as a port of entry for poor immigrants is continued, its ethnic ghettos are hardly examples of urban dilapidation. And although the city is losing population and supporting an expanding CBD, it still maintains a satisfactory level of public services. Last but not least, although it is the homeland of corporate banking, the local government has maintained a liberal political orientation in the midst of America's conservative tide of the late 1970s – a trend that accounts for the municipal policy of some social redistribution through public services.

This is, then, the enigma, the workings of which we will try to unveil. Our study of San Francisco is an inquiry into the social roots of urban vitality. It is an attempt to understand how a city with world-wide economic connections can still be shaped by the social interests of its neighbourhoods to achieve the quality of life millions of visitors have come to appreciate.

It is our hypothesis that the unique urban scene of San Francisco has been produced in the last two decades through the interaction of three major socio-political processes:

1 The rise and fall of the pro-growth coalition in the city government and the contradictory development of urban policies that it has put forward.[23]
2 Minority neighbourhood's protest and mobilization, first against urban renewal and displacement, and then to improve living conditions.[24]
3 The emergence of a new urban middle class as a major social force in the local society, a middle class which has been committed to values of urban life, environmental quality, cultural identity, and decentralized self-management, instead of reproducing the social order supported by the corporate organizations that tend to be their employers or clients.[25] Although gays cannot be singled out as an exclusively middle class phenomenon (since homosexuality is evenly distributed across the social spectrum), the gay community in San Francisco has played the role of a social vanguard struggling to change the city, culturally, spatially, and politically.

Because of our general interest in the pattern of relationships between urban development and the mobilization of neighbourhoods, this analysis will focus on the second and third elements. Nevertheless, their effect on the urban system would be incomprehensible without referring to the local political background against which they have taken place, and most of this will be established in the context of our case studies. But some general description of the changing pattern of San Francisco's local politics must be introduced as it relates to the evolution of urban policies and the transformation of the city.

The Changing Pattern of San Francisco's Local Politics

Perhaps the most striking local political trend is the importance of the broad and loose coalitions on which city government is based.[26] Californian law requires a non-partisan candidacy for local elections. A candidate, in order to have a reasonable chance of success, must obtain a variety of endorsements. Although these may incorporate political parties and personalities, they must rely on economic, social, ethnic, and cultural institutions of local society. In the case of San Francisco this trend is further amplified by the extreme fragmentation of power, established by the city's charter of 1932. A weak mayor shares power with an 11-member, elected board of supervisors. This power is then fragmented among a variety of commissions that, although approved by the mayor, remain largely autonomous. Furthermore, the whole system is constrained by the iron hand of a powerful, immovable civil service under the leadership of a chief administrative officer who enjoys a *de facto* life tenure. The origins of this complex and somewhat paralysing system are generally attributed to the reformist effort to control the wide spread corruption that characterized San Francisco's government for the first 50 years of its life, under local bosses such as Christopher Buckley and Abe Ruef.[27]

Our hypothesis is that this system of checks and balances reflects a compromise between two social blocs that fought for the control of the city until the 1960s. On the one hand, corporate business wanted a technocratic government based on an appointed city manager and a chief administrative officer. On the other hand, labour and the Catholic Church, representing Irish and Italian working class neighbourhoods, demanded institutions that would increase citizen representation, starting with an elected mayor and city council.[28] The general strike of 1934 in San Francisco, its bloody repression, and the Longshoremen Union's final victory dramatically highlighted the unstable political domination of business over labour in the city.[29]

In San Francisco's complicated system of local government, political scientists are apt to see a demonstration of pluralism. Historians, however, are more likely to recognize yet another instance of the social basis of weak government institutions: when a social class is unable to impose its will, alliances within an elected body will surely begin to change. This situation does not preclude class domination. In reality it paralyses the public institutions, while dominant classes still impose their conditions on the economy, on the cultural institutions and on the social patterning of daily life. The real problem with this unstable and fragile political domination is that it prevents local governments taking any major social or economic initiatives. Any undertaking by local government is likely to be stalled because of the mayor's inability to negotiate in a labyrinth of decisions rooted in a variety of social interests. All these phenomena manifested themselves in the politics of San Francisco's urban development plans.[30]

Urban renewal was proposed in the 1950s for San Francisco, as in other American cities, as an adequate instrument to provide a favourable setting for the new service economy, to renovate blighted areas, to displace the poor and minorities, to improve the urban environment, to keep middle class residents, and to reduce the flight of high income taxpayers to the suburbs.

The first serious move towards urban renewal came in the late 1950s when Mayor George Christopher, a Republican businessman, backed the efforts of the Redevelopment Agency, and began the first phase of the Western Addition project (A–1), planned the second phase (A–2), prepared the programme for the Yerba Buena Center (in the South of Market Area), and supported plans for BART.[31] The effort was too great for a political coalition relying solely on business support and Federal grants. Organized labour opposed the Yerba Buena Center on the grounds that it would displace industrial jobs. The conservationist movement stopped the highway progamme.[32] The black minorities, stimulated by the Civil Rights Movement and suffering the first displacement in the Western Addition, started to mobilize (a development that eventually led to the Hunter's Point riot in 1966). A politically significant incident was the picketing, in 1963, of Mel's Drive-In, a chain of restaurants owned by conservative supervisor Harold Dobbs, during the period in which he was running for mayor, supported by the business community. The isolation of the conservative group led to a narrow victory by the labour-backed candidate, John Shelley, a Democratic congressman and former president of the San Francisco Labour Council. It was time for negotiation. In the midst of increasing black militancy, particularly in the A–2 section of Western Addition, where 8,000 families were about to be displaced, the business community understood the need to reach a compromise with labour, as well as to make some concessions to ethnic minorities.

In the next election a new coalition was formed which, due to the death of the nominated candidate shortly before the election, came to have Joseph Alioto, a Democrat millionaire lawyer, as its candidate. He succeeded in defeating both the conservative Republican and the liberal Democrat opponents in 1967. Thereafter the city took on the development strategy but now the pie had to be shared. Labour received the promise of construction jobs, as well as more public employment, wage increases, and social benefits. The port of San Francisco came under city control, and Harry Bridges, the historic leader of the 1934 strike, was appointed to its board.[33] Labour now backed redevelopment. As we shall see with the Latino Mission District, the minorities succeeded in stopping any attempt of a new redevelopment project in 1966. Although the black-dominated Western Addition was almost entirely demolished, 1,300 new public housing units and 2,600 subsidized units were subsequently built to curtail the displacement.[34]

The Mission District, with the black ghetto, Hunter's Point, became part of the Model Cities Programme which, although it caused continuous conflicts, also allowed Mayor Alioto an increasing control over the minorities' autonomous organizations. In sum, by bringing together business groups and organized labour, Alioto established a strong basis from which he was able to negotiate with protesters, and, although conceding on some points, he went on to lay the foundations for San Francisco's service economy. During his two terms from 1967 to 1974, skyscrapers multiplied, most urban renewal was accomplished, rehabilitation and beautification programmes were begun. BART was constructed, downtown business boomed, the port was reorganized, and new tourist and commercial facilities were built along the waterfront.[35] To be sure, some projects had their problems – particularly the port – and others, like BART, were begun for reasons that were not only related to the city. But Alioto's time in power saw the higher point of the pro-growth coalition. Nevertheless, the victory of this coalition was not complete. The Yerba Buena Centre was paralysed for many years because of the mobilization of elderly tenants supported by neighbourhood groups.[36] Conservationists expanded their influence, although they were defeated in their legal initiative to limit the height of new buildings.[37] But the main counterbalance was the stimulation of neighbourhood associations which developed in a variety of urban and social situations to control their own development.[38]

The brutality of redevelopment policies triggered local self-defense, particularly because the success of the pro-growth policies undermined labour's presence in the city by bringing in new professional and clerical workers employed in the service-orientated organizations. The pro-growth coalition's final disintegration came in 1974 under the combined impact of fiscal austerity and public employee demands. Richard Nixon's decision in 1973 to cut off Federal programmes including Model Cities and Urban Renewal programmes, deprived the coalition of the patronage that fuelled it. The tightening of fiscal policies led, in 1974, to a confrontation between public labour unions asking for wage increases, and a fiscally conservative board of supervisors. Alioto backed labour efforts while business sided with the supervisors. The social basis of the coalition disappeared while the economic crisis seriously limited growth. In the 1975 election, the successful liberal candidate, George Moscone, apparently inherited the Democratic machine, but in reality gained his support from very different sources, of which the business sector only represented a tiny proportion.

Moscone tried to put together a new coalition comprising labour, the black community, and the new neighbourhood associations, led mainly by middle class activists. The leader of the Western Additions's resistance to urban renewal, Hannibal Williams, had already been appointed to the board of the Redevelopment Agency, provoking the resignation of its director. Another prominent black leader, Willie Brown, was given influence over the Housing Authority, and blacks found better opportunities in the public sector.[39] But the most important initiative was the support given by the mayor to the attempt by neighbourhood associations and left wing activists to change the electoral system of the board of supervisors, from city-wide elections to district representation. This initiative meant a major effort to bypass the control of the elections by business interests through media advertising as well as to decentralize city government by direct contact between each supervisor and his or her constituency. In November 1976, a referendum approved the reform, and the subsequent elections provided a much more liberal board of supervisors. San Francisco's business circles became seriously concerned and called for another referendum in 1977. In spite of a major financial effort led by the chamber of commerce, a very militant grassroots campaign by neighbourhood groups succeeded in maintaining the district elections system. In 1980, however, a new referendum, held at the same time as Ronald Reagan's landslide conservative victory, reinstated the system of city-wide elections. Nevertheless, most of the incumbent supervisors were re-elected, maintaining a liberal majority on the board. Among the eleven members were two pro-labour black women, two progressive white women, a socialist gay leader, and a well-known civil rights lawyer.

The recurring issue of district elections revealed not only the variations of San Francisco's political moods but also the emerging coalition behind San Francisco's local power, with minorities and middle class neighbourhoods incorporating a weakened, organized labour into an alliance from which corporate business was largely excluded. One of the most striking changes was the election to the board of supervisors, in 1977, of the leader of the gay community, Harvey Milk, who ran as a gay candidate. Mayor Moscone welcomed his presence in the city government and collaborated closely with him. The gays, who constituted the best organized and most mobilized single voting block of the new coalition, became the most solid supporters of progressive initiatives in the city government.

The reversal of local power relationships in a very short time was as dramatic as the crisis it prompted. In November 1978 a conservative supervisor, former policeman Dan White, shot and killed Mayor Moscone and Supervisor Harvey Milk. When, several months later, he was sentenced to a mild seven year term, the sentence provoked violent protest from the gay community which was answered in kind by the police. Mayor Moscone's death meant the end of his unusual, loose, and personalized coalition. Diane Feinstein, an upper class moderate Democrat, was elected mayor with the support of the same constituencies, but her ties with the business circles were much closer, and between 1979 and 81 San Francisco's local government became, once again, open so that each group could negotiate only on an *ad hoc* basis.

The significance of such a political evolution for the urban process was that the disintegration of the pro-growth coalition prevented the city from continuing on the path of development at all costs, even if the projects already programmed were to be completed. Instead, the growing strength of the neighbourhood groups, both in social influence and in their presence in the local government, shifted the emphasis toward rehabilitation, environmental conservation, and revitalization of urban life. Ethnic minorities preserved their status quo, albeit in a very defensive manner, potentially threatened, as they were, by individual gentrification and new waves of Asian immigrants. Local cultures organized their territories. The gay community presented the most striking symbol of the search for an alternative life style. San Francisco increasingly fragmented into different worlds: the downtown business centre; the tourist and recreational areas; the different ethnic neighbourhoods; the gay territory; corridors of gentrified houses; the established areas of middle class-based alternative life styles; the defensive pro-family home owned residences; and the aristocratic hills of old San Francisco.

Since no single group was able to dominate the city's development, and no stable coalition came into existence, the city became a space of co-existing interests and cultures, unthreatened by any major project although isolated from any great collective enterprise. Leaving the banks to deal with the rest of the world, most San Franciscans concentrated on their local existence, on their neighbourhood's life, and on their home's comfort and beauty. Perhaps the absence of central urban policy is the secret of the new urban quality attained in San Francisco, along with the maximization of the neighbourhoods' autonomy in a situation where cultural values tend to match market pressures and where community organizations still are a deterrent to any kind of heavy-handed political authority.

In order to explore this major hypothesis, the formulation of which suggests the theme of our analysis without indicating the full complexity of is implications, we must be a good deal more specific. So we will try to understand the urban dynamics of San Francisco through the detailed analysis of two community mobilizations that appear to have provided major contributions to the city's evolution. They are the Latino-based Mission District's process of community organization and the San Francisco gay community. They represent, in their own distinct ways, the main social trends underlying San Francisco's urban quality: the search for cultural identity and for political self-reliance.

13

Urban Poverty, Ethnic Minorities and Community Organization: The Experience of Neighbourhood Mobilization in San Francisco's Mission District

Introduction

The largest urban popular mobilization in San Francisco's recent history took place between 1967 and 1973 in the predominantly Latino Mission District. The movement brought together a variety of social interests and ethnic groups into a multi-issue community organization, the Mission Coalition Organization (MCO), whose structure and tactics were largely inspired by the Alinsky model of community action. At the peak of its power, in 1970–71, the MCO probably involved upto 12,000 people[40] (in a neighbourhood of 50,000), who participated in over 100 grassroots committees of various types. Although the organization disbanded in 1973, after a highly significant and self-destructive process, it brought to the neighbourhood a series of improvements as well as a constellation of neighbourhood organizations and social agencies that survived the crisis and transformed the Mission into a vital urban scene.

The observation of the Mission's social dynamics, the reconstruction of the MCO's history, the analysis of its crisis, and the study of its social and urban outcomes provide privileged ground for the consideration of some major research questions suggested by the American urban experience: the relationship between community organizations and public programmes of social reform; the intertwining of poverty and ethnicity; and the complex articulation between neighbourhood self-reliance and local politics. These are all major themes of the social practice we observed, or reconstructed, in the Mission. On the basis of both existing historical records and our field work in 1980 (see the Methodological Appendix, pp. 346–55), we have been able to provide some tentative answers to the question, fundamental to American life, relating to the interaction between ethnic minorities and urban structure. Let us first recall the social profile of the experience before undertaking its theoretical analysis.

The Background

San Francisco's Mission District has been, for the last 30 years, the gateway to a new world of promises and fears for most Latino immigrants arriving in the Bay Area.[41] The sunny flatland of this old working class neighbourhood was the location of the first Spanish Mission settlement in 1776 and is now the setting for one of the most diverse, ethnic scenes of urban America.[42] (See Map 13–1 for its location in San Francisco.) It was one of the few areas preserved from the fire that followed in the wake of the 1906 earthquake. The Mission housed the Irish and Italian working class families displaced by the disaster, as well as many of the retail stores which moved away from the downtown area. The working class emigration to the suburbs during the 1940s and 1950s freed a considerable amount of old, though sound, housing units that became a shelter for the incoming Latin and Central American population, migrating for the most part from Nicaragua and El Salvador. During the 1960s and 1970s Mexicans, Puerto Ricans, Cubans, South Americans, Samoans, American Indians, and Filipinos also moved into the Mission transforming its 50,000 population into a 'world city' of many cultures.[43] By 1980, young middle class whites were also settling in the area, renovating some of its Victorian buildings,[44] upgrading its social status, and changing the local ambiance somewhat.

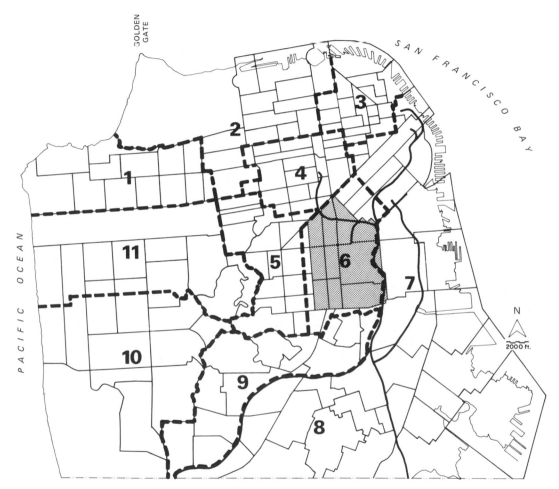

Map 13.1 Location of the Mission neighbourhood in the city of San Francisco.
(*Source*: Mission Housing Development Corporation.) The thick dotted lines indicate supervisorial districts (which are numbered) and the thin lines census tracts.

But the Mission still is the *Barrio* (the Latino Ghetto): the family income is far below the city's average;[45] the educational[46] and occupational[47] status is at the bottom of the scale; the public services do not equal those available elsewhere in San Francisco;[48] and the proportion of overcrowded and dilapidated housing, although relatively low, is much higher than in most areas of the city.[49] The Latino culture is present all over the neighbourhood, particularly in the Inner Mission sections, from restaurants to cinemas, from bookshops to grocers, from night bars to political posters. The current process of limited gentrification and the exodus of second generation Latinos to the suburbs is largely compensated for by the continuous arrival of new immigrants.[50] The neighbourhood is also the scene for various deviant behaviour and social protest – a mix of prostitution, drugs, 'street kids', joyful celebrations and political demonstrations. In 1980, on Friday and Saturday evenings, the low riders slowly paraded along Mission Street filling the night with their music, stopping to arrange parties or to share drugs and drinks.[51] On the pavements, usually around the BART stations,[52] flags and banners call for solidarity with the revolutionaries in Nicaragua and El Salvador. They also protest police brutality, often anticipating their arrest by police officers who constantly patrol the streets of the Mission, particularly during the evenings. And yet, unlike most American ghettos, this agitated ambiance has not discouraged white middle class people from walking around the Mission, enjoying its colourful life and even looking forward to their own life in the District.

Plate 13.1 Morning shopping in Mission Street, San Francisco. Notice the traffic sign: 'No left turn on Fridays and Saturdays from 9 p.m. to 4 a.m.'; this is to control the weekly parades by the low riders (see pages 120–21). (Photograph: F. Sabbah.)

This urban vitality is not stage managed and organized behind the lights of the bars and Mexican restaurants, but is the expression, in spite of poverty and deficient public services, of a very diverse network of neighbourhood-based activities, of a continuous flow of newcomers, and of an active community of small businesses. In the same way that Chinatown highlights the Asian roots of San Francisco, so the Mission underscores the city's deep Latin American connection. As in most major American cities, the reality of the international social and economic system emerges from behind the curtains of San Francisco's old-fashioned bourgeois charm. And the Mission, like Chinatown, is a combination of slums and lights, remodelling and overcrowding, drugs and politics, real estate speculation and community organization, middle class gentrification and the open door to Latin American immigrants. That evolution, we should note, does not hold true for the black community in San Francisco (either displaced or disorganized in the Western Addition, or kept isolated in the ghetto areas of Hunter's Point and Ingleside), for the East Oakland ghetto, or for San Jose's predominantly *chicano* popular wards.[52bis]

The Mission presents a unique case of a *Barrio* that remains a centre of attraction for urban life, improving the real estate values while still maintaining most of its character as a neighbourhood for immigrants and the poor. Some of the trends of this urban achievement (the characteristics of which will be presented in our study) seem to be related to the popular mobilization that has taken place in the Mission District since the mid-1960s. At least, this is the argument we will try to develop in the following pages.

Furthermore, the characteristics of neighbourhood mobilization account not only for the urban revival but also for the shortcomings of this urban situation, as a consequence of the contradictions and pitfalls of the grassroots movement. In other words, the community struggles and organization in the San Francisco Mission District account both for the persistence of an autonomous Latino culture and for the incipient process of middle class gentrification. They are also at the basis of the improvement of social services as well as at the roots of the housing crisis. The complexity of the Mission's urban reality is in fact the result of the tortuous path undertaken by the neighbourhood's mobilization.

The Mission Story

The MCO was, between 1967 and 1973, one of the most successful examples of an Alinsky-style community movement, showing a remarkable capacity to combine grassroots organization with institutional social reform. In a different but simultaneous initiative, Latino radical youth, searching to establish Brown Power, united in 1969 to defend *Los Siete de la Raza* in a notorious trial against a group of youth accused of killing a police officer.[53] Behind the activist front, day-to-day social and political work by a variety of agencies and neighbourhood-based groups built up a community network of activities, solidarities, conflicts, and debates. The fragmented and contradictory character of such a powerful and diversified movement resulted in an equally contradictory social outcome. Its internal diversity, its incapacity to become associated with the new local political coalition around George Moscone in 1975, and, above all, the difficulty of bringing some cohesion to demands for improved conditions, class issues, and ethnic identity, led to a highly differentiated social situation where failure and success, co-opted reformism and confused social change, interwined in a pattern as complex as the Mission's urban scene.

This is the theme of our story, one that we must give in full before we can analyse its components so that we may understand how ethnic revolt and urban protest affect society and politics.

The Beginnings

As in most American inner cities the first grassroots mobilization in the Mission was triggered, in 1966, by the potential threat of an urban renewal programme. The urban renewal project was initially presented as a study proposed by the San Francisco Redevelopment Agency (SFRA) to foresee, and possibly encourage, urban change induced by the construction of the BART line along Mission Street, with two major stations in the very core of the neighbourhood. Quite apart from the fact, however, that some private development projects were being considered as extensions of the adjacent downtown area, the concern of the Mission residents was more than understandable given the SFRA's record as a major instrument of demolition and displacement, and the future context of increased accessibility to the Mission from the entire Bay Area as a result of the new mass transit system. A conservative Anglo[54] Home Owners Association and a radical Mission Tenants Union[55] simultaneously called the attention of the neighbourhood to the potential danger. But neither of them had the power or the political legitimacy to mobilize and represent the community. The Churches, particularly the Presbyterians, the Episcopalians, and the Roman Catholics, seized the chance to lead a vast coalition to stop the urban renewal study. To do so, they relied on the organizational web already existing in the Mission, including at least four different types of neighbourhood groups:

1 Social service orientated agencies, like *Obeca-Arriba Juntos*, initially funded by the Roman Catholic charities and managed by a group of liberal Mexican-Americans with connections with the poverty fighters of the Democratic party.
2 The Latino wing of the San Francisco labour movement organized around the *Centro Social Obrero*, connected to the Construction Workers Union (AFL-CIO Local 261).
3 The Church-supported groups, particularly the Roman Catholic council for the Spanish speaking residents.
4 Local chapters of socio-political traditional Latino organizations such as the Mexican American Political Association (MAPA), and League of United Latin American Citizens (LULAC).

Additional support eventually came from the Economic Opportunity Council (EOC) organizers[56] who were at the same time trying to attract popular constituencies to implement the Federal social programmes under the classical premise of 'maximum feasible participation'[57] So, from the very beginning, the two major triggers of the American urban movements of the 1960s, urban renewal and the war on poverty, were the underlying causes of social mobilization in the Mission.

After some argument with the labour group, initially attracted to a redevelopment project by the possibility of obtaining construction jobs, a coalition was formed in the neighbourhood to stop urban renewal. This was the Mission Council on Redevelopment (MCOR) which successfully opposed the approval of the study project, organizing a major campaign of grassroots protest and public opinion support that swayed, in December 1966, the board of supervisors of the city of San Francisco to a six to five vote, overriding the mayor's approval of the SFRA's proposal. After its victory, the *ad hoc* coalition dispersed, proving too diverse to agree on anything but the preservation of the neighbourhood. Yet the success of this coalition realized the idea that urban renewal could be stopped and that an alternative pattern of social and urban policies could be developed in opposition to the one inspired by the usually predominant downtown interests. Under these circumstances, the ground was laid for the potential convergence, into an umbrella community organization, of the three powerful groups already active in the Mission's turbulent scene in the late 1960s:

1 The urban-based Churches, struggling to maintain their influence among the popular

sectors, threatened by spatial displacement as well as by the growing influence of radical ideologies.

2 The radical political groups, formed in the anti-war movement and the campus revolts, and identifying with the involvement of ethnic minorities in the process of Third World liberation.

3 The traditional Latino organizations (both the ones that were service-orientated as well as those politically motivated) trying to benefit from the war on poverty and aware of the challenge presented by the new Latino radical nationalism, one of whose most extreme expressions, the Brown Berets,[58] began to make themselves evident on the streets of the Mission.

Nevertheless the crucial event in the formation of a broadly supported community organization, came from high-up the institutional ladder. In February 1968, the newly elected mayor Alioto – probably looking to consolidate his influence among the city's ethnic minorities – unexpectedly announced his intention to apply for a Federally-funded, multi-million dollar Model Cities Programme.[59] The two basic target areas (model neighbourhoods) were going to be Hunters' Point (a black ghetto), and the Inner Mission (the Latino *Barrio*). The choice of these two areas was a striking demonstration of the implicit synonimity between troubled ethnic minorities and urban problems in the terminology of American social policy.

A very broad coalition was formed out of the existing organizations, both to qualify for a series of programmes that would meet the pressing demands of Mission residents and to develop new, more relevant grassroots groups that would control and/or administer the funds, jobs, and institutional resources to be delivered by the Model Cities Programme.

Thus two major factors appear to have been decisive in the process of formulating of the incipient MCO:

1 Although grassroots mobilization against urban renewal predated the Model Cities proposal, the organization was formed to represent the residents' interests in the Federally-funded urban programmes, administered by city hall. The MCO was, therefore, a carefully thought-out project of citizen participation, even though some of its leadership tried to use it to build a powerful and autonomous grassroots organization. Most participating organizations and agencies intended to preserve their autonomy and saw the MCO as a coalition of existing organized constituencies, without any capacity for initiative beyond the mandate of each participating organization.

2 However the MCO leadership saw in this process a chance to build up a new grassroots movement that could expand to be a multi-issue, multi-ethnic community organization representative of the entire neighbourhood, and would eventually bypass the indigineous leaders who they considered to be too close to the public bureaucracies and too narrowly defined as Latino notables.

These two conflicting views of the MCO's role led to continuous internal fighting in the neighbourhood mobilization, many of the differing interests finding expression in the electoral tactics for the annual MCO convention, and in the bureaucratic manoeuvring to win control of the key committees within the coalition. The movement was, from its inception, dominated by an organizational schizophrenia: on the one hand, the attempt to create an autonomous grassroots movement took place within the framework of mandated citizen participation in the local bureaucracies; and on the other hand, the political will to become a multi-issue, single-structure organization was confronted, again and again, with the reality of the MCO's origin as a coalition comprising many organizations, structured around a single issue – the control and management of a Model Cities Programme.

The First Conventions

The fragile unity of the MCO, as well as the complexity of the movement it expressed, were apparent at the organization's very first convention, held on 4 October 1968. Although the attendance of 600 delegates on behalf of 66 neighbourhood-based groups established the representativeness of the organization, the convention was disrupted from the opening session. Some delegates led by the black youth Mission Rebels, accused the Alinskyite leadership of secretive manoeuvring to ensure the control of the coalition's elected board, denied the necessity of an umbrella organization, and called for a more radical stand on truly political issues. In the midst of the shouted confrontations and at a point when many delegates were beginning to leave, a telephone call came from Cesar Chavez[60] praising the founding of the new organization. Order was restored and the convention was saved by being adjourned for one month to repair the damage. The MCO was born, but not, however, with all the participants who had been present at the opening session of the convention. The Mission Rebels, the Marxist-Leninist Mission Tenant Union, *La Raza*, (a radical Nationalist Latino party) and other radical Latinos walked out of the organization. The predominantly white middle class Home Owners Association never joined the MCO, distrustful of the Latino predominance. So although the MCOR had provided the organizational drive, the MCO came out with a more community-orientated strategy that went far beyond a merely defensive reaction to urban renewal.

When the first convention was finally reconvened, in November 1968, only 250 delegates appeared. Nevertheless the organization began to progress. By-laws were approved, *ad hoc* committees were set up, a budget was established with contributions coming largely from the Churches, and a president was elected: Ben Martinez, a 24 year old *chicano* college student working in one of the EOC programmes in the Mission. He soon became the charismatic leader of the Community (too charismatic for some of the member organizations). A limited staff was hired and a staff director appointed.[61] He was Mike Miller, an experienced community organizer, trained by Saul Alinsky himself, and introduced to the Mission by the Presbyterian Church. Miller it was who developed the strategy of the neighbourhood mobilization.

So as to remain open to the radical wing of the community, the convention took a very firm stand on the future relationship with public urban programmes and city hall, voting 13 non-negotiable demands to be fulfilled by the Model Cities Programme as a prerequisite for the MCO's participation. The most important demand was to reserve the MCO the right to veto any initiative coming from the Model Cities Administration. The most apparent reason for such an extreme position was the popular feeling that Model Cities would slip in a new programme of urban renewal. But also implicit in this stand was the ideology of community control, predominant among most grassroots committees: the feeling that the community itself should take care of the management of the urban programmes, removing them from the bureaucrats' hands. Neither Mike Miller nor Ben Martinez were convinced that the strategy would work and favoured what they called institutional change, that is, forcing the public institutions to modify their policies under pressure from the grassroots, but without actually involving the community organization in the daily management of the urban programmes. The conflicting approaches of community control and institutional change introduced an additional split into the jungle of feuds and alliances that already underlay the MCO.

Before it could debate its strategy, however, the Coalition had to prove its capacity to mobilize and organize people, to solve problems, to win demands, and to establish a favourable power relationship *vis-à-vis* city hall, business, and real estate interests.

Throughout 1969 a series of actions in the neighbourhood started to root the organization to its constituency. Actions were initiated such as creating new playgrounds, installing community representatives in the new Mission Mental Health Centre, and banning pawnshops in the neighbourhood. Unable to take a clear stand in relationship to the strike at San Francisco State College[62], the Coalition lost its appeal for the most radical Latinos and blacks, but reconciled itself with some of the predominantly moderate working class families in the Mission. The controversy between different Latino nationalities was handled by establishing *ad hoc* representation in the executive committee for each national or ethnic group.[63]

So, thanks to some internal and external groundwork, the second convention, in October 1969, was able to provide the image of a mature, broadly representative, and well-martialled grassroots organization. 800 delegates attended the meeting on behalf of 81 organizations, including national and ethnic groups, Churches, block clubs, tenants unions, youth committees, civil rights organizations, labour unions, social service agencies, business circles, merchants associations, and a few home owners associations. The MCO came into its own from this time, mainly through the militant activities and successful demands of its issue-orientated committees. The two most prominent issues that triggered social struggles were housing and employment. Absentee landlords were singled out, picketed in their suburban homes, and forced to sign fair agreements with their tenants on rents, repairs and maintenance. In one year the housing committee was able to win upward of 100 such actions. So other landlords refrained from indiscriminate rent increases or from the use of eviction. This campaign contributed, with similar struggles in other neighbourhoods in the early 1970s, to the legislation of a mild form of rent control in San Francisco. Another major outcome of the MCO housing campaign, which was instrumental in organizing the community, was a network of building stewards to handle the tenants' complaints on behalf of, and supported by, the entire Coalition.

The major field of action for the MCO was, however, to fight discrimination against minorities and youth in the workplace. The Coalition forced companies and shops to provide jobs for unskilled workers and special summer jobs for youth by picketing or disrupting normal operations, sometimes with an imaginative and humorous display. For instance, the Hibernia Bank in the Mission was forced to hire Latinos after its Latino clients started to withdraw their funds by writing one dollar cheques on a *tortilla*,[63bis] a perfectly legal device in California. Once again the emphasis was on simultaneously obtaining jobs and organizing people through carefully planned job allocation. People were given points according to their commitment to work, and committee activities (attendance at the meetings, picketing, leaflet distribution, etc.). On the basis of the number of accumulated points, they were entitled to apply for a job on behalf of the Coalition. The companies were supposed to hire the person proposed by the MCO, as selected by the employment committee, regardless of the persons' professional qualifications, and the employer had to provide the job and the training. This scheme could obviously work only on a limited basis and relied on the strong bargaining position of the Community. In fact, during the peak of the MCO's mobilization, the practice did work, and hundreds of jobs were obtained from Pacific Telephone and from Sears. This approach to employment, however, created serious friction with the more cautious and traditional manpower and employment programmes used by the established Latino social agencies, which were also important members of the Coalition.

In a parallel development, a community maintenance committee took care of a variety of local issues such as obtaining stop signs and traffic lights; seeing that burned and abandoned buildings were torn down to avoid squatting; improving mail deliveries; and picketing a cinema on Mission Street that showed pornographic films, forcing it to close, and then coming to an agreement with the theatre whereby it would only show films for the family and that the MCO members could obtain 25 cents discount on all tickets. The activities of this committee ensured the good reputation of the Coalition among the conservative home owner's sector in the Mission.

A planning committee, on which the Anglo middle class was well-represented, collaborated with the city planning department in the formulation of a new land-use plan for the District.

The MCO tried to establish a broad base across the community at the price of losing the support of the more radical youth groups, as well as at the cost of playing down specific Latino cultural demands, an issue that soon caused major criticism from some of the Coalition's more important members. The major task, however, still had to be undertaken – to obtain a substantial Model Cities Programme and to make sure that it would benefit the whole community.

The Model Cities Programme

The mayor had supported, in principle, the provision of a Model Cities Programme for the Mission, but the important issue under discussion was the power relationships that it would create. Model Cities was for the mayor the channel through which funds and jobs could be distributed to the blacks and Latinos in exchange for their political allegiancy. For the MCO, the first convention had instructed the leadership to exercise a veto over the programme and to administer it autonomously in relation to city hall. The conflict took the form of a major disagreement over the new institution to be set up to operate the programme. The mayor wanted a Community Development Administration, located within city hall, but allowing participation of blacks and Latinos on its board of directors. The MCO felt it should be created as a neighbourhood-based, private corporation, controlled by the community and operated with funds directly allocated to it from the Model Cities Programme. Mayor Alioto refused to give away control of the operation. The MCO engaged in battle and mobilized strong support for its position. In addition to demands from its grassroots committees, it obtained favourable public statements from a very broad spectrum of religious, business, labour, and political leaders ranging from San Francisco's Archbishop to a top aide of Governor Reagan. After the MCO organized a massive march on city hall, the mayor accepted the Coalition's proposal. The board of supervisors confirmed the agreement after a public hearing where the MCO impressed the audience with its display of support and discipline, when each representative of 78 local organizations gave a one and one-half minute speech presenting a co-ordinated and scheduled collective presentation of the Coalition's position.

Nevertheless, the state does not stop at the city hall level, not even in America. The Federal funding agency, Housing and Urban Development (HUD), refused to allow community control over public funds, arguing that the MCO's insistence on veto power was illegal because it constituted power without commensurate responsibility. In spite of the MCO's momentum, HUD's declared position to reject Model Cities under the conditions already accepted by city hall rekindled the debate among the MCO leaders over the notion of community control. Both the president, Ben Martinez, and staff director, Mike Miller, feared the loss of organizational autonomy and of the transformation of the movement into a high-powered social agency, which would involve them in managing what would be a private, neighbourhood-based corporation. They had previously agreed, however, on the strategy of involvement in the administration of the programmes under pressure from a variety of members of the Coalition as well as from the widespread opinion of a community distrustful of public bureaucracies. Now that they were faced with a 'choice', as suggested by HUD, of 'Take it or leave it', the social agencies and the majority of the membership were ready to accept a compromise that would provide access to the desperately needed public resources. In the formula that was finally established, and approved by city hall, the legal requirements imposed by HUD were respected, but the MCO was allowed to designate 14 of the 21 members of a new public agency, Model Mission Neighbourhood Corporation (MMNC), in charge of the administration of Model Cities Programmes in the Mission. A similar public agency was created to manage the urban programmes for the black community in Hunter's Point.

A Model Cities grant was approved in June 1971 for the Mission neighbourhood, respecting these conditions and allocating a sum of 3.2 million dollars per year for a period of five years. The MCO, however, was given only six months to draft the proposal, with little technical expertise and serious internal fighting. Grassroots participation was thus minimal in the elaboration of the goals and procedures that were settled upon for the urban programmes by the MCO's leadership. But the proposed organizational model for the new neighbourhood corporation turned out to be a very sophisticated scheme that basically tried to ensure the objectives of community organization and grassroots enforcement through the resources provided by the programmes.[64] Power and independent organization were considered the most important resources to be obtained from Model Cities.

The organizational scheme was based upon the principle that the MMNC would be tightly controlled by the MCO, whose 14 delegates would meet at a caucus before each meeting and vote as a single group on each issue. Priority would be given to low-income housing programmes and job-finding efforts for the Mission's residents. The main activities of the MMNC would be governed by the main targets already set by the MCO: employment, housing, education, and child care. The main purposes of the programme would be to transform the local power system by asking local governments to be more responsive to people's demands, and to encourage grassroots mobilization and organization centred on the use and control of the granted public resources. A series of procedures were designed to infuse this spirit into the programmes. For instance, a hiring hall was set up to ensure that employers hired job candidates from the Mission on the basis of the non-discriminatory criteria established by the MMNC and with reference to the recommendations of the MCO's employment committee. The educational programme proposed to give money to the school district to improve the schools' facilities on the condition that the school district board would encourage parents' participation in the schools' management, and introduce a series of pedagogic reforms in the schools' curricula. On housing, given the difficulty of obtaining approval for low-income housing projects, the MMNC established a seed-money fund to influence local bank grants, in an effort to end red-lining loans in the Mission.[65]

The reality of managing urban programmes and simultaneously fostering community organizations proved even more difficult than foreseen in spite of the leadership's awareness of the problems. Bureaucratic routine slowed down the programmes at the moment when expectations and demands were mounting. HUD turned down several proposals for housing projects, limiting the total of new constructions to 89 housing units. The strategy of the educational programme was made obsolete when the city desegregation programme through busing broke the relationship between the School District and Mission residents. Additional difficulties came from the insensitivity of the Model Cities Agency to requests by the Latino cultural associations for bilingual education and bi-cultural programmes. The child care programme, although successful, fell under the management of city hall and so lost its close ties to the MCO. Finally, the innovative hiring practices used by the employment committee were declared illegal, and the companies refused to honour them as soon as they felt strong enough to resist the community's pressure.

Throughout the formation of the MMNC, most of the MCO's original leaders were absorbed into managing the programmes. When cultural, political, and personal divisions developed within the Coalition, the internal split took the form of a confrontation between the MCO and its supposedly controlled public agency, legally responsible for the administration of the resources aimed at improving the neighbourhood. The social agencies that existed in the Mission before becoming a part of the MCO were particularly bitter about the new public agency that bypassed them to take over control of the funds that they had been awaiting for such a long time. As a result, the confrontation between the MCO, now controlled by the Latino social agencies, and the MMNC, now managed by the Alinskyite cadres, replaced the anticipated confrontation between Mission residents and city hall. The MCO militants started to picket their fellow MMNC representatives, as they had formerly done against the speculative landlords. Mayor Alioto, reassured by his re-election in 1971, and having carried the Mission vote with the MCO's support, presented himself as a mediator between the rival factions, taking advantage of the community's division to reject the requests for neighbourhood improvement from both groups. When Richard Nixon made the decision in 1974 to shut down all Model Cities Programmes, funds were cut off in San Francisco. The Model Cities Programme in the Mission had, however, already died from wounds inflicted by internal conflicts whose social logic we shall try to explain.

The Coalitions' fifth convention, held in November 1972, had the largest attendance, at least on paper, in the organization's history with 1,600 delegates representing 202 neighbourhood groups and agencies. In fact, many of these organizations were only labels prepared for the convention to increase the voting power of the different quarrelling factions. Instead of a social movement, the MCO had become an organizational battleground. Every formal or informal caucus was struggling to win power within the MCO which would then grant them access to the resources of Model Cities as well as to the power centre of city hall.

The first major conflict in the leadership had appeared in the third convention in 1970 when the president decided to run for a third term, at the cost of changing the MCO's by-laws that had forbidden more than two terms. As a result he faced the opposition of one of the founders of the movement, a Puerto Rican woman, outraged by the personalization of the leadership. After her candidacy was defeated, she withdrew from the movement, pulling out with her several grassroots committees.

At the same 1970 convention, Ben Martinez also faced more substantial opposition in the shape of the Latino national groups dominated by the middle class, such as LULAC, arguing that in spite of Martinez's ethnic background, the Coalition was dominated by an Anglo Alinsky-inspired staff, insensitive to the Latino culture: the MCO was using a Latino image, so the argument ran, to win power in city hall for a non-Latino organization.[66] Although they lost the 1970 contest, the Latino nationalists received a major boost in 1971 when the chicano-based social agencies in the Mission sided with them to join the Alianza Caucus within the MCO for the purpose of taking control of the organization which up until then was in the hands of the Alinsky cadres, themselves organized as the Unity Caucus.

In 1971, Ben Martinez finally stepped down from the presidency to become staff director.[67] The Unity Caucus, supported by Church groups, Latino Youth groups and tenants, managed to choose his successor and obtain a majority on the coalition's steering committee in 1971 and again in 1972. But the new president was unable to hold together the complex, effective puzzle that the MCO had become over the previous three years. Meanwhile the Alianza Caucus gained the support of the Latino-based labour groups, the Obreros, as well as social agencies, the powerful Mission Language and Vocational School, and the Latino Nationalists. The result was one of organizational paralysis and self-destructive in-fighting. The Alinskyite cadres used their position of control over the Model Cities Agencies to fire several prominent members of the Alianza Caucus from the staff. Then internecine war broke out amongst the various factions of the MCO including personal attacks, lawsuits, and militant tactics. The tension was heightened by the withdrawal of funds, particularly by the Churches that had become sceptical about the character of such a strife-ridden movement. In its last active year, 1972, the MCO only survived with the help of a 42,000 dollar grant from Stanford University, to train its students in community development so that they may write their Ph.D. theses on urban social movements. In January 1974, after a final series of conflicts and personal attacks had been gleefully reported in the local press, the MCO, to all intents and purposes, collapsed.

Yet the entangled network of social interests and neighbourhood-based organizations that had formed the MCO survived and expanded on its own, sometimes coming together for a particular event, but more often competing for political power, social representation, or financial resources.

Further Mobilizations

The Alinskyite-branch of the MCO survived through the activity of the Mission Planning Council (MPC), whose opinions and demands were seriously considered by city hall in all decisions concerning the neighbourhood's urban development. In 1975, allied with *La Raza*, the MPC mobilized hundreds of residents to oppose the zoning of a section of the Mission, a change that would have permitted the conversion of family residences into commercial areas, making the displacement of low-income families legal. The zoning was halted as a result of the pressure brought to bear by the neighbourhood and the residential areas were preserved. Nevertheless, the MPC had by 1980 really come to represent the Anglo middle class residents, to the point that the founder, Luisa Ezquerro, a highly respected schoolteacher and leader of the Latino community, left the Council to avoid being identified with its increasingly anti-Latino stand. The last spin-off from the MCO had faded.

The traditional Nationalist-Latino organizations went through serious difficulties to mobilize support for themselves, torn as they were between cultural identity and middle class interests, against the background of the Latino poor. LULAC concentrated on administering some educational programmes, and its membership declined to about 35. MAPA, in spite of good connections with the broader political system, did not have enough strength to take the initiative single-handed, and its only successes came as a result of joint efforts with other community forces, such as the effective campaign against racial discrimination with Latinos for Affirmative Action.

In the late 1970s the two basic grassroots related activities in the Mission District were, on the one hand, the social programmes orientated towards the community, and, on the other, the political solidarity with liberation struggles in Latino America.

Among the social agencies, Obeca-Arriba Juntos established itself as a dynamic multi-purpose corporation with a one million dollar a year budget, largely used on manpower programmes. The Mission Hiring Hall, developed on the basis of the Model Cities Programmes, specialized in obtaining jobs for the Latinos. The Mission Language and Vocational School expanded, employing a staff of over 200 people, and was the major channel through which the continuous waves of Latin American immigrants passed, enabling them to integrate into the Mission and subsequently settle in northern California. The Mission Community Legal Defense, also a spin-off of Model Cities, provided free legal assistance to Mission residents who faced criminal charges, and made a point of protecting Latino youth against unjustified police harassment. The Mission Health Neighborhood Centre, funded by Federal programmes, became an important and well-equipped public health facility, although its work was continually interrupted by violent conflicts between the board, speaking for the Latino Community Organizations, and the Centre's staff and health workers, who were influenced by a radical left wing group called The Rebel Workers.

In 1979 the Latino Unity Council (LUC) was established, along the lines of the most prominent social agencies and with the support of some notable people in the Latino community. The Council functioned through a network of reciprocal support, including 12 community-based agencies and about 100 individuals. The interactions, organization, and tactics of this coalition radically and deliberately departed from the model incarnated by the MCO. The LUC avoided any by-passing of its member organizations and fully represented its fragmented interests so that its activities were highly dependent upon volatile but evenly-weighted compromises.

Another set of social programmes, mainly funded through United Way,[68] tried to deal with the problems experienced by Mission youth. Real Alternatives Programme (RAP) articulated an effort to meet youth demands on jobs, education, recreation, and counselling, with a strong socio-political commitment expressed through hard day-to-day work to serve the people. Given the increasing incidence of hard-drug abuse among the Mission youth, RAP introduced specialized programmes to deal with this sensitive issue. They created *Centro de Cambio*, a rehabilitation programme partly managed by youths who had formerly been drug addicts. They also built *La Casa*, a residential drug-free centre for youths wanting to escape drug dependency, obtain a high school education and find a job with the staff's support.

The youth-orientated social programmes also had to cope with the friction between the youth, challenging the status quo, and the police, who reacted harshly to that challenge. Efforts such as the Mission Community Alliance emerged to protest police beatings of youths and the juvenile courts' attempts to impose Anglo, middle class social and cultural standards on Latino youths.

While dealing with the problems of poverty and unemployment, those residents of the Mission who were Latino, particularly the youth, tried to emphasize their cultural identity and their ties with political activity in Latin America. They had left behind them the extreme romanticism of the 1960s, best exemplified by the Brown Berets who wanted to expel both Anglos and blacks from America, and to then negotiate the sharing of the country with the American Indians. In San Francisco the efforts to provide a political content to the ideology of Latino solidarity was made easier by the Mission's strong Central American connections, at a time when that region was exploding. The revolutions in Nicaragua and El Salvador provided an opportunity for self-affirmation for hundreds of immigrants attracted by a series of activities and events co-ordinated by *La Casa de Nicaragua* and *La Casa del Salvador*. But their stand was too political to obtain massive support from a community living, in many cases, with an uncertain legal status. The convergence between Latin American solidarity and the cultural identity of the San Francisco's Latinos was actually provided by the Mission Cultural Centre, created and funded by city hall in 1975 under pressure from community groups and Latino personalities. Since that time it has become one of the most controversial institutions of the Mission District given its consistent support for left wing politics in Latin America, as well as its campaign for the fostering of the Latino and Chicano cultures in California. This search for such a new source of identity has seemed to be the most fruitful axis of development for the Latinos in San Francisco, since, paradoxically, the movement for political solidarity was undermined by the successes of the revolutions in Central America. The arrival in 1979–80 of so many Nicaraguans escaping the Sandinista Revolution, as well as terrified middle class Salvadorenos, and the newly exiled anti-Castro Cubans, was reversing the political atmosphere in the Mission, forcing the Latino community in California to face up to the reality of their own social and political background.

The old Marcusian dream, incarnated in the San Francisco State College strike of 1969, of bringing together the revolt of the American minorities with the Third World liberation movements had faded. The Brown Berets did not survive their model, the Black Panthers. The solidarity movement organized around *Los Siete de la Raza* disappeared in time to avoid witnessing the personal failure of its defendants who were unable to escape the clash between police and individual, violent revolt. Significantly enough, the main leader of the solidarity movement organized around *Los Siete de la Raza* was a brilliant poet who became an organizer of *La Casa de Nicaragua*. He tried to join the Sandinista army and finally became the first cultural attaché in Washington of the Nicaraguan Revolutionary Government. Many realized, as he did, that the Latin American revolution had to be accomplished in Latin America, although support for it could be voiced in the streets of the Mission.

Perhaps one of the most significant developments of the radical Latino student movements, formed in the late 1960s, was its gradual transformation into what, in 1980, seemed to be one of the most active community organizations in San Francisco: *La Raza en Accion Local*. Its name clearly expresses its two-fold character: an ethnic-cultural community (*La Raza*) orientated towards local action, and the social demands of a territorially defined group. Coming, as it did, after the San Francisco State College strike, and the early split with the MCO, *La Raza* took a careful stand, concentrating on its legitimacy as defenders of the Latino community – both on cultural grounds and on the basis of their urban demands – and only confronting the system step by step. We should note that they did not follow the model of a grassroots organization, but built social programmes which were funded by the Catholic and Baptist Churches and some liberal-minded foundations. Militant groups were formed around these programmes and each group in each programme elected the programme's board, that in turn, elected the general board. The organization was extremely careful in selecting its membership, and required each voting member to have been an active participant in one of the programmes for at least two years. From 1970 onwards, the realm of *La Raza's* activities expanded steadily, to include the La Raza Information Centre, a tutorial programme to improve the education of Latinos, a legal centre for counselling, a silkscreen centre, a credit co-operative, and a Housing Development Corporation which supported co-operative housing, its first venture being to build a 50 unit housing project for low-income residents, solar-heated and built above a public parking area in the very core of the Mission.

The driving force behind this long term effort – maintained in spite of so many failures – was that the community had to learn to rely on its own economy and organization before it could engage in wider confrontations that might bring general acceptance. From time to time, however, the networks established by the programmes were used to mobilize people on specific issues. The 1975 campaign in collaboration with the Mission Planning Council, for example, succeeded in preserving residences for some 4,000 people, and protecting family life along the way, closing down some bookshops and theatres trading in pornography. They attacked, and ran out of business, a bar on 24th Street in order to prevent gentrification of the neighbourhood. They were also influential in redirecting city hall funds for beautifying the urban landscape into more pragmatic uses such as sanitation, public transportation, and traffic regulations. And finally *La Raza* participated effectively in a coalition with all the neighbourhoods in San Francisco to obtain approval for a new zoning ordinance that would preserve the residential character of the city.

All these actions were, nevertheless, skirmishes from *La Raza's* point-of-view. They were waiting for the moment when the city would be ready for such a large mobilization by all the poor neighbourhoods that it would be capable of imposing a new strategy for urban development. This situation would, however, require the transformation of the local political system. So *La Raza* members were much in evidence in the 1976 and 1977 referendums that modified the way the board of supervisors were elected. Once District elections were established in 1977, *La Raza* began a drive to have its candidates elected as representatives of District 6 which included the Mission. They tried to form a broadly-based Latino coalition around one of its leaders, Gary Borvice, a *chicano*, who was running as a Latino candidate, and they succeeded in obtaining widespread support within the community. Most of the social agencies and several of the former leaders of the MCO sided with Borvice. His opponent was Carol Ruth Silver, a liberal, white lawyer. She ran with the double support of the Anglo middle class and the growing lesbian and gay population of the District, particularly those voters from the section that was not part of the Mission neighbourhood. A few minor Latino candidates diverted some votes from *La Raza* but the race looked as if it would be close run.

In the month before election, however, Larry Del Carlo entered the competition – a former vice president of the MCO and a respected and well-known community leader with a mixed Anglo-Latino background. He ran on a fairly conservative platform and was backed by some of the remaining MCO constituency. He came third in the election[69] but his presence was enough to split the Latino vote, so that Gary Borvice lost to Carol Ruth Silver. Our sources suggest that it was quite possible Del Carlo's candidacy may have been encouraged by Mayor Moscone who wanted both to support the candidate backed by the gay community and to fight the *La Raza* candidate, who was considered politically too radical but culturally too conservative.

Two years later Bob Gonzales, the last Latino supervisor and one of the last vestiges of Alioto's political machine, was defeated by a black woman in the District's election, and with him went the last of the Latino power in the local political arena. Many of the Mission leaders, particularly in *La Raza*, adopted a different strategy to recover some of that power. In the 1979 mayoral election, they supported the conservative challenger to the incumbent mayor, the moderate liberal, Diane Feinstein, in exchange for promises of programmes and positions favouring the Latino community. The conservative lost and the Latino influence declined still further, in a city where they represented approximately 15 per cent of the population. To be sure, they accounted for much less of the actual voters (perhaps as low as 6 per cent), an example of the key difference between a people's existence and their political representation.

A Time of Uncertainty

The failure of all the Latino-based political initiatives, as well as little grassroots mobilization in the Mission, heralded a period of social uncertainty in the late 1970s. The number of community-based organizations, however, was still high (approximately 60), and most remained quite active. Their achievements nonetheless have been relatively limited and the preservation of the neighbourhood has not been able to alleviate seriously the poverty of its residents. So the contradictions became increasingly acute between the quality of the neighbourhood and the day-to-day survival of immigrants and poor Latinos. Disenchantment set in and drugs swept through the Mission, with hundreds of teenagers swallowed in a 'storm of angel dust'.[70] A more positive attempt at self affirmation though began to express itself in a new form of Latino youth culture: the low riders. Latino youths bought old cars, installed hydrolic jack-up devices, lowered the bodies, modified the engines and painted the exteriors in pink, green, silver and blue with religious and hippie motifs. They stayed in groups, listening to rock music. On Friday and Saturday nights groups of low riders paraded their cars slowly down Mission Street between 24th and 20th Streets, revving the engines, raising and lowering the chassis, playing their stereos, and stopping from time to time to exchange passengers. Surrounding them on the pavements and in the adjacent streets were hundreds of teenage *cholitos* and *cholitas* (young Latinos), each carrying a radio tuned into the same station. Beer drinking, dancing, smoking, and the urgent need to express pent-up violence was apparent everywhere. From time to time a car, taking advantage of a traffic jam, would stop, the windows open and a dozen youths would run over to grab plastic bags, hand over a few dollars and disappear into the crowd before the police could react. Violence erupted occasionally, encouraged rather than prevented by an overwhelming police presence.

In fact, most of the low riders did not live in the Mission. They were the sons of the Latino immigrants who came to the Mission and were then dispatched to the suburbs of the Bay Area, predominantly to the Southern Peninsula. But the second generation returned to the Mission, and, although they did not grow up there, claimed it as their territory (analogous to the American Indians claiming the Alcatraz Island in the San Francisco Bay). An Anglo-based conservative group (the Mission Action Team) asked for police protection and the mayor quickly provided it so that today the Mission is continuously patrolled by police cars, and frequently visited by the 'tactical' squad. On Friday and Saturday nights, traffic is diverted and police cars block the entire street, and arrests and confrontations have become more and more frequent.

Almost the entire Latino community, including the mainstream social agencies and the progressive Mission Cultural Centre, sided with the low riders and vowed to protect their youth in their territory. Hundreds of youths united to 'stop police brutality' and to seek new forms of autonomous organizations. The merchants were split on the issue. The Mission Street Merchant's Association, representing Anglo absentee owners, called for police rein-forcement and asked for the closing of the Centre. The 24th Street Merchants Association, stronghold of the Latino-owned retailers supported the dialogue with the youth, looking for solutions to such an explosive situation.

Ten years after the Mission Coalition experience, the community organizations have largely failed to solve the social problems or to change the political system. But they have improved the neighbourhood and have succeeded in keeping Latino culture alive in its own territory. The minority youth, because they have been denied the right to the memory of their community's struggles, have revived the process of revolt in their own way, finding new forms to express their cultural identity and their social demands. History does not repeat itself, but when contradictions remain unsolved, they become more acute.

The Rise and Fall of a Neighbourhood Movement: An Analytical Model to Explain the Social Process Underlying the Evolution of the Mission Coalition Organization

The MCO's legacy in the Mission District and the Latino community of San Francisco will be evident for a long time. When we conducted our research, almost eight years after its disinte-gration, traces of the MCO were everywhere, like a meteorite that has exploded in the sky over San Francisco leaving pieces scattered in the streets of the *Barrio*. People continue to argue over the issues that the MCO raised and its leaders discuss over and over again what happened. Many of them, along with the most active participants, have suffered severe exhaustion from their involvement as frustration mounted. For the ones who have remained politically active, the old divisions that define friends and enemies still exist which goes to show that the MCO was the most intense social experience for those men and women who were part of it, besides being a major urban mobilization. This experience is common to any significant social movement which has sudden and glorious life and death.

Part of the continuing obsession with the MCO lies in the mystery surrounding both its startling surge and its relatively rapid crisis, at the very peak of its achievements. To be sure, every witness of the movement has his or her own interpretation, but most of them point to the clashes in character; to bitter internal fighting to obtain money, jobs and power; to organizational manoeuvring; and to the lack of leadership. And yet we know that these factors are present in all social mobilizations, without, necessarily, the same results. Personal conflicts and ambitions are only a precipitating factor in the crisis of a movement, the underlying causes of which must be found, as we will try to show with the MCO, in the process itself. Furthermore we will seek an explanation for both the success and failure of the MCO, since only a comprehensive scheme can provide us with some understanding about the formation and decline of urban social movements. Only then will we be able to understand why 'heroes' become 'villains', that is, why the social context allows people to more easily express one or the other of the many contradictory dimensions we all carry in ourselves.

The Context of the MCO and a First Theoretical Construction

Certain factors created a very favourable atmosphere for the emergence of the MCO in 1968, but when reversed in 1972, provided a more difficult framework for community organization and progressive urban policies. As we have pointed out, the MCO appeared as a simultaneous response to two major public programmes that acted as a trigger for most community mobilizations in America during the 1960s: urban renewal and the social programmes funded by the Federal government. The fear that the San Francisco Redevelopment Agency (SFRA) would transform the Mission into another field of action for its bulldozers and developers first motivated people to form a coalition. Once the threat of displacement had been removed, the possibility of obtaining a variety of urban programmes and social benefits through the Model Cities grant pushed the movement onto the offensive. In this sense, the MCO was an archetypical movement arising from the urban heritage of the 1960s. By 1972, the picture had changed greatly with respect to Federal policies. Urban renewal had been stopped because of the neighbourhood opposition and the shrinking resources and influence of the San Francisco Redevelopment Agency. Furthermore, the cutting of social programmes, including Model Cities, by President Nixon's administration dried up the Federal funds, and severely limited the majority of programmes. The channelling of social demands through Model Cities was no longer possible and the MCO, in order to survive and develop had to find other resources and targets. It failed to do so. Thus, it is clear that there was a strong connection between public policies and the formation of neighbourhood movements. Community organizations developed to improve people's living conditions by taking advantage of the Federal social programmes. However, the conservative stand of the Nixon administration prompted a backlash in those programmes, most of which were severely reduced and submitted to tighter controls; and funds dried up, limiting the organizational capacity and undermining the political legitimacy of the urban poor. The new policy emphasized the role of city hall over the grassroots organizations.[71]

So, in spite of the MCO's strength and militancy that by 1972 had gained the respect of its adversaries and of public authorities, it was unable to operate within the relatively open institutional context that had supported its development. However it did not have consequently to fall apart. For the new conservative urban policies to have caused the MCO's collapse, the

MCO could only have been a camouflage set up to receive money from the Model Cities programmes (an accusation in fact levelled at the organization by its critics). All available evidence, however, disproves this interpretation.[72] The MCO had hundreds of active members and dozens of grassroots committees, and although they did take advantage of public funds and programmes, generally took a militant stand on their demands. In fact, even given the favourable situation in 1968, the MCO was created because a group of neighbourhood activists, supported by the Churches, wanted to transform the defensive MCOR into an autonomous grassroots organization. It is true, nevertheless, that by 1972 most of the original Alinskyite leaders had become deeply involved in the management of the Model Cities programmes, forgetting, for the most part, the grassroots committees, except to support their own election onto them in the MCO's annual convention. But why? How could the same persons with the same ideas, who had successfully imposed a tight control by the people over the content and management of public programmes for the neighbourhood, allow themselves to become lost in a bureaucratic jungle and consequently isolated from their community. We must try to find a social explanation of the process that led to the precipitating factor in the MCO's crisis – its absorption into social programmes, and its subsequent disarray once the social programmes were dismantled by a Federal administration recovering from the assaults it had suffered in the 1960s.

We need, first, to introduce a few elementary concepts which will enable us to understand the structure and dynamics of an urban movement with the characteristics of the Mission-based mobilization.

Urban movements, and indeed all social mobilizations, happen when, in their collective action and at the initiative of a conscious and organized operator, they address one or more structural issues that differentiate contradictory social interests. (We will develop a broader and more systematic presentation of the underlying analytical model in Parts 5 and 6.) These issues, or their combination, define the movement, the people they may mobilize, the interests likely to oppose the movement, and the attitude of institutions according to their political orientation. So the issues encapsulate the potential significance of a movement to its society. We call these social issues 'goals' of the movement's structure and to be so, they must be present in its practice. For example, if a movement is to be defined as 'Latino', it must act in such a way that there is an affirmation of 'Latino ethnicity' with a set of corresponding demands and goals that are defined and put into practice. Of course, the movement's 'goals' do not entirely determine its development, outcome, organization, success, or failures. Social mobilization includes the organizational arrangement of these 'goals' and the operators – their interaction and their interplay with larger social structures and with other social actors. These 'goals' constitute the raw material of a movement, and the understanding of their basic structure affects the explanation of the movement, making it a social process that extends beyond its history and social circumstances.

The social issues providing the 'goals' of an urban movement represent the connection in action between the movement and the whole society. The issues are the translation of one into the other, and therefore they are specific to each society as it is historically determined. In the American experience of urban mobilization there seem to have been three main structural issues underlying the popular movements:

1 *Neighbourhood.* The preservation and improvement of residential neighbourhoods at the level of their physical space, at the level of their urban services, and at the level of their economic value. (We exclude from the meaning of *neighbourhood* the social networks or sub-cultures that are sometimes attached to neighbourhoods. We prefer to describe these as a *community*, to distinguish the urban and cultural dimensions of a neighbourhood.)

2 *Poverty.* The economic and social demands of the most deprived sectors of the population in terms of jobs, income, education and social benefits. We also include in this category a diversity of social problems that (it can be demonstrated) are systemic consequences of the socio-economic deprivation, such as street crime, juvenile violence, and widespread drug traffic and consumption (different from the 'drug problem' which is socially broader).

3 *Oppressed ethnic minority.* The specific demands of oppressed ethnic minorities who, besides suffering poverty and urban decay, have problems linked to racial and cultural discrimination. (We do not therefore consider ethnicity in general here, since Irish or Italians do not face similar problems in American society. We would, however, have proceeded differently at the turn of the nineteenth century . . .)

If we want to relate these three basic issues to the overall social structure, we have to remember, first, that specific *neighbourhoods* express the general dynamics of the *city*; second, that *poverty* is the consequence, at the distribution level of a basic pattern of relationships of production organized by *class*; and, third, that the oppression of ethnic minorities originates in an asymmetrical social structure differentiated by *race*. So the immediate experience of an urban movement concerns only the first level of a broader structure, along three different but interrelated dimensions:

Dimensions	Level of Local Experience	Level of Social Structure
Urban-spatial	Neighbourhood	City
Socio-economic	Poverty	Class
Socio-cultural	Minority	Race

What generally characterizes the American experience of *social mobilization* is that:

1 It tends to happen at the level of immediate experience without relating to the corresponding level of a broader social structure (so that 'poor people' will mobilize to obtain more welfare benefits without challenging the general employment policy or the taxation system).

2 It tends to isolate each element which means, therefore, that a single objective is pursued. (Mexican Americans, for example, will try to obtain social benefits for themselves as Mexican Americans without considering other ethnic minorities. This pattern of behaviour is defined, in sociological terms, as that of an *interest group*.)

What generally characterizes the experience of *social movements*[73] in America, and even more so in Europe, is that they develop one-dimensionally according to a pattern that we would describe as 'horizontal':

From	*Neighbourhood*	to	*City*
From	*Poverty*	to	*Class*
From	*Minority oppression*	to	*Racial liberation*

In addition social movements tend, on the basis of each mobilization, to challenge the overall social structure by attempting to change the political institutions. Thus their dynamics affect a fourth, and most important dimension of the social structure: *state power*. Specific to and original in the 'community mobilization' model found in the Alinsky-inspired ideologies and tactics,[74] is that the elements on which the movement relies are deliberately confined to the immediate experience while, at the same time, they are connected to a multi-dimensional movement dealing with all aspects of the social structure by virtue of bringing together all sorts of popular organizations; and they base their counter-power on this wide support, a power that is called a *community organization*. A community organization theoretically remains autonomous from the political system; yet by mobilizing the grassroots and politicizing the immediate experience, it brings about institutional change that puts pressure on the state. If we represent in our diagram the dynamics of the three theoretical models of social mobilization (interest group, social movement, Alinsky-inspired community movement) we obtain the following:

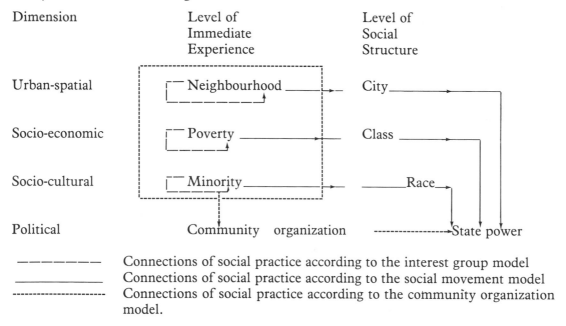

Dimension	Level of Immediate Experience	Level of Social Structure
Urban-spatial	Neighbourhood	City
Socio-economic	Poverty	Class
Socio-cultural	Minority	Race
Political	Community organization	State power

— — — — —   Connections of social practice according to the interest group model
——————   Connections of social practice according to the social movement model
- - - - - - - - - -   Connections of social practice according to the community organization model.

However simple this theoretical construction may be, it is a helpful tool for deciphering the mystery of the brilliant life and dramatic death of the MCO. It is our hypothesis that the development of the MCO as a community organization came from a successful combination in its practice of *neighbourhood*, *poverty* and *minority* (Latino) issues yet without reference to the higher elements of *city*, *class*, and *race*. Its failure can be blamed on the relationship established between the MCO (*community organization*) and city hall and Model Cities (*state power*) – this crucial relationship failed precisely because of the MCO's refusal to challenge the higher levels of the social structure. The sources of its strength were also the factors that determined its crisis. Let us develop our interpretation, try to prove it and elaborate on its meaning.

Deciphering the Rise and Fall of the MCO

The methodology of this demonstration requires a somewhat complex mechanism that organizes in a systematic way the detailed information we gathered on the actions, organization, and evolution of the MCO. (See the Appendix, p. 351, for this formal analysis.) If our hypothesis is true, then:

1 The different elements of the proposed model had to be present in the practice of the Mission mobilization.
2 The elements will have varied during the evolution of the MCO, so that different combinations will have developed compared to the original matrix and the permutations will have been meaningful, and able to have been coded in terms of the basic elements.

3 There will have been a system of significant correspondences between the variations in the structure of the MCO and the variations in its outcomes and functioning.

To observe the evolution of the movement in a systematic way, we have chosen to observe the interests that were present and the positions taken during the five annual conventions of the MCO. Far from being pro-forma meetings, the conventions were the source of power for the leadership and openly expressed the interests and programmes of each member organization. We will be able to test our hypothesis (and to base the proposed analytical model on the experience under observation) by examining the clustering and splits between the different interests and by assessing the impact upon the process of urban mobilization of the new structure that the MCO formed in each convention. Since we have already described the sequence of events in the Mission, and since we will present a systematic summary of information in our Methodological Appendix (see pages 346–55), the analysis here will concentrate on the synthetic theoretical explanation of the social process under consideration.

In defending the neighbourhood against urban renewal before the MCO existed, MCOR called on the broadest possible range of interests and elements. Many home owners, tenants unions, block clubs, and Churches defended the neighbourhood, particularly the Mission Tenants Union, and challenged the urban policy for the entire city. Social agencies, administering Federal programmes, were basically interested in the poverty issues. The Latino branch of the labour unions tried a coalition of class, poverty and Latino elements. The Latino Nationalist groups of different countries introduced the consideration of the Latino minority, and some of them went on to call for Third World liberation and Brown Power. The Coalition tried to rest almost everything on a single issue – the arresting of urban renewal. But once this fight was won, the coalition fell apart. The first convention of the MCO in 1968 tried to bring together all these elements and ended in total disruption. The best formula for a movement to begin in the Mission District did not appear to lie with the combination of all dimensions at all levels. The formula that finally worked was one that the MCO put together between 1968 (first convention) and 1970 (third convention), the period in which specific demands were won, a community-controlled Model Cities grant was obtained, and a series of committees and grassroots organizations got underway. During this period it was formed by:

1 MCO-inspired grassroots committees addressing a variety of social issues: employment, education, housing, in the Mission (*neighbourhood and poverty*).
2 Church organizations playing a very similar role to the grassroots committees (*neighbourhood and poverty*).
3 Latino-based social agencies (*minority* and *poverty*).
4 Latino national groups emphasizing the Latino culture (*minority* and *race*).
5 Latino branch of the labour movement (*minority* and *class*).
6 Strong staff organization such as the MCO (*community organization*).

Reduced to its basics, this structure reproduces the model of community organization as postulated, with the addition of a second order element such as class, and a strong component of racial self-affirmation on the basis of the Latino culture. (In fact the *Centro Social Obrero*, although a part of AFL-CIO Local 261 (construction workers), was much more significant as the Latino branch of the union, than as the union. Its strength came from the language school which was basically a social agency.)

The latter 'goal' became the breaking point for some organizations in the third convention, in 1970. Although the MCO fully recognized the Latino's self-affirmation as a major component of the movement, it was not and did not want to be a Latino organization. In the third convention, the fourth 'goal' split from the MCO, both in its moderate (*minority*) and radical (*race*) components.

The immediate result was a weakening of the MCO's influence, but this was largely compensated for by the boost given to the organization by the beginning of the Model Cities programmes in 1971. So a seventh 'goal' was added: MMNC's staff representing, as it were, a portion of state power. This staff was, significantly enough, headed by the Alinskyite leaders who, in so doing, left behind them the sixth 'goal' (*community organization*) that was then operated by the remaining MCO forces.

The major split came at the fourth convention in 1971. The Latino-based social agencies, joining forces with all recipient Latino-orientated groups opposed the candidate from the Alinskyite circles. Although he was elected, with the support of the grassroots committees and Churches, the two blocs became warring factions: on the one hand, *neighbourhood and poverty* and on the other hand, *minority and poverty*.

Latino labour found itself in the middle. The two blocks organized. The first one, the Unity Caucus, had 50 per cent Latino members while the second one, the Alianza Caucus, was 100 per cent Latino. In the fifth convention (1972), Latino labour finally switched to the Alianza Caucus and the Latino president of the MCO changed loyalty to be re-elected this time against his former supporters. While the Alinskyites still retained control over the Model Cities institution, the Latino-based organizations and agencies won the leadership of the MCO. The result was conflicting structures as follows:

Unity Caucus	Alianza Caucus
Neighbourhood	Latino culture (*minority*)
Poverty	Latino *poverty*
Some *state power*	Latino *labour*
	Community organization (staff)

The split between neighbourhood issues and minority issues was fatal for the MCO. When, finally, 'community organizers' picketed 'city hall bureaucrats', and 'city hall bureaucrats' fired 'Latino militants', the end of the movement had arrived.

Thus, apparently, ethnic divisions and absorption into bureaucracy account for the disintegration of the movement. But why? After all, the MCO was supposed to control MMNC, and the Alinskyite leaders always supported Latino culture. Is it impossible, in America, for a movement to bring together poor people, neighbourhood problems and oppressed minorities in the same community organization? The answer must be 'No' by nature, but 'Yes' in this particular case. The disintegration came not so much because of the split between Latino and Non-Latino people as the use of this real difference to represent more fundamental and contradictory interests.

In truth, the MCO experienced three different but successive splits, apparently related to the division between urban poor (including Latinos) and the Latino cultural self-definition.

The first one, at the initial stage of the organization, clearly distinguished the MCO from the radical nationalists identified with the Third World Liberation Movement. The 'reformist' stand of the MCO – trying to 'come down to people's real issues' – preferred to distance itself from an ideological radicalism that might compromise its chances of becoming a widely supported grassroots movement.

The second split was more embarrassing. The middle class Latino cultural and political organizations, such as LULAC or MAPA, largely cut the MCO off from the traditional political elites of established Latinos, until they finally eroded its ethnic minority component.

But the real blow came when the Latino-based social agencies, dealing with the poverty issues on behalf of a Latino constituency, opposed the 'All People United' stand of the Alinskyites and took over the MCO, regaining control over the grassroots organization. In this context we can state that although the Latino versus non-Latino division was a real one, it only became a disruptive one when it was used as the flag to rally support in the battle over the control of the Model Cities programmes, and beyond, over the representation of Latinos and Mission residents *vis-à-vis* the public social policies. This self-definition of the community-based poverty agencies was not a matter of tactics: it was their very essence. Only by being the socio-political brokers of an ethnic minority, defined in the terms of the dominant culture as 'Latinos' or 'Spanish-speaking', could they maintain their institutional existence, economic resources, and political influence. And, anyway, their Latino identity was not only organizational self-interest but also the expression of basic distrust towards the artificial uniformity of a culture in which all citizens are equal, except that the decision-making bodies comprise male, white privileged groups as against a constellation of fragmented minorities.

If the economy and institutions discriminate against a particular group, like the Latinos, the reaction will be one of self-preservation, which in this case was to organize a group based around the Latino culture and to address the demands of this group to the powers that be. This is the process by which social needs are converted into *interest groups*, and this was the way the Mission's social agencies were born and grew up. 'Mission District' in San Francisco was the code word for the 'Latino minority', and this was why they obtained a Model Cities Programme and why the MCO had an immediate impact on the city's social policies. Thus, when the Alinskyite leaders, with a broader vision that stretched across ethnic lines and poor people's interests, took over the social programmes provided by Model Cities, the established Latino agencies felt threatened and decided to end the MCO in favour of the old system of being the intermediaries between their ethnic constituency and the public institutions. Their behaviour was motivated, at one and the same time, by the will to keep their position as broker and by the defense of the borders that would guarantee them at least the share that Latinos could obtain in American society. In other words, once people are institutionally segmented in different interest groups, it is impossible to reconcile the different demands competing for the distribution of increasingly scarce resources.

The confrontation was made more sudden and more acute by the Alinskyite cadres seizing power in the Model Cities agencies, the very same people who were advocating the construction of grassroots organizations as the only real source of help for the poor people. The reason had nothing to do with personal corruption or unrestrained ambition, but was related to the strategy underlying the Alinsky model of community organization which was systematically implemented in the Mission. On the one hand, the community's activists had to rely in the initial stages on the existing social agencies, whose constituency was based upon patronage and who provided the natural ground on which community organizations could grow. On the other hand, if the activists intended eventually to bypass the influence of the agencies and build up autonomous militant organizations, it was necessary to establish their own legitimacy with the neighbourhood residents, including the Latino majority. The legitimacy of the new community organization would only replace the old ties from clients using one of two premises: either people's consciousness would be raised to a higher level so that the defense of their immediate economic interests was not the first and only concern, or they would have to satisfy their immediate demands through new organizational channels that would become the new source of legitimacy.

The MCO's leadership chose the second way, and decided to take over the programmes themselves on the basis of their influence on the grassroots committees to prevent Latino social agencies from reinforcing their power through the resources obtained by grassroots struggles. To keep their influence they needed to fulfil the condition of satisfying people's immediate material needs through the delivery of jobs, services, and money. So, ultimately, they became a 'super service' agency, and the MCO was transformed into a battleground between the two sets of agencies fighting over the resources that would buy people's allegiancy, once 'people' had been reduced to a definition in terms of immediate economic interests. In a case like this, once the driving force of an interest group is accepted, the self-definition of each group tends to be stated in terms of the cultural categories of the dominant ideology. So 'Latinos' ended up fighting 'non-Latinos' over the control of resources that finally disappeared once the community organizations had become too weak to impose a redistributive policy on the representatives of the state.

But why was it that the community organizers, who had a clear awareness of the need both to respect the identity of different popular sections and to bring them all together in their common interests, were unable to raise the level of self-definition and organization to a point that would have created unity? The reasons for such a crucial outcome are most significant for our understanding of the relationship between urban poverty and ethnicity, and they mainly concern the obstacles existing in most American cities, and certainly in San Francisco, against raising the practice of an urban movement over and above one of the four dimensions we have previously differentiated.

For the neighbourhood issues posed in the Mission to be transformed into an urban policy for the entire city, it was necessary to seek an alliance with a middle class-based neighbourhood movement whose emphasis on urban conservation, environmental quality, and low-density zoning was far removed from the basic concerns of poor Latinos – decent housing and construction jobs. The demand for rent control was the only clear, common ground but it was insufficient to establish an alternative model of urban development taking into consideration both urban quality and living conditions. Thus neighbourhood demands in the Mission remained narrowly defined to local issues.

To connect the poverty problems with a broader strategy of class struggle stronger ties were needed to the labour movement. But the Latino component of the labour movement was dependent on the construction workers, who were only interested in redevelopment and the construction of new high-rise buildings as a source of jobs and income. When the Latino leader of the *Centro Social Obrero* tried to play a major role in the Construction Workers' Union, he ran into bitter conflict with the established Union leaders and had to leave San Francisco in 1971 (at gun point, so the story goes).

To shift from defense of Latinos against economic and social discrimination to the self-affirmation of Latino culture as a process of national liberation connected with the Third World was unthinkable for a community organization based on the unification of poor people's interests in a given city. Therefore all self-definition that might alienate other ethnic groups was to be excluded.

Finally, to transform the community organization into a political force (as the gays did in San Francisco) was impossible for a neighbourhood where at least 20 per cent of the residents were not legal residents, and where the majority of the poor people, particularly Latinos, were not registered voters. The lack of confidence in the responsiveness of the political institutions encouraged political alienation, which in turn increased the likelihood of discriminatory practices in public policies which, as ever, sought to reinforce the status quo.

So, constrained to limit their initiatives to the level of people's immediate interests, the community activists who created the MCO were very successful in establishing the link between urban demands, grassroots organizations, and social programmes. Distrustful of radical ideologies, and believing only in what they could take into their own hands, the neighbour-hood populists were able to establish themselves as the citizen's representatives and genuinely speak for the poor and minorities. But, having established their legitimacy exclusively on the basis of their capacity to deliver immediate rewards they reproduced the social fragmentation of different interest groups fighting for the diminishing pieces of an unquestioned pie of dubious taste.

People's unity does not result from an ideological statement. It has to be built, as the MCO activists rightfully argued, through a common collective practice originating from the different situations of its participants. Nevertheless, people's unity neither results from the piecemeal satisfaction of different demands that are taken for granted nor by excluding any process of cultural transformation aimed at the redefinition of needs. The social logic of interest groups is not superseded by their coalition. The Mission Community organizers learned too late the crucial historical distinction between popular unity and political trade-offs.

And yet, in its life and death, the MCO decisively shaped the Mission District as well as San Francisco's social policies. As we shall see, the profile of this transformation closely follows the characteristics and shortcomings of a major neighbourhood mobilization, the social logic of which we tried to discover behind the facade of the discourse of its social actors.

A Place to Live: The Urban Impact of Grassroots Mobilization in the Mission District

Urban decay in the Mission District was, as in most American inner cities, the consequence, not the cause, of the white working class flight to the suburbs during the 1950s. Tables 13–1 and 13–2 show a parallel evolution of an increasing Latino population in an urban environment whose quality was consistently below the San Francisco average, and which deteriorated as the landlords were able to avoid repairs and maintenance due to the weak bargaining position of the new Latino immigrant-renters.[75]

Similar downward trends could be observed in most public services and physical facilities, according to the study prepared by the Mission Housing Development Corporation, 'Compared to San Francisco's averages, the Mission District public schools show lower student learning achievement, and serious reading problems; higher drop-out rates; lack of innovative teaching methods and less parents' participation in secondary school activities. Child care centers have waiting lists totalling about 1,000 children; preventive mental and dental health care are insufficient'.[76] Also, while the Inner Mission accounted for 7 per cent of

Table 13.1   Evolution of Spanish-surname population in the Mission District of San Francisco, 1940–1970.

	1940	1950	1960	1970
Total population	52,000	53,000	51,000	51,870
Spanish-surname population	NA	5,530	11,625	23,183
(% over total population of the District)		10·4%	22·8%	44·7%

(NA: Not Available)

Source: Noelle Charleston, Robert Jolda, Judith Waldhorn: *Summary of Trends in Housing and Population in the Mission Model Neighbourhood, 1940–1970* (Stanford: Stanford University Community Development Study, 1972, mimeographed).

Table 13.2   Housing trends, 1940–1970, Mission Model Neighbourhood (MN) and San Francisco (SF)

	1940		1950		1960*		1970	
	MN	SF	MN	SF	MN	SF	MN	SF
Total units	18,379	222,176	19,288	265,726	21,330	331,000	21,000	310,383
Vacancy rate	5·8%	7%	1·3%	2%	4·7%	5%	4·6%	3%
Owner-occupancy rate	17%	29%	19%	36%	16%	33%	14%	31%
Average value	$4181	$5503	$9646	$12,209	$15,913	$17,300	$25,877	$30,600
Percentage renter-occupied	83%	71%	81%	64%	84%	67%	86%	69%
Average rent	$25	$32	$34	$44	$66	$68	$105	$135
Percentage crowded (1·01 + persons per room)	10%	7%	9%	8%	9%	6%	13%	7%
Percentage of un-sound housing units	4%	NA	9%	NA	16%	NA	16%	NA

*A different definition of 'unfit' was used in 1960; see study.

Source: Stanford University Community Development Study.

the city's population in 1970 and 9 per cent of the city's youth, they only had 0.004 per cent of San Francisco's 3,452 acres of open and recreational space.[77]

Community organizations in the Mission mobilized to halt the trend towards housing dilapidation and to obtain better urban facilities for the neighbourhood. At the same time they tried to prevent the classic process of a deteriorated area being improved for new residents once the poor and minority families have been displaced, either by redevelopment, 'code enforcement' programmes,[78] or higher rents.[79] In fact, the movement started, as we have noted, as a mobilization to prevent the threat of an urban renewal programme.

Thus, the first and major urban impact of neighbourhood mobilization in the Mission was to preserve the neighbourhood physically. The grassroots' opposition to any potential course of displacement prevented future projects from being implemented or even formulated. Such was the case for the Okamoto Plan prepared by the City Planning Department, or with the attempt to rezone the District to change it from residential to commercial uses. When speculators tried to use 'other methods' to make gain out of increasingly valuable land, taking advantage of fires in the 16th Street area in 1974–75 for example, block clubs were formed, in this case to prevent arson and to (successfully) counter their tactics.[80] The impact that BART was supposed to have materialized in terms of increasing accessibility to and from the Mission, as well as upgrading its potential as a commercial and leisure centre. But it did not trigger any major private development projects or even gentrifying renovation on a scale large enough to change the social or physical character of the neighbourhood.

A good indication of the extent of the preservation of housing stock in the Mission is its very high stability compared to the number of housing units demolished or constructed. According to a survey of the city Planning Department between 1968 and 1971 (that is just before and after the mobilization we have studied) only 283 units were demolished in the Mission, and only 461 new units were built. Related to the 21,000 housing units in the Mission in 1970, this represents a low 1·3 per cent and 2·1 per cent of the housing stock. Relative figures for the rest of San Francisco are much higher: 6,657 demolitions out of 310,383 units represents a 2.1 per cent demolition rate, and 16,588 new constructions out of 310,383 units a 5 per cent construction rate. As a point of contrast, in the black Western Addition area, for the same period, 3,119 housing units were demolished and 3,450 constructed; and in the other major black area (South Bayshore) for the same period 1,161 units were demolished and 757 new units built. Thus it seems that community mobilization prevented the Mission from undergoing the physical destruction that other minority residential areas in the city suffered. The reason, again, was that the impressive community organization of the early 1970s, widely publicized by the media, discouraged many realtors and developers from risking investment in an overly volatile, although desirable urban spot. In the words of a realtor, '. . . unless the Latinos get rich or we get rid of them, there is no way to make money there . . '[81]

In fact this was not true. The Mission preserved its physical setting[82] and its cultural identity, while attracting a growing number of Latino immigrants,[83] and improving the economic vitality of small business. Even in the midst of the disruption caused over several years by the construction of BART, the Mission kept its place as the second major retailing centre in the city. A survey of the 24th. Street merchants (the core of the small Latino businesses) at the end of 1975, in a period of economic decline, showed that 50 per cent were making profits similar to those of 1973, and that 20 per cent actually improved their benefits.[84] The housing quality seems at least to have been maintained and probably upgraded.[85] The evaluation of the Stanford University Research Team on the evolution of the housing stock indicates a proportion of 85 per cent sound housing units for 1972, up from the 1970 figure of 84 per cent, and therefore reversing for the first time the downward trend that started during the 1950s. The property values also improved and by 1979 an average three bedroom unit in the Mission was valued at over 100,000 dollars.[86] To be sure, some gentrification had occurred but by all accounts it was less important than the reinforcement of ethnic minorities with Filipinos, Cubans and Peruvians joining the Central Americans, and Mexicans in the late 1970s. How was this possible?

It was certainly not the direct result of the housing demands and policies supported by the MCO, the major result of which was the creation of the Mission Housing Development Corporation (MHDC) in 1971, supposedly aimed at constructing and managing low-rent housing units and providing affordable loans for rehabilitation and home buying in collaboration with the local banks. In fact, as soon as the MCO fell apart, the MHDC suffered all kinds of limitations from HUD, including the rejection of a proposal for a low-income housing project in the Mission on the grounds that there were already too many low-income housing units in that area and more units of this type would encourage urban segregation. Caught between rising prices of land and construction costs and little financial or institutional support, the MHDC, reassigned to the mayor's office, barely survived with a budget of 200,000 dollars per year. In its nine years of existence it could only build 101 housing units (39 for elderly), provide house ownership loans to 80 families, and help with the rebuilding of 331 units using loans that totalled an average of 3,000 dollars each. Even these modest achievements, however, seemed dubious successes to the MHDC's director given the problems of drugs, violence and delinquency that plagued its main achievement, the 50-unit Betel Apartments. He felt that this overall failure was attributable to the fact that the MHDC's only source of strength was the MCO. Once the community was disorganized, the MHDC could not challenge the prevailing housing policy.

What preserved the Mission, both from redevelopment and housing dilapidation, was the neighbourhood's capacity to organize defensively and to take care of its inner space. On the one hand, any major attempt of widespread displacement was tackled, albeit with a confused but firm defense that resisted with equal spirit the redevelopment plans, a rezoning proposal, or a lesbian bar. On the other hand, the neighbourhood was cared for on a point-to-point basis, through individual rehabilitation, maintenance by families, or, sometimes, co-operative housing projects. One such project that *La Raza en Accion Local* was trying to build in 1980 used solar energy technology for the first time in a low-income housing project. With this pattern of behaviour, the settlement of young middle class couples or even of lesbian households did not meet with open hostility, as long as they fitted into the neighbourhood, collaborated on its upgrading and got along well with the predominant Latino culture, keen on its family life. As one neighbourhood group in the Mission put it, 'We choose to live here because there are more positives than negatives. Our neighbourhood is a lively place rich with sounds, the colours, the scents, the languages and styles of many cultures, a warm place of sunshine almost every day, where neighbours talk to each other on the street and look out for one another, a dynamic place where people are actively working towards collective improvement and community pride, where change is always in evidence and stagnation is impossible'.[87] This was the major contribution of the community mobilization of the Mission, the transformation of a decaying ghetto into a vital neighbourhood. The improvement of the urban quality was the result of the day-to-day action of many groups and individuals that had needed a place to live, found it, kept it and cherished it.

The Mission experience demonstrated that there was a third way out of the conservative-inspired dilemma between free-market and urban decay: a combination of defensive organization and care for the neighbourhood. But in spite of the success, there were dark clouds on the horizon. The Mission was not only a neighbourhood but also a poverty-stricken area, with the usual characteristics of low-income, unemployment, drugs and violence.

Community and Poverty

A major issue underlying community mobilization in the Mission was poverty. The struggle for economic well-being was the driving force behind the residents' motivations. Once the neighbourhood had been protected against renewal, employment became the main concern, and the movement succeeded in obtaining thousands of jobs, either by bargaining with firms (from Pacific Telephone to local shops) or through training programmes that made low-level service jobs accessible to people without education or without English language skills. The struggle was for the extension of the right to work to deprived ethnic minorities. In a parallel effort, the residents claimed, and largely retained, a variety of social services (health, child care, cultural and recreational facilities, youth centres, drug-counselling programmes), and they improved the quality of the schools, also adding some bilingual educational programmes. Out of the MCO experience came an array of social programmes and non profit community agencies, initially funded and administered by Model Cities, and later on kept alive by Federal and local funds. Existing agencies, such as *Obeca-Arriba Juntos* or the Mission Language and Vocational School, expanded tremendously throughout the 1970s. An impressive list of social programmes were still alive in 1980 as can be seen in the Appendix, page 355. Thus community action considerably improved the living conditions of the Mission residents.

The particular organizational form through which improvement was channelled is very significant from the point of our research. Instead of changing the employment policies, expanding bilingual education, providing for public health care, taking care of the specific problems of incoming immigrants, or controlling police brutality, the Federal government and city hall reacted in the traditional American way: they created a piecemeal constellation of *ad hoc* programmes, funded on a year to year basis, in those areas or for those problems where the community was strong enough to command a response to its dramatic needs. Furthermore, the management of all these programmes was left in the hands of community leaders who obtained jobs and funds for becoming a cushion between the people they represented and the public administration responsible for the social policies.

This practice had a devastating effect on the community's capacity to preserve its unity and strength since it encouraged corruption, personal power, and the formation of cliques, and divided people's energies with fights between different groups to win control over narrowly defined programmes that framed popular needs into bureaucratic categories. In the final stages, once the community was divided, demobilized and disorganized, many programmes were suppressed or severely curtailed. In 1979, the Mission-based social agencies tried to defend themselves by organizing a Latino Unity Council, representing 12 programmes and a network of local 'notables'. However they did not have any organized popular support behind them and so had little voice in the administrations' offices. With blue collar jobs disappearing in San Francisco, the public schools deteriorating, and social services reduced, the drug culture found a susceptible population in the late 1970s. Many young Latinos began dropping out of the incomprehensible educational programmes, and, without opportunities to find jobs or invest their energy constructively, they reverted to hanging around on the street corners of the Mission in groups that the police hastily named 'gangs'. Poverty again became associated with 'street crime', depriving any potential revolt from the community of a legitimate name. Unable to foster institutional change, the limited improvement obtained by community mobilization faded with the exhaustion of the neighbourhood militants, allowing poverty and despair to increase in a dramatic, vicious circle.

And yet, in spite of all, life goes on in the Mission today in a continuous self-affirmation of neighbourhood vitality and Latino culture.

Community, Ethnicity, and Culture

The physical preservation of the urban environment and the maintenance of the poor minority population through a variety of social programmes kept the Mission as a very distinctive ethnic community, filled with street life, social contact, and activities of all kinds. In spite of the crisis of the MCO, literally dozens of voluntary associations, with interests ranging from art and music to Latin American liberation or urban planning, maintained the neighbourhood as a strongly self-organized community. The CORO Foundation listed 91 community organizations in the Mission in 1974, more than double the average figure for other San Francisco Districts.[88] In 1980 we discovered some 60 grassroots organizations that were active in their own specific field, as shown in the list presented in our Appendix (p. 355), an astounding figure for an area with slightly over 50,000 inhabitants. It is very significant, however, that this grassroots vitality followed a highly fragmented pattern, covering precisely those issues that the MCO failed to put together: neighbourhood, poverty, labour, and Latino culture.

Of the variety of splintered neighbourhood organizations, the Mission Planning Council and Operation Upgrade were the most active ones in the period from 1975 to 1980. They tried to follow up the issues concerning housing, rehabilitation and urban equipment. The 24th Street Merchants Association also developed some new ideas for neighbourhood life by organizing public events, such as the Annual Street Fair which attracted 25,000 people to its first celebration in 1979.

In a separate action, the social agencies (including *Obeca*, the Mission Language and Vocational School, the Mission Neighbourhood Health Centre, the Mission Hiring Hall, the Mission Legal Community Defense, etc.) were mostly co-ordinated through the Latino Unity Council, and continued to alleviate poverty in an exhausting daily struggle to solve, at the individual level, the wider social problems of inequality and discrimination.

Latino labour changed its influence and its orientation in the late 1970s. With industrial and construction jobs rapidly disappearing in San Francisco, the *Centro Social Obrero* lost most of its former grip on the local unions. On the other hand, the public employees union (Local 400-AFL-CIO) became the pivotal element between organized labour and the political system, as a result of the shift of the job market towards the service sector. Therefore the main problem of the Latinos was how to take advantage of the new public jobs whilst fighting ethnic and language discrimination in job allocation. A new coalition of organizations and individuals was formed, under the label of Latins for Affirmative Action, to overcome the employment–ethnicity problem.

The cultural dimension of the Latino community developed very strongly on its own along three different though inter-related paths:

1 National groups preserved their identity through their kin networks, customs, and internal fights, something they continue to do today. The Mission is probably the only place in the world where the daily newspapers of Nicaragua or El Salvador are sold outside those countries; organizational expressions of such national identity, such as *La Casa de Nicaragua* or *La Casa del Salvador* are, at once, a reminder to the immigrants of their origins and a major source of division and rivalry in the emerging local society.

2 There was and is a very strong tendency, particularly among the youth, to relate to Latin American revolutionary movements, encouraging a culture of liberation in which themes from Latin America and the Third World prevail. In this sense some attempt is made to convert the Mission into an enclave within the 'enemy's territory'. This Utopia, however, finds itself contradicted by a growing flow of conservative political refugees from Latin America as the process of liberation goes on in the homeland . . .

3 This is why a third cultural trend becomes increasingly significant in the Mission – the new culture of Latino-San Franciscan teenagers who cannot sympathize with liberation movements of countries that have become foreign to them, but also realize that they are different from other Americans. Symbolized by the low rider phenomenon, prone to drink alcohol and take drugs, and under constant pressure from the police, the 'kids' try to maintain a street life and make the Mission their real home. Social programmes for the youth, like *Centro de Cambio*, provide support for the most desperate cases. The Mission Cultural Centre tries to relate their experience to the broader Latino liberation through the arts, music, and the organization of the new Mission Carnival. The Mission Community Alliance mobilizes the street culture of the young, socially and politically, around its basic social issue of police harrassment.

Thus, the explosion of the MCO has left a new heritage of community action, whose dynamics explains the preservation today of the ethnic identity and cultural vitality of the neighbourhood. But such an intense local life follows a fragmented pattern that strikingly mirrors the divisions of the earlier grassroots mobilization.

Only one effort was made in the late 1970s to co-ordinate urban demands, poverty programmes, and Latino culture in the form of a community organization – *La Raza en Accion Local* which we have already described. But no major movements followed, partly because of unhealed wounds resulting from the in-fighting during the MCO-led mobilizations, and partly because of the very political stand of *La Raza*, which contradicted the weakness of the Latino community in San Francisco's local politics.

The Powerlessness of a Mobilized Community

The experience of the Mission offers the paradox of a highly mobilized community that achieved substantial changes at the urban, social and cultural levels, while being totally unable to become politically influential in the local power system. The only Latino supervisor appointed by Alioto's patronage system was defeated in 1979 and was not re-elected. In the 1977 District elections, the liberal woman lawyer who defeated the several Latino candidates relied on the support of the gay and lesbian communities on the fringes of the Inner Mission. Very few Latinos now hold public positions in the local government, and the Latino community appears to be the most deprived of access to municipal power of all ethnic minorities, considering that they make up about 15 per cent of the city's resident population.

The most usual explanation for such an anomaly concerns the high proportion of non-American citizens among the Latinos (probably around 50 per cent of the adult Latino residents) which considerably weakened their electoral chances. But there were more important factors. A major reason for the defeat of Latino candidates in 1977 and 1980 was the split in the votes among different candidates on the lines of the split observed in the community mobilization. In 1977 the two Latino candidates opposed ethnic self-definition as an issue·in the representation of the neighbourhood. Also many of the Latino-American citizens did not register as voters. This sceptical attitude diminished the chances of the community becoming an influential element in the city's coalition politics. What are the roots of such scepticism? The general answer, common to other countries, is the demoralizing experience of not obtaining anything substantial through electoral mobilization.[89] But in San Francisco this has not been the reaction of other oppressed minorities who have suffered similar defeats, such as the blacks and gays. Why, then, should Latinos have behaved differently?

The answer lies, again, in the history of the MCO mobilization. In spite of the low registration by voters, Latinos (and the Mission Neighbourhood) had a strong influence on the political system in the 1970s because of their capacity for grassroots organization and militancy. But this strength was devoted not to changing the political system or the social policies, but to obtaining programmes or services whose delivery became the only proof of the Latino's political effectiveness that could maintain popular support. When the community organization suffered a crisis, it lost momentum and allowed the programmes to be phased out. And without any benefits to deliver, the crisis of the grassroots organizations deepened. But the people did not retire. They continued to mobilize and organize themselves around a variety of issues ranging from land-use planning to mural painting. But they had lost the only established connection with the political system. Deprived of their citizenship, many of them also distrusted the potential of their citizenry, given the frustrating experience of having their needs channelled into the bureaucratic labyrinth of the local welfare state. The power of the grassroots missed its chance of transformation into grassroots power.

Conclusion: The Limits to Urban Change

The threat of urban renewal, the injuries of urban poverty, the suffering of ethnic discrimination: all triggered a powerful grassroots mobilization in the San Francisco *Barrio*, where a team of community organizers supported by the Churches took advantage of the favourable atmosphere provided by the Federal programmes of social reform. The neighbourhood- based collective action preserved the physical space of the Mission District and improved the urban quality while keeping its cultural identity as the main focal point of the Latino minority in San Francisco.

This process of urban revival was more the indirect consequence of a very dense network of community organizations than the result of public housing programmes or of planning initiatives. The network acted both as a deterrent against displacement and as a stimulus for individual rehabilitation and collective maintenance of the urban environment. Through grassroots pressure a variety of community-controlled, Federally-funded social programmes directly benefited thousands of residents. Nevertheless, the absorption of most of the leadership into the management of the programmes and the subsequent in-fighting within the community over the control of public resources, decisively weakened the grassroots organizations, allowing a gradual shrinkage both in the funds and in the scope of the social programmes.

From the beginning, the dilemma of whether to define the community as a poor neighbourhood or as a Latino minority introduced the major division which was deepened when it became necessary to establish the social criteria determining how much of the public resources each faction of the community should receive. The subsequent divergence of the various lines of action in response to urban problems, poverty needs, and ethnic liberation, considerably weakened the social pressure brought to bear on the urban policies dealing with the Mission District. The political marginality of the Latino community, both as a result of the immigrant status of most Latinos and as an expression of their frustrating relationship with the political system, increased the distance between the potential of popular mobilization in the neighbourhood and its actual impact on public policies and living conditions.

The Mission's urban scene expresses the two-fold outcome of this contradictory urban mobilization: on the one hand, a valuable space whose residential quality, cultural vitality, and economic dynamics have considerably improved while preserving its original physical form; on the other hand, the occupation of this space by a deprived and segregated ethnic minority, proud of its culture, although subjected to the increasing pressure of poverty, drugs, crime and police surveillance. The tensions and contradictions between these two realities, both defining the Mission's urban dynamics, became unbearable and remain so today.

Thus the contradictory neighbourhood mobilization that we observed decisively contributed to the preservation of a particular spatial form and the definition of specific urban issues: it shaped the urban scene of the *Barrio* and influenced the urban policies dealing with it. In the Mission, city lights and urban darkness emerge from a common matrix: the achievements and failures of the people.

14

Cultural Identity, Sexual Liberation and Urban Structure: The Gay Community in San Francisco

Introduction

San Francisco has become the world's gay capital, a new Mecca in our age of individual liberation where homosexuals migrate for a few hours or for many years to find themselves and to learn a language of freedom, sexuality, solidarity, and life – to 'come out' and to become gay. Numbers are significant but not crucial. An estimated 115,000 gay men and women, about 17 per cent of the city's population,[90] they represent a much less important number than the large concentration of gay people in New York or Los Angeles. Furthermore, the modern gay liberation movement was triggered by the Stonewall Revolt in New York, on 27 June 1969.[91] Although the gay experience of New York has been more radical and militant, San Francisco has been the city where gays have uniquely succeeded in building up a powerful, though complex, independent community at spatial, economic, cultural, and political levels. And, on such a basis, gay people, particularly gay men, have been able to achieve a certain amount of power within the institutional system. Because of their age, level of education, and militancy, gays represent about 25 per cent of registered voters, and in decisive elections, their high turn out may approach 30 per cent of the voters. Since 1977 San Francisco has elected a supervisor who publicly ran as a gay candidate and no mayor can afford to risk openly opposing gays in the election. Also, they have come to have some influence through public appointments – the police department, for example, now recruits gay men and lesbians in informal consultation with the gay community.

However striking these developments may be in the context of our homophobic culture[92], it is only the expression of a deeper and more significant social process: the emergence of a social movement and its transformation into a political force through the spatial organization of a self-defined cultural community.

Spatial concentration, as the basis of a search for self-reliance, is a fundamental characteristic of the gay liberation movement in San Francisco, which makes it more than a human rights movement trying to end legal discrimination on the basis of sexual preferences. (In our interviews with Harry Britt the political leader of San Francisco's gay community, he went on record as saying that, 'When gays are spatially scattered, they are not gay, because they are invisible'.) The crucial step for gay people was, as the movement said, to 'come out of the closet', to publicly express their sexuality, and on the basis of such recognition (namely on the basis of a social stigma), to reconstruct their socialization.[93] But how is it possible to be openly gay in the middle of a hostile and violent society increasingly insecure about its fundamental values concerning virility and family? And how can one learn a new behaviour, a new code, and beyond that a new culture, in a world where sexuality is implicit in everybody's presentation of self and where the general assumption is heterosexuality?

In order publicly to express themselves, gays have always met together – in modern times in night bars and coded places. When they became conscious enough and strong enough to 'come out' collectively, they have earmarked places where they could be safe together and could develop new life styles. But this time they selected cities, and within the cities they traced boundaries and created their territory. These boundaries were to expand with the increasing capacity of gay people to defend themselves and to build up a series of autonomous institutions.[94] Levine has shown the systematic patterning of spatial concentrations of gay people in the largest American cities.[95] He, and others, consider such a culturally significant cluster to fit the traditional sociological definition of a ghetto.[96] But whatever coincidence there may be between the characteristics of the ghetto, as defined by the Chicago School and the gay experience of spatial organization, the argument is a purely formal one and, in any event, misleading. Instead, gay leaders tend to speak of 'liberated zones', and there is a major theoretical difference between the two notions, the difference being that gay territories, unlike ghettos, are deliberately constructed by gay people.[97] Of course, they cannot choose the urban space they want because of discrimination against them and because of the limited income of many gays. But they do choose to live together as a cultural community settled in a well-defined territory.

Two major consequences follow for the relationship between the gay movement and the city:

1   The gay territory is not the consequence of forces usually dominating the social and functional patterning of space, particularly the urban land market. Although constrained by economic factors, the gay territory develops according to the relationship between the emerging movement and the counteracting forces, a relationship that reshapes the whole urban fabric.
2   Gays need a spatially defined community for a long period, where culture and power can be reformulated in a process of experimental social interaction and active political mobilization. By virtue of an alternative life style in a spatial sub-set of the urban system, a 'city' emerges within the city (not outside the existing city and not necessarily against other communities) in a process that transforms established cultural values and existing spatial forms.

This is the process we want to understand as a major step in our intellectual journey across the web of connections between social movements and urban forms. Why San Francisco? What made this city so attractive to gay people and how did they manage to survive the repression in a setting that was not always tolerant of them, until they established a relatively self-protected territory? What are the social and spatial profiles of this territory? What are the cultural themes of the community, the forms of its social organization, the waving flags of its political battles? And, above all, what are the effects of the process, as triggered by the gay liberation movement, on the city's spatial forms, urban policies, cultural values, and political institutions? Is the gay movement, as reflected by the experience in San Francisco, an agent of urban social change, or on the contrary, does it exhaust itself behind the walls of an artificial paradise? What are the elements favouring one direction or the other in such a dramatic dilemma?

These are the questions we are about to answer by using the results of the field work we conducted in San Francisco, between 1980 and 1981 with the collaboration of the gay community, the characteristics and methodology of which are presented and justified in the Appendix to this chapter (pp. 355–62).

Let us point out two major and deliberate limits of our analysis:

1   We do not discuss the origins, evolution, organization or orientation of the gay movement as such. Although we have obviously tried to understand it in order to be able to establish a

significant connection between gay liberation and urban change, it is this latter question that concerns us in this book. Thus all our general understanding of gay culture as a social movement is directed towards the study of its relationship to the city as a social construction.[98]
2   Our analysis solely concerns gay men. The reason is a profoundly theoretical one. Lesbians, unlike gay men, tend not to concentrate in a given territory, but establish social and interpersonal networks,[99]. On the whole they are poorer than gay men[100] and have less choice in terms of work and location, and their politics is less directed towards the established political system. For all these reasons lesbians do not acquire a geographical basis for their political organization and are less likely to achieve local power. And there is a major difference between men and women in their relationship to space. Men have sought to dominate, and one expression of this domination has been spatial. (The same desire for spatial superiority has driven male-dominated cultures to send astronauts to the moon and to explore the galaxy.) Women have rarely had these territorial aspirations: their world attaches more importance to relationships and their networks are ones of solidarity and affection. In this gay men behave first and foremost as men and lesbians as women. So when gay men try to liberate themselves from cultural and sexual oppression, they need a physical space from which to strike out. Lesbians on the other hand tend to create their own rich, inner world and a political relationship with higher, societal levels. Thus they are 'placeless' and much more radical in their struggle. For all these reasons, lesbians tend not to acquire a geographical basis for their political organization and are less likely to achieve local power. As a consequence of all these trends, we can hardly speak of lesbian territory in San Francisco as we can with gay men, and there is little influence by lesbians on the space of the city. The situation is, in fact, the consequence of a more fundamental reason for not analysing the experiences of gay men and lesbians as a similar social process. The man/woman distinction as a source of oppression is largely reproduced within the gay universe, and although male gay leaders are clearly anti-sexist and seek alliances with lesbians, the cultural, economic, and political status of gay men and lesbians is clearly unequal, and results in paths of liberation specific to each situation. While spatial communities and local power seem to be fundamental to gay mens' liberation, in San Francisco at least, they are clearly not so for lesbians who are more concerned with the revolution of values than with the control of institutional power. Since our research purpose concerns the relationship between socio-cultural revolt and the city, we will deal only with the experience of gay men in San Francisco. It is an experience with long-standing historical roots that must be recounted in order to understand the role of the city as a potential source of personal freedom.

Why San Francisco? The Historical Development of the Gay City

An instant city, a settlement for adventurers attracted by the gold fields, San Francisco was always a place where people could indulge in personal fantasies and a place of easy moral standards.[101] The city's waterfront and Barbary Coast were a meeting point for sailors, travellers, transients, and lonely people – a milieu of casual encounters and few social rules where the borderline between normal and abnormal was blurred. San Francisco was a gateway city on the western limits of the Western world, and in the marginal zones of a marginal city homosexuality flourished. But in the 1920's San Francisco decided to become respectable, to emerge as the moral and cultural capital of the West, and to grow up gracefully, under the authoritative shadow of the Catholic Church, fuelled by its Irish and Italian working class legions. So 'deviants' were repressed and forced into hiding. The reform movement reached the police in the 1930s[102] and forced a crackdown on prostitution and homosexuality, the twin evils in the eyes of puritan morality.

Thus the pioneer origins of San Francisco are not enough to explain its destiny as the setting for gay liberation. The major turning point seems to have been the Second World War.[103] San Francisco was the main port of embarkation and disembarkation for the Pacific front. An estimated 1·6 million men and women passed through the city: young, alone, suddenly uprooted, living on the edge of death and suffering, and living with people of their own sex. The average ten per cent of homosexuals found in all human populations[104] found themselves more easily and rapidly in this context, and others discovered their bisexuality. Many service men and women were discharged from the military for homosexuality. Many of them were serving in the Pacific area and were ordered to disembark in San Francisco. Since they did not wish to return home bearing what society deemed to be the stigma of homosexuality, they stayed in the city, and were joined at the end of the war by many others who had discovered their sexual and cultural identity. They met in bars, particularly in the Tenderloin area. Bars were then the focal points of social life for gay people;[105] and networks were constructed around these bars: a specific form of culture and ideology began to emerge.[106]

One particular bar has become a legend in San Francisco – The Black Cat (situated on Montgomery Street). It played a major role in the early stages of the gay movement, because of the initiative, courage, and imagination of its entertainer, Jose Sarria, a famous drag queen, and a living symbol of the gay movement. Jose Sarria was born in San Francisco. His mother, a Nicaraguan, was a descendant of the Counts of Sarria, from Barcelona, Spain. He worked as a waiter in The Black Cat, a bohemian bar owned by a straight Jewish man. One night he played 'Carmen' for a few minutes, with some variations on the theme. In his rendition, Carmen appeared as a drag queen hiding from the police in the bushes of Union Square (the main, fashionable public square in downtown San Francisco). The performance was very successful and Sarria was hired to perform his show on Sunday afternoons because this was the quiet time of the week. For 15 years, each Sunday afternoon, 250 people would pack themselves into The Black Cat to watch Sarria dressed as Madam Butterfly, and listen to his 'sermon' about homosexual rights, after which they would end the show by joining hands and singing 'God Save the Nelly Queens'.

However remote such an image might seem from a liberation movement, the bars and the drag queens were fundamental to the creation of networks, making gay people visible, and stating their right to gather in public places. The Black Cat was, in fact, under continual threat from the police and had to defend its existence through many lawsuits which were finally settled in 1951 when the California Supreme Court declared that it was illegal to close down a bar simply because homosexuals were the usual customers. The first right to a public space had been won. However, after continual harrassment from the Alcoholic Beverage Commission, The Black Cat was finally closed in 1963, but not before it had established a tradition, a network, and a fundamental dimension of the gay culture – fun and humour. (This is something that many hardline gay militants seem to be ashamed of, but both Jose Sarria and Harry Britt consider it a crucial aspect of the cultural transformation still to be undertaken. They relish the capacity to enjoy life, turn oppression into creation, and subvert established values by emphasizing their ridiculous aspects. Bars, feasts, and celebrations should be, they believe, the nest of gay culture, as they are one of the primary sources of a vibrant city life.)

The critical moment, nevertheless, was the transition from the bars to the streets, from nightlife to daytime, from 'sexual deviance' to an alternative life style. Gays were able to negotiate this change on the basis of another specifically San Franciscan experience: the

Beatnik culture and the literary networks through which it expressed itself in the 1950s. Allen Ginsberg's 'Howl'[106] provoked a legal action in 1957 against City Lights, the most famous 'beat' bookstore, accused of selling 'obscene' publications. Kerouac's *On the Road*[107] won an international audience, and the Black Mountain poets were becoming well-known to the literary critics. A beat culture emerged as a reaction against several things: McCarthyism, the institution of the family, and suburbanism.[108] This culture concentrated spatially in the old Italian North Beach area near the red light tourist zone of Broadway, and gays were accepted in this tolerant, experimental ambiance, and were able to find common interests in an alternative milieu that was concerned with broader issues than sexual differences and boundaries. When the media focused its attention on the San Francisco beatniks, it pinpointed tolerance of homosexuals as evidence of their deviance. In so doing, the media reinforced the attraction to the city for thousands of isolated gays all over the country. On the basis of the bar networks and of the counter-cultural movement, the human rights orientated, respectable gay associations, with an interest in legal rights, found a favourable environment in San Francisco. The conservative, well-to-do Mattachine society moved its headquarters from Los Angeles to San Francisco in 1955, and some time later began to publish *The Advocate* which became the only gay magazine with a national audience. Also in 1955 the first openly lesbian organization, The Daughters of Bilitis, was founded in San Francisco, and started *Ladder Magazine*. These open expressions of the taboo subjects of sexuality and homosexuality, coinciding as they did with the ideological rebellion of the beatniks, caused much consternation among the conservative sectors of San Francisco. In the 1959 mayoral race, conservative candidate Russell Wolden, accused the incumbent, Mayor George Christopher, of allowing the city to become '. . . the national headquarters of organized homosexuals in America.' But the establishment and local press criticized Wolden for harming the image of the city and he was defeated.

The newly acquired fame of their growing community gave the gay bar owners the resolution to challenge police harassment by publicizing some cases of corruption and intimidation to which they had been subjected. After minor sanctions, the police responded during 1961 with more repression, including massive raids against gay bars and the revoking of licenses for 12 of the city's 30 gay bars, including that of The Black Cat. But the movement was already strong enough to develop its own autonomous organization, reinforced not long afterwards by the anti-war and counter-cultural movements. In 1962, in order to protect themselves against police harassment, the owners of the gay and Bohemian bars organized the Tavern Guild which became one of the basic financial and political supporters of all gay activities in San Francisco, and had well over 100 members in 1980. To protect gay rights in law, the same network of bar owners and some prominent gay figures such as Jose Sarria and Jim Foster founded, in 1964, the Society for Individual Rights. This organization soon had over 1,000 members. The hippy culture of the 1960s, which was particularly strong in the Bay Area, was also a sympathetic milieu for gays and influenced their developing cultural identity.

The single event, however, that marked the development of a gay liberation movement in San Francisco, as it did in the rest of the country, was the Stonewall Revolt of 27 June 1969. On that day the police raided, with customary violence, the Stonewall, a gay bar in New York's Greenwich Village. The gays resisted, fighting the police in a three day battle. The entire gay network reacted across the nation. In 1969 there were only 50 gay organizations; in 1973, there were over 800. In San Francisco the movement grew even faster because of the existing foundations. From the Circle of Loving Companions, created in 1966 as a spin-off of the hippy movement, many organizations evolved into more militant forms, such as the Pink Panthers, the Gay Liberation Front, and the Gay Activist Alliance. In 1971, the movement was strong enough in California to organize a march on Sacramento in defense of gay rights.

In an effort to connect with the extremely powerful current of lesbian liberation, the major theme of the movement was to overcome 'invisibility' by 'coming out'. The objective was to force society to revise standards on sexuality and individual behaviour: homosexuality not only had to be tolerated by a liberal culture, but also accepted as normal and legitimate behaviour by a society that was already questioning fundamental values and institutes such as the family, heterosexuality, and patriarchal authority. Superseding the human rights movement represented by the traditional homophile organizations, gays were asking for their identity to be recognized, and for dominant societal values to change, rather than being forced to adapt to such values. The more radical wing of the movement suffered the same crisis as the political movement of which it was a part. Confronted, after the Cambodian Spring, with stern repression from President Nixon's administration, and divided and weakened by in-fighting and dogmatic ideologies, the student-based organizations ceased. The gay movement, however, continued, and made an exception of itself on the basis of spatial concentration and social networks, building up its own institutions, and discovering its own collective identity as well as the consciousness of its individuals. The gay movement realized that between liberation and politics it first had to establish a community in a series of spatial settings and through a network of economic, social, and cultural institutions. It also discovered that such a community could not be built up as a new Utopian phalanstery. Some gays tried to start a new society in a rural environment by buying property in Alpine County in the California Sierra area. They quickly abandoned the project after several homes were destroyed by arson.

Major metropolitan areas such as New York, Los Angeles, Toronto, Seattle and the Bay Area became places of freedom that other cities could not equal. Yet San Francisco was tradi-tionally the most liberal environment where years of struggle by labour, minorities, students and counter-culture movements, as well as a concentration of gay people, had created the conditions for a gay community. So they created a gay community by living in certain neigh-bourhoods, by operating businesses, by meeting in bars (numbers jumped from 58 in 1969 to 234 in 1980), by inventing feasts and celebrations; in short by organizing socially, culturally and politically. It was against this background that Harvey Milk decided in 1973 to express the political strength of gay people by running for supervisor. A graduate of New York State University at Albany, he was not able to teach because of his discharge in 1956 from the Navy for homosexuality. Like many other gays, he migrated in 1969 to San Francisco. After leaving his job as a financial analyst, he opened a photography business, Castro Camera, on Castro Street which soon became the unofficial headquarters for the new political force growing up in San Francisco. When Jose Sarria ran for supervisor in 1961 in his drag queen dress, he obtained 7,000 votes. The goal for Sarria was not to win, but to show that gays were citizens. For Harvey Milk, however, the point was more than self-affirmation. His plan was to go from community, to business, to power. He called for 'gays to buy gay', so that Castro would not just be a cruising place, as Greenwich Village in New York, but a space owned by gays, lived in by gays, and enjoyed by gays. If gays could 'buy gay' and 'live gay', they would also vote gay. And they did. In his first election race, in 1973, Harvey Milk attracted 17,000 votes and came eleventh in a field of 33 candidates. Although it was an excellent showing, it was, at the same time, a sign that he also had to address a broader liberal constituency. In his second electoral attempt, in 1975, while he was still a gay candidate, he also dealt with the more general issues, particularly emphasizing the need to control real estate speculation. He assumed a 'straight image', and his support jumped to 53,000 votes, but he still lost.

In spite of these loses, it was nevertheless clear that the gay vote had become decisive in the city. In the 1975 mayoral election, liberal California Senator George Moscone was elected in favour of his conservative opponent by the very narrow margin of 3,000 votes. Moscone, who was politically astute, appointed Harvey Milk to an important city hall post as a member of the Board of Permit Appeals. For the first time an openly gay leader became a public official. At the same time the Neighbourhood Movement, boosted by the new progressive coalition emerging around Moscone, was attempting a major drive to make local government more democratic. In 1975, over 50 neighbourhood groups, including representatives of the gay community, met in a San Francisco Community Congress, to promote a programme of social change for the city. A major objective was to make it politically possible to effect urban and social reforms advocated by the grassroots, and to establish an electoral system ensuring accountability of supervisors to local constituencies. A campaign was initiated for district elections which were approved in two referendums (in 1976 and 1977), in spite of the multi-million dollar campaign that the Chamber of Commerce launched against the neighbourhoods' initiative.

Then, on the basis of the territory that the gay community had organized in the Castro area, Harvey Milk was elected supervisor in the 1977 election as a representative of District 5. It was just in time. The homophobic backlash was gaining momentum all over America. A campaign orchestrated by fundamentalist conservatives and publicized by Anita Bryant (an ex-Miss America and a Florida-based singer who appeared in orange-juice advertisements) had succeeded in winning a popular referendum to retain legal discrimination against homosexuals in Miami. Other cities followed suit. Other people expressed their homophobia in a different way. In June 1977 Bob Hillsborough was murdered in San Francisco by a gang of youths who stabbed him repeatedly, shouting 'Faggot. Faggot.' Even in California the conservatives believed the moment had come to regain control over public morality. In June 1978 Senator Briggs put on the state ballot a proposition banning homosexuals from teaching in public schools. The gay movement mobilized all its support and Harvey Milk became a major political figure due to his success with the media in this campaign. With the help of liberal Democrats, left wing militants, and neighbourhood activitists, gays won a major victory against conservative forces. In November 1978 Briggs' proposition was rejected by 58 per cent of the Californian voters and by 75 per cent of San Franciscan electors (the proposition being defeated in almost all precincts of the city). The local political culture had thoroughly supported the cause of gay rights. In April 1978 the board of supervisors approved a very liberal Gay Rights Ordinance. At the same time, two lesbian leaders, Del Martin and Phyllis Lyon, holding city hall posts, received from the city of San Francisco a certificate of honour for their civic services – including support for lesbians – and for their 25 years of living together. The beginnings in The Black Cat seemed far away: the gays had come a long way, from bar culture to political power. But such power proved precarious. On 27 November 1978 a conservative supervisor, Dan White, an ex-policeman who had campaigned against the tolerance towards 'sexual deviants', shot and killed Mayor George Moscone and Supervisor Harvey Milk in their offices at city hall. He later surrendered to his former colleagues in the police department. The mourning of Moscone and Milk was the most impressive political demonstration ever seen in San Francisco: 20,000 people marched with candles, in silence, after listening to speakers who called on the movement to pursue the struggle in the way shown by Harvey Milk.

The new mayor, Diane Feinstein, appointed another gay leader, Harry Britt, a socialist, to replace Harvey Milk, following instructions Milk had left recorded on a cassette in case he was murdered.[109] A few months later, on 21 May 1979, a jury sentenced Dan White to seven years in prison, the lowest possible penalty. As *Playboy* reporter Nora Gallagher wrote: 'What the jury stands for, in this unfolding drama, are the people who, like White, are growing invisible in San Francisco'.[110] Gay visibility had made 'invisible' the open will to repress sexuality and life-styles not centred on the family. The sectors representing conservative moral values had cause to be alarmed and when the dominant forces in a system become frightened, violence is their most likely response. But, as in New York ten years before, the gays reacted with rage, and after a public meeting in front of city hall to condemn the verdict, they smashed the building's windows, burned police cars, and there followed violent clashes with the police. A new stage of the gay movement had begun. Society was responding to the threat posed by gay values to the fundamental institutions of our civilization, such as family life and sexual repression. And so, in turn, the gay territory could not remain a cultural, Utopian community; either walls had to be elevated around the free city or the entire political system had to be reformed. This dilemma was still facing gays at the time of our research.

The gays' power was apparently most uncertain but nonetheless they possessed it, based on a spatial, cultural community whose profile and formation, and relationship to the political process, we will now examine.

The Social Making of a Gay Territory

Space is a fundamental dimension for the gay community.[111] Social prejudice, legal repression, and political violence have forced homosexuals throughout history to be invisible. Such invisibility is a major obstacle to finding sexual partners, discovering friends and leading an unharassed, open life. To overcome this obstacle, gays have always tended to establish their own space where encounters would be possible on the assumption of common sexual and cultural values. Bars were usually where gay social networks developed, the bars themselves being located in certain urban areas where police zoning would implicitly allow some 'deviant entertainment' under close surveillance. During the cultural revolts of the 1960s, when certain traditional values began to break down, the gays of San Francisco took advantage of the greater latitude to broaden their space. From bars and street-cruising, their spatial organization shifted to specific neighbourhoods, and from there to larger areas of the city that became, in the mid-1970s, gay free communes.

The urban residential structure was profoundly altered. The gay territory expanded according to a logic the understanding of which will be a key element for establishing the relationship between cultural transformation and urban form.

To proceed with this analysis we had to determine the spatial areas of gay residences and activities in San Francisco at different points in time. Such information was not reported and no empirical research had been done on this matter, so we were forced to find out for ourselves. The Methodological Appendix carefully describes this particular research (pp. 355–57). Let us at this point say what the data bases is and on which ones the following observations and analyses are based.

Given that we could not rely on a single source of information, we established five different means of determining the areas where gays were concentrated in San Francisco:

1   A map drawn by a team of key informants from the gay community on the basis of their experience as pollsters for gay electoral campaigns (Map 14–1). The map was established according to the sequential development of gay residence at different points in time.
2   A map representing the proportion of multiple male households on the resident population in the area, (Map 14–2) in 1977. (The census does not have such information, so we obtained it from the San Francisco Voter Registration Files. Therefore, the adequate description of the

Map 14.1 Gay residential areas.
(*Source*: Gay Community Informants.)

indicator is the proportion of registered voters living in multiple male households, by precincts (see Methodological Appendix (pp. 357–59).) Remember that in San Francisco, a high proportion of gays are registered voters. Obviously the assumption was not that all such households are formed by gays or that all gays lived in such a way. But the assumption is that the spatial distribution of adult males living together should follow the spatial distribution of gay residences. The fact that Map 14–2 closely follows Map 14–1 in its basic trends rather confirms our hypothesis. Thus, we only kept Map 14–2 as a reasonable quantitative indicator of the gay territory, after it had been reinforced by cross-checking from our additional sources of information.

3   A map representing the gay bars and other gay social gathering places (Map 14–3).

4   A map representing self-defined gay businesses, stores and professional offices (Map 14–4).

0-1.9%   2.0-2.9%   3.0-3.9%   4.0-5.9%   6.0-9.9%   10.0-13.9%

Voter registration household median = 3%

1970 census nonrelative households citywide = 3.6%

Map 14.2 Gay residential areas as indicated by the proportion of multiple male households over the total of registered voters in each census tract, 1977.
(*Source*: 1977 Voter registration tape/computer programme prepared by Doug De Young.)

5   A map representing the highest concentration of votes for Harvey Milk, the gay candidate in the 1975 supervisorial election (Map 14–5).

Observation of these maps leads to two conclusions:

1   The general spatial pattern tends to evolve along the same lines in all five maps obtained from five different sources, so there is reciprocal reinforcement as to the value of each indicator. While each one by itself would be doubtful as an expression of gay residential areas, the similar spatial distribution in the five maps strongly supports the validity of the residential profile we have obtained. Rank correlation coefficients confirm the covariation between the different indicators of the spatial distribution of gays as shown by Maps 14–1, 2, and 5. (See Methodological Appendix.)

■ 1964-66   ● 1969-71   ★ 1973-75   △ 1980

Map 14.3 Places where gays gather, 1964–1980 (including bars and social clubs) showing a sequential and cumulative development.
(*Source*: Bob Damron's address book. The map is based on series of maps by Michael Kennedy.)

2   If 1 is accepted, then there is a gay territory that includes residences, social places, business activities, as well as the ground for political organizing.

We are now able to define the spatial boundaries of San Francisco's male gay community *as of 1980*. Also, given the verification as to the accuracy of our key informants, we may, unless contrary evidence is provided, consider the spatial sequence described by the boundaries over time.

Having established the spatial profile of the gay community, we are also able to relate it to the social and urban characteristics distributed across the city, so that we may understand the factors fostering or counteracting the patterns of settlement inspired by gay culture. On the basis of the 1970 US Census and of the 1974 US Bureau of Census' Urban Atlas,[112] we selected

Map 14.4 Golden Gate Business Association members, 1979.
(*Source*: GGBA Buyers' Guide/Directory, Autumn 1979-Autumn 80.)

11 variables considered to be relevant to our analysis (see Table 14–1, page 152).

Yet we must keep in mind that all we have is a series of converging indicators of gay location and that the only thing this particular data basis tells us about gayness is where gays are or tend to be. We do not have any indicator of gayness and we are therefore unable to infer anything about gay individuals. In sum, we can only analyse gay versus non-gay spatial units and to proceed in such a way we have carried out two different analyses:

1 On the basis of our key informants map (Map 14–1) we have divided the city into two categories of spatial areas: those with gay presence and those without. For each selected variable we have calculated the mean value of its distribution in the census tracts corresponding to each of the two categories of space. The T test provides the statistical significance of the differences observed for the mean value of each variable in each one of the two categories of spatial units. The extent and direction of such differences will provide the clue for the social and urban specificity of the gay territory.

Map 14.5 Gay voting pattern that indicates two top ranking precincts in support of Harvey Milk in the 1975 supervisorial race.
(*Source*: Harvey Milk Campaign Office.)

2   We have tried to establish some measures of correlation between the spatial distribution of the gay community and the spatial distribution of selected social and urban variables. Since we are looking for correspondence between spatial organization in relationship to two series of criteria (rather than co-variation of characteristics across space), the usual regression analysis is inadequate for our purpose. Instead we have proceeded to calculate rank-correlation coefficients (Spearman test) between, on the one hand, the distribution of all census tracts in a six-level scale of 'gay space', constructed on the basis of the proportion of multiple male households; and, on the other hand, the distribution of all census tracts in a series of six-level scales on the basis of selected variables. Only variables that the first step of the analysis (as described in 1) showed to be discriminatory were considered in the construction of the scales of social and urban differentiation in San Francisco. Furthermore, one of the findings of our analysis is that these selected variables are likely to effect gay location patterns jointly, instead of having individual effects, since their spatial distribution does not overlap. To test our analysis we

constructed an additional special scale, classifying the census tract units in a scale that built into its criteria the three variables considered to have some effect on gay location. The Spearman coefficient between the ranks obtained by the census tracts units in this scale and the ranks they obtained in the multiple male households scale, provided the final test for our tentative interpretation of the social roots of gay location patterns.

The most important result of this study is the definition of the spatial organization of the gay community as presented in Maps 14-1-5. All converge towards a largely similar territorial boundary. Thus, the first finding is that there is a gay territory. Furthermore, it is not only a residential space but also a space for social interaction, for business activities of all kinds, for leisure and pleasure, for feasts and politics. It was on this spatial basis that the gay community succeeded in electing both Harvey Milk and Harry Britt with the largest and best organized single voting block, using the decentralized electoral system by Districts that existed in San Francisco between 1976 and 1980.

What were the characteristics of this space? Table 14-1 provides a tentative answer according to the methodology just described.

Of the 11 selected variables examined only two appear strongly negatively associated with the presence of gays: the proportion of owner occupied housing units and the proportion of the resident population under 18 years. In other words, property and family were the major walls protecting the 'straight universe' against the gay influence. It is our hypothesis that fundamental to this relationship was the cultural dimension of the rejection and the capacity of a given neighbourhood to oppose gay immigration either because of the control over real estate property or because of the local organization of a family-orientated community. The latter has been the case, for example, in the Latino Mission District and in the black Bayview-Hunter's Point areas – they have remained outside gay's location patterns. Variables in housing value, family income, or blue collar occupation have not differentiated gay and non-gay areas. Neither gay location nor gay rejection have directly appeared as economic processes: these seem to have come basically from cultural distances. Two other variables show some significant differences between the city and the gay city: gay areas have tended to carry a concentration of more educated population; and non-gay areas have tended towards higher rents. It should be remembered that San Francisco's housing stock was 65 per cent rental and that the areas of highest social status included the likes of Pacific Heights where the proportion of owner-occupied housing was below the average. Thus a new barrier was established in areas exclusive enough to keep gays out through high rents.

These findings are reinforced by the second method we have used to measure our observations. Table 14-2 shows that, as expected, the rank-correlation between the spatial distributions of our indicator of gay residence and each one of those for the four variables obtained by our previous analysis is very weak.

A simple observation of Map 14-6 provides the reason for such a result: gays have not resided in the western zone of the city because of the nature of the property; in the eastern side because of the predominance of the family-orientated community; and in the northern hills because of the high rents. Only when we combine the effects of the three variables in one scale (property, family, and high rents) do we obtain a significant -0·38 rank-correlation between this scale and the scale constructed on the basis of the indicator of gay residence.

To provide a clearer expression of these results we have constructed Map 14-6 where the three variables and the proportion of multiple male households (indicator of gay residence) are mapped *together* according to the description in the map's caption. Map 14-6 shows a striking autonomy between the territories defined by the four variables, with only limited overlapping.

Table 14.1 Statistical difference in the values of selected variables for spatial areas with significant gay residence and without significant gay residence, San Francisco, circa 1970.

1	2	3	4	5	6	7
	Cultural-			*Pooled Variance Estimate*		
Variable	*Spatial Area*	*Mean*	*Standard Deviation*	*T Value*	*Degrees of Freedom*	*2-Tail Probability*
Family % of the resident population under 18	Non-Gay	22·8	10·56	4·25	146	0·000
	Gay	15·9	8·43			
Property % of housing units owner occupied	Non-Gay	40·54	31·51	4·41	146	0·000
	Gay	20·93	18·02			
Education % of high school graduates among residents aged 25 and over	Non-Gay	57·21	20·05	−1·55	145	0·123
	Gay	61·73	13·08			
Housing Rents Median contract rent, dollars, 1970	Non-Gay	135·04	44·36	1·37	144	0·174
	Gay	126·16	29·76			
Housing Value Median housing value, dollars, 1970	Non-Gay	26,886	12,003	−0·26	122·5	0·795
	Gay	27,384	9,360			
Income Median family income, dollars, 1970	Non-Gay	9,858	3,989	0·82	144	0·415
	Gay	9,322	3,804			
Blue Collar % of blue collar employed among residents	Non-Gay	22·73	12·44	0·54	146	0·588
	Gay	21·72	9·32			
Black Population Blacks as % of total population	Non-Gay	16·17	25·98	1·10	146	0·273
	Gay	11·96	17·98			
Elderly % of total population over 65.	Non-Gay	14·66	9·51	0·15	146	0·879
	Gay	14·45	6·29			
Housing Dilapidation % of housing units lacking some or all plumbing	Non-Gay	7·68	18·09	−0·39	145	0·695
	Gay	8·75	13·81			
Housing Decay % of housing units lacking kitchen facilities	Non-Gay	7·66	18·45	−1·07	145	0·288
	Gay	10·89	17·60			

Note: Basic criterion for the statistical significance of the observed differences between mean values of each variable has been the 2-tail probability threshold as provided by the T test. $p < .000$ has been considered significant. p values between $< .1000$ and $< .200$ have been considered moderately significant. p values $> .2000$ have been considered randomly produced, although they do exist as trends of the urban reality of San Francisco.

Sources: 1 US Census, 1970, San Francisco.
　　　　　　2 Gay and non-gay areas have been defined by classifying in two separate categories all census tracts, according to information provided by key informants of the gay community, and checked with four other sources as described in the Methodological Appendix (pp. 357–58).
　　　　　　3 Our own calculations.

Table 14.2 Spearman correlation co–efficients between the rank of census tracts of San Francisco ordered in a six levels, scale according to the proportion of multiple male households among registered voters residents in 1977, and five other scales as indicated

	Spearman R
1 Scale according to the proportion of residents under 18 in 1970 (FAMILY) (6 levels)	−0·11
2 Scale according to the proportion of owner-occupied housing units in 1970 (PROPERTY) (6 levels)	−0·16
3 Scale according to the proportion of high-school graduates among residents over 25, in 1970 (EDUCATION) (6 levels)*	−0·18
4 Scale according to the median contract rent, in dollars, in 1970 (6 levels) (HIGH RENT)	−0·17
5 Scale of FAMILY, PROPERTY and HIGH RENT (Scale in 6 level constructed by combination of scores of census tracts in scales number 1, 2, and 4. It reads as follows: top level in scale 5 = top level in scale 1 *or* in scale 2 *or* in scale 4, and so on throughout all the levels of the scale)	−0·38 (p < 0·001)

*The ranking for *education* has been inversed in order and in relationship to the other scales, to be consistent with the hypothesis of a *direct* correlation with gay presence.
Source: Our own calculations on the basis of scales constructed by us; See the Methodological Appendix, pp. 357–59.

We are in the presence of four spaces: property land, family land, rich land (defined by the proportion of high-rent housing), and gay land. Gay settlement was opposed by property, family, and high class: the old triumvirate of social conservatism. Map 14–7 provides confirmation of this conclusion. Our informants (the accuracy of whose information was established through cross-checking with four other sources) forecasted the expansion of the gay community throughout the 1980s in the areas presented in Map 14–7, without any previous knowledge of our analysis. They are precisely the zones that appear to be contiguous to the gay territory and where the three variables proposed as deterrents to gay location score relatively low values.

Before proceeding towards any further elaboration of these results, we need to introduce a historical perspective into the analysis. The spatial setting of the gay community in San Francisco has developed along a series of progressions whose dynamics are the clearest way to understand the connection between alternative culture and spatial form. We have two sources, expressed in Maps 14–2 and 14–3, to study the sequence of expansion of the gay territory after the Second World War: on the one hand, the areas established for each period by the same team of informants whose information appeared accurate when contrasted to other indicators; and on the other hand the sequence of expansion of gay bars at four points in time on the basis of our reliable source, as cited in the Methodological Appendix. From the observation of these maps, and on the basis of the knowledge of the characteristics of the city as expressed in the US Census Urban Atlas and the CORO Foundation Districts' Handbook[113], we can propose the following spatial history of San Francisco's gay community.

The spatial history of San Francisco's gay community

At the 'beginning', in the 1940s, gays still had to be invisible, and for the most part met in bars,

Top rank in the proportion of multiple male households (indicator of *gay residence*)

High proportion of population under 18 (*family*)

High level of high rent in rental housing (*high rent*)

High proportion of house ownership (*property*)

Overlap of *property* and *high rent*

Map 14.6 Family, property, high rents, and gay residential areas.
(*Source*: Our study on the basis of US Census data and the voter registrar.)

particularly concentrated in the Tenderloin area, a red light zone adjacent to downtown. So gays were forced to be a part of the (relatively) tolerated milieu of individual 'deviant' behaviour. There were networks, but no community-places, but no territory. In the 1950s an alternative life style and culture flourished in the cafes and bookshops of North Beach, that of the beatniks. Gays found there a receptive, tolerant atmosphere and they became a part of the rebel residential community that established itself in that area. Without developing a com-

Map 14.7 Informant basemap, gay residential expansion areas (1980s).
(*Source*: Key informants mapping, February 1980.)

munity themselves, gays enjoyed relative freedom as a sub-set of a highly intellectual, fashionable counter-culture. In the 1960s gays' network expanded and took advantage of the atmosphere of liberalism imposed by the anti-war and civil rights movements. In addition to Tenderloin and North Beach, bars flourished around a new axis, Polk and Van Ness, that were more integrated into the city. For the first time, an independent gay residential area developed around the meeting places opened on Polk Street. The adjacent ghetto of the Western Addition was designated for redevelopment and some gay households started buying property in the renewed area in the late 1960s.

The gay liberation movement was given a dramatic impetus by New York's Stonewall Revolt of June 1969. Gays 'came out', and many of them migrated from all over the country to the cities where they could express themselves, especially New York, Los Angeles, and San Francisco. The new militants were not content just to be close to social places where there were sexual networks, but tried to develop, symbolically and politically, a life style defined as gay. They tried to establish a community. Others joined the effort in a somewhat confused frame of mind, to be socialized in a new culture more suitable to their needs and behaviour, a culture that they needed to feel part of by being, physically, in a given neighbourhood, for only then would they be able to rub their old classroom slates clean and learn for the first time about themselves in their rightful surroundings. So a collective movement, informally organized, began to take over a well-defined area (the Castro Valley in the geographical centre of San Francisco), an area characterized by two main features: it was traditionally a beautiful Victorian neighbourhood partly vacated by its Irish working class dwellers moving to the suburbs; and it was a very middle-level area in terms of income and education with much affordable housing to rent. Gays purposely started businesses and shops in the area and neighbourhood associations that forced other businesses in the area, particularly banks, to collaborate with them. Bars and social places followed the residential concentration, so reversing the usual sequence.

At the same time, in the 1970s, two very different trends were expressing other spatial and social orientations of gay people, trends that attracted less attention than the garish lights of the Castro territory. While sharing the aspirations to a self-controlled 'private territory', many gays could not afford the high rents that landlords were forcing them to pay if they were to have that kind of freedom. So they started another colonization in the much harsher area, South of Market, where transient hotels, warehouses, and slums waited for redevelopment. Their marginality to the gay community was not only spatial, but social: they tended to reject the politicization and positive counter-culture of the new liberation movement. Instead, they emphasized the sexual aspects of gay life, and the more the gay community strove for legitimacy the more an individualistic minority, who were generally poorer and less-educated, evolved new sexual codes, many of them joining the sado-masochist networks. The South of Market area became the headquarters of the leather culture.[114]

A growing proportion of middle class gays, however, rejected the militant stands of the liberation movement and ridiculed the idea of setting up in a ghetto. They believed it was necessary to obtain personal freedom and legal rights without challenging a system that was otherwise highly favourable to their sex, class, and race. This orientation, which we will examine as one of the main debates within the community, has also a distinct spatial expression. Since the early 1970s, according to our informants, some middle class gays had wanted to live in a friendly gay neighbourhood, but not in the Castro ghetto, and they began to locate themselves, in a very pointed move, in the lower sections of the fashionable Pacific Heights, literally on the threshold of San Francisco's elite.

In the mid-1970s, two major spatial developments characterized the gay community:

1   The Castro ghetto grew and expanded dramatically in all adjacent areas. A very dense gay network of bars, health clubs, stores, businesses, and activities developed on the basis of a growing population. Immigration from the rest of the country accelerated the rate that gay households bought property in the neighbourhood, taking advantage of the conversion of rented buildings into condominiums. They moved westward to more affluent sections. The expansion also reached the Dolores Corridor on the border with the Latino Mission District. Friction developed and there was some anti-gay violence from the Latino youth.

2   In a different development, gay households (particularly lesbian) developed in the working class areas of Bernal Heights and Potrero Hill, within what we have called 'familyland', taking advantage of relatively sound, cheap housing. The major reason for the tolerance shown towards the households was the existence in those areas of very large counter-cultural communities established by young white students and professionals who maintained a good rela-

tionship with working class families – their common ground being the strength of feeling about the neighbourhood. Gay men and lesbians were generally welcomed into this milieu of 1960s rebels, with which they had associated from the outset.

In the late 1970s, on the basis of the newly acquired (though uncertain) protection through political power, a new expansion of gay residences took place on the borders of the middle class areas such as Inner Richmond and Inner Sunset in the western part of the city, where home ownership was generally required. While still preserving their basic territory, gays had started to dismantle the last barriers to their spatial presence. The contradiction implicit in this move was that either gays would lose their identity to adapt to prevailing patterns of behaviour, or they would have to obtain from the entire city a degree of tolerance that would have demanded society to change its fundamental values with respect to the family and sexual repression – demands that were unlikely to be met without fundamental social change. For the moment we can only point to this question since we will have to introduce additional analytical elements to answer it. But suffice to say now that it is significant that a historical overview of the expansion of gay territory should introduce this debate.

The evolution and characteristics of gay residential space cannot answer the basic research questions we have asked about the relationship between alternative cultures and the production of urban forms. But because spatial structures do show the trace of social processes we are able to introduce some of the basic themes of our analysis on the basis of the results presented here.

The gay community expressed (and continues to express) a diversity of interests and social situations that always overlapped in reality and that we are only able to separate analytically. At the same time it represented a sexual orientation, a cultural revolt, and a political 'party'. In the case of San Francisco, young professionals and small businessmen who emigrated to the city because of its cultural tolerance and character as a headquarters of an advanced service economy comprise a very important sector of gay people. In fact all these aspects were present in the spatial history of the gay community but with different weights for each period.

When the gay identity had to be reduced to its hard core because of fierce social repression, sexually orientated networks were the basic instrument of communication and solidarity. But gayness is more than a sexual preference: it is an alternative way of life, characterized by the domination of expressiveness over instrumentalism and by human contact over impersonal competition. Such values were very close to the beatnik and hippy cultures of the 1950s and 1960s, and this is why gays moved into the territories of these alternative life styles. But gays were different and represented more than a counter-culture. Not only did they have a sexual network to preserve, they had also to win their right to exist as citizens, they had to engage in political battles, change laws, fight the police, and influence government. But how could they organize within the political institutions only on the basis of bars and of the marginal counter-cultures? To be a society within a society, they had to organize themselves spatially to transform their oppression into the organizational setting of political power. This is why the building of the Castro ghetto was inseparable from the development of the gay community as a social movement. It brought together sexual identity, cultural self-definition, and a political project in a form organized around the control of a given territory. This is why those who rejected the idea of a social movement left the 'commune', either to rejoin conventional society in exchange for some tolerance, or to cut all communication and attempt instead to affirm the potency of individualistic sexual pleasure. The ghetto preceeded the movement towards institutionalization and provided the basis, particularly through the decentralized District elections, to obtain enough power to live in the city instead of having to seek self-protection within a community. But as long as gays are beaten and killed because of whom they love, even in a city where they share institutional power, they will need the ghetto. The territorial boundaries of a cultural community are required for the same reasons that Jewish people in Europe, black people in America, and oppressed ethnic minorities all over the world have always needed them – for everyday survival.

The Renovation of Housing and Urban Space by the Gay Residential Communities[115]

Every incoming urban group has an impact on its housing and physical space. The gays of San Francisco definitely improved the quality of housing through repairs, remodelling, and excellent maintenance. Most gay households established themselves by renting or buying houses in middle-level neighbourhoods, worked on them, and upgraded both the buildings and the surrounding environment. The process of urban renovation in San Francisco has been largely, although not exclusively, triggered by gay people. As a result, property values in gay residential areas have been considerably improved, far above the already impressive average for the entire city. Commercial and business development has spread effortlessly through the gay residential areas.[116] The aesthetic quality of most houses renovated by gays has greatly helped San Francisco to preserve its historical heritage of beautiful old Victorian buildings, many of which had been condemned during the 1960s by the technocratic San Francisco Redevelopment Agency (SFRA). The gay community opposed the renewal strategies presaged by the SFRA's bulldozers during the period of the pro-growth coalition with an alternative model – that of rehabilitating the existing city – in which housing stock was to be reused and valuable architectural structures remodelled.[117] In fact, the spectacular urban renovation in San Francisco during the 1970s, with the new gay households as the driving force, was the result of a more complex pattern (as is clearly shown by the typology of renovation agents established by Don Lee on the basis of his study of gay realtors).[117bis] Three different types of interventions appear to have contributed:

1   Affluent gay professionals, desiring to move into the gay territory, hired skilled renovators to do the job for them once they had bought the inexpensive houses, the basic structure of which was sound and whose old Victorian shape offered a great potential for architectural beauty.
2   Gay realtors and interior decorators discovered the possibilities of a new housing market and decided to use it as a way to earn a living. Using their commercial and artistic skills, they bought property in low-cost areas, and repaired and renovated the buildings in order to sell them for a high profit. (This, incidentally, is the process that accounts for some of the renovation taking place in the predominantly black area of the Western Addition.[118]) It would be simplistic to label this activity as 'real estate speculation'. What in fact happened was that gays, discriminated against in the labour market, discovered the hard way how to survive the tough San Francisco housing market, and then decided to use their newly learned skills as a means of earning a living. A few of them became realtors and greatly contributed to urban rehabilitation and gentrification, most of them taking part as hired, skilled workers, carpenters, decorators and painters. Don Lee estimates that '. . . the gay community provides 90 per cent of labour in renovation and restoration in central San Francisco neighbourhoods.'[119] Some of the most prominent restoration enterprises such as the San Francisco Victoriana and the San Francisco Renaissance are spin-offs of initiatives by gays.

3   At the same time, the majority of the gay community could not afford to buy a house in San Francisco.[120] So they formed collectives to either rent or buy inexpensive buildings, and fixed them up themselves. This practice was not only an expression of an economic need but a tradition initiated by the counter-cultural collectives of the 1960s, in an attempt to supersede the role of the family in the traditional household structure.[121] These collectives have probably accounted for a large proportion of San Francisco's housing rehabilitation and maintenance in recent years.[122]

Plate 14.1 An example of the renovation carried out by gays on Victorian houses in Castro Street, San Francisco. (Photograph: F. Sabbah.)

The impact of the gay community on the urban space went far beyond the walls of the restored buildings. The adjacent streets burgeoned with stores, bars, public places and miscellaneous businesses from clinics to launderettes. The monograph by Don Lee, *Castro Street Commercial District* has clearly established the decisive commercial, physical, and aesthetic improvement of a neighbourhood that was being abandoned by its Irish working class who were moving to the suburbs. To be sure, Castro Valley was – and still is – the core of the gay community and has therefore had much higher chances of urban improvement because of the high expectations in terms of real estate. But this is precisely the argument: unlike other oppressed communities, gay people have raised the physical standards and economic value of the space they have occupied. Are we then in the presence of typical gentrification? Were gay people the middle class vanguard pushing urban poor and minorities out of a newly discovered space picked out by the well-to-do in the so-called 'back to the city' movement?[123] This has been the accepted wisdom. Analysts, including Don Lee, have tried to dissociate the gay community from the renovation process, saying that renovation was going on independently of the gays and they took their opportunity. Furthermore, the reference to the contribution by gays to the aesthetics of renovation is rejected as a 'sexist prejudice' on account of the supposed 'femininity' of gays.[124]

Reality is more complex, but the issue must be discussed because it is fundamental for our research purposes. Has there been a contribution by the gay community to the quality of their urban space or has it been a more general gentrification and a 'back to the city' movement by the middle class, part of which happened, in San Francisco, to be gay? Have gays been improving the city or gentrifying the working class neighbourhoods? Our answers to these questions contain several findings.

Firstly it is a fact that gays improved the quality of housing and urban space, mainly through renovation and maintenance.[125] Secondly, it is clear that most neighbourhoods that are now residential areas for gays were in a declining condition. Gay location in those neighbourhoods (particularly in the Western Addition, Haight Ashbury, Potrero Hill, Bernal Heights, Castro) was a decisive element in improving the housing stock and the neighbourhoods' commercial vitality. Thirdly, it is not true that all gay, or even a majority of them, were high-income, middle class professionals. In addition there were poor gay people who lived in the marginal areas, particularly in the South of Market and Tenderloin areas (San Francisco's skid row).

Many gays were able to live in their neighbourhoods because they organized collective households and they were willing to make enormous economic sacrifices to be able to live autonomously and safely as gays. Besides, many gays were more likely to be able to choose their space because they were single men, did not have to sustain a family, were young, and connected to a relatively prosperous service economy. All of these characteristics together made it easier for them to find a house in a tight housing market.

What the gays have had in common with some non-family heterosexual groups is an alternative life style that had close ties with gay culture – a middle class movement that preferred residence in San Francisco, not because they were predominantly middle class, but because they valued personal experience and an active, social street life. In this sense, gays appear to have been a cultural vanguard for these people. Other groups and institutions started upgrading their neighbourhoods as a result of the renovation initiated by gays. In this context the new policy from the banks located in the Castro area was particularly significant: not only did they lend money to would-be private renovators but they remodelled their own buildings, to improve the physical image of the street. The decision of the Surf Theatre Chain to renovate the Castro Theatre building, the main cinema in the gay territory, was the most symbolic at the time; a very old-fashioned structure in the Hollywood-Babylon tradition, the theatre was declared a Registered Landmark in the city after its renovation in July 1977.

Urban renovation in San Francisco reached proportions far above those of any other American city. Unlike other cities, the 'back to the city' movement has not just been the wealthy people inhabiting the central city on the basis of new profitable trends in the housing market.[126] Most renovators have been gay people who have come to San Francisco in the last decade. They have intentionally located themselves, individually or collectively, to build up a new community at a financial and social cost that only 'moral refugees' are ready to pay. They have paid for their identity, and in doing so have most certainly gentrified their areas. They have also survived and learnt to live their real life. At the same time, they have revived the colours of the painted facades, repaired the shaken foundations of the buildings, lit up the tempo of the street and helped to make the city beautiful and alive, all in an age that has been grim for most of urban America.

Gay Society and the Urban Culture

When we use the phrase 'gay community' we are implying something more than a gay territory and an open gay life style. We are referring to a deliberate effort by gay people to set up their own organizations and institutions in all spheres of life.[127] The first efforts, such as the Tavern Guild, came from the bar networks, mainly as a defensive reaction against harassment, violence and legal intimidation. During the 1970s, when gays felt relatively safe in their space and in their city as a result of the political influence they had acquired, they founded a whole range of gay organizations. Many of these were artistic expressions of a culture struggling to emerge: the Gay Freedom Marching Band, The Lavender Harmony Band, the Lesbian Chorus, the Chrysanthemum Ragtime Band, the Quattro Quartet, and a whole series of dancing groups, orchestras, poetry clubs, and art galleries, most of which were co-ordinated and supported by an umbrella organization, the Golden Gate Performing Arts Inc. At another level, counselling clinics and institutions were started, offering psychological support. Operation Concern tried to provide the necessary milieu for people to adapt to their new social milieu, particularly for the young gays who had just arrived in the city. Gay groups were also placed in different Churches according to their beliefs. There was even an openly gay Church, the inter-denominational Metropolitan Community Church, started by a former Pentecostal pastor. Even with spiritual experiences, such as EST,[128] gays organized their own circle with the support of *The Advocate*, the major national gay magazine.

The most visible and sometimes most controversial of the attempts to rebuild the society on the basis of gay institutions was and remains the Golden Gate Business Association (GGBA), a federated network of more than 500 businesses (in 1980), only five years after its foundation.[129] Since it was able to mobilize some financial support for gay activities and celebrations, as well as for political campaigns, the GGBA has become the target of gay radicals who see it as the symbol of a desire by the more affluent gays to win acceptance within the established capitalist order, instead of furthering the transformation of that order's fundamental values. In fact, a look at the membership[130] reveals that a great majority are small firms and individual businesses such as lawyers, business consultants, realtors, small merchants, bars, financial consultants, decorators, advertising specialists, photographers, tourist agents, entertainment organizers, and so on. This in no way represents the world of San Francisco's financial establishment. The real business elite is, and will continue to be, profoundly homophobic, and while a few individuals are tolerated as homosexuals they will not be accepted as gay, namely, as involved in the promotion of an alternative life style. The GGBA has very little possibility, therefore, of allowing the takeover of the gay movement by capitalist forces, and, in fact, expresses the profound desire for individual autonomy and personal freedom that gays feel are the basis of their own development. Such autonomy in American society relies on the ability to earn a living by being self-employed, and there is a real chance for the more educated gays of finding such positions in the changing margins of San Francisco's characteristic service economy. They tend to specialize in providing services for the growing middle class of the city, and in taking intellectually demanding jobs for the government and private corporations. They work also in the expanding market of the gay community. Thus we are in a merchant world and in a world of urban freedom, in a world of autonomy, exchange, interaction, and cultural experimentation. We are almost in the world of the Renaissance city where political freedom, economic exchange, and cultural innovation, as well as open sexuality, developed together in a self-reinforcing process on the basis of a common space won by citizens struggling for their freedom.

To push this image even further, we are also in a world of merchant fairs and street feasts. The gay community is one of the main organizers of popular celebrations in San Francisco, some of which come from the merchants' interests that provide the economic support for the community, such as the Annual Castro Street Fair, initiated in 1972 by Harvey Milk, and which attracts over 100,000 people each year to exhibitions, songs, eating, drinking, playing, and meetings to debate politics. Other feasts are gay versions of traditional customs like Christmas carolling, the Beaux Arts Ball, and Halloween. Halloween in particular has become a major festival where straight and gay people share their fantasies of 'crossing over', dressing as in a contest of imagination, aesthetics and humour, and parading along Polk and Castro streets in a night of joy, drinking, laughing and dancing in the streets under the outraged eyes of a nervous police force that must trust the gay community's autonomous security service to take care of its own people. Costumes and witchcraft are precisely what people need to walk happily on the uncertain edge of blurred identities. But the interesting phenomenon is not only the appropriation by gays of a tradition usually associated with children, but the joy and pleasure of tens of thousands of Bay Area residents who participate in the event in the Castro area, happy to celebrate the gay's sense of humour and life by joining in the fun, dressing in drag or just enjoying the spectacle.

Other major gay celebrations are new, created by the tradition of the movement itself and established to commemorate major social struggles, one of the most important of which is the Gay Freedom Day Parade, a week-long programme of activities to celebrate the anniversary of the Stonewall Riot of 27 June 1969. Initiated by a spontaneous demonstration in 1970, it has become an institution, the major social event for the gay community, when all cultural and political tendencies meet to express the power, joy, and contradictions of an increasingly liberated community. But the colour, imagination, and verve of the celebration are so strong that many people from San Francisco, as well as from other parts of the world, come to join the gays in what has become the major popular event in San Francisco. (In recent years, between 200,000 and 300,000 people have attended the parade.) Other commemorations have another dimension, such as the yearly Memorial March for Harvey Milk and George Moscone, when thousands of mourners march, carrying candles; or the Harvey Milk Birthday Party celebrated in Castro Street since 1979. The gay community has done more through these increasingly diverse array of events than project its values or have fun: it has shown the city that streets are for people, that urban culture means gathering together to play in public places, and that music, politics and games can intertwine in a revitalizing way, creating a new media for messages and establishing new networks of communication. At the Columbus Day

Parade (a non-gay celebration) the Gay Marching Bank and Twirling Corps appear to be the most cheered performers. This is not only because there are many gays in the city or because of the truly exceptional quality of their performance; it is also because there is a vague consciousness that gays have greatly reinforced the San Francisco tradition of urban life, largely missing in most American cities, such as feasts in the streets and public celebrations – the feeling that a city is not just a combination of capitalist functions and empty streets patrolled by police cars.

Of course, the recognition of this fundamental contribution stops short of the acknowledgement that life could be better if lived their way. But there is the beginning of a connection between gay values and a more general cultural transformation. To consider gay society as a short-sighted, separatist ideology would be misleading. The building of a gay community with its own institutions in the midst of a heavily heterosexual, central city is itself a major transformation, and is highlighted by the fact the gay celebrations have become San Francisco's most popular and brilliant events. But such feasts do not come only from the free expression of a rich culture. They are, as their origins shows, symbols of political battles and demonstrations of the strength and militancy of the gay community in its own territory. This is the other side of the parade. Each time there is a major defeat of gay rights in the voting polls of middle America, gays take to the streets in San Francisco chanting 'Civil Rights or Civil War'. The streets of San Francisco continue to be public places, unlike most American urban streets, partly because of the impact of the gay culture. But for public places to be public, political rights have to be heightened. The gay culture has been able to enrich the urban culture because it has been able to substantially modify the political system. Gay culture is inseparable from gay politics.

Gay Power? The Transformation of the Local Political System by the Gay Community

On a warm spring evening of 1980, middle America was shocked to learn through a CBS nation-wide special report that gays were about to seize power in San Francisco, '. . . everybody's favourite city'.[131] It is true that a disciplined and mobilized block of about 20 to 25 per cent of the city's registered voters[132] was making a difference in the local political system. But the process of power-building was far more complex than just adding gay immigrants to San Francisco's declining population. To understand this process may also explain the profound impact that gays had on city politics and the fragility of that power.

The first apparent connection between the emerging gay community and the political system came in 1972, when George McGovern's presidential campaign opened the way for the expression in an election of many of the social issues arising from the movements of the 1960s. Gay rights were among them.

In the drive to obtain support for McGovern in California, a group of gay, liberal organizers of the homophilic Society for Individual Rights, under the leadership of Jim Foster, founded a gay-orientated political organization affiliated to the Democratic Party, the Alice B. Toklas Democratic Club.[133] It was a very effective campaign organization: the club was rapidly recognized as the responsible gay connection to democratic politics, and prominent straight San Francisco Democrats such as John Burton and the black leader, Willie Brown, joined it. Using the club's influence, Willie Brown sponsored, and obtained approval for, a bill in 1975 that legalized homosexuality in California. The basic political understanding was that the California Democrats would protect the gay community from discrimination and repression in exchange for its votes, channelled through the Democratic Party. This was not, as it transpired, how the majority of the gay community behaved politically in San Francisco. In a parallel effort, Harvey Milk had initiated his own campaign to establish an autonomous political platform for gays. Coming from the anti-war movement, he was distrustful of the national political parties, and was anyway orientated towards grassroots support from the community as the only way of insuring the political accountability of representatives. Taking his Castro Village as a base and using the tactics of a ward politician, Milk attended neighbour-hood meetings, shook hands at the bus stops, and spent hours in the local bars.[134] His Castro Camera store became the political meeting place for the local gay community. He obtained 17,000 votes in the 1973 supervisorial election, and 53,000 in 1975. The first major confronta-tion with the Democratic Party, supported by the Alice B. Toklas Democratic Club, came in 1976. Harvey Milk, a registered Democrat, ran for a State Assembly seat against the official Democratic candidate; he lost the election having received only 45 per cent of the votes cast but carried District 5 which was his territory.

In the midst of this confrontation, the most militant wing of the Alice B. Toklas club seceded to form a new Gay Democratic Club, where explicit gayness became the symbol of their manifesto. The club stressed the importance of gays organizing themselves within the political system and the Democratic Party. In 1979, the club became the Harvey Milk Gay Democratic Club; with a membership of over 1,400 and a militant core of over 200 it was the largest and most active single political organization in San Francisco.

But the key to Harvey Milk's political success in 1977, and with him an autonomous gay community, was the connections he established with the emerging political system. On the one hand, he could only be elected because of the new District-based electoral procedure, itself the expression of the growing influence of neighbourhood associations and grassroots politics of which the gay community was a significant component. On the other hand, he exercised some influence (and so the gay community could win some respect) in the local governing coalition, since it was being reorganized around Mayor Moscone. To replace declining labour presence in the city and to confront pro-growth conservative policies from business, middle class progressive neighbourhoods and blacks needed the support of the gay community which leant politically to the left. Several supervisors elected in the period from 1975 to 1980 (Carol Silver was one) relied on the gay vote as did Moscone himself. Thus the rise of gay influence represented a total recomposition of local power provoked by grassroots pressure, including the gay community, in which the gay community would be a significant member of the new local alliance, relying on its territorial and cultural constituency.

Harvey Milk's political testament, tape recorded ten days after his election, was a clear expression of the continuing conflict between gay politics as an expression of the local com-munity and gay politics as a subordinate wing of the Democratic Party. He clearly designated the names of four persons who could replace him as supervisor in the event of his murder. They were, in order of priority: Frank Robinson, a writer and a close friend; Anne Kronenberg, a lesbian militant; Bob Ross, publisher of the BAR[135] and 1978's Emperor of San Francisco;[136] and Harry Britt. Of even greater importance was his naming of the people who should not be nominated to his post. All of them were prominent, established Democrats who would be the most likely appointees of a moderate Democratic mayor such as Diane Feinstein. Harry Britt, who was the more politically experienced of the four, was appointed.

A declared socialist, close to the left of the Democratic Party, Harry Britt became one of the most active supervisors on a variety of progressive issues, always trying to establish his plat-form on a broader base. Although highly respected by the gay community and clearly repre-senting gays, Britt did not have the charisma of Harvey Milk which was the crucial element for the political self-definition of the community since the Harvey Milk Club was supported by the bar culture and the Tavern Guild. The club's systematic support and endorsement allowed Britt to be easily elected in 1979 and re-elected in 1980.[137] In spite of his presence on the board of supervisors, the influence of gays in the political system did not correspond to its political strength, as measured by the number of appointees nominated by the major to city hall posts. Their main influence was in terms of the threat of their opposition. In the 1979 mayoral race, the incumbent, Diane Feinstein, was forced into a run-off against her conservative opponent because of the presence of a gay candidate, and she was elected only when gay leaders called in their votes for her in exchange for a series of promises, noticeably to give them some influence in the recruiting within the police department.

This cautious attitude was symptomatic of the unstable political situation in San Francisco following the assassinations in 1978 of Harvey Milk and George Moscone. The incipient new coalition disappeared at the same time that a right wing current was sweeping the national political scene. A new coalition of neighbourhood groups, ethnic minorities, women's organizations, gays, and public employees unions was formed, under the name of Action for Accountable Government (AAG). Although influential through its contacts with various communities as well as with Democratic Party leaders, AAG could not control the mayor nor field a new political candidate. So San Francisco became an example of coalition politics, with alliances between different groups forming and disappearing according to the political issues of the moment. In this situation, the initiatives of the gay representatives were consistently progressive, defending social programmes and neighbourhood conservation against the proposals of the downtown business sector and fiscal conservatives. The importance of the gay's contribution to the formation of progressive urban policies in San Francisco is demonstrated by the series of proposals presented by Harvey Milk and Harry Britt to the board of supervisors including the suggestions to favour rent control, fight real estate speculation, oppose high-rise developments, and defend the city's urban quality. (See the list of these initiatives presented in the Methodological Appendix p. 360–2.) Significantly enough, Dan White, Harvey Milk's murderer, was the strongest advocate of redevelopment programmes, and a defender of the controversial and speculative development for tourists known as Pier 39.[138] In this sense, gay leadership sought to establish a broader political legitimacy by embracing the defence of popular interests in urban development, sometimes at the expense of a significant gay real estate sector which was opposed to rent control. We can therefore say that gay political influence in San Francisco has been a major factor since 1975 in undermining the control of business interests over city politics.

Nevertheless, the inability of the various components of this alternative political scheme to establish one platform and a common leadership led to a succession of *ad hoc* alliances and compromises between interests that were not always easy to reconcile when very narrowly defined. For instance, the neighbourhood opposition to high-rise development was criticized by labour unions looking for jobs, both in the construction process and in future office buildings. Gays' desire for urban restoration was viewed by blacks as a threat of intensified gentrification. Police control of anti-gay violence was often considered as a potential source for a crackdown on Latino youth. The protection of family-orientated public services was often met with indifference by the predominantly single gay population, and so on. Thus, in spite of conscious efforts by the leadership to establish strategic alliances, the reduction of the groups' interests to the logic of interest groups led to an increasing fragmentation and to the weakening of the emerging urban popular alliance at a time when it had to face up to a powerful offensive from business interests.[139]

The difficulty that the gay community has had in articulating its interests to a heterosexual society pinpoints the fragility of gay power, even in a city that so clearly wears its political imprint.

The Transformation of the City by the Gay Community and the Limits of Gay Self-determination

The development of a gay community, in support of a political movement to defend civil rights and to foster an alternative life style, has been a major factor of urban change in San Francisco during the 1970s. Most of the changes triggered by the expansion of gay culture have been major contributions to the improvement of the city's quality of life. New gay households account for a significant proportion of the renovation of old buildings, for the repair and maintenance of many sections of the city, for the upgrading of property values, and for the dynamism of the real estate market. Although gay people have operated in a very attractive urban environment, they have also been pioneers in taking unusual risks to live in decaying areas, as well as making innovations in collective co-habitation, enabling an intensive residential use of the city that has resulted in a definite improvement in housing maintenance. Although some of this action took place within the broader context of middle class, childless professionals desiring to live in the city, a very significant proportion of housing renovation and neighbourhood improvement seems to have been the result of moderate – income gays making a special effort to invest their own work and time to share a limited dwelling space in exchange for the feeling of freedom, protection, and self-expression provided by a gay territory.

Furthermore, the artistic talents of many gays has accounted for one of the most beautiful urban renovations known in American cities. The effects on urban aesthetics have gone beyond the careful painting of the original Victorian facades. Apart from the impressive interior decoration of the imaginatively remodelled flats the impact can be seen in the well-designed treatment of semi-public spaces – between the front door and the pavement for example; in all, a very unusual architectural improvement in the highly individualistic world of American cities.

Some gays have denounced this evaluation of their talent as renovators and of their care as urban dwellers, perceiving in it a typical prejudice of heterosexual culture. It is clear however that gay culture has this particular talent, a talent that constitutes an invaluable resource in the preservation of urban beauty. Besides which, there is nothing wrong with recognizing artistic ability, as long as the judgment is not used to maintain a social stigma associated with that image.

There is, in fact, a theoretical social explanation for such a talent. Gay men are in the midst of two processes of socialization, each one leading to a specific set of values. On the one hand, they grow up as men, and therefore are taught to believe in the values of power, conquest, and self-affirmation, values that in American society tend to be expressed through money or, in other words, through the dominance of exchange value. At the same time, because of the feelings that many have had to hide for years, and some for their entire life, they develop a special sensitiveness, a desire for communication, a high esteem of solidarity and tenderness that brings them closer to women's culture. This is not, however, because gays are 'feminine', but, like women, their oppression and discrimination creates a distance from the values of conquest and domination which they are supposed to share as men. Thus, they tend to consider the use value of their personal lives as important, or worth more than the exchange value that could be acquired without even obtaining the greatest reward of all – to be themselves. And yet power and money still matter for many gay men. The spatial expression of this two-fold desire for exchange value and use value is, in our opinion, housing renovation. On the one hand they occupy a building, and make it distinctive and valuable. On the other hand, there is something else going on in the restored building: it has beauty, comfort, and sensuality, and it is saying something to the city while expressing something to its own dwellers. And when a space becomes meaningful, exchange value is no longer the dominant issue. This is perhaps the most important contribution of the gay community to the city: not only housing improvement but urban meaningfulness.

As often happens in the process of social change, groups inconvenienced by the progress of another are not properly recompensed. So there has been little urban improvement for the black families forced to move out from the Hayes Valley,[140] or help for the Latinos suffering high rents along the Dolores corridor because of real estate speculation from the increasing influx of gays. These hardships have been at the root of the hostility of ethnic minorities against gay people, a hostility often translated into violence. Class hate, ethnic rage, and fear of displacement by the invaders have clearly held greater sway than prejudices from family traditions or machismo ideology. This contradiction cannot be solved by contacts between the communities. There is too much need on both sides and too much self-definition as interest groups to enable people to relate to broader social perspectives. There have been exceptions. Willie Brown, a black political leader, was the sponsor of the Gay Rights Bill in California. Harry Britt is one of the most active defenders of low-income housing on the board of supervisors. But to really make the interests of gays and ethnic minorities compatible a new urban policy would be needed, emphasizing the use value of residential communities, imposing the public interest before the profit of real estate interests, as well as allowing the downtown business provide non-skilled jobs through construction work, services, and so on. Since ethnic minorities actually need these downtown jobs and many gays are involved in real estate speculation, the limits of the alliance are increasingly narrow, and the feeling of hostility increasingly bitter. The improvement of the urban space by the gay community might therefore represent a new form of residential displacement and social inequality.

There seems to be a parallel contradiction in the improvement by the gay community of urban culture. We have pointed out how decisively street life, popular celebrations, and joyful feasts have increased during the 1970s as a direct consequence of the gay presence. Although the appreciation could be somewhat subjective, most urbanists seem to value public life, street activity, and intense social interaction as one of the most distinctive positive dimensions of city life. Cities, all through history, have been spaces of diversity and communication. When communication ends, or when diversity is swallowed by social segregation, as in the uniform backyards of American suburbs, the urban culture is endangered, – the sign, perhaps, of a sick civilization.[141] Thus the intensity of San Francisco's urban culture, certainly highlighted by gays' sense of urban theatre, seems to be an effective antidote against meaninglessness and broken communication. And yet this urban culture is incomprehensible to the elderly people who feel like strangers in their own sedate neighbourhoods. For straight San Franciscans, the Castro ghetto, as well as many of the gay celebrations, seem to be from another world with a distinctive dress code[142] aimed to isolate and exclude the 'voyeur'. The visibility that gays have created has had very positive consequences for the community, including the defensive device of identifying almost immediately who is and who is not gay. But what for gays increases their protection and communication creates for straights a major barrier, limiting the effects that gays may have on urban culture. If only gays benefit from the revival of street life and urban happenings, San Francisco will become a functional and impersonal city like most other American cities, the only difference being that in addition to Chinatown or the

Fisherman's Wharf, tourists will be able to visit the gay territory as another curiosity, spatially segregated and culturally distant from the rest of city. A major barrier to the gay community being heard in a broader urban culture seems to be the necessary emphasis on sexual liberation. Western society in general, and the American society in particular, is based on sexual repression. Individuals and institutions are deeply fearful of, and profoundly disturbed by, sexuality. For gays on the other hand, it is a major element of self-definition. We could say that the encouragement that the gay movement gives to the assumption and expression of sexuality is in fact a major contribution to the values of society. And yet, the issue is made more complex by the fact that sexual liberation is continually challenged by the predominance of heterosexuality. So both sexuality and homosexuality have to be affirmed against the psychological frontier between 'normal' and 'abnormal', as well as against basic rules of social interaction implicit in all organizations and institutions. The daily contradiction is so untenable that gays tend to live more and more within their own walls. But this limit, the need to continuously reinforce relationships, the difficulty of learning new values, and their self-discovery make a fertile ground for the development of esoteric sub-cultures, severing ties with society to explore alternative sources of meanings and feelings through a new sexual code, based on the continual crossing of whatever borders become established. The sado-masochist culture was the most rapidly growing component of the gay community in 1981 and also the most ideologically committed, attacking the gay leaders because they were trying to define norms that were 'socially acceptable'. For the sado-masochists the journey had no limits. So violence, humiliation, slave auctions, leather dress, Nazi uniforms, chains and whips were much more than sexual stimulii or games. They were cultural expressions of the need to destroy whatever moral values straight society had left them with since these values have traditionally been used to exploit and repress homosexuality. Although it is true that S-M culture represents a tiny part of the gay community and that most S-M practitioners are heterosexuals, the considerable embarrassment that this issue causes to most aware, gay people is revealing, suggesting that this is an important issue.

Left to itself, in its cultural ghetto, the gay community is unlikely to accomplish the sexual revolution which is, implicitly, its major social project. To make homosexuality acceptable, society has first to accept its own sexuality, and such a cultural transformation provokes panic in most minds and institutions. This is why gay celebrations, no matter how brilliant and humorous they are, can only be city celebrations in part. There is always an underlying sexual dimension that is untenable for many people, not only because of its homosexuality but its sexuality. Unable to build bridges towards a broader and deeper cultural transformation, the gay community is in danger of internal destruction by introspective forces that might cause the community to forget that human experience has to be a social experience if it is going to last and grow. Between the transformation of the city's culture and the sado-masochists' back rooms, the gay community still hesitates and confines itself within the spatial limits of its free village.

It would appear that the bridges between the gay community and social change could be built by the political movement. And we have observed how the power obtained by the gay leadership through the community's capacity for electoral mobilization and social organization was used to contribute to and to support many politically progressive causes, particularly in the field of urban policies. As Figure 14–1 shows, District 5 (the Castro area) appears to have been by far the most liberal in terms of political attitudes and voting behaviour. Gays were the backbone of left wing initiatives in San Francisco's political system. So the gay community transformed the local political system, making it very difficult for conservatives to control the city, and creating an alternative power base relying on neighbourhood associations, public workers' unions, and oppressed ethnic communities. At the same time, as we have already pointed out, the obstacle to such an alliance were conflicting immediate interests between groups defined by very different social situations.

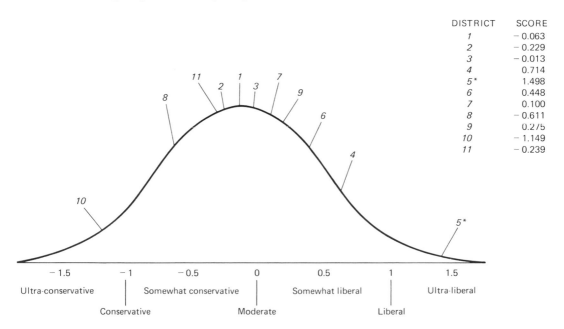

DISTRICT	SCORE
1	− 0.063
2	− 0.229
3	− 0.013
4	0.714
5*	1.498
6	0.448
7	0.100
8	− 0.611
9	0.275
10	− 1.149
11	− 0.239

*District 5 is the predominantly gay district

Figure 14.1 San Francisco supervisorial districts ranked by Liberal/Conservative score. See Map 13.1, p. 107 for the location of the supervisorial districts.
(*Source*: Computronics Research, 1977.)

In fact there were two possible forms of political collaboration between these groups. One was the American custom of coalitional politics in which interests are defined and everybody tries to benefit from the political bargain. The experience of San Francisco made it almost impossible situation for the gay community to reconcile its interests to those of all the other organizations and institutions. The daily contradiction was also apparent within the other groups, producing the stalemate in local politics that we have observed in 1979 and 80. On the other hand, a political alliance could have been established on the basis of long-run political interests, for instance based on the common and essential concern of transforming a cultural-economic structure which was at the same time sexist, homophobic, sexually repressed, racist, and capitalist. Only in such a long-term perspective could gay men and Latinos, for instance, have common interests.

But the gay community in San Francisco has not proceeded in such a direction. Instead of building a new hegemonic culture, including homosexuality, based on an ideologically and politically – led transformation, it tried to develop autonomous power to negotiate its demands within the institutional and political system. This strategy could have been successful if the demands and interests of the gays were compatible with the dominant American culture. They have not been so because they implicitly attack a basic social institution: the family. Only if gays are strong enough to replace the family with another form of human organization would they be able to expand at a social level. But to do so, they would need to articulate their struggle to the only major social movement that is oppressed by the family and ready to replace it: the women's movement. And yet lesbians have tended to be excluded from most positions of power within the gay community, and the community has remained dominated by gay men's problems and perspectives. The reason is not only that gay men are first of all men. It is also because lesbians tend to be politically much more radical and willing to make the connection of personal issues to the transformation of society, to be the marching wing of the women's liberation movement. Lesbians know that there is no way they can accommodate this society. Gay men still have some illusions, particularly if class and race join their sex as a potential source of privilege. Harry Britt, in the interview he gave us, considered gay liberation as a 500 year process. So thinking, he clearly associated himself with a process of social transformation, in which gay men would be play a major part. But this is not the perspective of the community as a whole. The lack of any clear connection to the women's movement as well as the secondary role that lesbians play within the community are clear signs of a separatist male mentality that severs any link with the major agent of cultural transformation in our society, the women's movement.

Given these conditions, self-destructive tendencies have appeared in San Francisco's gay community, and a very serious homophobic backlash is developing in the media and amongst the family orientated, popular sectors. The improvement of San Francisco's urban quality by the gay community will last only if gays are able to articulate their interests concerning social transformation instead of bargaining specific issues within an incompatible scheme of interest groups. They will have to shift from the coalition politics to strategic and historic alliances, particularly with lesbians and with the women's movement, if they are to transform society. If they ignore these alliances they will overcrowd a ghetto instead of enhancing a city.

The last weeks of Harvey Milk's life were a dark period for him. His friend, Jack Lira, committed suicide. His reasons were apparently not related to Milk or to other people, but caused mainly by his own reflections on the gay universe. When he decided to die, he left at his side the book that he had been obsessed with for months: *Holocaust*. This was not Harvey Milk's message. His efforts, on the contrary, were based upon hope – upon the capacity of gays to free themselves from oppression and while doing so, to free society. This was the profound reason for his commitment to improve the city. The transformation of the city into a space of freedom was a major element in the creation by the gay community of social hegemony. But gays can not forget that a free city is also everybody's place. The survival of the gay community is closely tied to the overall process of social change.

15

Conclusion: The Richness of Diversity, the Poverty of Pluralism

Our studies of the Mission Neighbourhood and of the gay community in San Francisco have shown the specificity and the depth of influence of grassroots mobilization on spatial form, urban politics, and the city's culture. We have also revealed the limits of such an influence.

And we have been able to trace the connection between the profile of each urban mobilization and the characteristics of their outcomes as expressed in San Francisco's urban experience.

The urban movement in the Mission was able to preserve the neighbourhood's Latino character, and still upgrade its physical and social conditions. At the same time, it was unable to impose substantial change on housing and urban service policies. The social programmes that were obtained for the poor residents were severely curtailed when the organizations divided and weakened. The limits of the success of the Mission mobilization stemmed from its inability to transform the coalition into something other than an accumulation of interest groups. Some of this inability came from the unwillingness of some community organizers to recognize ethnic and cultural identities, and class divisions as the unavoidable, differential starting point in the shared practice of protest and organization. A more important obstacle for the effective merger of the different identities into a popular movement was the desire of other community leaders to maintain the definition of each group in such a way that the established channels of representation could still function *vis-à-vis* the state institutions. In this context, what has really seemed decisive in the experience of community organizing in the Mission, as well as in America in general, was that the local, state, and Federal governments set up the basic framework defining social interests. That framework was generally accepted by most social actors despite the fact that the underlying social structure was functioning along contradictory lines defined by specific interests.

In other words, if people are defined by the state as Latinos, gays, blacks, women, Asians, conservationists, drug addicts, dropouts, juveniles, Moonies, or middle class, there is no other way, as far as the definition is concerned, than either to submit to the demands of the state on behalf of all the others, or to play coalition politics at the grassroots or institutional level. Once such a game is started, each player defines him/herself as having to pursue his/her own interests in a remarkable mirror image of the ideal model of the free market.

No group would accept a broader definition in terms of 'historical interests of social change', unless its own interest coalitions became highly unstable and the struggle for power within became as important as the confrontation with the system. Furthermore, the differences in identities are real (Latinos are different from blacks). Yet difference need not imply conflict except when some identities are placed in structurally contradictory positions, such as capital and labour, or the masculine role and the feminine role (not men versus women) within the patriarchal family. By equalizing all identities as single definitions, and redistributing the cards among all the players who are socially redefined as individual players, the state is actually undoing the social structure, and restructuring it according to the model of a free market where, potentially, all political trade-offs are possible. Such a process obviously is not a conscious manipulation but it is just the institutionalized reproduction of a society dominated by capitalist corporations with the ideology of endless competition.

In a similar way, if grassroots pressure is strong enough to obtain redistribution without challenging the operation of the system, the state will acknowledge this new source of power and will modify the policies. But it will do so in such a way that each interest group will be targeted through defined policies (programmes), and be rewarded in accordance to its capacity to mobilize. Thus a competition is started between the different groups and, obviously, the competition is most acute when the groups are in need. As they destroy each other in this battle, the social pressure slows down, and redistribution is halted. When people lose power, they also lose access to resources and therefore their right to represent their constituency, since this position is based on their ability to bargain for the resources in the process of redistribution. What remains from people's efforts is a series of scattered fragments: some programmes, many different grassroots groups, a place to live, and the right to keep their identity.

Also, on the other side, the 'powers that be' are made aware that pushing too hard could backfire, a cautious attitude that provides some protection for the people, their culture, and their neighbourhood. This is, in essence, the Mission story.

An even more striking and parallel result derives from our study of the gay community. In order to be themselves, gays colonized a territory, set up their own economy, social places, feasts and celebrations, and political organizations. They built up a community. In the process, their efforts were decisive in helping to improve San Francisco's urban quality. They renovated large sections of the city, beautified their neighbourhoods, highlighted popular celebrations, and contributed to the city as a public place. And they greatly strengthened progressive local political decisions, particularly in the sphere of urban policies.

At the same time, in spite of the awareness of some of their leadership, gays remained distrustful of a society that was distrustful (and in some sectors scared) of them. So they became an interest group, increasingly feared as their power grew, which in turn triggered all kinds of strong defensive reactions within the gay community. Defining themselves only on the basis of their gayness, their contribution to urban improvement became closely associated with gentrification. Their construction of a highly distinctive, sexually orientated sub-culture set off destructive tendencies within the community itself. Their political separatism led to an increasing marginality in relation to the lesbian sector of the community, and largely cut them off from the women's movement. This prevented them from joining the radical political stream which represented their only chance to bring about some basic socio-political changes without which it is unlikely that society will ever accept the challenge that gays present to such fundamental institutions as the nuclear family and sexual repression.

San Francisco has emerged from urban mobilizations such as the ones we have studied, those led by the Western Addition blacks in the 1960s in protest against urban renewal, and the middle class neighbourhood associations in the 1970s, as an incredibly diverse, contradictory and alive city. Neighbourhoods have been preserved, minorities have remained in the city, urban services have been improved, housing has been renovated and maintained as real estate values have rocketed, and a tolerant and local culture has been strengthened by the sustained, relatively liberal orientation of the local power system.

At the same time, because of the inability of different sources of popular protest and cultural innovation to unite over decisions concerning alternative urban policies, the financial district made plans for further expansion, the gentrification process accelerated, local elections were centralized again, fiscal austerity was initiated, and the unifying political expression of the city's liberal majority disappeared with the slaying of Mayor Moscone.

So the city lights shine brighter than ever. The sun still plays on the ornately painted facades of the Victorian buildings. Chinatown still feeds tourists and weaves garments. The Mission in 1980 still welcomes Salvadorans and low riders. Gays still discover themselves and enjoy their free city. Yet there is a feeling of uncertainty, as if the city was more a delicate pathern of coloured laser beams than a solid patchwork quilt sewn by a patient woman's hands. Behind the urban décor preserved by the neighbourhood movements, San Francisco seems to await a social earthquake.

Part 4

The Social Basis of Urban Populism: Squatters and the State in Latin America

16

Introduction: Squatter Communities and the New Dynamics of the World System

The fastest and most dramatic process of urbanization in human history is taking place in the squatter settlements and slums of the metropolitan areas of developing countries.[1] Engendered by uneven development and the new international division of labour in the world economy,[2] it forces millions and millions of people to live in physical and social conditions that are reaching the point of ecological disaster.[3] Yet, contrary to the expectations of those who believe in the myth of marginality and in spite of the fears of the world's establishment, social organization seems to be stronger than social deviance in these communities, and political conformism seems to outweigh the tendencies towards popular upheavals.[4]

Our hypothesis is that both trends can be explained by the same crucial social phenomenon: the local self-organization of squatter settlements and its particular connection to the state and the political system at large in the shape of urban populism. We mean by urban populism the process of establishing political legitimacy on the basis of a popular mobilization supported by and aimed at the delivery of land, housing, and public services. While this is a very traditional mechanism that has existed for a long time in many countries, its quantitative importance and its qualitative meaning has been enhanced in recent years by the rhythm and forms of urbanization in dependent societies.[5] Thus the relationship between the state and the popular masses in the Third World in general, and in Latin America in particular, is increasingly shaped by the new forms of interaction between the city and the grassroots. Furthermore, the growing social concern for the squatter settlements actually reflects the evolving pattern of political relationships between the state and the unorganized urban popular sectors in Latin American societies.[6] Such a relationship is itself constrained by the integration of all economies into a world system while accelerating the disintegration of national economies.[7] Urbanization in Latin America, as elsewhere, is determined by the interplay of economic trends, political power, and cultural values.[8] Such an interaction takes place, largely, in a world network which has been, from the beginning, the operating unit of the capitalist system.[9] Nevertheless the historical variations within the system are as important as the system itself in the production of social effects, contrary to what the dogmatic statements of the centre-periphery theory would have us believe.[10] So, what is crucial to our understanding of the world system is the interaction between the large trends shaping its evolution and the social processes which are historically and spatially rooted in particular societies.[11]

At a very general level we can say that three major historical tendencies are currently shaping the world system:

1 The increasing internationalization of capital in the form of multinational corporations which have set up a new pattern in the social division of labour, creating a highly fluid and interconnected system of production, distribution, management, and circulation across the entire world.[12]

2 The increasing challenge to the power of the dominant corporate interests by organized labour and social movements in the advanced capitalist societies[13] and by the national governments and liberation movements of dependent societies, a challenge which, in this last case,

transcends different interests and viewpoints.[14] As a result of such challenges, the world capitalist system has entered into a period of structural crisis which will last as long as the centres of decision-making remain unable to organize a new model of accumulation suitable to the current circumstances.[15] Inflation is merely the economic expression of the system's inability to creep away from a confrontation with these basic social contradictions.[16]

3 The military power of the Soviet Union and the possibility of an alliance between state-planned societies and Third World nationalism in the age of nuclear weapons makes it more difficult for the core capitalist governments to use crude military force to restore the system's equilibrium, as was common in colonial or neo-colonial times.[17] In this context, the lesson of Vietnam made the revolutions in Angola, Iran, and Nicaragua seem possible. The massacres in El Salvador and the invasion of Afghanistan, however, remind us that the struggle against intervention is not over.

The major consequence is that, at the moment when the economic capitalist system is over-expanded across the world and needs to increase its control, the political power of the centre over the periphery is weaker than ever, even if it still plays a decisive role. For corporations to produce commodities in Korea for the American market, it is crucial that the political conditions which made Korea a more convenient location be preserved. And yet all over the world two phenomena are deeply transforming the power structure of developing societies:

1 Grassroots activity, generally organized by left wing leadership, is taking place against dictatorships that are based on an increasingly narrow social support.[17bis]
2 But such a political radicalism (which also existed in the 1960s and was clearly defeated all over Latin America) is now converging with a second, newer, and far more important trend: that of national societies, particularly those shaken by the new processes of industrial growth or energy production, becoming more complex, more diversified, more powerful, and therefore more likely to establish their own specific relationship with the multinational corporations.[17ter] The reinforcement of the national states in the Third World parallels the declining role of national governments in the West. At the same time, the general demand for the establishment of a new international economic order, backed by countries as different as Brazil and Cuba, clearly shows what the new stage of world development should be: if the future of the capitalist economies is to lie with the multinational corporations, the operational capacity of these corporations will ultimately depend upon their relationship with the nation-states of developing countries.

The dramatic change has been that those very states have themselves become the expression of societies in the midst of increasing turmoil as a consequence of a rapid, disruptive, and externally induced economic change that very often contradicts the rules of their political system, forcing them to become increasingly pluralist in order to allow a sharing of power amongst a much more diversified society. For instance, once industrial development starts on a large scale, some kind of union organizing and freedom to strike almost inevitably follows. Even more important, the traditional cultural values of a society cannot be wiped out in a few years, even by as powerful medium as the colour television (something that, in another cultural context, the Shah of Iran forgot and Ayatollah Khomeini did not).

As a result, the dominance of a given set of economic or political interests can no longer rely on the exclusive use of military power but has to take into consideration the complexity of a plural and unstable society, as well as the fundamental values which provide psychological security for people in a period when the amount of new information received exceeds an individual's ability to absorb it. Therefore, the battleground moves to the actual relationships being established between the state and the 'people' (that is, the whole structure of social classes) in a period of rapid change and uncertain alliances.

Where are 'the people' in Latin America? Increasingly, they are located in cities[18] and particularly in the threshold areas of the large cities: the slums and the squatter settlements.[19] Table 16–1 illustrates this point for a selection of Third World cities, including Latin America.

Table 16.1 Incidence of slums and squatter areas in selected cities of developing countries

Country	City	Slums and Squatter Settlements as Percentage of City Population
Sub-Saharan Africa		
Cameroon	Douala	80 (1970)
	Yaounde	90 (1970)
Ethiopia	Addis Ababa	90 (1968)
Ghana	Accra	53 (1968)
Ivory Coast	Abidjan	60 (1964)
Kenya	Nairobi	33 (1970)
	Mombasa	66 (1970)
Liberia	Monrovia	50 (1970)
Madagascar	Tananarive	33 (1969)
Malawi	Blantyre	56 (1966)
Nigeria	Ibadan	75 (1971)
Senegal	Dakar	60 (1971)
Somalia	Magadishu	77 (1967)
Sudan	Port Sudan	55 (1971)
Tanzania	Dar es Salaam	50 (1970)
Togo	Lome	75 (1970)
Upper Volta	Ouagadougou	70 (1966)
Zaire	Kinshasa	60 (1969)
Zambia	Lusaka	48 (1969)
Middle East/Mediterranean		
Iraq	Baghdad	29 (1965)
Jordan	Amman	41 (1971)
Turkey	Ankara	60 (1970)
	Istanbul	40 (1970)
	Izmir	65 (1970)
Lebanon	Beirut	1·5 (1970)
Morocco	Casablanca	70 (1971)
	Rabat	60 (1971)
Low Income Asia		
Afghanistan	Kabul	21 (1971)
India	Calcutta	33 (1971)
	Bombay	25 (1971)
	Delhi	30 (1971)
	Madras	25 (1971)
	Baroda	19 (1971)
Indonesia	Jakarta	26 (1972)
	Bandung	27 (1972)
	Makassar	33 (1972)
Nepal	Katmandu	22 (1961)
Pakistan	Karachi	23 (1970)
Sri Lanka	Colombo	43 (1968)

Table 16.1 (*continued*)

Country	City	Slums and Squatter Settlements as Percentage of City Population	
Middle Income Asia			
Hong Kong	Hong Kong	16	(1969)
Korea	Seoul	30	(1970)
	Busan	31	(1970)
Malaysia	Kuala Lumpur	37	(1971)
Philippines	Manila	35	(1972)
Singapore	Singapore	15	(1970)
Latin America and Caribbean			
Brazil	Rio de Janeiro	30	(1970)
	Belo Horizonte	14	(1970)
	Recife	50	(1970)
	Porto Alegre	13	(1970)
	Brasilia	41	(1970)
Chile	Santiago	25	(1964)
Colombia	Bogota	60	(1969)
	Cali	30	(1969)
	Buenaventura	30	(1969)
Ecuador	Guayaquil	49	(1969)
Guatemala	Guatemala City	30	(1971)
Honduras	Tegucigalpa	25	(1970)
Mexico	Mexico City	46	(1970)
Panama	Panama City	17	(1970)
Peru	Lima	40	(1970)
	Arequipa	40	(1970)
	Chimbote	67	(1970)
Venezuela	Caracas	40	(1969)
	Maracaibo	50	(1969)
	Barquisimeto	41	(1969)
	Ciudad Guayana	40	(1969)

Definitions vary from country to country and from city to city. Therefore these data only present the roughest of impressions regarding the housing problem in these cities.
Source: Orville T. Grimes, *Housing for Low Income Urban Families* (Baltimore: The Johns Hopkins University Press, 1976) as presented by Johannes F. Linn, *Policies for Efficient and Equitable Growth of Cities in Developing Countries* (Washington, DC: The World Bank, 1979, pp. 35–6).

We must, furthermore, establish the nature of the crucial relationship between the new state and these popular sectors for two major reasons. First, these are 'unknown', potentially volatile sectors, unlike the peasants still under the control of well-established social rules and unlike public employees or unionized workers whose whereabouts are identifiable and negotiable. And second these are sectors that seem capable of setting up new social and cultural rules which could be translated into political demands. In fact, this potential could go either way: it might happen or it might not, depending upon circumstances that research should be able to establish. But in any case this very openness, the possibility of these sectors becoming a bank for an alternative political scheme, makes them at once dangerous and necessary, both for the existing political system as well as for any attempt to establish new political institutions. Thus our hypothesis is that the nation-states tend to be the mediators between the multinational corporations dominating uneven economic growth and the local communities trying to rebuild a new urban world on their own from the debris of their disrupted rural past and from the memory of their cherished traditions.

Therefore the political dimension of the squatter settlements in Latin America is crucial. This dimension, however does not depend only on the political behaviour of urban dwellers *per se*, but is bound up in the phenomenon of a developing country establishing a nation-state with a presence in the international financial networks at the same time as representing the different cultural traditions and social interests of the local communities on which it ultimately relies, a phenomenon that engenders both the confusion and the interest in social research on urbanization in the Third World.

We cannot, obviously, treat such a major issue at the same level of generality at which we have posed it, but we will try to approach the problem with as much as empirical evidence as possible by focusing on the relationship between squatters and the political system in three Latin American countries (Peru, Mexico, and Chile) for which we can rely on field work. Our analysis will try to explore the dialectics between social integration and social change, since urban populism always walks on the thin edge between clientelism and the triggering of urban social movements. This is why we will focus particularly on the experience of Chilean squatters during the Allende government, to probe the potential and the limits of squatters' participation in a revolution. The Methodological Appendix (pp. 362–65) describes our sources and presents and justifies our own research. Before we can give our observations and analysis of squatter movements we need, first, to discuss the state of the evidence regarding the social structure and the urban-spatial characteristics of squatter settlements, to clarify an urban condition whose profile has been repeatedly blurred by the 'theory of marginality'.

17

The Social Dimensions of Marginality

Community mobilizations in Latin American cities take place in a very precise socio-political context.[20] Their significance comes, mainly, from the fact that they generally represent the collective organization and action of the so-called 'marginal sector'. We will therefore attempt to specify what this social position is and how it relates to the overall dynamics of society.

We will not repeat the critique of the ideological assumptions of the 'marginality theory' nor the need to recognize it as a symptom of a new type of social structure in dependent societies. Rather, we will refer here to the theoretical findings already obtained on both issues, particularly since they have been sufficiently summarized by Janice Perlman's criticism of the myth of marginality[21] and Alain Touraine's fundamental reflection on the specificity of the social structure of dependent societies.[22] To facilitate the understanding of our analysis, we must remember that the ideology of marginality merges and confuses in a single dimension the positions occupied by individuals and groups in different dimensions of the social structure – the occupational structure, the spatial structure, the stratification system of individual consumption, the process of collective consumption, income distribution, the cultural structure, the psychosocial system of individual behaviour, and in the power structure. Assuming (without any evidence) the empirical covariation of the low-level positions occupied in these different dimensions, the 'marginality theory' proposes an explanation of society in which rural migration and ecological marginality appear as unexplained independent variables affecting the cultural attributes of people living on the urban margins, such as psychological anomia, deviant behaviour, and political apathy.

In fact, a scientific analysis of the variety of issues addressed by the 'theory of marginality' should start with the theoretical and empirical distinctions of all the dimensions of social structure. Only after we have described these distinctions can we empirically observe the existing links between them so that, in turn, we can explain the theory of the social process underlying these relationships.

Given our specific interest in the relationship between locally-based communities and the transformation of social structure, let us examine the degree of overlap between what has been called urban or ecological marginality and the positions of 'marginal residents' in the occupational structure, as well as their cultural level and geographical origin.

It is obviously impossible to address the issue in a way which could take into account the whole variety of empirical situations, but we will provide some material on two different cities: Santiago de Chile in 1966, and Caracas in 1978. As a matter of fact the overwhelming

Table 17.1   Socio-economic characteristics of residents in the deteriorated urban areas as compared to the average value of each characteristic for the whole metropolitan population Santiago de Chile, 1966. (Differences in percentage points *vis-à-vis* the value of each variable for the whole metropolitan population.)

Socio-Economic Characteristics as Percentage of:	Type of Deteriorated Urban Area		
	Poblaciones (Provisional State housing projects)	Callampas (Shanty towns)	Conventillos (Urban core slums)
Unemployed	+ 1·7	+ 0·1	− 1·2
Occasional unemployment	+ 0·5	+ 1·2	+ 1·6
Active population in the primary sector	− 0·7	+ 0·6	+ 0·1
Active population in manufacturing	+ 5·7	+ 10·1	+ 6·4
Active population in construction industry	+ 5·3	+ 7·1	− 2·5
Active population in trade	− 4·0	+ 1·5	− 0·6
Active population in personal services	− 3·0	− 8·6	− 8·2
Active population in 'other services'	− 3·3	− 12·0	+ 4·9
Active population in unspecified activities	+ 0·1	+ 1·4	0
Active population in the tertiary sector	− 10·3	− 19·1	− 3·9
Active population who are employers	− 2·1	− 2·1	− 2·1
Active population who are salaried	− 14·1	− 24·7	− 13·0
Active population of self-employed	+ 5·1	+ 6·4	+ 6·3
Manual workers	+ 13·4	+ 21·1	+ 10·1
Family workers	− 2·2	− 0·6	− 1·6
Illiterate	+ 2·5	− 1·2	− 0·1
Families earning below minimum wage	+ 1·7 (average for three types)	+ 1·7	+ 1·7
Recent immigrants	− 8·5	− 4·3	− 4·2

Our calculation, on the basis of these data, was made according to the formula:

Value of the variable (percentages) in the defined urban dwelling type   −   Value of the same variable (percentages) in Santiago Metropolitan Area

Obviously, (a) Value 0 means no difference and (b) Since the marginal settlements are a part of the metropolitan area, the differences are underestimated.
Source: DESAL, *La Marginalidad Urbana* (Santiago de Chile, April 1969, 2 volumes.)

majority of empirical studies in other Latin American cities shows a similar tendency as has been demonstrated, for instance, in the classic article by Anthony Leeds, summarizing the social characteristics of squatter settlements in Latin America.[23]

In the case of Santiago (as a part of our study on the squatter settlements carried out with colleagues[24]) we summarized the most reliable statistical information on the characteristics of a representative sample of dwellers in slums, shanty towns, and self-constructed, state-organized housing (*conventillos*, *callampas*, and *poblaciones*, according to the Chilean terminology). We used the data gathered by DESAL,[25] and we compared a series of key variables for the 'urban marginal' population to the population of Santiago as a whole. The findings, as presented in Table 17–1 are quite striking: although the percentage of families with income above the minimum wage was 1·7 points higher in the marginal settlements than in Santiago, the percentage of illiterates varied randomly, as did the percentage of unemployed. The population working in industry was over-represented in the marginal settlements, while the proportion in the ill-defined 'service sector' was under-represented. Even more striking, the percentage of recent immigrants was lower than in the city as a whole.

By examining the data closely, and relating them to other empirical studies as presented in Table 17–2, we were able to specify the dominant social group living in self-constructed settlements: they were not the unemployed street vendors of Third World mythology, but mainly the industrial and construction manual workers of the small companies. At the same time, the slums and squatter settlements appeared to be the home of people with a broad range of occupations and social positions. Thus, social, economic, and cultural heterogeneity were dominant characteristics.[26]

Yet one of the most complete statistical surveys in Latin American 'marginal' settlements came to very similar conclusions for Caracas in 1978.[27] Relying on a stratified random sample of Caracas' 'marginal' areas, that is 1,095,631 people, Ricardo Infante and Magaly Sanchez showed that while the urban situation worsened considerably for the marginal dwellers, their employment and economic situation improved; the unemployment rate was a low 9·1 per cent in those 'marginal' sectors covered by the survey. The data collected by a survey on the residential areas of *ranchos* showed a high percentage of salaried workers (56·3 per cent) and a low level of the famous 'independent worker' typical of most Latin American postcards (13·6 per cent). Yet the population was highly diversified (see Table 17–3), and mixed clerical and civil service employees who enjoyed relatively high income and job stability with industrial and construction workers suffering low incomes and high job–turnover rates.

What really matters was the internal diversity of the 'marginal settlements' and the fact that many of their dwellers came from other sectors of the city and not from impoverished rural areas. Urban marginality did not correlate with occupational marginality. People in Caracas lived in these self-constructed settlements because they were the only ones that they could afford. Even during a period of sustained economic growth, 1970–77, the rise in family income, in nominal terms, was 196 per cent but the cost of living increased by 300 per cent. The employment situation was not the cause of urban deterioration. Although the different dimensions of marginality do relate to each other, this relationship is a social process which has to be revealed by research and explained by adequate theory.

As we said above, several studies have shown the lack of empirical support for assuming covariation between residential, occupational, cultural, and political marginality.[28] At this point, we would like to provide a more precise idea as to the social content of the different situations contained in idea of marginality, and then try to show how, basically, the political process links them. If we can do this, then it would suggest that the marginality phenomenon is not a political determinant but a political outcome.

Table 17.2 Social composition of 11 urban popular settlements, Santiago de Chile, 1968 and 1969.

	Year 1969					Year 1968						Average % for Settlement 1-5 and 6-11	
	Urban Population Settlements												
	1	2	3	4	5	6	7	8	9	10	11		
	Villa 4 Sep.	R. Kennedy	Sta. Olga	M. Rodr.	Lo Ferrer	Sta. Mónica	La Faena I	La Faena II	Herminda o la Victoria I	Herminda o la Victoria II	Valledor Norte		
Social Groups	%	%	%	%	%	%	%	%	%	%	%	%	%
Lumpenproletariat	18	8·5	8	8·5	45	37	25	25	33	17	17	18	26·5
Unskilled working class	58	48	48	35	18	33	38	45·5	35·5	49	22·5	41	36·5
Skilled working class	14	21	31	39·5	25	13	20	20·5	23	23	34	26	21·5
Clerks and lower middle class	9	23	13	12	12	17	17	9	8·5	11	27	15	15·5
	100	100	100	100	100	100	100	100	100	100	100	100	100

Sources: a) We established the categories and re-calculated the figures. For definitions and justification see: M. Castells, *La Lucha de Clases en Chile* (Buenos Aires: Siglo xxi, 1974, pp. 43–124)

b) Data collected by Franz Vanderschueren in 'Significado Politico de las Juntas de Vecinos', 1971.

Table 17.3 Distribution of residents among occupational categories in four major, deteriorated urban settlements, Caracas, 1978. (Percentage calculated on the total population of each zone.)

OCCUPATION	ZONES				
	Total 4 Zones	Barrios (Shanty towns)	Barracas (Shanty towns)	Casco (Slums)	Banco Obrero (Public housing)
Artisans	0·6	1·1	–	–	–
Workers	56·3	61·6	72·3	42·9	27·8
Industry	22·3	23·2	33·9	16·9	9·7
Services	25·7	27·3	33·0	23·4	12·5
Transportation	8·3	11·1	5·4	2·6	5·6
Self-employed	13·6	12·6	19·6	16·9	7·0
Industry	1·2	1·8	0·9	–	–
Commerce	7·6	6·2	10·7	13·0	4·2
Services	4·8	4·6	8·0	3·9	2·8
Clerical Workers	27·0	22·3	1·8	39·0	65·2
Government	10·8	6·2	–	20·8	33·3
Private	16·2	16·1	1·8	39·0	65·2
Professionals	0·2	–	–	1·2	–
Domestic servants	2·2	2·2	6·3	–	–
Illegal Activities	0·1	0·2	–	–	–
TOTAL	100·0	100·0	100·0	100·0	100·0

Source: Ricardo Infante and Magaly Sanchez, Survey of Caracas's segregated Residential Areas, 1980 (as cited in Methodological Appendix, p. 000)

The main reference supporting the myth of marginality concerns the occupational structure of dependent societies.[29] This structure is a consequence of uneven capitalist development, combined with a disintegration of existing productive forms which is not matched by the creation of new sources of employment.[30] In fact, the structure of occupations for a dependent society presents a series of conditions that we cannot organize under a single concept. Paradoxically, we could say that the only occupational situation which is almost non-existent in a dependent society is unemployment because, strictly speaking, unemployment (that is, the absence of a regularly paid labour activity) is a 'privilege' of advanced capitalist countries, as well as of a tiny labour aristocracy of developing countries, strong enough to obtain 'unemployment insurance'. The average person in Venezuela, Mexico, Chile and Peru, cannot live without working – something must be done to earn money to survive. And, in fact, everybody does some kind of work although only a minority receives a regular paycheque.[31] These are, in fact, the basic dynamics of the so-called 'informal sector' or, as it also described, of occupational marginality which has four main components, each of which is entirely different from the others:[32]

1 *Salaried workers of the 'traditional' sector of the economy* that is, the sector which is only loosely linked to the functioning of capital acccumulation at the world scale. We could also include in this category many workers employed on the spot under subcontracting arrange-

ments, a particularly frequent practice in the construction industry. From the characteristics of this 'traditional' capital one can deduce the characteristics of the labour it employs:

a Exploited above the social average, yielding a higher rate of absolute surplus value through lower wages, longer working time, worse working conditions, and lack of social benefits. According to Mesa-Lago, 77 per cent of the economically active population of five Latin American nations were excluded from any coverage under the national social security system.[33]

b Instability of employment and uncertainty of labour contracts.

Here we are dealing with the working class proletariat of the small business sector of the economy, structured around the interests of 'fringe capital' (as opposed to corporate capital) and quite similar to the backward and 'underground' sectors of advanced capitalist economies. Yet the crucial historical difference in Latin America is the much greater importance of this sector, both as a source of employment and as a source of income.

2 *Small merchants and handicraft persons* occupied in activities of exchange and petty commodity production which express the cultural values and economic needs of a given society. For instance, in Mexico City we found in the popular neighbourhood of El Tepito a great number of families living off a very original skill: the transformation of dirty street dogs into luxurious 'pure bred' animals to be sold in the fashionable city centre pet shops. In a similar way we could refer to all kinds of street vendors selling a variety of commodities from religious medals to chewing gum whose main characteristic is to sell in very small quantities (one mango fruit in one morning seemed to be an acceptable trade in Mexico City in 1976). Such trade and handicraft activities correspond, in fact, to the structure of consumption in large sectors of dependent societies. In this sense, they are not 'marginal' but basic elements of a commercial structure geared to popular consumption, as well as key elements for the cheap reproduction of labour power in the overall economy.

3 *Sellers of their labour to people* for the personal service and consumption of the buyers, instead of using this labour power to obtain a surplus value. Here we could include all domestic service, as well as an endless variety of personal services (shoeshine boys, porters, guides, *recaderos*, etc.). We call all these occupational positions a 'subproletariat': 'proletariat' because there is a selling of the labour power and 'sub' because this selling is not included in the production or circulation of the surplus value.

4 *Sellers of their bodies* what we could call 'skin sellers', that is, the provision of a service by virtue of the 'purchase' of their body. Prostitutes, beggars, bodyguards, delinquents exchange their survival against the possibility of potential destruction (total or partial) or trade their deterioration (in the case of the beggars). This situation (which is one that the classical works of Marxism named 'lumpenproletariat') apparently contradicts the institutionalized social norms. In fact, their different activities are absolutely necessary for the existence of such norms and institutions because they maintain the borderline between the social dilemma of society and the underground, of normal and abnormal behaviour, of the existing order and urban chaos.

Outside the occupational structure *stricto sensu* we can also find many people involved in self-subsistence agriculture, able to feed themselves without entering the commercial networks of goods distribution. Most of this 'urban farming' takes place within the squatter settlements.

These are the main occupational situations to which marginality refers. And, in fact, they represent a substantial proportion of the Latin American population. But they are not the source of urban marginality because the urban-spatial dimension of marginality refers to the majority of the population's inability to have access to the private housing and private urban services markets (and even those of the public sector). In Mexico 65 per cent of the national population (47 per cent in Mexico City) is included in this category[34] and, of course, among them we find families from all four types of occupational marginality that we have distinguished. But there are also in the same situation a great proportion of workers from the formal economic sector, as well as clerks and civil servants of the public sector. So urban marginality suggests something broader than occupational marginality and the overlap between the two is only partial. Let us now, therefore, turn to consider the profile of so-called 'urban marginality'.

18

The Structural Causes of Urban Marginality

Urban marginality can be defined as the inability of the market economy, or of state policies, to provide adequate shelter and urban services to an increasing proportion of city dwellers, including the majority of the regularly employed salaried workers, as well as practically all people making their earnings in the so-called 'informal' sector of the economy.

If we consider the situation in Caracas, according to the survey conducted by Ricardo Infante and Magaly Sanchez, Table 18–1 shows clearly that families were living in 'marginal areas' because of lack of housing (39·78 per cent) or because they were displaced by some of the urban programmes such as urban renewal and highway construction (42 per cent). Only a small minority (18·16 per cent) referred to their critical housing situation as a consequence of their low level of income or their lack of a stable job. And yet most of these families lived in the

Table 18.1 Segregated residential zones of Caracas, 1978, residents over ten years; reasons for moving from their former residence.

REASONS FOR MOVING	TYPE OF RESIDENTIAL SETTLEMENT					
to the Settlement	*Barrios*	*Barracas*	*Banco Obrero*	*Casco*	*Urbanizaciones*	*Total*
Low income and unemployment	1,231 (15·66%)	–	53 (27·04%)	428 (35·76%)	134 (14·87%)	1,846 (18·16%)
Housing problems	3,135 (39·89%)	14 (100%)	52 (26·53%)	398 (33·25%)	446 (49·50%)	4,045 (39·78%)
Displacement and others	3,493 (44·45%)	–	91 (46·43%)	371 (30·49%)	321 (35·63%)	4,276 (42·06%)
TOTAL	7,859 (100·0%)	14 (100·0%)	196 (100·0%)	1,197 (100·0%)	901 (100·0%)	10,167 (100·0%)

Source: Ricardo Infante and Magaly Sanchez, *Reproduccion de la Fuerza de Trabajo es la Estructura Urbana la Condicion de la Clase Trabajadora en Zonas Segregadas de Caracas* (Caracas: Universidad Central de Venezuela, Instituto de Urbanismo, 1980, 4 Volumes).

Casco, that is, the slums of the urban core. Thus, dilapidated housing and self-constructed settlements can be identified as the product of the crisis in the urban system, and not of the absence of industrialization causing widespread unemployment.

There is a great diversity of housing situations within the 'marginal settlements'. In the Caracas survey, the following typology was established:

1 *Barrios de ranchos* – self-constructed housing on useless urban land.
2 *Barracas* – poor quality, state-produced, public housing, mainly used to relocate tenants displaced by urban programmes.
3 Slums concentrated in the *Casco* (urban core), using all kinds of physical structures, ranging from abandoned industrial sites to dilapidated old housing.

Plate 18.1 Squatter settlements – a way of urban life in Latin America. Barrio La Vega, Caracas, 1977. (Photograph: F. Molina.)

4 Public housing, produced by the Public Housing Agency, *Banco Obrero*, which was mainly for the lower middle class strata in spite of its substandard condition. The acceptance of such bad quality housing by relatively well-to-do families is a clear indication of the depth of the housing crisis and its impact on a broad range of social groups.

The interesting feature of the Caracas survey is that it expands the image of urban marginality beyond the arbitrary definition of squatter settlements. The study shows that only about 36 per cent of 'marginal housing' in Caracas was self constructed, 30 per cent having been built by the state, and the remaining stock being produced under some form of private builder's contract. And yet the lack of urban services, the unhealthy conditions, the lack of public transportation (when 58 per cent of the families in Caracas do not own a car) was all very similar.[35]

We can, therefore, make two basic conclusions, according to the findings of the Caracas study:

1 Urban marginality does not coincide with occupational marginality. It is, rather, the consequence of the crisis of the urban system, unable to respond to the needs of a majority of the population.

2 The situation of the so-called marginal settlements, although very similar in terms of the critical level of deterioration of housing and urban facilities, is highly diverse as regards the type of buildings, the location in the spatial structure, and the legal status of each settlement. To consider the urban world of all these very different settlements as a unit is a mistaken empirical statement. In fact, the common factor in these wide-ranging situations of urban decay is a social construction whose logic owes a great deal to state policies, as we will see in a later stage of the analysis.

The situation in Caracas is by no means unique. It parallels very clearly the results of a study we made on the housing crisis of Mexico City using data provided by three different research teams (El Colegio de Mexico, Centro Operacional de Politica y Estudios sobre Vivienda (COPEVI) and Equipo de Sociologia Urbana (EQUISUR)) which were completed more or less at the same time in 1976, as the most accurate assessment of urban marginality and public policies in Mexico.[36]

As in Caracas, the urban crisis in Mexico had two major aspects: first, the shortage of housing units for the majority of the metropolitan population, and, second, the lack of services (water, sewerage, etc.) for a high proportion of the existing housing stock (see Table 18–2).

Table 18.2 Characteristics of housing in the metropolitan area of Mexico City 1960 and 1970. (Percentage of total housing units in the area.)

	% with less than 3 rooms	% with non-paved floor	% with no reliable walls	% without water	% without sewerage	Total Number
1960						
Housing units	65·9%	no data	28·1%	45·6%	45·1%	902,083
Dwellers	62·1%	no data	25·4%	49·4%	45·7%	4,870,876
1970						
Housing units	54·3%	5·8%	11·7%	36·0%	21·5%	1,219,419
Dwellers	51·3%	6·4%	12·1%	37·3%	22·5%	6,874,165

Source: Secretaria de Industria y Commercio, *Censo General de Poblacion*, 1960 and 1970.

According to the study of El Colegio de Mexico, the shortage in housing units in the Mexican cities in 1970 amounted to 1·6 million units: 40·2 per cent of these units were families in dilapidated housing and 27·1 per cent were families living in overcrowded conditions. The predictions of the team for the decade 1970–80 clearly demonstrated the inevitable worsening of the situation gives the circumstances of the time: to cope with population growth and to reduce the deficit 12·3 million housing units should have been built in those ten years, while the entire housing stock of Mexico in 1970 was 8·3 million units.[37]

The causes of such a situation are the same for most Latin American societies: the private market required prices or rents that could only be afforded by 9·5 per cent of the population of Mexico City; the state-subsidized housing asked for a level of income or of job stability which could only be met by 43·5 per cent of the population. Therefore, 46·5 per cent of the metropolitan dwellers had no chance of obtaining any housing. Furthermore, the public housing programmes were very limited, and most families eligible for these were excluded from real access to available housing.

As a result of this situation, the overwhelming majority of housing in Mexico City was produced and distributed neither by 'normal' capitalist firms nor the public agencies, but by what was called the 'popular housing sector' based upon three interlinking elements: first, a considerable amount of work provided by the housing occupants themselves (self construction, land clearance, maintenance and repair); second, the state's tolerance of the illegal status of most housing settlements; and third, investment by speculative private capital operating outside the legal limits through a variety of intermediaries. Such capital was not marginal although it was invested through some 'straw firm' realtors. In reality it had strong ties with the most powerful real estate financial networks. Table 18–3 shows the sustained importance of the 'popular' (self-constructed) sector of housing for the whole country.

Table 18.3   Production of housing units according to different sectors Mexico, 1950–1974. (Thousands of new housing units.)

	1950–1960		1961–1970		1970–1974	
	Units	%	Units	%	Units	%
Total	1,150	100·0	1,877	100·0	1,204·3	100·0
Public sector	62	5·4	175	9·3	223·7	18·0
Private sector	331	28·8	503	26·8	205·7	16·5
Popular sector	757	65·8	1,199	63·9	810·9	65·5

Source: Hugh Evans, *Towards a Policy for Housing Low Income Families in Mexico 1950–1970* (Department of Architecture, Cambridge University, 1970–74). Estimates by G. Garza and M. Schteingart, El Colegio de Mexico.

A wide variety of housing forms could be found, as in Caracas, within the 'popular sector'. A careful study by the COPEVI team has established a reliable quantitative evaluation of dwellers living in the various kinds of houses in Mexico City. There were three major types of 'marginal' settlement:[38]

1 The *colonias proletarias* made up of self-constructed housing units, generally illegally settled. 60 per cent of the population of the metropolitan area of Mexico City was in such housing in 1975. Squatters' invasions of land were generally not spontaneous moves. They were organized by professional squatters, connected with the local authorities as well as with the illegal private real estate developers. The squatters were then allowed to settle there

illegally under the protection of the organizers, as long as they paid a regular amount of money, according to the market price of illegal settlements.[38bis] Therefore, what the *colono* was paying for was the capacity of the illegal developer to win tolerance from the public authorities for the settlement. The *colonos* were very often expelled from their houses as a result of this unstable situation, in order to start the game again with new squatters. The illegal developers had their own network of local bosses to control the situation in the settlements, as well as their own 'private militia' to enforce whatever decisions they took. Most of the settlements were on public or communal land (*terrenos ejidales*). According to the Mexican Constitution, such land may not be sold or transferred meaning that squatting was not only a way to house people by taking advantage of their critical need, but also a way to introduce a huge stock of land into the legal private market that could not otherwise be urbanized, or would have to be developed under severe public controls after open, planned land-use reallocation.[39]

2 A second type of popular housing were the *vecindades* or slums: multi-family rental housing units, privately owned and generally located in the oldest portion of Mexico City. Many of the houses were subjected to rent control, discouraging any repair by the owners. These were, arguably, the most dilapidated shelters in the city, and tended to crumble during the rainy season. Two million people were living in the slums in 1975.

3 Finally, the shanty towns or *ciudades perdidas*, illegal settlements organized by the squatters themselves in the middle of the existing city unlike the peripheral *colonias proletarias*. The main difference between this type and the first was that they were relatively autonomous and tried to connect themselves to the existing urban services. They were the only really uncontrolled settlements, and this was why they were systematically demolished and, as a result, accounted for less than 100,000 people in Mexico City in 1975.

The most dramatic condition common to all types of 'popular housing' was the almost complete lack of collective urban facilities. In the peripheral area of Ciudad Netzahualcoyotl, most of the approximately two million inhabitants did not have water or sewerage in 1976. In the illegal settlement of Ecatepec, where 400,000 people lived, the rainy season meant almost continuous flooding, while during the dry period dust and wind caused a high rate of lung infection. This was because Ecatepec has been built on the dried portion of the old Vaso de Texcoco lake, which was uninhabited except for the 'invisible' shelter provided by 'illegal developers' who relied on the tolerance of public authorities.

Thus, again and again we find at the roots of 'urban marginality' the state employing different policies for different social groups, and the abuse of this attitude by economic groups or political forces taking advantage of a deadlock situation over the marginality of urban dwellers.[40] Which is why we should like to reverse the argument and ask what are the socio-political processes leading to the production and management of the urban crisis, instead of considering the crisis as an almost natural catastrophe with its own political consequences.

Nevertheless, in spite of all empirical evidence gathered against it, the 'marginality theory' persists, relying on the merger of occupational and ecological marginality, and the consequent production of a cultural type, the 'marginal personality'. The reason for the social persistence of such a theory, even though it has been dismantled by ten years of research and criticism, is that it is in fact highly functional for the new political strategy of the state in many dependent societies. To adapt to new international economic conditions, the state tries to organize and mobilize popular sectors around its development policies and to overcome any social class divisions. The merging of the two dimensions of 'marginality' allows the state to treat workers, clerks, and popular sectors as 'marginals' and to expand this single-minded category to all 'urban marginals', that is, to the majority of people unable to solve the problems of housing and services created by uneven development and metropolitan concentration. The world of marginality is in fact socially constructed by the state, in a process of social integration and political mobilization in exchange for goods and services which only it can provide. Thus the relationship between the state and the people is organized around the institutional distribution of urban services coupled with the institutional mechanisms of political control.

Now this process, like all political projects, is shaped, transformed, and sometimes reversed by the dynamics of social conflicts. The politics of marginality depends upon political constraints and historical variations, but its evolution will result from the form and orientation of urban mobilizations triggered by urban needs and state policies.

19

Squatters and the State: The Dialectics between Social Integration and Social Change (Case Studies in Lima, Mexico, and Santiago de Chile)

The conditions of urbanization in Latin American societies force an increasing proportion of the metropolitan population to live in squatter settlements or in slum areas. This situation is not external to the structural dynamics of the Third World, but is connected to the speculative functioning of some sectors of capital as well as to the peculiar patterns of popular consumption in the so-called informal economy.[41] On the basis of their situation in the urban structure, the squatters tend to organize themselves at the community level. Their organization does not imply, by itself, any kind of involvement in a process of social change. On the contrary, as we have pointed out, most of the existing evidence points to a subservient relationship with the dominant economic and political powers.[42] Nevertheless, the fact of a relatively strong local organization is itself a distinctive feature which clearly differentiates the squatters from other urban dwellers who are predominantly organized at the work place or in political parties, when and if they are organized at all.

Furthermore, the state's attitude towards squatter settlements predetermines most of their characteristics. Thus the connection between the squatters and the political process is a very close one. And it is precisely in this way that urbanization, and its impact on community organization, becomes a crucial aspect of political evolution in Latin America. Let us, therefore, explore the relationship between squatters and the state in three major Latin American countries: Peru, Mexico, and Chile.

Squatters and Populism: The Barriadas of Lima[43]

Lima's spectacular urban growth has mainly been due to the expansion of *barriadas*, peripheral[44] substandard settlements, often illegal in their early stage, and generally deprived of basic urban facilities. The population of the *barriadas* came, on the one hand, from the slums of central Lima (*tugurios*) once they had reached bursting point or when they were demolished, and on the other hand, from accelerated rural and regional migration,[45] the structural causes of which were the same as for all dependent societies.[46] And in Peru, this particular form of urbanization – the *barriadas* – cannot be explained without reference to the action of political forces as well as to the state's policies.[47] Given the illegal nature of land invasion by population of the *barriadas*, only institutional permissiveness or the strength of the movement (or a combination of both) can explain such a phenomenon. More specifically, given the way power has been unevenly distributed within Peruvian society until very recent times, the land invasion must be understood to have been the result, in part, of policies that originated from various dominant sectors. Very often landowners and private developers have manipulated the squatters into forcing portions of the land onto the real estate market, by obtaining from the authorities some urban infrastructure for the squatters, thus enhancing the land value and opening the way for profitable housing construction. In a second stage, the squatters are expelled from the land they have occupied and forced to start all over again on the frontier of a city which has expanded as a result of their efforts.

Nevertheless, the main factor underlying the intensity of urban land invasion in Lima has been a political strategy consisting of protection given for the invasion in exchange for poor people's support. Table 19-1, constructed by David Collier on the basis of his study of 136 of Lima's *barriadas*, clearly shows the political context for the peak moments of urban land invasion between 1900 and 1972.[48] The political strategies and their actual effects on the squatters were really very different from one land invasion to another.

Table 19.1 Number and population of *barriadas* (squatter settlements) formed in Lima in each presidential term, 1900–1972.

President	Number of Cases	% of cases	Population	Percentage of population
Before Sánchez Cerro (1900–30)	2	1·5	2,712	0·4
Sánchez Cerro (1930–31, 1931–33)	3	2·2	12,975	1·7
Benavides (1933–39)	8	5·9	18,888	2·5
Prado (1939–45)	8	5·9	6,930	0·9
1945 – Information uncertain	5	3·7	24,335	3·2
Bustamante (1945–48)	16	11·8	38,545	5·1
Odría (1948–56)	30	22·1	203,877	26·9
1956 – Information uncertain	2	1·5	11,890	1·6
Prado (1956–62)	30	22·1	93,249	12·3
1962 – Information uncertain	2	1·5	22,377	2·9
Pérez Godoy (1962–63)	2	1·5	1,737	0·2
Lindley (1963)	3	2·2	11,046	1·5
Belaúnde (1963–68)	15	11·0	93,407	12·3
Velasco (1968–1972 only)	10	7·4	217,050	28·6
Total	136	100·3	759,018	100·1

Source: David Collier, *Barriadas y Elites: De Odria à Velasco* (Lima: Instituto de Estudios Peruanos, 1976; updated 1978).

The most spectacular stage in the history of land invasions corresponds to the initiative of General Odria's government in 1948–56. At a time of political repression against the Communist Party, and particularly against Alianza Popular Revolucionaria Americana (APRA – which was trying to seize power to implement an 'anti-imperialist programme'), Odria's populism was a direct attempt to mobilize people on his side by offering to distribute land and urban services. The aim was to dispute APRA's political influence by taking advantage of the urban poor's low level of political organization and consciousness, and by mobilizing people around issues outside the work place where the pro-APRA union leaders would be more vulnerable. Nevertheless, APRA's reaction was very rapid: they demanded that Odria keep his promises to the squatters' organizations by accelerating the invasion, and the final outcome was a political crisis and the downfall of Odria's government.

We can understand, then, why Prado's government, supported by APRA, continued to be interested in the *barriadas* in order to eliminate the remaining pro-Odria circles and to widen its popular basis. Instead of stimulating new invasions, Prado launched a programme of housing and service delivery for the popular neighbourhoods, trying to integrate these sectors into the government's policy without mobilizing them. In a complementary move, APRA started formally controlling the organizations of squatters (the *Asociaciones de Pobladores*) in order to expand its political machine from the trade unions to the social organizations centred on residential issues.

Belaunde's urban policy was very different. Although he also looked for some support from the squatters, allowing and stimulating land invasions, he did not limit his activity to the struggle against the APRA, but tried a certain rationalization of the whole process. His Law of *Barriadas* was the first attempt to adapt urbanization to the general interest of Peruvian capitalist development without adopting a particular set of political interests. The activity of his party, Accion Popular, was aimed at modernizing the *barriadas* system and facilitating an effective connection with the broader interests of corporate capital. The social control of the squatters was then organized by international agencies, Churches, and humanitarian organizations, which were closely linked to the interests of the American Government.[49] Belaunde's strategy was quite effective in weakening APRA's political influence among the *pobladores*, but it was unable to provide a new form of social control established on solid ground. This situation determined a very important change in the government's strategy after the establishment of a military junta in the revolution of 1968. At the beginning, the military government tried to implement a law-and-order policy, repressing all illegal invasions and putting the *asociaciones de pobladores* under the control of the police. Nevertheless, its attitude towards the *barriadas* changed dramatically on the basis of two major factors: first, the difficulty of counteracting a basic mechanism that determines the housing crises in the big cities of dependent societies, and second, the military government's need to obtain very rapidly some popular support for the modernizing policies once these policies had come under attack from the conservative landlords and business circles.

The turning point appears to have been the *Pamplonazo* in May 1971. An invasion of urban land in the neighbourhood of Pamplona was vigorously repressed and provoked an open conflict between the Minister of Interior, General Artola, and Bishop Bambaren, nicknamed the '*Barriadas* Bishop', who was jailed. The crisis between the state and the Catholic Church moved President General Velasco Alvarado to act personally on the issue. He conceded most of the *pobladores*' demands, but moved them to a very arid peripheral zone close to Lima, where he invited them to start a 'self-help' community supported by the government. This was the beginning of Villa El Salvador, a new city which in 1979 housed up to 300,000 inhabitants recruited among the Lima dwellers and rural migrants looking for a home in the metropolitan area.

The military government learned a very important lesson from this crisis: not only did it discover the dangers of a purely repressive policy, but also realized the potential advantages of mobilizing the *pobladores*. Using the Church's experience, the military government created a special agency, the *Oficina Nacional de Pueblos Jovenes* (New Settlements' National Office), charged with legalizing the land occupations and with organizing material and institutional aid to the *barriadas*. At the same time, within the framework of Sistema Nacional de Movilizacion Social (SINAMOS), the regime's 'social office', a special section was created to organize and lead the *pobladores*. Under the new measures, each residential neighbourhood in the *barriadas* had to elect its representatives who would eventually become the partners of the government officials, controlling the distribution of material aid and urban facilities. At the same time, the new institution relied on the existing agencies and voluntary associations (most of them linked to Churches and international agencies) to tailor their functions and co-ordinate their activity to the parameters set by state policy. This policy would develop along several paths: economic (popular savings institutions, production and consumption co-operatives); legal (laws recognizing the squatting of urban land); ideological (legitimizing of the *pobladores'* associations, propaganda centres for the government); and political (active involvement in the Peruvian 'revolution' through SINAMOS). The *barriadas* became a crucial focus of popular mobilization for the new regime.

As a consequence of the successive encouragements given to squatter mobilization by the state, as well as by the political parties, the *barriadas* of Lima grew in extraordinary proportions: their population grew from 100,000 in 1940 to 1,000,000 in 1970 and became an ever larger proportion of the population in most of Lima's districts.

Nevertheless, it would be wrong to conclude that all forms of mobilization were identical save for different ideological stances. In his study, Etienne Henry makes clear some fundamental differences in practice. Odria's and Prado's policies expressed the same relationship to the *pobladores*, patronizing them to reinforce each's political constituencies. In the case of Belaunde, the action to integrate people was subordinated to the effort of rationalizing urban development. The military government's policy between 1971 and 1975 represented a significant change in urban policy. It was not an attempt to build up partisan support for a particular political machine but was, in fact, a very ambitious project to establish a new and permanent relationship between the state and urban popular sectors through the controlled mobilization of the *barriadas* now transformed into *pueblos jovenes* (new settlements). This transformation was much more than a change in name: it expressed the holding of all economic and political functions of the *pobladores'* voluntary associations by the state in exchange for the delivery and management of required urban services. The goal was no longer to obtain a political constituency but to build a 'popular movement' mobilized around the values promoted by the revolutionary regime. In this sense, the *barriadas* became closely linked to Peruvian politics and were increasingly reluctant to adapt to the new government's orientation resulting from the growing influence of the conservative wing within the army.

The picture of the Lima squatters' movement appears as one of a manipulated mob, changing from one political ideology to another in exchange for the delivery (or promise) of land, housing, and services. And this was, to a large extent, the case. The *pobladores'* attitude was quite understandable if we remember that all politically progressive alternatives were always defeated and ferociously repressed. So, as Anthony and Elizabeth Leeds[50] have pointed out, the behaviour of the squatters was not cynical or apolitical, but, on the contrary, deeply realistic, and displayed an awareness of the political situation and how their hard-pressed demands could be obtained. Thus it appears that the Peruvian urban movement was, until 1976, dependent upon various populist strategies of controlled mobilization. That is, the movement was, in its various stages, a vehicle for carrying the social integration of the urban popular sectors in the same direction as the political strategies of the different political sectors of the dominant classes.

Now this process, like all controlled mobilizations, expresses a contradiction between the effectiveness of the mobilization and the fulfillment of the goals assigned to the movement. When these goals are delayed as a result of the structural limits to social reform and when people's organization and consciousness grow, some attempts at autonomous social mobilization occur. A sign of this evolution was, in the case of Lima, the organization of the *Barriada Independencia* in 1972. When the autonomous mobilization expanded, the government tried to stop it by means of violent repression as it did, for example, in March 1974. In spite of repression, the movement continued its opposition, making alliances with the trade unions and with the radical left, as was revealed in the *barriadas'* massive participation in the strikes against the regime in 1976, 1978, and 1979. After the dismantling of SINAMOS by the new military president, Morales Bermudez, the political control of the *barriadas* rapidly collapsed. Ironically, Villa El Salvador became one of the most active centres of opposition to the state's new conservative leadership.

This evolution supports a crucial hypothesis. The replacement of a classic patronizing relationship, ruling class to popular sectors, by controlled populist mobilization expands the hegemony of the ruling class over the popular sectors which are organized under the label of 'urban marginals'. But the crisis of such an hegemony, if it does happen, has far more serious consequences for the existing social order than the breaking of the traditional patronizing ties of a political machine. In fact, it is this type of crisis that enables the initiation of an autonomous popular movement, the further development of which will depend on its capacity to establish a stable and flexible link with the broader process of class struggle.

Our analysis of the Lima experience, although excessively condensed, provides some significant findings:

1 An urban movement can be an instrument of social integration and subordination to the existing political order instead of an agent of social change. (This is, in fact, the most frequent trend in squatter settlements in Latin America.)
2 The subordination of the movement can be obtained by political parties representing the interests of different factions of the ruling class and/or by the state itself. The results are different in each case. When the movement has close ties with the state, then urban policies become a crucial aspect of change in dependent societies.
3 Since urbanization in developing countries is deeply marked by a growing proportion of squatter settlements (out of the total urban population), it appears that the forms and levels of such urbanization will largely depend upon the relationship established between the state and the popular sectors. This explains why we consider urban politics to be the major explanatory variable of the characteristics of urbanization.
4 When squatter movements break their relationship of dependency *vis-à-vis* the state, they may become potential agents of social change. Yet their fate is ultimately determined by the general process of political conflict.

Between Caciquismo and Utopia: The *Colonos* of Mexico City and the *Posesionarios* of Monterrey

Mexico's accelerated urban growth is a social process full of contradictions.[51] An expression of these contradictions during the seventies were the ever increasing mobilizations by the popular sectors and urban squatters to obtain their demands in the *vecindades* (slums) and *colonias proletarias* (squatters settlements on the periphery) of the largest Mexican cities.[52] The potential strength of this urban mobilization must be seen in the context of a political system that was perfectly capable of controlling and integrating all signs of social protest.[52bis]

In traditional squatter settlements on the periphery of big cities, the key element was a very strong community organization under the tight control of leaders who were the intermediaries between the squatters (*colonos*) and the administration officials. In its early stages, this form of community organization maybe considered to be dominated by *caciquismo*, that is, by the personal and authoritarian control of a leader, himself recognized and backed by local authorities. Therefore illegal land invasion, by itself, did not present a challenge to the prevailing social order. Indeed, economically, it represented a way to activate the capitalist, urban land market, and politically, was a major element in the social control of people in search of shelter. What must be emphasized is that *caciquismo* was not an isolated phenomenon, but had a major function to fulfill within both the political system and the state's urban policies. The local leaders were not neighbourhood bosses living in a closed world: they were representatives of political power through their relationships with the administration and with the Partido Revolucionario Institucional (PRI) – the government's party – from which they obtained their resources and their legitimacy. So Mexican squatters have always been well organized in their communities, and this organization has performed two major functions: on the one hand, it has allowed them to exert pressure for their demands to stay in the land they have occupied and to obtain the delivery of urban services; on the other hand, it has represented a major channel of subordinated political participation by ensuring that their votes and support goes to the PRI. Both aspects have, in fact, been complementary, and the *caciques* (the community bosses) were the agents of this process. They were not, however, the real bosses of the squatters, since they exercised their power on behalf of the PRI. To understand this situation we must remember the historical and popular roots of the PRI, and the need for it to continuously renew its role of organizing the people politically while providing access to work, housing, and services in exchange for loyalty to the PRI's programme and leadership.

Thus the new urban movements that developed in Mexico during the 1970s derived from a previous network of voluntary associations existing in the *vecindades* and *colonias* which were, at the same time, channels for expressing demands and vehicles of political integration with PRI. Taking into consideration the ideological hegemony of the PRI and the violent repression exercised against any alternative form of squatter organization, how can we explain the upheaval caused by autonomous urban movements since 1968? And what were their characteristics and possibilities?

Two major factors seem to have favoured the development of these movements:

1 President Echeverria's reformism (1970–76) to some extent recognised the right to protest outside the established channels, while legitimizing aspirations to improve the living conditions in cities.[53]
2 Political radicalism among students, after the 1968 movement, provided militants who tried to use the squatter communities as a ground on which to build a new form of autonomous political organization.

This explains how the evolution of the new urban movements came to be determined by the interaction between the interests of the squatters, the reformist policy of the administration, and the experience of a new radical left, learning how to lead urban struggles.

From the outset of urban mobilization, radicals tried to organize and politicize some squatter settlements, linking their urban demands to the establishment of permanent bases of revolutionary action and propaganda within these settlements. These attempts were often unable either to overcome the squatters' fears of reprisal, or to uproot the PRI's solid political organization. When the radicals did succeed in their attempt to organize a squatter settlement as a revolutionary community, the state resorted to large scale violence having taken prior care to undermine the movement by claiming it had subversive contacts with underground guerillas. The most typical example was the *colonia* Ruben-Jaramillo in the city of Cuernavaca, where radical militants organized more than 25,000 squatters, helped them to improve their living conditions, and raised the level of their political awareness. The *colonia's* radicalism prompted a violent response by the army which occupied and put it under the control of a specialized public agency to deal with squatter settlements.

Nevertheless, other settlements resisted police repression and survived by maintaining a high level of organization and political mobilization. The best-known case is the Campamento 2 de Octobre in Ixtacalco in the Mexico City metropolitan area. Four thousand families illegally invaded a piece of highly valued urban land where both private and public developers had considerable interests. Students and professionals backed the movement and some of them went to live with the squatters to help their organization. The squatters kept their autonomy *vis-à-vis* the government, and used their strong bargaining position to call for a general political opposition to the PRI's policies. They became the target of the most conservative sectors of the Mexican establishment. After a long series of provocations by paid gangs, the police attacked the campamento in January 1976, starting a fire and injuring many of the squatters. Some days later, several hundred families returned to the settlement, reconstructed their houses, and started to negotiate with the government to obtain the legal rights to remain there. But if repression could not dismantle the campamento, it succeeded in isolating it by making it too dangerous an example to be followed by other squatters. When the Ixtacalco squatters tried to organize around themselves a Federacion de Colonias Proletarias to unite the efforts of other settlements, they obtained little support given their image of extreme radicalism. In fact, their demands were relatively modest, consisting of the legalization of the settlement and a minimum level of service. But the repression was very severe because the government saw a major danger in the movement's will to autonomy, its capacity to link urban demands and political criticism, and its appeal to other political sectors to build an opposition front, bypassing the political apparatus of the PRI within the communities. At the same time, police action was made easier by the political naïveté of some of the students, who at the beginning of the movement thought of the settlement as a 'liberated zone' and spent much of their energy on verbal radicalism. In this sense, Ixtacalco was an extraordinarily advanced example of autonomous urban mobilization, but was also a very isolated experience which went forward by itself without considering the general level of urban struggle in elsewhere Mexico City.

In fact, the most important urban movements in recent years have taken place in northern Mexico, particularly in Chihuahua, Torreon, Madero, and above all in Monterrey, where the movement of the *posesionarios* (squatters) was perhaps one of the most interesting and sizeable in Latin America. Let us examine this experience in some detail.

Monterrey, the third largest Mexican city with a population of 1,600,000, is a dynamic industrial area with an important steel industry. It is dominated by a local bourgeoisie with an old and strong tradition, cohesively organized and closely linked to American capital. The so-called Monterrey Group is a modernizing entrepreneurial class, politically conservative and socially paternalistic. It has always opposed state intervention, often criticized the PRI, and succeeded with its workers through a policy of social benefits and high salaries. In Monterrey, the powerful Confederacion de Trabajadores Mexicanos (CTM), the major labour union controlled by the PRI, is relatively unimportant since most workers have joined the *sindicatos blancos* (the white unions) which are manipulated by company management. The city, which is proud of maintaining the highest living standards in Mexico, has experienced a strong urban growth rate since 1940: 5·6 per cent annual growth 1940–50 and 1950–60, and 3·7 per cent in 1960–70. Urban immigration has been the result of both industrial growth and accelerated rural exodus caused by the rapid capitalist modernization of agriculture in northern Mexico. This urban growth has not, however, been matched by the increase in housing and urban services. The big companies have provided housing for their workers, but for the remaining people (one third of the population) there has been no available housing. The consequence has been, as in other Mexican cities, the invasion of surrounding land and massive construction of their own housing by the squatters. Three hundred thousand *posesionarios* have settled there. The underlying mechanisms were similar to those already described: speculation and illegal development on the one hand, and the role of the PRI's political machine as intermediary with local authorities on the other.

It was against this background that the student militants acted, trying to connect urban demands to political protest in the same mould as the university-based radicalism which began in 1971. The students led new land invasions contrary to the agreement with the administration. To differentiate themselves from the former settlements, the students called the new ones *colonias de lucha* (struggle settlements). In 1971 they founded the first settlement, Martires de San Cosme, in the arid zone of Topo Chico. The police immediately surrounded them, but withdrew after a month of violent clashes. Then the squatters built their houses and urban infrastructure and established a very elaborate social and political organization. The same process was renewed in the following years, and the cumulative effect made it extremely difficult to use repression as a means of halting their progress. The participants of each land invasion included not only its beneficiaries but also squatters already settled elsewhere who considered the new invasions as part of their own struggle. The timing of each invasion was extremely important as a means of averting repression: one of the most courageous invasions, in San Angel Bajo, succeeded in occupying good open space close to the municipal park without suffering reprisals because it was carried out on the eve of President Lopez Portillo's arrival in Monterrey during his electoral campaign of 1976. Once the invasion was accomplished, people raised the Mexican flag, running the red flag up a few weeks later. In similarly ingenious ways Tierra y Libertad, Revolucion Proletaria, Lucio Cabanas, Genaro Vasquez, and 24 other settlements were born and eventually combined in an alliance, the Frente Popular Tierra y Libertad, representing, at the time of our field work in August 1976, about 100,000 squatters.[54]

A key element in the success of the movement was its ability to take advantage of the internal contradictions of the ruling elite. For example, the Monterrey bourgeoisie openly opposed President Echeverria's reformism, and launched a major attack against the governor, who replied by trying to obtain support from the people. Using the themes of the governor's populist speeches as justification of their actions, the squatters made open repression against them more difficult. Nevertheless, the embittered local oligarchy, which controlled the city police, reacted by organizing continuous provocations. In one of the police actions, on 18 February 1976, six squatters were killed and many others wounded. The movement's protest was impressive, and signs of solidarity came from all over the country. There were street demonstrations in Monterrey for 15 days, some of them attracting over 40,000 people, organized jointly by squatters, students, and workers. For two months, the squatters occupied several public places. Finally, they were personally entertained by President Echeverria in Mexico City. Victims' relatives obtained economic compensation, an official inquiry was opened, the city police chief was ousted, and the government provided strong financial support for the revolutionary squatter settlements.

So, in a critical moment, the movement clearly displayed its strength and political capacity. But it also revealed its limits. To understand this crucial point, we must consider the organizational structure and the political principles of the Monterrey squatter's movement.

The basic idea, shared by all the squatters' leaders, was that struggles for urban demands were meaningful only as far as they allowed people to unite, to be organized, and to become politically aware, because (according to these leaders) such political strength was the only base from which to successfully plead for demands. On the other hand, they wanted to link the squatters' actions to a collective theme aimed, in the long term, to the revolutionary transformation of society. Only if these principles are remembered can some surprising aspects of the movement be understood. For instance, the squatters strongly opposed the legalization by the government of their illegal land occupation. Their reasons were threefold: economic, ideological, and political. Economically, legalization implied high payments for a long time under conditions that many families could not afford. Ideologically, the movement could be transformed into a pressure group *vis-à-vis* the state instead of asserting their natural right to the land. Above all, politically: legalization, by individualizing the problem and dividing the land would create a specific relationship between each squatter and the administration. Thus, the movement itself could be fragmented, lose its internal solidarity and be pushed towards the integration with the state's machinery. Therefore, to preserve their solidarity, cohesiveness, and strength (which they considered to be their only weapons), the squatters refused the property rights offered by the state, and expelled from the settlements those squatters who accepted the legal property title. A similar attitude was taken towards the delivery of services.

The squatters believed in self-reliance and rejected the state's help in the first stages of the movement. They did not, however, avoid contact with the state, since they were continuously engaged in negotiation, but wanted to preserve popular autonomy in a Mexican context where the political system is quite capable of swallowing up any initiative by a grassroots organization. So they stole construction materials or obtained them by putting pressure on the administration, but they collectively built the schools, health services, and civic centres, with excellent results (unlike most Mexican squatter settlements). Houses were built by each family but in lots of a collectively-decided size, in proportion to the size of the family and following a master plan approved by the settlement's General Assembly. Water, sewerage, and electricity were provided by illegal connections to the city systems. It is interesting to note that several settlements refused electric power in order to avoid television because it was considered a source of 'ideological pollution'. To overcome transport problems, the squatters seized buses on several occasions, finally forcing the bus company to adapt to the new urban structure. Schools were integrated into the general educational system and paid for by the state, but were controlled and managed by the Parents' Association in collaboration with the children's representatives. A similar organization managed health services. There was also in each settlement an Honour and Justice Committee which passed judgement on conflicts, the most serious of which were handled by the General Assembly. Alcohol and prostitution were strictly forbidden. Settlement leaders organized vigilante groups to protect the squatters. The general organization was based on a structure of block delegates which nominated the settlement committees which, in turn, reported to the General Assembly. There were a variety of voluntary associations, the strongest of which were the Women's Leagues and the Children's Leagues. The ideology of collective solidarity was reinforced. On Red Sundays – in 1976, every Sunday – everybody had to do collective work on shared urban facilities. There was also a high level of political and cultural activity run by 'activist brigades'.

Nevertheless, in spite of this extraordinary level of organization and consciousness, the *posesionarios'* movement in Monterrey suffered from the shortcomings of its isolation, geographical, social, and political. Geographically, it was the only urban movement of such size and character in the whole country. Socially, the squatters' population consisted almost entirely of unemployed, migrant peasants, having little contact with Monterrey's industrial workers. Politically, the leaders had no national audience and were only important at a local level.

The movement's leaders were well aware of this situation and of the danger of closing themselves into a new kind of communal Utopia. To break this isolation they tried to launch a scrics of actions to support 'fair causes': for instance, each time a worker was unjustifiably fired, the squatters occupied the manager's homeyard until the worker was reappointed. Each individual repression was faced by the whole movement, and so it became increasingly politicized. But such political radicalism based only on the squatters' support carried two major risks: first, increasing repression, chiefly from the army; and second, political infighting within the movement.

Two crucial elements emerge from the analysis of this extraordinary experience:

1 The speed and development of an urban movement cannot be separated from the general level of organization and consciousness in the broader process of political conflict.
2 The relationship to the state is not exhausted either by repression or integration. A movement may increase its autonomy by playing on the internal contradictions of the state. Monterrey was able to go further than Ixtacalco mainly because of the type of relationship which the *posesionarios* were able to establish with the state.

Such political, urban movements as Monterrey or Ixtacalco are only able to stabilize if the power relationships between social classes change in favour of the popular classes. But this does not seem to have been true of Mexico, so that the survival of these community organizations ultimately required some alliance with a sector within the state. Thus the experience of Mexico shows, again, the intimate connection between urban movements and the political system. We will now turn to the most important political squatter movement in recent Latin American history – Chile during the Unidad Popular – so that we may study this relationship in detail.

Urban Social Movements and Political Change: The *Pobladores* of Santiago de Chile, 1965–73[55]

The historical significance of urban movements in Chile between 1965 and 1973 has been surrounded by a confused mythology. Our respect for the Chilean popular movement requires a careful reconstruction of the facts, as well as a rigorous analysis of the experience.

The squatter movement in Chile was closely linked with class struggle and its political expressions,[56] and this explains both its importance and shortcomings. While invasions of urban land had always happened in Chile,[57] they changed their social implications when they became entrenched with the political strategies of conflicting social classes: urban popular movements reached a peak as a consequence of the failure of the Christian Democratic programme for urban reform.[58] The reform, initiated under Eduardo Frei's presidency in 1965, relied on three elements:

1 A programme of distribution of urban land (Operacion Sitio) combined with public support for the construction of housing by the people.

2 The formation of voluntary associations of *pobladores* and of housewives (*centros de madres*) linked to a series of public agencies, organized around the government's Department of Popular Promotion.

3 The decentralization of local governments after the creation in 1968 of advisory neighbourhood councils (*Juntas de Vecinos*), elected by the residents of each neighbourhood.[59]

In fact the programme of urban reform failed because of two constraints: the first from the structural limits of the system (the difficulty of redistributing resources without affecting the functioning of private capital),[60] and the second from the pressure of interest groups (mainly the Chilean Chamber of Private Builders, and the Savings and Loan institutions) which used the programme as a means of producing profitable housing for middle class families.[61]

As a consequence of this failure, the Christian Democrats lost control of the *pobladores'* movement and the neighbourhood councils became a political battlefield.[62] The movement started then to put pressure on the government in two ways: on the one hand, the residents of the popular neighbourhoods started asking for the delivery of promised services, and on the other thousands of families living with relatives or in shanties gathered to form Committees of the homeless (*Comites Sin Casa*). These committees, in the late 1960s, took the initiative of squatting on urban land to force the government to provide the housing and urban services promised in the reform programme.[63] In the first period of the movement, between 1965 and 1969, the government responded by repressing the invasions, even causing a massacre (Puerto Montt, March 1969) and partially succeeded in stopping the process.[64] But the presidential elections were scheduled for September 1970, and in the Christian Democratic Party the left had won endorsement for its leader, Tomic, against the wishes of the incumbent President Eduardo Frei. Therefore, an open repression of the *pobladores* might have been politically costly among the urban popular sectors, whose vote had been crucial for the electoral victory in 1964. So, when in 1970 the police were restricted in the use of violence, mass squatting was launched in most cities of the country, taking advantage of the new leniency to establish a new form of settlements called *campamentos* to symbolize their political ideology (see Table 19–2).

When the newly elected socialist President Salvador Allende took office in November 1970, more than 300,000 people were living in these *campamentos* in Santiago alone. At the end of 1972, by which time the number of urban invasions had stabilized, more than 400,000 people were in the *campamentos* of Santiago, and 100,000 or more in the other cities.[65] The main

Table 19.2 Illegal invasions of urban land, Chile, 1966–1971, by year. (Units are acts of land invasion, regardless of the number of squatters involved.)

	1966	1967	1968	1969	1970	1971	Sept. 1971– 31 May 1972	1 Jan. 1972– 31 May 1972
Santiago	0	13	4	35	103	NA	88	NA
Chile (including Santiago)	NA	NA	8	23	220	560	NA	148*

Source: for Chile: Direccion General de Carabineros (cited by FLACSO).
for Santiago: FLACSO Survey on Chilean Squatters, 1972 (as cited in Methodological Appendix pp. 364).

*Source references for these particular figures: Ernesto Pastrana and Monica Threlfall, *Pan, Techo, y Poder: El Movimiento de Pabladores en Chile, 1970-3* (Buenos Aires: Ediciones SIAP, 1974). (They also relied on the Direcion General de Carabineros.)

NA: Not Available.

characteristic of these *campamentos* was that from the beginning they were structured around the *Comites Sin Casa* that led the invasion, each of which were in turn organized by different political parties[66] – so much so that we can say that the Chilean *pobladores'* movement was created by the political parties. Of course, to do so they took into consideration the people's urban needs, and they were instrumental in organizing their demands and supporting them before the government. But we can by no means speak of a 'movement' of *pobladores*, unified around a programme and an organization; it was not, for instance, like the labour movement, which in Chile was unified and organized in the Central Unica de Trabajadores (CUT), in spite of political divisions within the working class.

The majority of the *pobladores* were organized by the Comando de Pobladores de la Central Unica de Trabajadores (the urban branch of the trade unions), linked to the Communist Party, and by the Central Unica del Poblador (CUP), dependent on the Socialist Party. A very active minority constituted itself as the Movimiento de Pobladores Revolucionarios (MPR), a branch of the radical organization Movimento de Izquierda Revolucionaria (MIR). Almost 25 per cent of the *campamentos* were still under the control of the Christian Democratic Party, and a few settlements were even organized by the National Party (radical right). This whole situation had two major consequences:

1 Each *campamento* was dependent upon the political leadership which had founded it. Political pluralism within the *campamento* was rare, except between Socialists and Communists (for instance, the largest *campamento*, Unidad Popular, had a joint leadership of both parties).
2 The participation of the *campamentos* in the political process very closely followed the political line dominating in each settlement. We should actually speak of the *pobladores'* branch of each party, rather than of a 'squatters' movement'. While all the parties always spoke of the need for unifying the movement, such unity never existed except in moments of political conflict, such as the distribution of food and supplies during the strike in October 1972 launched by the business sector against the government.

This key feature of the movement explains the findings of the field work study we conducted on 25 *campamentos* in 1971.[67] The social world we discovered did not present any major social or cultural innovation. The only exception was the organization of police and judicial functions,[68] which due to the absence of state legal institutions within the squatter settlements allowed (and forced) the *pobladores* to take a series of measures representing a beginning of popular justice. Yet, concerning the urban issues, the *pobladores'* massive mobilization made it possible for hundreds and thousands to obtain, in a few months, housing and services, against the prevailing logic of capitalist urban development. The urban system was deeply transformed by the *campamentos*. But experiences aimed at generating new social practices were limited by the political institutions where the old order was still the strongest force. A good example of such a situation was the Christian Democrats' congressional veto in 1971, opposing Allende's project to create Neighbourhood Courts (*Tribunales Vecinales*) based on existing experiences of grassroots justice.

The dependency of the *campamentos* upon the political parties opened the door to their use by each party for its particular interest, lowering the level of grassroots participation. The most conclusive demonstration on this subject is the careful case study done by Christine Meunier on the Nueva La Habana, one of the most mobilized and organized of all *campamentos*, under the leadership of MIR, where she lived and worked between 1971 and 1973, until the military coup.[69] We crosschecked her information with our own observation and interviews in Nueva La Habana in 1971 and 1972, as well as with the demographic and social research conducted also on the same *campamento* by Duque and Pastrana in 1970 and

1971.[70] All the findings by the three independent research teams converge towards a similar picture, the significance of which explore in some detail impels us to the social universe of a *campamento* in order to analyse as conclusively as possible the complex relationship between squatters and parties in the midst of a revolutionary process.

Nueva La Habana was one of the most active, well organized, and politically mobilized *campamentos*. And it certainly was the most highly publicized, both by the media and by the observers of the Chilean sociopolitical evolution, the main reason being that it was considered the 'model' *campamento* under the leadership of MIR. The Ministry of Housing expedited its settlement in November 1970 by relocating 1,600 families (10,000 people), with their consent, from three previous MIR-led land invasions (*campamentos* Ranquil, Elmo Catalan, and Magaly Monserato). MIR accepted the relocation of the three *campamentos* in a new 86 hectare urban unit as a challenge that would demonstrate its capacity to organize, ability to obtain housing and services, and effectiveness in transforming the squatters into a revolutionary force. If there was potential for an urban social movement in the *campamentos* of Santiago, we could expect to see it emerge from the mud and shacks of Nueva La Habana.

The strength of Nueva La Habana came from its tight grassroots organization and militant leadership. All *pobladores* were supposed to participate in the collective tasks of the *campamento*, as well as in the decisions about its management. All residents were included in a territorial organization on the basis of *manzanas* (blocks) that delegated one of their members to a board that elected an executive committee (*jefatura*) of five members. At the same time, the most active *pobladores* were invited to form a functional structure, the 'fronts of work', both at the level of each block and in the *campamento* as a whole, to take care of the different services that had to be provided for the residents on the basis of resources made available by the government: health, education, culture, police and self-defense, justice, sports, and so on. As a matter of fact, the capacity of the MIR to agitate and the deliberate purpose of Allende's government to limit confrontations with the revolutionary left, led to the paradox that Nueva La Habana received preferential treatment for housing and social services compared to the average squatter settlement.[71] On the basis of the legitimacy acquired by its very effective delivery of services, particularly in the field of health care, MIR frequently asked the *pobladores* to show support for its policies outside the *campamentos*, and it was usual, in all major political demonstrations, to see buses and trucks from Nueva La Habana loaded with *pobladores* waving the red and black flag of the Movimiento de Pobladores Revolucionarios. A few dozens of Nueva La Habana's residents were dedicated MIR militants under the leadership of a charismatic and thoroughly honest *poblador*, Alejandro Villalobos, nicknamed El Mike.[72] For the majority of residents, though they were sincere supporters of left wing politics, involvement in the political struggle depended upon issues like the access to land, housing, and services.

The ideological gap between the political vanguard and the squatters was the cause of continuous tension inside the *campamento* during the three years of its life.[73] This tension was expressed, for instance, in the resistance of the residents to the efforts for a cultural revolution in the children's schools, set up by MIR using old buses as classrooms. When the young teachers tried to change the traditional version of Chilean history or to recast the teaching to follow Marxist themes, many parents threatened to boycott the school, forcing the staff to preserve the 'official' teaching programme. The reason was not that they were necessarily anti-Marxist, but rather that they did not want their children to become exceptional by virtue of a different receiving education from the rest of the city. The *campamento*, with its revolutionary folklore, its popular theatre group and its 12 metres high Che Guevara portrait, was clearly seen by most residents as a transitory step towards a more 'normal' neighbourhood, a neighbourhood where one could receive visits from friends and relatives from the outside world, who for a long time had been scared to come and visit the squatters living in areas reported as 'dangerous' by the press and proclaimed as 'revolutionary' by their leadership.

The careful observations by Meunier about the social use of space and housing by the squatters provides a striking illustration of the individualism of the majority of squatters. Most houses, though tiny (with ground measurements of six by five metres), tried to enclose a piece of land, to mark a front yard as a semi-public space, while refusing space for common yards. The shack itself was divided between the main room, where the man could receive visits, and the kitchen-toilet, the private domain of the woman. Only the more enlightened leadership tried to make some space available for public use, but this practice led to spatial segregation: the shacks of the leaders tended to be concentrated towards the centre of the *campamento*, close to the shacks used for public purposes. The discrepancy between the level of involvement and consciousness thus became expressed in the spatial organization of the settlement. Individualism was even more pronounced when the residents were called to decide upon the design of their own houses. While asking for architectural diversity (three types of houses were built to fit the different sizes of families), they emphasized the desire for a standard design, utterly rejecting high-rise buildings. They also asked for the individual connection of each house to the water and electricity supply, restated the convenience of individual yards, and specified that the conventional domestic equipment, including television sets and individual electric appliances, would have to have enough room in the new houses. The real dream of most *pobladores* was that Nueva La Habana would one day cease to be a *campamento* and become an average working class *poblacion*.

Plate 19.1 Pobladores at work in the early stages of the *campamento* Nueva La Habana, Santiago de Chile, 1971. (Photograph: C. Meunier.)

Yet it should not be deduced that cultural conservatism and political opportunism were the reasons for this attitude. In fact the residents of Nueva La Habana were ready to mobilize in defense of their houses and in defense of their political beliefs each time it was required. They invaded land against police repression during the hard months of 1970. They worked hard to dig sewerage trenches, connect electricity, provide water, build shacks, set up public services, administer their 'city', and help each other when required. When, in October 1972, the economic boycott from external and internal capitalist forces halted the distribution of basic foods, the entire *campamento* mobilized to obtain supplies from the factories and the fields, and to distribute a basket to each family for weeks, without asking any payment from those who could not afford. They also established a new popular morality, banning prostitution, alcohol and alcoholism in the *campamento*, protecting battered women, and taking care of each other's children when the parents were working or involved in political activity. In sum, Nueva La Habana did not refuse its share of mobilization or cultivate a hypocritical attitude towards socialist ideals in exchange for urban patronage. But what was clear to every observer was that such a struggle was a means, and not a goal, for the great majority of the *pobladores*, that Nueva La Habana was an introspective community, dreaming of a peaceful, quiet, well-equipped neighbourhood, while MIR's leadership, conscious of the sharpening of the political conflict, desperately wanted to raise the level of militancy so that the entire *campamento* would become a revolutionary force. Their efforts in this direction proved unsuccessful.

On the basis of 20 focused interviews with residents, Meunier hypothesized the existence of three types of consciousness in the *campamento*:

1 The *individual*, focused upon the satisfaction of urban demands through the participation in the squat.
2 The *collective*, whose goals were limited to the success of the *campamento* as a community through the collective effort of all residents, closely allied to the government's initiatives.
3 The *political*, emphasizing the use of the *campamento* as a launching platform for the revolutionary struggle.

Although her sample is too limited to be conclusive, similar observations can be drawn from the survey by Duque and Pastrana, as well as from our own study. It would seem that the political level was only reached by MIR's cadres, that the mainstream of residents had some kind of collective consciousness while a strong-minded minority maintained an individualistic attitude, though sympathetic to left wing politics. It is crucial for our analysis to try to understand some of the reasons behind each level of consciousness, since Meunier's study concludes with the connection between levels of consciousness and the behaviour of social mobilization. While the 'collective consciousness' appears to have been randomly distributed among a variety of social characteristics, the two other types tended to be connected with a few significant variables: the 'political consciousness' seemed more likely to happen among men than among women, among individuals with lower income, and among unemployed workers (although the fact of being unemployed in 1971's Chile might be a *consequence* of being a revolutionary worker). The 'individualists' seem to have been associated with higher income, better than average housing conditions before coming to the *campamento*, and women.

On the basis of these observations, two complementary themes can be noted:

1 The mainstream of the working class in Nueva La Habana probably followed the same pattern found elsewhere, collectively defending their living conditions but leaving the task of general political leadership to the government. A minority group of higher income families joined the invasion to solve their housing problem without further commitment. The radical

vanguard of MIR was composed of unskilled workers whose political leanings could surface more easily through the *pobladores'* movement, given the tight political control by communists and socialists in the labour movement (the CUT). This argument, specific to Nueva La Habana, confirms one of our basic general theses on the *pobladores* movement in Chile. A support for this interpretation can be found in the comparison of the occupational structure between Nueva La Habana and the *campamento* Bernardo O'Higgins, the model squatter settlement organized by the Communist Party. Table 19–3, constructed by us on the basis of the census that Duque and Pastrana took on four *campamentos,* shows that the Nueva La Habana's residents had a lower proportion of well-educated people, a lower proportion of workers in the 'dynamic sector' (modern industry), and a much higher proportion of unemployed (33·2 per cent against 19·5 per cent in Bernardo O'Higgins), and a much lower proportion of unionized workers.

Table 19.3 Social composition of four campamentos, Santiago de Chile, 1971. (Percentage of residents over the total of each campamento who have the listed characteristics.)

	Campamentos			
	Fidel Castro	*26 de Julio*	*Nueva La Habana*	*Bernardo O'Higgins*
Low income	39 %	29 %	18 %	NA
High level of education (primary completed)	15 %	20 %	18 %	24 %
Self-employed workers	11 %	13 %	15 %	17 %
Manufacturing workers	39 %	35 %	48 %	53 %
Service workers	21 %	27 %	24 %	36 %
Workers in modern industrial companies	16 %	25 %	25 %	28 %
Workers in large companies (over 50 employees)	36·6%	46·8%	42·9%	37·4%
Unemployed workers	37·6%	22·3%	33·2%	19·5%
High level of urban experience	56·7%	65·9%	64·6%	66·5%
Urbanized workers	30 %	43 %	35 %	44 %

Source: Joaquin Duque and Ernesto Pastrana, *Survey of Four Campamentos* (Santiago de Chile: Facultad Latinoamericana de Ciencias Sociales, 1971).

NA: Not Available. But other sources indicate that the income levels in Bernardo O'Higgins seems to be noticeably higher than in the other three *campamentos.*

The apparent contradiction that Nueva La Habana came higher in the proportion of workers it had from large factories is a simple statistical artifact: a substantial number of those from Bernardo O'Higgins were skilled and well-paid bus drivers who could not be counted as working in factories. In sum, Bernardo O'Higgins and the Communist Party seem to have relied on the support of the organized working class while MIR and Nueva La Habana seem to have been more successful among the workers of the informal urban economy. We will develop this argument at a more general level, once the profile of Nueva La Habana is complete.

2 Another major factor in Nueva La Habana was that women appear to have been the most reluctant group to follow MIR's revolutionary ideology and the ones who emphasized the satisfaction of basic needs before general political commitment. In fact, this is the main reason advanced by Meunier for explaining the gap in consciousness and mobilization between the vanguard and the majority of the squatters. Meunier lists many examples about the absence of any real transformation in women's roles and lives. She describes how women cooked and ate in the kitchen while serving their husbands and friends in the main room. She describes the sexual domination some cadres and the difficulty that women faced because their participation in the running of the *campamento* gave rise to suspicions of infidelity. She goes on to describe the difficulties women had in taking advantage of contraception services provided by MIR because the men felt their virility to be threatened. As a result, in 1972, a majority of the women in Nueva La Habana were pregnant. Furthermore, unable to fully participate in the political mobilization, women saw the absence of the men from the house, their unemployment and their political commitment as threats to family life. Separations were common among political leaders and their women as a result of these tensions. This, in turn, widened the gap between single men, who became full-time political activists, and the majority of families, dominated by women's fears and pragmatic feelings. The situation was paradoxical if we consider that MIR, given its strong student basis, was perhaps the one Chilean party that tried the hardest to liberate women and to integrate them fully into politics. But in Nueva La Habana the form that this liberation took deepened the divide between MIR's militant women and the majority of residents. MIR organized a women's militia that took care of a variety of tasks, particularly to do with health but also in matters of self-defense. But this initiative was not supported by a change of attitude of men towards 'their women', who were still unable to participate in the collective activities. So it further isolated the few political women and exposed them to the criticism and distrust of the housewives. Such a dramatic contrast can be illustrated by two events:

a The general blame put by almost the entire *campamento* on a woman whose unguarded child drowned while she was working at the health centre

b The rejection by women of MIR's proposal to close down the mothers' centres (an inspiration of the Christian Democrats) where women met to learn domestic skills, and to replace them by women's centres which would emphasize women's militant role. Most women felt that such a change would politicize their free space, depriving them of their capacity to autonomously decide how to use these centres. Thus, the mothers' centres continued to function in the heart of revolutionary squatters' settlements.

Although they were unable to challenge the machismo prevalent in the settlements, most resident women rejected MIR's heavy-handed politicization of women's issues and became the prime mover for the use of urban mobilization strictly for the improvement of their conditions.

So Nueva La Habana lived entirely under the shadow of MIR's initiatives. New housing was built, urban infrastructures were provided, health and education services were delivered, cultural activities were organized, goods were supplied, prices were controlled, moral reform was attempted, and some form of democratic self-management was implemented, although under the unchallenged leadership of the *miristas* (MIR militants). Yet the social role of the *campamento* shifted according to the political tasks and priorities established by MIR at the national level. In the first year, MIR supported urban demands as a means of consolidating its position in the squatter movement so as to reinforce its militant power. In May 1971, in the congress of Nueva La Habana residents, the leadership announced that top priority should be given to the penetration of the organized working class by MIR, to counteract reformist forces in the labour movement. So most of the cadres of the *campamento* were sent to other political duties, leaving the *pobladores* in a support role for the main struggle being fought in the work places. The working class ideology of MIR came into open contradiction with its militant presence among the squatters, and there followed in 1971–72 a period of disorientation in the *campamento*, leading to demobilization and in-fighting.

The general mobilization in October 1972 against the conservative offensive in Chile led to a new role for the *campamento*, first, in the battle over distribution and, later on, in the support of the construction of *cordones industriales* (industrial committees) and *comandos comunales* (urban unions) as centres of revolutionary, popular power. Militants from Nueva La Habana tried on 3 April 1973 to occupy the National Agency of Commercial Distribution (CENADI) as a gesture in favour of this strategy: they built barricades in Santiago's main avenue, Vicuna Mackena, and clashed fiercely with the police for a whole day. Nueva La Habana subsequently kept its subordinate role as a branch of a political party, adopting a variety of tactics, corresponding to the different directions taken by MIR's political activity. So if the 'model *campamento*' was an expression of the militant squatters' capacity to build their city and to try new communal ways of life, it was also, above anything else, an organizational weapon of a revolutionary party.

In our own research with the CIDU team we came to a similar conclusion: for all *campamentos*, whatever their political orientation, the practice of the squatters was entirely determined by the politics of the settlement, and the political direction of the settlement was, in turn, the work of the dominant party in each *campamento*.

The same finding was obtained by studies on mobilization in the *conventillos* (central-city slums)[74] and in the neighbourhood-based demand organizations.[75] Perhaps the only exception consisted of the committees organized to control prices and delivery of food, the *Juntas de Abastecimientos y Precios*, where a high level of popular autonomy was observed, cutting across the political membership. Even so, the practice of these committees was very different: they either aimed to reinforce the socialist government or to structure a dual power, depending upon the political tendency of their leadership.[76]

The political stand of the *pobladores* was a decisive element in enabling the formerly passive popular urban sectors to join the crucial political battle, initiated by the working class movement, for the construction of a new society. Thus we could speak, in this case, of an urban social movement because the popular masses were mobilized around urban issues and made a considerable political contribution to the impetus for social change.

Nevertheless, the partisan and segmented politicization of the *pobladores* made it impossible for the left to expand its influence beyond the borders of the groups it could directly control. The different sympathies held in each *campamento* hardened into political opposition among different groups, a situation quite unlike that of the trade unions, where Christian Democratic workers often backed initiatives from the left such as the protest against the boycott of Chile by the international financial institutions. Furthermore, the separating of political forces in the squatter settlements led each group to seek support in the administration, splitting the whole system into different constellations of state officials, party cadres, and *pobladores*, each with its own political flag.

The social effects of this development became evident in the changing relationships between the *pobladores* and Allende's government. During the first year (November 1970 to October 1971) the difficulties of putting the new construction industry to work made it impossible for the government to satisfy the *pobladores'* demands, and the only thing it could do was to accept the land invasion and provide some elementary services by putting the squatters in touch with public agencies. In spite of the government's inability, the *pobladores*, including

Christian Democrats, collaborated actively with the administration. In contrast, at the end of the second year, when 70,000 housing units were under way and when health, education, and other services started to be delivered, some serious signs of unrest appeared among the *pobladores*. Finally, after October 1972, when the political battle became inevitable, each sector of the *pobladores* aligned with its corresponding political faction, and the squatters movement disappeared as an indentifiable entity.

To understand the evolution of this attitude towards the government, we must consider the social class content of the political affiliations in the Unidad Popular as well as the social interests represented by the squatter settlements. In the first year the government, taking advantage of the political confusion in business circles, successfully implemented a series of economic and social reforms which substantially improved the level of production and standard of living. This policy obtained important popular support, as did the preservation of political freedom and social peace. The political debate was kept within institutional boundaries, and the opposition of the Christian Democrats was moderate.

During the second year, however, the economy deteriorated rapidly, due to the sabotage of the economy by the Chilean business sector and landlords, the international boycott, and the end of the benefits of using formerly idle industrial capacity. The political alliance between the centre and the right isolated the Unidad Popular. The radicalization of some popular sectors exacerbated the situation and was used as a pretext for political provocation. International pressure against Allende was reinforced. There was one popular working sector that was particularly sensitive to political alienation, especially in these conditions: workers in small companies, the reason being that, although not included in the nationalized sector, they were asked to restrain their own demands to preserve the alliance with small business. This sector of workers was actually non-unionized since Chilean laws before 1970 prevented union membership in companies with less than 25 employees, with the result that they tended to be politically less conscious than the unionized working class. So the Unidad Popular government asked for a more responsible effort by this less organized and less conscious segment of the working class. The reaction was a series of errant initiatives, sometimes very radical, sometimes conservative, and generally out of tune with mainstream policy of the popular left. Now all surveys show that this sector of small companies' working class – the workers of the 'traditional sector' or 'informal economy' – represented in Chile the most important share of the squatter settlements (see Tables 17–2, page 182 and 19–3, page 205), and therefore the *pobladores'* movement organized the main expression of this social group. But as we have just noted, the squatters' movement was split into political factions and so reflected the disorientation of this group. Instead of becoming factions and so a focus for organization and mobilization the movement only occasionally enabled them to manoeuver against the Unidad Popular government.

During the third year, the left of the Unidad Popular, as well as MIR, tried to build up a people's power base strong enough to oppose the ruling classes by developing territorially-based organizations which combined both the *comandos comunales* and *cordones industriales*.[77] But because many people actually leant towards the centre-right, and most workers were following the government, this grassroots movement only gathered a vanguard of industrial workers in some sectors of the big cities, particularly in the area of Cerrillos-Maipu in Santiago. In fact the squatters' movement disappeared as an autonomous entity in the decisive moments of 1973, and was less than ever the unified movement around which the left might have organized some popular sectors, people who in the event supported the centre-right as much as the left. Not only did the political influence of the *pobladores* movement wane but, as part of the right wing offensive, the far right organized some middle class neighbourhoods along sociopolitical lines (the Proteco organizations), linking the provision of local services to preparations for the military coup. The disappearance of the *pobladores'* movement, then, in 1972–3 was the consequence of the logic of party discipline replacing the search by the left to establish political hegemony.

The only moments of mass participation in the squatters' movement were those where political parties of the left gathered around a clear-cut common cause: the first year of Allende's government, and the mass response to the business strike of October 1972. In both situations, the squatters' movement started to produce a new urban system corresponding to the political transformation of the state by Allende's government. On both occasions, we could observe its potential as a mass movement and as a social movement. As a mass movement, it gathered and organized a larger proportion of people than the left wing parties could. As a social movement it started to produce substantial changes to urban services and the local state institutions because of its capacity to mobilize people. Both moments were exceptional but too short-lived: the unity and the cultural influence of the squatters' movement did not survive the polarization of the political opposition existing inside it.

The squatter movement in Chile was potentially a decisive element in the revolutionary transformation of society, because it could have achieved an alliance of the organized working class with the unorganized and unconscious proletarian sectors, as well as with the petty bourgeoisie in crisis. For the first time in Latin America, the left understood the potential of urban movements, and battled with populist ideology on its own ground, planting the possibilities of political hegemony among urban popular sectors. But the form taken by this political initiative, the overpoliticization from the beginning, and the organizational profile of each political party within the movement, undermined its unity and made the autonomous definition of its goals impossible. Instead of being an instrument for reconstructing people's unity, the *pobladores'* movement became an amplifier of ideological divisions. Yet its memory will last as the most hopeful attempt by Latin American urban masses to improve their social condition and achieve political liberation.

20

Conclusion: The Social Making of the Dependent City

Evidence provided from our case studies and those of others in Latin America, as well as by reliable research in other cultural areas,[78] suggests that urban squatter settlements have become an increasingly sensitive political issue in most developing nations. The major reason is that the provision of shelter and urban services by the state to a large proportion of a deprived urban population is one of the major channels for political participation and community organization in the new institutional system, emerging from a revival of nation-states struggling for control in a context provided by an international economy and in a world dominated by fierce competition between the super powers.

The specificity of the urbanization process in the Third World is creating a major gap between the spatial conditions of living, dominant economic interests, and people's experience. For the multinational corporations, space and distance have been dissolved by transportation technology, the mobility of capital, and the permeability of most political boundaries to their decision-making bodies. The world's corporate elite becomes placeless. For people uprooted by the disruptive trend of uneven economic growth and thrown out into uncontrolled urbanization as a consequence of new peripheral industrialization and economic integration into the world system, the quest for a new secure space is a major step in their search for preserving cultural identity, improving their living conditions, and ensuring political self-determination. The growing urban population of the Third World is clearly orientated towards the building and preserving of spatially defined local communities.

In between, the nation-states of most developing countries are increasingly dislocated by conflicting pressures from the traditional oligarchies and the new international economic powers, at a time when popular masses shift from demands for survival to political claims requesting a broader participation in the process of decision making. Many states try to adapt themselves to the situation by modernizing the economy and legitimizing the institutions using the leverage of a subordinated popular mobilization aimed at overcoming the resistance of traditional groups and at re-negotiating the current patterns of economic dependence within the world capitalist system. Urban squatters appear as a target social group, potentially able to be both solicited and mobilized by the new, modernizing state institutions. But the response of squatter communities to this strategy varies according to the overall pattern of social conflict in each particular society, as has been shown by the empirical studies.

It appears, on the basis of research findings summarized in this part, that the expansion of squatter settlements in Latin American cities is mainly the outcome of the political process we have described. Of course, such a political process operates on the grounds of dramatic urban needs generated by uneven development, widespread migration, demographic growth, and income inequality. Yet, the 'solution', adopted to cope with the urban crisis in developing countries seems to be orientated and conditioned by the relationship between the state and the urban popular masses, since the tolerance of squatter settlements depends upon the political will of public authorities. Furthermore, the process is a self-spiralling one: the more the state, or a powerful political agent, uses land invasions to establish their influence, the more the squatter settlements expand, as the case of Lima strikingly illustrates. On the other hand, once squatter settlements, in their different ecological forms, become a major component of the urban social structure, their permanent connection to the political system has to be set up, both for them to survive and for the political system to be able to maintain social control over the popular sectors, as the observation of Mexico City reveals.

The political meaning of such an urban mobilization depends upon specific historical situations. A movement tends to be the instrument of reformist elites aiming to modernize the state and looking for support in their attempt improve the patrimonial way their nation's economy is run so that it may gain by the new international order. But the structural limits imposed on reform by the unwillingness to confront the multinational capitalist interests sometimes encourages, as in Chile in 1970, a left wing-led squatter movement that participated in the struggle for socialism, but under the tight control of the Chilean left wing parties. In other circumstances, as with the movement of Rojas Pinilla in Bogota in the early 1970s, a classical populist agitation brought the squatters into the centre of the political area when the mainstream parties were unable to respond in any way to pressing urban demands. But in all cases, the explanation of the dynamics and orientation of the squatter movement, as well as the level and meaning of their community organizations, are essentially determined by the political system and by the characteristics of the political agent to which squatters relate. This is the most important social trend to consider for our analysis, namely, the dependency of squatter settlements upon state policies and the heteronomy of the squatter movement *vis-à-vis* the political system.

Let us make it clear that we are not opposing the situation we described to an ideal model in which the autonomy of the squatters in relation to politics would ensure their capacity as a social movement. There is no such thing in reality as a politics-free society. And, in any case, it is not our purpose here to evaluate the Latin American squatters' movement, but to understand its social meaning in the production of the city and in the changing of society. The heteronomy of the squatter communities must be put into perspective by considering the relative autonomy of labour unions, peasants' organizations, or ethnic liberation movements in relation to political parties. While most of these movements have very close ties to some political agent, they also generally preserve their identity and consciousness, and have political influence on their own, so that their relationship with political parties is hardly one of mere subordination. Thus, the relevant point is not whether squatters are politicized or whether they have political connections, but that their very existence and identity as collective actors are entirely defined and enhanced by the political system in a patronizing relationship *vis-à-vis* the franchise of their right to settle in the city. It is in this precise sense that our observations provide the basis for identifying the social heteronomy of the squatter movement. But why such a specific mode of collective behaviour? There is nothing that could justify such a dependent consciousness in terms of the social composition of squatter movements, of their subculture, or of their level of political participation. The studies cited and the data provided have dismissed once again the image of a specific universe separated from the mainstream society: the squatter settlements are the urban form, provided by the state, indirectly or directly, where an increasing proportion of the working population in Latin American cities lives.

The main reason for the squatters' dependency on the political system appears to be the vulnerability of their status as urban dwellers. Without the state's tolerance, or without some effective political support, they would not even have the right to their physical presence in the city. Their territoriality, as an exception to the formal functioning of the economy and of the legal institutions, is by itself, a patronizing relationship. Only their reliance on the state's permissiveness entitles the squatters to the spatial basis of their daily existence. To some extent, this analysis could be considered to be parallel to the argument we proposed years ago about the lack of citizenship of immigrant workers as their most 'valuable' characteristic, given their potential docility towards their employers in the absence of any political rights.[79] In a similar way, the squatters' lack of citizenry provides the political system with an ultimate weapon for controlling and enforcing their political allegiance: often the squatters do not have any legal rights to the land they occupy. But the argument also holds in the case of legal provision of an urban site, since the entire system of service delivery still depends on state agencies, and urban renewal plans and arbitrary displacement can be exercised at any moment. Thus squatters are the guest-citizens of Latin American metropolises, as foreign immigrants are the guest-workers of advanced capitalist economies.

This analysis must be pursued further. The territorial exceptionality of squatter settlements is not only a foothold for their dwellers in the metropolitan world; it is also a necessary material condition for the performance of their role in the informal urban economy. As Alejandro Portes and John Walton have demonstrated,[80] squatter settlements are crucial as a means of consumption that allow for a cheap reproduction of labour power, itself making possible the lowering of the social wage assumed by capital or the state in the economies of developing countries. When squatters refuse to live in high-rise buildings, it is not only because of their 'essential traditionalism' – they also need to raise poultry and cultivate vegetables as a basic element of their subsistence. Furthermore, a whole system of economic activities known as 'informal' (though extremely productive and directly connected to the 'formal' sector of the economy) can only grow on the basis of a territory that somehow escapes the legal rules of the game and is yet strictly controlled by a parallel network of institutions. From motor repair shops to drug dealers, passing through subcontractors of the building industry and occasional bodyguards, a substantial proportion of urban income is generated on the basis of a self-preserved space organized in and around the squatter settlements. So squatters need to preserve their 'exceptionality', while at the same time maintaining a close connection to the political system in order to protect the material and spatial basis of their way of life.

So the squatters, the state, and the informal economy, in intimate relationship with the 'formal' sector, are elements of the same system: the dependent city, the dependent state, the dependent economy. The social heteronomy of squatters, their location, their emphasis on community and territoriality, are not symptoms of a special type of psychological personality. Their dependency upon the political system is at the very core of their social condition. Their lack of identity as a social movement is the accurate expression of their experience of being unable to find avenues of protest outside the protection of established political forces. By perpetuating their relationship with the state and by expanding their settlements at an ever-increasing rate, squatters are in fact the driving force in the social production of the urban form known as the dependent city: a city where most workers must themselves take care of a substantial proportion of the reproduction of their labour power; where to do so, the state must disregard its own institutional rules; where to obtain such a tolerance squatters must find powerful protectors on whom to depend; and where the resulting urban form develops into an inarticulate constellation of functions and places, related through invisible networks to the underlying mechanisms of such urban dynamics, from the transportation technology imposed by the multinationals to the patterns of land invasion programmed by illegal developers.

Dependency, at the international level, is not only the exercise of the power of a nation-state over another nation. Dependency is a social relationship according to which the dynamics of a dominant society basically shape the process and structure of a dependent society that are interconnected in an asymmetrical way. Similarly, the dependent city is not just a city of poverty, or a city with a general housing crisis. It is a city whose space is produced by its dwellers as if they were not the producers of such a space, but the temporary builders of their master's *hacienda*. The dependent city is the ecological form resulting from the residents' lack of social control over urban development because of their forced submission to the good will of the state and to the changing flows of foreign capital. The dependent city is a city without citizens.

Part 5

The Making of an Urban Social Movement: The Citizen Movement in Madrid towards the end of the Franquist Era

21

Introduction

The social mobilization around urban issues that occurred in the neighbourhoods of most Spanish cities throughout the 1970s was, to our knowledge, the largest and most significant urban movement in Europe since 1945. For several years (approximately 1970–9) it actively involved hundreds of thousands of residents in Madrid, Barcelona, and almost every major city in the country. The neighbourhood became an organizational base where most struggles, though triggered initially by a particular problem, gave rise during the mobilization to neighbourhood associations aimed at dealing with all matters of everyday life, from housing to open spaces, from water supply to popular celebrations. Although the most militant protest originated in working class wards where the Movement started, neighbourhood associations encompassed a wide range of the social spectrum. Middle class areas mobilized around their own issues and subsequently joined the popular neighbourhoods to fight for such basic, common goals as freedom of association or the enjoyment of entertainments such as street parties. Furthermore, neighbourhood mobilization was not a mere fact of a politically isolated, activist vanguard. In spite of the ideological radicalism that generally characterized their leadership, neighbourhood associations enjoyed the sympathy and support of most sectors of society, particularly among professional groups, architects and lawyers being the most prominent. A decisive factor in the formation of this acceptable image was the importance given to neighbourhood protest by the media, particularly by the press. It was this connection to all of Spanish society – not just to a limited association with left wing opposition and the most exploited classes – that largely accounts for the striking paradox that characterized the Spanish neighbourhood Movement: its development, organization, and impact occurred in spite of the total restriction of human and political rights, and, in particular, the heavy police repression used to uphold the keystone of General Franco's dictatorship – the denial of any organizational capacity to popular classes and to the Spanish democratic sectors.

Thus the observation of neighbourhood mobilization in Spain should allow us to understand the apparent mystery of how a civil society that had been so shunned by the state took its revenge by developing such a prolific social tissue that the political institutions became increasingly obsolete in relation to the reality they were supposed to shape. Even more important for our research is that, given the circumstances under which the Movement grew up, it always kept a close connection to the political goals of democracy, and sometimes of socialism, as well as to specific interests of underground left wing parties who realised that the neighbourhood associations could provide a marvellous opportunity to reach people while allowing the parties to remain less exposed to police repression.

The subtleties of the interaction between political strategies and urban social movements can also be observed and hopefully deciphered in an almost experimental situation: one in which the political parties needed autonomous social movements since, without their presence and protection, the parties were exposed to systematic and institutional repression. Urban movements, as well as all social movements, need the institutions of a democratic state but in Spain faced the political system of one that denied the right of any autonomous grassroots organization to exist and crudely served dominant economic interests without any mechanism of social control. Any movement was bound to be in confrontation with the state by virtue of their very existence and therefore needed political operators capable of opposing the state with a feasible, alternative political strategy. Parties and movements had consequently to reciprocate support and respect: without the movements, parties remained condemned to underground agitation and without the parties, movements could not expect a major change in the status quo (a basic condition for the fulfillment of their demands on a relatively stable basis). Out of this complex interdependence a process flourished in which cities and neighbourhoods became at the same time a stake for power and a social experiment.

Over and above its special relationship to politics, the most significant aspect of the Spanish neighbourhood Movement was its performance as an agent of social change. Under its impact or, more precisely, under the influence of social processes to which it contributed substantially, Spanish cities changed, political institutions were turned upside down, social relationships in the neighbourhoods dramatically improved, and perhaps most significantly, the urban culture, namely, society's conception of what a city should be, was fundamentally altered. To be more specific (but without entering into the detailed analysis that will be presented later in this part) living conditions were improved in the mobilized popular wards: demolition was halted; rehabilitation and renovation programmes were promoted for the benefit of slum dwellers; shanty towns were redeveloped and replaced by low-cost public housing to be allocated to the squatters; open space was provided; urban services were improved; some environmental protection was legislated for; and public transport was either nationalized or municipalized and given priority. The city itself changed: neighbourhoods organized celebrations; cultural and popular traditions were restored and others were invented in the newly built urban areas; a whole network of associations and activities were established; the metropolitan area became a public place, enriched with street life, cultural activities, and community and city gatherings. Urban policies shifted even before democracy had been established: the betterment of urban amenities was given priority over more profitable new development; community life was enhanced and the neighbourhood associations won *de facto* recognition in most public programmes. The crisis of the dictatorship was deepened by closely related political opposition and social movements, including neighbourhood associations as well as the labour movement and the Basque and Catalan nationalist movements. Eventually, after Franco's death, national democratic institutions were established in 1977 and local ones followed in 1979, the result of strong pressure from the community organizations. While the urban movement was obviously not solely responsible for bringing democracy to Spain, it was nonetheless an essential component in the creation of a new political culture which won widespread popular support for democratic opposition by relating politics to everyday life, by reaching middle class sectors, and by denying the only argument left to Franco's supporters (the argument that the regime bettered living conditions was now clearly challenged by the flow of protest from many urban communities). Furthermore, the political parties themselves were shaken in their rather instrumental view of social movements, and were forced to entertain the idea of participatory democracy in city halls and planning agencies.

To observe and analyse the neighbourhood Movement in Spain between the late 1960s and late 1970s is a privileged position from which to ask questions and suggest answers about the relationship between urban mobilization and social change, between parties and movements, between city and culture. This is the task we are about to undertake on the basis of systematic field work on Madrid's Citizen Movement (the name the movement gave itself), whose characteristics and circumstances we describe and justify in the Methodological Appendix (pp. 000–000). Let us just say that Madrid was selected not only because of the size and intensity of the urban mobilization occurring in the neighbourhoods, but also because it was the city where the political dimension of the conflict was most directly felt given its role as the capital of a highly centralized state.[1]

To understand the structure, emergence, effects, and social meaning of Madrid's Citizen Movement, we must first establish the basic trends of the urban crisis and of the political crisis which gave birth to it. This is necessary not only for placing the Movement 'in its context', but also for identifying the raw materials that constituted this social process. We will then present the basic social characteristics and evolution of the Movement as a historical phenomenon, and turn later to a detailed analysis of some of the 23 neighbourhoods studied in our research. After showing the impact of the Movement on the urban, political, and cultural systems of Madrid, we will explore some hypotheses about the Movement by studying the set of relationships between the Movement and the class structure, the basic urban issues and the political system, and by including a careful consideration of its interaction with the political parties. We will finally try to summarize our main hypotheses in the form of an analytical model which we will confront with the collected empirical evidence.

22

The Crisis of a Political Model of Urban Development

The Citizen Movement of Madrid developed around the problems and contradictions resulting from an urban crisis in the city which had close ties to an increasingly conflictive political process. When we say 'crisis' we do not refer to the pressing needs of most dwellers or to the poor urban services. The fact that in 1974 54 per cent of the 4·3 million people of metropolitan Madrid lived in inadequate housing,[2] while 8·1 per cent of the housing stock remained empty for reasons to do with speculation, did not constitute a crisis in itself. In fact, during the 1940s, during the poverty and repression after the Civil War, Madrid was not in crisis. People were living in misery and terror, but the city's fate was consistent with the functions and goals assigned to it by the socially dominant interests whose overwhelming power could not be challenged or modified by outsiders. Thus, insomuch as the new political institutions of the dictatorship could be consolidated by building ministries, housing bureaucrats, erecting self-glorifying monuments, and developing exclusive residences in a few restricted sectors, the city could apparently function without rural immigrants, many of whom were sent back to their impoverished villages by the police who kept a close eye on the railway stations.

However cynical this observation might seem, we can generalize and say that an urban crisis is not defined by human suffering or lack of shelter, but by the extent to which the basic goals expected of an urban system cannot be achieved by a dominant set of social interests, either because of internal contradictions between some of the goals or because of mounting challenges from alternative social interests. The Citizen Movement represented such a challenge: its growing impact on the city and on urban policies called into question the whole logic of the model of urban development. But if the Movement was able to rely on widespread support when it came to full fruition in the 1970s, this was because many latent issues that had arisen through a series of earlier crises connected with the evolution of Madrid's urban system went without their proper social expression due to the constraints imposed by an authoritarian state.

Therefore, we will proceed to analyse Madrid's urban development since 1940,[3] its stalemates, and the alterations imposed to find ways out of each critical situation as well as the contradictions triggered by such new urban policies. The purpose of this analysis is not merely to introduce the urban context in which our research took place but also to outline and explain the basic issues that gave rise to the Citizen Movement.

The basic factor commanding Madrid's urban development was not the economy but the state.[4] Even at the peak of uncontrolled capitalist exploitation of urban needs, banks and developers took advantage of the situation, safe in the knowledge that the political ruling elite could be relied on to play the rapid economic growth 'card' for the benefit of large corporations – its major chance for survival in a political and ideological context that increasingly contradicted the very foundations of the regime. This is the crucial argument in the understanding of Madrid's peculiarities at the time: the state organized the economy, and the economy shaped the city in such a way that the people were forced to adapt. For about fifteen years this one-sided mechanism worked smoothly. Between 1940 and 1950, only 275,000 migrants settled in Madrid, in spite of hunger, misery, unemployment and agricultural crisis in most of what was still a predominantly rural Spain. The city remained, for the most part, a bureaucratic and service centre. Urban growth was limited and the specific needs of the small elite were easily met by an omnipotent administration, whose 1946 master plan for Madrid mainly emphasized the symbolic aspects while clearly asserting the right of the state to decide on the use of most land, channelling speculation through the patronage system of Franquist bureaucracy.[5]

In the early 1950s, some basic changes were under way at a very slow pace. Having physically destroyed the internal opposition, the dictatorship had been consolidated by the politics of the Cold War and American support. The time had come to move ahead, abandoning economic isolationism at the price of watering down Fascist ideology. The public sector undertook the building of basic industrial infrastructure in energy, transportation, telecommunications, heavy industry, and unprofitable but necessary investments, as well as a policy of grants, subsidies and joint ventures aimed at large, private corporations. A major decision was made on purely political grounds concerning the territorial shape of future economic growth: Madrid should become a major industrial centre to counterbalance the peripheral industrial power of the Basques and Catalans whose nationalistic feelings were being curbed by state repression. A series of measures was taken to this effect: fiscal exemptions, favourable transportation fares, easy supply of electric power, and concentration of public investments, all in the Madrid area. So industry started to arrive. So did people, after an easing of official hostility towards the dismantling of the eternal values of rural Spain. Between 1950 and 1960, 440,000 newcomers came to Madrid. Workers found low-paying jobs but no housing – they were still too few and too poor to be considered an attractive market. The construction industry was building 'subsidized housing' exclusively reserved for middle-level civil servants. Since workers had to stay in the city because the only jobs were there, they created their own housing market: shanty towns spread all around the city's periphery which accounted, in 1956, for 20 per cent of Madrid's population.[6] These settlements were, of course, illegal but tolerated: by the landowners who, besides obtaining high rents in the short term, had expectations of rising land values after years of urbanization by shanty town dwellers who would improve their neighbourhood; by the police, accepting money and co-operation in exchange for indifference; and by the administration, relieved of the duty of providing housing for workers who were required by the new industrial policy. As long as the workers contented themselves with the shanty towns or with the overcrowded slums of central Madrid, it seemed that self-regulatory mechanisms would work to sustain urban harmony. The shanty towns were denounced, however, as a scandal by the government-controlled press, and for the first time housing received the treatment usually reserved for political crises, leading to new urban policies for Madrid. An emergency programme of low-cost public housing was hastily designed and implemented between 1954 and 1962. Provisional units were built with light materials and to low standards in the unequipped periphery and housed thousands of shanty town dwellers who were removed from their shacks and settled there while waiting for their future homes. (In the event, they waited forever. . . .) Some massive high-rise public housing estates were built by the government and sold or rented to tens of thousands who were sub-letting, living with relatives, were housed in shanty towns or knew some friend in the housing administration. Such sudden generosity could be easily explained. On the one hand, construction companies and private developers were preparing for new, more promising times. A higher rate of urban expansion was foreseen, as well as the opening of some limited markets. To start operating, to create the basis for the new stage of urban development, they first needed a profitable captive market of thousands of housing units, built on the millions of square metres of land they had wisely bought years ago. The state provided such a market: it bought the land, lent the capital, paid for the construction, channelled the demand, granted fiscal exemptions, and 'forgot' to control the standards and legal requirements of the urban infrastructure. A new real estate network emerged from the public housing bonanza, along with a booming construction industry – big developers absorbed most of the demand and created some of Spain's largest firms, soon connected to the top banks. The ground was laid for the subsequent more profitable stage of business control over urban growth.

But however significant the public housing programme proved for the burgeoning developers, the main reason for its launching, once, again, originated with the state, particularly from the confrontation between the populist ideologists of the Phalange and the new technocrats of the Opus Dei, climbing into power with Franco's support in 1957. Two major issues were at stake in 1956: for the first time massive political demonstrations took place in several major cities, particularly in Madrid, initiated by students to demand democracy. While supporting repression of the protesters, the 'old-guard' fascists of the Phalange Party, their attitude dictated by a position of weakness, asked for some popular measures, including social benefits with which to keep people quiet. The regime wanted to change its face, to put aside the fascist symbols, espouse economic growth instead of imperial dreams, to open relations with Western democracies, to modernize institutions, and to attract the urban middle class. Although defeated in the conflict, the Phalangists kept a few positions for some-time, including the most valuable 'card' in their hands, the housing ministry which had been created for them in 1956, and they attempted to obtain some popular support through its housing policies. To this extent, the public housing programme was a token concession created for the Phalange but the programme's key positions were left to the new generations of Franquists.[7] In fact, the Phalangists were unable to use their position to attract people given their total lack of credibility and instead secured personal benefits by actively participating in the speculators' network.

As a result, tens of thousands of houses were built in the periphery of Madrid but, because of low budgets, corruption, incompetence, bad planning, and disregard for people's needs, the newly built estates began to crumble from the moment they were occupied. The houses were soon nicknamed the vertical shacks by the residents, a *double entendre* playing on their high-rise shape and the vertical (Fascist) trade unions responsible for their management. To aggravate the situation further, a new dimension of the urban crisis appeared in the midst of this development: people had been promised the ownership or life tenure of brand new housing, but thousands of them were being concentrated into huge instant ruins in the middle of nowhere. This new twist, however, appeared only as a minor pitfall when set beside the grandiose schemes dreamt up for the city at the beginning of the 1960s.

The Spanish economy was booming,[8] offering cheap labour and a fiscal haven to foreign capital, beautiful beaches to the tour operators, and Common Market jobs to one million Spanish migrants. The GNP grew at an average cumulative rate of 6·5 per cent per year. Madrid took the largest share of this expansion and imploded: almost 700,000 immigrants came to Madrid between 1960 and 1970; its population jumped from 2·4 million in 1960 to 3·6 million in 1970; about 40 per cent of all housing units existing in the Madrid metropolitan area in 1975 were built after 1960.[9] Most of the countryside, which lacked jobs, was deserted, with its population migrating to Europe, Madrid, and to a lesser extent Barcelona and the Basque region. Workers came to Madrid by the hundreds of thousands, looking for housing. In the wake of a militant, though unlawful, labour movement which had won higher wages, albeit in exchange for exhausting working conditions, this new urban population had some money – they were a market – and the developers were prepared, having bought land all over the city, concentrated capital, contracted hundreds of small subsidiary construction companies, and established a new legal foundation as a result of the 1963 master plan. Above all, they were counting on the good will of the mayor of Madrid, a personal appointment of the dictator himself.

So, the developers built hundreds of thousands of flats in compact groups in the middle of the Castilian plains, leaving empty spaces of several kilometres between clusters of blocks in order to raise the value of the land in between which they also owned. They only built housing – no amenities, no paved streets, no lighting, little sewerage, little water, and poor transportation. They used existing facilities as much as possible for legally required institutions such as schools and health care centres, and to help themselves in this respect often located blocks of flats in villages peripheral to the metropolitan areas. These villages grew in just ten years from 5,000 inhabitants to 150,000, without having their urban services altered. All housing was privately built, privately developed, and bought by an incoming population that was a captive market, given the concentration of job opportunities in Madrid. Families paid, on average, 30 per cent of their income over 15 years to buy a poorly constructed 70 to 100 square metre flat with no basic urban facilities. Many of them had to purchase their flats one or two years before construction was completed, based solely on sight of a model flat. Needless to say, the whole development was riddled with abuses, massive defaults, and bankruptcies, and caused a great deal of misery and hardship.

Although housing in Madrid did provide jobs and homes for industrial workers, one of its most important functions was as a major instrument of capital accumulation. The real estate business which was controlled by the largest banks obtained very high benefits from the conditions it was able to impose due to the tight market conditions created by the increasing urban and industrial concentration. The result was a new Madrid made up of massive, extremely dense high-rise complexes, where the main problem was the absence of all the proper elements of urban life with the natural exception of people. New schools, health care, open space, cultural facilities, a basic urban infrastructure, transportation, and so on, were totally lacking. And some times the water supply also failed.

While the periphery was being built, large sectors of the city were destroyed[10] in the downtown area to allow the expansion of department stores, to relocate office buildings, to establish hotels, and to develop expensive high-rise housing. The demolitions all over the city made way for the high-speed urban express ways that, since their creation, have been jammed by the growing number of cars which were increasingly necessary for daily commuting because public transport had become inadequate and obsolete for the expanded city. The bulldozers erased tree-lined boulevards, old neighbourhoods, cultural traditions, and local networks. Madrid became a city of strangers, with the remnants of the old neighbourhoods emptied of their dwellers and the newly urbanized areas unable to generate its own society as long as they were facing daily problems of survival. Cultural frustration and environmental damage resulted. When the major parts of the extensive urban development were completed, the real estate industry, always in close contact with both the banks and the administration, turned its attention to selected targets to create new markets. The remaining shanty towns which, as a result of the rapid urban growth, were now located in relatively central places, had to be removed. These were areas urbanized by squatters for many years but had to be yielded up to the force of redevelopment for more profitable uses. But a potentially explosive contradiction emerged between the use-value to the shanty town dwellers of this urban land and its exchange-value that they themselves had increased through their efforts to make their shacks inhabitable.

The developers also built new suburban housing in the suburbs of a better quality for the middle class, and marketed these, promising a new life on the fringes of the 'the city that is too hectic'. So the middle class were to discover the reality of suburban isolation, lack of urban life, and false hopes of public amenities. The economic crisis and political uncertainty of the 1970s caused the urban developers to alter their sights. With peripheral development halted by reluctant banks and a shrunken homeowners' market, real estate and builders turned to operating within the city. The large and recent housing estates were added to, to take advantage of the urban services and neighbourhood life that were at last beginning to take root there. But by building new blocks in the middle of a crowded area, developers created a new set of problems associated with a declining environmental quality: the sacrifice of open spaces, increased traffic and pollution, and overcrowded schools and public services.

At the same time rehabilitation policies were linked to new strategies of urban speculation in the city centre. These policies were beginning to force tenants out of rent controlled houses either by allowing the old buildings to crumble or by official declarations from city hall of their 'imminent ruin'. New land-use plans were designed to allow the demolition of entire neighbourhoods and their replacement by higher and more dense construction. Some limited gentrification began in the historic areas of Madrid. Hundreds of architecturally valuable buildings were threatened with destruction, while thousands of families were menaced with displacement, and the entire centre of the city appeared to be on the edge of the same fate as befell the nineteenth century boulevards ten years earlier. From uncontrolled high-rise urban expansion, Madrid was now moving towards on-the-spot demolition of its historic areas.

This was the ultimate extension of a model of urban development that was based on three premises:

1 The centralization and spatial concentration of economic activity on the basis of accelerated industrialization, leading to a massive exodus from the depressed regions, notably in the countryside, and to the location of companies, services, activities, and therefore jobs, in the Madrid metropolitan area.
2 The total control of this process by corporate financial capital, both in terms of industries and in the provision of housing and public works.[11] The banks, with close ties to the land-owners, set up urban development firms which were able to use a captive housing market as a

major source of profit. The total domination of capitalist interests on urban policy and the absolute lack of social control over urban development were key factors in explaining the rapidity of Madrid's urban growth, the brutality of its conditions, and the sharpness of its contradictions.

3 The basic underlying condition that could allow such urban development was the existence of an authoritarian state, founded on systematic police repression, the institutional ban of any voluntary association not controlled by the Phalange, and undemocratic administration at both national and local level.[12] Defenseless, people had little choice but to migrate, work ten hours a day for low wages, to commute for two hours, and buy expensive houses of poor quality in the middle of nowhere. The administration exchanged its favours with business groups for political allegiancy and active support. Widespread corruption among civil servants and plenty of 'mutual understanding' between public officials, big landowners, bankers, and developers made life easier for everybody.[13] So, the ability to keep all social protest under control by whatever political means were necessary was the fundamental prerequisite both for imbalanced urban-industrial growth and the use of Madrid's gigantic housing needs as the most profitable source of short term capital investment. The model of urban growth that shaped modern Madrid was based on specific political foundations, and the contradictions that it presented were soon expressed in political terms.

When the political structure finally came under serious attack, both from popular opposition and internal conflicts, state repression was somewhat slackened. As a result, a series of neighbourhood protests took place representing the entire range of urban problems engendered by Madrid's metropolitan development. The shanty town dwellers first demanded the improvement of services and later sought the redevelopment of their neighbourhoods for their own benefit. The repair of dilapidated public housing was required. Inhabitants of large peripheral housing estates struggled to obtain schools, health care centres, transportation, and other urban facilities. Residents of the new and massive concrete complexes claimed open space and green areas. Old neighbourhoods wanted to be protected from the bulldozer and gentrification, and demanded their improvement. Public opinion mobilized to save the remaining city, protect its monuments, and revitalize its traditions. All over Madrid, neighbourhoods, old and new, organized feasts and celebrations in a conscious effort to overcome their anonymity and social isolation. And because all claims and activities needed freedom to organize, franchise of political rights was demanded and the campaign to obtain an elected, democratic local government won overwhelming support from all social groups.

While the various contradictions brought on by the model of Madrid's urban development fuelled neighbourhood mobilization, such protest could only happen because of a loosening of the government's tight grip over its civil society. In other words, the political crisis commanded the expression of the urban crisis. This political crisis came from the internal contradictions of the regime as well as from increasing resistance from social movements and public opinion.[14] Internally, an increasingly diversified, industrialized, and modernized society clashed with a highly rigid, bureaucratic, and incompetent state apparatus, crippled by corruption and undermined by its obsolete fascist ideology.[15] Business circles, regional bourgeoisies, new managerial and professional sectors – all wanted access to power, and, particularly, a reliable procedure whereby major policy questions could be debated and decided upon. While they would have agreed on merciless authoritarianism in the event of serious danger or social revolution, there was no such danger in sight. So they called for limited democracy that would allow some civil rights and political plurality among the centre-right, while curbing popular opposition that, although it might not endanger social stability, could limit the extremely advantageous conditions for business in Spain.

The trouble however with this strategy was that the most active push for democratic institutions came from the grassroots. Foremost among the new social movements were the militant labour organizations which emerged spontaneously in the factories in the early 1960s in response to the need to represent workers' interests during rapid industrialization. Relying on Christian and communist leadership, the workers' commissions were able to infiltrate the official fascist trade unions, stage strikes and demonstrations, and become a major social force, respected and even recognized by the factories' management in spite of their illegal status which often led to police reprissals. Basque and Catalan nationalism won overwhelming support from their homeland population and across the entire political spectrum, as did labour unrest, so enabling the dissidents to challenge administrative centralism and cultural oppression. Militant Basques resorted to armed resistance destroying the myth of the invincible political police, and literally blowing up Franco's Prime Minister and personal confident, Carrero, who was killed by a Basque bomb. Student activists echoed in 1968 the French and Italian movements with open political rebellion on the nations' main campuses, trouble which required the permanent occupation of the classrooms by riot police. So the remaining argument for the regime's authoritarian outlook, namely its ability to enforce law and order and keep popular protest under control in order to preserve an easy way of life for business, was seriously undermined. The Church, middle class, press, as well as large sectors of the bourgeoisie began to wonder if it was worth suffering under such a heavy-handed state when it was clearly ineffective, and its repression more the residue of history than the means of insuring current interests. As a result, large and influential groups aspired towards democracy, and the administration had to cope with the new mood by informally tolerating popular organizations and collective protest as long as the political institutions and ideological values of the regime were not immediately and explicitly at stake.

It was in this context of political crisis, mounting social protest and fading support for the regime in the late 1960s that neighbourhoods started to mobilize and organize on a large scale. But this does not imply that the Citizen Movement was simply a response to a political crisis nor that the dictatorship was about to be overthrown. On the contrary: Franco, feeling threatened by political opposition, declared in 1969 a 'state of exception' in the entire country, jailed thousands of his enemies, dismantled popular organizations, issued long-term prison sentences to dozens of militants, killed a number of Basque activists, and restored order in the short-term. Underground parties and influential democratic leaders realized that, however shaken, the dictatorship could not be toppled unless massive political support could be won at the grassroots level. So began the reconstruction of a more cautious and less ideological labour movement, and the development of neighbourhood associations concerned with neighbourhood problems and community life. In this sense, we could argue that the Citizen Movement was allowed breathing space to express the acute urban problems by subjecting the authoritarian state to political pressure. But its resulting development, in turn, widened popular protest and self-organization, laying the ground for a broader and more legitimate attack against a system that, besides being fascist, was not supplying water to people's houses and was not preventing speculators from cutting down the city's trees.

The administration had to negotiate and accept some level of social control over urban development because of the growing strength of neighbourhood protest and organization. When the death of the dictator (November 1975) removed the main unifying pin behind the army's ability to maintain its authoritarian rule, the pressure for democracy greatly increased and opened the way for a democratically elected local government. Although the first free municipal elections had to wait until April 1979, the simple fact of having to confront public opinion in the polls destroyed the political basis on which the entire model of urban development was based. From then on, urban facilities were required, demolition was forbidden, price and standards were subject to discussion, extensive development had to accept planning directions, and community life burgeoned on top of the dust of quasi-military municipal ordinances. The people soon made their aspirations felt all over the city as they flourished under the first rays of light over their neighbourhoods and began a process of mobilization that gathered its own momentum. We will now turn our attention to the social characteristics of that mobilization.

23

A Social Profile of Madrid's Citizen Movement

To grasp the meaning of Madrid's neighbourhood Movement, we must first examine some of its basic characteristics, such as its historical evolution, organization, urban and political demands, and social and spatial specificity; in short, its profile as a social phenomenon. Only on this basis can our analysis of the Movement's emergence, dynamics, and effects be fully understood.

The urban mobilization that began in Madrid in the late 1960s developed around a series of demands that roughly corresponded to the main problems that gave rise to the urban crisis. It follows that, although urban protest was fostered by political initiatives, problems arising from the model of urban development nourished the Movement, provided its content and shaped its goals. Demands expressed by different neighbourhoods at different times covered a wide range of issues, but the most frequent and the most deeply felt were the following:

1 *Housing* – asking for newly built, decent and affordable public housing; protesting against the bad quality of public housing estates and demanding their redevelopment; demanding repairs and maintenance of new, private housing developments as well as of old dilapidated housing; requiring compensation for legal irregularities in the conditions of payment or in the state of the housing; asking for relocation of families displaced as a result of demolition or of urban renewal.

2 *Schooling* – especially for more public school places and better educational facilities; for control of the high fees of private schools; for cheaper textbooks; and for a better quality of teaching.

3 *Public health* – both in terms of health care facilities (dispensaries, rest homes, emergency medical services in the neighbourhood, an effective ambulance service), and good sanitary conditions (rubbish collection, an improved sewerage system, rat extermination, control of water pollution, etc.).

4 *Transportation* – including demands for improved and expanded public transport (undergrounds, buses, and suburban trains); improvement of access from the highways to neighbourhoods; and better traffic safety, brought about by overpasses and traffic lights to avoid the frequent accidents that bedevilled the newly built urban areas.

5 *More open space, preservation of parks, conservation of tree-lined streets* and general environmental protection.

6 *Preservation of the historic city* – its monuments, spatial form, population, and cultural traditions. This involved the opposition of demolition and requests for conservation and restoration.

7 *Improvement of social life in the neighbourhood* – promoting local associations, increasing opportunities of the social life, organizing cultural events, celebrations, street parties, song festivals, sports competitions, children's parties, Christmas parades, Spring picnics, and so on. These demands represented the people's desire (and ability) to overcome the loneliness and boredom of their metropolitan life.

8 *Political demands* – concerning the right for the neighbourhoods to organize voluntary associations, elect their board, call meetings, stage mass rallies, and more. The neighbourhoods often had to mobilize to obtain the freedom of some of their leaders, jailed under conspiracy charges, or to protest the banning of an association or meeting. Fired by their self-interested commitment for democracy, the Citizen Movement ultimately demanded political freedom, amnesty for political prisoners, and the unrestricted right of association and expression.

In the event of political democracy (1977–79) the Citizen Movement forwarded a new and more audacious demand: the request for grassroots participation in the elected institutions of local government, in the planning agencies, and in public programmes for urban redevelopment through the *ad hoc* representation of neighbourhood associations. They also asked, without success, that the new Spanish constitution (1978) recognize, as it had with labour unions and business associations, the degree to which neighbourhood associations were in the public interest.

We should emphasize that the expression of these demands developed in a distinctive way: a given neighbourhood, when successful, tended to shift from defensive demands (resistance against gentrification and displacement) to offensive demands (public redevelopment for the benefit of residents) in order to assert a local culture (fairs, celebrations, support of local networks), and then to raise the level to institutional reform (asking for participation in the local government). This progression and the ever-widening goals that came with it are crucial to our evaluation of the Citizen Movement as an agent of social change.

Thus, although each neighbourhood first mobilized around a particular issue, the subsequent development of collective action led to a continuous overlapping of demands in the majority of neighbourhoods. This was perhaps one of the most important characteristics of Madrid's urban Movement – it was composed of organizations that were concerned with all sorts of issues, and each was based in and responsible for one territory. Once a particular problem had succeeded in temporarily mobilizing people in a given area, the active wing of the Movement, often led by political militants, worked to establish a neighbourhood association that would eventually take care of organizing and mobilizing the residents around all kinds of problems concerning their living conditions, cultural activities, and social life as well as, from time to time, their political stands. As a result of this shifting from one issue to another, from one struggle to another, a permanent organization would emerge in one of three possible shapes:

1 The most usual form emphasized the role of a steering committee, elected yearly by a general assembly of all the membership. The committee designated permanent working groups on topics such as schools, housing, health, planning, women, and youth. The working groups were formed by the most militant members, meeting every week, and asking for the

support of the entire neighbourhood when needed. The critical moment in the life of the association came on election day, since several political factions would try to win support for their candidates, often leading to bitter controversies and blocking tactics by the losing side.
2 Some associations combined the preceding scheme with a decentralized organization consisting of block clubs and street delegates to foster participation and create a more intense involvement in the association's initiatives. This model was usually related to a burning problem that concerned most of the neighbourbood.
3 Other neighbourhoods mobilized themselves around regular general meetings that everybody could attend. This approach was often accompanied by a strong personal leader who was able to act on decisions reached in tumultuous circumstances. This alternative was basically a response to the immediate danger of police repression and relied on collective solidarity as a deterrent to institutional violence.

Whatever specific forms the associations took, two major characteristics must be noted. First, they were in most cases, *de facto*, illegal organizations given the institutional ban on all voluntary associations outside the Franquist Party, although a few neighbourhoods, particularly in the early times of the Movement, managed to present their organization as part of the legal structure of the Franquist Party (for example, Asociaciones de Cabezas de Familia, linked to the Movimiento Nacional). So for the overwhelming majority of neighbourhood associations, the very fact of their existence was a breakthrough for democracy against an authoritarian state. Aware of this, residents were extremely cautious when they participated, always counting themselves as representative of the entire ward's population, picking on sensible popular issues, and limiting their political stance to the affirmation of the right to exist. An association going any further was inviting trouble.

Second, each association was territorially defined, and in many cases borderlines were drawn on a map to clarify areas of responsibility (border disputes sometimes ensued). This territoriality is absolutely crucial to understanding both the emergence of the neighbourhood Movement and the political challenge it represented. In spite of the absence of legal recognition, the associations, by describing their competence over a specific territory, were staking claims beyond their immediate struggle. Even though one basic urban issue always remained the principal focus of the associations' activity, as well as the *raison d'être* for its initiation, they were asking for residents' self-reliance in the definition and management of all their problems, from housing to prices, from schools to women's conditions.

When in 1977 the government agreed to legalize the neighbourhood associations, it significantly imposed a major condition: the name of each association should be unique, generally with a religious meaning, and should not indicate the name of the neighbourhood (so the Association of St. Joseph instead of the Association of Hortaleza). An association was clearly not supposed to represent the residents of the neighbourhood, but only those who were voluntary members of it. The associations accepted the conditions, but continued to consider themselves representatives of the entire neighbourhood. Sometimes it was an obvious overstatement, but often as not the associations represented a militant vanguard which expressed the main concerns of its neighbourhood. At the time of our survey, in mid-1977, there were about 110 associations in Madrid, counting on some 60,000 members with a hard core of about 5,000 militants. Certainly, in statistical terms, they could not pretend to represent 4,300,000 people, but in the neighbourhoods where they were active, could claim to voice the main concerns of the residents, more or less in the same way that a small minority of unionized workers in a factory may represent the collective interests of all the workers. This notion of social representation on the basis of territoriality is what made the Citizen Movement so

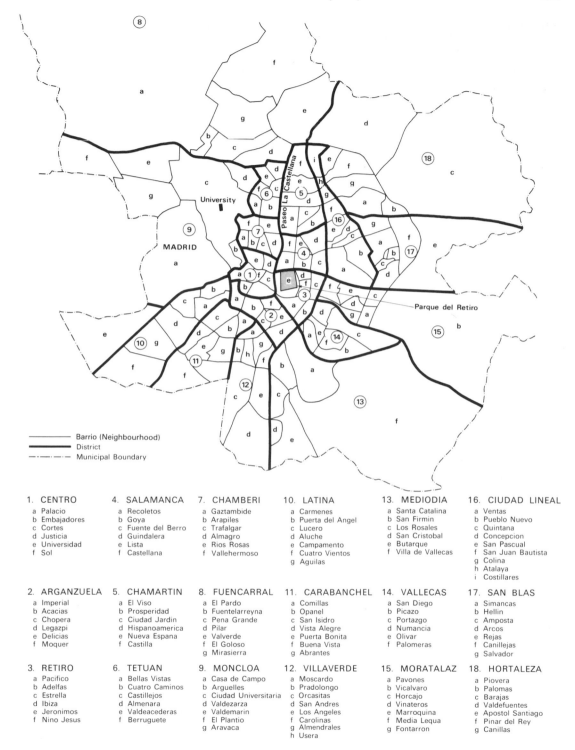

Map 23.1 The location and names of the neighbourhoods of Madrid.
(*Source for all the maps of Madrid*: Our study.)

Legend:
——— Barrio (Neighbourhood)
━━━ District
—·—·—· Municipal Boundary

1. CENTRO
a Palacio
b Embajadores
c Cortes
d Justicia
e Universidad
f Sol

2. ARGANZUELA
a Imperial
b Acacias
c Chopera
d Legazpi
e Delicias
f Moquer

3. RETIRO
a Pacifico
b Adelfas
c Estrella
d Ibiza
e Jeronimos
f Nino Jesus

4. SALAMANCA
a Recoletos
b Goya
c Fuente del Berro
d Guindalera
e Lista
f Castellana

5. CHAMARTIN
a El Viso
b Prosperidad
c Ciudad Jardin
d Hispanoamerica
e Nueva Espana
f Castilla

6. TETUAN
a Bellas Vistas
b Cuatro Caminos
c Castillejos
d Almenara
e Valdeacederas
f Berruguete

7. CHAMBERI
a Gaztambide
b Arapiles
c Trafalgar
d Almagro
e Rios Rosas
f Vallehermoso

8. FUENCARRAL
a El Pardo
b Fuentelarreyna
c Pena Grande
d Pilar
e Valverde
f El Goloso
g Mirasierra

9. MONCLOA
a Casa de Campo
b Arguelles
c Ciudad Universitaria
d Valdezarza
e Valdemarin
f El Plantio
g Aravaca

10. LATINA
a Carmenes
b Puerta del Angel
c Lucero
d Aluche
e Campamento
f Cuatro Vientos
g Aguilas

11. CARABANCHEL
a Comillas
b Opanel
c San Isidro
d Vista Alegre
e Puerta Bonita
f Buena Vista
g Abrantes

12. VILLAVERDE
a Moscardo
b Pradolongo
c Orcasitas
d San Andres
e Los Angeles
f Carolinas
g Almendrales
h Usera

13. MEDIODIA
a Santa Catalina
b San Firmin
c Los Rosales
d San Cristobal
e Butarque
f Villa de Vallecas

14. VALLECAS
a San Diego
b Picazo
c Portazgo
d Numancia
e Olivar
f Palomeras

15. MORATALAZ
a Pavones
b Vicalvaro
c Horcajo
d Vinateros
e Marroquina
f Media Lequa
g Fontarron

16. CIUDAD LINEAL
a Ventas
b Pueblo Nuevo
c Quintana
d Concepcion
e San Pascual
f San Juan Bautista
g Colina
h Atalaya
i Costillares

17. SAN BLAS
a Simancas
b Hellin
c Amposta
d Arcos
e Rejas
f Canillejas
g Salvador

18. HORTALEZA
a Piovera
b Palomas
c Barajas
d Valdefuentes
e Apostol Santiago
f Pinar del Rey
g Canillas

controversial, since it presented a challenge to the new democracy which was based on political parties. Although the neighbourhood associations, led by political militants, always presented themselves as a complement, and never as an alternative, to representative democracy, the politicians never overcame their distrust of an organization that was, in practice, drawing too subtle and too dangerous a distinction between citizenry and citizenship. We will return in detail to the crucial issue of the relationship between parties and movements, between democracy and grassroots participation. What matters at this point are the consequences of the territorial definition of the Citizen Movement.

The most important of these consequences was that, given the specificity of the urban problems of different neighbourhoods, the Citizen Movement developed various ploys to suit a variety of urban situations, a strategy that built up for the Movement an array of issues, contradictions, and processes of mobilizations to work on. This was another major feature of the Movement: its organizational and cultural unity was built upon a highly diverse urban and social universe. Basic differences in urban situations led to different forms of neighbourhood movement, the profile of which can be reduced to following typology of urban mobilization:

1 *Shanty town mobilizations* – starting in the mid 1960s, they were mobilizations to win broad support, particularly in the working class areas of southern Madrid (Vallecas, Orcasitas). Formed by unskilled construction workers, and relying on the support of Catholic parishes, they usually went though three stages of struggle, each one with specific demands. First, they tried to obtain a basic level of sanitation and urban services, as well as the right to improve their shacks. Second, when the improvement in the shanty town area made it desirable for profitable private redevelopment, they had to oppose urban renewal projects that would have displaced all shanty town dwellers. Third, turning the official argument for shanty town clearance on its head, they mobilized to obtain public urban redevelopment programmes for their own benefit.

2 *Public housing estate mobilizations* – a number of massive protests took place in the large public housing estates managed by the Ministry of Housing, as well as by the Franquist Trade Union Housing Programme (Obra Sindical del Hogar). Protests were aimed mainly at the appalling quality of housing construction, asking first for repairs and maintenance and later, when the blocks started to crumble, requesting the entire rebuilding of the project (San Blas).

3 *Protests over the urban facilities in the privately developed, large housing estates* – the largest urban mobilization of the Madrid metropolitan area, in terms of numbers of participants, took place in the huge new developments built by private real estate corporations, both in the immediate periphery (Mortatalza, Aluche, El Pilar), and in remote suburban locations (Leganes, Getafe, Alcorcon, Mostoles, Parla, Alcala-de-Henares). While most of these developments were inhabited by industrial workers, a significant proportion of their population was made up of young middle class couples who predominated in some areas (Santa Maria, Hortaleza). And yet the basic issue underlying most mobilizations was the same: the need for urban facilities, particularly education, health, urban infrastructure, and water supply.

4 *The revolt of middle class residential neighbourhoods* – even some upper middle class suburban neighbourhoods inhabited by engineers, professionals, high level civil servants (for example Alameda de Osuna) actively participated in the Citizen Movement. Having dreamed of a 'new life' in the exclusive residential condominiums as promised by real estate advertisements, they discovered the mediocre environmental quality of these new quarters, the lack of facilities, the boredom of anonymous urban settings, and ultimately, the overcrowding as open space was consumed by new housing to enhance profitability. So they

asked for environmental preservation and better urban facilities, while using the neighbourhood association as a way to foster communal life.

5 *The preservation and revitalization of central Madrid* – a major component of the Movement developed from 1975 on, originating with the opposition by various social groups to the transformation of central Madrid by real estate speculation. New urban development suggested the demolition of buildings, the destruction of historic neighbourhoods, and the displacement of most of the people who had lived there over many years. The Malasana Plan, seeking inroads into the heart of the city, was successfully opposed by the residents who had the support of public opinion and the architects. Downtown neighbours fought eviction and forced landlords to repair and maintain the buildings, halting the deliberate running-down of areas. Students, small merchants, the elderly, professional and service workers joined in efforts to preserve the city and to rehabilitate its aging quarters. A striking development in the same direction was the massive (and successful) defense in 1977–78 of middle class garden cities in central Madrid against a land-use municipal ordinance inspired by real estate interests that would have permitted new construction and less open space.

The Citizen Movement covered in its practice the entire range of urban issues, from satisfying basic housing needs to preserving historic quarters. This fragmentation of the Movement represented one of its major strengths, since it allowed a very disparate spectrum of interests and local cultures to feel represented in each neighbourhood without being committed to one broad programme the social basis of which would probably have been felt to be missing. But this argument did not satisfy the political vanguard of the Movement. In the traditional socialist conception (social democratic, as well as Leninist), a mass movement only becomes a force to be reckoned with when it has a centralized and well-articulated organization. Thus, in 1974 a handful of neighbourhood groups, feeling the Movement to be strong enough, created Madrid's Provincial Federation of Neighbourhood Associations (FPAV), electing a board and a president on the basis of a vote for each participating association. From the outset, the struggle was on since the government declared it illegal and jailed its president. To free him and to maintain the right to organize a federation, the neighbourhood associations took to the streets, clashed with the police, and obtained *de facto* tolerance for the Federation; this heroic origin kept the Federation alive. In practice it was always a superstructure using the grassroots strength to take stands and issue public appeals on behalf of the neighbourhoods, but also (and importantly) it fulfilled the political strategies of the Partido Comunista de España (PCE) and of the Organizacion Revolucionaria de Trabajadores (ORT),[16] the two main parties that had agreed to share power in the executive committee of the Federation, so excluding it from all other social influences. For most associations, including those led by the PCE and ORT, participation in the Federation was a matter of political discipline in which party instructions were to be followed rather than a belief in the Federation usefulness to the Movement.

This attitude did not imply a territorial approach. Each time the Movement needed to appear as a single entity it did so easily, staging major demonstrations on a particular issue with which many people from many neighbourhoods could identify. Thus, in 1975, 20,000 people gathered in Cuatro Caminos to maintain the pressure for more and better schools; in May 1976, 60,000 people demonstrated in Calle Preciados against the cost of living; in September 1976, 100,000 filled up the Moratalaz area to protest fraud in the making of bread . . . and to ask for political democracy; in Spring 1977, dozens of public meetings were held to obtain the legalization of neighbourhood associations; in September 1978, 70,000 people demonstrated in Vallecas to ask for effective measures to solve the housing crisis. Each time, an informal network of militants of different associations started the necessary co-ordinating; the Federation acted as sponsor, but its role was always limited to a series of telephone calls to the media by its only representative, its president. In fact, thousands of people attended the meetings and participated in the campaigns because they were committed to the issues and because, by virtue of their mobilization, they were asserting their right to exist as an autonomous social force.

If, however, we emphasize the parasitic nature of the organizations which tried to act as 'umbrellas' for the neighbourhood associations we are not simply engaged in an ideological debate over the 'nice grassroots' and the 'nasty bureaucrats'; it is crucially important for our research to observe that all attempts to encapsulate the territorial organizations under a unified strategic command similar to the one of the trade unions failed and actually damaged the Movement by triggering sectarian in-fighting. Furthermore, when the neighbourhoods were required to agree on issues determined by a given leadership (instead of a programme), they refused to confine themselves to their local strongholds and attempted to mobilize the entire city. In fact, the tension between neighbourhoods and city-wide organizations did not represent the opposition between local and national approaches to the urban and political programmes, but the thin edge existing between urban corporatism and political instrumentalism. Our analysis will have to deal with this issue as a major element for the understanding of the overall urban change.

Thus territoriality was an essential element of Madrid's neighbourhood movement. All attempts to transcend these spatial attachments were mainly motivated by strategies of political control which ultimately weakened the Movement. Neighbourhood associations were then closely linked to specific spatial units. How specific were those units? Were neighbourhood associations typical of all sorts of urban space? Or were they fostered by certain social and functional characteristics that happened to be concentrated in specific areas? The answers to these questions are crucial, since we are asking whether the neighbourhood Movement responded to specific social interests and functional needs or if, on the contrary, it was the expression of a new form of collective action across all the social and urban spectrums. A systematic treatment of the topic requires the introduction of some analytical tools, but we may start by studying the relationship between Madrid's neighbourhood associations and the characteristics of the areas in which they were located.

To proceed, we have carried out three research operations:

1 To locate the neighbourhood associations in the 120 administrative boroughs of the city of Madrid.
2 To determine the urban and social characteristics of Madrid's spatial units.
3 To study the relationship between the characteristics of spatial units and the presence and level of mobilization of neighbourhood associations.

The Methodological Appendix (pp. 365–94) provides technical explanations and detailed justification of the procedures we have used. Let us simply explain a few elements to make our analysis comprehensible. We first listed 77 of Madrid's 92 neighbourhood associations on which we had accurate information. (As we will justify in the Appendix, the statistical analysis only concerns the city of Madrid, representing 3,300,000 people and 92 of the 110 neighbourhood associations of the metropolitan area.) We classified them at three levels of mobilization according to their relative strength and representativeness. Then we mapped the address of their headquarters, always a focal spatial point in their area of activity. To determine Madrid's social and urban characteristics on a disaggregated spatial basis, a more complex mechanism was required, given the total absence of analysis on this matter at the time of our research. So we did two factor analyses, one on the basis of all existing population and social data, another on the basis of all available functional, economic and urban data. Each factor analysis provided us with four factors concentrating in themselves all of the basic social and functional characteristics of the city. According to the value scored by each spatial unit on each factor, we ranked the boroughs into eight different scales. Following the ranking from each scale we defined six levels for each factor, enabling us to classify Madrid's spatial units in six categories for each factor. The eight criteria (based on the factor analyses) for classifying and differentiating Madrid's spatial units were the following:

1 Social status
2 Recent immigration
3 Aging population
4 The residential space of the bureaucracy
5 Quality of housing and urban facilities
6 Level of consolidation of urban structures (old city)
7 Importance of recent urban development (urban dormitory)
8 Importance of productive activities in the spatial unit (space of production)

To avoid any pitfalls due to the excessive synthetic emphasis of factor analysis techniques, we also classified Madrid in relationship to the values scored by each spatial unit on three additional and simple variables:

9 Proportion of manual workers over the resident population
10 Proportion of technicians over the resident population
11 Alternative life style (measured by proportion of divorced and/or separated people)[17]

On the basis of these eleven criteria we drew ten maps of Madrid (Maps 23–2–11) classified on six levels. On each of these maps we have represented the neighbourhood associations, symbolized in three levels of strength. To make the analysis less intuitive, we calculated an elementary statistical measure: the rank-order correlation coefficient (Spearman Test) between the score obtained by each spatial unit at the three levels of neighbourhood mobilization and each one of the eight scores obtained in the six-level scales constructed on the basis of the eight resulting factors from our correlation matrixes (Table 23–1). The results were as follows:

Table 23.1 Rank-order correlation (Spearman Test) between level of neighbourhood mobilization

And:	
1 Social status	−0·37
2 Recent immigration	−0·01
3 Aging population	−0·12
4 Residence of bureaucrats	−0·06
5 Quality of housing and urban facilities	−0·33
6 Consolidation of urban structure (old city)	−0·20
7 Recent urban development	0·34
8 Production-oriented space	0·09

What can we conclude on the basis of these series of maps and coefficients? The most striking factor is the highly scattered location pattern of neighbourhood mobilization activities,

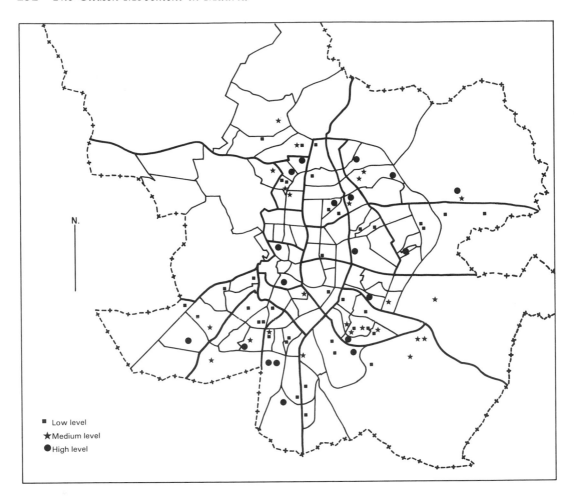

Map 23.2 Location of neighbourhood associations classified according to their level of mobilization, *c.* 1979.

both in terms of their organization and strength. The working class sections of southern Madrid were certainly more organized and militant than elsewhere. Nevertheless, this trend is overshadowed by the main discovery of our research: neighbourhood organization, at least at the peak of its development in the period 1977–79, was apparently ubiquitous and only subsided in the most exclusive residential areas (except for a few notable exceptions, like Salamanca and El-Retiro).

The rank-order correlation coefficient expresses this pattern in a more synthetic way, and there are five basic conclusions:

1 Most social or urban factors do not seem to have been distributed along the same spatial sequence of neighbourhood mobilizations.
2 There are only three significant correlation coefficients but they express a moderate spatial overlapping between social-urban characteristics and urban struggles. With these qualifications, it is important to consider what the tendencies were.
3 The higher the social status of residential space was, the lower the level of urban mobiliza-

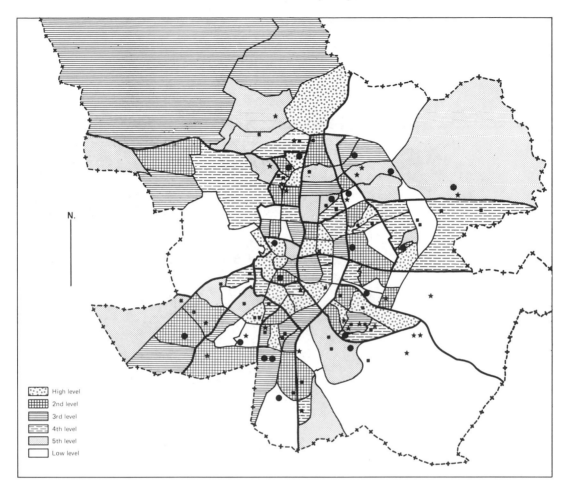

Map 23.3 Location of neighbourhood associations, in areas ranked in six levels according to their social standing, 1978.

tion. Thus, while the neighbourhood Movement cut across most social contexts, its main support tended to remain in the working class wards.

4 The more recent the urbanization, the greater likelihood there was to find an active neighbourhood organization. Madrid's Citizen Movement seems therefore to have been a response to the rapidity and brutality of the urban growth. This figure also suggests (without being too conclusive) a quite important observation: while the search for community was apparently a driving force for the Movement, the existence of a well-established social network does not seem to have been a necessary prerequisite.

5 The lower the quality of housing and urban facilities were, the higher the level of neighbourhood mobilization. The Citizen Movement was fostered by acute urban needs while not being limited to these causes.

The analysis of the urban and social characteristics of the spatial units where neighbourhood associations lived and fought points towards a two-fold conclusion:

1 Social needs (as measured by a low social status) and urban needs (as measured by low

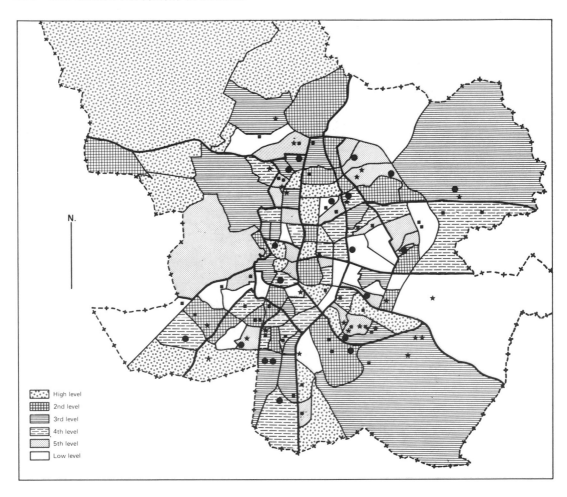

Map 23.4 Location of neighbourhood associations in areas ranked in six levels according to the numbers of recent immigrants among the residents of each neighbourhood, 1978.

residential quality and recent urban development) had an influence on the Movement's fermentation. So it was not merely a political movement but also took place as a response to social and economic dimensions of the urban crisis.

2 At the same time, neighbourhood associations and urban protest developed in a variety of urban situations and social contexts. The Citizen Movement was not mechanically determined by the social characteristics of a given territory. Neighbourhood mobilization occurred in Madrid as a series of locally-based convergent responses to a wider urban crisis, a series that followed in the wake of increasing political tension.

In terms of its historical evolution, the starting point of the Citizen Movement in Madrid was the aftermath of the repressive move in 1969 by the Franquist government.[18] Political opposition learned that direct confrontation with the dictatorship was suicidal. Thus, the crucial ploy was to allow claims for political democracy to find broad social support, founded on people's needs. While the Workers' Commissions had been a major step in this direction, they were confined to the militant labour movement and were too closely connected with com-

Map 23.5 Location of neighbourhood associations in areas ranked in six levels according to the proportion of aged among the residents of each neighbourhood, 1978.

munists to be supported by a majority of the population. So the PCE, as well as the radical left parties, being the only organized and active left wing forces in Spain at that time,[19] posted some of their militants to organize and mobilize neighbourhood protest founded on dramatic urban needs. They often used the incipient work done by the Church on such issues. (The second largest party within the Citizen Movement, the Maoist ORT, was a spin-off of militant Jesuits located in both the factories and the shanty towns.) The Movement gradually overcame repression by always presenting itself as only being interested in the satisfaction of immediate urban needs. There were three major phases in its development:

1 From 1969 to 1974 the Movement consolidated its neighbourhood bases, particularly in the shanty towns and in the public housing estates, and established its credibility by fighting the abuses of the speculators whose correction was requested by the administration.
2 From 1974 to 1977 the Movement fought major battles to obtain legal recognition as part of the final popular assault to end authoritarian rule. When the state became less able to control neighbourhood activities, dozens of new organizations arose and many communities won

N.

High level
2nd level
3rd level
4th level
5th level
Low level

Map 23.6 Location of neighbourhood associations in area ranked in six levels according to the proportion of bureaucrats (civil servants, military and police) among the residents of each neighbourhood, 1978.

substantial victories for housing and urban services by taking on a demoralized and confused administration which was trying to regain lost political ground as it stood on the threshold of the new democratic era.

3 Once recognized and consolidated, the Movement expanded from 1977 to 1979 to encompass a greater variety of urban situations and social classes. At the same time, given the essential role played by political militants in its leadership, it entered into a series of major conflicts to defend its autonomy against partisan control, and to survive the attacks from socialists and centre parties that refused political recognition to grassroots organizations because they could not claim electoral support. The Movement survived this crisis by making new demands, mainly focused on housing and urban renewal and by advancing the concept of participatory democracy in local government and planning institutions. But when, in April 1979, the first democratic municipal elections in forty years gave the government of Madrid to a socialist-communist coalition, the Citizen Movement fell apart, unable to absorb the contradiction between its political origins and its autonomous stand as a social movement.

Thus, direct observation of the Movement does not allow us to draw any firm conclusion

Map 23.7 Location of neighbourhood associations in area ranked in six levels according to the proportion of separated and divorced people among the residents of each neighbourhood, 1978.

about its social meaning. Here and there some hints appear. But neither the urban-social characteristics of the neighbourhoods nor the evolution of the political struggles can explain its dynamics, concerns, and effects. To understand Madrid's Citizen Movement as a process of social change, we need to undertake an analytical journey, and for such a journey to be fruitful we need to enter into the Movement's everyday life, to involve ourselves in some of its experiences, and to discover the diversity behind the general description we have so far provided. By closely examining a few case studies we will be able to see some of the social processes at work that our analysis attempts to explain at the end of this part.

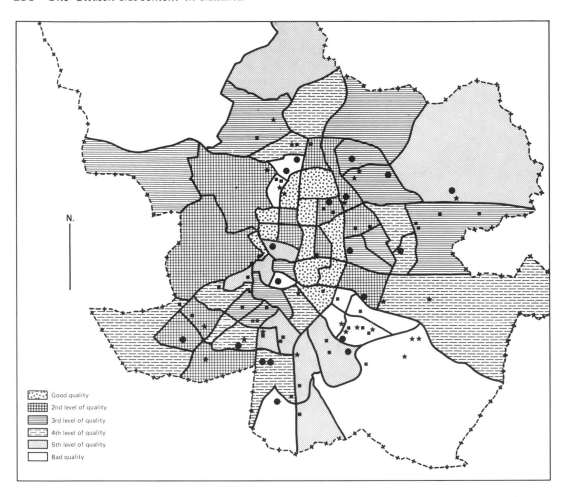

N.

Good quality
2nd level of quality
3rd level of quality
4th level of quality
5th level of quality
Bad quality

Map 23.8 Location of neighbourhood associations in areas ranked in six levels according to the quality of housing in each area, 1979.

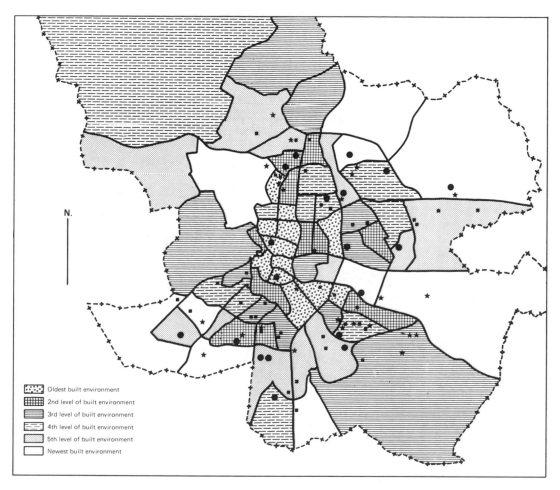

N.

Oldest built environment
2nd level of built environment
3rd level of built environment
4th level of built environment
5th level of built environment
Newest built environment

Map 23.9 Location of neighbourhood associations in areas ranked in six levels according to the age of the built environment in each area, 1979.

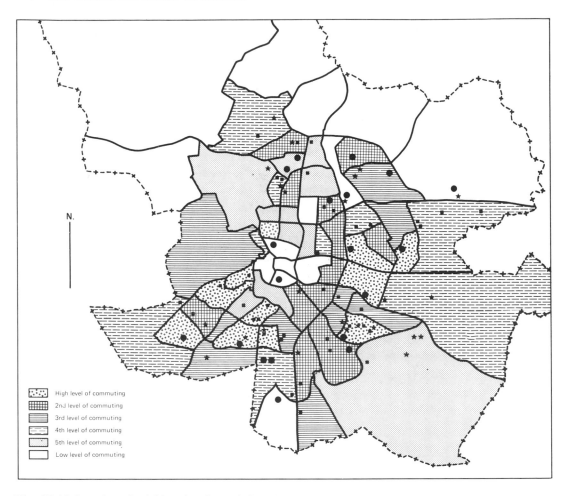

Map 23.10 Location of neighbourhood associations in areas ranked in six levels according to the proportion of people commuting among the residents of each area, 1979.

Map 23.11 Location of neighbourhood associations in areas ranked in six levels according to the importance of productive activities in relation of the land-use pattern of each area, 1979.

24

Inside the Neighbourhoods: Selected Case Studies

The Madrid's Citizen Movement was so diverse, active and important that it is difficult to do it justice. Indeed we will not reconstruct the experience and all its passions, colours, struggles and dreams, for our intention is not to convey feelings but to understand. And yet we must watch the Movement's operations, appreciate the connections between its different elements, be sensitive to the rising consciousness it represented and reveal the skullduggery behind the organizational manoeuvring since our research, as stated, is based on a detailed observation of 23 neighbourhood associations and their activities. We have already charted the main lines of the Movement's collective action and provided a tentative explanation of its birth, structure development, achievements and failures. We will present the final results of our analyses at the end of this part, once our account has provided a solid enough foundation to do so.

However some familiarity with Madrid's neighbourhood Movement is necessary and this is best done by entering the neighbourhoods themselves. Rather than discuss all the neighbourhoods, we shall select a few cases that represent the variety of urban situations underlying different mobilizations and cover a wide range of political influences, social class interests, and effects on the urban system. We will outline the fundamental trends of mobilization occurring in a shanty town (Orcasitas); in a large suburban working class housing estate (Alcala de Henares); in a large, socially mixed high-rise housing complex, fighting to prevent major commercial development on its last vacant spot of land (El Pilar); in the oldest historic neighbourhood of the downtown area (Lavapies); and in the middle class garden cities of central Madrid (Colonias de Hotelitos). Our journey will still be too brief but it will nevertheless offer us an opportunity to listen to the residents' voices and make the connections between experience and theory easier to draw when the time comes.

Orcasitas: The City For Those Who Built It

Orcasitas: two thousand shacks built by immigrants during the 1950s in the southern area of Villaverde, relatively close to Madrid's centre. Their origin follows the pattern of expansion already described. Their story tells how they went from a disorderly conglomerate of miserable dwellings to an organized community able to control its own urban development.

At first, the struggle was for individual survival: how to obtain tolerance for self-help construction from landowners and from corrupt officials. Then there were some steps towards collective survival: bringing water supply, paving the streets, disposing of the rubbish, and connecting the electricity. In 1970, to make sure that nobody would be left without water supply, the first informal neighbourhood organization was created, a spontaneous and apolitical gesture.

Once the neighbourhood had obtained, however, a minimum level of facilities, the problems worsened. A new land-use plan, backed by the landowners and approved by the administration, proposed clearance, promised relocation to undisclosed housing, and supported private redevelopment of new housing for medium income families. This plan was resisted at first by the residents who claimed their right to stay in an area that they had cultivated over many years. But then the shanty town dwellers decided to take a more positive stance. They did really not like their shacks, nor did they object to the development of new housing, and improvement to urban services and environmental quality, but they wanted to guarantee all of this for themselves by asking the administration to relocate them in new, affordable housing, in the same area. What was therefore at stake in Orcasitas was public acknowledgement that the occupants of the illegal shanty town settlements who were, after all, responsible for utilizing the area and increasing its value should be the first to benefit once the area had been redeveloped.

The residents added another important request: they should be active participants in the redevelopment as well as in the design of the buildings. To do so, they asked that their advocacy planners be appointed by the administration to operate the redevelopment pro-gramme. They also established their own channels of social control over the architects and planners they proposed. While these professionals added crucial support to the movement, they were always kept at a distance from the leadership which was indigeneous to the neigh-bourhood. The militants and leaders were no different from the residents: all were con-struction workers coming to Madrid in search of jobs from the impoverished rural regions of Andalucia, La Mancha and Extremadura. Many became unemployed in the 1970s and as a result (successfully) fought for the privilege to be employed in the construction of their own houses.

The neighbourhood association started around a group of six residents who, in 1970, got together to ensure the equal distribution of all urban services to the entire neighbourhood, and when there was a danger of displacement the group was easily able to organize the neighbour-hood; by 1977, 1,400 families were formal members of the association. They met once a year to elect a committee; it was always only one collective candidacy which, at the beginning at least, was entirely apolitical. The committee met once a week and the meeting was open to all on one condition: that each person should be prepared to share the tasks to be performed. A general meeting also took place once a week with attendance oscillating between 100 and 900 people. Theoretically, only this assembly could make decisions, the committee being its executive arm. But another informal power centre developed on a day-to-day basis around the neighbourhood's natural leader, a young jeweller who became president of the association, spokesman and negotiator with the administration, and counsellor and educator for his fellow residents. Working at home, his shack became the community's meeting place and his advice was requested on many issues, a role that should have been fulfilled by the local priest but he was distrusted and counted too conservative.

An important factor in the neighbourhood's success was the judicious combination of dif-ferent tactics, and particularly crucial was the use of legal action against eviction. They took their case in 1974 to the Supreme Court and won, having obtained effective advice from plan-ners and lawyers. The main line of attack was to repeat the usual statement in redevelopment schemes that 'redevelopment should be orientated towards social goals', and in so doing, they were able to sustain that the most important social goal was the well-being of the current residents which meant, among other things, staying put. This argument only worked because it could count on the residents' mobilization as well as the support of public opinion. The people of Orcasistas, aware of the administration's unwillingness to concede that it favoured real estate speculation, caused considerable embarrassment by pointing to the scandal of shanty towns in a modern, affluent city. The association also cleverly played on the incon-sistencies within the administration while avoiding local antagonisms, allying with the technicians and pointing all criticisms in the direction of the major authority, the delegate of the Ministry of Housing. After four delegates in 14 months were successively removed from their post because of their inability to handle the shanty town problem, negotiations became easier. But before it was ready to bargain, Orcasitas first had to demonstrate before the Ministry of Housing, invade city hall, organize sit-ins in several public buildings, fill the press with news for several years, publicize their cause in the university colleges, and win support from architects and planners, as well as from the Church, labour unions, and political parties.

The relationship to politics was a special one. The neighbourhood association expanded, relying on residents who had lived in the shanty towns a long time, an exclusive attitude that was maintained in terms of recruitment and commitment, even though the association was not apolitical. In 1974, when the Movement expanded in Madrid and tried to obtain legal recognition, Orcasitas took part in the creation of the Federation of Neighbourhood Associations, came to share the Federation's more politicized views on the need to fight for democracy, amnesty, and political freedom, views that were strengthened as a result of contact with the advocacy planners. The Federation's most prominent leader joined the PCE in 1976 and after him the core of the leadership also became communists; but although actively participating in political campaigns, they always made a point of distancing the associations from any given political stand. The most striking expression of this fierce political autonomy came in 1979 when the PCE offered the position of an alderman in Madrid's local government to the leader of Orcasitas. Although he continued to support the PCE, he refused in order to remain in close proximity to his neighbourhood during the crucial time in which it was to be transformed as a result of the general success of the Movement.

Community mobilization in Orcasitas did produce major urban, political, and cultural transformations in the neighbourhood as well as in the city. The neighbourhood was redeveloped. Shacks were demolished and all the dwellers were rehoused in the same place in new, good, affordable government-sponsored housing (all families were charged the nominal price of 2,000 pesetas a month – about 70 American dollars – over twenty years). By 1980, 1,500 housing units had been built and 760 additional flats were underway, enough not only to serve the Orcasitas' families but also several hundred from surrounding shanty town settlements.

The important aspect of the programme was the legal constraints imposed by the neighbourhood association and finally approved by the Ministry. Land and shacks were expropriated, but land was to be valued at its original rural price, while the shacks were to be valued at their market price after the shanty town's development. The rationale was, again, that residents should be compensated for their efforts, while landowners should not be rewarded for mere speculation. As a result, the impact of land on the cost of housing was very low, while shanty town dwellers received a large sum that could be used as the main payment for their new housing.

Furthermore, the residential complex was better equipped than most middle class neighbourhoods in Madrid, including a new school, kindergarten, civic centre, health centre, sports facilities, and funds and support for cultural and recreational activities. Residents also obtained a sizeable public park (about 70 hectares) close to the neighbourhood, large enough for the population of southern Madrid which had been deprived until that time of any open space.

The Orcasitas model had an impact on urban politics beyond the successful redevelopment of its own neighbourhood, and was adopted as the pattern to be followed. By 1979 the government had agreed to implement similar procedures for all shanty towns in Madrid, affecting about 30,000 families. Some of the programmes were under way in 1980, mainly in the highly

Plate 24.1 The new high-rise public housing estates of Orcasitas, Madrid, 1981, obtained by the local residents after a 10 year struggle. The people were previously living in shacks constructed by themselves, similar to the one in the foreground of the photograph. This shack housed the residents' association and so was saved from demolition. (Photograph: E. Cachafeiros.)

mobilized areas of Vallecas, but others would probably have to be fought for again. But, from our point of view, the breaching of the apparently unalterable logic of speculative develop-ment was decisive. The state at last recognized the right to channel urban value to those who had built the city – not to those who owned the land, nor to the would-be developers seeking profit from urbanization. So use value as opposed to exchange value was established as the legitimate source for benefiting from public programmes. And urban policy was redesigned to ensure that the inner ring around the core of Madrid would be inhabited by the shanty town dwellers after the disposal of their shacks: urban renewal, but not social removal. By reversing this universal trend, Orcasitas and the shanty towns succeeded in achieving a major urban change.

Another innovative aspect was to impose residents' participation in the design and imple-mentation of the land-use plan and in the construction of housing blocks. In fact, architectural innovation was somewhat limited and the neighbourhood's landscape was most traditional, but, as one of the leaders put it, 'It is our right to decide our ugliness . . .' When, in 1977, the Madrid Metropolitan Planning Authority instigated a new procedure of participatory planning, Orcasitas was in the minds of all former technocrats who had learned that the residents' input was not only a question of democracy, but also one of effectiveness in assessing needs and finding adequate solutions. The same level of participation was intended to continue in the running of all neighbourhood services, fostering the idea of urban self-management supported by public funds.

The urban impact of the Orcasitas movement would have never been achieved without its capacity to profoundly transform the cultural patterns of the neighbourhood. Its search for community created a network of solidarity that was the best possible protection against repression and the most immediate reward for day-to-day involvement in the activities of the association. It was not, as can be argued, the expression of a community attacked from the outside; on the contrary, Orcasitas, in common with most shantytowns in Madrid and elsewhere, was a fragmented, hostile, and alienated world, made up of individuals fighting each other for survival. One of the first initiatives of the association was to break down these inner social walls and to establish a cultural bond (for instance, an annual religious parade was organized to honour a Saint who, the leaders said, was going to protect Orcasitas from then on). A major element in this strategy was the building of the association's public hall in the centre of the neighbourhood, using the residents' voluntary labour on their Sundays off. The hall became the centre of a new communal life, a place where you could take a warm shower, drink beer at a reduced price, play cards, attend meetings, hold discussions with neighbours, and make friends. Children also fostered friendships and all kinds of activities were arranged for them. The association organized outdoor trips at weekends, taking children to the municipal swimming pools on hot days, arranging soccer competitions, and showing films on Sunday afternoons. This way a new social world evolved for the neighbourhood with celebrations, picnics, and in shared mobilizations. At the end, Orcasitas had become a community in the precise sociological meaning of the word, primary relationships at the neighbourhood level being more frequent and more significant for most residents than anything else.

In this sense we can speak of a cultural transformation, but not in terms of a general change in values. The workers of Orcasitas' were, in fact, quite conservative – for instance, the conditions of women were hardly considered as an issue. While most women supported mobilizations, they attended very few committee meetings, their membership was included on their husbands' card, and they were usually overwhelmed by domestic work and their children. An anecdote will clearly illustrate the point. A strong, active young woman whose husband was one of the association's leaders complained about the difficulty she had in attending the meeting since one of them had to stay home with the children in the evening. To discuss the issue 'objectively', her husband brought the matter before the general assembly, and it was finally stated that on grounds of expediency, given his greater contribution to the neighbourhood's struggle, the wife should stay home so he could attend the meetings. If the cultural transformation was 'real' it was also a one-dimensional one, specifically related to the expansion of community feelings and solidarity among neighbours.

This community culture was founded on the shared experience of struggle. After the new buildings had been finished, the Movement's proposals for street names caused a lastminute row with the administration. The residents wanted to name their streets in honour of their struggles, so: Avenue of Land Expropriation; Street of the Sit-in in the Ministry of Housing; Square of the One Thousand Delegates; and so on. After a heated debate in the Madrid City Council, the names were approved, with the left wing majority winning the day and indulging the romanticism of the grassroots militants. And yet the issue was more than outdated symbols: it was an attempt to keep alive community values in the new spatial structure, since the association was aware that once the struggle was over, their local culture might be eroded.

Politically, Orcasitas showed the rapid transition of a populist revolt, first to left wing politics and then, with an increasingly critical approach, to institutional politics. Leaders who were formerly apolitical joined the PCE while residents became more radical. In the first elections of June 1977, the Centre Party (UCD) obtained 40 per cent of the vote, whereas in the municipal elections of April 1979 its share shrank to 5 per cent, while the PCE obtained 50 per cent (well above its Madrid average of 15 per cent), and the PSOE collected 40 per cent. It is important to note that this changing attitude did not represent the influence of interest groups at work – the Franquist government in 1975 and the UCD government in 1977 had conceded the main elements of the reworked programme. The evolution was more the result of the neighbourhood's general identification with the left wing programmes for social reform. This identification, however, proved controversial.

The neighbourhood association had fought hard for participatory democracy and was highly dissatisfied with the token gesture implemented in this direction in 1979 by the left wing local government. Most of the leadership left the PCE, and the growing ties between neighbourhood struggle and general political change were halted – this after major progress had been made between 1970 and 1979. Orcasitas was in danger of becoming introverted – secure in its urban affluence and nostalgic for its historic moments.

Alcala-de-Henares: A Suburban Hell for the Working Class

Alcala-de-Henares was a historic city, twenty kilometres east of downtown Madrid, that became an industrial zone during the intense and disorderly economic growth in the late 1960s. Tens of thousands of workers looked around the factories for housing. Private developers quickly took advantage of the situation, providing bad, high-rise buildings that workers were forced to buy in order to stay in a promising though difficult, labour market. The city jumped from a population of 30,000 to 150,000 in ten years (1965–75), with densities of about 400 housing units per hectare. This urban growth was entirely due to housing but services remained at their previous level. The local government, in the hands of a clique of corrupt Phalangist officials, ignored the new social needs and refused to consider the slightest democratization. On the contrary, most of its members, including planning officials and municipal architects, played an active role in the real estate firms and construction companies that controlled the urban development. The council broke legal planning rules and building standards, and concentrated the incoming immigrant workers into high-rise housing blocks that started deteriorating within the first year of their occupancy.

Given the housing conditions and the general crisis of urban services in an area where strikes and working class organizations developed quickly in the factories, urban mobilizations flourished as soon as a militant group took the initiative. The Maoist ORT created the first neighbourhood association, starting in 1974 with 50 residents who had begun adult evening schools. By 1977 there were four co-ordinated associations in the city, each one with a membership of over 600. The main targets were urban facilities, education being a priority as there were 2,000 children without schools in 1976, and 70 pupils per classroom for those who were fortunate enough to go to school. The neighbourhood association organized their protest effectively on 4 October 1976. 20,000 people demonstrated in Alcala, asking for more and better schools and more teachers. Similar protest campaigns were launched for health services (they only had one emergency doctor for the entire city) after several people died for lack of medical attention. Water pollution was another issue as the river and canals of the Venice area of the city were being used for dumping industrial waste with very serious consequences to hygiene in the high-rise housing which surrounded them, particularly in the contamination of drinking water. The city was in fact deprived each summer of water because the projected depuration plan was not completed as the public funds appropriated for it disappeared into the labyrinths of local democracy.

But it was the intimate ties with the labour movement that really characterized the neighbourhood mobilization in Alcala. The city, with a concentration of several large factories as well as an overwhelming proportion of working class residents (around 75 per cent), became one of the most active areas in terms of labour struggles. Furthermore, the local society made a point of interlinking all its interests, and therefore all its problems. For example, private schools were organized by a local industry for the children of its workers as part of their social benefits. When the workers went on strike, the factory's management ordered the schools to expel the strikers' children. The neighbourhood associations mobilized in response and put pressure on the schools and on city hall to prevent the repressive measures. Furthermore, other neighbourhoods supported the factory strikers (there were strikes in sympathy in Ibelsa and Fiesta) by collecting money, offering meeting places for the workers and participating in demonstrations called by labour unions.

In fact the neighbourhood associations of Alcala saw themselves as part of the labour movement, taking care of the living conditions of the working class outside the workplace, rejecting any divisions in the class struggle as artificial. This is not to say that they limited themselves alone to economic demands. On the contrary, they organized celebrations attended by thousands of residents as did most neighbourhood associations, collaborated with the student movements of the local university, were one of the few associations to organize activities for women (although they did not risk audacious topics such as abortion rights) and organized a youth group with its own programme. But while expanding the range of its activities, the overall aim remained that of developing the class struggle (understood as working class-led struggle). To some extent, the neighbourhood associations' attitude was a reflection on the local ruling elite. Factories' management, private developers and the local authorities represented an interconnected cluster of interests, as well as a single body, whose decisions were implemented by a particularly brutal and repressive police force whose harassment and violence far outweighed that of the Franquist political police operating in other areas of Madrid.

This polarized class confrontation explains perhaps the most striking feature of the Citizen Movement in Alcala – its almost total lack of achievement in spite its militancy, mobilization and popular support. Almost none of the urban demands were met: housing was not provided; services were not improved; the depuration plant did not materialise; industrial pollution went uncontrolled; and working class struggles still met with a harsh response in the factory in spite of the city's solidarity. The Movement, however, did successfully raise the level of popular organization and consciousness. The hope was to translate mobilization not just into demands but also into political change, and to some extent that happened. A left wing local government was elected following the municipal election of 1979, and some progress was made with the problems highlighted by the Movement. Yet the new political leadership came from the Socialist Party which had not been active in the neighbourhood associations, while the militants of ORT and PCE were forced to play a very minor role in the new municipal government. In other words, by defining the Citizen Movement as a component of a general class confrontation, and aligning sectors of opinion and social forces accordingly, the militant neighbourhood movement of Alcala was forced to place most of its hopes into the lap of political change, since only a dramatic shift in power would stop the capitalist interest groups from exploiting the workers both in the workplace and in their neighbourhoods. But since in the working of the political system depended on factors beyond the control of Alacala's residents (for instance, the unaggressive image of the left wing Socialist Party), the ultimate political outcome was not exclusively ordered by the working class, but was instead the democratic and progressive management of local urban policies.

While they fostered community life and supported working class mobilization, Alcala's citizens did not improve their urban conditions in the short term. By arguing for political change as the only means to fulfill their demands, they delegated their power and became totally dependent upon the future evolution of local politics. Needless to say, this approach and its almost inevitable outcome, was neither the choice nor the effect of a somewhat narrow ideology. It was, in fact, the result of acute class conflicts where capital and labour faced each other across a multitude of issues and where the city became the battleground for a class struggle.

The implications are obvious: social and urban change will necessarily occur in clear-cut situations where the needs and the mobilization are fully developed, and it is doubtful whether the goals of collective action in spite of the awareness and militancy of a movement can successfully transfer outside their original framework of social contradictions. The lessons of worker's struggles in Alcala should be carefully considered in our analysis of the relationship between class conflict and urban social movements.

Urban Utopianism and the Struggle for Open Space: La Vaguada es Nuestra

La Vaguada: sixteen hectares of vacant land in the middle of a high-rise housing estate that crammed 160,000 residents into concrete buildings to reach one of the highest urban densities in Europe: 15,000 persons per hectare. The El Pilar residential complex was built between 1967 and 1975 by one of the largest private developers in Madrid, Banus, using privileges conceded by city hall to expropriate the land and build 'socially useful housing', privately built, sold and managed. Located in the immediate periphery of northern Madrid, it received tens of thousands of industrial workers who flocked into the city and were forced to accept whatever housing conditions they found. Later, when the zone had been urbanized by the mid-seventies, some better housing was built for middle income families. As usual, housing construction was not supported by urban facilities, and residents complained about the lack of schools, health centres and transportation. But from the very beginning, the major disappointment focused on the total absence of open spaces and parks. Packed with increasing density into a limited urban spot, these new immigrants sorely missed the countryside and when, in 1974, neighbourhood mobilizations began all over Madrid, a group of residents took several initiatives to call public attention to their plight. To dramatize their problem some people planted trees in a concrete plaza while others distributed paper flowers to passers-by. City hall asked Banus to make some kind of gesture towards answering the demands. A small urban garden was planted and opened to the public.

At about the same time, in 1975, a major decision was announced for Madrid's future urban growth: a mammoth metropolitan shopping centre was to be built in the middle of El Pilar using the remaining vacant land (nicknamed La Vaguada because of its valley-like landscape), with a new motorway access that would cut its way across the residential complex. This proved too much for the local residents. Commerce was about the only adequate facility that El Pilar could boast with 1,500 small stores in the complex and a commercial density higher than downtown Madrid. So the project was rejected on the grounds that it would increase traffic congestion, ruin small merchants, and use for speculative purposes the only vacant land that could be assigned to open space, public gardens, and community services. City hall refused to recognize their rejection. Banus had, in fact, already sold the land to a multinational consortium led by a chain of French department shops. Confrontation was inevitable and started in Autumn 1976. Residents tried to make their protest as joyful as the circumstances allowed, sponsoring folk-song festivals, painting murals, and repeatedly using La Vaguada for picnics and celebrations, and clashing with the police whenever they tried to prevent these events. To gain popular and professional support, the neighbourhood association presented its own landuse plan, was given good coverage in the press, showed a film in private sessions, filed a legal complaint, wrote to the king, petitioned the government, and when the self-appointed mayor of Madrid refused to see them, sent youths with guitars to sing under his windows to remind him of the residents' wishes. Neighbourhood leaders also established an alliance with the local merchants and with Madrid's merchants association to draw them into the efforts to prevent vast shopping centres from both destroying local businesses and increasing urban congestion. Thus a new dimension was added to the conflict: the defense of small shops with character against gigantic anonymous supermarkets controlled by financial capital – a clash of opposing urban styles. In this instance the neighbourhood won a strong ally. On 27 April 1977, the city council was scheduled to approve the building permit for the shopping centre and in response to a call by the residents and merchants of El Pilar, 80 per cent of Madrid's small shops closed their doors – a gesture against 'dehumanized urbanization' as the manifesto put it. The city council adjourned its decision. The French corporation owning the license to operate the shopping centre was threatened with legal action that could have cost the city over ten million American dollars.

The Movement had scored a major victory. The problem was where to go from there in order to obtain the use of the open space, and it was at this point that the Movement's basic flaw became apparent – its internal division and political in-fighting.

The initiative for the protest originated with a group of grassroots, Catholic militants, organized by the local priest who were distrustful of all political parties. They were reinforced by a group of loosely organized young anarchists with whom they shared both their hostility for the disciplined Marxist parties as well as their dreams of an alternative life style organized around the ecological myth. The defense of nature, cultural self-expression, community relationships, and rejection of alienating urban growth became major themes of the association. This strong ideological commitment explains the particular forms of their action – feasts, songs, culture, and jokes. Although the majority of the residents shared the concern for open space and fear of main road traffic, they were quite removed from the radical ideological stand of this group much of whose support came from Maoists, socialists, and communists, the last being crucial in establishing the connection with the merchants association where PCE and PSOE members were quite influential.

The point for these parties, with a more traditional approach to urban demands, was to obtain social services and open space while protecting small merchants, in such a way that a new kind of urban programme could be implemented. Furthermore, the first municipal elections were approaching. Left wing parties needed to present realistic electoral programmes both in respect of their voters' wishes and what they could hope to achieve if elected. Given the legal rights of the shopping centre company in relationship to the existing planning schemes, communists and socialists decided to pull out of the strategy of direct confrontation and negotiate with the corporation's representatives. The result was an agreement on a new project. The shopping centre would be built in La Vaguada, but part of the building would be underground with two stories above ground level, and the city would receive a substantial payment from the French corporation to build a public park as well as a cultural and civic centre on the other half of La Vaguada. The motorway would be partially driven underground into a tunnel to avoid noise and pollution. In 1979, the left coalition won a majority in Madrid, the communists took control of city planning, and the informal agreement became official policy. Needless to say, the confrontation between the militant group and left wing parties worsened during the electoral campaign, the communists in particular being accused of betraying the Movement. The conflict weakened the ability to mobilize either residents or public opinion. What most local residents wanted was to obtain more open space and urban facilities, and the plan to construct the shopping centre was unpopular because it obstructed such improvements; this hostility was however considerably reduced when it became the possible vehicle for their implementation. An opportunity was found for small merchants to integrate some of their stores into the new centre, and price and product agreements with the department stores were deemed possible. Compatible interests could be plainly negotiated within the prevailing model of urban development while considerably improving the facilities and the availability of open space. And so the influence of these 'urban utopians' shrank to within the boundaries of their local community, and their impact on municipal decisions was also greatly reduced.

Nonetheless these militants remained as an informal force: they were still covered by the media, and were carefully listened to by large sectors of public opinion, particularly the youth, which was increasingly receptive to blueprints for alternative styles of urban life, and disenchanted with left wing claims that the key issue was better urban facilities. La Vaguada never became an open land for free-living neighbours, but its myth awoke new possibilities of how to project the city, as well as making a clear distinction between the improvement of urban management and the visionary anticipation of new urban communities.

Preserving History and Saving the City: The Struggle for Urban Rehabilitation in the Old Neighbourhoods of Central Madrid

Urban problems changed significantly with the economic crisis that in Spain became serious in 1975. Given the slower growth rate in a period of economic and political uncertainty, new suburban development was halted and real estate investment began to favour urban renewal operations in the central city. The strategy implied the exploitation of existing urban facilities, the demolition of old housing (most of it in sound condition) and its replacement with higher and more dense construction for office space, entertainment, exclusive shops, and high – income residential units. A similar plan, undertaken on a large scale in the mid-1960s, had succeeded in bringing down large sections of Madrid. The situation ten years later was substantially different. The new targets were the old historic neighbourhoods whose cultural value was increasingly seen as commercial value in the fresh concern for the preservation of historic quarters and in the reawakened appreciation of city life. By attacking old consolidated neighbourhoods, moreover, real estate was pitting itself against the discontent of well-rooted popular communities, strongly attached to their areas and quite ready to defend them against landlords who allowed housing to become dilapidated and then emptied them for their own gains having declared them 'in danger of imminent ruin'. Another crucial development was the growing development of the Citizen Movement. A group of communist and socialist militants, anticipating the clash of interests in the old historic quarters, created in Autumn 1976 a new neighbourhood association in Lavapies, one of the oldest sectors of Madrid, a labyrinth of seventeenth century streets populated by the elderly, craftsmen, small merchants, grocers, bars and cafés, petty bureaucrats, manual service workers, and, more recently, a handful of

Plate 24.2 La Corrala, the historic building in the old neighbourhood of Lavapies in Madrid, 1981, which became the symbol of the resistance by local residents to their displacement and to the destruction of Madrid's architectural heritage. (Photograph: M. Alvarez-Bullia)

students and young professionals. It constituted a neighbourhood with its own community life built around its physical charm and folk culture, as well as its poverty and dilapidation. The militants named the association La Corrala,[20] to associate it from the outset to the preservation of historical architecture and a cultural and popular tradition.

Three issues were at stake. First, the relocation of residents who had been forced out of their homes because of the dilapidation and demolition provoked by landlords and supported by city hall. Second, to stop the urban decay and obtain a programme of urban rehabilitation for the benefit of the residents, avoiding displacement and improving their living conditions. Third, to preserve the architecture and culture of the historic city. The last was, perhaps, the most significant dimension of this mobilization. Starting from very narrow social demands, La Corrala successfully triggered in about three years a vast body of public opinion to save Madrid's traditions and architecture which were declared inseparable from the residents who had lived there for many years, and their handicrafts and celebrations.

Nevertheless, La Corrala was not only a cultural movement. The commitment of its militants to defend the rights of the low-income population determined a three-step strategy from relocation to rehabilitation, then to urban revitalization.

The first campaign around which La Corrala built popular support was the move to obtain adequate relocation of 300 families who, having been displaced by demolition, were being kept by city hall in miserable hotels. They were offered some public housing in distant suburbs, like Alcala-de-Henares, but only 20 families accepted in spite of their poor and overcrowded conditions. They wanted to remain in the neighbourhood which held so many sentimental attachments, job opportunities, and networks of solidarity. To relocate them La Corrala proposed two measures: first the building of 300 housing units for families already displaced, on the condition that the units would be located in downtown Madrid using existing plots of municipally owned, vacant land; and second the prevention of any further displacement by the implementation of a public programme of rehabilitation, forcing the landlords either to co-operate in maintenance and repairs or to sell their property to the city at a lower price, while preserving the tenure of the tenants under all circumstances. Most of the popular mobilizations and active protests led by the association throughout 1977–79 were aimed to obtain approval from the government and city for this ambitious programme.

La Corrala subsequently extended the scope of its activity to the preservation of the historic centre, calling for co-operation between cultural associations, neighbourhood militants, professional organizations, political parties and distinguished intellectuals to save Madrid's artistic monuments, valuable architecture, and popular traditions.

Thus, instead of choosing on the one hand between historic preservation through gentrification and on the other residents' tenure of a dilapidated housing stock, La Corrala's strategy gradually raised the level of urban demands while broadening its social basis. The original population of the elderly, service workers, and small business families allied themselves with young professionals who shared the common interest of preserving the neighbourhood, improving housing conditions, and stimulating local culture. The association rapidly expanded. While in the early stages of its existence the annually elected steering committee would centralize all initiatives, numerous working groups were soon taking care of specific campaigns. Each time a major decision was needed, a general assembly of several hundred members would make it. La Corrala grew from 600 formal members in 1977 to 1,600 by mid-1979.

The association employed all kinds of action, from demonstrations of nearly 10,000 people in downtown Madrid to legal complaints. The impact on public opinion was particularly important in this case, achieved mainly through the media. To attract attention, La Corrala employed the local culture with great imagination to show what kind of city could be achieved by developing the life of old neighbourhoods instead of suffocating it under gentrification and office development. So mural paintings covered the municipal land that was claimed for housing sites, theatre and popular parades took to the streets from time to time, and a whole series of traditions and celebrations were revitalized, the most prominent being the *verbenas* – evenings of dance in costumes, with the traditional music, drink and *cuisine* of Madrid. People from all over the city loved this revival, especially the *pièce de résistance* when La Corrala's inner patios were revived as sites for feasts, fairs and celebrations. It became increasingly difficult to reject the demands of a movement whose legitimacy was built upon the joy that it brought to the residents of central Madrid by reviving popular traditions, and all of this under the broken crust of Franquist bureaucracy.

The effects of the neighbourhood Movement in central Madrid were extremely important, particularly in transforming the city and modifying urban policy. The Ministry of Housing finally agreed to build 300 public housing units for the relocation of families in central Madrid. City hall initially provided a portion of the municipal land and once the left wing government took office, it relinquished all the necessary land. Thus, by 1980, the first 100 public housing units in downtown Madrid were under construction, employing a careful architectural design intended to improve the city's aesthetic quality. In 1978 the Ministry of Housing approved a demonstration project at an initial cost of eight million American dollars to rehabilitate old housing while maintaining the legal and financial status of the occupants.

Demolition was halved by 1977 and under pressure from the Citizen Movement, the new democratic government asked for an evaluation of the architecture in central Madrid, and for a suspension of demolition permits in the meantime. In Autumn 1978, the still unelected city council approved a Special Master Plan for the Conservation of Madrid that made demolition almost impossible. The local government elected in 1979 approved and perfected the Special Plan, making it more flexible but banning most demolition of sound housing, forbidding any displacement, and forcing landlords to repair and maintain their property with the support of municipal services and public funds. La Corrala was justly proud of its victory and took good care to enforce it, establishing a surveillance service that prevented several illegal demolitions. Defaulting landlords were also denounced and many of them fined, including the owner of the historic La Corrala who was fined the equivalent of 200,000 American dollars and forced to restore it. Although the La Corrala association was not the only catalyst behind the Special Plan, it was the driving force. It organized a coalition of the neighbourhood associations based in historical quarters, which was joined by cultural clubs, ecology groups and arts centres. By sending more than 500 legal and technical comments to support the Special Plan, La Corrala provided powerful evidence and political arguments that eventually overcame the opposition of real estate interests whose failure was not such a mystery – the first democratic local elections were only six months away . . .

The preservation of the old neighbourhoods had an impact far beyond programmes designed for them. The entire policy dealing with central city development was changed. From now on, the existing city had to be preserved: urban conservation without gentrification became the officially accepted aim. The time of uncontrolled urban 'modernization' at any cost was over.

La Corrala's activities also had a major impact on the cultural level. Besides awakening residents' individual consciousness as to their right to the city, the association was a decisive factor in the revival of old Madrid's popular traditions. From *verbenas* and children's games, to mural paintings and street theatre, to finally and triumphantly the reinstatement of Madrid's official spring San Isidro celebration, paid for and supported by city hall after many years of silence in public places, the neighbourhood mobilization of old Madrid linked urban demands and cultural change, pulling together the interests and desires of a very broad range of social groups.

The political impact of the movement was less obvious. La Corrala's leadership was always in the hands of communists, not so much because of the Party's activities as the strong personality of the neighbourhood's leader, a hard-line and imaginative female sociologist. The left wing vote, and especially PCE votes, increased in the neighbourhood between 1977 and 1979, although the tendency which cannot be precisely measured needs qualification, since downtown Madrid had a strong majority of moderate and right wing voters. Nevertheless, the association was not a transmission belt for the PCE and it clashed with the party's local organization during and after the electoral campaign because La Corrala maintained the pressure on the new local government as it had previously to obtain its demands. By refusing to submit to party rules and by asking for citizen participation in the rehabilitation programme, La Corrala clearly sided with an alternative political model based on participatory democracy. The decisions by city hall to set up neighbourhood councils in central Madrid in 1980 reflected the pressures of a movement proud of its strength and distrustful of the old friends now seated 'on the other side of the desk'.

The political impact of movements such as La Corrala is wrapped up in the political consequences of cultural and urban transformations such as we have described, because only when the bureaucratic city, the merchant city, the professional city, and the working class city will agree on an alternative model of government can a city such as Madrid rely on a stable majority supporting social change. And these very diverse interests can only be reconciled when a new set of cultural values are shared. La Corrala opened the way to that sharing by recovering common history and by pointing towards a new communal life. Although limited and embryonic, these few steps were perhaps the most striking political progress in the struggle by old neighbourhoods to take charge of the future on the basis of past.

Middle Class Values and the Preservation of Urban Environment: Garden Cities Versus Redevelopment

Urban movements, while basically expressing the protest of working class neighbourhoods against their living conditions, are potential sources of collective action and urban change. How true is this proposition for Madrid? We will carefully examine this matter at a more general level, but some crucial glimpses to help answer the question can be provided if we observe a powerful and active mobilization between 1977 and 1979 in the so-called Colonias de Hotelitos. They are what might be called garden cities in another context: a series of one family residential units, built during the 1930s in the Madrid periphery. Their design, modest but tasteful, clearly expressed two things: a love for open space and a desire for urban marginality. Living on the fringe of the city, its residents were both part of the city, and yet separate. The *colonias* attracted a variety of people: artists and railway workers, musicians and prostitutes, students and petty bureaucrats. Urban facilities were limited, transportation was scarce and the houses were modest enough not to attract speculators.

But the city began to grow at an increasingly rapid rate and by the 1970s the *colonias* had been fully integrated into the urban core. Given the jungle of concrete high-rise building typical of new Madrid, the *colonias* appeared as the only oases in the city, and their property value rocketed. Their population had already changed without the usual invasion-succession process; that is, their social status was considerably higher, not by displacement of the old timers, but because of the social promotion of the second generation. Thus, sons of railway workers had become clerks and professionals; musicians' sons had become teachers and civil servants. Also, a few newcomers, attracted by the environmental quality, hastily filled the vacant spots – architects and intellectuals being most prominent among them. So, with the exception of the traditionally aristocratic Colonia El Viso where liberal, establishment families resided, most of the 25 *colonias* improved their social status without gentrification.

Community leaders described themselves as, '. . . very middle, middle class'. They were liberal but apolitical, generally uncommitted to social conflicts and political militancy, although well-informed and deeply interested in social issues, the arts, and intellectual debates. In fact, politics appeared distant from the almost village-like quality of the *colonias*. Strong neighbourhood relationships and intense community feelings reinforced this rather introverted social life. Several *colonias* refused to have their streets paved in order to keep traffic out of their neighbourhood – they would rather walk or risk their own cars.

This urban paradise hoped to be forgotten by the surrounding world. It was not. A low-density area, right in the middle of the urbanizing mass of Madrid, in a fine location, well-equipped by then with facilities, it offered a wonderful opportunity for private developers who were running out of lucrative investment.

Someone spoke to the city hall's Planning Department. In 1972, a municipal ordinance declared that the *colonias* contradicted the land-use patterns established for their location, in spite of the fact that the *colonias* had existed long before the 1963 Master Plan was finalized. But the legal situation was settled. Capital could start moving in once the Planning Department had launched a public redevelopment programme to force the residents out. The operation was risky politically and for several years critical battles kept the mayor busy. But in the summer of 1977, it was apparent after the parlimentary elections that the neo-Franquist party had no chance of staying in power either nationally or locally; they therefore made several last minute initiatives on the *colonias*, trying to take advantage of their control of the city's administration.

The *colonias* turned to the Citizen Movement in some trepidation since the relative privilege of their urban situation could have counted against them. Why should the Movement, whose main leaders were living in shanty towns, central slums and suburban public housing, care about the deprivation of evironmental quality for the well-to-do? And yet they were given huge support. Neighbourhood associations and political parties (including this time the government party, Union de Centro Democratico, UCD) declared that it was necessary to preserve the *colonias* in recognition of their inhabitants and as a public utility for the entire city. The *colonias* organized their own coalition. The media placed all its power behind the neighbourhoods: in two months nearly 180 articles appeared in newspapers and magazines and television broke its usual silence on such matters and screened a very favourable report. The residents themselves mobilized, demonstrating in the streets, painting their demands on the city walls, writing thousands of letters, sending delegations with signed petitions, and waving protest banners all over the place. The mayor of Madrid, confronted with such unanimous popular protest and with only a few weeks left before his enforced resignation, suspended the controversial ordinance. Months later, the Special Master Plan for the Conservation of Madrid was approved as a result of the pressure from the historic centre's neighbourhood associations, and included the Colonias de Hotelitos as part of the urban heritage. (In fact, the paragraph concerning the *colonias* in the Special Master Plan literally reproduced the measures stated by the *Colonias* Coalition's Advisory Task Force.) So the residents could quietly go back to their village life.

But the Citizen Movement had transformed the villages. Now that neighbourhood associations had been created, the *colonias* found themselves organized into a whole set of collective activities: fairs, feasts, public talks, and weekly neighbour meetings that began to take care of their problems as well as those of others. The struggle for survival reintegrated the *colonias* into the city.

The struggle of the *colonias* had important effects on the future municipal elections. Given that the mayor was the main candidate of the right wing party Alianza Popular, the poor publicity provoked by this affair ruined his electoral chances. As a result, the right wing party did not present any candidacy in the 1979 municipal elections and asked its electorate to vote instead for the Centre Party. These tactics proved misguided. Many right wing voters abstained, the Centre Party did not attract all the potential centre-right votes, and a socialist-communist coalition was elected to office. Thus, although the *colonias* were not led by political activists, their movement had significant political consequences. The active support of left wing parties and the Citizen Movement to a middle class cause won political sympathy for the left from traditionally moderate sectors. But the *colonias* were jealous of their autonomy and rejected any attempt by any party to draw their support. They believed in community and tried to preserve their unity by avoiding political divisions.

This particular urban mobilization was significant on two grounds. First, the receptiveness of the whole population to the themes of urban ecology and to the defense of green areas and community life suggested that an alternative physical and social model of the city could be developed. Second, the fact of middle classes mobilizing effectively in a context of class conflict constituted a new phenomenon in Spain. This second feature represented a major broadening of the Citizen Movement's social basis so that, although it may have had to face corporate capital and top-level bureaucracies it was by no means confined to the poor for its support. The preservation of the garden cities pointed the way to the possibility of urban self-management and, beyond the improvement of the city, to an alternative life style for its people.

25

The Transformation of City, Culture, and Politics by the Citizen Movement

Social struggles often appear to observers as efforts to project grassroots interests and desires that, because they are powerless, never obtain their goals. This was not the case in Madrid. The Citizen Movement decisively changed the city, both revived and fostered new cultural activities, and actively participated in the transformation of the political system.

We have pointed out many of the Movement's innovations while describing it or referring to local mobilizations. The interested reader can also find more precise details about the impact of the selected 23 neighbourhood associations in the condensed empirical observations included in the Methodological Appendix (pp. 365–94). But it is crucial for our analysis of urban change to summarize the major transformations resulting from the Movement as a whole, over and above the achievements of its associations. The Movement's impact was in fact so fundamental as to be more than the sum of its parts, and can be best described as fostering an alternative urban, cultural, and political model that had many different aspects, reflecting the Movement's diversity.

Let us therefore summarize the main outcomes of the Movement.

Effects on Space, Urban Services and Urban Development

1 *Redevelopment of all shanty towns* through public programmes that would relocate the residents in the same location at an affordable price or rent. Expropriation procedures included a different method of calculating the compensation payment for both landowners and residents. The latter were favoured by defining their role in urbanizing the land as being a major source of land re-evaluation. Housing was either sold or rented to the residents under public control. The quality of the housing projects was far above the average, and the level of services (particularly in educational facilities and open space) was better than in many middle class residential areas. Between 1976 and 1980, around 5,000 units were built (or were being constructed), particularly in Vallecas, Villaverde and Hortaleza, fulfilling all the programme's conditions. On paper (meaning on the Ministry's written agreement), all the remaining shanty towns (about 25,000 additional families) were scheduled to undergo the same process between 1980 and 1990.

2 *Rehabilitation and redevelopment of several large public housing estates,* where the buildings were extremely dilapidated. One of the most important cases, involved the 100,000 occupants of San Blas, where entire blocks were demolished and reconstructed on the same location, to house the same residents without any additional cost to them.

3 *Preservation of the entire area of central Madrid,* as well as of some specific areas, accounting for almost 50 per cent of the population of the city. Although the main legal measure for this policy was a municipal Special Conservation Plan, approved in 1978 and revised in 1980, the first steps toward it were taken in 1977 by the Artistic Preservation Authority of the central government. According to a series of measures, demolition was, with few exceptions,

forbidden; over 10,000 buildings were classified and protected; the legislation on ruins was revised to ensure its effectiveness; landlords were forced to repair and maintain; entire sectors of the city were preserved on the grounds of their historical and urban value; and rehabilitation projects were approved to upgrade the old neighbourhoods.

4 *Use of municipal land in central locations to build small public housing projects in different places of central Madrid, to relocate formerly displaced families.* These housing projects would be carefully designed to improve the architectural quality of the surrounding environment, and some of the most famous architects were appointed to the work. By the end of 1981, 400 of these units were already under construction and more were being planned by the City Planning Department.

5 *Improvement of urban services and delivery of basic facilities to the most peripheral, large private housing developments.* This included, for instance, bringing schools to Moratalaz; open space and cultural facilities to El Pilar; water to Mostoles; a health care centre to Leganes; and so on. As a general rule all under-equipped housing complexes began to feel the benefit of this programme at a rate that reflected the effectiveness of their mobilization.

6 *Planning was democratized and decentralized.* The Metropolitan Planning Authority, under pressure from the neighbourhoods, introduced in 1977 a procedure known as *Plan-de-Accion Inmediata* (PAI) which had three major characteristics new to Spanish planning:

a There were plans for specific areas of the city, aimed at identifying and solving the most urgent problems in each area. Metropolitan Madrid was divided into 21 zones and planning staff and resources were correspondingly decentralized.

b Each PAI was prepared and drafted by a committee on which special interests and popular organizations of the zone could be represented so that political parties, neighbourhood associations, and labour unions could, along with planners and government officials, argue over and influence the planning process. Furthermore, the draft document, once completed, was submitted to the entire population of Madrid by a variety of means, ranging from public talks to video tapes to mailed leaflets.

c The revision of the Master Plan of Madrid was to be undertaken through a similarly decentralized procedure, the basic aim being to experiment with a new form of planning that was to be generated from grassroots, but supported at all stages by technical expertise.[21]

7 Beyond the measures put into effect in Madrid between 1975 and 1980, there was a *total rectification of the model of urban development as well as of official urban policy.* The existing city was given priority over peripheral developments; conservation and rehabilitation overshadowed the construction of new projects; gentrification and displacement were denied as necessary consequences of urban renewal; the facilities for existing housing estates commanded most of the available public money; the building of urban motorways were stopped; sudden and dramatic changes of land-use were avoided (for instance, the railway stations remained in the centre of the city); the underground was municipalized and its network extended; public transport was given priority by adding bus lanes and by putting more buses into service, while parking facilities were decreased and traffic discipline severely enforced; private parks were opened to public use, the garden at the Royal Palace being the first; pedestrian zones were extended; and architectural design codes were improved and enforced. And at the broadest level, Madrid stopped growing as real estate business, and the construction industry, unable to adapt to the sudden reversal, dramatically decreased their activity.

The city had by 1980 halted its accelerated race to unchecked urban concentration. The new urban values shared by most sectors emphasized the need to first deal with existing urban problems before starting any new development. The reluctance of the real estate business to follow this strategy and the inability of the public sector to inherit the entire economic burden of urbanization constituted the first and major problems to be faced.

As always, urban change that does not produce a corresponding social and structural change is likely to bring on a crisis of some kind . . . But for our purposes, the important point is that urban change had happened and in the innovative manner just described.

The Modification of Urban Culture and the Overall Cultural Patterns of Local Society

Perhaps the most striking effect in this respect was the revitalization of street festivals and popular fairs. Madrid had had a historical tradition of folk culture and had been a society focused on its neighbourhoods which were full of traditions and celebrations. But for almost 40 years, celebrations had been abandoned, traditions forgotten, and popular gatherings banned as potential threats to public order. Furthermore, new Madrid was populated by immigrants living in newly-constructed suburbs where community life did not exist, traditions were unknown, and personal gain was emphasized as the only path to progress. And yet the Citizen Movement revived old traditions and invented new ones. The historic neighbourhoods of Madrid organized their *verbenas*. The residents of the new peripheral developments instituted new occasions which all could enjoy; for instance, the president of the association in Hortaleza was a native of the northern province of Asturias and established one of the oldest rural Asturian traditions, the Feast of Bread, as one of his neighbourhood's main celebrations. By 1978, nearly all of the neighbourhoods in Madrid had their own annual feast, a feast being a week's celebrations, including children's galas, cultural activities, sports competitions, musical parades, public places for eating and drinking, and of course, several *verbenas* held at night. Taking all the neighbourhoods together, there was a daily celebration in Madrid in Spring and Summer. At Christmas time, the famous *Cabalgata de Reyes*[22] that had been reduced to one, very formal and commercial celebration in downtown Madrid suddenly increased in number so that there were 20, each zone of the city organizing its own through voluntary work by residents' committees.

City hall, shamed into action, finally took the initiative, and in May 1978 began organizing all over Madrid the traditional fair of San Isidro, having prohibited it for years. In addition neighbourhood associations were granted funds and permits to organize their own feasts. More than a million people participated. The celebrations and revived traditions were certainly fun for the residents but were also the expression of a rich and diverse local culture. Each neighbourhood had its own particular feast, responding, for instance, to the regional background of the majority of its population. All celebrations were arranged to recall a particular theme, so that the feasts expressed urban demands (but not political programmes). The celebrations also recovered public places, and so worked against the loneliness of city life and the loss of open space.

In less than five years the city had revived its popular traditions, added new ones and had learnt to express its diversity against a background of anonymous bureaucracy and cultural barrenness, both of which had dominated for forty years. This was the first major cultural effect of the Citizen Movement.

The second concerned the strengthening of local networks and the development of community life, both of which can be put down to the arranging of a number of social activities that did not exist before: public talks, sports competitions, Sunday markets, activities for children, and many informal meetings. In addition, neighbours in the most mobilized communities were socializing more than anywhere else, particularly in the small scale neighbourhoods such as shanty towns or garden cities. In organized neighbourhoods, the development of social networks led to a sharp drop in crime and violence. Furthermore, in some areas, such as Hortaleza, the high rate of juvenile delinquency noticeably declined. 'Solidarity means Safety' was one of the slogans of the Citizen Movement, and it was true.

What has to be remembered is that in most cases, community life did not exist before the urban protest. Community-building was, in fact, a goal and a product of the Movement, obtained through sharing the mobilization and built upon a network of activities and organizations. The struggle for community created a communal foundation on which to base a broader fight.

Political Effects

The effects of the Citizen Movement were clear in the first stage of its development, but later became more complex. Given that between 1970 and 1977 its very existence was conditional to civil rights and freedom of association, the Movement became a major factor in the popular mobilization for democracy and against the Franquist government. In this respect the Citizen Movement, because of its appeal to the middle classes and the legitimacy of its demands, was essential in the conversion to the idea democracy of those people still afraid of withdrawing their support from Franquism because of the threat presented by the left wing. Hence the Movement contributed in 1976 to some of the largest political mobilizations against the continuation of Franquism after Franco's death.

Once a democratic Parliament was created in 1977, the Citizen Movement exerted strong pressure for democratic local elections. In the subsequent municipal elections of April 1979, socialists and communists scored a major victory, winning control of the city government while in the parliamentary elections, held one month earlier, conservative and centre parties had obtained a majority of the vote in Madrid. The Movement provided some popular candidates to the left wing parties and although its autonomous stand prevented it from openly campaigning for any one party, the themes it had been popularizing for years formed the basis of the leftist municipal programmes. Moreover the popularity of the neighbourhood associations was such that all parties, including the UCD, promised in their campaign that they would support some form of participatory democracy, thus opening the way for the Citizen Movement.

The UCD and PSOE, however, added the condition that the Citizen Movement should first have to be purged of its excessive political partisanship. Political culture had been largely transformed from authoritarianism to democracy and then to participatory democracy. The neighbourhood Movement played a major role in this evolution, mainly because of the debate it maintained with its traditional supporters among left wing parties, as we will try to explain in our analysis of its relationship to politics. In fact, the Citizen Movement also had an impact on the political parties themselves as they were suddenly confronted with the reality of having to put into practice party ideologies which had insisted on autonomy for social movements. Leninism was badly battered by this same concept but the socialists had to admit to it, so that once people had voted, it was up to the parties alone to take care of public matters. The debate triggered by these political views led the Madrid city council to experiment with a decentralized structure of neighbourhood councils that included representation of parties and all kinds of voluntary associations. Thus the demands for participatory democracy actually reshaped the institutions of city government while opening a serious debate on the meaning of democracy within the political parties themselves.

The Transformation of the Social Concept of the City

Although, neighbourhood mobilization in Madrid led to a series of major and related urban, cultural, and political changes, perhaps its most important impact was on the social concept of the city. Madrid had been an instrument of power (the bureaucratic city), a mechanism of profit (the capitalist city), a necessary evil for survival (the labour market city), and the ambivalent symbol of modernization (the great metropolis). In the wake of the Citizen Movement, it still remained all of these things but another dimension had been introduced into the social debate: the city as a use-value. If the historic city was to be preserved, if people's effort to urbanize vacant land was to be rewarded, if suburban expansion should be discontinued until all the urbanized children could be educated, if feasts were more important than traffic, and if citizen's participation had to become a crucial element in the planning process, then it followed that economic profit and bureaucratic power could not be the ultimate goals. Now there were new priorities: pleasure mattered; environmental quality was not simply an additional item of individual consumption; and the city was a collective good, a shared experience, and should be governed by its own grassroots. As a result the city was opened to a variety of projects searching for new spatial forms and patterns of life.

Can we be confident of this truth? Have we accurately described the transformations which occurred in Madrid under the influence of the 1970s Citizen Movement, or are we romanticizing about spatial and political trends that were under way in any case because of the more general social evolution in Spain? In more methodological language, can we infer causality from a sequence of events so broadly exposed to a variety of social contextual influences? Our answer is that we have done justice to the changes wrought by the Movement but, at the same time, the question, however logical and generally posed, seems theoretically inadequate. Because of the strategic role that the definition of the social effects of an urban movement plays in our analysis, we need to discuss this issue of the Movement's impact in some detail.

To pretend that the Citizen Movement was the major factor in producing the series of effects we have summarized seems particularly audacious if we recall that between 1975 and 1977 Spain underwent a major socio-political change after Franco's death in November 1975, as well as a particularly acute economic crisis which was only partially the result of world-wide stagnation. And yet, social contexts do not by themselves set things in motion. Social action and its outcome is the result of collective behaviour whose form, characteristics and orientations depend upon their own structure and dynamics as much as on the influence of the contextual variables within which they take place. What this means is that the Citizen Movement of Madrid, while occurring at the end of the Franquist era, was also a factor in provoking that end. And, in the case of Madrid's cultural and political structure, the Citizen Movement was the self-conscious social sector within which could be found the whole diversity of structural contradictions and social goals necessary to bring about urban change.

At the level of specific urban effects, the major causal argument is that all the themes – from shanty town redevelopment, to historic conservation, to the re-equipment of peripheral housing estates – had been promoted alone by the Citizen Movement. The Franquist administration not only had followed an entirely contrary policy, but the opposition parties, including PCE and the radical left, never took the urban programme seriously, only considering neighbourhood mobilization as a matter of political agitation the revolutionary outcome of which would far outweigh all its demands. So, chronologically speaking, all the topics and concepts that became the common wisdom of leftist and centre administrations, as well as of the media, in the second half of the decade originated with the Citizen Movement through neighbourhood mobilizations. The municipal programmes of political parties were drafted by the cadres of the neighbourhood associations, and the media headlines on city's problems were determined by events provoked by the neighbourhoods' popular mobilizations.

To be sure, the election of a left wing local government in Madrid in April 1979 made the implementation of many measures proposed by the Citizen Movement easier, and therefore helped to transform the city. However this victory was by no means the decisive factor. In fact, the most spectacular victories scored by the Movement had been signed on paper, and some of them put into practice, by the Franquist administration as well as by the transitional UCD administration of 1978. The shanty town redevelopment scheme was obtained in 1975–77 in some local areas and in 1978 and 1979 confirmed at the general level by an agreement with the UCD's Ministry of Public Works. The policy to preserve historic areas was obtained in 1977 from the most conservative Ministry of Culture of all the UCD governments, and the Special Plan of Conservation was approved in 1978 by a right wing UCD mayor. The new 1979 city government stabilized the situation by integrating these victories into feasible programmes while postponing further progress until a new and balanced framework for urban development could be decided on.

Feasts and celebrations were entirely an initiative of the neighbourhood associations and could not be rivalled by those of the labour unions or political parties that had to ask permission from the neighbourhood to be present with their stands. One of the first actions of the left wing local government was to organize by itself the neighbourhood feasts, accepting participation of voluntary associations but keeping the operation under control. Local networks developed only where powerful neighbourhood associations existed, since local party chapters could only organize a handful of residents and could not generate other collective activities.

It would be simplistic to pretend that urban movements alone overthrew Franco's dictatorship and ushered in a democratic administration. But it would be equally simplistic to say that any other popular movement or opposition party did so single-handed. The dictatorship crumbled, as we have said, because of the combined pressure of internal contradictions and popular opposition. While the main opposition came from the labour movement and the nationalist revolts, these were also the ultimate enemies of the system, provoking cohesion within the establishment against any potentially revolutionary movement. Only when other social groups and a more diversified range of issues, such as the ones posed by the Citizen Movement, sided against the authoritarian state, did the reformist forces within it see the necessity for, and the possibility of, ensuring a peaceful transition to democracy. It is in this sense that the Citizen Movement had a specific and crucial political effect, opening the way for a new political culture with its demand for participatory democracy – a position which distinguished it from the more traditional model of partisan politics still supported by the labour movement.

The Citizen Movement undoubtedly transformed the city of Madrid – its space, culture, and politics – as well as the social perception of what the city was and should be. At this point, we do not know how lasting these effects will be, but the important point is that they were brought into existence at all. And the proper historical role of a social movement, unlike political forces, is not the cautious administration of its cultural heritage, but the momentum for innovation that it gives an established institution. We have observed Madrid's rising sun – her neighbourhoods – but for the moment we will not describe their demise.

26

City, Class, Power and Social Movements

Madrid's Citizen Movement produced significant changes in urban structure and policies, as well as in cultural values and political institutions. Given its scope, broad constituency, widespread influence, and lasting organizational presence, it can be considered a major urban social movement whose internal structure and historical development we should now carefully analyse in order to detect some of the underlying social mechanisms that relate the city to social change.

But before we proceed, we must examine a fundamental issue: have we been observing a specific type of social movement? Or, on the contrary, was it merely the expression of some broader social mobilization, such as the working class struggle, a political strategy, women's liberation, or some other social revolt? The question is not a rhetorical one because we have to assess the specificity of the urban contradictions, and therefore of mobilizations orientated towards urban issues, in relationship to other sources of social change. Furthermore, since no social movement happens in a social vacuum, we need to examine the relationship in Madrid between the Citizen Movement and the social contradictions that, according to historical experience, have triggered collective action aimed at social change. We need not only to show the specificity of the Citizen Movement, but also to comprehend the complex systems of relationships that formed its basic structure. In other words, while being fundamentally defined by the contradictions of urbanization, the Citizen Movement also emerges as a conscious mobilization for social change as a result of its connections with class structure, the political system, and continuing social movements. Let us then proceed, step by step, examining both the Movement's autonomy and connections in relationship to the basic social dimensions of class, power, and culture.

City and Class

For some observers, urban movements in general and the Madrid experience in particular were an extended manifestation of class struggle, understood as the process of social confrontation between capital and labour.[23] For others, the struggle was limited to distribution and, as such, was basically 'reformist' because the Movement's demands concerned consumption and outside relationships of production.[24] Our proposition is that the Citizen Movement occurred in a class structured society as a movement not defined by class which affected the overall structure of society, and therefore relationships between classes, through its organization, mobilization and demands. Instead of re-entering the general theoretical debate, let us observe what happened in Madrid.

There are different ways of looking at the 'class context' of the Citizen Movement. The most immediate one is to determine its members and the classes to which they belonged.

First of all, in almost every neighbourhood there was practically no difference between social base and social force: leaders, militants, and residents were, broadly speaking, of similar social origin. When the leader was significantly above the average, as in La Corrala, it was because she was representative of a potential sector of the community (middle class professionals) that, although being a minority among the militants, represented an important sector of the constituency.

If we look at the frequency and intensity of neighbourhood mobilization at the level of the entire city, a significant negative rank-correlation ($r = -0.37$) can be observed between these characteristics and the social status of the neighbourhood as measured by factor analysis (see the findings on page 231). Although the correlation is only moderate (explaining 13.69 per cent of variance), there is a negative relationship between urban mobilization and social stratification.

To move from social strata to social class, we have observed the distribution of neighbourhood associations, classified by levels of mobilization, into the space of Madrid ranked according to the proportion of manual workers, and to the proportion of salaried technicians among the residents. Maps 26–1 and 26–2 and Tables 26–1 and 26–2 show the findings. There was a clear, positive relationship between the importance of manual workers and the frequency of neighbourhood associations. There was also a positive relationship with the intensity of neighbourhood militancy – the stronger and more active the association, the more

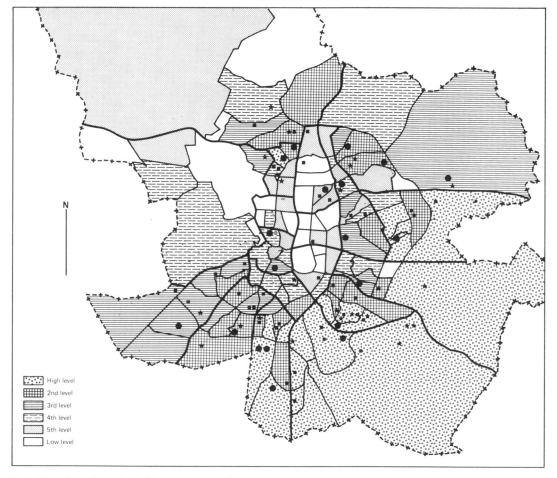

Map 26.1 Location of neighbourhood associations in areas ranked in six levels according to the proportion of manual workers among the residents of each neighbourhood, 1978.

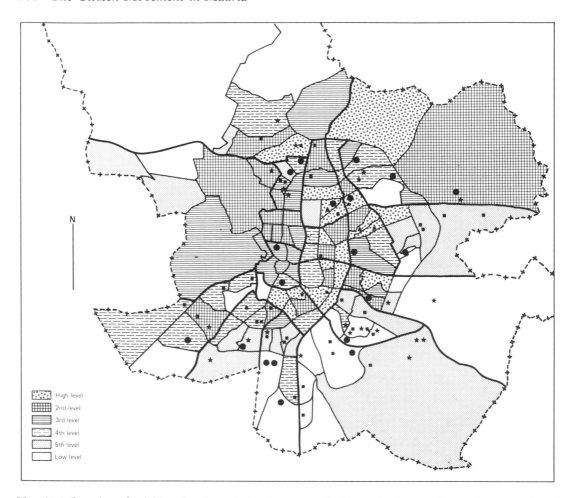

Map 26.2 Location of neighbourhood associations in areas ranked in six levels according to the proportion of salaried technicians among the employed residents of each neighbourhood, 1978.

frequently it appeared in a working class neighbourhood. There was also a negative relationship between the proportion of salaried technicians (the best discriminatory variable to be used as an indicator of middle class residence) and the presence of neighbourhood associations, the relationship being similar for all levels of militancy. Thus, there is no doubt that working class neighbourhoods were the most organized and the most militant on urban issues.

At the same time, the Movement as a whole was highly diversified across the social spectrum. For instance, if we divide the spatial areas of Madrid in relationship to the proportion of salaried technicians among residents (Table 26–2), one-third of the highly mobilized associations were located in the 'Over-represented technicians' category. Of course, since two-thirds were in the 'Under represented technicians' category, we still find the established statistical association between variables, but for the Movement as a historical phenomenon this one-third of middle class association was a fundamental feature.

Some of the most significant cases we have observed (Hortaleza, Alameda de Osuna, Colonias-de-Hotelitos, La Corrala, Aluche etc.) relied on very diverse non-working class con-

Table 26.1 Spatial distribution of neighbourhood associations ranked by their level of mobilization among the boroughs of Madrid ranked according to their proportion of *manual workers* on the total resident population of the area.
Units: Neighbourhood Associations

		Level of mobilization of neighbourhood associations.			
		High	Medium	Low	Total
High +	1	7	8	11	26
Proportion of manual	2	4	9	9	22
workers	3	5	3	5	13
among	4	2	4	3	9
residents	5	1	1	6	8
Low –	6–	0	0	1	1
	Total	19	25	35	79

Source: a Our study. b Municipal census of Madrid, 1978.

Table 26.2 Spatial distribution of neighbourhood associations ranked by their level of mobilization among the boroughs of Madrid ranked according to the proportion of *salaried technicians* on the total resident population of Madrid.
Units: Neighbourhood Associations

		Level of mobilization of neighbourhood associations.			
		High	Medium	Low	Total
High +	1	2	3	6	11
Proportion of salaried	2	2 = 6	3 = 8	4 = 13	9
technicians	3	2	2	3	7
among	4	5	4	7	16
residents	5	2 = 12	7 = 16	10 = 24	19
Low –	6	5	5	7	17
	Total	18	24	37	79

Source: a Our study. b Municipal census of Madrid, 1978.

stituencies, and the Federation of Neighbourhood Associations linked most of such organizations across the social spectrum. Furthermore, since Madrid was a highly socially segregated city, many neighbourhoods tended to be dominated by one of the following social groups: manual workers, low middle class (clerks and professionals), and old urban population (merchants, elderly, artisans, civil servants). So, each neighbourhood mobilization tended to be based on a single class, but the Movement as a whole, in its collective organization campaigns, ideology, image, and collaboration to produce urban, political and cultural impacts, comprised a plurality of social classes. Therefore, class allegiance was a major dimension in defining each mobilization, as well as in fostering its dynamics in working class neighbourhoods. But the Movement as a collective appears to have been segmented into a variety of social classes and could not therefore be simply defined as the expression of a class struggle, even if the potential of class struggle tended to reinforce its existence and militancy. Nevertheless, we have used a narrow, static vision of social classes. Most analysts of social class tend to consider classes as historical actors using peoples' class conscious collective action as the principal clue for recognizing a particular class position. Thus, the relationship of neighbourhood associations to the labour movement should be the most specific sign of class membership or class orientation. From this point of view, the experience in Madrid is clear: there was no connection. Of course, statements of mutual solidarity were frequent, but there was almost no organizational co-ordination, joint struggle, common demand, or shared strategy, in spite of a generally common political leadership and ideology. Organized labour largely ignored the urban movements: on only one occasion did it support a public demonstration by the neighbourhood associations (the housing campaign of September 1978), and only because of a peculiar internal fight between political groups within the Workers' Commissions that brought them into the campaign at the last minute. There were a few cases where neighbourhood associations acted, by their own choice, on behalf of the labour movement, closely linking themselves to workers' struggles (Alcala de Henares, Leganes) and developed a specific and atypical urban mobilization, as we will show in our final analysis. On the whole, however, the pattern was different. Labour and neighbourhoods fought different battles, even if they often clashed with the same police and exchanged messages of solidarity inspired by a common political matrix: they were allies, not comrades.

Now, even if movements are organizationally diverse and only partially overlap in their social base, they can still be differential expressions of a common class struggle if they address issues that are inter-related but at odds, one with the other: such is the relationship, for instance, between capital and labour. And perhaps here we can find the most specific distinction between class struggle and a social movement such as the Madrid Citizen Movement. The demands expressed by the Movement encompassed many facets of urban life including housing, health, urban facilities, transportation, celebrations, culture, participation, open space, and children's games. They embraced all aspects of life except work. Only occasionally were requests made that the unemployed be employed in the housing programmes obtained by the neighbourhood, and generally speaking the Movement avoided issues like wages, work conditions, and economic policies. It had, in fact, an awareness of its separateness from the only other existing and recognizable movement which was labour. So, the Citizen Movement took care of all other aspects of life. City and labour became two separate, although inter-related, dimensions in the social practice of Madrid.

It does not follow that the Citizen Movement had nothing to do with social classes. The interests it fought in opposing the consequences of a given model of urban development were ultimately class interests. Spanish financial capital, connected to the multinationals, was the driving force behind the accelerated metropolitan growth and industrial concentration in Madrid. Banks, real estate firms, landowners, and developers, all closely organized in a top business network, were the agents of urban development based on speculation, exploiting workers and residents in the process of collective consumption, by imposing conditions in a situation of urban scarcity. An authoritarian state, closely tied to business circles through social support and individual corruption, provided the class-dominated instrument of urban policy opposed by neighbourhoods. Thus the Citizen Movement confronted class interests by arguing in favour of use value against exchange value, and by claiming local independence against centralized dictatorship. In weakening the capitalist domination over the city it also had a major impact on class struggle. But it was not a class-defined mobilization in terms of its social base, organization, and the issues in which it was involved. The Movement was then a non-class, social movement challenging the structure of a class society.

City and Culture

The Citizen Movement in Madrid went beyond urban issues to challenge basic cultural values embedded in the framework of Spanish society. Could it then be considered as a cultural revolt taking place in the shape of the territorially-based neighbourhood associations?

The question requires careful treatment because it raises the broader issue of the relationship between urban movements and the culturally orientated social movements emerging in advanced industrial societies. This is, indeed, one of the main areas of our exploration in this book: whether urban movements, in different historical circumstances, could have represented fundamental revolts, like women's struggles, but have not been identified as such. We have pointed out earlier how the role of women in the organization of everyday life has often been extended by their role in struggles over material conditions and social patterns, often understood as urban problems. Therefore, many urban struggles have been, and still are, women's struggles, although they generally do not reach the heights of active feminist movements. How true is this hypothesis in the case of Madrid? Two different aspects must be considered: the issues raised by the Citizen Movement and the actual participation of women in neighbourhood mobilization.

Feminist themes were almost absent in the programmes, demands, and debates of the Citizen Movement, and this is true of all kinds of social classes and urban situations. By feminist we understand demands and topics that addressed women oppressed in their condition as women, and not such demands as housing, schools, and health that, although often directly linked to women, appeared from time to time in neighbourhood activities. Kindergartens were required as a basic neighbourhood amenity, particularly for working women. And some associations set up women's committees where the main activity was to organize talks for women on a variety of topics. In some instances, family planning and contraception issues were discussed, but more controversial issues such as divorce, abortion, and women's rights were carefully omitted due to the unanimous belief of the leadership (including women) that such subjects would shock most women, and so provoke their hostility. From time to time neighbourhoods supported important women's struggles, particularly working women striking for their rights. But even then, the struggles were external to the neighbourhood and the support was addressed more to the workers than to women. For instance, in 1976 young women working in the Fiesta sweet factory in Alcala struck to obtain equal pay for equal work. The neighbourhood association of Alcala, led by a woman who was a self-proclaimed feminist, took an active part in the campaign in support of the strikers. It did the same thing, however, for other strikes and no differentiation was ever established. So feminist themes, women's problems and women's struggles did not become an active component of Madrid's Citizen Movement.

Nevertheless, women are sometimes active participants in movements which do not directly relate to their own conditions. This was only partially true in the case of Madrid. The Federation of Neighbourhood Associations did not keep records from which such an evaluation could be made. But on the basis of our own survey of 23 associations, we can establish a profile that is probably accurate for the whole Movement. As Table 26–3 shows, 11 associations had a very low level of women in the rank and file, while in another only ten women had a significant role in the leadership. Women were also the main leaders in four associations, including three of the ten most active movements in Madrid.

Table 26.3 Classification of a selected sample of 23 neighbourhood associations in relationship to the role played by women in their leadership and in their membership:

	Significant Role in the Leadership	A Significant Proportion of the Leadership	No Leadership but a Significant Proportion of the Membership	No Leadership Role and Weak Participation
	(Being the Main Leader or at the Same Level than any Other Leader)	(1/3 at least)	(40% at least)	(Less than 25% of the Membership)
Names of Associations	Alcala-de-Henares El Pilar* Colonias de Hotelitos* La Corrala*	Alcorcon Moratalaz* Aluche Alameda de* Osuna Salamanca Santa Maria*	UVA-Hortaleza* Malasana*	El Olivar Palomeras Orcasitas* Pozo* San Pascual Orcasur* San Blas* Quintana Concepcion Arganzuela Leganes
Total	4	6	2	11

*Indicates the most active and powerful neighbourhood associations in the entire metropolitan area.
Source: Our study.

So, we have a diversified picture that cuts across the spectrum of social class and urban situations. Women were not the main basis of the movement: they were a minority of the active members, representing around 30 per cent of the whole militant population. But they did participate in the Movement and took a significant part in the leadership of some key neighbourhood mobilizations. Why, then, did they stop short of fighting for their own problems, either as a feminist movement or in terms of their legal or material situation?

The explanation does not lie in the structure or orientations of the Citizen Movement, but in the history of women's organization in Madrid. The potential was there for a powerful alliance of women's demands, urban mobilization and feminist themes, at a moment when both the Citizen Movement and an autonomous feminist movement were emerging in Spain. But women were separately organized into the Housekeepers Associations (*Asociaciones de Amas de Casa*), under the leadership of militant communist women. These Housekeepers Associations could have become the driving force of a powerful womens' movement based on neighbourhoods. In the event, they did not and could only manage to place a handful of women in positions of influence in the PCE, and they were used mainly to mobilize protests against the government on bread and butter issues.

Furthermore, they were paralysed by a major internal contradiction. While the militant women rightly argued that they should organize their own gender, they always refused to introduce feminist topics, or even controversial issues such as divorce or abortion, for fear of scaring off others. Instead they focused on issues concerning women as organizers of family consumption, their main campaigns being against rising prices which were fought by staging periodic shopping boycotts. Also schools, kindergarten, and all issues related to children were considered to be the most important and the ones most likely to mobilize working class women. So the Housekeepers Associations diverted women from participating in the Citizen Movement and yet addressed the exact same issues, refusing to concentrate on women's goals so that they would avoid being labelled as feminists. Torn between their will to affirm their own movement on the basis of their specific condition as women and the refusal to develop a corresponding struggle, the Housekeepers Association became a mass organization of a political party, eventually dismissed by the PCE when it decided to look to the more promising feminist current. The parallel development of neighbourhood mobilization on urban issues and of a powerful feminist movement taking women's conditions as a source of struggle and liberation ultimately superseded the Housekeepers Movement. But its existence seems to be the key factor behind the phenomenon we have observed: the division between women and the city in goals of social transformation proposed by the new Spanish social movements.

Other potential dimensions of cultural revolt were also present in the Citizen Movement without being able to shape it or clearly use the neighbourhood as a launching platform for alternative ways of life. Youth-inspired culture offers a good example. In 1980, the revolt of the youth in Zurich and other Swiss cities dramatically showed the underlying connection between the debate on living styles and policies of urban facilities. There was nothing comparable in Madrid. In fact, the youth committees of the neighbourhood associations were one of the most controversial activities. Youths were often expelled from the association and their initiatives censored under charges of drug use, sexual misconduct, or political radicalism. Youth committees tended to be the refuge for the most radical Maoist, Trotskyite, or libertarian political stands, and did not share the apprehensions of the associations' leadership in using the neighbourhood as a basis for political agitation. So in Hortaleza, Lavapies, Arganzuela, Quintana, Malasana, Aluche, and in many other places, a series of incidents and confrontations, sometimes violent, totally alienated the youth from the mainstream of residents, particularly in the working class neighbourhoods. The rift appeared most strikingly in the popular feasts and street parties organized by the neighbourhood associations. Youths would come from all over Madrid to enjoy the new opportunities for self-expression, a welcome contrast to the exclusive and repressive culture of most urban institutions. But they arrived displaying their particular brand of explosive behaviour, smoking pot, drinking too much, singing revolutionary chants, dancing in large groups, going half-naked, clashing with the police, or just 'looking bizarre'. This made most residents uncomfortable and many would leave the celebrations. The neighbourhood associations became upset, since the feasts were intended, in the first place, to attract families, and the considerable presence of children at these gatherings was considered a major success. But children and youths became increasingly incompatible, with the Movement trying to portray itself as representative of the normal resident as opposed to the radical and deviant fringe, labels generally associated with youths and their culture.

Can we then speak of the Citizen Movement as being culturally conservative? Yes and no. Yes, in the sense that, being extremely close to popular culture, the Movement generally reacted negatively to the disruption of traditional ways of life, particularly family life and patriarchal authority. But no, in the sense that it fundamentally altered the dominant cultural patterns of urban life, by substituting communication for loneliness, solidarity for aggressiveness, and local customs for mass media's monopoly of the message. In sum, it triggered community-building. But the nature of the communication had to be limited since the further its cultural content departed from current values, the more difficult it became for people to involve themselves in this community-building. So the lowest common denominator was generally adopted, and challenges and experimentation were not welcome. And yet to introduce new sources of information and expression, revive local culture and establish neighbourhood networks represented a major cultural transformation. We could say, paraphrasing McLuhan, that, here also, the medium was the message: people meeting in their neighbourhoods, feasts and fairs challenging the media, recalling history in folk traditions performed on demolition sites in the old city – all, by virtue of their existence, were understood to be new messages. In this context, the youths' own culture, events, political confrontations, and even commercial manipulation of the new local life were taken to be facets of a new pattern of communication. The search for community was the one, truly original, fundamental, cultural dimension of Madrid's Citizen Movement.

City and Power

The Citizen Movement was, from its foundation, a political movement. (By political we mean the explicit connection to domination and legitimation by state institutions.) From the start, Spain's situation to some extent forced neighbourhood protest to place its demands within the broader political context. Authoritarianism was the intrinsic element of the urban development to which residents were so opposed. And the existence of the Movement was in itself a challenge to a system founded on the banning of all uncontrolled voluntary organizations. Furthermore, most of the initiatives to organize protest and to set up neighbourhood associations were the output of political militants, trying to obtain grassroots support for their democratic struggle against Franquism.

We say militants instead of parties because no party ever had a clear strategy about using urban issues as sources of protest and organization. What militants did do was to put into practice a more general strategy: to use all possible forms of popular pressure to organize people and to fulfil their demands as a means of showing the necessity for a system that would allow socially and politically autonomous organizations, so putting an end to the dictatorship. Different blueprints emerged behind this strategy: for the radical left, grassroots protest was the beginning of a revolutionary process; for the PCE it was an additional factor in a massive popular peaceful protest (the Political General Strike) that would lead to the overthrow of the dictatorship and to a progressive coalition government; for the PSOE and Christian Democrats it was a demand for pressuring the system to open itself up in a process of gradual democratization. In all cases, some way had to be found to connect the pieces into a feasible strategy of building popular organizations, a way that would satisfy the differences in those perspectives, elude daily police repression, and improve the hard living conditions.

This was the task facing grassroots political militants, disciplined enough to their party's line but sensitive enough to popular needs and new sources of discontent. Without their effort, the neighbourhood movement would have never existed in Madrid: repression was too harsh, organizing efforts demanded too much energy and perserverance, and co-ordination with other neighbourhoods was too difficult to be carried out without some underlying project, ideology, or hope that all this smale-scale work would some day become part of a broader mobilization where one could find political and ideological rewards and some form of organizational support on a day-to-day basis. In fact, support was almost non-existent and, such as it was, mainly took the form of putting neighbourhood militants in touch with professionals, media, and other grassroots organizations. Unlike some American or North European experiences, Madrid's Citizen Movement was based entirely on voluntary militant work by people already working eight to twelve hours a day in their own jobs. Not only did it not have any financial or material support, but party chapters and political propaganda printing shops were often housed in the neighbourhood associations' front rooms. This situation was not only the consequence of a lack of resources and interest, but was mainly the result of the Citizen Movement's formal rejection of any form of support that implied some kind of dependency upon one party's organization. For instance, when in 1977 the PCE decided to include on its payroll the elected president of the Federation of Neighbourhood Associations of Madrid, the decision was kept secret in order to avoid the Movement's total distrust. Secrecy was, however, useless given this president's sectarian behaviour and his systematic alignment to PCE instructions. He was always considered a traitor to the Movement by most militants, including PCE cadres linked to the neighbourhoods, and was forced to resign in 1979 at the next election.

Thus the origin of the Citizen Movement established a peculiar relationship between political goals and urban issues. On the one hand, its leaders were fully political: they introduced political motivations and consciousness into the Movement and connected it to leftist politics in the broadest sense. On the other hand, they were able to develop a widely supported Movement because they focused it primarily on urban issues, maintained unity of action at the grassroots level, and, unlike Chile, refused to link the neighbourhood associations to a single party structure even when a given party, PCE or ORT often as not, held the majority in the elected steering committee. When they did not proceed in this independent way, the association would shrink and the Movement decline as soon as the residents discovered that they were not organizing themselves but supporting a political stand that they did not necessarily share. This was the continuous tension that characterized Madrid's Citizen Movement: it was based, at once, on the self-organization of residents to foster their urban interests and on the connection of their demands to the political struggle against the urban crisis, while keeping their autonomy in relationship to partisan politics. The ambiguity of the situation was both a source of creation and destruction: it was a creative tension because it allowed the Movement to expand, to find powerful allies, to shift from local and piecemeal demands to alternative models of urban policy, enabling citizens to have a decisive impact on the political mechanisms that were prerequisites for the transformation of the city. It was also the major source of crisis and, ultimately, of destruction. Partisan goals and the Movements' orientations became increasingly divergent. Until 1977, the frictions were minor. Everybody agreed that the priority was to re-establish political democracy. Everybody also realized that legitimate forms of grassroots organization, such as neighbourhood associations and informal labour committees, offered the best opportunity to mobilize people, linking their immediate interests to broader political goals. Once a democratic parliament was elected, in June 1977, the tension between broad social representation and specific political influence dramatically increased. For the big parties, UCD and PSOE, alternative forms of territorially-based organizations were a potential challenge to their overwhelming electoral superiority, on the grounds that democracy already offered a channel for participation (parties and elections) and the Citizen Movement was a platform manipulated by communists and radicals.

For the radical left, the problem was the opposite one. Having become marginal in an electoral system, the only power left to it was its agitational capacity on the basis of unsolved, pressing social needs, and it was strategically imperative that neighbourhood protest be fostered and led by the radical left. But since radicals were divided into many parties and since the PCE was still the main force in the Citizen Movement, most of the militants energy had to be redirected to winning control over the neighbourhood associations, therefore weakening and splitting the Movement.

For its part, the PCE entered into a profound crisis in relationship to the Citizen Movement as it was internally torn between three different needs or motivations. First, its will to reaffirm its party structure by organizing local chapters tended, in practice, to conflict with existing neighbourhood associations, pulling out the PCE militants to use them in reinforcing the party's influence, propaganda, fund-raising, and membership. Second it was nevertheless clear that the prestige and strength of the PCE in the neighbourhood associations could be an important asset in electoral politics, both for obtaining votes and for countering UCD's and PSOE's superior electorate, with its capacity to organize protest and (or) major support in relationship to city hall. So the official line was to preserve and develop the Citizen Movement, recognizing its autonomy, while finding forms of articulation between representative democracy and grassroots democracy. Third, fostering social movements was for the Utopian wing of the PCE (in reality the majority of cadres extracted from the Movement) *per se* a major task for any revolutionary party. So these idealists stayed in the Movement and activated it without paying much attention to the party's apparatus. While their activity was accepted, even praised, by the party's leadership, they clashed daily with the party's local chapters and mid-level cadres, until they discovered the impossibility of using a communist party structure as an organizational tool for fostering social movements.

When, in April 1979, a socialist-communist coalition took control of Madrid's city hall, the crisis between parties and Movement became apparent. The scheme of residents' participation that had been asked for by the neighbourhood associations and accepted by the electoral programmes was transformed into decentralized district councils, formed by representatives from the three political parties elected to the city council, along with the district's advisory boards where neighbourhood associations would be present, together with sports clubs, cultural centres, local fishermen, and other civic forces. Many neighbourhood associations, missing the historical connection between politics and local life, disappeared. Others retreated into their neighbourhoods to become demand-orientated community organizations and (or) local networks for socializing.

In the increasing tension and contradiction between urban struggles and political militancy, most neighbourhood leaders ceased to be party militants and some ceased to be neighbourhood activists. A few personal examples would help to illustrate the analysis. The leader of Orcasistas was offered a PCE's seat on the Madrid city council. He refused in order to stay in his neighbourhood where his main voluntary activity, in 1980, was to organize sports competitions for children. In a contrary example, the former president of the Federation of Neighbourhood Associations, once disavowed and dismissed by the Movement, became a PCE alderman and spent most of his time running the district's council in the same area where years ago he had founded a neighbourhood association. The story was even more complex for the president of Hortaleza, perhaps the Movement's most prestigious and aware leader. While a member of the Madrid's PCE provincial committee, he was under strong personal attack in his own neighbourhood from the local PCE chapter on the grounds that he gave too much attention to the Citizen Movement, forgetting the vanguard role of the party. Unable to live with the daily schizophrenia of enacting three roles, he resigned from the PCE in 1978 to become vice president of the Federation of Neighbourhood Associations, and went on to reactivate the Movement quite successfully. When, in April 1979, the PCE was elected to run the key City Planning Commission, he was offered the post of Madrid's director of City Planning, and accepted on the condition that he would not have to re-enter the party. So by 1980, he had become neither a neighbourhood leader nor a party cadre, but instead an honest urban manager overwhelmed by the bureaucratic machinery.

To end on a rather sad note, we shall tell about two intimate friends, Luis and Angel. Luis was a political cadre, a former priest who became a journalist. In the late 1960s he went to live in a shanty town to organize the neighbourhood. He succeeded, and his neighbourhood was one of the most active, organized, and conscious in all of Madrid. He was an articulate leader, loved and respected by the shanty town dwellers. He became good friends with Angel who was a young worker, exceedingly bright and militant who became the natural leader of the neighbourhood; and they built a shack together which they shared. They also shared their lives and struggles. They married, had children, and always lived there, expanding the shack when necessary. They both joined the PCE and both strongly supported the Citizen Movement against the bureaucracy of the party, obtaining some recognition for their positions. In 1979, Angel became the newly elected president of the Federation of Neighbourhood Associations. Luis became a PCE alderman of Madrid and was given a very important position within the city government. Both appointments were considered by observers as a major boost to the Citizen Movement. Yet, for a year Luis failed to receive any delegation from the neighbourhood in his city hall office, refused to participate in any local meetings, and sent instructions to the district council to include a variety of representation on its advisory board without recognizing the role of the neighbourhood association. In fact, Luis was submerged in paper work and had to submit to the common rules established by PSOE and PCE for the management of Madrid. Angel tried for a while to defend the Movement's autonomy and initiative, recalling the promises of participatory democracy. Then he became increasingly nervous and violent, lost his job, entered a period of psychological depression, resigned from the PCE and withdrew to his neighbourhood to control the accomplishment of the housing programme they had won. Luis and Angel still shared the same shack in 1980, but no longer spoke to each other.

These stories offer no lesson; neither are they intended to induce romantic compassion for a nice 'Miss Red Riding Hood' neighbourhood movement devoured by the 'Big Bad Wolf' of political parties. Instead they strikingly signal the tension between social movements and political strategy that characterized Madrid's Citizen Movement. We do not even suggest that there could have been a different scenario: this would be the task of a political strategist and not of an urban analyst. What should be concluded in relation to our research is that the Citizen Movement strongly articulated urban demands and political issues, linking city and power in the neighbourhood's mobilization, but, at the same time, it was not a purely political movement, nor was it, in contrast to Chile, a politically controlled process. It was an autonomous combination of urban and cultural practices, irreducible to any one dimension or dominance by one factor. When the tension became too acute, when politics took over, the Movement resisted, and ultimately collapsed, not because it was apolitical but because it was the expression of a new politics, relating issues of everyday life to power processes without submitting to the rules of the institutionalized political system. While on the wane as an historical experience, Madrid's Citizen Movement took something else with it to the deep: the century-old dream of revolutionary parties as agents simultaneously expressing both social movements and political strategies.

27

City, Community and Power: An Analytical Model to Evaluate the Citizen Movement in Madrid as an Urban Social Movement

The experience of the Citizen Movement in Madrid was one of urban, cultural, and political change, accomplished through neighbourhood mobilization and protest. Our research has systematically explored the main characteristics of this process as a way to understand historical and structural rules linking city and society in their patterns of change. We have found that although working class areas and urban poor were more likely to be active and organized, the Movement occurred in a diversity of social groups and could not be considered as a mere extension of the class struggle between capital and labour. Neither was the Citizen Movement an organizational manifestation of cultural revolts against oppression, such as of women or youth, even if the cultural dimension was a fundamental one in the form of a collective search for a new community-orientated life. While it challenged the prevailing power structure and incorporated as an essential element a political stand, the Movement cannot be seen as a spin-off from political conflicts. When parties tried deliberately to manipulate neighbourhood associations, they resisted or they quickly exhausted their appeal to local residents.

The Citizen Movement appeared to be deeply rooted in the structural features of the urban crisis. It was, first of all, a social response to the crisis of urban goals and services, triggered by a particular model of economic growth and metropolitan concentration. In this sense, it was an urban movement: it referred primarily to the conditions of living in the city and it opposed itself to the crisis of collective consumption, proposing a series of urban demands as well as an alternative functional, social, and spatial model of urban life.

Nevertheless, if this was the basis of the Movement, it only successfully achieved the transformation it was looking for when it articulated the three fundamental dimensions that characterized it: city community and power. In a situation where politics shapes the basic structure of the urban system, and both largely condition the prevailing cultural patterns, only a movement articulating urban demands, cultural aspirations, and political challenges would be able to become an agent of social change at a variety of levels. The fact is that the subject matter of the Movement – its issues, demands, interests and adversaries – expressed the search for a new city, a new community, and a new power. We are not debating the values of the Movement, but its behaviour. We do not mean, at that level, the necessary presence of the three elements of city, community and power in the consciousness of the residents, but rather the social practice of the neighbourhood associations.

It does not follow that consciousness is an unnecessary element to produce effects of social change. On the contrary, our general assumption and our observation in the case of Madrid is that there is no social movement without a self-conscious definition by the movement of its own role. For a neighbourhood association in Madrid to become a social movement that could produce social change in the urban system, in the culture of the city, and in the political institutions, it had to consider itself a party of the Citizen Movement, not necessarily as an organizational form but as a legitimate and specific source of social change and collective representation. Thus, the consciousness of the Movement – any movement – is an essential element in urban change, but it must be distinguished from the three obligatory dimensions in the practice of the movement (i.e urban demands, cultural aspirations, and political challenges), and not only at the level of self-representation.

Once a movement is potentially structured around these three dimensions, and once it recognizes itself as a potential source of change, it still needs an organizational means with which to relate to society as a whole. We use the term operators for the organizational forms generated outside the Citizen Movement that allow its three-dimensional practice. In the case of Madrid, we have observed three major operators at work: the media, the professionals, and above all, the left wing political parties. The media allowed the Movement to communicate to different sectors of public opinion, so overcoming its local base. Thus a given neighbourhood was able to identify an image of the existing city, criticize it, and to disseminate a new one through the demands it fostered in its struggle. The professionals made it possible to redefine alternative forms of urban development, both by breaking down the technocratic rationale behind the exploitative metropolitan growth and by providing legitimacy for a new city, as expressed in the demands and desires of neighbourhoods.

The left wing political parties brought together the different elements of the Movement in the effort to overcome the power structure that was at the very basis of the city against which the Citizen Movement was rebelling. They provided the strength and militancy necessary to address the major issue of an urban structure relying on the policies of an authoritarian state. As we have seen, the relationship between the Citizen Movement and political parties was particularly complex. The action of a party, or of a political nucleus within the Movement that had originated from one political stand, was an indispensable element for the transformation of neighbourhood mobilization into a social movement. At the same time, absorption of the Movement by the party's structure and strategy always led to tension, and eventually, to the Movement's destruction. Thus, the political operator had to play a very peculiar role in Madrid. On the one hand, he had to make (without confusing them) the different dimensions of the Movement articulate against the antagonistic power structure, then playing a crucial role in the dynamics of the Movement. On the other hand, he had to play his role as an element of the Movement, without absorbing the neighbourhood association's urban protest within the realm of its political and organizational interests. Thus the political operator had to exercise leadership while respecting the autonomy of the movement. His role as an active agent had to be combined with the placing of some distance between himself and the Movement, for without this distance the Movement would have been absorbed. But without the presence of the operator, the Movement would have been powerless when confronted by the state-enforced urban model.

The relationship between the dimensions of the Movement and its operators was a structural one. These dimensions did not necessarily precede the action of the operators, nor did operators always provide missing dimensions to a given neighbourhood. How the structure of a movement is generated is a crucial matter for our research, but must be treated at a different analytical level; we will examine the issue in the final pages of this chapter. What we are considering now is the proposition about the existence of a structural formula underlying the formation and development of an urban social movement as observed in Madrid.

In such a formula there are no unessential elements, and neither is there a sequential nor a causal order between the components. Our research is not accurate enough to establish the network of causal relationships between elements. We have, however, enough reliable information on Madrid to advance a precise combination of dimensions and operators as characteristics of an urban social movement. If this formula is adequate, all its elements must be present to produce social change, whatever the sequence of their articulation in a collective social practice.

By urban social movement we understand a conscious collective practice originating in urban issues, able to produce qualitative changes in the urban system, local culture, and political institutions in contradiction to the dominant social interests institutionalized as such at the societal level. We have already presented the urban, cultural, and political changes that took place in Madrid due to the Citizen Movement. We now want to synthecize the social factors appearing in the structure of the Movement that led to the change of the city at these three levels. On the basis of the observed neighbourhood mobilization and bearing in mind the discussion in the preceeding paragraphs, we may advance the following proposition.

The Citizen Movement in Madrid constituted an urban social movement characterized by the social change it brought on the city, culture, and state as a result of collective action triggered by urban demands. Social change was achieved through the links in the transformation simultaneously produced on the urban system, the local culture, and the political system. To accomplish this social innovation, neighbourhood protest had, in its practice, to articulate urban demands, the search for community, and political goals challenging the state's institutions. It also had to define its own mobilization as part of a broader social movement led by citizens, and had to be related to society through several operators, requiring at least the support of the media, professionals and political parties. While the presence of political militants within the Movement was a fundamental condition to achieve social change, the Movement had to keep its organizational autonomy, as well as its capacity to define its own goals. Given these conditions, one neighbourhood's mobilization had to achieve urban change, political change, and cultural change, regardless of any other factor such as the composition of social class, type of urban issue, or ideological orientation. Therefore, the proposed formula defines the necessary and sufficient conditions for a neighbourhood mobilization to become an urban social movement, taking the process observed in Madrid.

This proposition is demanding. If true, it would imply that all cases of neighbourhood mobilization meeting the proposed structural formula should produce social change on city, culture, and the political system. It would also imply that all cases of three dimensional transformation observed in Madrid had been produced by, and only for, this combination.

The obvious problem then, as in all systematic research on social movements, is to analyse what happened in those cases of mobilization (actually the majority of cases) where overall change did not occur. We will try to show that the same analytical model that explains the production of urban-political-cultural change also accounts for other possible outcomes of neighbourhood mobilization. In other words, there is a relationship between the changing internal structure of an urban movement and different types of outcomes, as reflected in the city, culture, and political system. When a given movement has reached the proposed structural formula, it should have produced social change at the three noted levels. If some element(s) is (are) missing, social change will be confined to some levels and some dimensions, and not to others. The relationship between what has been achieved and what is missing must be significant from a theoretical point of view. Thus the analytical model we propose is a comprehensive one since it must account for the proposed relationship between the structure of a movement and its capacity for producing social change, but must also provide connections between each modification of the basic structure and each outcome diverging from the desired pattern of change. In so doing, we can discover not only the structure of an urban social movement, but also the underlying mechanisms leading to a typology of urban movements.

To be sure, the discovery of this formula and its variations does not provide, by itself, a theoretical explanation. Once the formula is established on the basis of empirical evidence, we will then have to relate its characteristics to a broader analytical framework, enabling us to fully understand the meaning of the observed mechanism. But before we can go onto this, we need to demonstrate the accuracy of the proposed formula and its variants as actual sources of the effects produced on the urban, political, and cultural systems of Madrid.

To do so, we have constructed a relatively complex analytical procedure, whose justification and detailed operations are presented in the Methodological Appendix (pp. 000–00). Nevertheless, we need to provide some explanation of the model to make our findings intelligible.

The model is specifically designed to test our proposed formula and its variants. It does not summarize all possible information on neighbourhood mobilization, but only that needed to determine the proposed structural formula and to test its effects on city, culture, and the political system. While we have provided enough information for the Citizen Movement to be known and analysed under different alternative theoretical approaches, here we organize the empirical evidence in a way that relates to our research question to which we have yet to find adequate answers.

Our basic proposition establishes a systemic relationship between the structural dimensions composing an urban movement, the operators through which it relates to society, and its effect. Therefore, we have analysed each one of the observed 23 neighbourhood mobilizations, coding them in relationship to four series of characteristics:

1 The urban, cultural, and political dimensions present in the Movement as shown by its demands, the targets of its mobilization, the themes of its debates, the interests attacked and defended, and so on. We have called city (CY) the dimension related to urban issues. We have called power (PW) the dimension referring to political issues. We have called community (CM) the cultural dimension present in the Movement, since the results of our analysis have shown that this, and not other sources of cultural revolt, was the source of mobilization in Madrid's Citizen Movement. In addition to the three basic dimensions we also examined the Movement's consciousness.

2 We observed the role of the operators: the media (MD), the professionals (PF), and the parties (PT). In relation to the last, we distinguished between two kinds of situations: the presence of a political party in the movement (PT_1) and the type of relationship established between the party and the Movement, particularly in terms of autonomy or subordination (PT_2).

3 We also coded the effects produced by each neighbourhood-based collective action in Madrid's urban system (U), political institutions (P), and local culture (C). For each area where there was a potential outcome, we distinguished two levels (U_1, U_2), (P_1, P_2), (C_1, C_2), in accordance with the discussion of observed social effects. Level one refers to the effect on the Movement's target: in other words, the immediate urban demand, the reinforcement of democracy and the increased support for left wing parties,[25] and the improvement of neighbourhood-based social interaction. Significant social change only happens at level two in each area: the modification of basic premises underlying the model of urban development (U_2); the transformation of political institutions (e.g. obtaining democratic municipal elections, establishing mechanisms for participatory democracy (P_2); innovation of cultural patterns with reference to the city with reference (C_2) (e.g. fostering the notion of the city as a public place, recovering history through the newly affirmed urban culture).

4 To improve the demonstration we also introduced control variables: factors that are normally suggested as sources of the effects of social change produced by urban movements.

Three such variables were carefully considered: the class position of the Movement (CP), coding (+) the dominance of working class in the neighbourhood as opposed to middle class or socially mixed neighbourhood; the class consciousness of the Movement when represented by itself as a working class movement (+) more than a citizen movement; and the solidarity with other social movements when the neighbourhood association closely related itself to other social struggles (e.g. labour, women, youth) (+). If our formula is correct these three variables should not have major influence on the production of social effects. The coding of observed neighbourhood mobilizations in relationship to each one of the cited elements and effects takes a dichotomic form: only presence (+) or absence (–) of the element is recorded.

Criteria for coding are presented and justified in the Methodological Appendix with the basic empirical observations for every code of every element of every neighbourhood mobilization. Let us just emphasize here that the information and criteria used for each element are entirely independent from each other. This is fundamental to preventing contamination in the definition of variables that are supposed to be causally related. For instance, the coding of the urban, political and cultural dimensions of the neighbourhood mobilization, and the coding of its urban, political, and cultural effects, are founded on totally different empirical information. The former refer to the demands and concerns of a movement. The latter refer to the actual effects produced in the urban system, political institution, and cultural categories by that movement.

Once every neighbourhood mobilization has been coded on the basis of a sheet reconstructing the different elements of the proposed formula, we obtain a profile for each urban movement. Every profile must fulfill the rules as postulated by our structural formula. Therefore an urban social movement, defined as having an effect of social change on the city, the culture, and the political system (namely: U_1+, U_2+, P_1+, P_2+, C_1+, C_2+) can only be produced by a structure of neighbourhood mobilization: C_y+, P_w+, C_m+, $M+$, PT_1+, PT_2+, $MD+$, $PF+$, no matter what values are taken by CP, CC and SSM.[26] So we postulate a model of mechanical causality as opposed to statistical causality: namely, all observation must fit within the model as proposed. It must be possible to integrate all effects resulting from other forms of structural arrangement into the model, while reinforcing the model's logical consistency and without altering the substance of the theoretical interpretation underlying the original formula.

On the basis of these assumptions and explanations, we can now examine our research findings as presented in Table 27–1.

Since reading this chart is difficult, we will proceed by grouping different neighbourhood mobilizations according to the pattern of social effects they have produced.

We should immediately say that, on the basis of our empirical findings, a small but crucial modification to our analytical rule will have to be introduced, as follows: when a given formula works in the entire profile of a neighbourhood mobilization with the exception of one element that does not fundamentally effect the analytical model, we will include the case in the group in which it tends to fit. This practice, the legitimacy of which is defended in the Appendix (pp. 365–94), allows us to consider small accidental variations without losing the main line of our argument.

We will now proceed with the analysis, step by step.

1 We first identify the cases of *urban social movements*: cases number 3, 4, 7, 18, 21, 22. We could also incorporate case 6 into this group by virtue of the tolerance threshold we have introduced.[27] The profile reads in all cases as follows:

$Cy+$, $Pw+$, $Cm+$, $M+$, PT_1+, PT_2+, $MD+$, $PF+$, U_1+, U_2, P_1+, C_1, C_2+

CP and CC vary randomly. SSM has equal value in all cases, without discriminating among them and other processes.

Even more important: all movements with the proposed structural formula produced an effect of a social movement. There is only one way to produce social change at three levels and the same structure, when it occurs, always produces this change.

2 A second group of cases, as defined by the pattern of social effects, is characterized by the low level of change produced but, at the same time, by their impact at three levels. More precisely, they were movements that obtained their immediate urban demands without modifying the urban system; they fostered the strength of left wing parties' without changing the institutions; and they improved neighbourhoods' social networks without redefining the urban culture. Their effects formula is: U_1+, U_2-, P_1+, P_2-, C_1+, C_2-, and we call these movements *urban reform*.

Cases 5, 9, 10, 13, 16, 20, are included in this group. We now compare their structural formula to the one giving an urban social movement. The observation is complex but shows some coherent development if we combine several observations. In cases 16, 20, and 10 the movement did have the basic structural combination: $Cy+$, $Pw+$, $CM+$, but did not lead to an urban social movement. In fact 16 and 20 were under the control of a political party (PT_2-) and 10 did not consider itself a citizen movement ($M-$) but an expression of the labour movement (SSM). Cases 9, 5, and 13, in addition to being politically heteronomous (PT_2-), as in the preceeding cases, lacked the community dimension in their basic structures ($Cm-$). This is why 9 and 13 did not have any cultural impact (C_1-, C_2-).

Therefore it seems that the absence of the need and search for community impoverished the cultural output of the movement, and, most importantly, when the basic dimensions to foster social change were present but were orchestrated by a political party, the level of change was lowered and reform substituted for social movement.

3 A third group is provided by movements that produced a high level of urban and cultural change, but did not alter the political system (so: U_1+, U_2+, P_1-, P_2-, C_1+, C_2+). We name this outcome *urban Utopia* because of the assumption, particular to Madrid, that without political change there cannot be lasting urban-cultural change. This is not to say that they are impossible – they do exist – but the label is to describe a fundamental variant in neighbourhood mobilizations: movements that cannot be projected on to the entire city because of their political alienation, but in their local area accomplish substantial changes that suggest an alternative city and culture.

Cases 17, 19, 12 fall into this category. When examined, their particular attribute was to reproduce the basic structural formula of a social movement with two fundamental differents: power was not a dimension of their practice, and no political party appeared as operator. Apolitical mobilizations do not challenge the political system, but, as we shall see, it does not follow that strictly political actions challenge institutional power.

4 A fourth group consists of movements that only produce urban effects: U_1+, U_2+, P_1-, P_2-, C_1-, C_2-. We name them *urban corporatism* because of their limited scope. By examining the only two cases that produced this outcome (1, 8), it becomes apparent that they have an idea in common distinguishing them from other cases: a narrowed dimensional structure (only urban issues in 1; urban and political issues, but not community in 8) connected to a powerful party structure (PT_2-). A political party becomes an urban trade union to defend residents' interests without connecting its practice to other realms of society.

5 Finally, a fifth group is formed by movements unable to produce a single transformation: U_1-, U_2-, P_1-, C_1-, C_2-. We describe these movements as *urban shadows*. They include Cases 11, 14, 15, 23. Interestingly enough, they were characterized by two things: they did not

Table 27.1 Record of Presence/Absence for selected components of the structure of neigbourhood mobilization in 23 observed neigbourhoods.

Characteristics of Neighbourhood Mobilization	Structural Dimensions of the Movement				Control Variables		
	City	Power	Commu-nity	Conscious-ness as citizen movement	Class position	Class consciousness	Solidarity with other social movements
Association Number	Cy	Pw	Cm	M	CP	CC	SSM
1	+	−	−	−	+	−	−
2	+	+	+	+	+	+	+
3	+	+	+	+	+	+	+
4	+	+	+	+	+	+	+
5	+	+	−	+	−	−	+
6	+	+	+	+	+	+	+
7	+	+	+	+	+	+	+
8	+	+	−	+	+	+	+
9	+	+	−	−	+	+	+
10	+	+	+	−	+	+	+
11	+	+	−	−	−	−	+
12	+	−	+	+	−	−	+
13	+	+	−	−	−	−	+
14	+	+	−	−	−	−	−
15	−	+	+	−	−	−	−
16	+	+	+	−	−	−	−
17	+	−	+	+	−	−	−
18	+	+	+	+	−	−	−
19	+	−	+	+	−	−	+
20	+	+	+	−	+	−	+
21	+	+	+	+	−	−	+
22	+	+	+	+	−	−	+
23	−	+	−	−	−	−	+

Source: Our study.

Effects on Social Structure

Operators				Urban Effects		Political Effects		Cultural Effects		
Political party	Type of relationship to political party	Media	Professionals	Level of satisfaction of urban demands	Transformation of the urban system	Gains of the left without changing political institutions	Change of political institutions	Improving quality of neighbourhood life	Producing a new type of urban culture	
PT_1	PT_2	MD	PF	U_1	U_2	P_1	P_2	C_1	C_2	Association Number
+	+	−	+	+	+	−	−	−	−	1
+	−	+	+	+	+	+	−	−	+	2
+	+	+	+	+	+	+	+	+	+	3
+	+	+	+	+	+	+	+	+	+	4
+	−	−	+	−	−	+	−	+	−	5
+	+	+	+	+	+	+	+	+	−	6
+	+	+	+	+	+	+	+	+	+	7
+	−	+	+	+	+	+	−	−	−	8
+	−	−	+	+	−	+	−	−	−	9
+	+	−	+	−	−	+	−	+	−	10
+	−	+	+	−	−	−	−	−	−	11
−	−	+	+	+	−	−	−	+	+	12
+	−	+	+	+	−	+	−	−	−	13
+	−	−	−	−	−	−	−	−	+	14
+	−	−	−	−	−	−	−	−	+	15
+	−	−	+	+	−	+	−	+	+	16
−	−	+	+	+	+	−	−	+	+	17
+	+	+	+	+	+	+	+	+	+	18
−	−	+	+	+	+	−	−	+	+	19
+	−	+	+	+	−	+	−	+	−	20
+	+	+	+	+	+	+	+	+	+	21
+	+	+	+	+	+	+	+	+	+	22
+	−	−	+	−	−	−	−	−	−	23

present the three basic dimensions of city, power, and community; and they existed only because a political party (PT_1+, PT_2-) used the neighbourhood as a pretext for political agitation. Thus parties may try to invent a domesticated neighbourhood movement, but they will end by projecting urban shadows, instead of fostering urban change.

All surveyed neighbourhood mobilizations have been included in this grouping, except case 2 the profile of which our model does not satisfactorily explain. Possible reasons for this failure are discussed in the Appendix (pp. 365–94). But for all other cases, the proposed formula appears to suggest an urban social movement, and variations in their structure accordingly produce coherent variations in the outcome of their action. Such effects are by no means self-evident. Some observers have suggested, for instance, that radical political leadership, if strictly followed by a movement, should lead to the highest possible level of social change, but in the case of Madrid we find the opposite. Instead of commenting on the empirical findings one by one, let us summarize the main trends in a schematic way that will allow us to develop a more general analysis:

1 An urban social movement, as defined by effects on urban, political, and cultural change, appears when a movement articulates city, community and power, develops its own consciousness, and operates through a political party, while keeping its autonomy and continuing to relate to society through the support of professionals and the images transmitted by the media.
2 When the movement has no autonomous consciousness or when it closely follows a partisan leadership, while still keeping the basic structure necessary for social change, it produces *urban reform*.
3 When politics does not enter into the structure of the movement it leans towards *urban Utopia*.
4 When a party structure links upto particular urban demands without relating them to a more general level, the movement becomes *urban corporatism*.
5 When neighbourhoods are purely a political arena for partisan organizations, movements are nothing but *urban shadows*.

Let us now put these findings into a broader explanatory framework. The social change accomplished by the Citizen Movement in Madrid appears to have been shaped by a formula expressing the internal structure of the Movement. The formula, with all its components, certainly was present if we take the Movement as a whole. But what our detailed analysis shows is that when we break the Movement into neighbourhood mobilizations, only those that stand by the general formula effected social change on the urban system, culture, and the state.

Why is this so? What is the theoretical meaning of the proposed formula? Let us examine its composition.

First of all, a movement must, in its practice, be based upon three dimensions which we have named as city, community, and power. City relies on the presence of urban demands that reject production and management of urban space and services as profitable commodities. People struggle for housing, services, and location on the basis of their living requirements. These people appear to the capitalist city (organizing the urban space in terms of its exchange value) as opposition since they demand a city determined by use value.

Community addresses the fact that neighbourhoods affirm their will to become social entities, based on face-to-face interaction and territorially defined cultures that are part of their heritage. So they oppose placeless networks of a technocracy that does not care for its history with place-specific traditions and uses of local communities, and the mass media with personal communication.

Power refers to the reaction against increasing bureaucratic forms and the authoritarian style of an increasingly centralized state. Neighbourhoods appeal to democracy against the political enforcement of socially dominant interests. To oppose the centralization and insulation of public authorities, they call for local government, self-reliance, and citizen participation.

Thus an urban social movement, on the basis of the Madrid experience, emerged from the affirmation of urban use value in opposition to the capitalist city; from the search for space-based cultural communities in opposition to the technocratic city; and from the defense of local autonomy and citizen participation against state centralism and bureaucratic politics. The crucial finding is that these three dimensions must be connected and present to produce social change. In fact they reinforce each other. Urban demands based on use value tend to create an alternative economic basis of community-orientated social relations, and, at the same time, their satisfaction could provide a new source of legitimacy for decentralized political power. Community-orientated neighbourhoods could become the social fabric required for a more effective functioning of urban services through self-management, while they could establish the political institutions in the grassroots by bringing the state down to the community level. Participatory democracy appears to be the political prerequisite for achieving both economic redistribution by means of urban services as well as the revitalization of popular culture.

This web is not an urban dream, but rather a projection of what maybe possible in the event of the three levels underlying the structure of the social movement interweaving successfully. That is why the effect of social change supersedes the system where it occurs. In Madrid it affected the city as a whole historical construct, since the currently segmented urban-political-cultural system was challenged by the projected image of a reunified city, orientated towards use value, based on a local culture, and administered by a decentralized, participatory democracy. These were the embryos of alternative social organization conceived by the urban social movement in Madrid, a movement triggered by the city's urban-political crisis.

We have seen that operators are crucial if such embryos are to grow. The Movement needs the media, to oppose the monopoly of messages by the media. The Movement needs alternative sources of legitimacy to oppose the economic rationality of capitalist city, provided by the professionals, the holders of knowledge and expertise. And the movement needs a political instrument to oppose a centralized state, capable of democratizing the polity and ensuring new and broader channels of citizens' representation (but not the kind of political instrument that would replace one centralized state with another, only with a different class content). The practice of an urban social movement must therefore dispense with the traditional distinction between regrettable means and justifiable goals.

Different sets of effects are produced when the basic structure of the social movement is altered in the development of a collective action. We have seen that the lack of consciousness and (or) of organizational autonomy reduces the level of social change. No social movement can exist without an independent and conscious social actor to lead it. When the movement does not integrate power structures into its practice, it may still produce some urban and cultural changes but is unable to affect the institutions and the relationships between them that are at the root of the urban development we have observed. In these cases, urban change is likely to be limited, and cultural change will probably reach only some particular sectors of the cultural vanguard (ecologists, for instance).

When political operators use urban demands on purely defensive grounds, they achieve at the most some limited effects upon the city's living conditions without ever projecting their practice onto other dimensions of social change, in spite of the fact that they are interdependent within the urban system.

Thus our analytical model does explain the urban social change in greater depth than would be possible by a series of systemic mechanisms. Each dimension – the articulation of the three dimensions, the function of the operators, the modified structures of the social movement – are the elements of broader social processes: the opposition between exchange value and use value, mass culture and personal communication, centralized apparatuses and decentralized self-management, political leadership and politicized social movements.

It must be remembered that this explanation is specific to Madrid, even if general concepts and processes have emerged. Furthermore, the three basic dimensions of an urban social movement are the reverse side of the three roots of the urban crisis in Madrid: a wild capitalist model of urban development; an authoritarian and centralized state; and an accelerated territorial concentration rapidly destroying existing local communities. We do not mean to imply that the underlying dimensions of an urban social movement are reactions to the specific manifestations of Madrid's urban crisis. The crisis does not produce the movement, as the movement does not cause the crisis. They are both faces of the same historical process articulated in a dialectical way by a series of contradictory couples: capital denies the city as a living place and the city denies capital's capacity to commodify space; the state denies that people are its legitimate source and people deny the state's authority; mass culture overwhelms popular traditions and local networks switch to personal communication. As with all contradictory relationships their evolution can emphasize one pole or other within each couple. Our finding is that to favour the social movement pole, the three contradictory relationships must be connected. This is not necessarily due to an universal rule or by accident, but because of this particular model of urban development, itself a striking expression of the characteristics of the advanced capitalist city. As we have seen, the particular nature of metropolitan growth in Madrid lay in the dominance by corporate capital of both urban concentration and of the profitable use of new urban needs, relying on unlimited support from a dictatorial state. Politics, territory, and urban needs were thus closely connected, but were also contradictory expressions, and this situation was reflected in the need of the urban movement to articulate all these dimensions in its struggle. So the reaction and surpassing movement generated by urban protest in each one of the three contradictory dimensions points not only to a reversal of dominance between the two poles within each dimension, but also to the city emerging around a relationship of equality between the three levels, and all that this implies. Instead of replacing the dominance of capitalist profit by the priority of residential quality, the urban social movement in Madrid leaned towards new cultural definition of the city that required both a well-equipped urban space as well as a vital community with self-reliant power. In this sense, it was more a citizen movement than an urban one in that it sought to propose a new city while improving the existing one.

Thus, the structural formula we have proposed in order to understand the social change brought about by Madrid's Citizen Movement is not only empirically adequate and logically consistent, but also has significant things to say at a theoretical level. Nevertheless, we have not explained what produces the producer, or, in other words, what the social sources of the elements composing the formula are, and what their variations and articulation are. By studying the social production of the basic structure that, in turn, produced social change, it should be possible to explain the entire process, and our research would then have succeeded in connecting social structure and social change at the three levels of city, politics, and culture by tracing the interaction between urban issues, social movements and political operators.

In fact, we cannot yet provide a general theory concerning the social production of structural formulae for urban social movements. If the research can and must establish the conditions for a movement to produce social change, the evolution of these conditions remains a matter of history. In other words, if our analytical model is correct within the context of the Citizen Movement, each time a neighbourhood mobilization reaches the structural formula proposed, social change must happen. But the advent of the elements of the structural formula, as well as of their interaction, is a product of their history. Therefore, on the basis of our Madrid study alone, we cannot provide a comprehensive analytical framework, and we may only refer to the historical mechanisms building the structural combination that underlies the social change produced by urban social movements. We have already provided all the empirical information on this historical context, as well as many clues as to how it shaped the Citizen Movement and its effects. We will now finish by strengthening the argument.

Madrid, as the capital city of Spain, condenses and concentrates the main trends of Spanish society, a society secularly dominated by the state and the Catholic Church in close institutional association. The Spanish state has never been democratic and has perpetually struggled to centralize power while denying indigenous cultures that existed before the merger of different states into a single, Castilla-dominated state. As a consequence, cultural traditions were curbed and local autonomy ignored. The city of Madrid, under direct control of the central government, was the first victim of centralism, and the richness of its neighbourhood life has always had to face the harassment of distrustful bureaucracies. The Civil War considerably worsened the situation: the people of Madrid resisted for three years the assault of the elite forces of the Franquist army. When finally conquered, in March 1939, the city was severely punished. For the following 40 years the central government appointed a dictatorial mayor to concentrate all power on its behalf. Local cultures and popular traditions were deliberately exterminated. Cultural anonymity and political authoritarianism opened the way for the repressive urban development we have described. On the basis of state repression, capital transformed the city into a gigantic source of exploitation and profit, both in the process of work and urban consumption.

So, the three basic levels of the structural formula of the Citizen Movement were the three basic elements of urban development in Madrid as determined by history. Their close interdependency expressed the dominance of the state over the entire conditions of capitalist accumulation, cultural oppression, and urban concentration. Only a three dimensional challenge could defy this tight structure. The Citizen Movement incarnated this challenge, and staged it on the basis of three operators, also specific to the Spanish social evolution in the late Franquist era: a press struggling to be free; a generation of professionals ideologically liberal and technically competent; and a new generation of political militants who learned through practice that autonomous social movements were the only effective antidote to an omnipresent and overpowerful state. Thus the most exploitative model of urban development of any European capital was coupled with the most powerful and innovative neighbourhood movement. But it happened this way because the state was in open confrontation with the civil society, and capital was simply destroying the city. On the basis of this, a major structural division, the connection between powerless militant parties and neighbourhood-based urban protests, led to the formation of the Citizen Movement by opposing city and society to capital and the state. Such a complex network of social elements, systemically expressed in the structural formula we have discovered, fostered social change at the urban, political, and cultural levels. We cannot, however, rely exclusively on the study of Madrid if we are to understand on a more theoretical level the historical process that, in this case, led to the structure of an urban social movement. To achieve this we need a comparative perspective able to observe the variation in production of social change by urban movements under different historical conditions and socio-spatial contexts. Such will be the task of the last part of this book, which brings together the lessons provided by the analysis of various experiences of urban mobilization.

Thus, the study of Madrid's Citizen Movement cannot be concluded by a general theoretical statement. The formula we have discovered summarizes only the essence of the potential of the Movement for social change, and the findings have to be placed in their own social context. But the raw materials uncovered by our observations form the social nuclei through which cities are produced as social forms and cultural categories: collective services, community cultures, local governments, neighbourhood organizations, communication networks, political parties, and spatial settings. And all are filled and shaped by people. People are the roots of cities.

Part 6

A Cross-Cultural Theory of Urban Social Change

' "As life is disorderly, so is the city . . . .'

[*Through the Chaos of the Living City*], Baudelaire
'A great motto for the study of urban disorder.'

Charles Tilly, 1974[1]

'The control of space is important to environmental quality in any social context. . . . But it is particularly critical in a changing, pluralistic society, where power is unequally distributed and problems are large in scale. . . . Making community control of community space a reality will require drastic changes in our economy, political power, and way of life.'

Kevin Lynch, 1981.[2]

'Social movements are not dramatic and exceptional events.
They are, in a permanent form, at the very core of social life.'

Alain Touraine, 1978.[3]

28

Introduction: In Search of a Theory

The basic purpose of this book is to further our understanding of the relationship between cities and social change. As stated in the Introduction, the major hypotheses that have inspired our analysis are:

1 The city is a social product resulting from conflicting social interests and values.
2 Because of the institutionalization of socially dominant interests, major innovations in the city's role, meaning, and structure tend to be the outcome of grassroots mobilization and demands. When these mobilizations result in the transformation of the urban structure, we call them urban social movements.
3 Yet the process of urban social change cannot be reduced to the effects produced on the city by successful social movements. Thus a theory of urban change must account both for the spatial and social effects resulting from the action of the dominant interests as well as from the grassroots' alternative to this domination.
4 Finally, although class relationships and class struggle are fundamental in understanding urban conflict, they are not, by any means, the only primary source of urban social change. The autonomous role of the state, the gender relationships, the ethnic and national movements, and movements that define themselves as citizen, are among other alternative sources of urban social change.

What our perspective affirms, and what empirical research shows, is that technology *per se* or the structure of the economy itself are *not* the driving force behind the process of urbanization.[4] Economic factors and technological progress do play a major role in establishing the shape and meaning of space. But this role is determined, as well as the economy and technology themselves, by the social process through which humankind appropriates space and time and constructs a social organization, relentlessly challenged by the production of new values and the emergence of new social interests.[5]

In our series of case studies, we have already examined the relationship between society and urbanization from a variety of angles. In particular we have focused on grassroots mobilization as it relates to the forms and functions of the city and *vis-à-vis* the state's policies for managing the urban system. Our observations have not strictly been empirical research monographs. We have already attempted in each chapter to theorize most of our findings, and deal with a number of analytical issues for the explanation of particular processes. Thus, at a semi-organized level, a theory of urban change, with a particular emphasis on urban social movements, has taken shape as the book has progressed. Yet, once we have sufficiently grounded our main interpretation in historical experience and tested some of the crucial hypotheses on the basis of our empirical research, it seems useful to organize the analysis in a more systematic and theoretical form. Nevertheless, as was stated in the introduction and will be justified in the Methodological Appendix, we do not intend to construct a formal theory whose concepts and relationships are supposedly valid for all societies and cities, and which precludes major adaptations of its general framework as a result of the singularity of each social context. We do intend, however, to provide a general view of the interaction between cities, societies, and historical change, so that a fruitful research perspective can be developed on the basis of the experience of our investigation. Thus we will try to place this research perspective within an analytical framework broad enough to do justice to the richness of the urban experience.

To undertake this task we have tried to support our elaboration with the existing body of theoretical knowledge. But, as usually happens with exploratory research, we found little groundwork directly useful to our theoretical purpose, in spite of some intellectual efforts of exceptional quality from which we derived some basic ideas and from which we learned the necessary caution in approaching our research matter. When we looked for case studies on urban movements or community action we found an enormous number of monographs, many of which have been integrated into the empirical background of this book. But when we tried to explore more systematically the connection between cities and social change in the theoretical literature of the social sciences, we could only rely on a few experiences whose contribution to our own framework we would like to make explicit before presenting our theory, itself the product of the interaction between our research and the exchange of ideas and analyses provided by other authors from different intellectual traditions.

To some extent the scarcity of a theoretical body relevant to our subject is the consequence of our special perspective, involving the asking of research questions that were hardly the concern of the sociological tradition or major themes in the field of urban studies. For instance, we know that classical urban sociology, organized around the tradition of the Chicago School, was (and is) more concerned with the problem of social integration than with the problem of social change, the latter viewed mainly as the source of disruption of the established moral order. This perspective can be understood in the context of the rapid urban growth and economic dislocation experienced by American cities in the first third of this century. In this period the acculturation of a largely immigrant working class was the major social problem posed to the stability of a society trying to discover its own rules of co-existence in a culture marked by merciless capitalist competition.

But the classic integrationist approach of urban sociology, easily prone to considering social conflict as a form of deviance, is no longer tenable in a new situation in which the management of the entire urban system by the state has politicized urban problems, and so translated the mobilization of local communities into a new and significant form of social challenge to established values.[6] Under these conditions, the pluralist theory of political science developed a new approach to the urban problem and started dealing with the question of conflict and protest, even if such processes were considered as steps towards the inexorable bargaining that would re-equilibrate the system at a new level without altering its substance.[7] But, as Gamson says in one of the classic works on American protest movements:

'To operate properly pluralist political institutions require an underlying pluralist social structure and values as well. (p. 6) . . . It is a game that any number can play. The only rule of entry is that the contesting group must agree to behave itself. (p. 9) . . . Pluralist theory is closely connected to the collective behaviour tradition; it is the other side of the coin. Its actors are groups that engage in bargaining to achieve goals. The central process of pluralist politics is exchange . . . Besides this kind of essentially rational, interest-oriented politics there is the other kind – an irrational, extremist politics, operating on a symbolic level with distant and highly abstract objects. The analysis of this kind of politics is left for the social psychologists whose intellectual tools prepare them to understand the irrational.' (p. 133)[8]

We have, ourselves, developed in our earlier work a critique of the metaphysical assumptions of the pluralist paradigm (namely: the rational profit-orientated individual as the basis of the entire social organisation), as well as of the historical fallacy of considering the political process as an open game where the actors can play, and lose or win, without considering (except in a very remote way) the connection of the rules of the game with the structural rules and institutions of society.[9]As David O'Brien (one of the most coherent representatives of pluralist analysis in the field of neighbourhood politics) writes, with some *naïveté*: 'The basic unit of analysis is the rational self-interested person. The central task of the organizer is to find incentives to induce this individual to pay for nondivisible collective goods (that is, public goods).'[10]

At this extreme of the analysis, societies have disappeared and we are left with markets. But because of the changing conditions of the economy and the necessary recognition of the increasing importance of public or collective goals[11] (whose value, and therefore, price is indivisible), instead of changing the philosophical postulates of individual rationality and profit-searching as motives of behaviour, the neoclassical theory prefers to extend its empire by providing an explanatory framework for non-market and collective processes under the same a-historical assumptions of free market competition.

The best expression of this theoretical perspective is the elegant model constructed by Mancur Olson to explain group behaviour in the book that has rightly become a jewel of neo-classical theory in public economics, *The Logic of Collective Action*.[12] Particularly striking in his analysis is what has come to be known as the free-rider dilemma. In his own words:

'A common, collective, or public good is here defined as any good such that . . . those who do not purchase or pay for any of the public or collective good cannot be excluded or kept from sharing in the consumption of the good, as they can when noncollective goods are concerned. Students of public finance have, however, neglected the fact that the *achievement of any common goal or the satisfaction of any common interest means that a public or collective good has been provided for that group* . . . It follows that the provision of public or collective goods is the fundamental function of organizations generally. A state is first of all an organization that provides public goods for its members, the citizens; and other types of organizations similarly provide collective goods for their members . . . The individual member of the typical large organization is in a position analogous to that of the firm in a perfectly competitive market, or the taxpayer in the state: his own efforts will not have a noticeable effect on the situation of his organization, and he can enjoy any *improvements brought about by others* whether or not he has worked in support of his organization.'[13]

In other words, the free-rider is the individual who takes advantage of what groups or organizations do, while minimizing his personal involvement. So the main problem for Olson and for O'Brien is how organizations can induce their members to participate by providing them individually with extra rewards.

Olson's problem is not wrong – it is simply in the theoretical Antipodes as far as the questions we are posing in this research. We are concerned with the understanding of how cities and societies change on the basis of collective projects and societal conflicts generated through history. Olson is concerned with how the rational individual can take advantage of collective mobilization without being too much involved in it. In fact, there are three kinds of actors in history: the dominant elite, the creators of a new social order, and the rentiers of any social organization. Our questions address the issue of how and why the creators challenge the dominants, and we leave the study of the rentiers' behaviour for the neoclassical economists.

Nevertheless, most pluralist theorists do not make this extreme metaphysical assumption of the rationality (defined in economic terms) and individuality of players who intervene in an established game. Furthermore, the most perceptive of them, such as Michael Lipsky[14] or John Mollenkopf,[15] consider a major element in the transformation of the political system to be social protest, precisely the process through which the system is enlarged and somewhat modified. From this point of view, the flexibility and openness of the system is seen as a fundamental feature, necessary to preserve the legitimacy of the institutions and their responsiveness to new challengers, to adopt Gamson's terms.

Yet, this perspective is incapable of explaining social transformation other than through a gradual modification of the established institutions, a hypothesis that is rejected by most historical experience.[16] The problem with this perspective when it treats social movements in general and urban movements in particular is that it considers them in terms of the impact they are able to have on the political system, in which they are considered as some kind of basement in a hierarchical and architectural vision of political institutions. In fact the crucial theoretical element to be emphasized here is the distinction of levels in the social organization between social movements and the political system.[17] The political system is aimed at the state, is dependent upon the state, and is a part of the state.[18] Therefore to some extent it institutionalizes some forms of social domination and accepts the rules of bargaining within such forms.[18bis] At the other end of the scale, social movements exist, develop, and relate to civil society, and are not necessarily limited to, or bound by, the rules of the game and the institutionalization of dominant values and norms. This is why social movements are the sources of social innovation while political parties or coalitions are the instruments of social bargaining. When a social movement is at the same time a party, it forms a revolutionary party. Then, either the revolution happens or the party is only revolutionary in its ideology.[19] There is no hierarchy between the two kinds of actors in social change. Without social movements, no challenge will emerge from civil society able to shake the institutions of the state through which norms are enforced, values preached, and property preserved.[20] Without political parties and without an open political system, the new values, demands, and desires generated by social movements not only fade (which they always do, anyway) but do not light up in the production of social reform and institutional change.[21]

Thus the shortcomings of pluralist theory are two-fold:[22]

1 It tends to ignore the anchoring of political actors into the generally contradictory structure of social interests. The theory is therefore unable to take into consideration the biases of bargaining, the differential powers at stake, and the established relationships between the different actors.
2 Even when the realm of the pluralist analysis is separated from the metaphysical assumption of individual economic rationality, and the boundaries of the political system are extended towards social protest, the point of reference continues to be the state and the possibility of sharing power within a given social structure. In so doing, pluralist theory is unable or uninterested in understanding the transformation of the social structure and its values, and therefore cannot provide us with a theory for the study of social movements.

This need analytically to distinguish social movements from the political system is not only a theoretical argument, but also the result of the research gathered on movements and politics, even in America. As Seymour Martin Lipset says:

'A focus on the role of tactics and movements, as distinct from parties, must produce the conclusion that reliance on methods outside of the normal political game has played a major role in effecting change throughout much of American history. While most of the movements have not engaged in violence as such, some of the major changes in American society have been the product of violent tactics resulting from the willingness of those who felt that they had a morally righteous cause to take the law into their own hands in order to advance their cause. By extreme actions, whether violent or not, the moralistic radical minorities have often secured the support or acquiescence of some of the more moderate elements who came to accept the fact that change was necessary in order to gain a measure of peace and stability. To some extent, also, the extremists on a given side of an issue have lent credence to the arguments presented by the moderates on that issue. Extremists, whether of the right or left, have often helped the moderates to pass through reforms.[23]

While this distinction of levels of analysis is absolutely crucial precisely to study the interaction between social movements and the political systems most pluralist theorists (unlike Lipset who comes from a tradition of class analysis, however ideologically mutated) consider social movements as special forms of resource mobilization for entering into the system. As Gamson puts it, 'In place of the old duality of extremist politics and pluralist politics, there is simply politics.'[24]

Paradoxically enough, when Gamson tries to criticize the pluralist tradition by reducing it to a half-truth[25] he pushes it over a major hurdle, by broadening its scope to all forms of collective, purposive mobilization.

Similarly, the well-known research on social movements in the United States, that of Oberschall[26] and of Roberta Ash[27] for instance, pays attention to a phenomenon largely ignored by classical sociology, namely the social movement, but does so at the expense of denying it as having a reality of its own and immediately incorporating it into the political process aimed fundamentally at the state.

In his introduction to the best cross-cultural collection of essays from all schools of thought on social movements and collective action, Alberto Melucci clearly points out the necessity of maintaining the autonomy between the analysis of the social structure – that of political systems and social movements. And he establishes a major difference between collective action ('. . . the ensemble of conflictual behaviour within a social system . . .') and social movements ('Conflictual behaviour that does not accept the social roles imposed by institutionalized norms, supersedes the rules of the political system and/or attacks the structure of class relationships of a given society.'[28]) Only on the basis of these distinctions can we then study the reciprocal impact of political systems on social revolts, the transition of revolts to social movements, and the reform of the state, as well as the transformation of society under the direct or indirect impact of social movements.[29]

In our field of research, only Frances Piven and Richard Cloward have consistently applied this perspective to the study of the formation of protest movements and their subsequent impact on political institutions and social reform.[30] While their writings are enlightening about social history and the mechanisms of insurgency and co-opting in America, their theory is so oversimplified and their ideological bias so overwhelming that their contribution is limited for any theory-building on the relationship between cities and people. To take, for instance, the theoretical self-portrait at the beginning of their most important book:

'Common sense and historical experience combine to suggest a simple but compelling view of the roots of power in any society. Crudely but clearly stated, those who control the means of physical coercion, and those who control the means of producing wealth, have power over those who do not. This much is true whether the means of coercion consists in the primitive force of a warrior caste or the technological force of a modern army. And it is true whether the control of production consists in control by priests of the mysteries of the calendar on which agriculture depends, or control by financiers on the large scale capital on which industrial means of production depends. Since coercive force can be used to gain control of the means of producing wealth, and since control of wealth can be used to gain coercive force, these two sources of power tend over time to be drawn together within one ruling class. Common sense and historical experience also combine to suggest that these sources of power are protected and enlarged by the use of that power, not only to control the actions of men and women but also control their beliefs. What some call superstructure, and what others call culture, includes an elaborate system of belief and ritual behaviors which define for people what is right and what is wrong and why; what is possible and what is impossible; and the behavioral imperatives that follow from these beliefs.[31]

This trans-historical concept of an entirely coherent, closed system of multi-dimensional oppression by a unified elite effectively distinguishes people's movements from the inside processes of the state apparatus. But this distinction becomes a wall of China that can only be penetrated by the unorganized, disruptive popular outbursts, and yet only for as long as they remain unorganized and their tactics continue to be disruptive. Even under these conditions, the fate of the movements is predetermined by the stages of social evolution and the overall political framework: Piven and Cloward say that (their italics), '*Protesters win, if they win at all, what historical circumstances have already made ready to be conceded.*'[32]

In this perspective, therefore, humankind is not the subject of its own history, but the actor of a play whose script has been written in advance (by whom?) and whose performance will invariably end up in bloodshed and co-opting. This is neither our perspective and experience, nor is it what we have observed in ten years of research in the cities of a variety of societies.

The question remains how can we use our observation and elaboration to fill the theoretical vacuum that is evident when we look for cumulative investigation and the communication of knowledge?

Our intellectual matrix, the Marxist tradition, was of little help from the moment we entered the uncertain ground of urban social movements. In terms of classical Marxism, the major effort by Henri Lefebvre[33] to reconstruct the main contributions of the founding fathers into an analysis of the city shows that such contributions are limited to the study of the relationship between city and countryside, as characteristics of different modes of production, based on some passages of the *German Ideology*[34] and of the *Grundrisse*.[35] They also include the pamphlet by Engels attacking the housing reforms of bourgeois social paternalism[36] and his impressive research monograph on the living conditions of the English working class, with a very detailed study of the industrial city of Manchester in 1845[37]. But, as Lefebvre says, there will at a later stage be some sort of reduction of Marxist thought, even for Marx and Engels, because, pressured by the urgent task of providing theoretical tools for the labour movement and popular insurrections, they were compelled to place the accumulation of capital and domination by the state at the forefront of their work as revolutionary intellectuals. As Lefebvre writes, 'Revolutionary thought will become cautious, carefully tactician. It will lose in the process. Its focus will move away to be located on the places of work and production. Yet, such was not the perspective, nor the prediction in 1845. Could it not be the result of an ex-post *reduction* of the Marxist revolutionary thought accomplished in the twentieth century?'[38]

In any case, such a reduction had its lasting effects on any effort to renew Marxist thought on urban problems. When, in the late 1960s, both Lefebvre[39] and ourselves[40] called attention, on different and even opposite lines, to the need to introduce a class conflict analysis into the new realm of problems identified as urban, so developing the heritage of Marxist theory, we were delighted to observe the expansion, first in France, later in other countries, of a major research effort in that direction. This did not happen necessarily because our call was so powerful or influential, but rather because the time was right. The growing urban contradictions and conflicts in advanced capitalist societies required a refurbishing of the prevailing currents of urban theory.[41]

Yet, with some fortunate exceptions, Marxism as a whole has been unable to stand up fully to the challenge, as has been intelligently shown by Peter Saunders.[42] To the physical determinism of human ecologists, or to the cultural idealism of the Wirthian tradition, Marxists tended to respond by reducing the city and the space to the logic of capital.[43] The reintroduction of economic factors under the conditions of capitalism into the analysis of urbanization has been a useful reminder of a too often neglected aspect of the analysis of space.[44] Yet many works have been overwhelmed by dogmatism and flawed by an insufficient attention to the most elementary methodological rules of empirical research. In some more subtle analyses, the state was identified as the major actor in urbanization, a fact that, particularly in France, could hardly be neglected. Yet, as in the work of the most representative author of the orthodox Marxist school, Jean Lojkine, the state was simply an apparatus fulfilling the single-purpose interests of the dominant class: profit maximizing for monopoly capital.[45] Thus, in line with the pseudo-theory invented by the French Communist Party to justify its political isolation (the theory of monopoly state capitalism),[46] the city was simply the result of the continuous efforts by the state to foster the interests of financial capital, whether in Paris,[47] Lyon,[48] or in the capitalist system in general. As a matter of fact, since it was difficult to ignore the efforts towards social reform in non-communist municipalities, a new research effort was directed to show the other face of capitalist domination in those cities governed by the Socialist Party: *Classe Ouvrière et Social-Democratie: Lille et Marseille*.[49] Unfortunately for their authors, this book was published in 1981, only weeks before the Socialists won control of the government of France and allowed the Communists, despite their poor performance, symbolic representation in it. Since transport was one of the ministries obtained by the PCF, a safe prediction can be made about the launching of a research project to test the hypothesis of a new and successful transport policy under the guidance of the working class, or in other words, of the Communist Party, so continuing a shameful pattern of constructing theories according to the party line.

These remarks are not a political detour,[50] but are at the very core of what we are trying to contribute to: a theory of urban social change. On the one hand, they illustrate the importance of rejecting the intellectually inadmissible practice of adjusting theoretical approaches to the variations of any party's line. On the other, and more importantly, they demonstrate the difficulty in using Marxist theory as codified by the Third International or the French Communist Party (which is the same) to understand the city or urban social movements, or even more simply, to propose the concept of social movements. During the last ten years we have obviously been aware of the production of urban forms and issues as a result of conflictual processes between social actors that we named social classes, following the Marxist tradition. But we were also aware of the necessity to relate the forms of conflict to the social and economic structure, or, in other words, to connect class structure and class struggle. In fact, we kept the tension between the two poles without ever being able to fully integrate both processes. We wrote *Luttes Urbaines* (1973)[51] to call attention to the new forms of social struggles emerging from the city without much reference to their determination by the overall social structure. And we wrote *Monopolville* (1974) with Francis Godard[52] to show how the intertwining logic of capital and the state were at the roots of the production of the urban system. To demonstrate this hypothesis empirically (and we think we succeeded) the only city in France (Dunkirk) was selected where the state and the big corporations (particularly steel and oil) had decided to launch a major joint venture that would double the urban area and triple its productive capacity in a few years. Yet, when we tried, with a courageous and intelligent team of researchers, to bring together all the aspects, namely, the logic of capital, the action of the state, and the formation of urban social movements, in a highly formalized and systematic empirical way, we produced what we consider the only major fiasco we have had in empirical research: *Crise du Logement et Mouvements Sociaux Urbains: Enquête sur la Région Parisienne* (written in 1974, published in 1978).[53] The reasons for this failure, in spite of the exceptional quality of the information we obtained and of the intelligence of the researchers with whom we collaborated, lie deep in the core of the Marxist theory of social change. To be sure, a highly formalistic file for coding social movements made things worse, inherited as it was from the abnormal cross-fertilization between our early Althusserian paradigm and the standard procedures of empirical sociology. But we would have been able to correct the instruments, and even to completely change our method, if we had been able to grasp the crucial theoretical problem. In fact, we could not succeed because we were attempting what the Marxist theory had never been able to accomplish, except through a particular solution, which was precisely the one that we rejected at that stage of our research. Let us explain. Marxism has been, at the same time, the theory of capital and the development of history through the development of productive forces, while also being the theory of class struggle between social actors fighting for the appropriation of the product and deciding the organization of society, since '. . . history summarizes the production of human beings by themselves.'[54] Leninism (including Trotsky, Mao and Stalin) added some elements to a theory of the state, but this theory was a by-product of two basic elements: either the state was an instrument of class domination or else it was the result of a new stage of capitalism (or of a new mode of production).

Marxism was never a unified theory, neither explicitly nor in the practice of political struggles. It was enriched and developed by this practice, but was also deformed and used as an instrument of manipulation, and, later on, as the object of ideological propaganda and state religion. But, as a theoretical body, its intellectual tradition and its political heritage was always dominated by these two emphases that are equally Marxist, and may even be found in the same author. And it is not a matter of opposing the young Marx (pro-class struggle) versus the mature Marx (focusing on capital). Rosa Luxembourg wrote both *The Accumulation of Capital*[55] and *Strikes, Party and Unions.*[56] Only perhaps Lukacs, Gramsci and the Italian historicist school clearly leaned towards the class struggle tradition.[57] To be sure, we know that the accumulation of capital includes exploitation, and therefore some form of class struggle. But in the Leninist tradition, when reduced to fundamentals, capital accumulation and the development of productive forces operate at the level of the infrastructure (the basis of society). At a different level, classes, defined by their place in the production process, struggle politically, culturally, and militarily to win control of society and to reorganize it according to their interests.

But how is the connection established between the structure and the practices, between the mode of production and the historical process of class struggle? According to Marx, through class formation and class consciousness: a class in itself becomes a class for itself. But how does this occur? Marx has no answer. Lenin and the Third International provided the answer: through the revolutionary party. Why is the party revolutionary though?[58] Because it represents the historical interests of the working class. And how do we know that? Because it makes the revolution, seizes power, and establishes the power of the proletariat. How do we know that the proletariat is in power? At first, for a brief period, because councils, the vanguard of the working class, seize power. Later, because new state institutions appear to foster these interests and will, in the long term, dissolve themselves. But in all cases the guarantee of the proletarian character of the soviets in the socialist state, and of the entire practice of the working class, is their way of following the correct party line, defined by the party itself. Thus the working class is revolutionary when it follows the party line, and the party's victories are the verification of this line and its revolutionary character, precisely because its triumph substantiates that it is the conscious agent of an historically predetermined development.[59] Leninism became an integral part of Marxism, not only because of the triumph of the Soviet Revolution, but because only the theory of the party can establish a bridge between structures and practices in the Marxist construction. The development of productive forces and the class struggle come together into the action of an exploited class transformed into a party that speaks both for the workers and for the unlimited development of the productive forces.

Therefore, by definition, the concept of social movement as an agent of social transformation is strictly unthinkable in the Marxist theory. There are social struggles and mass organizations that revolt in defense of their interests, but there cannot be conscious collective actors able to liberate themselves. The motto of the First International, proposed by Marx ('The emancipation of workers will be accomplished by the workers themselves') is not only contradictory with the historical practice of communism, but also with the essentials of the Marxist-Leninist theory. It actually reflects the sensibility of Marx and Engels who were revolutionary intellectuals, capable of seeing around them the burgeoning of consciously orientated workers' struggles that represented the origins of the labour movement. But to sustain this position, they had to abandon their social Darwinism and their confidence in the natural movement of history towards progress guided by the rails of the development of productive forces, aboard a train accelerated by capital whose engine was about to be driven by the proletariat. They never imagined that the proletariat might prefer bicycles to trains and therefore never accepted that the working class could decide its own destiny in terms different from those earmarked by the historical development of productive forces.

Thus classical Marxism was ambiguous about the existing social movements: they were the living proof of class struggle and resistance to capitalist exploitation. And yet the movements had to accept – so the argument went – that they could not produce history on their own but, rather, were instrumental in the implementation of the next stage of a programmed historical development. The ambiguity of Marxism was superseded by Leninism. On the one hand, a new theory of uneven development was added as a postscript to justify the possibility of socialism breaking out in the most backward capitalist country, instead of in the most advanced ones. On the other hand, the emancipation of workers would be the role of the party, and social movements were degraded as spontaneous trade unionism (Britain) or denounced as the work of provocateurs (Kronstadt, Makhno). As for the working class, as long as it had political freedom to express itself, it struggled for social reform and the preservation of its liberties while observing its unions and parties become integrated into the political systems (at least this was the case in most of the dominant capitalist countries). In sociological terms, the working class movement was (sometimes reluctantly) institutionalized.

So why still worry about social movements? And why urban? First of all, because of experience, both contemporary and historical: May 1968 in France; the Autunno Caldo in the Italian factories in 1969; the 1960s in America; the worldwide mobilization against the Vietnam War; the Spanish Resistance against Franquism; the German Student Movement; the national liberation movements in the Third World; the Unidad Popular in Chile. the uprising of the feminist movement; all over the world conscious people have continued to mobilize collectively to change their lives and propose new ones against those who want to preserve the old order. People mobilized, in a variety of historical contexts and social structures, without parties, beyond parties, with parties, against parties, and for parties. The parties' role has not been a discriminatory variable; the crucial phenomena have been self-conscious, self-organized social movements. So although Marxist theory might not have room for social movements other than the historically predicted class struggle, social movements persist. So experience was right and Marxist theory was wrong on this point, and the intellectual tradition in the study of social change should be recast.

Second, why should the issue be urban social movements? In addition to the arguments presented in the introduction to this book, we will simply recall that the increasing contradictions in the process of urbanization, the growing number of social conflicts aimed at urban policies, and the embryos of some powerful urban protests in the early 1970s led us to believe that a new form of social struggle was arising, a conviction that grew because we would not consider separately the development of the urban contradictions and the emergence of new social actors.[60] Furthermore, since our intellectual interest has been to understand the city as a social process and since our perspective connects the organization of society to the characteristics of the underlying social change, we tried to discover the mechanisms involved in the formation of social movements aimed at the city in order to contribute to the general knowledge about the new material forms of our social life.

We could count on an enormous amount of experience and information to undertake this task (some of which has become empirical research as presented in the preceding chapters) but could only rely on a limited amount of intellectual support. The work by Lefebvre on the urban revolution[61] was very stimulating without providing instruments of research, given the speculative character of his philosophical perspective. Richard Sennett's[62] perceptive analysis on the connection between cultural contexts and urban forms was certainly decisive in the development of our hypotheses between the public domain and the private sphere, encapsulating one of the main historical debates involving urban social movements. Jean Remy and Liliane Voye's last book, *Ville, Ordre et Violence*,[62bis] was a source of inspiration on the role of territoriality in social organization. Neil Smelser's classic work, *Theory of Collective Behavior*,[63] helped our understanding of social movements as agents of social transformation, especially his chapter on what he calls 'the value-oriented movement'[63bis], while discouraging us from looking to functionalism for a fresh intellectual outlook that we felt to be lacking in the Althusserian circle. Charles Tilly's American-based, European-orientated, major empirical work helped considerably in our typology of urban movements and convinced us of the need to emphasize the comparative character of the analysis throughout history.[64] The sharp criticism of our theory by Ira Katznelson in his last book[65] provided the groundwork for the attempt to integrate the general characteristics of urban social change and the historical context in which movements develop. Norman and Susan Fainstein's work on *Urban Political Movements*[66] called attention to the importance of community control, and enabled us to see its connection to the more general theme of self-management, one of the crucial goals posed by the new social movements. John Rex and Robert Moore, with their pathbreaking book, *Race, Community and Conflict*,[67] laid the ground for our understanding of the relationships between ethnicity, class, and community, something that we could hardly have developed from our experience in France. The continuous remarks by Chris Pickvance on the inconsistencies of our formal models for the study of urban movements helped us to break the final links of our obsession with formalism.[68] Jordi Borja's insistence on treating urban movements and urban structure in compatible theoretical terms pointed out the crucial theoretical and methodological question that had to be solved.[69] Our careful study of Kevin Lynch's *magnum opus* provided an intellectual basis for establishing the connection between the study of historical change and the meaning of urban forms, a basis that the reader may recognize throughout this part[70]. The research seminar we gave with Claude Fischer at Berkeley in Spring 1981 provided a dialogue with a different tradition of urban sociology, leading to the final formulation of our concepts[70bis].

However, the theoritical framework we have tried to construct is mainly indebted to the most systematic and thorough work ever undertaken on social movements in the entire history of sociology, that of Alain Touraine.[71] We rely on him, for example, for the definition of a social movement as '. . .the organized collective action by which a class-actor struggles for the social definition of historicity in a given historical ensemble.'[72] But we do not see any reason (except in Touraine's internal coherence) for a social movement to be based on a class relationship: either we extend excessively the concept of class or we must reject collective action as social movements, for there are many such actions – the feminist movement for instance – that without being based on a class have made major contributions to the redefinition of the goals and values of a society. Yet the reader should be aware that our convergence on Touraine's perspective comes more from years of intellectual interaction and debate over his work than from a reliance on his highly formalized and precisely defined theory. We should say, in fact, that we start with similar questions about society and social movements, and take advantage of his experience in the development of new concepts and methods to approach a problem, without actually using his theory. The main reason for this cautious attitude is that we think Touraine's theory is still at an experimental stage, and that he is the only one really able, at this point, to carry out the experiments to test it, since what he learns about the theory continuously reorganizes the conceptual framework being tested. Therefore, while strongly influenced by the approach to social movements proposed by Touraine, and, more generally, to social change, the theory that we will elaborate in this part, synthesizing the theoretical hints obtained throughout our empirical studies, is not an application of Touraine's theory of social movements and should not be considered as such. This does not mean that we reject the Touraine's invaluable teaching, but simply refuse to let him be responsible for our own complicated reading of history, cities, and society, arrived at through the glorious ruins of the Marxist tradition, the methods of American sociology, and a continuous dialogue with urbanists and planners, as well as with the desire for history that Touraine has permanently imprinted on our soul.[73]

It is apparent that there was more intellectual support than at first appeared for our work on urban social movements. We should therefore proceed further with the exploration of the relationship between cities, societies, and historical change, bearing in mind the support on which we have relied while, of course, accepting full responsibility for the results.

29

The Process of Urban Social Change

Societies only exist in time and space. The spatial form of a society is, therefore, closely linked to its structure and urban change is interwined with historical evolution. This formula, however, is too general. To understand cities, to unveil their connection to social change, we must determine the mechanisms through which spatial structures are transformed and urban meaning is redefined. To investigate this question based on the observations and analyses presented in this book, we need to introduce some fundamental elements of a general theory of society that underlie our analyses. But for these elements to be considered as the effective tools used in our research, we must first be more precise about our research questions.

Our goal is to explain how and why cities change. But what are cities? Can we be satisfied with a definition like, spatial forms of human society? What kind of spatial forms? And when do we know that they are cities? At which statistical threshold of density or population concentration does a city become a city? And how are we sure that, in different cultures and in diverse historical times, we are referring to the same social reality on the basis of a similarly concentrated, densely settled and socially heterogeneous population? Urban sociologists of course, have repeatedly asked the same questions without ever producing a fully satisfactory answer.[74] After all, it seems a rather academic debate, too far removed from the dramatic issues currently arising from the worldwide reality of urban crisis. And yet it seems intellectually dubious to undertake the explanation of change in a social form whose content we ignore or whose profile could be left to a category that is ill-defined by the Census Bureau. In fact, our basic theoretical perspective supersedes the question by studying the city from the viewpoint of historical change.

Let us begin, at the risk of appearing schematic, with the clearest possible statement. Cities, like all social reality, are historical products, not only in their physical materiality but in their cultural meaning, in the role they play in the social organization, and in peoples' lives. The basic dimension in urban change is the conflictive debate between social classes and historical actors over the meaning of urban, the significance of spatial forms in the social structure, and the content, hierarchy, and destiny of cities in relationship to the entire social structure. A city (and each type of city) is what a historical society decides the city (and each city) will be. Urban is the social meaning assigned to a particular spatial form by a historically defined society. Two remarks must immediately qualify this formulation:

1 Society, as we will discuss a few pages below, is a structured, conflictive reality in which social classes oppose each other over the basic rules of social organization according to their own social interests. Therefore the definition of urban meaning will be a process of conflict, domination, and resistance to domination, directly linked to the dynamics of social struggle and not to the reproductive spatial expression of a unified culture. Futhermore, cities and space being fundamental to the organization of social life, the conflict over the assignment of certain goals to certain spatial forms will be one of the fundamental mechanisms of domination and counter-domination in the social structure.[75] For instance, to achieve the establishment of the city as a religious centre dominating the countryside is to obtain the material support for the exploitation of agricultural surplus by exchanging symbolic legitimacy and psychological security for peasant labour. Or, in another instance, declaring the city a free space for common trade and political self-determination is a major victory against feudal order. Thus, the definition of the meaning of 'urban' is not the spatialized xerox copy of a culture, nor the consequence of a social battle fought between undetermined historical actors in some intergallactic vacuum. It is one of the fundamental processes through which historical actors (social classes, for instance) have structured society according to their interests and values.

2 The definition of urban meaning is a social process, in its material sense. It is not a simple cultural category in the vulgar sense of culture as a set of ideas. It is cultural in the anthropological sense, that is, as the expression of a social structure, including economic, religious, political, and technological operations.[76] If the city is defined by the merchants as a market it will mean street fairs and intense socializing, but it will also mean the commodification of economic activity, monetarization of the work process, and the establishment of a transport network to all potential sources of goods and to all markets that maybe expanded. In sum, the historical definition of urban is not a mental representation of a spatial form, but the assignment of a structural task to this form in accordance with the conflictive social dynamics of history.

We define *urban meaning as the structural performance assigned as a goal to cities in general (and to a particular city in the inter-urban division of labour) by the conflictive process between historical actors in a given society.* We will examine below how societies are themselves structured around modes of production. Thus, the definition of urban meaning might vary both with different modes of production and with different outcomes of history within the same mode of production.

The historical process of defining urban meaning determines the characteristics of urban functions. For instance, if cities are defined as colonial centres, the use of military force and territorial control will be their basic function. If they are defined as capitalist machines, they will subdivide their functions (and sometimes specialize them in different cities) between the extraction of surplus value in the factory, the reproduction of labour power, the extraction of profit in urbanization (through real estate), the organization of circulation of capital in the financial institutions, the exchange of commodities in the commercial system, and the management of all other operations in the directional centres of capitalist business. So we define *urban functions as the articulated system of organizational means aimed at performing the goals assigned to each city by its historically defined urban meaning.*

Urban meaning and urban functions jointly determine urban form, that is, the symbolic spatial expression of the processes that materialize as a result of them. For instance, if the city is defined as a religious centre, and if the ideological control by the priests over the peasant population is the function to be accomplished, permanence and stature, mystery, distance, and yet protection and a hint of accessibility will be crucial elements in the buildings and in their spatial patterning in the urban landscape. Few architects believe that the skyscrapers in downtown America only concentrate the paperwork of giant corporations: they symbolize the power of money over the city through technology and self-confidence and are the cathedrals of the period of rising corporate capitalism.[77] Yet they also perform a number of crucial managerial functions, and are still major real estate investments in a space that has become a commodity in itself. There is naturally, no direct reflection of the urban meaning and function on the symbolic forms, since semiological research has established the complex derivations of the language of formal representation and its relative autonomy in relationship to their functional content.[78] In any event, we are not arguing that the economy determines urban forms but, rather, we are establishing a relationship and hierarchy between historical meaning, urban functions, and spatial forms. This is entirely different as a theoretical perspective. In certain urban forms, such as the early medieval cities for instance, the symbolic element of the cathedral was the major factor structuring urban form and meaning. But this was because the urban meaning was based upon the religious relationship between peasants, lords and God, with the Church as intermediary.[79]

Furthermore, urban forms are not only combinations of materials, volumes, colours, and heights; they are, as Kevin Lynch has taught us, uses, flows, perceptions, mental associations, systems of representations whose significance changes with time, cultures, and social groups.[80] For our purpose, the only important question is to emphasize both the distinctiveness of the dimension of urban forms and its relationship to urban meaning and urban functions.

We therefore define as *urban form the symbolic expression of urban meaning and of the historical superimposition of urban meanings (and their forms) always determined by a conflictive process between historical actors.*

In any particular situation, cities are shaped by three different, though inter-related, processes:

1 Conflicts over the definition of urban meaning.

2 Conflicts over the adequate performance of urban functions. These conflicts can arise both from different interests and values, within the same accepted framework, or from different approaches about how to perform a shared goal of urban function.

3, Conflicts over the adequate symbolic expression of urban meaning and (or) functions.

We call urban social change the redefinition of urban meaning. We call urban planning the negotiated adaptation of urban functions to a shared urban meaning. We call urban design the symbolic attempt to express an accepted urban meaning in certain urban forms.

Needless to say, since defining urban meaning is a conflictive process so is urban planning and urban design. But the structural role assigned to a city by and through the social conflict over its meaning, conditions the functions and symbolism through which this role will be performed and expressed.

Urban social change conditions all aspects of the urban praxis. The theory of urban social change therefore lays the ground for any other theories of the city.

Where does such a change come from? And how do we know that there is a change?

The crucial question here is to reject any suggestion that there is a predetermined direction of urban change. History has no direction, it only has life and death. It is a composite of drama, victories, defeats, love and sorrow, joy and pain, creation and destruction. We now have the possibility of enjoying the most profound human experiences as well as the chance to blow ourselves up in a nuclear holocaust. We can make the revolution with the people or trigger the forces of revolutionary terror against the same people. If we therefore agree that the outmoded ideology of natural human progress must be abandoned, we must also proceed similarly with urban social change. Thus by change we refer simply to the assignment of a new meaning to the urban realm or to a particular city. What does new mean? On the one hand, the answer is specific to each historical context and to each city we have observed, but on the other, the answer is related to a more general and theoretical assessment of social transformation. So we must wait a few pages before settling this key question.

A major conclusion can, however, far be drawn from our definition of urban social change: its assessment is value free. We do not imply that change is improvement, and therefore we do not need to define what improvement is. As we have said before, our theory is not normative, but historical. We want to understand how processes happen that the most humanistic urban designers, such as Allan Jacobson and Kevin Lynch, would find positive for the well-being of our own environment. Although we generally agree with their criteria, our purpose is not to define the good city. It is rather to understand how good and evil, heaven and hell are produced by the angels and devils of our historical experience (our own feeling being that the devils are likely to be more creative than the angels).

Urban social change happens when a new urban meaning is produced by one of the four following processes (all of them conflictive and in opposition to one or more historical actors):

1 The dominant class in a given society, having the institutional power to restructure social forms (and thus cities) according to its interests and values, changes the existing meaning. We call this urban renewal (for cities) and regional restructuring (for the territory as a whole). For instance, if the South Bronx is deliberately abandoned, or if the Italian neighbourhoods of Boston are transformed into a headquarters city, or if some industrial cities (like Buffalo, New York) become warehouses for unemployed minorities, then we have instances of urban renewal and regional restructuring.

2 A dominated class accomplishes a partial or total revolution and changes the meaning of the city. For instance, the Cuban revolution deurbanizes La Habana,[81] or the workers of Glasgow in 1915 impose housing as a social service, not as a commodity.[82]

3 A social movement develops its own meaning over a given space in contradiction to the structurally dominant meaning, as in the feminist schemes described by Dolores Hayden.[83]

4 A social mobilization (not necessarily based on a particular social class) imposes a new urban meaning in contradiction to the institutionalized urban meaning and against the interests of the dominant class. It is in this case that we use the concept of urban social movement: a collective conscious action aimed at the transformation of the institutionalized urban meaning against the logic, interest, and values of the dominant class. It is our hypothesis that only urban social movements are urban-orientated mobilizations that influence structural social change and transform the urban meanings. The symmetrical opposite to this hypothesis is not necessarily true. A social change (for instance the domination of a new class) might or might not change the urban meaning; for example, a working class revolution that keeps the role of a city as the site for a centralized non-democratic state apparatus.

At this point of our analysis, it becomes necessary to make explicit some of our assumptions on social change to be able to establish more specific links between the change of cities and the change of societies. This task requires a brief and schematic detour into the hazardous land of the general theory of social change.

30

The Process of Historical Change

The meaning of the city is not produced arbitrarily by a particular social actor or by an undetermined conflict between many actors. The very process of social definition and the outcome of such a process relies upon the structure of society and upon that structure's particular mode of historical development. Therefore we must introduce some elementary concepts enabling us to locate our analysis of urban change in the broader context of a theory of social change. It must be noted, nevertheless, that this theoretical construction cannot be verified here and its usefulness exclusively relates to the fact that social themes and projects observed in the urban change we have studied explicitly refer to the values, interests, and conflictive projects providing the basic framework of our analytical scheme. Thus by presenting this scheme in a systematic form, we are trying to clarify further the explanation, without yielding to the already rejected temptation of presenting a comprehensive social theory, the foundation of which cannot be sufficiently sustained by our current knowledge of social structures and historical processes.

Yet, we know enough to be able to say that all human processes seem to be determined by relationships of production, experience, and power. Production is the action of humankind on nature (that is, on matter and energy) to transform it for human benefit by obtaining a product, consuming part of it (in an unequally distributed manner), and accumulating the surplus for future investment, according to socially determined goals. Experience is the action of human subjects on themselves within the multidimensionality of their biological and cultural entity. Power is the result of relationships between human subjects on the basis of both production and experience. On this basis, human subjects establish relationships of power between them that create and organize societies.

Therefore, history and society (actually arrived at through the same process) are formed by an articulation of experience, production, and power. In known societies, experience is basically structured around sexual gender relationships[84] (males dominating females); production is organized in class relationships (non-producers appropriating the surplus from the producers);[85] and power is founded upon the state (the institutionalized monopoly of violence ensures the domination of the power holders over their subjects).[86] The particular form through which non-producers appropriate the surplus, that is, the class relationships, defines a mode of production. For instance, capitalism is defined by the separation between the producers of the means of production, and by the appropriation by capital of both the means of production and of the labour power of the producers, forcing them to provide the owners of the means of production with their labour power in exchange for a share of their own production. It is on this basis that capital can organize production and structure society to reproduce social conditions that favour its interests and enhance its values. The formation of capital and labour, and therefore of capitalist social relationships, was not the result of technology or of some economic necessity. It was the historical outcome of the capacity of the bourgeoisie to construct social hegemony, to defeat and assimilate the feudal lords, to revolutionize the absolutist state, to subordinate the peasantry, and to expand its colonial domination over the world. Each new mode of production is the result of the victorious effort of a new class to reorganize society around the structural reproduction of its own interests and values. Consequently, each new mode of production establishes new forms of exploitation and domination that trigger new forms of class struggle.

We cannot undertake here the analysis of the sequence of modes of production in concert with the modes of gender relationships, particularly as the historical research we have on some areas of the world is so tenuous. We will only refer in our analysis to the two modes of production existing in the period of our observation, and we will in fact only enter into the dynamics of the capitalist mode of production since it is the only one that appears dominant in our research. But because of the worldwide relationships established in our contemporary scene, we must refer to the alternative and co-existing statist mode of production that is dominant in the so-called socialist countries.[87] By statist mode of production we mean a system where the appropriation of surplus from the producers is based upon the political domination of a state apparatus, itself controlled by a self-reproducing elite relying on the monopoly of violence and means of information. To be sure, the state is present in the capitalist mode of production, having a major repressive function and tending to represent the interests of the capitalist class.[88] Yet, under capitalism the state expresses class domination but under socialism is the basis for the new class domination.[89] As has been the case for all transitions, the statist mode of production[90] has resulted from the class struggle between exploiters and exploited, between capital and labour. In the struggle between capital and labour, the proletariat did not emerge as the new dominant class. This accords with a general historical trend: for instance, the peasants of the feudal order did not become the new masters after their struggle against the lords because the absolutist state mediated the transition and opened the way for the bourgeoisie to impose a new mode of production.[91] In the same way, parties and armies (that is, counter states ready to become states) of proletarian and peasant origin took to the forefront of the new historical epochs in exchange for economic development and social redistribution, and at the price of systemic political repression and ideological persuasion.

Another concept is crucial for the understanding of an analytical framework: mode of development.[92] It is often confused with mode of production, but must be carefully distinguished because it appears to be at another level of social relationships. It refers to the particular form in which labour, matter, and energy are combined in work to obtain the product.[93] Work is certainly related to social (class) relationships, but, in addition to the way through which the surplus is appropriated, it is also important to understand how the surplus is increased. Here again, we refuse to rewrite the entire history of humanity without a sufficient empirical basis. We need to introduce, however, the difference between the two modes of development which have become apparent in our field of observation and for the existence of which we already have adequate evidence.

There are two types of mode of development: the industrial and informational. In the case of the industrial mode of development, productivity (that is, the additional unit of output per unit of input arising from investment) results from an increase in the quantity of labour, matter, or energy, or else from an increase of all three elements. For the informational mode of production, productivity is based on knowledge and results from the organizational methods of combining the three elements of production. In other words productivity depends on the capacity to predict relationships between the characteristics of the elements and their recombination in the production process.[94] Each mode of development defines a new dominant social category (allied with and dependent on the dominant class, but having formidable bargaining power because of their particular expertise). Industry generates managers, that is, controllers of organizations. Information generates technocrats, that is, controllers of knowledge.[95] Modes of production and modes of development have principles of performance that are imposed as structural social goals that become their *raison d'être*. Thus capitalism is orientated towards profit maximizing, that is, increasing the amount and proportion of product appropriated from surplus value on the basis of the ownership of the means of production. Statism is orientated towards power maximizing, namely towards the increasing of the military capacity of political apparatus to impose the goals it assigns to itself on an increasing number of subjects and to deeper levels of their consciousness. Industrialism is orientated towards economic growth, that is, towards the increasing of output. Informationalism is orientated towards technological development, that is, towards the accumulation of knowledge.

All these goals defining organizations, societies, empires, and means of production and reproduction are neither accidentally generated by some event nor inexorably imposed by some iron law of technological evolution. They are material products from the human species, a form of matter that happens to be distinctive because of the endless development of the symbolic, communicative, and informational functions of the human brain. As a result of this mental capacity, our species continually redefines the social forms of its life and the relationship it establishes with the complex of matter and energy. Therefore the goals defining modes of production and modes of development are the result of the conscious action of historical actors establishing relationships of production (*vis-à-vis* other actors) and technologies of production (*vis-à-vis* matter and energy) that serve their interests and values. How a particular historical actor appears, and how a mode of production emerges, is a historical question that has to be answered by research, and not by reference to some general law of combination between a finite collection of structural elements. What we know is that this historical change is conflictive and takes place within the framework of the struggles and crises stemming from an existing mode of production. Yet the new mode of production will not be the symmetrically inverse image of the old one, but the historical product of classes and social actors fighting each other on the basis of the structural relationships that have antagonized them, and guided by the values and projects generated within each actor by their conditions of experience, production, and power. And the dominated classes? They live, resist, revolt, and attempt revolutions. Where successful, they disappear as a class to generate either a new form of social relationship or a new class domination generally imposed by a segment of the old, dominated class or by an instrument of the revolutionary process. Historically we do not know of any revolution where the dominated classes have succeeded in dissolving the existence of class domination or have even succeeded in gaining the new dominant position for themselves.

Yet we cannot rule out the possibility of such an occurrence. If we did, it would lead us to the metaphysics of a general law of human development that is incompatible with scientific research. Classless societies might someday exist, but they would result in the end of history, although not, however, in the end of humankind – quite the contrary. In fact, if we can speak of prehistoric societies, of societies whose main collective task was to survive against nature, we might also speak of posthistoric societies, whose collective task, within a communal relationship, will be to appropriate and explore nature, both towards the outside (matter) and towards the inside (our own inner experience).

This perspective has too often been dismissed as Utopian. But if we accept the premise that societies are produced by the combination of cultural goals by historical actors with the technological tools obtained by each mode of development, we must accept the possibility of such a posthistoric society as a projected outcome of the new struggles. If we observe the emergence of historical actors (not necessarily or uniquely from the dominated classes) calling for the dominance of use value against exchange value, we recognize that capitalism is challenged, as would be any other system orientated towards investment and the generation of surplus. If historical actors call for autonomy and self-management as a principle of collective decision, the statist mode of production is undermined, but so is any form of state. If the informational mode of development allows for the automation of most of production, including agriculture, and relies on both the intimate relationship between the producer-scientist and the process of work, and the communication and co-operation between producers, plus the close interdependency between production and consumption, then the technological basis exists for the fulfillment of the cultural goals of the new historical actors who are use value orientated and self-management prone. This fulfillment is therefore not Utopian, but a historical struggle, a possible (although unlikely) outcome of a terrible battle in which the multinational corporations and the empire-states will be ready to do anything to stop the process, including warring with each other or even blowing up the planet, not so much as a means to an impossible victory than as a way to keep their subjects occupied with the duty of killing or being killed.

These are the traces we want to find in our observation of the redefinition of urban meaning. This is not to say that they happen particularly in cities or in the debate over cities – they happen everywhere. The current historical change is multidimensional, and so are the forces reproducing and conserving the system. If this is true, if a new historical struggle to change the goals of society, and therefore cities, is already engaged, we should be able to find the signs of this fundamental transformation in the reshaping of spatial forms. As the reader knows by now, we have found scattered symptoms of the process, here and there, in different forms and with different fortunes. We are now in the process of bringing together all these broken fragments from the mirror of a new world in which people with enough hope and strength would like to see their children's faces. But before we start to reassemble the puzzle we need to add some new fundamental elements without which the mirror will give a distorted image or, more likely, will never shine in the light of history.

How does the dimension of experience and its basic dynamics, that is the sexual-gender relationships, relate to historical change as described? In fact what characterizes human history is that, in addition to the domination by men over women, the relationship of gender itself was determined, in its content and evolution, by production relationships (class position of males) and by power relationships (state enforced family relationships). Thus women's rebellions, as observed in our historical accounts of urban struggles in Part 1, dealt with the level on which their active participation affected class and power struggles – they mobilized on behalf of their families' needs. On the contrary, in our contemporary field of observation, one of the major socio-cultural changes is the growing connection between women's struggles and a feminist consciousness – that is, with the movement aimed at overcoming the structural domination of one gender by the other. It is our hypothesis that this fundamental phenomenon is part of a broader historical tendency: the calling into question of the hierarchy over the relationships of production, power, and experience. To be more precise, new social movements arise that try to establish the command of experience over production and power, instead of adapting experience in the best possible conditions to the structural framework created by production and enforced by power. In this particular sense, the redefinition of urban meaning to emphasize use value and the quality of experience over exchange value and centralization of management is historically connected to the feminist theme of identity and communication, in spite of ideological divisions and organizational barriers. Such is, in our hypothesis, the connection between the new role played by the gender relationships and our approach to the understanding of historical change.

We still have to introduce a last basic element into the discussion of our underlying theoretical scheme: cultures, nations, and their institutional expression in the form of states. For an overwhelming proportion of human history, societies largely developed in isolation in different regions of the planet, and when they made contact it was either on a superficial level (mainly through occasional trade) or in the destructive form of conquest, submission, assimilation, or extermination. Thus, although modes of production, modes of development, gender relationships and power relationships probably would help us in understanding the development of most historical societies, their combination in a particular society was always unique, as was their timing, struggles and, therefore, the historical actors who emerged in each society or regional set of societies to create and impose a new mode of production. A Marxist tradition uses the concept of social formation to indicate that any given society is the combination of different modes of production, and different stages of a mode, under the domination of one of them.[96] The concept calls attention to the complexity of any particular situation and reminds us that modes of production are simplified models whose dynamics vary according to the historical context.

Yet to treat the problem only from this approach could be misleading because once a given society is structured, if we accept that the combination underlying its structure is unique, so will be its evolution, dynamics, struggles, and change. Thus, instead of social formations, what we have are historical processes. This specificity produces historically defined cultures, in the anthropological sense. Cultures generate (in interaction with the modes of production they express) nations, that is socio-cultural communities sharing the acceptance of values and institutions, above the lines of gender, class, and power.[97] Of course, cultures and nations will also express these dominations by class, gender, and the state, but they will be a subset of this cluster of relationships, a subset in which a human group will find self-recognition through patterns of communication particular to themselves. When a nation becomes politically sovereign, it forms a state.[98] States also form on the basis of power relationships by incorporating other nations. Therefore history produces both the nation state and the state nation,[99] that is, a state that unifies politically several nations within the same political boundaries. When cultures do not develop as nations (that is, when they remain fragmented not only politically but also socially), they form ethnic groups, some of them called racial groups, however questionable the concept of race might be.[100] Power relationships are not only between state and society, but between the states themselves through war and conquest.

So throughout history, cultures and nations have been incorporated by force into the boundaries of a state that has created the ground for a multiethnic, multicultural and multinational society. Also, cultures and individuals have tried to escape oppression and poverty by migrating to new societies, where they have formed social subsets whose dynamics are fundamental to the understanding of historical change in our world. As Katznelson reminds us,[101] wihtout an understanding of the social diversity of national contexts, no analysis of social struggles and social movements can be accomplished. But this diversity cannot be the main line of our inquiry, otherwise we would be mere collectors of an infinite variety of singular contexts in human history. We need to establish the potential, structures, and themes of historical change in a given mode of production and a given mode of development, to then be able to assess the projects and challenges posed by the new actors entering the social scene, in order to determine if they are anticipating history or simply expressing their obsessions.

The diversity of cultures and power relationships between states introduces a major feature in the world under observation. The capitalist mode of production is based on a world system, as Fernand Braudel[102] and Immanuel Wallerstein[103] have been telling us for a long time. This process has commanded since its very beginning the dynamics of the system and has transcended the frontiers of the nation-states. Furthermore, as we have written in Part 4, the interpenetration of economies and societies has tremendously accelerated in the last decades.[104] The capitalist mode of production, and the industrial and informational modes of development are territorially differentiated and integrated at the world level in an asymmetrical manner. Not only is there a core and a periphery, but there are a series of levels in these inter-relationships, levels that shift from time to time and from dimension to dimension: the core-periphery relationship is not the same in the field of energy as it is in the field of finance, car production, or research into micro-electronics.[105] Thus we live in a world-wide system organized around relationships of dependency between societies,[105bis] and in a dependency of variable geometry according to the nation, the time, and the dimension on which dependency is considered. Because relationships of production are integrated at the world-wide level, while experience is culturally specific and power is still concentrated in the nation-states, our world exists in a three-dimensional space whose dynamics tend to be disjointed. The nation-states of dependent societies are the key elements in avoiding disintegration, but only on the condition that they mobilize (and if necessary construct) their nations to impose new relationships to the centre of the system.

So our observation of historical change has to take into consideration a new, major social challenge: the challenge of established power relationships between states. This challenge, expressed in terms of national development versus world-wide capitalist growth threatens not only the power of the dominant states but the capitalist relationships of production on which these states are based. The challenge of dependency by a project of national development is creating a new relationship between the dependent nation-states and their popular classes, one that we described, using a classic term, as populism, and whose urban dimension we showed as being a fundamental element of the political process.

This challenge stems from three different sources: first from the resistance to foreign domination by the national cultures; second, from the social mobilization generated in the periphery of the system by the new expansion of the industrial mode of development; and third, from the new power relationship established between the super-states regulating the two modes of production that compete in today's world – capitalism and statism. The latter is, of course, the main element, allowing for the challenge mounted by the dependent states against the core-states of the capitalist system. Capitalism tries to expand the basis of its profit, if necessary through military enforcement of the freedom to choose in the market-place. Statism tries to expand the number of its subjects, both as a defensive reaction against capitalism, and as the expression of a social logic in which domination tries to substitute for failures in technological development. Out of this competition, national, dependent-states play one super-power against another, trying to keep their autonomous path on the narrow edge between submission and subrogate confrontation.

So, to summarize, the pattern of historical change in our epoch is expressed, on the one hand, by historical actors who challenge the class relationships of production, the gender relationship of experience, and the power relationships of the state. But, on the other, it is also marked by the fact that for the first time in history, the would-be new historical actors try to challenge the determinant role of production-based class relationships over the other fundamental dimensions of social structure. The new emerging states demand a redefinition of power at the world level, on which new relationships of production will be established. The new emerging social movements call for the pre-eminence of human experience over state power and capitalist profit. In the middle of this new historic triangle, the eye of the cyclone may be found: two mutually exclusive modes of production ready to manipulate the new states and to suffocate human experience in order to transform all new sources of life into deadly weapons against the rival empire.

It is against this historical background of light and darkness, hope and fear, that new spatial forms are being produced and new urban meanings invented.

31

The New Historical Relationship Between Space and Society

On the basis of our understanding of the process of historical change, we can now undertake the exploration of its relationship to spatial functions and forms, and therefore to the production of urban meaning. It has been a custom in the recent literature of urban studies to use the formula according to which space is the expression of society. While such a perspective is a healthy reaction against the technological determinism and short-sighted empiricism too frequently predominant in the space-related academic disciplines, it is clearly an insufficient formulation of the problem, besides being too vague a statement.

Space is not, contrary to what others may say, a reflection of society but one of society's fundamental material dimensions and to consider it independently from social relationships, even with the intention of studying their interaction, is to separate nature from culture, and thus to destroy the first principle of any social science: that matter and consciousness are interrelated, and that this fusion is the essence of history and science. Therefore spatial forms, at least on our planet, will be produced by human action, as are all other objects, and will express and perform the interests of the dominant class according to a given mode of production and to a specific mode of development. They will express and implement the power relationships of the state in a historically defined society. They will be realized and shaped by gender domination and by state-enforced family life. At the same time, spatial forms will also be marked by resistance from exploited classes, oppressed subjects, and abused women. And the work of this contradictory historical process on space will be accomplished on an already inherited spatial form, the product of history and support of new interests, projects, protests, and dreams. Finally, from time to time social movements will arise, challenging the meaning of a spatial structure and therefore attempting new functions and new forms. Such are the urban social movements, the agents of urban-spatial transformation, the highest level of urban social change.

We cannot here use the proposed analytical model to explore the production of spatial forms and urban meaning across time and cultures. But we can introduce into the discussion some recent trends of the transformation of spatial forms that underlie the production of new urban meaning by urban social movements.

We know that the dominant interests of the capitalist mode of production, during its industrial model of development, led to a dramatic restructuring of the territory and to the assignment of new social meaning to the city. Four socio-spatial processes account for this transformation:

1 The concentration and centralization of the means of production, units of management, labour power, markets, and means of consumption in a new form of the gigantic and complex spatial unit known as the metropolitan area.[106]
2 The specialization of spatial location according to the interests of capital and to the efficiency of industrial production, transportation, and distribution.[107]
3 The commodification of the city itself, both through the real estate market (including land speculation) and in its residential areas triggering, for instance, suburban sprawl as a way of opening up construction and transportation markets, and of creating a form of household designed to stimulate individualized consumption.[108]
4 The basic assumption that the accomplishment of this model of metropolitan development necessitated the mobility of the population and resources, shifting to where they were required for profit maximizing. This assumption followed massive migration, disruption of communities and regional cultures, unbalanced regional growth, spatial mismatching between existing physical stock and need for housing and facilities, and a self-spiralling urban growth beyond the limits of collective efficiency and short of the minimum space-time requirements for the maintenance of patterns of human communication.[109]

This model led to a generalized urban crisis in housing, services, and social control, as we have shown and analysed elsewhere.[110] The action of the state to cope with the urban crisis led to the increasing politicization of the early type of urban movements.[111]

The response of the dominant interests of a given system to a structural crisis has always been two-fold: on the one hand, political – repression and integration (this was the experience in all capitalist countries between 1960 and 1980, with different results depending upon the social situations); and on the other, technological – shifting gears towards new systems of management and new techniques of production. Thus, the informational mode of development created the conditions for a new restructuring of a spatial form in crisis, and at the same time it needed new spatial conditions for its full expansion.[112] The main spatial impact of the new technology, based upon the twin revolution in communication systems and micro-electronics, is the transformation of spatial places into flows and channels – what amounts to production and consumption without any localized form.[113] Not only can information be transmitted from individual sender to individual receiver across distance, but consumption can also be individualized and transformed into the exchange of a cable television image against a credit card number communicated by telephone. Technically speaking, shopping centres are already obsolete. To be sure, shopping is more than buying, but the dissociation of the economic and symbolic functions leads to the differentiation of their spatial form and, potentially, to the transformation of both functions into non-spatial flows (entertainment through images and drugs at home; buying through advertising and home computers connected to the telephone).[114] There are four limits, from the point of view of the dominant class, to this tendency towards the de-localization of production and consumption.

1 An enormous amount of capital stock is in fixed assets in the gigantic concentrations created by them during the preceding phase. Manhattan or the City of London cannot be written off as easily as the South Bronx or Brixton.[115]

2 Some cultural institutions, historical traditions, and interpersonal networks in the upper echelons of the ruling elites must be preserved and improved, since capital means capitalists, managers, and technocrats; that is, people are culturally defined and orientated, and are certainly not ready to become flows themselves.[116]

The spatial process that the dominant class has designed to deal with these two problems is a well-known device: urban renewal. This is the rehabilitation, revitalization, improvement, and protection of a limited, exclusive space of residence, work and leisure, insulated from its immediate surroundings by a computerized army of bodyguards, and related to the other islands of the elite (including resorts) by increasingly protected air communication (private jets and airport VIP rooms) and tele-conference systems.

3 Yet the informational mode of development requires some centres where knowledge is produced and information stored, as well as centres from which images and information are emitted. So universities, laboratories, scientific design units, news centres, information agencies, public service financial centres, managerial units, with all their corresponding technicians, workers, and employees, must still be spatially concentrated.

4 Furthermore, the informational mode of development is inextricably intertwined with the industrial mode of development, including industrialized agriculture, mining, and crop-collection around the world. Thus factories, fields, housing, and services for workers and peasants must have some spatial organization.

The spatial process designed from the point of view of the dominant class to cope with these third and fourth obstacles to the dismantling of the structure of space places the emphasis on increasing hierarchy and specialization of spatial functions and forms, according to their location.[116bis] What the informational mode of development allows is the separation of work and management, so that different tasks can be performed in different places and assembled through signals (in the case of information) or through advanced transportation technology (standardized pieces shipped from very remote points of production). Work at home or in community centres, regional differentiation of production, and concentration of the units of management and production of information in privileged spaces could be the new spatial model of the capitalist-technocratic elite. Furthermore, the expansion and integration of the capitalist mode of production at the world level accelerates the international division of labour and hierarchically organizes production in a world assembly line, opens up a world market, imports and exports labour where it is convenient, and transforms the flows of capital in multinational corporations into the final, most powerful immaterial property of the capitalist system: money. The spatial project of the new dominant class tends towards the disconnection between people and spatial form, and therefore between peoples' lives and urban meaning. Not that people will not be in places or that cities will disappear; on the contrary, urbanization will accelerate in most countries and the search for housing and services will become the most dramatic problem facing people.

Yet, what tends to disappear is the meaning of places for people. Each place, each city, will receive its social meaning from its location in the hierarchy of a network whose control and rhythm will escape from each place and, even more, from the people in each place. Furthermore, people will be shifted according to the continuous restructuring of an increasingly specialized space. Unemployed blacks in Detroit are already invited to go back to their now-booming industrial cities in the deep South. Mexicans will be brought into America and Turks will remain in Germany until General Motors develops its production in Mexico, and Japan takes over the European market, once controlled by the German cars, by adopting such measures as acquiring ailing Spanish car factories. The new space of a world capitalist system, combining the informational and the industrial modes of development, is a space of variable geometry, formed by locations hierarchically ordered in a continuously changing network of flows: flows of capital, labour, elements of production, commodities, information, decisions, and signals. The new urban meaning of the dominant class is the absence of any meaning based on experience. The abstraction of production tends to become total. The new source of power relies on the control of the entire network of information. Space is dissolved into flows: cities become shadows that explode or disappear according to decisions that their dwellers will always ignore. The outer experience is cut off from the inner experience. The new tendential urban meaning is the spatial and cultural separation of people from their product and from their history. It is the space of collective alienation and individual violence, transformed by undifferentiated feedbacks into a flow that never stops and never starts. Life is transformed into abstraction, cities into shadows.

Yet this is not the spatial form to emerge or the urban meaning to be imposed without resistance by the new dominant class, because space and cities, as well as history, are not the products of the will and interests of the dominant classes, genders, and apparatuses, but, the result of a process in which they are resisted by dominated classes, genders, and subjects, and in which they are met by alternative projects of new, emerging social actors. So the spatial blueprint of capitalist technocracy is historically being challenged by the alternative urban meaning projected by labour, women, cultures, citizens, urban social movements, along a series of dimensions that we must point out before introducing the connection between the drama we are describing and the social processes observed in our research on urban movements.

Each spatial restructuring attempted by the new, dominant class, each urban meaning being defined by the capitalists, managers, and technocrats is being met by conflicting projects of urban meaning, functions, and forms, coming from a variety of social actors. To use the terms of Charles Tilly,[117] some movements are reactive to the disruptions operated in their space by the dominant class, while others are proactive by proposing new relationships between space and society. Let us outline the basic tendencies of this new struggle over the definition of urban meaning before entering into the analysis of the urban social movements we have observed and how they relate to historical change.

For the sake of clarity, we will enumerate the different contradictory relationships established between the spatial project of the dominant class and the alternative meaning proposed by popular classes and (or) social movements:

1 The adaptation of old spaces to new dominant functions through urban renewal, and the regional restructuring on the basis of a new specialization of the territory are resisted by neighbourhoods that do not want to disappear, by regional cultures that want to cluster together,

and by people who, previously uprooted, want to create new roots. At the time of writing, the most lucid publication of the American corporate establishment, *Business Week*, realized the problem. Its issue of 27 July 1981 is titled 'America's New Immobile Society', reporting that:

America's celebrated 'mobile society' is putting down roots. After a quarter-century in which 20% of the population changed addresses each year, the percentage is dropping. It fell to 17·7% in the last Census Bureau study in 1976 and is continuing to decline, according to census officials . . . Larry H. Long, the bureau's chief migration specialist, says the U.S. is very unlikely to return to the mobility of the 1950s and 1960s. That easy *mobility* – which had been both evidence and a cause of the nation's freewheeling ways and innovative economy – has ended. Dealing with the effects of this change will be one of the top challenges of the 1980s for U.S. industry. . . . Evidence that Americans are staying put is as close as the next house or office. Tied down by dual-career marriages, housing costs, inflation, and a growing emphasis on leisure and community activities – the 'quality of life' – workers are resisting relocation.[118]

Business Week dixit. Mobility, a major spatial prerequisite of the industrial mode of development and, to some extent, of the informational mode, is being challenged by the defense of neighbourhoods and the search for a quality of life.

2 A somewhat more complex pattern appears to be happening at the level of the new international division of labour. On the one hand, the penetration of the national economies by the multinational corporations, the green revolution, and the international financial networks, entirely disrupts the existing productive structure and triggers the accelerated rural-urban and urban-metropolitan migrations.[118bis] On the other hand, once in the big city, the newcomers try to settle in stable communities, build up neighbourhoods, and rely on local networks.[119] The world's rootless economy and the local co-operative community are two faces of the same process, heading towards a potentially decisive confrontation.[119bis]

3 The third major debate over the city concerns the spatial consequences of information and knowledge as a major source of productivity, founding a new model of development.[120] The major social problem with the reliance on information is that because of the power and class relationships that dominate the framework within which information develops, their monopoly becomes a major source of domination and control. Therefore in the context of a class and statist society, the more that information develops, the more the communication channels must be controlled. In other words, for information to become a source of control, information and communication must be disjointed, the monopoly of the messages must be ensured, and the sending of images must be programmed, as well as their feed-back. Here again, the source of the new form of domination is neither the computer, video, nor mass media. Interactive systems of communication and computerized dissemination of knowledge have developed enough to dramatically improve, instead of reduce, the communication and information among people, as well as the cultural diversity of their messages.[121] Yet the monopoly held by capital-controlled or state-controlled mass media, as well as the monopoly of information by the technocracy, has generated a reaction by local communities emphasizing the construction of alternative cultures and patterns of communication through face-to-face interaction and the revival of the oral tradition. The tendency towards communication and culture without any spatial form as a result of centralized one-way information flows is being met by the localization of communication networks on the basis of territorially rooted cultural communities and social networks. The cultural uniformity of mass media is met by the cultural specificity of spatially based inter-personal networks. The informational technocrats dissolve the space in their flows. Distrustful people increasingly tend to rely on experience as their basic source of information. The potential breaking of two-way communication would

create a dramatic gap in the legitimacy of our informational society.

4 The popular movements, triggered by the acceleration of the restructuring of space by the informational mode of development and the new international division of labour have come to rejoin urban protests stemming from other structural contradictions of the capitalist city. Foremost among these urban movements is what we have named collective consumption trade unionism. The economic and spatial concentration of production led to the socialization of consumption under conditions such that most of these collective means of consumption (like housing, schools, health centres, and cultural amenities) were insufficiently profitable for private capital investment unless the state provided the conditions for a risk-free market or took direct responsibility for the delivery and management of urban services. The conditions of living in the city became a crucial part of the social wage, itself a component of the welfare state. While these developments released pressure on demands over direct wages and created a framework of relative social peace between capital and labour, they also led to the formation of a new type of demand movement dealing with the standards, prices, and ways of living as conditioned by urban services. When the economic crisis of the 1970s expressed the structural limits of the contradiction of a capitalist economy relying increasingly on an ever-expanding state sector of service distribution,[122] the urban fiscal crisis in America[123] and the austerity policies in Europe[124] had to meet the popular demands for collective means of consumption that had become the material basis for everyday life. The recommodification of the city had to challenge the collective demand for a good city as a social service to which all citizens were entitled.[124bis]

5 Another major tendency of the capitalist mode of production in its new industrial development at the world level was to incorporate workers from different ethnic and cultural origins in such a way that they would be much more vulnerable, socially and politically, to capital's requirements than the native citizen workers of core countries.[125] Furthermore, the split introduced within the ranks of labour could lead towards the ethnic fragmentation of the working class that had been so successful in the formation of American capitalism, paving the ground for the complete victory of business over labour.[126] In fact experience has shown that immigrant workers were less submissive than anticipated and in some countries, like Switzerland and Germany, have been at the forefront of a new wave of social struggle.[127] Yet the economic mechanism of overexploitation of immigrants still works, both in America and Western Europe, in spite of widespread unemployment and the increasing militancy of immigrant labour. As a consequence the ethnic structure of major capitalist cities has undertaken another major transformation in the last two decades, and the process is expanding. Combined with the classical process of spatial segregation, racial discrimination, and segmented housing markets, territorially-based ethnic communities are increasingly in evidence. The recent development of an informal economy in the metropolitan area, based on cheap labour and illegal conditions of work and living, is self-perpetuating and adding to the harshness of the newcomers' existence. The basis of their usefulness for the new economy is their defenseless situation, which requires the maintenance of a situation of dependency and disorganization in relationship to the labour market, to state institutions, and to the city's mainstream life.

On the other hand, for the new city dwellers to survive, they need, more than ever, to reconstruct a social universe, a local turf, a space of freedom, a community. Sometimes the community is built on the basis of the reconstruction of the social hierarchy and economic exploitation of the society they left behind, as in San Francisco's Chinatown dominated by the six companies, or in Miami's Cuban community dominated by the exiled Cuban bourgeoisie. In other cases, ethnically-based community organizations have mobilized a neighbourhood, both for their urban needs and against institutionalized prejudice; Latinos in Los Angeles for example, Puerto Ricans in New York, or West Indians in London. Most often, the self-organization, particularly among the youth, takes the form of clubs, gangs, or groups, where in-group identity is tied to collective survival, where the drug economy and the underworld find their manpower, and where the territorial boundaries of a gang's turf become at the same time the material proof of their power and their shop-floor – the source of their income. Sometimes all these elements combine into major outbursts. The inner city communities combat the segregated space of ethnic fragmentation, cultural strangeness, and economic over-exploitation of the new post-industrial city with the defense of their identity, the preservation of their culture, the search for their roots, and the marking out of their newly acquired territory. Sometimes, also, they display their rage, and attempt to devastate the institutions that they believe devastate their daily lives.

6 Space has always been connected to the state. This is even more evident in the new urban forms and functions of the capitalist system. The management of urban services by state institutions, while demanded by the labour movement as a part of the social contract reached through class stuggle, has been one of the most powerful and subtle mechanisms of social control and institutional power over everyday life in our societies, as the researchers of the CERFI, a Paris-based research centre directed by Michel Foucault, have established both theoretically and empirically.[128] Furthermore, the centralization of the state, the increasing role of the executive branch, the shrinkage and bureaucratization of the political system, and the reduction of fiscal resources and legal power for local governments have led to a situation where the exercise of democracy is limited to some isolated, although crucial, votes, choosing between a limited number of alternatives the origin of which has been largely removed from public information, consciousness, opinion, and decision.

The gap between civil society and the political system is widening because of the rigidity of the political parties and the difficulty they find in being receptive to the values and demands expressed by the new social movements (for instance, feminists, ecologists, anti-establishment youths). The crisis of legitimacy for the democratic state[129] has convinced the experts of the Trilateral Commission that democracy should be restricted and limited, so that people will not take excessive liberties.[130] On the other hand, there is a growing tendency towards political tribalism, calling for the abandonment of democratic life and the withdrawal into the wilderness of squatter houses, free communes, and alternative institutions.[131] A fundamental debate over the state is going on at the core of our civilization and, surprisingly enough, it tends to use a territorial language. The new capitalist, technocratic elite calls for a state without boundaries, territories, limits: again, for a state that governs overflows. Its blueprint includes informational control over the entire population by electronic means and storage of files in interconnected memories; blurring national boundaries; state-centralization of energy in the form of nuclear power; concentration of decisions in small cabinets and *ad hoc* groups relying on powerful bureaucratic machineries, with local governments considered as parochial and incompetent to view the overall picture, and therefore undeserving of their responsibilities. This new form of enlightened despotism calls for a non-localized world order where the representation of citizens on the basis of the membership of their cities must be replaced by the controllers of know-how who take a broader look at the problems of this planet from the carpeted meeting room of a space shuttle.[132]

People of all *classes* have proposed views of the relationship between the city and the state that are opposite to this urban system, increasingly penetrated and controlled by a centralized state via insulated bureaucracies. On the one hand, when the German squatters asked for an urban reservation in which to live and a modest state allowance to survive in it, they were taking the ultimate step in the disintegration of the relationship between state and civil society.[133] The Christiania commune in Copenhagen, the Indiani Metropolitani in Italy during the 1970s, some of the Dutch squatters, parts of the Californian gay community, and certainly the youth of Zurich, all share a similar attitude: if the city cannot get rid of the state, let us seek the state's agreement to siphon off a small part of the city, on the condition that it should be a real neighbourhood, with an intense urban life and historical tradition, as opposed to a piece of land in some anonymous suburban apartment complex.

Yet the tendency towards state centralism and domination by the state over the city is being opposed all over the world by a massive popular appeal for local autonomy and urban self-management. The revival of democracy depends upon the capacity of connecting the new demands, values, and projects to the institutions that manage society (that is, the state) on the basis of its increasing penetration by civil society, starting where people can most actively participate in decision-making: the communal institutions of local government,[134] as decentralized as possible in neighbourhood councils a system begun 20 years ago in Bologna[135]. Between the state and its undifferentiated hinterland, on the one hand, and the demand for urban reservation, on the other, a new project of self-management appears able to reconstruct the relationship between the state and the city on the basis of their mutual grassroots.

This is, then, the historical framework in which our observation of emerging urban movements took place. Let us now turn to the integration of this general framework and our research findings, so that historical trends can be fleshed out, and the results of our observations fully understood.

32

The Alternative City: The Structure and Meaning of Contemporary Urban Social Movements

Cities and space are the unfinished products of historical debates and conflicts involving meaning, function, and form. We have observed throughout the different situations presented in this book how grassroots mobilization has been a crucial factor in the shaping of the city, as well as the decisive element in urban innovation against prevailing social interests. While the situations which we researched were carefully selected to maximize the impact of urban change fostered by social mobilization, it is our theoretical perspective to consider all cities as being shaped by the outcome of social conflicts and contradictory projects. The structurally dominant interests prevail more often than not, and so shape the city. Yet, as the continuation of capitalist management does not diminish the crucial role of labour in affecting production and distribution, the trace of urban protest and alternative projects can also be recognized in the spatial forms and the meaning of cities. Any theory of the city must be, at its starting point, a theory of social conflict. Our cross-cultural evidence supports this fundamental hypothesis.

Yet urban situations can be so diverse, and the specificity of the processes we have observed has deliberately been so exceptional, that the theoretical usefulness of our findings must be considered in a broader context. Our main proposition is that there is an intimate connection between the themes, goals, and experiences of urban social movements and the overall process of historical conflict and change in our societies. Not that urban movements are the new historical actors creating social change, nor the pivotal source of alternative social forms. Rather, our statement is that urban movements are not random expressions of discontent, varying from city to city, but that they bear, in their structure and goals, the stigmas and projects of all the great historical conflicts of our time. If such a statement is true, historical change and urban change are intertwined, as assumed in our general theory. If this hypothesis is a social fact, we must find the trace of these debates and conflicts in the urban movements we have studied. Furthermore, the themes of these debates must be the crucial factors in explaining the behaviour and effects of urban movements as recorded in our research.

So let us turn to our case studies to determine what were the main elements present in these urban movements. To avoid repetition, we will analyse only the essential trends detected in each city and refer the reader to the relevant part for the details and verification of the social trends now presented.

We have found that, in accordance to the general hypothesis posed in the Introduction, urban movements making their interests and values materialize, are structured around three basic goals.[136] By goals we mean purposive desires and demands present in the collective practice of the movement. They must be consciously expressed, but a declaration of intent or a list of demands is not sufficient to denote a goal, which must be collectively acted on, not just declared. Each goal opposes another project in the city, relying on a contradictory set of social interests and values. Therefore each goal defines an adversary whose power and characteristics will profoundly influence the movement. Not all the movements we observed had the three basic goals; nor did they pursue them with the same intensity. In fact the articulation (or lack of articulation) of the three goals in any given movement is one of the major elements that explains our theory about the relationship between movements and cities.

The three goals, are as follows:

1   To obtain for the residents a city organized around its use value, as against the notion of urban living and services as a commodity, the logic of exchange value. The content of this use value changed considerably from place to place, city to city, or between classes within a given city. It could be decent housing provided as a public service, the preservation of a historic building, or the demand for open space. But wherever mobilization occurred, it was for improved collective consumption, in contradiction to the notion of the city for profit in which the desirability of space and urban services are distributed according to levels of income. We name this type of mobilization *collective consumption trade unionism*. (Please note that this is a theoretical type, and therefore a movement can be focused on collective consumption while pursuing other goals; it would then be a combination of two types of movements, and research would have to determine the consequences of such a combination).

2   The second major goal we found present in the urban movements was the search for cultural identity, for the maintenance or creation of autonomous local cultures, ethnically-based or historically originated. In other words, the defense of communication between people, autonomously defined social meaning, and face-to-face interaction, against the monopoly of messages by the media, the predominance of one-way information flows, and the standardization of culture on the basis of increasingly heteronomous sources for the neighbourhood residents. We named the movement orientated towards this goal, *community*.

3   The third goal we discovered was the search for increasing power for local government, neighbourhood decentralization, and urban self-management in contradiction to the centralized state and a subordinated and undifferentiated territorial administration. We call the struggle for a free city, a *citizen movement*.

Our emphasis on goals stems from our general theoretical perspective that cities and societies are produced by the conflictive process of collective actors mobilized towards certain goals, that is, ways of structuring society and space. Therefore a movement is first of all defined by its goals (as expressed in its conscious practice) or set of goals. Each time a social actor defines or searches for a goal he finds an adverse one, as well as allies and enemies (that is allies of the adverse goal). Then both movement and adversary are moving towards a historically defined confrontation over the object of their goals, which in our case is the city. Thus the structure of an urban movement, while generated by the definition of a goal, appears to become complex as soon as it begins the same social process by which a movement defines its goal. On the basis of our case studies, we propose in Table 32–1 the social structure underlying the dynamics of contemporary urban movements.

But who are these urban actors? Are we not re-entering a structuralist paradigm, deprived of social actors and worked out by contradictions? Certainly not. The actors of the urban movements are the urban movements themselves, since we have defined movements by the goals they set up for themselves. The movements become social actors by being engaged in a mobilization towards an urban goal which is itself linked to the general struggle over the continuous restructuring of society. And the movements are different, according to the goals of each type of movement. Yet the question remains: who are they in terms of their social characteristics? At the empirical level, we have carefully answered the question in each observed situation. At the theoretical level, however, a major point needs to be made, based on our empirical observation: the movements are urban actors, defined by their goals and their urban condition. They are not, then, another form of class struggle, gender struggle, or ethnic struggle. The components of the urban movements come from a variety of social, gender, and ethnic situations, according to their urban and national contexts. And yet their urban themes are recurrent and the factors underlying their dynamics, successes, and failures are quite similar, as we were able to observe in our case studies. To be more specific, they are neither working class movements nor a middle class movement, as has been advanced, particularly by French researchers. First, this idea is empirically false, as witnessed by the American and British inner cities, the Spanish neighbourhood movements, and the Italian self-discount movement.[136bis] Even in Paris our research on the Grands Ensembles showed the social diversity of the movement's participants, including, but not predominantly, the middle class. Second, and more significantly, when Dagnaud and Mehl[137] among others, point out the role of the new middle class in the urban movements, they do not deny the participation of manual workers, or even unionized workers, in those movements, but emphasize the non-class basis of the urban movements, which is a fundamental and most useful observation. The fact that they can be associated with the petty-bourgeoisie, a non-class by definition in the classical sense of class, means that they are defined on another social dimension, cutting across the class structure. They are not middle class but multi-class movements for the very simple reason that they do not relate directly to the relationships of production, but to the relationships of consumption, communication, and power.

So the observed experience of urban movements points towards an alternative urban meaning, posing the alternative to the city emerging from the interests and values of the dominant class. The alternative city is therefore a network of cultural communities defined by time and

Table 32.1 The social structure underlying the dynamics of contemporary urban movements.

	The city as a use value.	Identity, cultural autonomy and communication.	Territorially based self-management.
Goal of the urban movement.	The city as a use value.	Identity, cultural autonomy and communication.	Territorially based self-management.
Ideological themes and historical demands included in this goal.	- Social wage. - Quality of life. - Conservation of history and nature.	- Neighbourhood life. - Ethnic cultures. - Historical traditions.	- Local autonomy. - Neighbourhood decentralization. - Citizen participation.
Goal of the adversary.	The city as exchange-value.	Monopoly of messages and one-way information flows.	- Centralization of power, rationalization of bureaucracy. - Insulation of the apparatus.
Social issues and ideological themes.	- Appropriation of land rent. - Real estate speculation. - Infrastructure for profitable capitalist production.	- Mass culture. - Standardization of meaning. - Urban isolation.	- Centralism. - Bureaucratization. - Authoritarianism.
Conflicting projects over the historical meaning of city.	City as a spatial support for life. *versus* City as a commodity or a support of commodity production and circulation.	City as a communication network and a source of cultural innovation *versus* Despatialization of programmed one-way information flows.	City as a self-governing entity. *versus* City as a subject of the central state at the service of world-wide empires.
Structural historical contradition of which the urban conflict refers.	Capital. *versus* Labour in the appropriation of surplus value and the decision over investment.	Information (excluding communication). *versus* Communication (that necessarily includes information).	Order and authority. *versus* Change and freedom.
Name of the adversary (historical actor).	Bourgeoisie.	Technocracy.	State.
Name of the urban movement by this particular goal (urban actor).	Collective consumption trade unionism.	Community.	Citizens.

space, and politically self-managed towards the maximization of use value for their residents; this use value is always decided and re-examined by the residents themselves. This new urban meaning is neither the ideal image nor the dream of a midsummer night: it is the set of goals that emerges from the practice of the urban movements we have observed, and its significance and existence is not contradicted by the amount of secondary data known about other urban movements in other cities and other societies. (We exclude the socialist countries because, as already stated, we do not have enough reliable information on them concerning our subject.) This urban profile is as real as the skyscrapers on the drawing boards of the corporate board rooms. The movements are projects of cities, social life, and urban functions and forms (predetermined by urban meaning) emerging from the capacity of the new urban dwellers to produce and control their own environment, space, and urban services. Another question, and a fundamental one, is the feasibility of such a city – the likelihood of its ever taking shape. In fact this outcome will depend on the conflict over the city and the conflict's links with social change and political struggle. This is the aim of our theoretical analysis: to unveil the mechanisms at work in the conflictive process that is shaping today's dramas, and tomorrow's heavens and hells.

The most important point, from this perspective, is to determine the conditions under which urban movements seem to achieve their maximum impact on the change of urban meaning. Or, in other words, under what conditions do they become urban social movements?

On the basis of a selected sample of major urban movements in four cultural areas in the last two decades, our research shows that the highest transformation of urban meaning occurred in Madrid, and we were able to establish the structural formula underlying the capacity of Madrid's Citizen Movement to become an urban social movement. To be sure, Madrid continues to be an extremely difficult city to live in, and therefore to say that urban movements accomplished a great deal might seem a subjective appreciation. Nevertheless, we provided enough empirical evidence in Part 5 to support a conclusion on the extent of the change in the urban meaning prevailing in Madrid, in spite of the setbacks experienced after 1980 (after our research had been concluded) because of the crisis in the Citizen Movement.[138] So, for reasons that will become more evident, we propose the structural formula we discovered in our research in Madrid as the general structural formula able to foster the fulfillment of an urban social movement across different cultures of the capitalist-informational mode of production and in our epoch. We have already presented and justified this formula in the section on Madrid, but let us remind ourselves of the four basic elements:

1   To accomplish the transformation of urban meaning in the full extent of its political and cultural implications, an urban movement must articulate in its praxis the three goals of collective consumption demands, community culture, and political self-management.
2   It must be conscious of its role as an urban social movement.
3   It must be connected to society through a series of organizational operators, three in particular: the media, the professionals, and the political parties.
4   A *sine qua non* condition: while urban social movements must be connected to the political system to at least partially achieve its goals, they must be organizationally and ideologically autonomous of any political party. The reason is that social transformation and political struggle, negotiation, and management, although intimately connected and interdependent, do not operate at the same level of the social structure. As Daniel Cohn-Bendit, the leader of the students' revolt in Nanterre in 1968, once said to his liberal professors, 'For you to be successful reformists, we have to be failing revolutionaries.'

On the basis of our observation of other experiences, we add a fifth rule for the development of an urban social movement: the first condition must command all the others. If the three basic goals are not interconnected in the praxis of the movement, no other element will be able to accomplish a significant change in urban meaning.

How is it possible to prove this major statement? We proved it for the case of Madrid at three levels:

1 The Movement as a whole produced a change in urban meaning and could be considered to be holding on to the four elements of our formula.
2 Bearing in mind for a moment the particular movements in Madrid, only the ones that fit the formula accomplished multidimensional change.
3 For the movements that did not fit, their outcome was systematically related to the absence from their practice of elements in the basic formula.

Does our theory, and therefore our structural formula, hold for the other cases under observation? We think so. In none of the cases did a complete transformation of urban meaning happen (unlike Madrid); but in none of these cases were the three basic goals articulated in the practice of the movement. Furthermore, there is a systematic correspondence between the missing goals and the profile of the urban outcome. On the basis of the empirical findings, we can formulate these correspondences in the following way:

a In the case of the *Grands Ensembles* of Paris, the collective consumption trade unionism never took into consideration the community dimension and split over its political role, for example at Sarcelles. Thus it obtained urban demands but disappeared as a movement when a left wing municipality was elected. In the case of Val d'Yerres, one sector of the movement was identical to the tenant union in Sarcelles and obtained a similar result. Another sector, around the GERB at Boussy, linked community and self-management and foreshadowed the new French urban movements, but failed because of insufficient emphasis on trade unionism.
b In the case of the *gay community in San Francisco*, the movement merged the defense of cultural identity with a powerful drive into the political system, actually accomplishing major improvements in the urban functions and forms of the city. Yet its specificity, isolation, unwillingness as a movement (in spite of its leadership) to commit itself to the struggles for urban demands eventually resulted in its isolation as a cultural community and it ended by being another interest group playing coalition politics.
c In the case of the *Mission Coalition in San Francisco*, the three basic goals of our proposed formula were present, but in a very perverse way: Latinos (community) and Urban Poor (consumption) were there, but fighting each other over the definition of the movement's identity in order to win privileged access to the power system, which in turn used the division of the movement to assert its development. This explains why the movement was successful as long as it maintained the ambiguity over the articulation of the three goals, and also why it collapsed so suddenly and so dramatically once the ambiguity turned into a crisis over the definition of the legitimate goals of the movement.
d The *squatter's movements in Latin America* offers an even more complicated picture. But to make things as simple as possible, let us say that the three goals were also present in most movements but in an asymmetrical way. To be more precise, movements were orientated towards urban services and tried to build up new cultural communities. But to do so, they subordinated themselves to the political system, be it the state or a party. In so doing, they were generally successful in changing urban functions and urban forms, but became entirely dependent on the fate of their political godfathers in the construction of urban meaning. When their political representatives suffered defeat and terror, as in Chile, they

disappeared together in the same bloodshed. When, as in Peru, the state decided to halt clientelism, they revolted but were unable to modify the role of the *barriadas*. Only in Monterrey, where the *posesionarios* attempted to maintain some autonomy in relationship to the state, did an embryo of an urban social movement appear, but under conditions of geographical and political isolation that made its development difficult.

In sum, our case studies do not falsify the structural formula developed on the basis of the more systematic research on Madrid. If anything, the application of the concepts and logic embodied in our formula to the different cases clarifies the social process we have reconstructed. The theoretical framework seems to be logically coherent and empirically consistent with the urban situations we have considered in a variety of social contexts.

Let us assume therefore that the structural formula underlying the formation and achievement of urban social movements is correct. Why should it be so? And where does it come from? These two fundamental questions require careful answers.

First, what is the process of formation of urban social movements? How, within the limits of our time and cultures, have urban movements come to integrate the goals and the means which have been discovered as necessary to produce a change in urban meaning? It is here that the contribution of Ira Katznelson[139], John Rex[140] and John Foster[141] are invaluable. They have all insisted on the necessity of considering the historical contexts in the formation of social classes in general, and social movements in particular. And that is in fact our answer: the production of the structural formula leading to urban social movements is specific to each national-cultural context, and any attempt to find a general formulation is to resort to metaphysics. Let us point out, at the same time, that we maintain there is a general structural formula in our historical epoch of urban social movements as processes aimed at a given outcome – the transformation of urban meaning. This is because we live in a world-wide mode of production (capitalism) developing through two world-wide articulated modes of development (industrial and informational). Therefore the raw materials of social change (and thus of urban change) are ubiquitous, while the social processes bringing together these raw materials are historically, and so nationally and culturally, specific.

How did the Citizen Movement in Madrid bring together the three basic goals aimed at multidimensional change? The answer is paradoxical: Spain was a society oppressed in a totalitarian way that integrated the different social subsystems. The state, blessed by the Church, was at the root of everything, destroying any remnant of political freedom or cultural autonomy. Multinational capital and local speculators took advantage of the freedom given to them to impose industrialization and urbanization at a cost that in Europe can only be rivalled by the early nineteenth century. The cultural backwardness of an illiterate army ensured that no popular cultural expression could flourish. Furthermore, the structure of Spanish society was not a historical accident linked to the Franquist dictatorship; it goes back to the Christian crusade, fighting for eight centuries to exterminate the superior Arab civilization; it goes back to the massive expulsion of over half-a-million Spanish Jews in the sixteenth century, throwing out forever the most enlightened Spaniards; it goes back to the Inquisition and the absolutist state; it goes back to the Catholic Church, the backbone of Spanish society, where bishops and priests ordered the kings to conquer more territories in order to determine whether their inhabitants' souls could be sent to paradise if they converted or to hell if they resisted. This context called for total, sudden, and violent revolution. The Spanish people tried several times in history until they learned that the institutions were so strong, so deeply embedded in the people themselves, any attempt to confront the system at its roots would cause civil war. This meant bloodshed and, in the European context, defeat. So they gave up the idea of total political revolution. But any movement knew, from the collective memory, that everything was linked. To have light in the city streets to which they were forced to migrate, they had both to fight the police and gather their neighbours to a street-dancing party where life could go on in spite of the harshness. This has been the Spanish way. And this was at the root of the Spanish urban movement.

In San Francisco things were very different. American society, and California in particular, is based upon ethnic fragmentation of the popular classes, a pluralist political system based on coalitions of interest groups, and a decentralized insulated state that works through integration and co-optation except when it feels threatened, in which case it uses the most extreme violence. The Mission Coalition collapsed because Latinos wanted to be ethnically defined in order to avoid sharing the benefits of social programmes with other communities, while the community activists, trying to unify all the poor people, became totally absorbed by the management of social programmes that would create their own power. Gays won their right to survival and their capacity to be themselves by concentrating spatially and mobilizing electorally. Yet, since they needed a space, they took it from the poor ethnic communities, triggering prejudice and hostility. They won their right to existence but at the expense of their capacity to transform the city and society in unison with the other oppressed minorities. Thus coalition politics led to a series of victories by different oppressed groups, but ended in a collective stalemate.

Paris was a different history again. From 1947 to 1978 French society has been characterized by three major trends. First, the state (namely the centralized state) was the beginning and the end of everything. Yet, since this was a democratic state, it was itself dependent on the political system. Second, all social movements were dominated by the labour movement – itself dominated by the Communist Party through the CGT – not only the largest union but the most militant and best organized on the shop-floor. Third, the Communist Party and, with it, the labour movement, were totally excluded from the political system and from the state, both because of the anti-labour and colonialist policies of the government and because of the sectarian messianism of the communists. Thus, what we saw in the Grands Ensembles was the development of a new movement that had immediately to confront the choice between labour-inspired economic demands and the attempt of autonomous communal politics. The contradiction destroyed it. We also witnessed the beginning of the process that led to the construction of the new Socialist Party and to the embryos of some dialectical relationship between grassroots' movements and a left wing dominated political system. In the Val d'Yerres, young professionals wanting to improve their quality of life and to change society without losing their privileges, were mobilizing for environmental preservation and local self-management, but still missing the connection, that came later, with the hard-core of demand-orientated urban trade unionism.

In Latin America overurbanization and the new international division of labour described in Part 4 led to the emergence of an urban populism in which squatters exchanged political allegiance and cultural heteronomy for urban services and the right to settle in the appendages of the world economic system. The movements followed a contradictory pattern of demand, negotiation, mobilization and integration, bound up in the fate of the political actors on whom the squatters always relied.

Thus each national-cultural context explains not only how but why different goals converged or became disjointed, as well as how the organizational operators of the movements connected, disconnected, or took over, the relationships between urban demands, state, and society.

Now the final and most important question. Are these goals constitutive of urban social movements and why do they generate a change of urban meaning? And why these goals as opposed to others? Could there be more or fewer goals? And why must they be clustered together in the praxis of the movement to produce a significant effect?

Here we must recall the general analysis of social change in our historical context. The three goals that are crucial factors in the fulfillment of urban social movements are precisely the three alternative projects to the modes of production and modes of development that dominate our world. The city as a use value contradicts the capitalist form of the city as exchange value. The city as a communication network opposes the one-way information flow characteristic of the informational mode of development. And the city as a political entity of free self-management opposes the reliance on the centralized state as an instrument of authoritarianism and a threat of totalitarianism.

Thus the fundamental themes and debates of our history are actually the raw material of the urban movements. Does this mean that urban social movements are the core of the new processes of historical change? Not at all; it is precisely because the alternative projects of change in the dimensions of production, culture, and power have come to a stalemate that urban social movements have been able to appear and play a major social role. Let us develop this idea that is the keystone of our analysis.

Cities in our societies are the expression of the different dimensions of life, of the variety of social processes that form the intricate web of our experience. Therefore people tend to consider cities, space, and urban functions and forms as the mainspring for their feelings. This is the basis for the urban ideology that assigns the causality of social effects to the structure of spatial forms. Yet when people experience an undefined force they react on one of several levels against the material form that transfers to them the force they feel. Thus the less people identify the source of their economic exploitation, cultural alienation, and political oppression while still feeling their effects, the more they will react against the material forms that introduce these experiences into their lives. Furthermore, the spatial form is not simply a transmitter of all these evils. It is an organizer of them and becomes an evil in its own right. So popular reaction is two-fold, both against the unrecognized structural source of their exploitation-alienation-oppression, and against the particular spatial form that expresses their condition as a daily reminder: the wild city.[142]

The source of urban movements in our societies is the absence of effective channels for social change for each one of the basic dimensions involved in the conflictive appropriation of production and history. The labour movement has been, by and large, unable to address the issue of the social wage and the negotiation of living conditions outside the work place. So urban trade unionism has had to take its place outside factories and offices. The overflow of one-way information has been met only by marginal, alternative cultures, leaving to people to try and spontaneously defend their autonomous networks on the most primitive basis: territoriality. The centralization of the state and the obsession of political parties with the instrumental dimension of power has led to a growing distance between civil society and the state. The revival of local autonomy, the call for political self-management, decentralization, and participation is the last chance before the dramatic split between bureaucratic apparatuses and irreducible identities.

Because all these potential sources of conflict in our society do not have autonomous means of expression, organization, and mobilization they have come together in a negative and reactive way in the shape of urban movements. When they are primitive one-dimensional reactions, they take the form of urban protest. When they have developed an alternative global vision, they form a counter-culture, and feel more comfortable if they define their alternative in a territory: they propose an alternative social organization, an alternative space, an alternative city. They become an urban social movement. But such a movement cannot be 'proactive', only 'reactive', except in its Utopian dimension. It cannot, however, be a social alternative, only the symptom of a social limit, because the city it projects is not, and cannot be, connected to an alternative mode of production and development, nor to a democratic state adapted to the world-wide processes of power. Thus urban social movements are aimed at transforming the meaning of the city without being able to transform society. They are a reaction, not an alternative: they are calling for a depth of existence without being able to create that new breadth. They project the profile of the world they want, without knowing why, or how, or if. When institutions remain insulated or unresponsive, banks maintain their high interest rates, police take over the streets again, and meaningful space continues to disintegrate, and urban social movements no longer call for an alternative city. Instead their fragmented elements undertake the destruction of the city they reject. We observed and analysed their hope for society as projected by their desired space and cherished city. If such appeals are not heard, if the political avenues remain closed, if the new central social movements (feminism, new labour, self-management, alternative communication) do not develop fully, then the urban movements – reactive Utopias that tried to illuminate the path they could not walk – will return, but this time as urban shadows eager to destroy the closed walls of their captive city.

33

The Social Significance of Contemporary Urban Movements

We have unveiled the structure and dynamics of the urban movements observed in a variety of cultural, economic, and institutional contexts. We have related these observations to a broader theoretical framework, whilst dealing simultaneously with the relationship between space and society, and with the formation and effects of social movements. A tentative theoretical framework has emerged, enabling us to understand the complex dialectics between the city and the grassroots.

We have therefore enough elements to address some more specific social and political concerns about the actual role that urban movements play in society. Are they marginal forms of protest, doomed to disappear as soon as parties, unions, and other institutionalized forms of social mobilization take care of the concerns voiced by urban movements? After all, several of the movements we studied disappeared or were seriously weakened after their defeat or victory. Furthermore, a number of very important movements, the Italian urban struggles of the early 1970s for example, have receded spectacularly in recent years. Nevertheless, on purely empirical grounds we could speak of the uneven development of urban movements, but of expansion to a broader geographical and cultural area. At the time the Italian movement was agonizing in the late 1970s, the Spanish neighbourhood associations strengthened and had greater impact. When, in 1980–81, the Citizen Movement in Madrid went through a devastating crisis, the squatter movements in Holland and Germany proposed many of the goals that had been forwarded by neighbourhood groups elsewhere. When the *pobladores* of

Chile crumbled under the terror of Pinochet, new urban movements started to develop in Brazil, Venezuela, and Mexico, with a broader social basis and a higher consciousness of their autonomous role as agents of social change. And after the end of collective violent protest of the American inner cities in the 1960s, a steady flow of community organizations and neighbourhood groups demanding public services quietly irrigated the country's urban geography through the 1970s, from Cincinnati to Los Angeles, and from Crystal City, Texas, to New York. In spite of the absence of reliable, systematic information on the development of urban movements in different countries throughout history, our own knowledge[143] as well as the amount of existing information[144] suggest a clear, comparative upward trend.

Although the size and ubiquity of this development are important to the evaluation of its historical significance, the decisive point is the role that urban movements have played in the overall dynamics of a society. Are they another form of interest group? Have they become a new form of alternative society, that is a major contemporary social movement? Or do they tend to be, as we proposed in the last chapter, reactive Utopias? And why so?

First of all, let us make clear that we believe we are considering, in general, a somewhat homogeneous phenomenon. To be sure, under the general term of urban movements (or urban struggles as we used to call them) we are considering very different forms of mobilization, from counter-cultural squatters to middle class neighbourhood associations and shanty town defense groups. Nevertheless they all seem to share some basic characteristics in spite of their diversity:

1 They consider themselves as urban, or citizen, or, in any case, related to the city (or to the community) in their self-denomination.
2 They are locally-based and territorially-defined, a feature that will be decisive in helping us to determine their significance.
3 They tend to mobilize around three major goals that we identified in our general overview and found to be crucial in our case studies: collective consumption, cultural identity, and political self-management. Futhermore, our tried and tested hypothesis is that only when the three themes combine in a movement's practice does it bring about social change, while the separation of any of the goals and a narrow self-definition turn it into an interest group that will be moulded into the established institutions of society, so losing most of its identity and impact. We also pointed out that these three goals were not arrived at by accident, but are the major points of opposition against the dominant logics of capitalism, informationalism, and statism.

Thus, we are convinced of some fundamental degree of homogeneity in urban movements in whatever societies they may occur. The diversity of their effects and development stems from the fact that their origin, social causation, and development are differential, according to the specificity of each historical context, and their singular pattern of behaviour. To some extent, this can all be said of the labour movement, a movement that is evident in all societies, but in different forms, behaving in divergent ways, and having diverse social effects.

Yet, while recognizing the generality of urban movements and their development, we have rejected the thesis that they might constitute a new central social movement able to transform our history. We have, furthermore, characterized urban movements as reactive Utopias. Why so?

The reason is not that they are incapable of being politically effective because of their distance to, or their subordination to, the political system. In fact, all social movements are unable to fully accomplish their project since they lose their identity as they become institutionalized, the inevitable outcome of bargaining for social reform within the political system. Such is the natural cycle of life and death in society so that the fate of urban movements is not unique. If they followed the experience of social movements, they would extinguish themselves in a struggle that would cause social change they would not survive to see. But this is not our thesis for today's urban movements. We argue that they are not agents of structural social change, but symptoms of resistance to the social domination even if, in their effort to resist, they do have major effects on cities and societies.

The reason for this defensive role is that they are unable to put forward any historically feasible project of economic production, communication, or government. Let us explain.

For any historical actor to handle satisfactorily the production and delivery of public goods and services, it has to be able to reorganize the relationship between production, consumption, and circulation. And this task is beyond any local community in a technologically sophisticated economy that is increasingly organized on a world scale and, at the same time, increasingly disguised within the labyrinths of the underground economy.

To maintain and develop cultural identity and autonomous forms of communication, communities and people must deal with the technology of mass media, as well as with the empires of image-producers that monopolise the codes, flows, and receivers, reinforcing the increasing impoverishment of inter-personal communication. The global village announced by Marshall McLuhan has become, instead, a collection of silent, individual receivers, and the lonely crowd[145] has gone over to high technology. How could local communities match this satellite-related network, so well-supported by economic resources and so directly enforced by the state?

Furthermore, how to advance grassroots democracy when the state has become an over-whelming, centralized, and insulated bureaucracy, when the power game is being played all over the planet with nuclear stakes, and when political parties represent social interests and cultural values which bear an increasingly narrow spectrum? The more locally-based urban movements aim at local governments, but local communities are, in reality, powerless in the context of world empires and computerized bureaucracies.

So, why urban movements? Why the emphasis on local communities? Have people not understood that they need an international working class movement to oppose the multi-national corporations, a strong, democratic parliament, reinforced by participatory democracy, to control the centralized state, and a multiple, interactive communication system to use the new technologies of the media to express (not to suppress) the cultural diversity of society? Why, instead of choosing the right ones, do people insist on aiming at the local targets?

For the simple reason that, according to available information, people appear to have no other choice. The historical actors (social movements, political parties, institutions) that were supposed to provide the answers to the new challenges at the global level, were unable to stand up to them. The labour movement generated by the capitalist mode of production has largely lost its capacity to control the economy, given the internationalization of production, markets, labour, and management, the attack of the informal economy, and the entry of women to work that has shaken the male-dominated foundations of the labour unions. As a result, the relationships between production and consumption, the individual wage and social wage, and the labour process and the welfare state are increasingly out of the control of the labour movement that was the key social actor of the class struggle of the last hundred years. Private corporations and debt-ridden governments take advantage of their newly recovered freedom to cast off the burden of their social responsibility for collective consumption. But if the mechanisms of the welfare state disappear, people are still in need of its benefits in their homes, neighbourhoods, and cities.

At the level of communication patterns and cultural identity, the philosophical rationalism of the political left and the one-dimensional culture of the labour movement led the social movements of industrial capitalism to ignore subcultures, gender specificity, ethnic groups, religious beliefs, national identities, and personal experiences. All human diversity was generally considered a remnant of the past, and class struggle and human progress would help to supersede it until a universal fraternity was arrived at that would provide, paradoxically, the ideal stage both for bourgeois enlightenment and proletarian Marxism.[146] Between times, people continued to speak their languages, pray to their saints, celebrate their traditions, enjoy their bodies, and refuse just to be labour or consumers. In fact, the real drift towards cultural uniformity did not originate with class consciousness or mass consumption, but with the new audio-visual technology, itself not a capitalist conspiracy, but the by-product of military communication that has been commercialized and used by some states for their propaganda.[147] Once again, the existing social movements and forces of political change ignored the potential of these developments, and either switched-off the television or used it in a purely instrumental way to get their message on it. But there was no attempt to connect people's life, experience, and culture to the new world of images and sounds. As a result the sources of communication dried up, interpersonal channels became obsolete, and the mass media took over everybody's imaginary world. Although people did not necessarily like this development they did not find an alternative source of communication and information. So they became accustomed to it, while taking every opportunity to express themselves outside the mass media.

The increasing gap, in terms of political institutions, between people's concerns on the one hand, and parties and the state on the other, grew even greater. All over the world, the state developed a voracious, independent machinery, technologically sophisticated, and bureaucratically self-reproductive. In most nations, this state apparatus repressed the people' coercing them through the policing of their souls and torturing of their bodies. In the few remaining parliamentary democracies, the tragedy has been the increasing distance between citizens and political parties. On the one hand, parties have been historically produced by very different social movements or social interests from the new values and projects so that the established parties and new movements are consequently mismatched. On the other hand, the dominant parties tend to dilute their programmes to capture the middle ground of the political spectrum. As a result, the differences between parties and political coalitions, while still important, tend to diminish, so that the chances of encompassing the electorate's variety of interests are, in fact, reduced, and the distance between everyday life and electoral programmes increased.

As a result we can perceive a growing pattern of electoral abstention (almost 50 per cent in America), that is only counterbalanced when the law enforces the vote (Italy), or when there is a dramatic choice (France and Spain). While national politics are still crucial for the future of the country concerned, the citizens in all cases think the national state is too far removed from their problems. They therefore tend to oscillate in their vote, hoping that the alternance of apparently moderate formulae will yield results. But each time that the pendulum moves and little happens, belief in the political system is further undermined, and people dig a little bit deeper into their local trenches.

So, faced with an overpowered labour movement, an omnipresent one-way communication system indifferent to cultural identities, an all-powerful centralized state loosely governed by unreliable political parties, a structural economic crisis, cultural uncertainty, and the likelihood of nuclear war, people go home. Most withdraw individually, but the crucial, active minority, anxious to retaliate, organize themselves on their local turf. They react against the exploitation-alienation-oppression that the city has become to represent. They may be unable to control the international flows of capital, but they can impose conditions on any multinational wishing to set up in their community. Although not against the television networks they do insist that some broadcasts are made in their language at peak-viewing hours; and they do keep their local celebrations to which the media takes second place. They will support representative democracy, but they go to the city council meeting *en masse* both to remind their representatives that they are there to represent them, and so to exercise some control. So when people find themselves unable to control the world, they simply shrink the world to the size of their community.

Thus, urban movements do address the real issues of our time, although neither on the scale nor terms that are adequate to the task. And yet they do not have any choice since they are the last reaction to the domination and renewed exploitation that submerges our world. But they are more than a last, symbolic stand and desperate cry: they are symptoms of our contradictions, and therefore potentially capable of superseding these contradictions. They are the organizational forms, the live schools, where the new social movements of our emerging society are taking place, growing up, learning to breath, out of reach of the state apparatuses, and outside the closed doors of repressed family life. They are successful when they connect all the repressed aspects of the new, emerging life because this is their specificity: to speak the new language that nobody yet speaks in its multifaceted meaning. When the vocabulary becomes too restricted (a single focus on rent control, for instance) the movements lose their appeal and become yet another interest group in a pluralist society. When they try to impose their programme, they become a counter-society, and collapse under the combined pressure of multinational capital, a mass media system, and the bureaucratic state.

Urban movements do, however, produce new historical meaning – in the twilight zone of pretending to build within the walls of a local community a new society they know to be unattainable. And they do so by nurturing the embryos of tomorrow's social movements within the local Utopias that urban movements have constructed in order never to surrender to barbarism.

34

History in the City

Cities are the products of history, both of the urban forms and functions inherited from the past, and of the new urban meaning assigned to them by conflictive historical change. While the former observation is generally accepted, the latter one is unusual and yet is fundamental to the understanding of urban change.

The observation of the five major urban social movements that occurred in different periods of history and in various cultural contexts provides support for this interpretation.

The revolution of the *comunidades in sixteenth century Castilla* expressed the attempt to historically define the city as a new political institution, as a new form of institutional organization of society, in opposition to the absolutist monarchy's project for building an imperial nation-state with the support of the nobility and the Church. Thus the conflict was directly connected to what seems to have been the major historical debate in late medieval cities and at the beginning of the Modern Age: what were the forms and institutions of the new European states to be when they were about to undertake global expansion which would lead in most cases to primitive accumulation for capitalism (although it could, as in the case of Spain, lead to the mercantile appropriation of wealth to finance wars and bureaucracies)? Fernand Braudel has correctly emphasized the novelty and importance of the conflict over the political meaning of the new cities:

> 'The West was, as it were, the luxury of the world. The towns there had been brought to a stan-
> dard hardly found anywhere else. They had made Europe's greatness. But although this fact is
> very well known, the phenomenon is not simple . . . The main, the unpredictable thing, was that
> certain towns made themselves into autonomous worlds, city-states, buttressed with privileges
> (acquired or extorted) like so many juridicial ramparts. Perhaps in the past historians have insisted
> too much on the legal factors involved, for if such considerations were indeed sometimes more
> important than, or of equal importance to, geographical, sociological, and economic factors, this
> last category did count to a large extent. What is privilege without material substance?
>
> In fact, the miracle in the West was not so much that everything sprang up from the eleventh
> century after having first been almost annihilated with the disaster of the fifth. History is full of
> those slow secular up and down movements, urban expansion, birth and rebirth: Greece from the
> fifth to second century B.C., Rome too; Islam from the ninth century, China under the Sungs.
> But these revivals always featured two runners, the State and the City . . . The State usually won
> and the city then remained subject and under a heavy yoke. The miracle of the first great urban
> centuries in Europe was that the town won entirely, at least in Italy, Flanders, and Germany. It
> was able to try the experiment of leading a completely separate life for quite a long time. This was
> a colossal event. Its genesis cannot be pinpointed with certainty, but its enormous consequences
> are visible.'[148]

In Castilla, the cities did not win their conflict with the state. And, as was pointed out in Part 1, this historical outcome marked Spanish society forever. Their struggle was aimed at the redefinition of urban meaning, and the transformation of the cities into communes, both as forms of state and as experiments in grassroots democracy. For the monarchy, on the other hand, the city should supply the support for an administrative machinery whose origin was in God, and close to Him, in the king, whose ultimate aim was to win the supply of American gold, and whose *raison d'être* was the conquest of the world and competition with the other empires for European soil. As we agreed in Part 1, the *comunidades* as a historical actor was not an incipient bourgeoisie, but the cities themselves. Nor was the Spanish monarchy the expression of the feudal order even if it relied on the nobility. The conflict was acted out by the city and state; and the definition of urban meaning was at the core of this conflict, because only by absorbing state functions would cities have been able to maintain a free space. Yet at the level of the imperial nation-state, it was imperative to have territorial domination over a world-wide hinterland conquered by the sword of its fanatic warriors. The two spaces were mutually exclusive, as were the two political forces that they were assigned to support. That is why, to some extent, the experience of the *comunidades*, while being a late medieval urban revolution, poses a debate closely connected to our current issues: the self-management of a free space versus the global reach of the new empires.

The *Commune of Paris* represents the transition between two forms of historical conflict: one, pre-capitalist, between the city and the state, very much in the same terms as the one expressed by the *comunidades* in Castilla centuries earlier; another one, proto-capitalist, between the people of Paris and the beginning of a proletarian vanguard, reacting against the evils of capitalism (the speculators, property owners, renters) more than industrial capitalism itself (the industrial bourgeoisie was never opposed as such by the *communards*). From the point of view of the adversary of the *communards*, both aspects (the all-powerful state and the real estate speculators) came together in the shape of city planning, represented by the public works and urban renewal undertaken by Haussmann, with the triple purpose of creating an urban grid determined by economic criteria, ordering the city to make easier the military repression of popular upheavals, and above all, cleaning, marking, and symbolically defining Paris with the new permanence and scale of the French state, thereby establishing anew the secular power of its bureaucracy over the turmoil of political representation that was part of the Parisians' revolutionary goal.

Thus the Commune was also a struggle over the urban meaning of Paris, and through it of modern French cities, both between local autonomists and state centralists, and between workers and women asking for use value (low rents, housing, services) and real estate speculators (petty landlords combined with financial interests) seeking the transformation of the urban space into an even more profitable commodity calculated on the basis of its exchange value.

La Commune, caught in the transition between two historical epochs, fought two different, although articulated, conflicts over the definition of urban meaning: the city as freedom and the city as use value, against the state's project for the city as a low level administrative outlet and the capitalists' interests in the city as a valuable space on which to make a profit.

The experience of Glasgow offers a more clear-cut case. Here we were in the core of industrial capitalism. The city as an autonomous, social or political entity had largely disappeared. What women and workers wanted was a decent city and economic security in their newly commodified social relationships. The state was no longer seen as the enemy, except by members of the scarcely influential communist vanguard. The movement remorselessly appealed to the state to impose on capital the respect of fair economic and social contracts. The city was considered by the (dominant) industrial fraction of capital in terms of production, but was desired by the working class in terms of consumption (or appropriation of use value). In between, the financial fraction of capital and their rentiers tried to use the city for profit, extracting from the workers not only their surplus value but also their wages. The strikers from Glasgow, and very soon from the rest of Britain, rebelled against this over-exploitation. They reluctantly accepted the capitalist relationships of production, but they wanted protection and security. They wanted the city to be part of a social wage for them. They appealed to the state to control the rapacity of the money-makers by rationalizing capitalist production and by reaching a social contract with the labour movement. So, from then on, the city came to represent production, circulation and management for capital and use value, translated into collective consumption for labour. And the residential segregation in space ensured the spatial support for the separate expression of class-based local cultures.

So, on the one hand the city disappeared in the economic process but on the other moved towards neighbourhood life. The conflict over urban meaning under industrial capitalism lead to relatively common ground: space and cities were secondary to production and classes. Yet history did not stop with early capitalist industrialization. New challenges to urban meaning, contracted in the relationship between capital and labour, appeared with the broadening of the definition of use value, and with the conflict over the social process of this definition.

Veracruz was a link between two worlds and this was reflected in the *movimiento inquilinario*. First, it represented, as in Glasgow, the revolt against the commodification of the living conditions by rentiers and speculators. It was not, however, an anti-capitalist movement, but a movement against the domination of exchange value over use value under the impact of capitalist expansion in Mexico. But second, and more fundamentally, the *inquilinarios* represented an anti-urban movement. While they sought to negotiate the level of rents, they did not, unlike the rent strikers of Glasgow, appeal to the state to intervene, in spite of the willingness of one sector to do so. At heart, they did not want a welfare system, but did desire a new society, free of foreigners, speculators, and policemen. Their adversaries were precisely those foreigners who were, simultaneously, the speculators. For the colonizers, Veracruz was still a colony and presented a simple chance to make money that would either be sent home or else invested to re-establish the colonial pattern. The Veracruz movement was at the same time an urban movement for the use value of the city against capitalist speculation and an anti-urban movement against the dependent city. In that sense it foreshadowed the squatter movements in Latin America that would construct their own social world on the periphery of the city, and would relate to the city only for instrumental reasons. So they still demanded housing and services – evidence of the dilemma they were in between the cultural autonomy they would like to have preserved and their desire to have a share of the product of the new urban economy into which they had unwittingly been absorbed. Yet, unlike most of the squatter settlements we have studied, the *inquilinarios* of Veracruz did not call upon the state, and distanced themselves from any political apparatus that could manipulate them into a relationship where they might be the client. In fact, this is why they were massacred, but is also the reason for their symbolic value to the few urban movements that are striving today in Latin America for autonomy in the development of an alternative definition of their own city.

The community-based revolts we observed in the *American inner cities during the 1960s* offer a much more complicated picture, and their conflictive pattern is also closer to the core of our research findings. Yet we can clearly distinguish, again using the helpful typology proposed by Tilly, between reactive movements that fought against the destruction of neighbourhoods and urban decay, and proactive movements that used the ghettos as a space for satisfying urban demands and developing a basis for autonomous power. In the first case, the conflict over urban meaning was between the new dominant class' attempt to adapt the space of inner cities to the new functions of the informational mode of development, and the working class neighbourhoods' defense of their rights to urban use value, the very goal upon which they had based their acceptance of the system.

In the second case, the restructuring of American space brought millions of blacks into urban reservations where they were supposed to feed into the informal economy. But they reacted by asking for jobs, welfare, and political self-determination. The conflict over urban meaning was between two different projects for relating urban space to residential ethnic communities:

1 For the new dominant class, either blacks had to accept their ghettos as they were (market solution), or they could be concentrated and controlled in public housing projects (state solution). In addition, some liberal ideologists called for desegregation, but without being able to take any measures (with the exception of the most unpopular one: busing) to enforce this ideal.
2 For the majority of blacks, the ideal was to keep their space of autonomy and freedom, while gaining the benefits of adequate housing and public services. Their project was a sound autonomous city within the city.

The stalemate led to a situation of effective spatial autonomy with the black community in the ghettos, as well as an increase in urban decay, marginal integration into the informal economy, and increasing violence, crime, and dominance of the drug culture. The unsolved conflict over urban meaning in American inner cities led to widespread meaninglessness and to the progressive disintegration of spatial forms and functions, as expressed by the continuing and massive residential abandonment.

Thus, at each point in history, the conflict over urban meaning observed in five major urban social movements expressed the major themes of the historical debate being fought between social actors. Sometimes the conflict was largely connected to the class conflict. On other occasions, it was the power relationship between alternative forms of the state that dominated. In none of the cases observed were the gender relationships at the core of the conflict, in spite of the decisive participation of women in the movements: a striking verification of our hypothesis about the historical hierarchy between relationships of production, power and gender. In all cases, the city was shaped by the historical struggle fought over its urban meaning, the basic source of its urban functions and forms. Beyond the observation of the evolution of the city in history, our analysis has been able to show how history has embedded in the city: that is, cities are not in history, they *are* history.

35

Conclusion: The Theory of the Good City and A Good Theory of the City

The result of our cross-cultural investigation is not a new formal theory of the city or society. It was not intended to be. Our purpose and our achievement has been to ask the right questions, to point at the sources of historical structures and urban meaning, and to discover the complex mechanisms of interaction between different and conflicting sources of urban reproduction and urban change. By considering cities as the result of an endless historical struggle over the definition of urban meaning by antagonistic social actors who oppose their interests, values, and projects, we have been able to understand urban change, as well as the limits of such change, in a deliberately selected variety of spatial situations and historical contexts.

The product of our research is not a formalized framework of abstract categories that should now be combined in different ways to code empirical situations, thus changing their labels without adding any new knowledge. Rather, we end up with a box of research tools with which we can explore in a particular manner the fundamental issue of social change. As a result of the use we have made of these tools in the observation of a variety of urban mobilizations, we have been able to propose a number of ideas about the relationship between social conflict and the production of urban meaning, and our case studies have not falsified the main ideas of our interpretative framework. Furthermore, by reconstructing the specific socio- cultural contexts in which urban processes take place, we have been able to demonstrate one of our basic hypotheses: that, although urban social change operates in a similar way at a general level, the bringing together of the elements of such change, as well as its outcome, closely depends upon the historical context in which it takes place. Therefore, instead of a general trans-historical theory of the city, we have presented theorized histories of the production of urban meaning. This is our answer to the question relentlessly asked by urbanists, planners, architects, communities, political officials, and people in general: what is a good city? Kevin Lynch, in his important book, *A Theory of Good City Form*, provides a detailed, specific and documented answer whose main normative criteria we basically share. Yet the obvious objection immediately rises: how, for whom, and by whom is such a city produced? Lynch ends his *magnum opus* with the recognition that his theory, as all normative theories of urbanism, '. . . has a number of deficiencies. Most glaring is the lack of a complementary theory on how cities come to be and how they function . . .'[149] And he adds that, 'No theory will be mature until it shows how performance tends to vary with political and social context'.[150]

In sum, we need a theory able to explain how city forms (and therefore good city forms) are produced. At the same time, we need a theoretical perspective flexible enough to account for the production and performance of urban functions and forms in a variety of contexts. Our book wishes to be a step in the construction of such a theory and such a perspective. It can only be a segment of a comprehensive theory, because we have focused our attention on the production of new urban meaning by urban social movements when most existing research has dealt with the management of urban functions (planning) and the creation of urban forms (design). Yet it is our belief that unless we uncover the secrets as to how cities come to historical life with a given social meaning, functions remain a matter of technological adjustment, and forms purely a question of subjective taste. Thus our research effort has tried to connect with two other major continuing projects in current intellectual endeavour. We have attempted to introduce in the analysis of social change the materiality of spatial forms resulting from the conflict between dominant classes and social movements. And we have also attempted to contribute to the understanding of how new urban meaning is produced, thus opening the way for the discovery of the historical process that could lead to the promising new urban forms envisioned by the most advanced urban designers.

Our hope and bet is that, notwithstanding the threatening storms of the current historical conflicts, humankind is on the edge of mastering its own future, and therefore of designing its good city. At last, citizens will make cities.

The Methodological Appendices

The Methodological Appendices

General Methodological Issues

The Strategy of Theory Building

This book intends to contribute to a theory of urban social movements, within the broader framework of a theory of social change and of a theory of the city. The selected case studies presented here are something else than empirical verifications of the theory. They have been used as steps in the process of theory building and have been chosen with this purpose in mind. Thus the theory has been partly generated (and not just tested) by the analysis of a series of urban mobilizations in a variety of socio-cultural contexts and historical movements. This explains the organization of the book, relying as it does on a series of analyses that integrate theory and observation around a particular, dominant theme and finishing with an attempt to merge the different but parallel elaborations in a final theoretical chapter.

This cautious strategy is the result of a serious effort to rectify the excessive theoretical formalism that has flawed social sciences in general and some of our earlier work in particular. As a healthy reaction against short-sighted empiricism that forbade human thought to go beyond those situations that were measurable by rudimentary statistical tools, a series of theoretical attempts have been made in recent years to construct a system of categories and propositions from which research could recode observations in a helpful, cumulative form. Yet all efforts (from functionalism to structuralism, or from symbolic interactionism to Marxism) ended up in constructing a series of formal models that were as sophisticated as they were irrelevant. Their application in research led to a painful recording of observed experience, in which the conceptual frameworks added nothing to the understanding of that experience. The source of these difficulties derived from the reluctance of the social sciences to accept the reality of their underdevelopment as sciences and to acknowledge the differential and tortuous path of their advancement in relationship to the natural sciences. Between the negation of the possibility of any objective knowledge of human action, and the idealistic attempt to construct a comprehensive general theory as a pre-condition for any significant effort of investigation, the reality of research throughout historical experience has always made its breakthroughs in a different way. Instead of reinventing a theory or proposing a new approach of doing research, our effort has been to follow, as closely as possible, the experience of the most fruitful studies, accepting in advance the primitive state of our knowledge and of our methods.

Thus, our strategy of theory building relied on a sequence of articulated research operations:

1 We started by asking some fundamental research questions (presented in the Introduction), themselves generated by the social issues arising from the historical experience.
2 We asked these questions at a very general and tentative level, by using concepts and approaches inherited from intellectual traditions adequate to the issues we were trying to understand. For instance, it would be difficult to undertake an analysis of social conflict without using, as a starting point, the Marxist tradition of class struggle; or to refer to state domination without recalling the Weberian arguments; or to undertake the analysis of the cultural determinants of spatial forms without considering recent contributions to the theory of urban design. In our theoretical chapter we made explicit the variety of intellectual sources with which we armed ourselves.
3 We then proceeded to construct a provisional theoretical framework that, without being a general theory of society, was comprehensive enough to stimulate our thinking and our observations along a variety of analytical dimensions.
4 On such a basis, we then selected the social situations (or cases) whose observation could potentially be most fruitful for generating substantive analyses aimed at constructing a theory of urban social movements. (We will discuss below how our research design fitted into this perspective.)
5 The following step was to carry out the actual empirical analysis for each case, and to construct *ad hoc* analytical models enabling us to answer the same general theoretical questions in each one of the empirical situations observed. As a result of this work, new questions arose, several concepts were modified, some propositions were rejected, and new ones were incorporated into the general framework of our tentative theory.

6 We then had the conditions to summarize our thinking in a more systematic form, as modified by experience. The theory of urban social change proposed in Part 6 represents the outcome of this effort.
7 With this theory in mind we reanalysed the specific cases, to verify some general propositions and to correct some of our *ad hoc* interpretations.
8 We finally integrated, at least in an indicative way, the theory and the analysis of the case studies, although we deliberately refused to formalize all the findings in a single systematic, theoretical framework (for reasons that we will explain shortly).

The process we have just described is not the reconstructed logic of our research, but represents the actual intellectual journey that we have undertaken in the writing of this book.

The epistemological assumptions embodied in such theory-building, as well as the actual process itself, have very important consequences on the theoretical outcome. While we were able to propose, at least tentatively, a general structural formula underlying the collective action defined as urban social movement, we strictly rooted the general formula in conditions that were historically specific. The elements of the formula were made up with the social problems specific to each social context. If the presence of the proposed formula was a necessary and sufficient condition for the existence of an urban social movement, the origins of the formula in the actual social practice must have been contingent upon specific historical processes. Finally, our theory of urban social movements was explicitly related to a broader theory of urban social change, and, implicitly, to a theory of history and society. Yet we did not develop the implications and elements of such a theory, although we hypothesized some basic social relationships that appeared to refer to the crucial issues posed by historical praxis, and that seemed to be congruent with the theory of urban social movements on which we grounded our cross-cultural observation.

Thus, from the outset we rejected the building of a formal theory of urban social change. By a formal theory we understand a theory whose main concerns are trans-historical comprehensiveness and logical consistency. We believe that social sciences have an historical and experimental character, unlike formal sciences, such as mathematics. Therefore the crucial test for a social theory is its adequacy rather than its coherence. (By adequacy we mean the capacity of a series of intellectual tools to generate new knowledge on a given phenomenon.)

As Gaston Bachelard pointed out, the most useful concepts are those flexible enough to be deformed and rectified in the process of using them as instruments of knowledge. It is this capacity of enabling us to understand social processes and situations, and not the endless exercise of recoding experience in a comprehensive paradigm, that is the test for the fruitfulness of a theory.

So, what we need is not trans-historical theories of society but theorized histories of social phenomena. This is not, and should not be, a general epistemological position. It is possible that we could reach a cumulative and comprehensive theoretical paradigm of history and societies, but our knowledge is not at that stage, nor will it be in the near future. Therefore we need humble but effective strategies of theory building able to take us away from empiricism without loosing us in the artificial paradises of the grand theory: a cautious path, maybe, but one that we have persistently tried to pursue.

The Procedures of Demonstration

The process of theory building expressed in this book relies on a series of interconnected empirical studies. These studies support a series of theoretical propositions verified according to standard methodological procedures generally used in social research. The description and justification of each procedure are presented in the appendix to each chapter. In fact, we have not used a general methodology, but have tried to maximize methodological rigour by adapting the procedures of demonstration to the technical problems posed by each case. So our actual methodology has to be found in the solution we give to the problem of demonstrating each statement in each empirical situation.

Nevertheless, there is a general methodological approach to the question of proof of our theoretical propositions that we consider useful to summarize here.

The general framework of our theory of urban social change appears to be compatible with our theory of urban social movements. Both theories are not only internally consistent but also provide some meaning for the historical phenomena under observation. Part 6 substantiates in detail these statements. Our theory of urban social movements is itself coherent and carries weight in relation to the theoretical interpretations of the processes observed in each case study. Finally, each case study is explained by an analytical framework the main propositions of which are not falsified by reliable systematic observation.

For each case study to fulfill the conditions of falseability, fundamental to all empirical research, they had to meet four conditions:

1 A systematic structure of unequivocal propositions establishing given observable relationships between given empirical facts.
2 Such a systematic structure of propositions had to carry meaning in terms of the overall theory that informs it.

3 All the facts had to be empirically established.
4 All the relationships between these facts had to be empirically verified in the sense postulated by the theory.

In order to meet all these conditions we have constructed analytical models for each case study. In fact, we only present in the book a semi-formalized model for the case of the Latino community in San Francisco and a somewhat more formalized model to analyse the Citizen Movement in Madrid. The reason for not presenting here all the models and for generally relying on an analytical discourse is that such a methodology would go beyond the level of accuracy of our theoretical analysis. It is senseless to provide highly formalized structures at the current level of tentative theoretical elaboration. In fact the social sciences are sick of formalism because they entered into the process of reproduction before reaching the minimum conditions of scientific production.

Nevertheless we have presented some analytical models (particularly for the case of Madrid) to indicate the general logic that underlies all of our research, a logic that can easily be unveiled behind the interpretative discourse referred to in each case study. In these models we outlined the specific proposition, established the rules of the demonstration, and showed the correspondence between our propositions and the observations. When some observation contradicted the model, we either rectified it or we provided an *ad hoc* explanation for the 'deviant case'. The final assumption of causality was sustained by the fact that our exploratory model was the simplest, most meaningful and comprehensive of those capable of organizing our observations around the issues posed by our research questions. Thus, as in all the best social research, we cannot say what is true, but what it makes sense to say without being false. We are not yet in a position to predict, but cumulative research on these lines will strengthen us enough in the future to experiment, that is, to predict and manipulate social practice.

To be sure, other questions would organize the same observations differently, to obtain different answers. For instance, where we see social movements, other researchers might see reward-maximizing strategies. This is not a problem. Our reading of reality, our concerns with society, are not the only ones. The crucial question is to know whether or not – *vis-à-vis* our questions – what experience shows is contradictory with our explanation. In all of the case studies presented in the book it seems that our analysis provides the simplest and most meaningful interpretation of the phenomenon under observation, for reasons specifically justified for each case.

The presentation of some formalized models is simply a device to help make clear the underlying logic of our demonstration. Formalization does not add any explanatory value to our analysis: it only provides more clarity to the presentation of our implicit system of proof. The reader should consider the analytical models as a primitive sample of what could be done by social research once the theoretical foundations are solid enough and the observational techniques for observation can be said to be fully reliable.

Yet, how accurate can a demonstration be, based upon a limited number of case studies? As we said in the Introduction, case studies have always been praised because of their capacity for allowing in-depth analysis, but blamed because of their singularity, making any extrapolation of the findings impossible. Nevertheless, we should remember that all social situations are unique. A representative sample of the residents of Madison, Wisconsin in 1977, or even of the American manual workers in 1980, is as singular a universe as the neighbourhood mobilization in the Mission District of San Francisco in 1971. The general value of any observation depends on the use to which it is put. If we want to predict the outcome of a political election, an opinion poll of potential voters is an adequate instrument (at least, sometimes). If we want to understand the new cultural patterns introduced by illegal immigrants, we will have to establish a typology of ethnic communities and weigh their differential evolution in relationship to mainstream society. And if we want to elaborate a theory of urban social movements on the basis of historical experience, we must observe unique situations in which a particular phenomenon, considered by our theory to be crucial, is amplified. This was the rationale that informed our research design. It is only when we have a grounded theory of urban social movements and a full understanding of how they relate to the evolution of cities, that we will be able to compare mobilized and passive neighbourhoods *vis-à-vis* their differential effect on urban functions and forms. Thus, while case studies cannot provide a systematic verification of accepted propositions, they are invaluable in the pathbreaking efforts towards new theories.

Finally, though the case study approach is at the core of our research, we have used in support of our demonstration a very wide range of methods, from participant observation to factor-analysis, and from social mapping to oral history. It is our conviction that all research tools are legitimate and useful when they remain tools at the service of the research purpose, instead of forcing a theory to adapt to the procedures bureaucratically defined as being the only scientific ones. Intellectual freedom includes the freedom to choose the adequate working tools.

Techniques of Data Collection

The research presented here is based upon a rich and diverse data basis. To obtain this base we used a pragmatic approach that maximized access to relevant, unveiled information. Within the limits of a clear, unambiguous and non-manipulatory attitude towards the subjects of our observation, we used every means possible to learn in detail what actually happened. Our approach combined three main techniques:

1 In-depth information on the observed situation through written sources and documents. We always exhausted the recorded information before turning to the field.

2 Extensive participant observation in the local situation for a long time. We had 16 months of field work in Paris, eight months in Santiago de Chile, 20 months in Madrid, and 12 months in San Francisco. We were fully involved in the processes we observed, yet always made explicit our role as researcher, and so maintained the necessary distance.

3 The most important source of our data was, in every case, interviews with key informants. It must be noted that we selected these informants on the basis of quite extensive knowledge of the situation before meeting them. Therefore, we were able, while interviewing them, to undertake three simultaneous operations:

a   Obtain all the information they would provide us with, while cross-checking it with other sources and other informants.

b   Learn the particular position of the person and therefore his or her particular bias.

c   Being able, towards the end of the interview, to engage in a debate with the interviewee, and therefore actually test his or her role in the social process to which the interview referred.

Our interview's guideline generally left aside individual attitudes of the interviewee, to focus only on two aspects: quality of the information through which we could reconstruct a given social process; and the interviewee's role as a social actor in the social process we were studying.

It has to be emphasized that each one of the interviewees or informants were fully aware of the research context of our interaction. This was not only an elementary professional rule, but also a specific research technique. Let us explain. They all knew that we were fully aware of the situation, and that we had many sources of information. So they could not hide information. Besides, they were willing to co-operate with the research without much reservation. They therefore generally engaged in a debate with us about their particular point of view, while still providing crucial information in support of their position. Thus, through the interviews we obtained two different and equally crucial elements:

1 Very detailed information that we cross-checked and verified from different sources until we were able to reconstruct unequivocally a particular social process.

2 The positions of solidly identified actors in a given debate that enabled us to reconstruct the interaction between different subjects in each process of urban mobilization.

It is obvious that the richness of our information and the accuracy of our observation were only possible because the social actors under study fully trusted us and our collaborators. Why was it so? And how was it compatible with the necessary distance and objectivity of any serious scientific research? The answer is a personal one, namely our schizophrenia between academic research and political commitment, and in all the situations observed we were considered as both researcher and political participant (less so in Paris, although the statement stands for the research team). So, communication continuously developed on two different, although closely entangled, channels. Afterwards the analysis, *in vitro*, made it possible to separate the elements that were necessary for the construction of a general explanatory framework.

We must insist that the actors of the movements we studied were perfectly aware of the nature and purpose of our research. Why were they so open and co-operative? Besides the basic condition of personal trust, the main motivation was their enormous need to understand their own experience, and the feeling that they required some distant research procedure able to provide them with the knowledge they could not distill from an experience that was too close to themselves. So, in fact, they wanted us to research in the hope of enhancing their understanding of their own practice, and so increase their effectiveness.

The Research Design

The book is organized around the attempt to build a theory of urban social movements. The core of our theory is to understand how urban movements connect collective consumption issues with cultural identity and political power. So we selected three cases that would maximize, separately, each one of these three dimensions. Suburban Paris was the field work for collective consumption-orientated trade unionism. San Francisco provided the ideal setting for studying the connection between diverse sources of cultural identity and urban mobilization. Squatters in Santiago de Chile, as well as in other Latin American cities, offered the test for the intimate relationship between urban movements and the political system. Finally, the Citizen Movement in Madrid gave us the opportunity of observing the conditions and effects of the link between urban demands, culture, and politics in the making of a social movement. The diversity of socio-cultural contexts we studied met the additional condition of a cross-cultural observation without which all proposed theories would be parochial and ethnocentric.

Finally, because of the historical perspective inherent in our theory, we wanted to observe the relationship between social movements and urban meaning in a variety of historical contexts, selected (within the scope of our knowledge) according to the transitional moments between modes of production and stages of a mode of production.

A Personal Note

This research design is not the rationalization of an accidental experience. I actually undertook to embark on cross-cultural research of urban social movements (as described in a theoretical paper delivered at the Seventh World Congress of Sociology meeting in Varna, Bulgaria) in 1970. Since then I have systematically explored the most innovative urban practices around the world. I went to Chile in 1970, 1971, and 1972, to work on, and with, the *campamentos*

during the Unidad Popular. I went to Madrid in 1977–79 to follow closely the high point of the Citizen Movement in the country's transition towards a democratic state. And I decided to study San Francisco, instead of any other American city, when I discovered its cultural diversity and the vitality of its neighbourhood movement. I must confess, however, that the only reason to study Paris was that I was living there, since the collective consumption unionism that I discovered was also present in most large cities around the world. So our research design issues from a deliberate, ten year effort to trace emerging urban social movements in different parts of the world. But it does also follow the reconstructed theoretical logic that informed the final project of this book when I undertook in Berkeley the analysis of data, theoretical elaboration and writing between 1979 and Summer 1982.

This, then, has been the progress of the study I present here: it is a combination of purposiveness and flexibility, programming and experience, theory and practice. It was born at the crossroads between research and politics.

Appendix to Part 2: The *Grands Ensembles* of Paris

The analysis of urban mobilization in the *Grands Ensembles* of Paris is based on the findings of field work carried on during two years by a team of four sociologists, including the author, in the suburban communities of Sarcelles and Val d' Yerres. At the same time a study was conducted on the evolution of housing policy using secondary data and interviewing of key policy makers. (The complete results of the research, including the analysis of squatters in Paris, as well as an exploratory study of 180 miscellaneous urban struggles in the entire area, have been reported in a research monograph: Manuel Castells, Eddy Cherki, Francis Godard, Dominique Mehl, *Sociologie des Mouvements Sociaux Urbains: Enquête sur la Région Parisienne* (Paris: CEMS, 1975, 2 volumes.))

The choice of Sarcelles and Val d' Yerres resulted from the preliminary study of housing policy. They were the first and the last *Grands Ensembles* built in Paris and clearly represented two poles of orientation in housing design and urban policy. The aim of the research was to compare the characteristics and outcomes of urban mobilization developing under two different realizations of a similar urban form. The

process of data collection combined three observational procedures:

1 Analysis of secondary data and written sources, including government documents; statistics and files provided by the developer (the SCIC); municipal archives; residents' associations bulletins and internal documents; and local newspapers.
2 Participant observation in the everyday life of the community, including neighbourhood meetings, for a period of one year in each community. (1973 in Sarcelles, 1974 in Val d' Yerres).
3 56 focused interviews with key informants on the *Grands Ensembles*, on Sarcelles' local life, and on Val d' Yerres social activity. All interviews were tape-recorded. The average length of the interview was 65 minutes. The list of interviews included all significant local actors: management of the *Grand Ensembles*; local officials; neighbourhood militants of all associations; political parties; labour unions; and cultural groups. We conducted group interviews with the most important associations, to include a variety of opinions in order to crosscheck the information. The list of interviews follows.

List of Interviews with Key Informants as the Basis of the Empirical Data for the Analysis of Urban Mobilization in the *Grands Ensembles* of Paris

Interviews on Housing Policy in Paris

1 Director of the *Direction Territoriale* of the SCIC (in charge of all decisions on new housing location).
2 Director of Land Policy, SCIC (*Gestion B* office).
3 Deputy Director of Public Housing (HLM), City of Paris.
4 Group of technicians of the Public Housing Office (HLM), City of Paris.
5 Director of Public Relations, SCIC.
6 Director of Psycho-Sociology Department, SCIC.
7 Director of SCIC for the *departement* (province) of Essonne (where Val d' Yerres is located).

Interviews on Sarcelles

8 Managing Director of the *Grand Ensemble* (SCIC).
9 Manager of the Young Workers Home.
10 Mayor of Sarcelles.
11 President of the Residents' Council.
12 Municipal City Councilman, former leader of the *Association Sarcelloise*, former elected member of the Residents' Council, member of the PCF.
13 Municipal Councilman, in charge, with the Neighbourhood Council, of Sarcelles 8.
14 Another City Councilman (PCF).
15 Leader of the *Association Sarcelloise*, former secretary of local Chapter of the PSU.
16 Militant of the *Association Sarcelloise*, former elected member of the Residents' Council. (Interviewed jointly with another militant of the *Association Sarcelloise*.)
17 Former president of the Residents' Council.
18 Group interview with leaders and militants of the local Chapter of the CNL.
19 Group interview with leaders and militants of the local chapter of *Association des Familles*.
20 Group interview with the Homeowner's Associations.
21 The Secretary of a Homeowner's Association.
22 Secretary of Parents Associations, local chapter, (*Federation Armand*).
23 Secretary of Parents Associations, local chapter (*Federation Cornec*).
24 Secretary of the local chapter of the PSU.
25 Secretary of the local chapter of the PS (Socialist Party).
26 Secretary of the local chapter of the Socialist Youth (PS).

27 Secretary of the local chapter of the PCF.
28 A leader of local chapter of the CGT (labour union).
29 A leader of local chapter of the CFDT (labour union).
30 Editor of *Villes Nouvelles* (local magazine).
31 A social worker (neighbourhood Vignes-Blanches).

Interviews on Val d' Yerres

32 Managing Director of the *Grand Ensemble* (SCIC).
33 Manager of La Ferme (Socio-Cultural Centre).
34 Chief architect of the Val d' Yerres.
35 Social worker, Boussy, (SCIC).
36 Social worker, Epinay, (SCIC).
37 Social worker, Quincy, (SCIC).
38 Municipal social worker, Epinay.
39 Group interview with leaders and militants of the GERB (a series of three interviews).
40 A militant from the GERB.
41 Group interview with leaders and militants of the CRI.
42 Group interview with leaders and militants of CNL chapter at Epinay.
43 Secretary of CNL Chapter at Quincy.
44 Secretary of *Association des Familles* at Epinay.
45 President of the Residents' Council.
46 Secretary of Association for Culture and Leisure.
47 Militant of Parent's Association (Quincy).
48 Militant of Parent's Association (Epinay).
49 Militant of Association for Solidarity with Immigrant Workers.
50 Secretary of the Family Planning Association.
51 Leader of Homeowners Association at Epinay.
52 Leader of Homeowners Association at Boussy.
53 *Animateur* of the Jardin de l'Aventure.
54 Mayor of Boussy.
55 Mayor of Quincy.
56 Mayor of Epinay.

On the basis of the material collected, three forms of analysis were undertaken for each *Grand Ensemble*:

1 We identified the main urban problems at stake and we carefully studied the process by which they were produced and the policies attempted to manage them.
2 We observed each key social actor (management, associations, local governments, political parties, institutions, etc.) and analysed its behaviour and internal structure.
3 We identified each urban struggle and studied it by summarizing existing information on all aspects of the struggle on a coded card for each struggle. We proceeded in such a way for 21 struggles in Sarcelles and 12 in Val d' Yerres.

A Note on the Relationship between Urban Mobilization and Voting for Left Wing Parties in the Local Elections in the Suburbs of the Paris Metropolitan Area

At the time of completion of this book (June 1982), the final results of the statistical study we are conducting with Michael Aiken on the determinants of voting for the left in French municipal elections are not available. Nevertheless, the first findings clearly support our hypothesis: that is, that suburban location in Paris and residence in rapidly growing suburbs (mostly the *Grands Ensembles*) favour the left, for reasons explained in Part 2.

The first report on our study is a paper by Michael Aiken, *Victory on the Left: Strategies and Correlates of Left Success in Local Elections in France* (Paper delivered at the Social Science Research Council Conference on Local Institutions in National Development, Bellaggio, Italy, March 1982).

The results presented in Table A–1 (that we have constructed to relate Aiken's findings to this specific hypothesis) seem to indicate a positive relationship between suburban location, rapid suburban growth, and voting for the left.

Table A.1 Pearsonian correlation coefficients between city characteristics and left success among 219 French of size 30,000 or more in 1971, by type of city. (N = 219)

Type of City	Left Voting 1977	Increase in Left Voting 1971–1977	Left Won 1977
– Central City of Largest 19 Metropolitan Regions.	–·17***	–·03	–·16***
– Independent City	–·25****	–·09*	–·04
– Suburb[a]	·35****	·11*	·13**
– Rapidly Growing Suburb	·26****	·10*	·14*

(a) 70 of the 97 suburbs of the study are located in the Metropolitan Area of Paris.

    * $p < 0.10$
    ** $p < 0.05$
    *** $p < 0.01$
    **** $p < 0.001$

Source: Michael Aiken, *Victory on the Left: Strategies and Correlates of Left Success in Local Elections in France*, Paper Delivered at the Conference on Local Institutions in National Development. Bellaggio, Italy, March 1982. (Table recontructed by ourselves on the basis of Aiken's data.)

These findings are particularly important when contrasted to other data presented by Aiken in his paper, in which he examines the relationship between the percentage increase in manufacturing labour force in a city in 1962–75 and the vote for the left in 1977, as well as the increase of votes for the left between 1971 and 1977. The figures show that the relationship is either negative or non-existent. Apparently, urban growth and not industrial growth is associated with left's success in local elections. In fact, the greatest gains for the left were in cities experiencing industrial decline. Local left wing voting in France appears to be the consequence of the defensive reaction of the old working class (in what Aiken calls independent cities) of the French province, and the result of the new political attitudes generated by the new social problems in the growing suburban areas of the big cities.

We emphasise the tentative nature of these observations and invite the reader to consult the results of the study when it is completed and published. Yet, we feel that it is important to point out this first indication of the relationship between urban mobilization and local politics on the lines suggested in our analysis of collective consumption trade unionism.

Appendix to Part 3:
The San Francisco Experience

Research Strategy in San Francisco

Our analysis of San Francisco focuses on the interaction between cultural identity and urban mobilization in the production of city's functions and forms. The subject matter of this part explains why we selected San Francisco as the urban scene to observe such a problem. Few cities in the industrialized world had such a diversity of urban sub-cultures, and few American cities were so neighbourhood-orientated and so prone to community organization. Within San Francisco we selected two communities that were very different but shared their emphasis on the affirmation of a cultural identity as the most important goal of their mobilization. (Here we use the word 'community' in a descriptive, non-theoretical sense, following the actors' own definition. Yet the term implies a self-proclaimed will of establishing cultural boundaries.) The study of the gay community was an obvious choice as it was the most visible, active, organized, and politically influential socio-cultural group in San Francisco. Besides, its experience was most unusual at the world level. On the other hand, we studied the Latino community in order to introduce a new, crucial element of the American scene: the poverty-stricken ethnic minorities. Although the black community in San Francisco was even more active and mobilized than the Latinos in the last two decades, it was unique to the Mission Neighbourhood mobilization of the period 1967–73 that we could observe the interaction between grassroots protest and the self-affirmation of an autonomous, largely immigrant culture. The purpose of the study was not to compare both communities, but to observe the interplay between culture and urban protest for two different cultures within the same city.

The methodology followed to study the two communities was very different. In the case of the Latino-based Mission Neighbourhood mobilization, we tried to reconstruct in all its details the process of urban protest and to understand the evolution of its internal structure through a formalized analytical model on which we could build, using information from one neighbourhood. By contrast, the main effort for the gay community focused on the analysis of its spatial organization and the role played by a culturally defined territory and the impact gays made on urban forms and local politics. We present in this appendix the research operations and data bases on which our analysis is founded.

Methodological Appendix to the Study of Urban Mobilization in the Mission District

Research Strategy

The study of the Mission was an in-depth case study of a relatively small neighbourhood whose experience of mobilization and community organization we examined in detail. The strategy of proof consists in reconstructing a 14-year span of social mobilization in such a way that the specific interpretation of the process became theoretically significant, logically consistent, and empirically sustained by a body of rich and detailed information.

To fulfil these goals we combined three different approaches:

1 The analysis of the neighbourhood, both in its urban and social dimensions, through the analysis of existing documentation and personal observation during one year of field work and research from November 1979 to December 1980.
2 The study of the community mobilization and organization in the Mission through a series of in-depth interviews by key informants.
3 The actual objective of the study was to understand the emergence and crisis of the Mission Coalition Organization (MCO) as well as to measure its impact on the city, in accordance with our theoretical concerns. This purpose was reinforced by the first two steps of the study, since it soon became apparent that the MCO's experience was the social background to which we were referring most of the current community-based activities. Besides, unlike the situation in 1980 when the Mission was not a particularly active community and even less an effective agent of urban change, the MCO used to be *the* large urban movement in San Francisco and its impact was still evident in the neighbourhood when we were there. Thus, understanding the MCO's history was the most fruitful contribution to the study of the relationship between minority neighbourhoods' protest and urban change.

To analyse the MCO experience we had, at the same time, a great problem and a major asset. We could not observe the process but only reconstruct it by calling on the memories of its actors, some of whom were impossible to locate. The asset was that, precisely because of time that had elapsed, we could reconstruct in our interviews the debates, alliances, conflicts, and projects that formed and destroyed the MCO. However these interviews could only take place successfully if we could obtain the basic information about the MCO from an independent source so that we could talk to its actors with a good deal of the information at our fingertips about the events which we wanted to debate, rather than just learn what happened. At this level we were extraordinarily fortunate to benefit, through Professor John Mollenkopf, from extensive documentation accumulated by Stanford University on the MCO, including very detailed research, in the form of an unpublished Ph.D. thesis by Robert A. Rosenbloom. Later on, Mike Miller, the main organizer of the MCO, gave us access to all his files.

Thus we combined two approaches: reconstruction of events on the basis of existing information, and analyses of the process on the basis of in-depth, carefully planned, interviews with key actors who could provide their part of the truth, and their view of the process. (Naturally they all were aware of the nature and purpose of this research.) Afterwards, it took months to assemble the pieces of such a small but incredibly complex world, by connecting information that previously had not been in one place since communication had broken down between the different sectors of the movement. Furthermore, the different views were exposed to us, free of implications, since the battle was over and we were an outsider. So we could check basic information from various independent sources, and we could also appreciate the different logics at work within a movement whose shadow was still present. Why were people so open to us? Besides the fact that they were nice people and had nothing to hide, we think they realized that what really mattered for us was to understand the process, and nothing else. And they too wanted to understand, since one of the great traumas of the experience was that the MCO fell apart without their people really knowing why, since they were totally involved in their struggle. On the basis of their trust and support, we could collect the most complete set of information and self-analyses we have ever had on any single urban movement. And on such a data basis, we developed our own analysis through the procedures described below.

Data Basis

The research on the Mission Neighbourhood mobilization was based on seven different, although interrelated sources, of unequal importance in terms of time and personal work, but equally crucial for the construction of the final picture:

1 Basic urban, economic, and social data, facilitated by the special collection of documents on the Mission,

gathered by the San Francisco City Planning Department. Its Mission Liaison Planner, Roger Herrera, generously provided me with all the information existing in 1980 on the Mission District. Most of the documents are cited as references in the footnotes to the chapter.
2 The reading and analysis of 10 years of the Mission-based Latino Magazine, *El Tecolote*, as well as of collections of local press clippings.
3 The analysis of an important fraction of the MCO's archives, that we could consult in the files still kept at the Organize Training Centre, in San Francisco.
4 The vast amount of information produced by the Stanford Community Development Study, and, particularly the extraordinary study by Rosenbloom on the Mission Coalition: Robert Arthur Rosenbloom, *Pressuring Policy Making from the Grassroots: The Evolution of an Alinsky-Style Community Organization* (Stanford: Department of Political Science, Stanford University, August 1976 unpublished Ph.D. thesis) In addition to the thesis itself, Professor Mollenkopf gave us access to internal memos of the MCO, budget documents, transcripts of interviews etc., that were kept in the Stanford study files.
5 Unpublished personal accounts of the process written by some of the main participants in the MCO, particularly, Mike Miller, *An Organizer's Tale* (San Francisco: 1976, 160 typewritten pages); and Leandro P. Soto, *Community Economic Development: More Than Hope for the Poor* (San Francisco, 1979, 76 typewritten pages). Of course, they were provided for us by their authors.
6 Personal observation of Mission's social life for five months, in a systematic way (January-May 1980) and for a year in a more casual manner. This included physical knowledge of the neighbourhood, meeting with the people, being around in the streets, spending time in the public agencies, drinking in the bars, eating in the restaurants, shopping in the area, low riding, attending community meetings, etc.
7 Yet, the core of our data basis came from 26 selected interviews with key community actors and informants in the period January-June 1980. The criteria for selecting the interviewees was: first all key actors and leaders in the Mission Coalition; second, leaders and members of other community organizations, particularly of *La Raza*, the only important community network that remained independent of the MCO experience; third, the most important community services and social agencies in the Mission; and fourth, experts with some crucial knowledge of the neighbourhood. Interviews were held in offices, people's homes, or bars. Some were accompanied by wonderful dinners, others were given during tours on foot, most took the form of a heated discussion on the past experience. Their average length was 70 minutes. 20 of the 26 interviews were tape-recorded, the others transcribed and summarized on tape. It was not an easy

task to find the key actors of a movement extinguished eight years before, but most were interviewed and, in fact, all the key tendencies of the MCO were represented. Of the leadership, only one major name was missing: Abel Gonzales, the boss of the Latino Labour Union (we were told that he was 'somewhere in Texas'). Yet we did discover the key actor, Ben Martinez, and went to see him in his house in the Los Angeles area. So, we give below the list of interviews that represent the basic material behind our analysis of the Mission. We have kept the names of the persons because the vagueness of their institutional role is more than balanced by their popularity in the San Francisco local scene. Thus, by giving the names we publicly guarantee the diversity and accuracy of our sources of information. To be sure, all agreed to have their names cited; the list is as follows:

List of Interviews Related to the Process of Community Mobilization in the Mission District, San Francisco

1 Mr Lee Soto, Director, OBECA–Arriba Juntos, founder of MCOR and of the MCO.
2 Mr Herman Gallegos, founder of MCOR and MCO, active leader of Community Services Organization, California.
3 Mr Ben Martinez, President of the MCO.
4 Mr Al Borvice, Director, *La Raza Centro Legal*
5 *La Raza en Accion Local*, staff members
6 Mr Celso Ortiz, *La Raza* law student, advocate planner.
7 Ms Luisa Ezquerro, Mission Planning Council, former MCO leader, former Model Cities manager.
8 Mr Juan Pifarre, Director, Mission Model Cities Neighbourhood
9 Mr Larry del Carlo, Mayor's Office of Community Development, Vice-President of the MCO, Candidate to Supervisor for District 6 (Mission).
10 Mr Mike Miller, Director, Organize Training Centre, Staff Director of the MCO.
11 Mr Manuel Larez, former president of LULAC (San Francisco), candidate for the presidency of the MCO, organizer of 24th Street Merchants' Association.
12 Mr Ed Sandoval, State President, MAPA.
13 Ms Flor Maria Crane, Vice-President, MCO, candidate for the presidency of the MCO.
14 Ms Rosario Anaya, Director, Mission Language and Vocational School.
15 Mr Bob Bustamante, MAPA (San Francisco), Latinos for Affirmative Action.
16 Mr Pedro Rodriguez, President of LULAC, San Francisco Chapter.
17 Mr Bob Dwight, Director, Mission Community Legal Defense.

18 Ms Norma Galvan, Real Alternatives Programme.
19 Staff, *Centro de Cambio*.
20 Mr Ricardo Hernandez, President, Latino Unity Council.
21 Ms Betty Anello, Operation Upgrade.
22 Mr Alfonso Maciel, Director, Mission Cultural Centre.
23 Dr Paul O'Rourke, Mission Neighbourhood Health Centre.
24 Mr Roger Herrera, Mission Liaison Planner, Department of City Planning, City of San Francisco (1980).
25 Mr Juan Gonzales, Director, *El Tecolote*.
26 Mr Jack Bourne, Director, Mission Development Housing Corporation.

An Analytical Model to explain the Social Logic Underlying the Urban Mobilization in the Mission

The interpretation of the Mission neighbourhood mobilization as presented in Part 3 relied on a systematic analysis of the information we collected, guided by the conceptual mechanism we constructed to understand this particular process. We explain this model below to communicate the research tools we have used. By presenting the model in a somewhat more formalized way, we do not add any explanatory value to what has already been demonstrated in Part 3, but we emphasize the main logical and empirical argument for the sake of clarity.

The logic of the demonstration can be summarized in two steps:

1 The choice of propositions implicit in our analysis, as formulated in terms of the categories proposed in our theoretical construction (Neighbourhood, Poverty, Minority, City, Class, Race, Community Organization, and State Power, from now on abbreviated as: N, P, M, CY, CL, R, CO, and SP).
2 The sequence of observed events in the community mobilization, whose logic should closely follow all the propositions on which our interpretation relies.

Let us consider both levels of the demonstration.

The System of Theoretical Propositions on Urban Mobilization as Related to the Mission Study

Before stating the system of propositions, let us keep in mind that:

1 Our theoretical construct, at this point of the analysis, is an *ad hoc* approach to the movement observed in the Mission. Although it obviously relates

to a broader theoretical framework, any generalization of the propositions requires a series of transformations, as formulated in Part 6.

2 The justification of the categories employed here (as well as of the relationships they are supposed to hold) have already been provided in Part 3. We only deal here with the formal expression of such relationships. The same argument applies to any substantive analysis of the proposed relationships.

Our analytical model of the Mission neighbourhood mobilization can be summarized by the following nine propositions:

1 The basic elements structuring the practice of the movement are N, P, M, CY, CL, and R. In fact they are intimate connections between pairs of elements: CY is the upgrading of N at the level of the overall social structure; so are CL for P, and R for M.

2 To relate to the overall social organization movements organized around these elements have to relate to SP in its different levels. Such a relationship must be mediated by organizational operators. When an organizational operator expresses N, P, and M, separately, we name it an interest group (IG); when they integrate N, CY, or P, CL, or M, R, to challenge SP, we name it a social movement (SM); when they integrate N, P, M, we name it a community organization (CO).

3 In the specific context of American inner cities, a direct articulation of N, P, M, CY, CL, R, cannot generate any CO, and therefore cannot jointly address SP, except for purely defensive single-issue purposes on which a coalition of interest groups may be formed.

4 A successful combination of N, P, and M, in the practice of a movement, creates a dynamic CO that will expand under two conditions:

a N, P, and M stick together.

b CO relates to SP in such a way that it affects SP's behaviour without coming under SP's control.

(It should be noted that condition a commands condition b.)

5 Although N, P, and M, may come together in a shared collective practice, they will not be able to stay together if they do not upgrade their social level (although consciousness raising) in the practice of the movement. Namely, N has to expand to CY, or P to CL, or M to R. If any one of the dimensions expands separately, CO becomes a social movement which integrates in its basic definition the other two dimensions under a subordinate form: an urban social movement (based upon CY), or a class struggle (based upon CL) or an Ethnic Social Movement (based upon R). If all dimensions simultaneously expand, CO becomes the basis for a multi-dimensional social movement challenging SP: it is what we used to name revolutions.

6 If neither element reaches the higher level of social practice, the basic structure of the movement

disintegrates, and therefore CO falls apart, and SP takes over.

Under the conditions of the Mission, neither N, P, or M were present as pure elements. There was actually a combination of NP and MP, with N and M as elements. Thus N could not rise to the CY level because of its P component that isolated itself from the mainstream of the N-based movement in the city. M was limited to shift towards a racial movement both by its P component (excluding broader M alliances) and by its specific ethnicity as *Latinos* (so that M in the Mission was actually M_1, within a potential $M_1 \ldots M_n$ range representing a variety of ethnic minorities). Under the two conditions described, the elements N, M, P, should split. Since P was a common element to NP and MP combinations, the split, according to our rules, should be between N and M components. Given the particular structure of the movement their opposition should take two forms:

a N versus M.

b Competition between N and M to appropriate the definition of P, as NP or as MP.

7 The more N and M oppose each other, through successive steps, the more CO is weakened, and the more SP tends to dominate CO. In the last stage the split between N and M (defined as conflicting NP and MP) is mirrored by the split between CO and SP: M is absorbed within CO and N is absorbed within SP. Under these conditions, the movement disintegrates.

8 The disintegration of a complex, powerful, and multisegmented urban movement leaves its trace in the urban scene where it took place, in the form of community-based, single-purpose organizations that represent the different dimensions of the movement, N, NP, P, M, MP. None of them becomes CO, and therefore all of them are submitted to SP without any real capacity of challenging its power.

9 The social outcomes of the movement express its articulation and the changing relationships between its elements. Thus, a movement whose pattern would follow the sequence as described (according to the logic we proposed), it should:

a Have a strong defensive relationship to SP because of the wide range of its interests groups (therefore, opposing those policies hostile to the neighbourhood's status quo).

b Be successful on poverty issues given the common ground between this element and the other components of the structure of the movement.

c Basically fail on urban or ethnic issues, given the contradictory relationship between N and M.

d Become powerless in relationship to SP, given the collapse of CO.

e Have the potential to prevent major disruptive initiatives in the neighbourhood because of the possible coming together of the multiple fragments of the movement as a new defensive reaction against an open threat from business, government, or other social group.

Let us now consider the correspondence between this theoretically meaningful, logically coherent chain of propositions, and the empirical observations we have gathered.

A Formalized Record of the Sequence of Events in the Process of Urban Mobilization in the Mission

The method we followed to observe the correspondence between the recorded information and the postulated model was the following:

1 We divided the process in several periods, according to major breakpoints of urban mobilization:
a   The pre-MCO period (MCOR mobilization).
b   The period between MCOR and the second half of MCO's First Convention (1968).
c   First MCO Convention to Second MCO Convention (1968–1969).
d   Second MCO Convention to Third MCO Convention (1969–1970).
e   Third MCO Convention to Fifth MCO Convention (1970–1972).
f   Process of Disintegration of MCO (1972–1974).
g   Fragmented community mobilization in the Mission (1974–1980).
    Remember that MCO Conventions were the occasion to openly express the strength and alliances of the different components of the movement.
2 For each period we established the basic internal structure of the movement, according to our theoretical codes. We also recorded, for each period, the strength of the community organizations, the relationships to the state, and the outcomes of the movement on urban, social, ethnic, and political issues.
    Table A–2 summarizes some of the basic information corresponding to each period. It is presented in this highly schematic way to better outline the argument, but the reader should be referred to the text of Part 3 (pp. 106–36) for additional information on the events of each period.
3 On the basis of such a periodized sequence of events, we can now compare each one of the propositions of our theoretical construct, with the recorded information:
a   Propositions 1 and 2 are mere definitions.
b   Proposition 3 is supported by three facts:
    i   N, P, M, CY, CL, R came together in a defensive coalition (MCOR), to obtain a defensive victory against SP, preserving the *status quo* of the neighbourhood.
    ii Yet, as soon as this victory was achieved, MCOR disappeared.
    iii In the First Convention of the MCO, in October 1968, the MCO tried to put together the same

combination that underlay MCOR, and the effort failed. The MCO could only start on a narrower basis one month later.
c   Propositions 4, 4a and 4b are positively supported by the structure of the MCO, its successful outcomes, and its advantageous power relationship in the periods 1968–1969 and 1969–1970.
d   Proposition 5 does not apply empirically to the movement observed in the Mission, although it must be kept in our theoretical construct as a logical step. Let us observe that it does not apply because of the verification of Proposition 6, whose premises exclude those of 5.
e   Proposition 6 and 7 are verified by:
    i   The gradual split between N and M in the periods 1969–1970, 1970–1972, and 1972–1974.
    ii The particular form of the split:
        —In 1969–1970 N, NP and MP versus M.
        —In 1970–1971 N, NP versus M, MP.
        —In 1971–1972 N, NP versus M, MP, and MCL.
        —In 1972–1974 SP and NP versus M, MP, MCL, and CO.
f   Proposition 8 is verified by the composite, fragmented scene of the Mission in 1974–80, along the separate dimensions of N, NP, M, MP, CL, and R, as described in the text. In addition to it, the failure of *La Raza* to bring together again all the dimensions seems to indicate that each element resulting from the disintegration of the MCO was still alive on its own, so that the dimension it represented in the Mission could be combined in a new collective practice by another operator (*La Raza*, for instance) until the genuine fragments coalesced again through a new social process.
g   Proposition 9 is verified by the outcomes resulting from the social dynamics in each period, as expressed in Table A–2, as well as from the presentation of urban, social and political effects, as exposed in Part 3.

The Social and Urban Profile of the Mission Neighbourhood

As a way of contributing to the understanding of the mobilization that we studied, we present here some basic data concerning the specificity of the urban setting where it took place (Tables A–3 – A–11). Notice that data are organized for District 6, which was broader than the Mission. Our study area concerned both the Mission and the so-called Inner Mission (the core of the Latino community), as shown in Map 13–1, p. 107 that locates the neighbourhood within the city of San Francisco. We have kept the District-basis for the data in order to make comparisons easier with other areas of the city. All data come from Coro Foundation, *The District Handbook* (San Francisco, 1979), the most

Table A.2 Analysis of the elements of the MCO's process of mobilization.

	Period of Action				
	1967-68 (Formation of MCO)	1968-69 (1st-2nd Convention)	1969-70 (2nd-3rd Convention)	1970-72 (3rd-5th Convention)	1972-74 (Process of Disintegration)

Issues present in the movement	–Defense of the neigbourhood against the potential threat of urban renewal
	–Search for funding from the Federal Social Programmes (Model Cities)
	–Emergence of a Latino culture as a source of identity and protest
		–Jobs for minorities (especially Latinos)
		–Educational programmes
		–Housing for the poor
		–Preserving family life
		–Building of a community organization
		–Emergence of student-based Third World radicalism
			–To expand programmes
			–To win a Model Cities Programme controlled by the community
			–To clearly separate from radicals
				–To run Model Cities under the strategy of community control (MMNC)
				–To improve neighbourhood conditions
				–To obtain more jobs for minorities by expanding the city's economic activity
				–To support Aliotto's power
					–Internal battle over:
					  * control of public funds
					  * access to the mayor
					  * control of apparatus of MMNC and MCO

Elements of the movement	–Neighbourhood preservation and improvement (N) –Remedies against poverty (P) –Latino culture (L) –Youth Counterculture (Y)	–Neighbourhood (N) –Poverty (P) –Latino labour (LLB) –Third World Liberation Radicals (TW) –Community Organization (CO)	–Neighbourhood (N) –Poverty (P) –Latino Labour (LLB) –Community Organization (CO) –Latino Culture (L) –Radicals (R)	–Neighbourhood (N) –Poverty (P) –Community Organization (CO) –Power (PW) –Latino Culture (L) –Latino Labour (LLB)	–Neighbourhood Poverty (P) –Community Organization (CO) –Latino Culture (L)
Operators of the movement	–MCOR (N, P, L, R) (no interaction) –Brown Berets and other groups (Y, R, P)	–Agencies (P, L) –Churches (N, P) –Latino nationalists (L) –Blockades and Tenant Unions (N, P) –Centro Social Obrero (LLB) –MCO, (CO)– –vs. Latino Radicals –vs. Homeowners	–Agencies (P, L) –MCO (N, P, CO) –Centro Social Obrero (LLB) –vs– –Latino Culture (L) –Third World (LR)	–Unity Caucus – –MMNC (N, P, CO, PW) –vs– –Alianza Caucus – –MCO (L-P, LLB)	–N, CO → MPC –L, P → Agencies –L (Latino Culture) –LR (Mission Cultural Centre) –LP, N, R (La Raza) –LLB (Labour Union, Centro Obrero)
Effects of the movement	–Stop urban renewal	–Neighbourhood improvement –Building grassroots organization and winning legitimacy in the institutional system	–Obtaining Model Cities –Winning battles over jobs, housing, education	–Obtaining the programmes of Model Cities –Split in leadership –Organizational crisis	–Disintegration of MCO –Active community organizing in the Mission –Planning-orientated activities

Source: Our study.

up-to-date synthesis on urban-social data on San Francisco's neighbourhoods at the time of our research. In fact most data are originated from the 1970 American census.

Also, as proof of the vitality of grassroots organization in 1980 – testament to the lasting effects of the earlier period of active mobilization – we include a list of neighbourhood groups and locally-based agencies present in 1980 in the Mission (Table A–12).

Statistical Profile of District 6 and Mission Neighbourhood, 1970

Table A.3

Ethnic Category	South of Market	Mission	Inner Mission	Total District 6	City-wide
White	39%	49%	26%	39%	57%
Black	10	2	7	6	13
Latin	33	37	55	42	14
Chinese	4	2	2	2	8
Japanese	–	1	–	–	2
Filipino	10	6	6	7	4
American Indian	1	1	1	1	·5
Other	3	2	3	3	1·5
Foreign stock*	51	55	60	56	45
Spanish-speaking	28	32	50	37	12

*Foreign born and persons of foreign born and mixed parentage

Table A.4   Family income levels*

Neighbourhood	Total Families	Under $4	$4–10	$10–15	$15–25	Over $25
South of Market	2,957	29%	44%	18%	8%	1%
Mission	6,169	20	42	24	12	2
Inner Mission	5,021	24	42	23	9	2
Total District 6	14,147	23	43	22	10	2
City-wide	165,295	14	33	26	20	7

*Annual income in thousands of dollars

Table A.5   Employment category

Neighbourhood	All Workers	Managerial/ Professional	Skilled	Semi- & Unskilled
South of Market	5,811	13%	57%	30%
Mission	11,675	15	60	25
Inner Mission	7,612	10	59	31
Total District 6	25,098	13	59	28
City-wide	318,324	25	55	20

Table A.6 Educational level

Neighbourhood	No School	Less Than High School	High School Only	Some College	College Graduate	Adults Surveyed
South of Market	4%	52%	24%	11%	9%	9,854
Mission	2	47	30	11	10	16,837
Inner Mission	5	58	23	8	6	11,796
Total District 6	3	52	25	11	9	38,487
City-wide	3	35	29	16	17	458,887

Table A.7 Land use

Neighbourhood	Residential	Commercial	Industrial	Other Use	Net Area (acres)	Gross Area (incl. streets)
South of Market	14%	24%	40%	21%	420	634
Mission	66	19	4	10	321	483
Inner Mission	49	11	13	27	474	698
Total District 6	42	18	20	20	1215	1815
City-Wide	39	6	6	49	23,367	30,329

Table A.8 Owners and renters

Neighbourhood	Owner Occupied	Renter Occupied	Vacant	Total
South of Market	5%	89%	6%	7,744
Mission	17	79	4	11,629
Inner Mission	26	71	3	7,259
Total District 6	16	80	4	26,632
City-wide	31	64	5	311,457

Table A.9 Distribution of the mission neighbourhood active resident population by occupational category, 1970

Type Occupation	No. Persons (Employed, 16 years or over)	Per cent
Professional, technical, kindred	1,571	7·8
Managers and administrators	753	3·8
Sales workers	758	3·8
Clerical and kindred	5,101	25·9
Craftsmen, foremen and kindred	2,263	11·5
Operators	2,282	14·3
Transport equipment operators	742	3·8
Labourers	1,385	7·0
Service workers	3,591	20·1
Private household workers	347	1·8
Total	18,793	100·0

Source: 1970 American Census

Table A.10   Votes for supervisor in 1977 election district 6

Candidate	Total Votes	% of Votes	Mission	Inner Mission	South of Market*
Silver (liberal white woman)	4,225	35·0	2,091	769	1,220
Borvice (*La Raza*)	2,376	23·0	1,011	897	380
Del Carlo (moderate, supported by some members of MCO)	1,693	16·5	593	726	256
Medina	417	4·0			
Rivera	361	3·5			
Mendelson	334	3·2			
Cullins	314	3·0			
Martinez	166	1·6			
Acido	159	1·5			
Sucheki	144	1·4			
Others (3)	147	1·4			
Total	10,336	100·0			

*Non-Latino area within the District.

Table A.11   Ethnic composition (white versus non-white) of districts in San Francisco, 1970

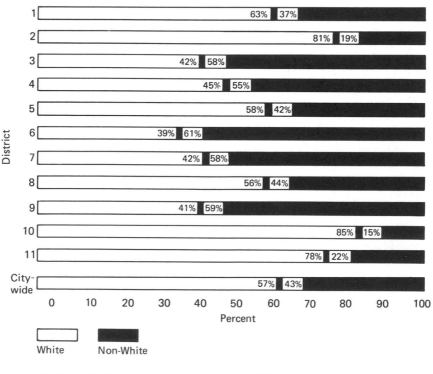

Source: CORO Foundation on the basis of 1970 American Census
Notes: a Latinos are here counted as non-White
          b District 6 includes the Mission

Table A.12 Mission-based community organizations and community-based social agencies identified as active in 1980*

1 American GI Forum	33 Mexican-American Political Assoc. (MAPA)
2 Arriba Juntos	34 Mission Adult Centre
3 Casa Hispaña de Bellas Artes and Casa Editorial	35 Mission Cultural Centre (MCC)
4 Catholic Council for the Spanish Speaking	36 Mission Language and Vocational School Inc.
5 Centro Cultural Guatemalteco	37 Mission Neighbourhood Health Centre
6 Centro de Cambio	38 Mission Outreach Centre
7 Centro Latino	39 Puerto Rican Organization for Women
8 Centro Social Obrero	40 S F Coalition
9 Centro Social Peruano	41 S F Inca Club
10 Club 'Alegria'	42 Spanish-American Political Institute
11 Comite Mexicano Civico Patriotico	43 Vetreach Office
12 Communidad Hispano-Americana de Corpus	44 Centro Communal de Buen Samaritano
13 Concilio Mujeres	45 Children's Rights Group
14 Council of Organizations Pro-Activities of	46 Mission Alcoholic Centre
P.R. Affairs, Inc. (COPAP)	47 Mission Child Care Consortium, Inc.
15 Defensores de la Juventud	48 Mission Community Legal Defense
16 Galeria de la Raza/Studio 24	49 Mission Education Centre
17 Hispanic Educational Congress of the U.S.	50 Mission Education Projects, Inc.
18 Horizons Unlimited of S.F., Inc.	51 Mission Head Start
19 IMAGE	52 Mission Hiring Hall
20 *La Raza* Centro Legal	53 Mission Mental Health Centre
21 *La Raza* Information Centre	54 Mission Neighbourhood Adult Centre
22 *La Raza* Silkscreen Centre	55 Mission Neighbourhood Family Centre
23 *La Raza* Tutorial Centre	56 Mission Neighbourhood Physical Development,
24 Latin American Fiesta, Inc.	Inc.
25 Latin American Mission Programme	57 Mission Reading Clinic
26 Latin American National Senior Citizens	58 Mission Rebels Health and Nutrition Programme
27 Latin American Republic Assoc.	59 Mission Rebels in Action, Inc.
28 Latin American Veterans Political Assoc.	60 Mission Senior Citizens Centre
29 Latino Family Alcoholism Counselling Centre	61 Mission Street Merchants Assoc.
30 Los Mayores de Centro Latino	62 Mission YMCA
31 LULAC Educational Service Centre	63 Real Alternatives Programme (RAP)
32 Mexican-American Legal Defense and	64 Mission Planning Council
Educational Fund (MALDEF)	65 Operation Upgrade

*This does *not* include churches, or non-Latino National groups such as Samoans of Filipinos.

Methodological Appendix to the Study of the Gay Community in San Francisco

Research Strategy

There were four objectives of this study, in accordance with the theoretical concerns underlying our research:

1 To reconstruct the historical origins of the gay community through interviews with key witnesses of the period 1940–1970.
2 Given the very crucial role played by the territorial identity of the community, we made a special effort in obtaining information about the non-statistically recorded locational residence of gay people, and identifying the social and urban characteristics of gay residential areas. The goal was to obtain maps of these areas as precise and reliable as possible. Given the potentially sensitive character of this information, we want to emphasize that the research was carried out with the support and approval of the political representatives of the gay community.
3 We also tried to evaluate the impact of the gay community on the city through the study of urban innovation, the analysis of the cultural events fostered by the community, and the study of political decisions they supported in local government.
4 Finally, since the gay social mobilization largely took the form of winning power within the local political system, we focused an important part of our study on gay politics through selected interviews with key informants and the analysis of available documentation. We should remind the reader that our

study is limited to the gay men community, excluding lesbians, for reasons given in Chapter 14.

Data Basis

Our study of the gay community relies on three different sets of information:

The **first source**, and by far the most important, is the field work research conducted jointly by Karen Murphy and the author, from February to December 1980, and pursued later by the author in 1981. Most of the interviews were done by Karen Murphy, although the research design and data analysis, as well as some key interviews, field work observation, and spatial analysis, were done jointly. The research included four different operations:

1 A survey of the literature and a review of the main gay publications. The following publications were analysed:

a   *The Advocate*, May 1975–1980.
b   *Daugthers of Bilitis San Francisco Newsletter*, April 1967–November 1968.
c   *Gay Sunshine* (San Francisco), Summer 1974–1980.
d   *Interim* (Mattachine Society), 1956–1965.
e   *Ladder* (San Francisco), 1956–1970.
f   *League of Civil Education Newsletter*, 1961–1962.
g   *Mattachine Review*, 1966.
h   *Vector* (San Francisco), 1965–1968.

2 Some personal observations of gay public meetings, social life, and street celebrations, such as the Castro Street Fair, Halloween, the Gay Day Parade, etc., as well as with meetings of the Harvey Milk Gay Democratic Club.

3 Information-gathering on the spatial structure of the gay community, as described in the paragraph below, presenting the methodology of our spatial analysis.

4 The most important source of information consisted of 27 in-depth interviews with key informants of the gay community as well as with experts in some of the key areas of our research (political consultants for the gay vote; urban geographers for the spatial structure; historians for the evolution of the gay community). Interviews included important gay leaders, such as Harry Britt, Jim Rivaldo, Jim Foster, Bill Krauss, Frank Fitch, Wayne Friday, and others, as well as such historical figures of the gay and lesbian movements as Jose Sarria and Phyllis Lyon. Interviews lasted between 30 minutes and five hours (Jose Sarria) with a median time of 65 minutes. Most of them were given in bars. Ten of the 27 are tape-recorded, the others were transcribed in written notes. The interviews were conducted between February and June 1980. The list of interviews, classified by dominant topics, is as follows:

List of Original Interviews with Key Informants on the Gay Community in San Francisco

Background

1   Sharon Long, aide to Supervisor Harry Britt.
2   Gwen Craig, community activist/Vice-President of the Harvey Milk Gay Democratic Club.
3   Jack Trujillo, community activist/aide to Supervisor Carol Ruth Silver.
4   Walter Kaplan, community activist/assistant to Supervisor Harvey Milk.
5   John McEnroe, CHEER, San Francisco State University.
6   Louis Flynn, Professor, San Francisco State University, Interdisciplinary Social Science Department.

Historical

7   Jose Sarria, entertainer/First Empress of San Francisco.
8   Jeff Escoffier, Alan Berube, Gail Rubin, members of the Gay History Project.
9   Phyllis Lyon, co-author of *Lesbian Women* and co-founder of the Daughters of Bilitis.
10   Stewart Loomis, Professor of Education, San Francisco State University.

Spatial

11   Dough DeYoung, private political consultant.
12   Les Morgan, private consultant/Co-ordinator of San Francisco Police Department's Gay Outreach Programme.
13   Dick Pabich, community activist/assistant to the Committee to Re-elect Supervisor Harry Britt/community informant.
14   Jim Rivaldo, community activist/aid to Supervisor Harvey Milk/community informant.
15   Terry King, community activist/Treasurer, Harvey Milk Gay Democratic Club.
16   Max Kirkeberg, Professor of Geography, San Francisco State University.
17   Richard DeLeon, Professor, San Francisco State University Public Sector Research Consultant.
18   Dick Solem, Jon Kaufman, Solem and Associates Political Consultants.
19   Bonnie Loyd, Editor, *Landscape* magazine.

Political

20   Richard Schlachman, political consultant/assistant to the Committee to Re-elect Supervisor Harry Britt/community informant.

21 Bill Krauss, President of Harvey Milk Gay Democratic Club.
22 Harry Britt, San Francisco Supervisor.
23 Jim Foster, community activist/co-founder of Alice P. Toklas Democratic Club.
24 Frank Fitch, President of Alice P. Toklas Democratic Club/San Francisco Charter Commissioner
25 Wayne Friday, President of the Tavern Guild.
26 Hugh Schwartz, Public Response, Survey Research.
27 Harry Britt, second interview (1981).

The **second source** on which we relied is the very important research carried out by Don Lee, for the Master Thesis in City Planning, University of California, Berkeley, that he completed under our supervision in June 1980. He particularly focused on the urban impact of the gay community through personal observation, extensive interviewing, press clippings, and data gathering. We did not consult his files, although we used extensively (with his consent) his final written material, summarized in his thesis, but also in a number of course papers. Detailed references for each information provided by his own research can be found in the endnotes to the text of Chapter 14. Unlike the joint research we did with Karen Murphy (that also led to her Master Thesis in City Planning, as well as to a number of joint and individual publications), we do not present the list of interviews or documents collected by Don Lee, since our interpretation does not rely on this material, but only on the summary and analysis provided by Don Lee himself.

The **third source** was the extensive readings of materials on gay issues and gay politics, both in general, and in San Francisco. The works and sources that have actually been used in our study are cited in the endnotes of Chapter 14.

Methodology for the Spatial Analysis of the Gay Community

There is no statistical source that provides information on sexual preferences of residents of particular urban areas (fortunately enough). Yet, such an obstacle appears overwhelming to the researcher trying to understand the spatial dynamics of the emerging gay culture. Thus, our first and main concern has been to establish, as realiably as possible, the precise spatial boundaries of the gay community in San Francisco. Once gayness is related to certain urban units, on the basis of reliable information, it becomes possible to search for potential associations between gay location patterns and different sets of

social and spatial variables. In this section we will start exploring some relationships between the characteristics of population and housing, and the settlement of gays. It is our hope that when the 1980 census data becomes available, a more thorough statistical and spatial analysis on the reciprocal influence between the evolution of the city and the affirmation of the gay culture will be conducted. This analysis will only be possible if it relies on an accurate estimation of the locational pattern of the gay community in San Francisco. To our knowledge such an estimation has never been attempted on any city in the world: it is an additional reason to be particularly cautious in our approach.

Unable to feel secure enough on any single source of estimation as to the gay spatial distribution, we have used five different sources obtained in an entirely independent manner. The fact that all five sources tend to show a similar spatial pattern of gay residence and activity reinforces the credibility of each particular source, and provides very solid support for the mapping that emerges.

The five sources were as follows:

1 A map of the concentration of gay residence established on the basis of key informants from the gay community. The main informants were the most qualified political pollsters for gay candidates in San Francisco's local elections. Following our request, informants indicated particular periods of time for gay settlement in each area. Gay residential areas, according to our informants, were cumulative over time. Once they became visible as gay neighbourhoods, they did not reverse their character, and, tended at least in San Francisco, to increase their proportion of gay residents as they consolidated as areas of cultural tolerance. On the other hand, it was impossible to obtain any reliable estimation of the number of gays in each area. Thus, the areas we characterized as gay might be so at very different levels, although it was to be expected that in all these areas there would be a substantial gay residence, and, what is more important, that the gay culture would be evident. Yet it is crucial to keep in mind that we did not quantify the presence of gays in particular areas, and that the entire analysis was based upon the degree of likelihood that each urban unit was a home for gay men, without considering their numbers.

2 In the second step of our analysis, we looked for a statistical indicator whose different values could be distributed all over the city. On the basis of direct observation of gay life style, we concluded that an accurate indicator would be the proportion of multiple male households in each urban unit. We rejected the proportion of a single male household as an indicator, because of the high percentage of non-gay elderly living alone. Census data did not provide such information, but the voters' registrar for the city

of San Francisco did. We used the 1977 Voters' Registrar data files, the most updated source providing such information. Obviously the indicator was the proportion of multiple male households to the total number of registered voters in each urban unit. If we were dealing with an ethnic minority population, we would suffer some uncontrolled statistical bias. But concerning gay men, the source was accurate enough, given their high level of voter registration in their drive to win electoral power in San Francisco. The assumption, of course, was not that all, or the majority, of multiple male households were gay. The assumption was that there would be a strong correlation between the spatial distribution of gay residence and the spatial distribution of the frequency of multiple male households. The difference was not merely a semantic one: it was to have major consequences for the selection of the statistical techniques suitable to any analysis on this particular data basis.

3　The third source we selected was the spatial distribution of the vote for the gay candidate in a city-wide local election. It was clear that not all people who vote for a gay candidate were gay. It was also clear that there was a close relationship between the number of gays in an area and the vote for the gay candidate in such area. And it was equally clear that such a relationship was closer in the early stages of gay mobilization as compared to the time when they had achieved some power on the basis of broader alliances and more diverse constituencies. Thus we selected as gay strongholds the areas of highest electoral support for the late gay leader Harvey Milk in the 1975 supervisorial race, his second attempt at city-wide elected office as a gay candidate and the first in which he obtained a significant number of votes widely distributed across the city (53,000).

4　The fourth source concerned the location of gay businesses. We mapped 250 businesses (most of them very small) listed in the directory of the Golden Gate Gay Business Association in 1979. Here again, the assumption, relying on our direct observation, was the close connection between gay residence and gay self-proclaimed activities.

5　The fifth source concerned the location of gay bars and public places as presented in the specialized publications.

To establish relationships between these five indicators of gay territory and all variables provided by the census, we also transformed the different counting units into census tracts. From now on, these will be our units of observation and analysis.

On the basis of these five different independent sources, we established five maps. The areas of gay concentration that resulted from the observation of the five different maps fitted closely on the whole, into a common spatial location within the city of San Francisco.

To rely on a somewhat less intuitive measure we calculated the zero-order correlation between the spatial distributions of the indicators of gay residence we proposed. To do so, we gave dichotomic values (1,0) to areas with gay presence or absence (Map 14–1, p. 146). We proceeded in a similar way classifying in 1 versus 0, the areas with high or low proportion of multiple male households (levels 6, 5, 4, versus 3, 2, 1, in the scale of census tracts in the city according to the proportion of multiple male households, as shown in Map 14–2, p. 147. We then calculated the correlation for all census tracts distributed in relationship to the values (1,0) of the two indicators. We proceeded in the same manner with the third indicator, namely the importance of gay vote (Map 14–3, p. 148). We also mapped the public places (including bars and social clubs) where gays met (Map 14–4, p. 149) and the location of gay businesses (Map 14–5, p. 150).

The correlations were highly positive: $r = 0.55$ ($p = 0.001$) between the areas designated by the community informants and the ones resulting from the spatial distribution of multiple male households. And $r = 67$ ($p = 0.001$) between the definition proposed by the informants and the distribution of the 1975 vote for Harvey Milk. Statistical measures confirmed what the simple observation of the maps suggested: we had a similar pattern of spatial location provided by different independent indicators whose credibility were mutually reinforced. We now were able to define the spatial boundaries of San Francisco's gay male community as of 1980. Also, given the verification of the accuracy of the estimation provided by our key informants, we could, unless contrary evidence was provided, consider as a probable trend the spatial sequence described by them over time.

Having established the spatial profile of the gay community, we were able to relate it to the social and urban characteristics distributed across the city, in order to understand the factors fostering or counter-acting the patterns of settlement inspired by the gay culture. On the basis of the 1970 American Census and of the 1974 American Bureau of Census' *Urban Atlas*, we selected 11 variables considered to be relevant to our analysis, as presented in Table 14–1, p. 152.

Yet we must bear in mind that the only thing this particular data basis told us about gayness is where gays were or tended to be. We did not have any indicator of gayness; the only thing we had was a series of converging indicators of gay location. Thus, we could not infer anything about gay individuals. We were only able to analyse gay versus non-gay spatial units. To proceed in such a way we carried out two different analyses:

1　On the basis of our key informants map, we divided

the city into two categories of spatial areas: those with gay presence and those without such a presence. We calculated for each selected variable the mean value of their distribution in the census tracts corresponding to each one of the two categories of space. The T test provided the statistical significance of the differences observed for the mean value of each variable in each one of the two categories of spatial units. The extent and direction of such differences provided the clue for the social and urban specificity of the gay territory.

2 We tried to establish some measure of correlation between the spatial distribution of selected social and urban variables. Since we were not looking for co-variation between characteristics across the space, but for correspondence between spatial organization in relationship to two series of criteria, the usual regression analysis was inadequate to our purpose. Instead we have proceeded to calculate rank-correlation coefficients (Spearman test) between, on the one hand, the distribution of all census tracts in a 6-level scale of gay space, constructed on the basis of the proportion of multiple male households; and, on the other hand, the distribution of all census tracts in a series of 6-level scales on the basis of selected variables. Only variables that the first step of the analysis (as described above, in 1) showed to be discriminatory were considered to construct the scales of social and urban differentiation in San Francisco. Furthermore, one of the findings of our analysis was that these selected variables were likely to affect gay location

patterns jointly, instead of having individual effects, since their spatial distribution does not overlap. Thus, to test our analysis we constructed an additional scale, classifying the census-tract units in a scale that combined in its criteria the three variables considered to have some effect on gay location. The Spearman coefficient between the ranks they obtained in the multiple male households scale provided the final test for our tentative interpretation of the social roots of gay location patterns.

Selected Information on the Gay Community

We shall now give some important information to which we referred in the text of Chapter 14 to support our analysis. Such information includes the most accurate unpublished data on sexual preferences of a representative sample of San Francisco's residents; our classification of gay businesses on the basis of the directory of the Golden Gate Business Association; and the list of proposals concerning urban policies presented to the San Francisco's board of supervisors by Supervisors Harvey Milk and Harry Britt, political leaders of the gay community. We constructed this list on the basis of information provided by the staff members of the Committee on Planning, Housing, and Development of the San Francisco's board of supervisors.

Table A.13 Sexual preference of a representative sample of San Francisco residents by age and sex (percentages on the total of each sex and age group)

| Sexual Preference | Total | | Male | | Female | | Age 18–29 | | Age 30–49 | | Age 50 and over | |
	N	%	N	%	N	%	Male %	Female %	Male %	Female %	Male %	Female %
Gay and Bisexual	226	17%	159	24·4%	67	9·6%	21%	13%	37%	9%	11%	7%
Heterosexual	1,111	83%	483	75·6%	628	90·4%	79%	87%	63%	91%	89%	93%
Total (N)	1,337	100%	642	100%	695	100%	243	215	249	222	150	258

Source: Richard DeLeon and Courtney Brown, *Unpublished Research Report* (San Francisco State University, Department of Political Science, 1980; Provided by Professor DeLeon)

Table A.14   Businesses registered as members of the gay business association by type of activity.

	N	%
Banking and Insurance	7	2·8
Real Estate	20	8·1
Advertising/Public Relations	13	5·3
Contractors and Building supplies	11	4·4
Retail stores	20	8·1
Restaurants and Hotels	10	7·7
Bars, Discos, Baths, Health Clubs	18*	7·3
Antiques, Art Galleries, Collectors	7	2·8
Hair Stylists	9	3·7
Lawyers	11	4·5
Architects and Interior Designers	9	3·6
Financial, Computer, and Business Consultants	25	10·1
Travel agencies and Tourism	10	4·0
Audio-Visual and Communications	2	0·8
Automobiles Sales, Repair and Service	2	0·8
Printers	10	4·0
Bookstores	1	0·4
Newspapers and Magazines	8	3·2
Doctors and Health Care	7	2·8
Counselling	11	4·5
Home Services (Janitors, cleaning, etc.)		
Personal Services (Chauffeurs, Maids and other)	5	2·0
Business Services (Secretarial support)	6	2·4
Employment Agencies	6	2·4
Miscellaneous	10	4·0
Total	247	99·7%**

  * Actually there are over 200 Gay Bars in San Francisco, although most of them are not members of the
    Golden Gate Business Association, since they tend to be organized under the Tavern Guild.
 ** Percentages add only up to 99·7% because of rounding up of figures.
Source: Our own study.

Legislation Introduced and Measures Proposed by Gay Representatives in the San Francisco Board of Supervisors on Matters of Housing and Urban Policy, 1977–1981

Harvey Milk's Sponsored Initiatives

— Authored anti-speculation ordinance designed to provide monetary disincentive for trading residential property for speculative purposes. Defeated 9–2 (in 1978).
— Sponsor of Prop. U, an unsuccessful ballot measure designed to force landlords to rebate their Prop. 13 tax savings to tenants (1978).
— Consistent opponent of downtown high-rises (1978).
— 1976–1978 opposed expansion of UC Medical Centre-related doctor's complexes into residential neighbourhoods; also opposed similar expansion of Franklin Medical Centre in Castro area. Both issues were popular and hard-fought and largely successful efforts of neighbourhood activists largely supported by Harvey Milk before he was Supervisor.
— Strong advocate of rent control (1978).
— Introduced moratorium on second-floor conversions from residential to commercial in November, 1978: passed. Preparatory to Special Use District legislation eventually passed under Britt's leadership. Also moratorium on new bars and restaurants in certain areas.

Some Legislative Background Information on Supervisor Harry Britt, appointed to the Board January 1979

1 *Chronology of Proposals*

1979
— Strongly supported rent control legislation.
— Introduced legislation for strong control on high-rise expansion.
— Supported the settlement of the suit brought against the Police Department by the Officers for Justice, the Chinese for Affirmative Action, the NAACP, NOW, etc.
— Authored the one-year moratorium on bars and restaurants on Haight and 24th Streets.
— Opposed the multi-million dollar sewer project as being too costly and too disruptive to the integrity of the neighbourhoods.

1980
— Introduced legislation to prevent discrimination against the disabled.
— Introduced the Residential Hotel Conversion Act to severely limit conversions of residential hotels to tourist use. This legislation helped to preserve low-income housing for the poor and elderly.
— Sponsored the neighbourhood special use district legislation – an ordinance that protects the integrity of neighbourhood commercial areas.
— Introduced legislation to regulate the transportation of toxic chemicals through residential neighbourhoods.
— Introduced legislation to close the loophole in the rent stabilization law, which will result in the elimination of vacancy de-control.

1981
— Re-introduced Mayor George Moscone's proposal for an Office of Citizens Complaints.
— Introduced legislation to establish registration of paid lobbyists.
— Co-sponsored legislation that would strongly regulate the conversion of rental units into condominiums.
— Held hearings regarding the possible need for some type of rent regulation for commercial property occupied by small merchants.
— Called for hearings on the concept of equal pay for comparable worth.
— Introduced resolution to put the City and County of San Francisco on record opposing off-shore oil drillings.

Supervisor Britt's Attitude on Selected Urban Issues

Condominium Conversion
— Since reappointment to the board of supervisors in January 1981, has voted against all proposals to convert rental units to condos. The board regularly must vote on each condo conversion proposal, and Britt's opposition is usually the minority position.
— June 1981 – sponsored a moratorium on condo conversions which was defeated by one vote.
— 1981 – supported a limit on condo conversions of 1,000 per year which passed and is law.

Special Use Districts
— Sponsor of legislation creating Special Use Districts, now in existence in seven neighbourhood areas, in which merchants and residents set standards for neighbourhood commercial development. Legislation is designed to prevent the excessive intrusion of non-neighbourhood orientated businesses into traditional neighbourhood commercial districts (1980).

Residential Hotel Conversion Ordinance
— Supported successful moratorium on conversion of residential hotel units to tourist use in 1979 – interim measure while long-term legislation was being drafted.
— December 1980 – sponsored Residential Hotel Conversion Law – adopted unanimously, which effectively prevented residential hotel units from being converted to tourist use. These units are one of the last remaining sources of low-income housing, particularly for the elderly in the tenderloin area.
— May, 1981 – resisted the rewriting of this law to weaken its enforcement and other sections, creating loopholes which make it much easier to convert. This watered-down bill passed with Britt and Supervisor Nancy Walker dissenting, and is now law.

High-rise Construction
— Opposition to downtown high-rises has been a long-time neighbourhood cause in San Francisco. They are seen by neighbourhood activists as exacerbating housing problems, impacting negatively on the neighbourhoods,

and creating tax and service burdens on the citizens.
Britt has followed the tradition of Harvey Milk in opposing excessive high-rise construction.
— Sponsor of the November 1979 ballot proposition placing strict controls on high-rises. The measure lost.

Rent Control
— May 1979 – sponsored rent control law, which passed and was signed into law, established rent control and fairly strict eviction controls – limited rent increases to 7 per cent yearly and established a Rent Arbitration Board.
— 1979 – supported strong rent control legislation which did not pass at the board.
— November 1979 – strong sponsor of Proposition R ballot measure for stronger rent control. Measure lost.
— Fall 1980 – sponsored an amendment to rent law opposing vacancy de-control which, in current law causes vacant apartments to escape rent control. Compromise version passed board and was vetoed by mayor.

Miscellaneous
— 1980 – unsuccessfully opposed use of city redevelopment funds to underwrite Opera Plaza, a condominium development in which units would sell for $100,000 – $350,000.
— May 1981 – opposed Performing Arts Centre Garage which would provide below market rate parking for patrons of the Opera and Symphony and result in the tearing down of several dozen low- and moderate-income housing units. Garage approved on 9–2 vote.
— Early 1981 – successfully lobbied for inclusion in Mayor's UDAG proposal for North of Market area of low-cost housing, largely in control of local neighbourhood and housing activists.
— Late 1981 – working with Latino-based community housing corporation to help create first subsidized housing project which integrates housing for the disabled, families, and seniors.
— Late 1981 – sponsor of legislation to create low-cost senior housing on top of Performing Arts Centre Garage.
Source: San Francisco board of supervisors' internal files, Committee on Planning, Housing and Development, 1981.

Appendix to Part 4:
Squatters and the State in Latin America

General Description of Sources

The analysis presented in Part 4 was based on a series of fieldwork studies in Latin American squatter settlements, whose circumstances and characteristics we will outline here.

Chile

Most of the information was gathered by a research team organised by the author during a period as Director of Community Research at the Centre for Urban Studies (CIDU), Catholic University of Chile, Santiago, 1970–72. Our main study consisted of an in-depth observation of a sample of 20 *campamentos* in Santiago in 1971. Other connected studies were carried on under our general supervision on slums and squatter settlements, as well as on a variety of grassroots urban organizations. Some of the studies were made by the CIDU researchers, and others by our Ph.D. students at the Ecole des Hautes Etudes en Sciences Sociales

(Paris) working in Chile. The most finished product was a series of interconnected Ph.D. dissertations in Sociology at the University of Paris wherein each individual researcher outlined his own piece of work. Perhaps Jaime Rojas' Ph.D. dissertation was the most complete report on the general urban social movement generated in the Chilean squatter settlements. None of these theses has been published. The interested reader must be referred to the University of Paris' Library, where copies of each dissertation are deposited. The dissertations are the following:

— Jaime Rojas, *La Participation Urbaine dans les Societes Dependantes: L'Experience du Mouvement des Pobladores au Chili* (Paris: Université de Paris, 1978, Ph.D., 400 pp).
— Christine Meunier, *Revendications Urbaines, Strategie Politique et Transformation Ideologique: Le Campamento 'Nueva Habana' Santiago, 1970–73* (Paris: Université de Paris, 1976, Ph.D., 321 pp).
— Francois Pingeot, *Populisme Urbain et Crise du Centre-Ville dans les Sociétés Dependantes*: Santiago du

Chili 1969–73 (Paris: Université de Paris, Ph.D., 1976).
— Franz Vanderschueren, *Mouvements Sociaux et Changements Institutionnels: L'Experience des Tribunaux Populaires de Quartier au Chili* (Paris: Université de Paris, Ph.D., 1979).

Other related publications are:
— Equipo de Estudios Poblaciones del CIDU, 'Revindicacion Urbana y Lucha Politica: Los Campamentos de Pobladores en Santiago de Chile', *Revista Latinoamericana de Estudios Urbanos y Regionales (EURE)* 6, (1972), Santiago de Chile.
— Luis Alvarado and Rosemond Cheetham, 'Movilizacion Social en Torno al Problema de la Vivienda', *Revista Latinoamericana de Estudios Urbanos y Regionales*, 7, (1973).
— Manuel Castells, 'Movimiento de Pobladores y Lucha de Clases en Chile', *Revista Latinoamericana de Estudios Urbanos y Regionales*, 7, (1973).
— Santiago Quevedo and Eder Sader, *Las Nuevas Formas de Poder Popular en Poblaciones* (Santiago: CIDU, Universidad Catolica de Chile, 1972, Working Paper no. 57).
— Rosemond Cheetham, Alfredo Rodriguez, and Jaime Rojas, 'Comandos Urbanos. Alternative de Poder Socialista', *Revista Interamericana de Planificacion*, Vol. VIII, 3, (July 1974).
— Manuel Castells, *La Lucha de Clases en Chile* (Buenos Aires: Siglo XXI, 1974).
— Enrique Pastrana and Monica Threlfall, *Pan, Techo, y Poder. El Movimiento de Pobladores en Chile, 1970–73* (Buenos Aires: Ediciones SIAP, 1974).

Mexico

1 A personal survey of the situation through our fieldwork study in the *vecindades* and *colonias* of Mexico City and Monterrey in 1976.
2 On Monterrey, a Ph.D. dissertation in Sociology completed under our supervision at the University of Paris: Diana Villarreal, *Marginalité Urbaine et Politique de l'Etat au Mexique: Enquête su les Zones Residentielles Illegales de la Ville de Monterrey* (Paris: Université de Paris, Ecole des Hautes Etudes en Sciences Sociales, 1979, Ph.D., 350 pp).
3 A series of studies on the housing crisis in Mexico with special reference to the popular sector. We worked with the members of the different teams, besides using the very good information provided by their research reports. The main written sources of information on these studies are:

— Priscilla Connolly, Enrique Ortiz, and Gustavo Romero, *La Produccion de la Vivienda en Mexico* (Mexico DF: COPEVI 1976, mimeographed, 600 pp).
— Gustavo Garza and Martha Schteingart, *El Problema de la Vivienda en Mexico*, El Colegio de Mexico, 1977.
— EQUISUR, *Significacion Social de la Politica de la Vivienda en Mexico* (Universidad Autonoma Metropolitana, Azcapotzalco, 1976, mimeographed, 620 pp).

Peru

Besides some personal observation in 1971 and 1972, we relied mainly on an extraordinary fieldwork study carried on over several years by our former student, Etienne Henry, later a professor at the Catholic University of Lima. He first completed his dissertation in Paris and then went back to Lima, producing a more up-to-date report on the *barriadas* and urban social movements in Peru. The written sources are:

— Etienne Henry, *Urbanisation Dependante et Mouvements Sociaux Urbains: Analyse Comparative des Experiences de Lima et Santiago du Chili* (Paris: Université de Paris, 1974, four volumes, Ph.D. in Sociology, 1300 pp).
— Etienne Henry, *La Escena Urbana* (Lima: Pontificia Universidad Catolica del Peru, 1978).

We cross-checked the information with the updated publication of the classical study by David Collier: *Barriadas y Elites: de Odria a Velasco* (Lima: Instituto de Estudios Peruanos, Lima, 1978).

For general data on Peruvian urbanization we relied on another Ph.D. dissertation by our former student, Jacqueline Weisslitz:

— Jacqueline Weisslitz, *Developpement, Dependance et Structure Urbaines: Analyse Comparative de Villes Peruviennes* (Paris: Université de Paris, Ph.D., 1978).

Caracas

We relied basically on data from a study carried on by Ricardo Infante and Magaly Sanchez, of the Institute of Urbanism, Universidad Central de Venezuela, with our collaboration, between 1976 and 1979:

— Ricardo Infante and Magaly Sanchez, *Reproduccion de la Fuerza de Trabajo en la Estructura Urbana la Condicion de la Clase Trabajadora en Zonas Segregadas de Caracas* (Caracas: Instituto de Urbanismo, Universidad Central de Venezuela, 1980, 4 volumes).

A further elaboration was provided by Magaly Sanchez, *La Segregation Urbaine à Caracas* (Paris: Université de Paris, Ph.D. in Sociology 1980).

We completed the information with some informed analysis drawn from Ester Marcano's Ph.D. dissertation in City Planning, *Caracas: Autoroutes et Bidonvilles*, (Paris: Université de Paris, 1979), as well as with our observation during visits to Caracas in 1979 and 1981.

The Study of *Campamentos* in Santiago

The study was conducted by a team of eight researchers of the Centre of Urban Studies (CIDU), Universidad Catolica de Chile, under the direction of the author, who participated in the interviews and observation of the *campamentos*. Names of researchers are omitted here because of the current political conditions in Chile.

The study had three phases:

1 Exploratory observation of four *campamentos* and interviews with leaders of the *pobladores* (November – December 1970)
2 Selection and systematic observation of 20 *campamentos*. Series of interviews to leaders and residents (June – September 1971).
3 Follow-up of the process of evolution of the 20 *campamentos*, focusing on the new popular organizations emerging in the *campamentos*, through systematic observation of the same 20 *campamentos* (July – October 1972).

For each *campamento* at least four interviews were conducted: first, interview with the spokesperson of the *campamento's* leadership; second, interview with a member of the *Comite Sin Casa* that originated the invasion; third, interview with a cadre of the dominant political party in the *campamento*; and fourth, group-interview to several residents, randomly selected, to cross-check the information obtained in the interviews.

Interviews were conducted on the basis of guidelines focusing on the following aspects:

1 History of the *campamento*.
2 Social organization and collective activities.
3 Urban situation (housing, transportation, services, etc.).
4 Political participation.

Table A.15   List of *Campamentos* studied in Santiago by the CIDU team in 1971, with reference to selected characteristics

Name of the Campamento	Number of Resident Families	Area of Location in Santiago	Predominant Political Party*	Date of Invasion
Junta De Adelanto	2,900	Barrancas	PC	August 1970
Fernando Quezada	192	Barrancas	PC	August 1970
Benite del Canto	1,800	La Cisterna	DC	August 1970
Unidad Popular	3,500	La Florida	PC and PS	January 1970
Ex-Che Guevara	176	Barrancas	PS	August 1970
Metropolitano	150	La Cisterna	DC	October 1970
26 de Septiembre	96	La Florida	MAPU	September 1970
Nueva La Habana	1,600	La Florida	MIR	November 1970 (on the basis of previous invasions in 1970)
26 de Julio	836	La Cisterna	MIR	July 1970
Fidel Castro	665	San Bernardo	MIR and PC, PS	July 1970
Che Guevara	850	Barrancas	PS	August 1970
Laura Allende	100	Curacavi	PS	June 1971
La Tencha	236	Nunoa	PS	October 1970
Rene Schneider	130	La Florida	DC	April 1971
Manzanar	40	La Cisterna	DC	August 1970
Tepual	95	La Cisterna	DC	November 1970
Bernardo O' Higgins	1,800	Barrancas	PC	August 1970
Venceremos	2,200	La Cisterna	PC	August 1970
Pedro Aguirre Cerda	465	San Bernardo	PR	May 1971
Lulo Pinochet	580	Nunoa	PS	October 1970

*List of Abbreviations of Political Parties with presence in the Compamentos of Santiago:
  PC Partido Comunista de Chile
  PS Partido Socialista de Chile
  MIR Movimiento de Izquierda Revolucionaria
  DC Democracia Cristiana
  PR Partido Radical
  MAPU Movimiento Accion Popular Unitaria

5 Relationship to the administration.
6 Formal organization of the *campamento*.
7 Social, economic and demographic characteristics of the resident population.
8 Participation in collective mobilizations.
9 Spatial structure.
10 Specific experiences of innovative social organization.

Information from the interviews was recorded in writing. On the basis of notes taken by *two interviewers*, a summary-file was established for all *campamentos*, following the same guidelines to classify the information. These 20 files represent the basic material of our own study of the *campamentos* in Santiago.

The selection of 20 *campamentos* (over the 75 that existed in Santiago in 1971) was decided according to the following criteria

1 All large *campamentos* were included.
2 All highly mobilized *campamentos* were included.
3 The entire political spectrum was covered.
4 The entire social spectrum was covered.
5 We included *campamentos* at a very different level of social organization and urban quality.

We reproduce in Table A–15 the *campamentos* we studied, identified by their name and characteristics in June – September 1971.

Other Studies on the Chilean Squatters' Movement

Although the analysis presented here is basically supported by our own study, as well as by the doctoral theses supervised by the author at the University of Paris, we also relied on information personally provided by several researchers working concurrently in the same field:

1 A research project conducted by Joaquin Duque and Ernesto Pastrana of the Facultad Latinoamericana de Ciencias Sociales, particularly on four *campamentos*: Nueva La Habana, Bernardo O'Higgins, 26 de Julio, and Fidel Castro. See Joaquin Duque and Ernesto Pastrana, 'Le movilizacion reivindicativa urbana de los sectores populares en Chile: 1964–1972' in *Revista Latinoamericana de Ciencias Sociales*, 4 (1973). Given our advisory role in this research, we had access to the data files, particularly to the census established by Duque and Pastrana on the four *campamentos* cited above. 2 A series of studies carried on by the Equipo de Estudios Poblaciones of the CIDU, Universidad Catolica de Chile, between 1970 and 1973, on aspects related to neighbourhood organization, popular justice, communal councils, price and supply committees, etc.

Much of the empirical data gathered were published as working papers by the CIDU between 1971 and 1973. In addition to the already cited papers, our analysis has also taken into consideration the following:

— Jorge Giusti, *Organizacion y Participacion Popular en Chile*: *El Mito del 'Hombre Marginal'* (Buenos Aires: FLACSO, 1973, 200 pp).
— Cristina Cordero and Monica Threlfall, *Consejo Comunal de Trajabadores y Cordon Cerrillos-Maipu*: *1972* (Santiago: CIDU, 1973, Working Paper 67, 140 pp).

The Data File

All information supporting our analysis is recorded and classified, but not published in a systematic way. It includes complete files for 17 *campamentos*, as well as 5000 pages of documents synthesizing the experience of Chilean squatters during the Allende period. Access to the documentation could be provided under certain conditions to those scholars engaged in independent academic research, as well as to the Chilean people, for whom the memory of their experience is a due patrimony.

Appendix to Part 5:
The Citizen Movement in Madrid

Research Strategy in Madrid

Our research strategy was consistent with the theoretical perspective of our study. We tried to establish the conditions under which urban issues triggered grassroots mobilization, to understand the

form taken by such collective behaviour, and to discover its relationship to social change by assessing its impact on the urban system, on the political institutions, and on the city's culture. We did not interview individual actors, but individual informants as subjects of a collective process. We did not observe only neighbourhoods' social life, but neighbourhood-based protests. The shape and content of local social networks were considered as a sociological variable, not as a research matter.

And yet our basic units of observation were neighbourhood associations. This option entirely relied on the specificity of the Movement in Madrid. It was a multi-issue Movement, unified around a territorial basis, so neighbourhood associations were the real empirical unit around which mobilization happened. There was no organizationally unified Movement, but instead a collective process, highly diversified and decentralized, that could only be reconstructed by articulating different local experiences. Thus we sample 23 out of 110 neighbourhood associations, including all the most active, and we studied each process in its local setting before integrating the main observed trends into a more general pattern.

The results are produced as a result of combining three different levels of observation and analysis:

1 The internal structure of neighbourhood mobilization and its differential impact on urban and social change.
2 The structure and history of Madrid's metropolitan area, spatial characteristics, urban growth, and the successive urban crises that took place throughout it.
3 The evolution of the Citizen Movement in the 1970s as closely related to social and political conflicts in Spain.

Each level of observation required sources of data and modes of analysis, as described below. The crucial research goal was to link different approaches around a unified theoretical model, proceeding by successive steps from the more general interpretation to the more specific and formalized analysis. We tried to show how different structures of mobilization were produced and what were the effects of each one of these structures on social change. But our analysis, although theoretically constructed, remained specific to Madrid's social context. To broaden its scope to a more general theory of social movement and social change, the Madrid findings have to be related to other experiences, enabling us to observe the creation of urban mobilization under different social contexts. However, such a comparative perspective requires, first, that we establish the specific social process observed within each context, and this is what we intend here. To lay the ground, theoretically and empirically, for the building of an historically supported theory of urban change. The validity of such a theory depends upon the validity of our historical observation, and that is why we examine now in detail our data basis and the techniques used at different levels of analysis. The tentative solutions we give to the serious methodological problems encountered are a fundamental element of our investigation.

Data Basis

The research on the Citizen Movement in Madrid was based on four different sources of information that have been used jointly to check and complement each other:

1 31 in-depth interviews with key informants (most of them leaders) of a selected sample of 23 neighbourhood associations.
2 Participant observation in the Movement, being an observer, for a total of 20 months, between January 1977 and August 1980.
3 Archives and organizational files of the Federation of Neighbourhood Associations, as well as of several neighbourhood associations, and of a major advocate consulting firm (DEINCISA).
4 Documents and research monographs (many of them unpublished) on Madrid's urban problems.

We will now describe the data basis in more precise detail.

Interviews of Neighbourhood Activists

Description

Interviews of key informants of a targeted sample of 23 neighbourhood associations – they were focused interviews, quite general in nature but always covering at least the range of topics as described in the interviews guideline. When possible it was a group interview, with representatives of different tendencies of the neighbourhood association. Most interviews concerned the neighbourhood's main leader, sometimes alone, sometimes with other militants. Information obtained through the interviews was systematically checked through direct knowledge of the neighbourhood, informal meetings with residents, and examination of Associations' internal documents and press clippings. Interviews lasted between 40 minutes and seven hours, with a median length of 75 minutes. Places where they took place were very diverse: militants' homes, headquarters of neighbourhoods' associations, parks, and, very often, bars and cafés. 26 of the 31 interviews took place in the period January – June 1977, the remaining five in February – April 1979. They were all tape-recorded, and were personally conducted by the author.

Sample

The following *criteria* were used to select the sample:

1 All very active, large, and successful neighbourhood associations were to be included, but a variety of levels of mobilization should be kept.
2 They should cover the whole range of urban situations, according to the typology constructed on the basis of our analysis of Madrid's urban crisis.
3 They should include the variety of political orientations in the leadership, although still reflecting the

Table A.16 Sample of neighbourhood associations directly observed.

		Social Status of the Neighbourhood			
		Low Working Class (Construction Workers)	Working Class (Industrial Workers)	Mixed Social Composition	Middle Class
Urban Situation	Shanty Towns	–Orcasitas –Pozo Tio Raimundo –Palomeras Bajas –El Olivar –San Pascual	—	—	—
	Public Housing	–Orcasur	–San Blas –Uva-Hortaleza	—	—
	Large Housing Estates (peripheral location within the city)	—	–El Pilar –Quintana	–Concepcion –Aluche –Moratalaz	–Santa Maria (Hortaleza)
	Large Housing Estates (suburban Periphery)	—	–Leganes –Alcala de Henares	–Alcorcon	–Alameda de Osuna
	Historic City	—	–Arganzuela	–Lavapies –Malasana	–Salamanca
	Garden Cities in the Urban Core	—	—	—	–Colonias de Hotelitos

overwhelming influence of the PCE within the movement.

4 They should cover all social classes participating in neighbourhoods mobilization. Therefore middle class neighbourhoods should be overrepresented to watch closely their dynamics, in spite of the fact that they were a statistical minority.

Using these criteria, 23 of the 110 neighbourhood associations that were in existence in 1977 were selected. We added a new case (*Colonias de Hotelitos*) in 1979. The final sample was composed in the following way.

Interview's Guidelines

1 History of the Association.
Where it was formed, why and how; social characteristics of: a) membership b) steering committee; membership number, number of active members; organizational force, legal status; relationship with different social groups; relationship

with the administration; relationship with the media; relationship with professional circles; relationship with other citizen organizations; relationship with labour unions; relationship with political parties; phases of evolution in the life of the association.

2 Urban and social characteristics of the neighbourhood.

3 Most important urban struggles led by the Association. Issue underlying struggle; demand by the association; focus(es) of the struggle; effects produced by each struggle.

4 Relationship to the political process.

5 Relationship to neighbourhood life.

6 Vision of Madrid and of urban policies.

7 Opinion of the Citizen Movement.

(The interviews were conducted in a non-directive way, so the sequence never followed the guideline. But, in the end, most aspects of it were covered in most interviews. Specific quantitative information, such as membership or precise dates for events, were obtained through documents of the association.)

Table A.17 List of neighbourhood associations interviewed with indication of selected characteristics*

Neighbourhood Association Identification	Approximate Average Membership for the period 1976–78	Predominant Political Influence	Characteristics of the Interview
1 El Olivar	200	PCE	Group of leaders, militants, and advisers.
2 Palomeras Bajas	1,000	ORT	Group of leaders, militants, advocates and neighbours.
3 Orcasitas	1,600	PCE	1 Group of leaders, militants, and residents. 2nd interview with leader.
4 Pozo Tio Raimundo	2,100	PCE	1 Main leader 2 Group of leaders and neighbours.
5 San Pascual	150	PCE	A leading activist.
6 Orcasur	900	ORT	Architect, adviser of the association.
7 Uva-Hortaleza	500	PCE	Group of leaders and militants.
8 San Blas	4,000	PCE	President of the Association.
9 Leganes	2,000	PCE	Steering committee of the Association, including the president.
10 Alcala de Henares	2,400	ORT	President of the Association and militants.
11 Alcorcon	200	PCE	President and militants.
12 El Pilar	500	Autonomous Radicals	Members of coalition's steering committee.
13 Moratalaz	2,000	PCE	Member of steering committee.
14 Quintana	100	PCE	President of Association.
15 Concepcion	60	PCE	Member of steering committee.
16 Aluche	500	PCE	Steering committee, including the president.
17 Alameda de Osuna	300	Apolitical	Steering committee, including the president.
18 Hortaleza (Santa Maria)	1,200	PCE, then autonomous	Steering committee and residents.
19 Colonias de Hotelitos	1,000	Apolitical	Several members of the coalition's leadership (group).
20 Arganzuela	200	PCE	Secretary of the Neighbourhood Association.
21 Malasana	600	PTE	Group of militants.
22 Lavapies	1,600	PCE	1 Main leader. 2 Steering committee and residents.
23 Salamanca	100	PCE	Militant.

*Information concerning urban situation and social status of the neighbourhood are presented in the sample chart.

Other extensive interviews were conducted with:
 –Secretary of the Federation of Neighbourhood Associations of Madrid (1977).
 –President of the Federation (1979).
 –Vice-President of the Federation (1979).
 –Members of the advocate Urban Centre CIDUR (1977).
 –Members of the advocate Urban Centre DEINCISA (1977).

Participant Observation

The author spent 50 per cent of his time observing the Movement from the inside, in the periods January – June 1977, January 1978 – April 1979, and in July 1980. The status was one of planning adviser: in 1977 with DEINCISA, an advocate firm of lawyers and planners working for the Citizen Movement; in 1978-79, with the Federation of Neighbourhood Associations. It was known by the Movement's leadership that the Movement's motivations and achievement was being researched along with the professional advisory role. Observation included participation in meetings of various neighbourhoods, attendance at general assemblies, an active role in preparing the Movement's campaigns, and presence at all the main demonstrations and protest actions.

Use of Archives

Additional information was provided by reading the archives and documentation gathered by DEINCISA, the Federation of Neighbourhood Associations, and several neighbourhood associations (Hortaleza, La Corrala, Orcasitas, Pozo Tio Raimundo). They included records of meetings, collection of manifestos, demand-programmes, and information bulletins from various associations. DEINCISA provided us with a precious collection of press clippings for all Citizen Movement's action in 1976 and 1977.

Documents on Madrid

To examine the Movement in its urban and social context, a documentary research was carried on Madrid in 1977 and 1978. Besides the usual bibliographic sources, some of which are cited, we consulted the following documents:

1 The basic collection of 12 research monographs produced by the Metropolitan Planning Commission (COPLACO or the Ministerio de Obras Publicas y Urbanismo, Comision de Planeamiento y Coordinacion del Area Metropolitana de Madrid) between 1977 and 1979, under the title *Analisis de Problemas y Oportunidades*, synthesizing all urban data and research existing on Madrid. The 12 volumes, published in 1979, were communicated to us by COPLACO as Draft Documents in 1978, thanks to the dedication of its Director, Professor Fernando Teran.
2 The best existing data sources on housing problems in Madrid is an unpublished manuscript by Eduardo Leira, *Desarrollo Urbano y Crisis de la Vivienda en Madrid* (1978, mimeographed, 400 pp.)
3 The special issue on Madrid of the journal *Ciudad y Territorio*, 2-3, (1976).
4 The two monographs by Alfonso Alvarez-Mora, *La*

Remodelacion del Centro de Madrid (Madrid: Ayuso 1978), and *Madrid: las Transformaciones del Centro-Ciudad en el Modo de Producion Capitalista* (Madrid: Colegio de Arquitectos, 1979).
5 The history of planning in Madrid by Fernando Teran, *Planeamiento Urbano en la España Contemporanea* (Barcelona: Gustavo Gili, Barcelona, 1978).
6 We undertook the study of urban, social, and historical characteristics of Madrid's neighbourhoods: M. Castells, A. Alvarez-Mora, N. Pascual, *Evolucion del Tejido Urbano de Madrid y Analisis Tipologico de Barrios* (Madrid: Gerencia de Urbanismo de Madrid, 1978, 400 pages, 108 maps, 5,000 tables, unpublished research report).

Method to Measure Social and Functional Differentiation of Madrid's Neighbourhoods

The research purpose was to differentiate Madrid's spatial areas along a series of scales, comparing them on basic social and functional characteristics. To construct these scales in a way that would gather together all existing data in the simplest and most synthetic possible way, we used factor analysis techniques. There was no data basis on Madrid that allowed for the inclusion of social variables in the same correlation matrix, along with urban functional variables. So, we used two data sources concerning different spatial units:

1 A social variables data basis, relying on the Municipal Population Census of the City of Madrid, as for 31 December 1977. On a correlation matrix of 68 variables, calculated for the 120 administrative neighbourhoods of the city of Madrid, we obtained four 'social' factors that jointly accounted for 65·9 per cent of the variance.
2 An urban-functional variables data basis, relying on the Urban Data Bank of the Metropolitan Planning Commission (COPLACO), the most comprehensive stock of information existing on Madrid. We selected 50 crucial urban functional variables, calculated on the 62 area analysis zones (broader than neighbourhoods) on which the Planning Commission divided the city of Madrid. From the correlation matrix we obtained another four 'urban-functional' factors, jointly explaining 49 per cent of the variance. On the basis of the factors defined, we obtained four factor scores for each one of the 120 administrative neighbourhoods, and four factor scores for the 62 planning areas. Therefore, we could differentiate the space of Madrid in eight scales, ranking spatial units in relationship to the scores of each factor. To make observation simpler, we grouped spatial units in six categories for each scale,

from the higher values (1) to the lower values (6), by grouping together in one structure every one-sixth of the spatial units, once they had been ranked according to the values they scored on the factor used to define each scale. Each one of the eight factors used to differentiate Madrid's spatial areas in six levels was graphically expressed by a map, as shown in the text (pp. 232–41).

The content of the factors (as represented by the names we gave them) was defined by the most loaded variables in each factor. We provide such information as follows (only correlation coefficients above |.30| in both directions were considered).

Social Factors (Population Census)

Factor 1

Most loaded variables on this factor, ordered by decreasing loading scores:

Positive Correlation
a Proportion of technicians and engineers (on resident population).
b Proportion of residents with high-school degree.
c Proportion of employed in managerial activities in private business.
d Proportion of salaried professionals.
e Proportion of salaried technicians.
f Proportion of college graduates.
g Proportion of managers, professionals, and top civil servants.

Negative Correlation
a Proportion not having finished elementary school.
b Proportion of manual workers.
c Proportion of construction workers.
d Proportion of textile workers.
We call Factor 1: Social Status.

Factor 2

Most loaded variables (decreasing order).

Positive Correlation
a Proportion of residents in undefined economic activities.
b Proportion working in agriculture.
c Proportion of unmarried residents.
d Proportion of residents in Madrid after 1972.
e Proportion of domestic servants.

Negative Correlation
a Proportion working in printing.
b Proportion of housekeepers.
c Proportion of active population.
d Proportion of salaried clerks.
e Proportion of all-time residents in Madrid.
f Proportion born in Madrid.
We call Factor 2: Recent Immigration.

Factor 3

Most loaded variables (decreasing order).

Positive Correlation
a Proportion of population of age 50–64 years.
b Proportion of retired.
c Proportion of population over 65.
d Proportion of residents since before 1939.
e Proportion of residents arrived between 1939 and 1952.
f Proportion of handicraftmen, merchants, and independent workers.

Negative Correlation
a Proportion of population between 0–14 years old.
b Proportion of students.
c Proportion of population between 30–40 years old.
We call Factor 3: Aging Population.

Factor 4

Most loaded variables (decreasing order):

Positive Correlation
a Proportion in military service.
b Proportion working in the Public Administration.
c Proportion of professional soldiers and policemen.
d Proportion of civil servants.
e Proportion of active women.
(No significant negative correlation.)
We call Factor 4: Bureaucracy.

Urban Functional Factors (Urban Data Bank)

Factor 1

Most loaded variables (decreasing order):

Positive Correlation
a Proportion of housing units equipped with domestic gas.
b High level of family income.
c High level of car ownership.
d Proportion of largest size of housing units.
e Proportion of housing units equipped with bathroom.

Negative Correlation
a Proportion of housing units without heating.
b Proportion of immigrant population.
c Proportion of housing units without hot water.
d Proportion of low-rent housing units.
e Proportion of housing units without water.
We call Factor 1: Residential Quality.

Factor 2

Most loaded variables (decreasing order):

Positive Correlation
a Proportion of housing units with only cold water.
b Proportion of small housing units.
c Proportion of population working as clerks.
d COPLACO Index of aging housing.
e Residential density.
f Proportion of rental housing units.
g Density of subway stations.

Negative Correlation
  a Proportion of housing units with bathroom.
  b Proportion of housing units rented between 1961 and 1965.
  c Proportion of residents immigrated between 1960–1970.
  d Proportion of house ownership.
We call Factor 2: Old City.

Factor 3
Most loaded variables (decreasing order):

Positive Correlation
  a Proportion of home ownership.
  b Index of daily commuting by private transport.
  c Index of daily commuting by mass transit.

Negative Correlation
Proportion of rental housing units.
We call Factor 3: Urban Dormitory.

Factor 4
Most loaded variables (decreasing order):

Positive Correlation
  a Density of office space.
  b Density of store space.
  c Density of industrial building.
  d Proportion of employment in industry as compared to other activities located in the area.

Negative Correlation
Density of cultural and social service facilities.
We call Factor 4: Space of Production.

The factors, as defined, account for the following proportions of variance between the distinction of social and urban variables among Madrid's spatial units.

Table A.18 Population data (68 variables, 120 neighbourhoods.), Madrid, December 1977.

Factor	Proportion of Explained Variance (factors alone)	Cumulative Proportion of Explained Variance on Total Observed Variance*
I	18·66%	26·28%
II	12·13%	43·36%
III	11·16%	59·08%
IV	4·83%	65·90%

Table A.19 Urban data bank (50 variables, 62 spatial areas.), Madrid, December 1977.

Factor	Proportion of Explained Variance (factors alone)	Cumulative Proportion of Explained Variance on Total Observed Variance*
1	9·29%	18·58%
2	7·40%	33·38%
3	4·44%	42·26%
4	3·35%	49·00%

*Includes proportion of variance explained by each factor and by its interaction with other factors, as well as variance already explained by the preceeding factor.

Ranking and Mapping of Neighbourhood Associations: Analysis of Spatial Distribution of Urban Mobilization in Relationship to Social and Urban Characteristics

To establish the relationship between the social and urban characteristics of the spatial areas and the presence and militancy of neighbourhood associations, we classified the associations in three levels of representativeness and activity, and we mapped them to include their sphere of action within the differentiated space of Madrid.

While our study actually concerned the entire metropolitan area, this particular analysis only referred to the city of Madrid, accounting in 1977 for 3,300,000 people out of the 4,030,000 of the metropolitan area. The reason for this decision was that only the city of Madrid kept relatively accurate statistical information on population and urban functions. Thus, our factor analysis had to be limited to the city, and our general information on neighbourhood associations had to match our statistically reliable spatial unit of observation. The city of Madrid contained, in 1979, 82 of the 110 neighbourhood associations formally in existence in the metropolitan area.

We obtained relatively accurate information on 77 of the 82 neighbourhood associations. We were unable to establish the existence of the five remaining ones. We obtained the list of addresses of all associations from the files of the Federation of Neighbourhood Associations. We added some important associations that were not members of the Federation (such as El Pilar, Malasana, a different *colonias de hotelitos*, Alameda-de-Osuna). We mapped each association by locating its headquarters' address in one of the 120 administrative neighbourhoods into which Madrid was divided. Given the functional self-definition of the associations' range of action, the decision seems to have been accurate enough: no association would act outside its neighbourhoods' territory, except for general campaigns, collectively called.

To rank the associations, we relied on three criteria: first, number of members; second, importance of their mobilizations; and third, major successes in their demands. We used three sources of information: our own knowledge; data from the Federation of Neighbourhoods Association; and independent subjective ranking by three key informants – the 1979 president of the Federation of Neighbourhood Associations the president of Hortaleza, and the president of *La Corrala*. They all fitted in the same evaluation. Actually, a three-level evaluation was an easy one: associations that were clearly known as strong, militant, and representative, having achieved major victories, were classified as level 1; associations that were clearly 'paper organizations' without any acknowledged record of activity or representation, were classified as level 3; associations in between or too difficult to describe were classified as level 2. Thus, we did not have equal numbers in each stratum. Unlike the statistical distribution of spatial units in the eight scales defined by factor analysis, classification of neighbourhood associations in three levels of mobilization was done on a largely qualitative basis, emphasizing their relative performance.

Once we ranked neighbourhood associations on the basis of their mobilization score (2 to 4), and spatial units in terms of their score (1 to 6) in eight scales according to their factor scores, we could calculate a rank-correlation coefficient (Spearman test) between the rankings of spatial units in relationship to social mobilization and in relationship to each one of the eight social and functional factors. The calculation was done as follows:

— Each spatial unit received a score of 1 to 6 on each one of the factor-based scales.
— Each spatial unit received a score of neighbourhood mobilization by multiplying each neighbourhood association located there by its level (1 to 4 multiplier factor, 1 being absence of neighbourhood associations), and by adding all weighed associations' scores within a given spatial unit.
— Rank-correlation was calculated between eight double-series of scores; the final mobilization score for each unit and each one of the eight rank scores received by the spatial units in the social and functional scales constructed on the basis of the eight factors.

We used rank correlation instead of regression analysis because of the uncertain quantification of our levels of neighbourhood mobilization. While we were pretty sure of the hierarchy between levels, we could not guarantee any empirical basis to shift to a metric level in our measurement. The Spearman test gives a reasonable measure of the association between the distribution across the space of two series of properties that rank spatial units in a non-metric but homogenous, decreasing order. At the level of our reasoning, any strong association between properties should have appeared in the form of a strong coefficient. The observed correlation between ranks of two characteristics in their spatial distribution could not have supported any inference of causality by itself. We did not pretend to propose in this study a casual analysis between variables. The aim of the procedure used was to qualify socially and functionally the spatial context where neighbourhood mobilization occurs.

Table A.20 Underlying rationale for the analysis of the citizen movement as an agent of social change.

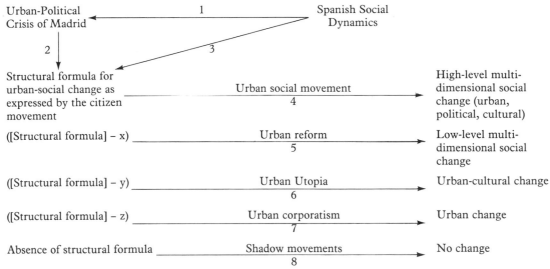

In relationship to this chart, our model attempts to:

1 Not consider explanation of relationships 1, 2, 3 in a systemic form. For epistemological and theoretical reasons, these relationships that are verbally examined in this chapter must be treated in a broader context in our general analytical model.
2 To define the 'structural formula' in a way coherent with our theoretical interpretation.
3 To define precisely what the 5 possible levels of change mean.
4 To identify x, y, z.
5 To prove relationships 4, 5, 6, 7, 8.

Methodological Issues in the Structural Analysis of Neighbourhood Mobilization

Methodological Criteria

The method of structural analysis used to construct our interpretive model of the causes of social change prompted by the Madrid's Citizen Movement was a logical apparatus that simply intended to lend some consistency to our propositions, to state them in a clear way, and to show that they account for a coherent organization of our empirical observation. Any challenge to our interpretation must provide an alternative model that, while being simpler, would be equally coherent and comprehensive.

The model, as proposed, responded to our approach, and could not have provided support for alternative interpretations. But it could have accepted or rejected our hypotheses. As we have seen, it was compatible with most of them. To understand its general logic, we should place it in the context of the underlying structure of our reasoning on the Madrid's Citizen Movement as described in Table A–20.

The model implies mechanical causality: once the context has been settled, all situations in which the formula happens, must produce the projected effects. Systemic variations must produce systematic projected effects. Deviant cases must be minor, and it must be possible to interpret them without altering the main theoretical proposition. Because all observations form a closed universe, there is no problem of statistical representativeness. On the basis of the model and of the relationships we want to establish, we must code the collected observations in an unequivocal manner.

Criteria for Coding

Each neighbourhood mobilization observed was coded, according to a uniform file in relationship to 15 elements. These elements synthesized the basic characteristics that our theory suggests are crucial to understand the structure, practice and effects of the Citizen Movement. We also added the most important control variables usually suggested by alternative interpretations.

The coded elements were defined as follows:

City (Cy)	Urban demands as expressed by the Movement in its active mobilization.
Power (Pw)	Political goals by the Movement's practice.
Community (Cm)	Search for communal social relationships in the Movement's practice.
Movement (M)	Explicit consciousness by the neighbourhood association of being a part of a broader social movement, identified as citizen, and distinct from other social movements.
Class Position (CP)	Social class composition of the neighbourhood (as defined by a clearly predominant class) working class = + ; others = −
Class Consciousness (CC)	Self-definition by the neighbourhood movement as being (+) or not being (−) a part of the working class movement.
Solidarity with other Social Movements (SSM)	Active and conscious involvement by the neighbourhood in struggles of other social movements.
Media (MD)	Expression (or not) of Movements' themes and activities in the mass media (daily newspapers, radio, TV).
Professionals (PF)	Support and advice by established and legitimate professionals (lawyers, architects, planners).
Party (PT)	Active involvement of political militants, acting within the Movement on behalf of a broader political commitment.
Party 1 (PT$_1$)	Presence of a political nucleus within the Movement.
Party 2 (PT$_2$)	Dominance (−) or autonomy (+) between the party and the neighbourhood movement.
Urban Change at the level of Immediate Demands (U$_1$)	When urban demands of the Movement are fulfilled.
Urban change at the level of the Urban System (U$_2$)	When demands imposed by the Movement modify the basic logic of the model of urban development as described.
Political change within the Political System (P$_1$)	Fostering the chances of opposition parties whose programmes reflect in a greater extent popular classes' interests and are traditionally voted by working-class citizens.
Political change and Institutional Change (P$_2$)	Expanding and broadening democratic institutions (reinforcing decentralization, participation, and grassroots control).
Cultural change in the Neighbourhood (C$_1$)	Improving community life and local social networks.
Cultural change in the City (C$_2$)	Transforming the urban culture; making the city a meaningful social setting. The city as a symbolic network for social autonomy.

All codes proceed in a dichotomic manner, by simply assessing the presence (+) or absence (−) of the element.

Using this file we classified the 23 neighbourhood mobilizations on which we had abundant information. Each coding of each element was established as the basis of a series of observations that we called *indicators*. We must make clear what we understood by this term. There was no fixed battery of observations equal for all cases. Coding depended on specific knowledge of specific situations, and in fact organized in a systematic way our own observation.

To evaluate the accuracy and meaning of coding in any research situation three questions must be assessed: the *reliability* of the information; the *validity* of indicators, and the *adequacy* of the coding. Our information was reliable, because it was based on recorded empirical observations whose sources we have carefully identified. Besides, all information was verifiable by checking our research material, as well as by consulting informants knowledgeable about neighbourhoods in Madrid.

By *validity* of indicators, traditional sociological methodology understands the unequivocal correspondence between a given concept and the empirical observation(s) used to measure it. In fact, in our research this question was a superfluous one; because we did not have coded concepts, but actual observable social behaviour whose presence or absence had to be theoretically analysed, our notions such as city, community, power, etc. were simply shorthand expressions to refer to specific empirical behaviour. For instance, if a movement mobilized around urban demands, we coded it City +, and if it did not, we coded it City −. In this case, the presence of urban demands among the Movement's goals was not an indicator of City, but was, in our theoretical language, a movement that had the element city as one of its goals. Thus our research did not need to establish the unequivocal one-to-one relationship between concepts and indicators, but to theorize the empirical behaviour we observed in a series of coded empirical categories, using our file described above.

More complex is the issue of the adequacy of our coding operation. Was our coding consistent for each category in each neighbourhood? Was there a subjective bias in our coding, so that another observer might have coded the same situation under a different value? These are traditional questions of empirical research to which social scientists have generally responded by the use of two complementary procedures:

1 By making available to the general public enough information to allow other researchers to check the logical consistency and empirical reality of the criteria used for the coding.
2 By proceeding to an independent coding by different observers, and cross-checking their judgement.

In our research on Madrid we were able to fulfill the first procedure, but not entirely the second. The reason was that there was not any other observer with the same empirical knowledge *and* theoretical training in relationship to the processes we were analysing in the neighbourhoods of Madrid. In this sense, we were quite close to the situation of an anthropologist who is the only one able to observe a particular culture. Instead of renouncing a systematic analysis, we have, because of the uniqueness of our observation, preferred to proceed as carefully as possible to a personal coding of all the neighbourhood movements we studied, at the same time trying to provide enough reliable empirical information for alternative explanations of the phenomenon we recorded.

Therefore, to satisfy procedure 1 and to go as far as possible towards 2, we summarize in this Appendix the main empirical criteria used to code every element in every neighbourhood. Interested readers might like to try and re-code each neighbourhood association on the basis of the information provided here, and then compare the results of their coding with the one carried out by the author. Interested researchers desiring to go further in the cross-checking operation may recode the original research material. Thus replication procedures are possible, and the limits imposed on our research by the conditions of observation do not reduce our study to mere opinion. Although the theoretical perspective is specific to our thinking, our empirical analysis can be studied objectively under the conditions presented here, and we give below a summary of the observations that led to the systematic categorization of each neighbourhood association.

Coding of Neighbourhood Mobilizations in the Categories Provided by the Analytical Model to Interpret the Madrid's Citizen Movement

Table A-21 List of Cases of Neighbourhood Mobilization

Number	Neighbourhood or Urban Area
1	El Olivar
2	Palomeras Bajas
3	Orcasitas
4	El Pozo del Tio Raimundo
5	San Pascual
6	Orcasur
7	Uva de Hortaleza
8	San Blas
9	Leganes
10	Alcala de Henares
11	Alcorcon
12	El Pilar
13	Moratalaz
14	Quintana
15	Concepcion
16	Aluche
17	Alameda de Osuna
18	Santa Maria and La Union de Hortaleza
19	Colonias de Hotelitos
20	Arganzuela
21	Malasaña (Amaniel-Noviciado)
22	La Corrala (Lavapies)
23	Salamanca

1 Coding Sheet for El Olivar

Element	Code	Indicators
Cy	+	Demands focused exclusively on: 1 Improvement of urban conditions (pavement, water, sewerage, lighting); 2 Avoid eviction from public housing; 3 Obtain re-allocation of empty public housing units to needy neighbours; 4 To obtain a new plan of urban redevelopment aimed at construction of new public housing given, at a very low cost in property, to the residents.
Pw	−	Any political issue could not even be mentioned to keep the association alive. People who were part of the elected steering committee removed as soon as they appeared politically involved.
Cm	−	There were several neighbourhoods, each of them highly differentiated, which became connected only because the activeness of the urban demand movement.
M	−	The only consciousness came from a small militant group. Most participants defended their very narrow material interests as residents.
CP	+	Manual workers, mostly in the construction industry. Some street sellers. High level of unemployment.

CC	–	Any specific statement as workers or working class avoided so as not to scare the residents.
SSM	–	There was deliberately no solidarity in relationship to the workers' unions, which seen as excessively political. Besides, there was some antagonism to the housekeepers women association which tried to foster women's issues, as defined by themselves (prices, schools, health).
PT	+, +	Association entirely created by a small group of CP militants. Nevertheless, rejected any kind of manipulation, disregarded party's instructions and organized street's delegates and open meetings to show unequivocally the movement's autonomy.
MD	–	No evidence of any exposure.
PF	+	A lawyer and an architect were key elements in supporting the association's activities.
$U_{1,2}$	+, +	They obtained, after two year period, full satisfaction of their demands, namely the repairing and rebuilding of public housing at a very affordable cost to relocate all residents.
$P_{1,2}$	–, –	Total apolitical activity.
$C_{1,2}$	–, –	Besides some isolated street party, there was no evidence of any change in the patterns of behaviour in the neighbourhood.

2   Coding Sheet for Palomeras Bajas

Element	Code	Indicators
Cy	+	Movement at various times to legalize squatter dwellings, to improve urban services in the neighbourhood, and to avoid displacement, to obtain public housing for dwellers and relocation on the same site at an affordable cost. Claiming the right to the city for those who built it.
Pw	+	This neighbourhood was the first one to address itself to the Franquist parliament to ask the recognition of its right to stay in its original location as a constitutional right. It also strongly backed different democratic political campaigns.
Cm	+	Strong locally-based social network, originally organized around the Catholic parish. The neighbourhood association was organized by street committees, its headquarters a shack built by the militants, was the physical

		centre for all kinds of social gatherings in the neighbourhood.
M	+	The above cited petition initiative to the parliament was exercised on behalf of the neighbours' movement and appeared – in 1975 – as one of the first manifestations of the Movement for a large sector of public opinion.
CP	+	Mostly, immigrant construction workers. Some gypsy. Some street merchants. Many unskilled service workers.
CC	+	Self-defined as a workers' movement in close connection with the unions, they primarily relied on their self-identification as neighbours.
SSM	+	Solidarity with workers' strikes in several occasions.
$PT_{1,2}$	+, –	Movement initiated by a highly militant group of CP members and, particularly, Christian militants who became Maoists (ORT). Attempts to control the movement from the partisan structure led to continuous in-fighting between the two groups as well as to quarrels with other radical splinter groups. Political debates and strategies always dominated the neighbourhood's mobilization around urban issues.
MD	+	This neighbourhood, as well as the Vallecas' shanty town protest movement, made the newspaper head-lines repeatedly during the 1970s.
PF	+	From the very beginning connected to Christian professionals, to the school of architecture, and to city planners who became, in fact, the main inspiration of the movement.
$U_{1,2}$	+, +	They succeeded: first, in stopping eviction; second, in improving services; third (1971) in obtaining low-income public housing, in a close location, for one third of the dwellers; finally, in 1977, together with all the shanty towns of Vallecas, obtained the expropriation of the squatter settlements by the Ministry of Housing and the commitment to build public housing to relocate, on the same site, all the squatters.
$P_{1,2}$	+, –	Supported the main political anti-fascist demonstrations, as well as the demand for local elections. Subsequently, participated, as most of Vallecas, in building a left-wing political voting constituency, mainly attracted by the Socialist Party,

although the CP and the Maoists scored above their city's average, particularly in the 1979 local elections. Nevertheless, the continuous in-fighting between different political factions seriously weakened the local organization and mobilization. Parties acted using the association as a transmission belt, and, subsequently, the demands for local government decentralization did not have enough strength to be met.

$C_{1,2}$ $-,+$ The frequent political feuds in the neighbourhood restrained the intensity of community feeling. There were almost no celebrations, no social activities nor cultural events. The neighbourhood started to dissolve into the new housing development. At the level of the city, the urban redevelopment struggles in Vallecas imposed a new concept about the rights of squatters and about the goals and procedures of redevelopment policies. Palomeras Bajas was one of the first neighbourhoods to propose the concept.

3 Coding Sheet for Orcasitas

Element	Code	Indicators
Cy	+	Movement originally aimed to obtain basic services (i.e. water supply) for a squatter settlement. Afterwards, the main demand appeared: to redevelop the neighbourhood, obtaining from the Ministry of Housing the expropriation of the land and the provision of low cost new housing in private ownership to the squatters. In addition the new neighbourhood should be fully equipped and its design controlled by the neighbourhood's association and executed by the association's appointed architects.
Pw	+	Participation in campaigns to demand civil rights and political freedom. Active opposition to the rule of local Phalange party cadres. Demands for decentralized local government and participatory democracy.
Cm	+	Existence of a strong local network of social interaction. Most people were immigrants from the southern regions (La Mancha and Andalucia). Local celebrations with active participation

of everybody existed before the association, particularly around a conservative Catholic faith.

M $+$ The highly charismatic leader of Orcasitas became the most respected spokesman for the autonomous movement of shanty town dwellers.

CP $+$ Immigrant construction and other manual workers.

CS $+$ Self-definition as neighbours and as workers.

$SS\ M$ $+$ Active solidarity with strikes and with Construction Workers Commissions.

$PT_{1,2}$ $+,+$ The movement self-generated by the squatters themselves. Afterwards, once the movement was consolidated, most of its leadership joined the CP. But they were always very independent in relationship to the partisan organization and eventually came into conflict with it. They actively participated in the campaign for local elections, cheering the victory of the left in the streets adjacent to the city hall building.

$U_{1,2}$ $+,+$ Obtained full recognition of its redevelopment strategy, building new housing for all dwellers on the same location with a much higher level of collective facilities than most sections of Madrid, the whole process being controlled by the association's own technicians. The experience provided the model for shanty town redevelopment, for organizing new public facilities (for instance, kindergarten, co-operative shops, etc.), and for popular participation in planning.

$P_{1,2}$ $+,+$ A traditionally apolitical immigrant population actively engaged in left wing politics, massively voting for the left parties, particularly in the local elections. They asked for a political model of participatory democracy and imposed some basic changes in that direction, both in the electoral programmes of the left and in the measures implemented by the newly elected city hall. They also imposed on the Ministry of Housing a new procedure of citizens' participation and control in the design and execution of public housing policies. Eventually, they conflicted with the CP when the demands towards participatory democracy were insufficiently met by the left-dominated city council. Thus, tendencially, they were one of the main promoters of a new relationship between the Movement and political parties, as well as between neighbourhoods and public authorities.

$C_{1,2}$ +, +   They strongly stimulated all kinds of local recreational and cultural activities in the neighbourhood, particularly for children. They created consumption co-operatives, they built a house to be the association's home, but also to use it daily as the centre of a miscellaneous set of activities. At a general level, the Orcasitas model, as described by the media, became an example of a neighbourhood-orientated city, with an active local participation and a highly moralistic integrative life style, where the neighbourhood natural leaders became also personal counsellors and controllers of the new social order, particularly to fight back problems of delinquency, drug addiction and juvenile disorder.

4   Coding Sheet for El Pozo del Tio Raimundo

Element	Code	Indicators
Cy	+	Movement focused upon: right to stay in the shacks established illegally; improvement of urban services in the neighbourhood; demand of urban redevelopment in the interest of squatters, expropriating land and providing low-cost public housing to the settlers on the same location. Demands included recognition of the right to the city for those who built it.
Pw	+	Demanded the recognition of free association, free meeting and free expression. Participation in campaigns for amnesty and political democracy. Demand of free municipal elections. Demand of participatory democracy.
Cm	+	Creation of a network of solidarity and mutual support on the basis of the existing Catholic parish activities. The association took the initiative of organizing popular celebrations, street parties, street market, cultural and sport activities.
M	+	The association gathers 2,100 members in a neighbourhood of 2,000 families. Considered themselves as a

part of the Citizens Movement and were among the first group of associations to organize the Madrid Federation of Neighbourhood Associations. Considered themselves to be the pioneers of the Movement in Madrid, breaking down the process of densification, high-rise building and systematic construction of all vacant open space which had characterized the city for the last 15 years.

$P_{1,2}$ −, −   There was no specific political effect. Democracy had already been established, there was no political repression, and the movement took care not to support one particular political force.

$C_{1,2}$ +, +   The neighbourhood took on a new life. Many neighbourhood associations which did not previously exist started to operate. From the existing personal networks, social interaction expanded to community life, incorporating street celebrations and neighbourhoods' gatherings. On the other hand, the hotelitos campaign and the broad support it received from all sectors of public opinion represented a major shift towards an urban ecological culture. The city looked at these private gardens as a clean area, and several colonias, inhabited by well-to-do families refused to have their streets paved in order to discourage traffic. An alternative city clearly emerged as a blueprint from the hotelitos' successful movement.

CP   +   They were all manual workers, immigrants to Madrid coming from the rural areas. The large majority were construction workers.

CC   +   Defined themselves as workers and considered themselves to be a part of the working class struggle.

SSM   +   Active involvement with the workers' struggles, particularly with the construction workers and with the main union. *Comisiones Obreras* (CCOO). They collected for the benefit of strikers. The association created an office for employment, in collaboration with the union, and also organized a training school for union cadres. Nevertheless, the association considered all these activities as acts of solidarity, and defined itself strongly as part of the Citizen Movement, being a differen movement in relationship to the union. Its initiatives always autonomously decided by the neighbourhood association.

$PT_{1,2}$ +,+ The association and the movement directed throughout its history by the same group, while expanding its number and influence. They started as a group of Christians, organized by a Jesuit priest. While the main priest always remained in his original conditions, others became Maoists and were a part of two militant groups, ORT first, then *Bandera Roja*. They finally joined the CP without basically changing their orientation towards the neighbourhood. They always imposed on the party the autonomy of the movement, leading to some confrontations, particularly with the CP.

MD + Was always one of the favourite stories in shanty towns for the media during the 1960s and 1970s, partly because of the legendary figure of Father Uanos, the priest who was living there. The association had also strong connections with the press and one of his main leaders, a former Jesuit, was a professional journalist.

PF + Architects, planners and lawyers admired and supported the neighbourhood demands, particularly in the late 1970s.

$U_{1,2}$ +,+ The movement succeeded, first, in stopping eviction, then in improving the urban services, forcing the local authorities to accept the right of the shanty towns to public facilities. Then it defeated existing redevelopment operation aimed at the transformation in the area into middle class private housing, and imposed public housing at a very low cost for the benefit of the settlers. The neighbourhood to be well-equipped and its development to be planned by a professional team appointed and controlled by the neighbourhood association, the whole budget being provided by the Ministry of Housing. The location of the neighbourhood in a relatively central and valued area contradicted the speculative trends dominating there. The notion imposed by the movement was that the squatters were entitled to major compensation for urbanizing with their effort for many years a desolated land in the urban fringe.

$P_{1,2}$ +,+ The neighbourhood had the highest percentage of Communist and Radical left votes in several elections. It also provided some key political cadres to the CP, among them a city councilman. On the other hand, the neighbourhood strongly supported the autonomy of the movement and the notion of participatory democracy with real effect. The president of the association became in 1979 the president of the Madrid federation of the basis of a programme calling for autonomy of the movement and participation in the local government. It was on the basis of the pressure from this association that some representation was allocated in 1979–80 to the neighbourhoods into the newly created decentralized institutions of the local government (District Councils).

C_1,C_2 +,+ The neighbourhood was full of local life and local activities (celebrations, street parties, sport competitions, public talks, etc.). Also, it opened itself up to the city by organizing a public market on Sundays, sponsoring cultural events, as well as social and political debates.

5 Coding Sheet for San Pascual

Element	Code	Indicators
Cy	+	Demands directed at improvement of urban space and public facilities (pavement, street lighting) as well as to avoid the eviction of squatters from their shanty towns, in a section of the neighbourhood.
Pw	–	While the initiative of creating the association was political, practice and focus of the neighbourhood association was deliberately apolitical.
Cm	–	Very diversified and uncohesive section of the city. No previous social network.
M	+	The attempt was explicitly to build up the Citizens Movement.
CP	–	Manual working-class neighbourhood. The association represented the lower strata.
CC	–	Association defined themselves more as neighbours than as workers.
SSM	+	Active involvement on issues of youth, as well as on women.

$PT_{1,2}$ +, − Association created as an extension of the CP section and tightly controlled by it.

MD   −   Nonexistent expression in the press.

PF   +   Legal assistance as the main device to attract support from the residents.

$U_{1,2}$ −, −   At the time of the survey, the association (being very recent) had not succeeded in any of its claims.

$P_{1,2}$ +, −   The association's activities strongly reinforced the CP in the neighbourhood, as well as other radical groups. Most of the effort was channelled then to electoral campaigning and through the party structure.

$C_{1,2}$ +, −   The association revitalized some neighbourhood life through exhibitions of pictures in the streets, children's activities in the schools, celebrations, public talks on subjects such as women's problems, health, etc. There was no sign of any connection to an upper level of cultural manifestation in the city.

6   Coding Sheet for Orcasur

Element	Code	Indicators
Cy	+	Movement orientated towards a redevelopment programme concerning a dilapidated public housing neighbourhood, asking for new construction to be provided at a very low cost to the same residents in the same location.
Pw	+	Participation in the main political campaigns. Open political radicalism in the practice and discourses of the Association (for instance, singing the International while meeting representatives of the Ministry of Housing).
Cy	+	Strong local network organized by and around radical priests from the local parish. The Church was the meeting point.
M	+	They considered themselves as the vanguard of the neighbourhood Movement.
CP	+	Mostly construction workers. High proportion of unemployed. Significant gypsy minority.
CC	+	They considered themselves as workers in struggle on issues outside the work place.
SSM	+	Solidarity with strikers.
$PT_{1,2}$	+, +	Leadership closely controlled by the ORT, with participation of other

radicals. Nevertheless, influence of the local leadership by the priests established the autonomy of the neighbourhood towards any conflicting guideline.

MD   +   One of the most popular stories by the press, particularly because of the spectacular and often violent expression of protest by Orcasur, was of the invasion of the Ministry of Housing building, demonstrating in downtown, clashing with the police in their neighbourhood, etc.

PF   +   One of the main leaders was a well-known architect. He was under threat of punishment by the Professional Architects' Association because of his participation in the protest. He was strongly defended by the movement, becoming one of the first cases where advocacy planners were sustained and protected by the neighbourhood they were advising on technical matters.

$U_{1,2}$ +, +   Their demands were fully met. They actually represented a major breakthrough in the logic of urban redevelopment: namely, the Ministry actually accepted to demolish its own housing estate and to provide new housing for nothing to the residents, in the same location and improving the quality of urban facilities.

$P_{1,2}$ +, +   Reinforcement of the radical left, strong support for a workers' central model of political democracy.

$C_{1,2}$ +, −   Creation of a cohesive neighbourhood with an intense local cultural activity, and face-to-face interaction. Nevertheless, they remained very isolated in relationship to the city as a whole.

7   Coding Sheet for Uva de Hortaleza

Element	Code	Indicators
Cy	+	Opposition to eviction of residents from public housing units, combined with specific demands to improve the physical condition and urban equipment of the neighbourhood (water, streets' pavement, school, health centre, public garden, street cleaning, lighting). Also the movement protested against the authoritarian style by local management of the public housing complex.
Pw	+	Connection to political campaigns together with other neighbourhoods

within the larger umbrella organization of *La Unita de Hortaleza* (rights of association, freeing arrested leaders, amnesty for political prisoners, free municipal elections).

Cm   +   One of the explicit goals of the movement was to reconstruct the network of social relationships existing among the residents in their former location in the shanty towns, lost after their move to public housing estates. Social meetings and reunion parties were purposely organized to re-establish some basic solidarity and develop new acquaintences.

M   +   As a part of *La Unita de Hortaleza*, they took an active part in the East Madrid Co-ordination of Neighbourhoods and in the Federation of Neighbourhood Associations.

CP   +   Mainly construction and factory workers.

CC   +   Close connection to the Workers Commissions, self-definition as workers.

SSM   +   Solidarity with strikers, close connection with activities of Housekeepers Association.

PT   +,+   Movement Initiated and led by a group of CP militants, who were also recruiting using the movement's participants. At the same time they carefully preserved their autonomy and finally entered into open conflict with the local chapter of the party.

MD   +   Continuous exposure to the press. Frequent stories about the neighbourhood in the Madrid newspapers.

PF   +   Close connection with a group of lawyers and architects.

$U_{1,2}$ +,+   They obtained all their demands. They fundamentally altered the logic of previous urban policy by transforming a unit of provisional public housing into a very well-equipped and well-maintained housing estate, while keeping the same residents and allowing them to participate in the management of the housing estate.

$P_{1,2}$ +,+   Full participation in the overall political process undertaken by *La Unita de Hortaleza*. Check corresponding coding sheet for indicators which are common to both movements (Coding Sheet 18, p. 000).

$C_{1,2}$ +,+   They rebuilt a neighbourhood network in terms of solidarity and interaction. They established several celebrations during the year (spring celebration, King's Cavelcade at Christmas time, etc.). Such celebrations became a major event, not only for the neighbourhood but for the anonymous and dense urban environment of east Madrid. In a broader sense, that impact is inseparable from the cultural transformation produced by *La Union de Hortaleza* (check description on Coding Sheet 18.)

8   Coding Sheet for San Blas

Element	Code	Indicators
Cy	+	Movement focused upon the remodelling and redevelopment of a public housing estate for the benefit of the residents without any additional payment.
Pw	+	This particular neighbourhood association was at the forefront of all political mobilizations in Madrid between 1974 and 1977, on campaigns such as the ones to demand political amnesty, civil rights and democratic elections. As a consequence, the association was temporarily closed down and its president jailed until he was freed by the massive protest organized in many neighbourhoods against his arrest.
Cm	–	The movement did not put any emphasis on the social interaction and neighbourhood life, although as a consequence of massive mobilizations and common struggles, some networks were created.
M	+	Was one of the initiators of the Federation of Neighbourhood Associations, and its charismatic leader became the first president of the Federation.
CP	+	Overwhelming majority of industrial working-class.
CC	+	The movement considered itself as part of the working class movement.
SSM	+	Close connection to the Workers' Commissions and active solidarity with different labour strikes.
$PT_{1,2}$	+,–	Movement initiated by an alliance between CP, socialists, Christians and radical militants, then tightly controlled by the local CP Chapter, and always submitted to violent in-fighting, particularly between the CP and the radical left.
MD	+	Given San Blas' prominence among the new urban periphery of Madrid,

		the press and local radio stations closely followed the evolution of neighbourhood's protest.
PF	+	Day-to-day connection with a group of advocacy planners and lawyers.
$U_{1,2}$	+, +	They obtained all their demands. This victory implied a dramatic correction of the Government's public housing policy. Not only did the large public housing estates have to be improved (instead of remaining pure instruments for the reproduction of labour power at the lowest possible cost) but, when needed, the rehabilitation and redevelopment of the blocks, for free, was officially recognized as being public duty.
$P_{1,2}$	+, −	The movement contributed a great deal to political protest in general and to the political organization and consciousness of San Blas, which later became one of the strongholds of the left, as measured by voting patterns. The CP took the largest share of the gain, although the socialist vote was more important, as in all districts in Madrid. On the other hand, all political commitment was channelled through the left wing parties, and the initiatives of the neighbourhood association always remained subordinated to the political strategies, feuds and alliances.
$C_{1,2}$	−, +	No significant impact on local behaviour of a neighbourhood which remained a largely anonymous and impersonal community.

9 Coding Sheet for Leganes

Element	*Code*	*Indicators*
Cy	+	Demand movement focused upon collective equipment for the city (schools, health centres), upon control on housing conditions (quality of the dwelling units sold by the private developers), and upon transportation (roads for private cars, demand for public mass transit system).
Pw	+	Active participation in specific political campaigns, particularly those called by the Democratic Junta led by the CP.
Cm	−	While Leganes was an anonymous instant city, there was no effort or intention to develop any cultural activity. One of the few attempts was to organize children as red pioneers in a highly politicized effort.
M	−	The neighbourhood leaders considered their action as an extension of political activity, closely subordinated to the party's strategy.
CP	+	An overwhelmingly industrial working class suburb whose social base was reflected in the association's membership.
CC	+	The neighbourhood Association considered itself as a special branch of the working class movement.
SSM	+	Total subordination to the strategy and aims of the Workers' Commissions.
$PT_{1,2}$	+, −	Association founded and tightly controlled by CP militants along with a few members of the radical left. Some opposition from Maoists and socialists lead to sharp in-fighting. The leadership used its influence to foster CP interests: for instance, the association's headquarters housed Worker Commissions' meetings while denying the same right to the UGT.
MD	−	Leganes' spatial and social isolation decreased its exposure to the media, contact with whom was not sought by the neighbourhood militants anyway.
PF	+	Some Labour Union lawyers, together with one advocacy planner, advised the movement in its demands and rights.
U	+, −	Succeeded in obtaining an improvement in transportation, along with some betterment in schools and other public facilities. The struggle was always aimed at services, without altering the pattern of urban development or the system of public services' delivery.
P	+, −	The Association succeeded in mobilizing a wide political support for left parties' initiatives, as well as preparing the ground for an overwhelming victory in the local elections. At the same time, all power was delegated to the party structure and the neighbourhood movement became increasingly weak, lacking any kind of voice in the new power structure.
C	−, −	There was no effect on neighbourhood life nor in the city's culture. In fact, the acute politicization of the movement increased the distance between the values of neighbourhood militants and those of the great majority of residents, who became even more apathetic.

10 Coding Sheet for Alcala de Henares

Element	Code	Indicators
Cy	+	Struggles over urban facilities and services (water, pollution of the river, quality of schools), as well as control of all city planning issues.
Pw	+	Active participation in all political campaigns (from amnesty to elections). Confrontation with the mayor. Demand for municipal elections.
Cm	+	Attempt to set up local networks of interaction and solidarity. Organization of popular celebrations gathering over 4,000 people for several days. Concern with education to raise the cultural level of poor and almost illiterate immigrants.
M	–	Considered itself part of the working class movement and an extension of class struggle, as a support movement in the mobilizations occurring around big factory strikes.
CP	+	An entirely working class city; the neighbourhood association recruited among unskilled industrial workers, newcomers to Madrid from the central and southern rural areas of Spain.
CC	+	Active solidarity with strikers. Connection between neighbourhood conflicts and industrial conflicts. Thus, factories paid the school fees for many children so when there was a strike, the school threatened to expel the students. The neighbourhood association successfully struck back, picketing the school and putting pressure on the mayor to avoid the measure.
SSM	+	Besides solidarity with factory strikes, there was active solidarity also with working women, with women's issues, and with the student movement.
$PT_{1,2}$	+,+	Association initiated and controlled by a group of Maoist and CP militants. Nevertheless, the leadership kept the autonomy of the movement, for instance refusing to be a propaganda platform during the electoral campaign.
Media	–	A very isolated movement.
PF	+	Support and advice from engineers (for the water supply campaign) and lawyers (in general).
$U_{1,2}$	–,–	None of the demands were obtained. Purely defensive struggles to avoid excessive repression had some effect.
$P_{1,2}$	+,–	Strong effect in developing a left wing vote, in mobilizing people for political purposes, and in challenging local authorities, to obtain a democratic municipality. Everything was, afterwards, channelled through the parties, particularly through the PSOE, largely absent from the movement.
$C_{1,2}$	+,–	Neighbourhood life was revitalized, some integration of immigrants in the urban milieu was obtained, cultural activities and public talks were held. All efforts remained limited to the neighbourhood, while the social divisions and oppositions in the city were sharp enough to discourage all cultural effort which would not address the political issues in the first place.

11 Coding Sheet for Alcorcon

Element	Code	Indicators
Cy	+	Mobilization in search of a minimum level of urban equipment in a mushrooming suburban high-rise development (mainly on water supply, heating, mass transit, pedestrian protection against heavy traffic, etc.).
Pw	+	The Association rapidly became a political platform, mobilizing for political amnesty and freedom, and giving priority to specific political goals.
Cm	–	The only cultural events and public talks were politically aimed. No action was undertaken to provide social life for a 180,000 people anonymous development.
M	–	The movement saw itself as an extension of the working class movement.
CP	–	Mixed composition: workers, clerks, low-level professionals.
CC	–	Association saw itself mainly as petty bourgeois.
SSM	+	Close connection (and even subordination) with the trade unions. Full co-operation with the Housekeepers Association.
$PT_{1,2}$	+,–	After a joint beginning by left Christians and the CP, the CP took over. All other political tendencies left the leadership, and the movement became closely linked to the CP's political campaigns.
MD	+	The press reported all problems in Alcorcon as well as the association

PF   +   *Deiveisa* and other professional advocacy agencies elaborated reports on different matters, such as transportation or water supply.

$U_{1,2}$ –, –   No significant demand was met, in spite of some very violent massive demonstrations. Only small improvements in transportation and traffic.

$P_{1,2}$ +, –   Alcorcon became a left wing stronghold. The appointed mayor was dismissed 'for cause of corruption'. The movement remained entirely subordinated to partisan structure and electoral strategy.

$C_{1,2}$ –, –   Remained a socially empty city. Only some political speakers attracted a sizable audience. Celebrations were rare and hardly ever the initiative of the neighbourhood association.

12   Coding Sheet for El Pilar (La Vaguada es Nuestra Coalition)

Element	Code	Indicators
Cy	+	Movement opposing the construction of a metropolitan shopping centre in the middle of a large and very dense high-rise housing estate, and proposing instead to keep the vacant lot as a sizeable urban park, as well as the site for a cultural and civic centre. It also defended small merchants' interests against the competition from big stores, particularly the French-owned chain building the shopping centre.
Pw	–	Most of the associations and militants active in the movement did not participate in any specifically political mobilization. Instead, they focused most of their criticisms against the left parties, considered too reformist in their approach to the problem. Yet this was a political stand, but the question of power as related to the institutions or parties was not posed by the movement, the whole mobilization depending upon the specific issue of the shopping centre as well as on the self-reliance of the neighbourhood as a social community.
Cm	+	Major emphasis on generating a self-sustained community. Continuous initiatives, in the form of parties, folk song and music festivals, neighbourhood newspaper, picnics,

activities, keeping regularly in touch by telephone.

celebrations, etc. The movement decided to establish an alternative culture and claimed its right over the future land development to obtain the spatial support for the neighbourhood's cultural expression.

M   +   Although unrelated to other neighbourhood associations, the coalition *La Vaguada es Nuestra* considered itself as the example of a new form of community mobilization, linking autonomous neighbourhood organization, ecological consciousness, and influencing the quality equipment of the urban setting.

CP   –   Although the urban zone of El Pilar was predominantly working class, the coalition as such brought together various social groups, with a very strong influence of small merchants as well as of young intellectuals and students.

CC   –   The movement explicitly defined itself in cultural terms more than as a class-based mobilization.

SSM   +   Active reciprocal solidarity with the small merchants movement in Madrid, as well as with the youth movement in the neighbourhood. April 1977 saw a general shutdown of small stores in Madrid to support La Vaguada's demands.

$PT_{1,2}$ +, +   The movement was started and animated by a group of Christian militants, allied to some anarchists and libertarian militants. A minority of CP members and Maoist militants opposed the predominant orientation and the coalition was continuously torn apart by political in-fighting. Nevertheless, the movement as such was largely autonomous and spontaneous, partly because nobody had enough power to control it, and partly because the self-reliance ideology of the leading militant group.

MD   +   La Vaguada was the most cited urban conflict in the Madrid newspapers for several years. Several radio programmes were also broadcasted, and major events, such as the occupation of the city hall during a decisive meeting, had a deep impact on public opinion.

PF   +   Several planners provided extensive advice and counter-planning strategies, which proposed an alternative land-use plan for the whole urban area.

$U_{1,2}$ +, –   Although the movement obtained a substantial modification of the initial project, by gaining a civic centre, urban facilities, some open space, and by forcing the commercial building to be done underground, the shopping centre was actually built, and the vacant land was not preserved for a park. Thus, while the quality of the neighbourhood was certainly improved, the challenge to the type of metropolitan commercial equipment and to the increasing densification was defeated.

$PT_{1,2}$ –, –   Given its radicalism again all forms of political representation, the movement did not have any political effect since the damaging impact on the city hall's image also extended to the left-wing parties. Refusing to participate in any local government institution, it slowly disintegrated as an organizational structure.

$C_{1,2}$ +, +   The movement dramatically increased the neighbourhood's life and interaction, as well as collective activities of all sorts, in a highly hostile environment. At the level of the city, some of the major themes of the movement (ecological preservation, keeping small stores, restoring community life, emphasizing street dancing and music festivals) became major popular desires of an alternative life style, to a large extent because of the extent to which La Vaguada's arguments were advanced by the public.

13   Coding Sheet for Moratalaz

Element   *Code*   *Indicators*

Cy   +   Movement to demand improvement of urban facilities and collective equipment in a large housing estate (mainly focused on schools, parks, and public transportation). Attack to illegal construction, criticism of new land-use plan, and mobilization to impose a new plan, reflecting priorities of residents.

Pw   +   Very close construction with all campaigns for political democracy and

amnesty, as well as with political parties and political goals set up by the highly militant leadership.

Cm   –   There was no deliberate effort of the association to set up neighbourhood activities. Cultural events were mainly aimed at political agitation.

M   –   It was one of the main promotees of the Federation of Neighbourhood Associations. Nevertheless, at the level of consciousness, their leaders said that both the association and the Federation were considered to be a platform of the CP and other left-wing parties to broaden their social influence.

CP   –   Mixed social composition (workers, clerks, and low-level professionals).

CC   –   They considered themselves citizens, many of the leaders being teachers.

SSM   +   Strong connection with the teachers' movement, as well as the Christian committees movement.

$PT_{1,2}$ +, –   The CP dominated the association and used it for its own political stances. As a consequence, radicals and independents left their positions in the steering committee. Although this weakened allegiency to the CP, the association also benefits from the strong militant presence of the CP in the neighbourhood.

MD   +   There was close and constant connection with the press, through some personal acquaintances. Madrid's newspapers regularly publish Moratalaz's demands and proposals. This exposure was a major factor in making the association a representative bargaining agent with the administration.

PF   +   Connection with lawyers and planners. Some of the leaders were professional planners.

$U_{1,2}$ +, –   Some of the demands on schools were met by the administration. But other demands, including the one to stop dense construction, were rejected. So, although specific struggles were won, Moratalaz remained a large, dense, underequipped housing estate, as many others on the periphery of the city.

$P_{1,2}$ +, –   The movement succeeded in mobilizing a large sector of the population against the Franquist Government, as well as in defending democratic rights. At the same time the instrumental use of the neighbourhood campaigns for political agitation weakened the movement and left all decisions in the hands of increasingly divided left wing parties.

$C_{1,2}$ –,– No significant effect on neighbourhood life, in striking constrast with other areas of Madrid at the same time.

emerging in the eastern area of Madrid, around the middle class sector of Arturo Soria. An extension of this connection was offered during the street parties organized by the association, but was met by a strong rejection from the residents who otherwise would have been interested in the group's activities.

14 Coding Sheet for Quintana

Element	Code	Indicators
Cy	+	The goals of the existing mobilization were almost exclusively concerned with public facilities, particularly with streets' pavement, open space and traffic signals.
Pw	+	The youth group of the association was exclusively centred on radical politics. As a whole the association participated in all campaigns for political rights.
Cm	–	There was no social cohesion or local network in a large neighbourhood of over 40,000 people.
M	–	They were aware that they were at the beginning of a narrowly focused demand-orientated association.
CP	–	Skilled industrial workers, clerks, civil servants, and army personnel.
CC	–	No definition.
SSM	–	No initiative taken in any sense.
$PT_{1,2}$	+,–	Association started by the CP, following a political decision of the party, and successful negotiation with the Socialist Party to work together. The movement was dominated by the confrontation with splinter radical groups. When there was some important political event all activities of the Neighbourhood Association was suspended, since the militants were too busy with their own parties.
MD	–	Since there were no actions, there was no news in the press.
PF	–	No connection with any advisory group.
$U_{1,2}$	–,–	No demand was met.
$P_{1,2}$	–,–	The Association did not have any specific effect beyond the sphere of influence of the political groups using it as a platform. They did not intervene in the electoral campaign.
$C_{1,2}$	–,+	While not producing any impact at the neighbourhood level, the youth group was linked to the 'dope culture'

15 Coding Sheet for Concepcion

Element	Code	Indicators
Cy	–	There was no one single, urban demand.
Pw	+	Main campaigns related to demand for political amnesty and political freedom. Most of the energy was dedicated to taking over the existing association, previously controlled by the Phalange party.
Cm	+	Street parties and cultural and social activities were basic targets, particularly among the youth, its main supporting group.
M	–	Appeared as a platform of agitation for the different political forces intervening in it.
CP	–	Mixed social composition, with predominance of clerks and low level bureaucrats.
CC	–	Total distance from low, middle class background of radical ideologies of most militants youth.
SSM	–	While political campaigns were the main target, the weakness of the movement did not allow any real mobilization on behalf of other causes. The only attempt, which failed, concerned the organization of a youth clubs' alliance.
$PT_{1,2}$	+,–	All kinds of radical left groups (CP, Maoists, anarchists, etc.) participated in the leadership and fought each other to obtain control of the association, formalizing all initiatives by their feuds.
MD	–	Never heard of this neighbourhood as the basis of any urban protest movement.
PF	–	There were no urban demands, so no contact with the professional milieu.
$U_{1,2}$	–,–	No impact on any urban matter, since there were no campaigns or struggles focused on such issues.
$P_{1,2}$	–,–	The movement isolated itself from the local population: the street parties it

organized scared people and were mainly taken over by youths and drug culture. The rivalries between different radical parties contributed to some political disaffection among a largely moderate social basis, according to the militants' own judgement.

C   −, +   The movement diminished neighbourhood cohesion and frustrated the embryonic social network by assimilating collective activities to social and political radicalism. Nevertheless, its utilization by some youth contributed to the expansion of the marginal youth counter-culture as a new and important aspect emerging in Madrid: the city for pleasure, whatever transgression it implied.

estate without changing either the policy or the functioning of the area.

$P_{1,2}$ +, −   Some effective political mobilization was obtained, strictly limited to partisan politics.

$C_{1,2}$ +, +   Significant improvement of neighbourhood life and popular collectives: children's activities and competitions; Christmas *Cabalgata*; several street merrymakings, one of them gathering over 20,000 people for two days. This change was of major significance in one of the most anonymous new developments of Madrid. Conflict during the merrymaking between families and counter-culture youths.

16   Coding Sheet for Aluche

Element	Code	Indicators
Cy	+	Movement organized around demands of urban equipment for a privately built large housing estate (schools, transportation, pavement, traffic signs, water supply).
Pw	+	Active political demonstrations organized by the association (against police repression, and the undemocratic mayor).
Cm	+	Conscious effort to bring together a large, recent urban zone, emphasizing family life and neighbours' interaction, initially using activities organized for children to build up the networks.
M	−	'Everything is mixed' was the leadership's statement, meaning that CP's initiatives were all connected and the community mobilizations were mainly a fact of an overall political strategy.
CP	−	Mixed social composition both in the association and the housing estate.
CC	−	Self-defined as neighbours.
SSM	−	No connection. A very isolated community, except for specific political mobilizations.
$PT_{1,2}$	+, −	Movement entirely organized, controlled and politically used by the CP.
MD	−	Little coverage in the press, given the low level of activity.
PF	+	Advice from lawyers and planners.
$U_{1,2}$	+, −	Some demands were met, particularly those concerning schools and traffic. The process came, in fact, to slightly improve the equipment of the housing

17   Coding Sheet for Alameda de Osuna

Element	Code	Indicators
Cy	+	Mobilization to improve urban equipment, obtain a park, and propose an alternative land-use plan, while slowing the unlawful construction of several housing blocks in the community.
Pw	−	Although there were some political interests expressed in the association, there was no specific approach to any political issue nor any mobilization on occasion of some political campaigns.
Cm	+	The main motivation behind the activity of the neighbourhood's association was to construct a community life to fill the empty lives of suburban families who were deeply disappointed after losing the urban life of central Madrid.
M	+	Being active in the organization of a neighbourhood co-ordination of east Madrid, the association considered itself a pioneer of both the community mobilization and a middle class perspective to urban problems.
CP	−	Middle class neighbourhood and upper middle class militants.
CC	−	They had a middle class consciousness
SSM	−	No sign of mobilization for other causes.
$P_{1,2}$	−, −	There were no organized political chapters in the neighbourhood. The association argued for participatory democracy, trying to relate the grassroots organization to democratically elected local governments. Thus an

MD   +   Frequent coverage of neighbourhood activities in the press, including reproduction of their alternative land-use plan in the most important of Madrid's newspapers.

PF   +   Several of the neighbourhood leaders were highly skilled professionals, including some in the planning field.

$U_{1,2}$ +,+   They obtained all their demands. Also, they broke down the speculative logic of new suburban development, requiring better equipment, challenging the illegal construction, and contributing to the halting of this form of development in the Madrid area.

$P_{1,2}$ -,-   There was no significant political impact of this association, except for its share in the general support of the Citizen Movement to democratic forms of government.

$C_{1,2}$ +,+   The neighbourhood came alive through all kinds of activities and celebrations. The association was a place to create social networks and to provide mutual support. The sub-urban world was transformed into an urban community in a highly publicized example for the entire city.

autonomous urban movement should have developed but without a partisan structure.

18   Coding Sheet for Santa Maria and La Union de Hortaleza

Element   *Code*   *Indicators*

Cy   +   Mobilization against rent increases and for tenants' participation in the management of the private housing development. Demands for urban equipment and urban facilities (kindergarten, civic centre, transportation, preservation of a park, etc.) Alternative plan under control of the neighbourhood.

Pw   +   Active participation in political campaigns for democracy, as well as on information of residents on local elections, inviting speakers from different political parties.

Cm   +   An explicit goal was to create social interaction, through all kinds of activities ranging from cultural events and street dancing to children's competitions, sports, and a neighbourhood street bookshop on Sundays.

M   +   La Union de Horteleza (with its leadership in Santa Maria) appeared as the symbol of an autonomous neighbourhood movement, and in 1977, 78, and 79 was the most rated association for the presidency of the Madrid Federation of Neighbourhood Associations.

CP   -   Santa Maria was a middle-class zone, and Hortaleza, as a whole, mixed all social groups in the same community organization.

CC   -   The explicit effort was to cut across class lines.

SSM   -   No evidence of any active solidarity.

$PT_{1,2}$ +,+   La Union de Hortaleza was initiated and led by a group of CP cadres, of middle class background, living in Santa Maria. Thus they closely linked the movement to the general orientations of democratic struggle and used the neighbourhood as a recruiting basis for the CP. Nevertheless, they always preserved the autonomous decision of the movement and fiercely opposed all attempts to use it as a transmission belt to the party. Ultimately the leadership came into open conflict with the local CP chapter, and the prestigious president of the Neighbourhood Association, who was also a member of the CP's Madrid committee, left the CP to show his autonomy in relationship to the sectarian manoeuvers of the CP's local chapter.

MD   +   The association had a permanent press service, a daily contact with the Madrid newspapers and radio stations, and a video-team, responsible for producing reports of the neighbourhood's mobilization.

PF   +   Several of the leaders of the movement were lawyers, sociologists and planners, who were putting together alternative proposals on each one of the urban issues at stake.

$U_{1,2}$ +,+   They won all their demands. In addition, they obtained from the private developer the right to control all issues of housing and equipment in the zone. They also obtained from the Metropolitan Planning Commission of Madrid the right to conduct an urban study, paid by the Commission, to determine the basic problems and policies in their area. Their experience was used as the model to set up a new procedure of participatory planning in the whole metropolitan area.

$P_{1,2}$ +,+   They created popular support for democracy, democratic local elections and massive left voting in Hortaleza, in spite of the District's middle class composition. Also, they set up a co-ordination of popular organizations, and imposed, both to the local government and to the partisan structure, an alternative model of participatory democracy.

$C_{1,2}$ +,+   The neighbourhood became the most alive of Madrid's periphery. They had up to a dozen major celebrations per year, as well as continuous cultural and sport activities and a neighbourhood newspaper. They undertook some major initiatives, initiated by the city as a whole, such as organizing a second-hand Sunday Street Market, or planting hundreds of trees and caring for them.

19 Coding Sheet for Colonias de Hotelitos

Element	Code	Indicators
Cy	+	Movement to stop the demolition of middle class single family dwellings located in the core of Madrid, opposing a multi-million speculative drift. To do so, the land-use plan had to be modified to preserve residential uses, low density and surrounding gardens.
Pw	–	Although political support was sought, any political implication of the movement was carefully avoided.
Cm	+	One of the main goals of the movement was to preserve and enlarge existing community relationships established on the basis of a family occupancy of most houses.
M	+	The movement constituted itself in a co-ordination of all single family dwellings' neighbourhoods of the city, and posted banners in the streets proclaiming its goal of defending the urban environment for everybody.
CP	–	Low and middle class, ranging from civil servants and clerks to professionals.
CC	–	They refused to assume any class label, including middle class, and proclaimed themselves simple citizens.
SSM	+	No sign of any joint action with other movements in any issue.

$P_{1,2}$ –,–   Entirely spontaneous and autonomous movement. Although some communists and socialists participate in it, they were not in key leadership positions and never played any role as political militants. The leadership was largely apolitical.

MD   +   There were, in 6 months in 1977, some 180 articles and press reports on the movement, in addition to a very favourable TV programme; all of this was unusual in the context of tight political control in Spanish television.

PF   +   The main leader was a female architect, teaching at the School of Architecture. Several leading planners and lawyers were also advising the movement.

$U_{1,2}$ +,+   They were entirely successful in their demands: a revision of the land-use plan was drafted by the Coalition, preventing any change of use, volume or height. It was then approved by the city council and a year later incorporated into the new Special Master Plan. As a consequence, Madrid could preserve its last low-density garden neighbourhoods.

20 Coding Sheet for Arganzuela

Element	Code	Indicators
Cy	+	Movement to stop eviction of poor and elderly as a consequence of renewal of an old central neighbourhood, and/or to relocate the displaced. Also to provide an alternative land-use plan for the projects of urban redevelopment in the lots of existing railway stations which are supposed to be moved from the downtown area. Neighbours opposed speculative and expensive housing, and asked for social services, open space, playgrounds, and some public housing for their eventual relocation.
Pw	+	The movement was initiated, organized and led as a political platform of the CP. The association intervened in democratic campaigns, electoral training, and supporting CP candidates and strategies concerning the elections.
Cm	+	One of the main goals of the association was to become a social centre connected to the hobbies of the

residents. First moves in that direction were the organization of popular holidays, a tradition that had been lost; a youth club; and a social club for the elderly.

M   –   It was an extension of the CP.

CP   +   Working class neighbourhood and militancy.

CC   –   There was a deliberate effort to represent citizens and to reach all the residents, without limiting the action to the working class.

SSM   +   Close connection to the trade unions, to the housekeepers' association, youth, and the elderly.

$PT_{1,2}$ +, –   Effective and tight CP leadership, without allowing much autonomy. Radical leftists were expelled from it. Socialists left the association. Voting for the CP was approved as an association stand.

MD   +   The press covered the mobilization against eviction. City hall and the association publicly debated in the newspapers.

PF   +   There was a group of lawyers advising the association. Also, some planners prepared the alternative urban redevelopment scheme.

$U_{1,2}$ +, –   Evictions were stopped in some areas, without obtaining the repair of houses. In other cases, eviction happened, but the association forced city hall to relocate the families in public housing in another sector of Madrid. Thus the specific demands were satisfied, but the social logic of urban renewal unchallenged.

$P_{1,2}$ +, –   The neighbourhood was politically mobilized around the left wing parties, and voted more to the left than other neighbourhoods with similar urban and social characteristics. The association was, nevertheless, a service for the residents, and all political participation was channelled through the parties.

$C_{1,2}$ +, –   There was some improvement in the social activities of the neighbourhood, particularly in the street celebrations and network around the youth club. Also, children were invited to participate in painting and writing competitions. The experience was, nevertheless, limited and isolated, and most activities were confined within the close circle of a politicized unity.

21 Coding Sheet for Malasaña (Amaniel-Noviciado)

Element	Code	Indicators
Cy	+	Movement against an urban renewal programme aimed at demolishing an old, popular neighbourhood. Movement for the rehabilitation of an historic palace and its use for public, cultural activities.
Pw	+	Active participation in political campaigns, both democratic and radical. Strong mobilization against fascist violence in the neighbourhood.
Cm	+	Movement's core was to develop an alternative life style (bohemian) together with the preservation of the traditional popular culture of the neighbourhood. Feasts and celebrations, particularly on 2nd May in the square of the same name, were key dimensions, in spite of the disruption caused by youth bands and drug culture.
M	+	Malasaña was the highlight of the convergence between the urban movement and the counter-culture's revolt (such was the self-definition of most participants in the movement).
CP	–	Old population of merchants and retired persons, along with a young group of students and intellectuals. Some marginal sectors, mainly connected with the drug culture and business.
CC	–	Consciousness of being more of a popular movement than a class-based mobilization.
SSM	+	Connection with ecologists, as well as with the student movement.
$PT_{1,2}$	+, +	Movement initiated and led by a Maoist party (PTE). Nevertheless, the movement was much broader: the CP and other radicals took over the leadership, and the PTE militants formed another association. But in spite of the split, the popular support went to the demands and goals of the movement, over and above any specific membership.
MD	+	Full coverage of problems every week in all major newspapers: many young journalists used the neighbourhood as their recreation space. . . .
PF	+	A decisive factor in mounting support was a legal action against the urban renewal plan undertaken by the

Professional Association of Architects. A permanent team, with a paid staff, helped the community to oppose the plan legally and to elaborate its own alternative.

$U_{1,2}$ +, +   The renewal plan was cancelled. All demolitions were stopped. The palace was rehabilitated for public uses. Malasaña became one of the most fashionable 'alternative culture' sections of Madrid. Then gentrification took place, but this slowed down because of street crime related to drug trafficing.

$P_{1,2}$ +, +   The neighbourhood became one of the most politicized and rebellious sections of Madrid. A new political model emerged, fairly critical of the establishment, both of right and left. Whatever ambiguous expression of libertarian individualism was represented, it clearly emphasized the need for the neighbourhood's control over the city hall, as well as self-defense tactics against frequent fascist attacks.

$C_{1,2}$ +, +   The neighbourhood became a live, active place, attracting many youths as well as curious professionals wanting 'another way of life'. Furthermore, it became the centre of the urban drug culture which, in turn, had an impact on the crime rate and police raids. But there was no culture of poverty: it represented a new mood of 'urban decay', while introducing innovation to the city.

22   Coding Sheet for La Corrala (Lavapies)

Element	Code	Indicators
Cy	+	Movement to stop demolition of old, historic neighbourhoods of central Madrid, to avoid the eviction of its residents, to preserve the city, and to obtain a public programme of rehabilitation, renovation and remodelling for the benefit of the resident population.
Pw	+	Active participation in campaigns for democracy. Open support for the left wing parties in the local elections. Established goal of obtaining participatory democracy in the local government.

Cm   +   One of the main objectives of the Movement was to revitalize the historic popular traditions of Madrid, from feasts to neighbourhood theatre and street dancing parties.

M   +   La Corrala sees itself as the vanguard of a new type of Citizen Movement related to the historic city and to the central wards, connecting the defense of people and the defense of the city as a spatial heritage of history.

CP   –   Mixed composition of retired people, merchants, handicraft men, service workers, students and professionals.

CC   –   It was a popular non-class movement.

SMS   +   Close connection with the ecologist movement, as well as with the merchants associations.

$PT_{1,2}$ +, +   Association tightly controlled by the CP, in collaboration with some socialists and Maoists. Nevertheless, the leadership stood for the autonomy of the movement, refusing to follow narrow partisan directives. At several points, there was conflict between the CP members of the neighbourhood association and the CP local chapter.

MD   +   Given the immediate exposure of any action in the historic part of Madrid, the movements' actions and communiqués received frequent exposure in newspapers, radio, and even on regional television.

PF   +   There was a permanent team of lawyers and planners working on a community's task force.

$U_{1,2}$ +, +   The movement tried to stop the evictions, to relocate families of buildings in ruin, to rehabilitate several houses, and to launch a programme of public housing in vacant municipal land of central Madrid aimed at relocating the 300 families evicted by previous demolition. In addition to its demands, the association was one of the main forces behind the mobilization which forced the government to approve a new special plan forbidding any demolition in central Madrid since 1977. Speculative, urban renewal was halted.

$P_{1,2}$ +, +   The neighbourhood evolved towards a less conservative voting pattern and traditional local bases lost their power in the neighbourhood. The association created a co-ordination for community groups of central Madrid and imposed a mechanism of participation in the decisions of the city hall as well as in planning.

$C_{1,2}$　+,+　All kinds of joyful activities blossomed in the neighbourhood, together with mural paintings and street celebrations. Historic buildings were repaired to accomodate plays. Furthermore, some of the most traditional celebrations of the entire city, which had been lost, were organized by this neighbourhood until the city hall finally took responsibility for it, in collaboration with the neighbourhood associations of central Madrid. The first massive celebration of that kind, the *San Isiduo* holiday in May 1978, gathered almost 1,000,000 people in different sectors of the city, with La Corrala being the foremost, popular organizor.

23   Coding Sheet for Salamanca

Element	Code	Indicators
Cy	–	There were no specific urban demands.
Pw	+	All initiatives of the association were linked to the general political campaigns of the Federation of Neighbourhood Associations, particularly the campaign to legalize the associations, as well as some general political democratic mobilizations.
Cm	–	Some cultural events were organized but in a limited way and always addressed to the political left-wing minority.
M	–	The association was a platform for political agitation.
CP	–	Upper and middle class neighbourhood, and student and intellectual militants.
CC	–	The attempt was to reach the middle class.
SSM	+	Connection with the housekeepers' association and with the Human Rights Defense Committee.
$PT_{1,2}$	+,–	From the beginning it was a political
MD	–	platform organized by the local CP. Its
PF	+	tight control alienated the socialists and other political forces. The association always followed the CP's political decision.
$U_{1,2}$	–,–	None
$P_{1,2}$	–,–	Actually, the Salamanca neigh-

bourhood was increasingly the Fascist stronghold in Madrid, following a trend that the associations could not reverse.

$C_{1,2}$　–,–　The only cultural expressions undertaken by the association were of the same upper class style as the traditional ones in the community, except their political orientation was different.

Structural Analysis, Typical Models and Deviant Cases

On the basis of the coding, as justified, of neighbourhood mobilizations, we obtained a series of correspondences between profiles of the different elements hypothesized as constituants of an urban social movement, and their effects. Table 27–1 on page 000 gave the results for all neighbourhood mobilizations. Tables A–22–A–6 offer the results classified by type of social outcome. They show a clearer picture of the analysis presented in Part 5.

The pattern remains an important outstanding problem. Some of the cases analysed here closely follow the predicted pattern, but not entirely. We call these *deviant cases*, to borrow an old, authoritarian tradition in sociology where methodologists used to be angry with those subjects that dared not to adapt their behaviour to the proposed theories. We will not fall into the same trap. Our analytical model is not intended to explain everything. History is diversified and accidental enough to make its path elusive enough for us to lose track at any given moment. Of course, if the difference between the empirical observation and our theoretically-based model, is too great, then history is right (and undeciphered) and it is our model that is wrong. This is, however, not the case here, as we have predicted closely enough: a series of neighbourhood mobilizations(9) miss the predicted pattern by one element. We decided that they were variants of our general model and any attempt to modify their behaviour or explain their aberrance seemed to be a formal game without any real connection to scientific research. Our model explains in a useful way the overwhelming majority of our observations, but more comprehensive, models will always be welcome! One case, however, out of 23 does not really fit our analytical model, and it should therefore be examined.

Case Number 2 Palomeras Bajas
Palomeras Bajas presents the following profile: Cy +; Pw +; Cm +; M +; CP +; Ce +; SSM +; PT +,–, MD +,PF +, $U_{1,2}$ +,+; $P_{1,2}$ +,–; $C_{1,2}$ –,+

The problem concerns an atypical pattern of effects on city and society:

$$U_1 +, U_2 +, P_1 +, P_2 -, C_1 -, C_2 +$$

Or in descriptive language: major urban change at all levels; support for left wing politics and democracy but not for participatory democracy; lack of achievement in neighbourhood life, but major impact on the cultural definition of what a city is and should be.

There are two major differences with our pattern of multidimensional change: P_2- and C_1-. P_2-'s effect is actually consistent with our hypothesis because this movement did not have the basic structural formula: it has PT_2-. The subordination to a party's direction forbade the drift toward participatory democracy:

Leninism was still in action. . . .

C_1- is more cumbersome. Its meaning cannot be formalized. We need to go back to the neighbourhood's experience which reflected the fact that a very innovative urban movement, able to produce effects of cultural change about how society perceives the city, was unable to create a local culture as it was torn apart by political in-fighting. Community-building was incompatible with internal, political war within a working class community. This finding does not fit our model, nor does it contradict it. Could it be serendipity?

Table A.22 Structure of neighbourhood mobilization *underlying the production of an urban social movement*

Cases of Neighbourhood Mobilization	Structural Elements	Effects of High Level Multi-dimensional Change (common to all cases)
(Identified by number)		
3	$Cy + /Pw + /Cm + /M + /PT_1 + /PT_2 + /MD + /PF +$	$U_1 + /U_2 + /P_1 + /P_2 + /C_1 + /C_2 +$
4		
7		
18		
21		
22		
6(*)		
*Variant		
6	$Cy + /Pw + /Cm + /M + /PT_1 + /PT_2 + /MD + /PF +$	$U_1 + /U_2 + /P_1 + /P_2 + /C_1 + /C_2 -$

Table A.23 Structures of neighbourhood mobilization *underlying the production of ubran reform*

Cases of Neighbourhood Mobilization	Structural Elements	Effect of Low-Level Multi-dimensional Change (typical)
5(*)	$Cy + /Pw + /Cm - /M + /PT_1 + /PT_2 - /MD - /PF +$	$U_1 + /U_2 - /P_1 + /P_2 - /C_1 + /C_2 -$
9(*)	$Cy + /Pw + /Cm - /M - /PT_1 + /PT_2 - /MD + /PF +$	
10	$Cy + /Pw + /Cm + /M - /PT_1 + /PT_2 + /MD - /PF +$	
13(*)	$Cy + /Pw + /Cm - /M - /PT_1 + /PT_2 - /MD + /PF +$	
16	$Cy + /Pw + /Cm + /M - /PT_1 + /PT_2 - /MD - /PF +$	
20	$Cy + /Pw + /Cm/M - /PT_1 + /PT_2 - /MD + /PF +$	
*Variants		
5		$U_1 - /U_2 - /P_1 + /P_2 - /C_1 + /C_2 +$
9		$U_1 + /U_2 + /P_1 + /P_2 - /C_1 - /C_2 -$
13		$U_1 + /U_2 - /P_1 + /P_2 - /C_1 - /C_2 -$

Table A.24 Structure of neighbourhood mobilization *underlying the production of urban Utopia*

Cases of Neighbourhood Mobilization	Structural Elements	Effect of Urban Cultural Change
17	$Cy + /Pw - /Cm + /M + /PT_1 - /PT_2 - /MD + /PF +$	$U_1 + /U_2 + /P_1 - /P_2 - /C_1 + /C_2 +$
19	$Cy + /Pw - /Cm + /M + /PT_1 - /PT_2 - /MD + /PF +$	
12(*)	$Cy + /Pw - /Cm + /M + /PT_1 - /PT_2 - /MD + /PF +$	
*Variants		
12		$U_1 + /U_2 - /P_1 - /P_2 - /C_1 + /C_2 +$

Table A.25 Structure of neighbourhood mobilization *underlying the production of urban corporatism*

Cases of Neighbourhood Mobilization	Structural Elements	Effect of Urban Change
1	$Cy + /Pw - /Cm - /M - /PT_1 + /PT_2 + /MD - /PF +$	$U_1 + /U_2 + /P_1 - /P_2 - /C_1 - /C_2 -$
3(*)	$Cy + /Pw + /Cm - /M + /PT_1 + /PT_2 - /MD + /PF +$	
*Variant		
8		$U_1 + /U_2 + /P_1 + /P_2 - /C_1 - /C_2 -$

Table A.26 Structure of neighbourhood mobilization *underlying the production of urban shadows*

Cases of Neighbourhood Mobilization	Structural Elements	Absence of Effects
11(*)	$Cy + /Pw + /Cm - /M - /PT_1 + /PT_2 - /MD + /PF +$	$U_1 - /U_2 - /P_1 - /P_2 - /C_1 - /C_2 -$
14(*)	$Cy + /Pw + /Cm - /M - /PT_1 + /PT_2 - /MD - /PF -$	
15(*)	$Cy - /Pw + /Cm + /M - /PT_1 + /PT_2 - /MD - /PF +$	
23	$Cy - /Pw + /Cm - /M - /PT_1 + /PT_2 - /MD - /PF +$	
*Variants		
11		$U_1 - /U_2 - /P_1 + /P_2 - /C_1 - /C_2 -$
14		$U_1 - /U_2 - /P_1 - /P_2 - /C_1 - /C_2 +$
15		$U_1 - /U_2 - /P_1 - /P_2 - /C_1 - /C_2 +$

Table A.27 Deviant Case

$Cy + /Pw + /Cm + /M + /PT_1 + /PT_2 - /MD + /PF +$	$U_1 + /U_2 + /P_1 + /P_1 - /C_1 - /C_2 +$

6   Access to the Research Files

Our research is based on a series of inter-related propositions whose implications for each case study are not falsified by the recorded empirical observations. Therefore, it is important for the proof that these empirical observations be reliable and unequivocal.

We have already provided detailed information for each case study in the text of each chapter as well as in the Appendices. Additional evidence is provided by the original information we gathered during the 12 year period of our research (1970–1982) in Paris, Santiago de Chile, Madrid, and San Francisco. All the data files of our research (including tapes, transcripts, notes, original documents, and working reports) will be deposited at a university library. Any interested researcher may have access to these files with the author's agreement. At the time of publication (summer 1983), negotiations are still underway with several libraries to ensure the proper custody of this research material and its accessibility. When a final decision has been reached as to the location of our data files, it will be announced in the *International Journal of Urban and Regional Research* (London: Edward Arnold).

Endnotes

Introduction

1   Lewis Mumford, *The City in History: its Origins, its Transformation and its Prospects* (New York: Harcourt, Brace Jovanovich, 1961), p. 93. Rousseau's quote is from his *Le Contrat Social* and may be found in J. J. Rousseau, *The Social Contract and Discourses*, (London: J..M. Dent & Sons, 1973, page 175, footnote 1).

Part 1 Cities and People in a Historical Perspective

1   See, for instance, Robert MacAdams, *The Evolution of Urban Society* (London: Weidenfeld and Nicolson, 1966).

2   See, for instance, William M. Bowsky, *A Medieval Italian Commune: Siena Under the Nine 1287-1355* (Berkeley: University of California Press, 1981); Jacques LeGoff, *La Civilisation de l'occident Medieval* (Paris: Arthaud, 1964); Jose Luis Romero, *Latinoamerica: las Ciudades y las Ideas* (Buenos Aires: Siglo XXI, 1976); I. Lapidus, *Muslim Cities in the later Middle Ages* (Cambridge, Mass.: Harvard University Press, 1967); and the classical work by Fritz Rörig, *The Medieval Town* (Berkeley: University of California Press, 1967. First published in German in 1955 by Propyläen Verlag).

3   See: T. Chandler and G. Fox, *3,000 Years of Urban Growth* (New York: Academic Press, 1974).

4   In the perspective of the classical work by Barrington Moore, *Social Origins of Dictatorship and Democracy: Lord and Peasant in the Making of the Modern World* (London: Peregrine Books, 1969, first published in 1966).

5   Joseph Perez, *La Révolution des Comunidades de Castille (1520-1521)* (Bordeaux: Institut d'Etudes Iberiques et Ibero-Americaines de l'Universite de Bordeaux, 1970. Read in the Spanish updated translation: Madrid: Siglo XXI, 1977.)

6   Jose Antonio Maravall, *Las Comunidades de Castilla* (Madrid: Alianza Universitaria, 1979; First edition, Madrid: Revista de Occidente, 1963.)

7   See Jose Antonio Maravall: *Carlos V y el Pensamiento Politico del Renacimiento* (Madrid: Instituto de Estudios Politicos, 1960).

8   The best source with which to identify the social composition of the *comuneros* is the list of rebels excluded from the royal amnesty because of their role in the revolution. On this point, see: Perez, *La Révolution des Comunidades de Castilla (1520-1521)* 1977 pp. 452-502.

9   *Op. cit.,* p. 501.

10 *Op. cit.,* pp. 509-522.

11 See, Pietro Ingrao, *Masse e Potere* (Roma: Editori Riuniti, 1971).

12 A world that has been magisterially reconstructed, along with the entire European society, by Fernand Braudel, *Civilisation Matérielle, Economie et Capitalisme 15ᵉ-18ᵉ Siecles* (Paris: Armand Colin, Revised Edition 1979, 3 volumes. For our purpose, see particularly volume 3, *Le Temps du Monde*; English translation of first two volumes of Revised Edition, London: Collins, 1981 and 1982, third volume forthcoming).

13 Gregorio Maranon, *Los Castillos en las Comunidades de Castilla* (Madrid: Espasa-Calpe, 1957.

14 See particularly Maravall, *Las Comunidades de Castilla* and also the summary of findings by Perez, *La Révolution des Comunidades de Castilla (1520-21)*.

15 The German historian Werner Sombart researched and prepared the classical analysis of the bourgeoisie as a historical actor. See Werner Sombart, *Der Moderne Kapitalismus* (originally published between 1921-1928).

16 A classical distinction, drawn from Italian urban history, opposes the *Popolo Grasso*, basically the rich merchants, to the *Popolo Minuto*, the manual labourers of the nascent urban economy – two groups with socially divergent interests that will often find themselves together in the defense of the free city.

17 Charles Tilly, ed., *The Formation of National States in Western Europe* (Princeton: Princeton University Press, 1975).

18 Maravall, *Las Comunides de Castilla* p. 55.

19 Manuel Castells, *La Question Urbaine* (Paris: Maspero, 1972 and 1976). *The Urban Question:*

A Marxist Approach (London: Edward Arnold and Cambridge, Mass.: MIT Press, 1977).

20   Max Weber, *The City* (Glencoe, Illinois: The Free Press, 1959).

21   Maravall, *Las Communides de Castilla*, p. 92

22   Lewis Mumford, *The Culture of Cities* (New York: Harcourt, Brace Jovanovich, 1938.)

23   Gideon Sjoberg, *The Pre-Industrial City, Past and Present* (New York: The Free Press, 1960).

24   Jorge E. Hardoy, *Pre-Columbian Cities* (New York: Walker, 1973. First published in Spanish in 1964).

25   Robert MacAdams, *The Evolution of Urban Society* (London: Weidenfeld and Nicolson, 1966).

26   Max Weber, *The City.*

27   See, for instance the special issue 'Histoire et Urbanisation', *Annales*, (September 1970).

28   Max Weber, *The City*, p. 104.

29   *Op. cit.*, p. 115.

30   Alessandro Pizzorno, *Développement Economique et Urbanisation* (Proceedings from the Fifth World Congress of Sociology of the International Sociological Association, Washington, DC, 1962).

31   Pierre Clastres, *La Société contre l'Etat* (Paris: Editions de Minuit, 1974.)

32   Karl Marx, *The Civil War in France, 1871.* (Read in the French translation, Paris: Les Editions Sociales, 1960). Also, J. Bruhat, J. Dautry, E. Tersen, *La Commune de 1871* (Paris: Editions Sociales, 1960).

33   V. I. Lenin, *The State and the Revolution* (Moscow, 1917). Read in the Spanish translation (Moscow: Ediciones del Progreso, 1958).

34   G. Bourgin, *La Commune, 1870–71* (Paris: Les Editions Nationales, 1939) and H. Lefebvre, *La Proclamation de la Commune* (Paris: Gallimard, 1965). Pierre Joseph Proudhon (1809–65), the great French libertarian philosopher, was a major source of inspiration for the *communards*.

35   H. Lefebvre, *La Révolution Urbaine* (Paris: Gallimard, 1970).

36   G. Bourgin, *La Commune* (Paris: Presses Universitaire de France, 1953).

37   J. Duclos, *'A l'Assaut du Ciel'. La Commune de Paris Annonciatrice d'un Monde Nouveau* (Paris: Editions Sociales, 1961).

38   Prosper-Olivier Lissagaray, *Histoire de la Commune de 1871* (Paris: Librairie E. Dentu, 1876. Consulted in the edition by François Maspero, Paris, 1976. All quotes will refer to the 1976 edition).

39   Jacques Rougerie, *Procès des Communards* (Paris: Gallimard-Archives, 1978).

40   *Op. cit.*, p. 131.

41   P.O. Lissagaray, *La Commune de 1871*, p. 172.

42   J. Rougerie, *Communards*, p. 129

43   P.O. Lissagaray, *La Commune de 1871*, p. 131.

44   *Op. cit.*, p. 110.

45   *Op. cit.*, p. 134.

46   *Op. cit.*, p. 211.

47   According to the *Communard* leader, Varlin, cited by Lissagaray, *Op. cit.*, p. 125.

48   The representative of the central government.

49   *Op. cit.*, p. 104.

50   Public institution lending money against the deposit of personal objects.

51   Louis Chevalier, *La Formation de la Population Parisienne au XIX Siècle* (Paris: INED, cahier 10, 1950).

52   David H. Pinkney, *Napoleon III and the Rebuilding of Paris* (Princeton: Princeton University Press, 1958).

53   Particularly Lenin and the Leninist tradition.

54   Manuel Castells, 'Théorie et Idéologie en Sociologie Urbaine', Montreal: *Sociologie et Sociétés, 2,* (1969).

55   They were, according to conservative estimates: 20,000 Parisians killed by the army; 40,000 arrested; nearly 50,000 exiled; 36,000 were tried in military courts, with 10,000 convicted. 93 received death sentences. More than 5,000 were deported to the French colonies. (See Rougerie, *Procès des Communards.*)

56   See our analysis of the relationship between urban renewal in Paris and the creation of political conditions for the domination of the capital by the conservative forces in Castells, *The Urban Question.* We wrote this analysis in 1971, and what we predicted eventually happened in 1977 . . .

57   For a description of the urban evolution of Glasgow, see Charles A. Oakley, *The Second City* (Glasgow and London: Blackie and Son, 1967).

58   See, for instance, S. D. Chapman, (ed.,) *The History of Working Class Housing* (Newton Abbot: David and Charles, 1971).

59   C. G. Pickvance, 'The State and Consumption', Course Unit 24 for *Urban Development* (D202) (Milton Keynes: Open University, 1982).

60   Iain McLean 'Popular Protest and Public Order: Red Clydeside 1915–1919' in J. Stevenson and R. Quinault, eds., *Popular Protest and Public Order* (London: George Allen and Unwin, 1974).

61   On this point, see: P. Wilding, 'The Housing and Town Planning Act of 1919. A Study in the Making of Social Policy' *Journal of Social Policy*, 2(1973).

62   Joseph Melling, *Scottish Industrialists and the*

Changing Characters of Class Relations in the Clyde Region, 1880–1918 in Tony Dickson, ed., *Capital and Class in Scotland* (Edinburgh: John Donald, 1982, pp. 66–142); 'Clydeside Housing and the Evolution of State Rent Control, 1990–1939, in Joseph Melling, ed., *Housing, Social Policy and the State* (London: Croom Helm, 1980); *Employers, Labour, and the Housing Market in Clydeside from 1880 to 1920* (Glasgow: SSRC – University of Glasgow Conference on Social Policy, May 1978, mimeo); *The Glasgow Rent Strike and Clydeside Labour 1914–1915: The Rise of a Social Movement* (Glasgow: Department of Economic History, University of Glasgow, 1978, unpublished paper); 'The Glasgow Rent Strike and Clydeside Labour. Some Problems of Interpretation', *Journal of the Scottish Labour History Society* 13(1979); and a fully revised study exists as *Rent Strikes and Working Class Politics: The Glasgow Rent Strikes and the Rise of Independent Labour in West Scotland, 1890–1916* (Cambridge: King's College Research Centre, University of Cambridge, 1982, unpublished).

63 Sean Damer, 'State, Class and Housing. Glasgow 1885–1919' in Melling, ed., *Housing.*

64 Melling, *Employers*, p. 9

65 The classical book on the subject is Enid Gauldie, *Cruel Habitations: A History of Working Class Housing, 1780–1918* (London: George Allen and Unwin, 1974).

66 See evidence cited by Damer, 'State, Class and Housing',

67 David Englander, *The Workmen's National Housing Council* (Warwick: MA thesis, University of Warwick, 1973) cited by Damer, *Op. cit.*

68 Melling, 'Non-Commissioned Officers: British Employers and their Supervisory Workers, 1880–1920', *Social History*, 5 2(1980).

69 Melling, *Employers*, p. 18.

70 Willie Gallagher, *Revolt on the Clyde* (London: Lawrence and Wishart, 4th edition, 1978) cited by Damer, 'State, Class the Housing', p. 93

71 Yet, factory strikes did happen, centred on the Clyde Workers Committee's initiative. They led to harsh repression and a costly defeat of the movement in early 1915. See Walter Rendall, *The Revolutionary Movement in Britain, 1900–21* (London: Weidenfeld and Nicolson, 1968).

72 Melling, *Employers*, p. 22.

73 Ann and Vincent Flynn, 'We Shall Not Be Removed,' in Laurie Flynn, ed., *We Shall Be All* (London: Bookmarx, 1978), cited by

74 Damer, 'State, Class and Housing'.

74 *Op. cit.*, p. 93.

75 Cited by Melling, *Employers*, p. 20.

76 *Op. cit.*

77 S. Marrett, *State Housing in Britain* (London: Routledge and Kegan Paul, 1979).

78 See particularly the four movements that Melling suggests may be distinguished in Glasgow in 1915, 'Glasgow Rent Strike'.

79 John Foster, 'How Imperial London Preserved its Slums,' *International Journal of Urban and Regional Research*, 3, 1(1979).

80 Manuel Castells, 'Vers une Théorie Sociologique de la Planification Urbaine,' *Sociologie du Travail*, 4(1969).

81 Melling, *Employers*.

82 James Hinton, *The First Shop Stewards' Movement* (London: George Allen and Unwin, 1973).

83 Melling, *Scottish Industrialists*.

84 Raymond Challinor, *The Origins of British Bolshevism* (London: Croom Helm, 1977).

85 Hinton, *Stop Stewards' Movement*, and John McHugh, 'The Clyde Rent Strike', *The Scottish Labour History Society Journal*, 12(1978). For a critique, see, Melling, *Glasgow Rent Strike*.

86 Melling, 'Non-Commissioned Officers'.

87 Cited by Damer, 'State, Class and Housing', p. 87.

88 *Op. cit.*, p. 87.

89 Manuel Castells, 'Advanced Capitalism, Collective Consumption and Urban Contradictions', in N. L. Lindberg et. al, eds., *Stress and Contradiction in Modern Capitalism* (Lexington: D.C. Heath, 1976).

90 Cited in the report published by *Women's Dreadnought*, (Glasgow, October 1915).

91 See evidence presented by Damer, 'State, Class and Housing', p. 98.

92 Helen Crawfurd, *Unpublished Autobiography* (typescript held in the Marx Memorial Library, London; cited by Damer, *Op. cit.*, p. 95).

93 Melling, *Employers*, p. 86.

94 John Broom, *John McLean*, (Loanhead, Midlothian: McDonald, 1933).

95 Damer, 'State, Class and Housing', p. 105.

96 See the systematic empirical evidence gathered on this point by Melling, *Employers* and *Scottish Industrialists*.

97 Melling, *Employers*, p. 30.

98 C. G. Pickvance, 'The State and Consumption'.

99 According to Damer, 'State, Class and Housing'.

99bis This contradiction is that of the level of workers' wages versus rent or house prices. The primary contradiction is, to follow the traditional Marxist formula, between capital and labour in the process of production.

100   For a critique of Engels conception of the housing crisis, see: Manuel Castells, 'Revisar a Engels', Madrid: *Argumentos*, July, 1979.

101   Manuel Castells, 'L'urbanisation dependante en Amérique Latine', *Espaces et Sociétés* 3(1971), pp. 3–19. For a presentation of the analytical perspective of dependency, see Fernando H. Cardoso and Enzo Faletto, *Desarrollo y dependencia en America Latino* (Mexico: Siglo XXI, 1969). The reader is referred to their expanded edition in the French translation, Paris: Presses Universitaires de France, 1979).

102   Third World is an ambiguous notion that refers, in fact, to dependent societies. See Alain Touraine, *Les Sociétés Dependantes* (Bruxelles: Duculot, 1976).

103   Octavio Garcia Mundo, *El Movimento Inquilinario de Veracruz* (Mexico DF: Sepsetentas, 1976).

104   Moises Gonzalez Navarro, *Poblacion y Sociedad en Mexico (1900–1970)*, (Mexico, DF: UNAM, Volume I, Serie Estudio, 42, 1974).

105   Manuel Perlo, 'Politica y Vivienda en Mexico 1910–1952', *Revista Mexicana de Sociologia*; 1(1980).

106   Rafael Ortega Cruz, *Las Luchas Proletarias en Veracruz: Historia y Autocritica* (Jalapa, Veracruz: Editorial Barricada, 1942).

107   Arturo Bolio Trejo, *Rebelion de Mujeres: Version historica de la revolucion inquilinaria de Veracruz* (Veracruz: Edicion del Autor, Editorial 'Kodo,' 1959).

108   According to Rosendo Salazar, cited by Perlo, 'Mexico 1910–1952'.

109   Ortega-Cruz, *Las Luchas*.

109bis   Mario Gill, 'Veracruz: Revolución y Extremismo' in *Historia Mexicana*, 8(1953), particularly pp. 619–620.

110   As reported by *El Dictamen*, Veracruz's conservative newspaper and the oldest in Mexico.

110bis   See: Romana Falcon, *El Agrarismo en Veracruz La Etapa Radical (1928–1935)*, (Mexico DF: El Colegio de Mexico, 1977).

111   See the evidence cited by Perlo, Mexico 1910–1952.

111bis   See: Heather Fowler, *The Agrarian Revolution in the state of Veracruz, 1920–1940* (Unpublished Ph.D. Thesis, Washington DC; The American University, 1970), particularly page 93 onwards.

112   Mundo, *Inquilinario de Veracruz*. Also, Erica Berra-Stoppa 'Estoy en huelga y no pago renta', *Habitacion* (Mexico DF: 1, 1, (1981), pp. 33–41.

113   Mundo, op. cit. Berra-Stoppa cites the figure of 500% in rent increases for the period 1910–1922, saying that a room rented for 3 pesos in 1910 was rented for 15 pesos in 1922; Berra, *Habitacion* p. 37.

114   Perlo, *Mexico 1910–1952*.

115   Mundo, *Inquilinario de Veracruz*.

116   *Jarocho* – native of Veracruz.

117   Mundo, *Inquilinario de Veracruz*.

118   Navarro, *Mexico (1900–1970)*, pp. 180–181.

119   Bolio Trejo, *Rebelion de Mujeres*, p. 53.

119bis   See Falcon, op. cit; Fowler, op. cit.; Mundo, op. cit.

120   Cruz, *Las Luchas*.

121   This is the title of the major book by a detractor of the movement, Bolio Trejo, who assumed that to describe a struggle as women-based was the best way to denigrate it, in a cultural context deeply marked by 'machismo'.

122   Reported by *The New York Times*.

123   Cited by Mundo, *Inquilinario de Veracruz*.

124   As reported by *El Dictamen*, cited by Mundo.

125   *El Dictamen*, 8 May 1922.

126   Daniel Bell and Virginia Held, 'The Community Revolution', *The Public Interest*, 16 (1969), pp. 142–177.

127   Harry Boyte, *The Backyard Revolution: Understanding the New Citizen Movement* (Philadelphia: Temple University Press, 1980.)

128   For an analysis of the characteristics and crisis of the American model of urban development in the period 1945–1975, see our analysis, 'The Wild City' in Joe Feagin, ed., *The Urban Scene. Myth and Reality*. (New York: Random House, 1979).

129   For a presentation of American social evolution in the 1960s, see Morris Janowitz, *The Last Half Century* (Chicago: University of Chicago Press, 1979). For a different view of the process see our book, *The Economic Crisis and American Society* (Princeton, New Jersey: Princeton University Press and Oxford: Basil Blackwell, 1980).

130   For an analysis of the structural conditions characteristic of American inner cities see Bennett Harrison, *Urban Economic Development. Suburbanization, Minority Opportunity and the Condition of the Central City* (Washington, DC: The Urban Institute, 1974).

131   For a detailed analysis of Urban Renewal in America, see Roger Friedland, *Crisis, Power and the Central City* (London: Macmillan, 1983). See also my own analysis in *The Urban Question*, pp. 283–304).

132   The best analysis of American social programmes during the 1960s is still Peter Marris and Martin Rein, *Dilemmas of Social Reform* (London: Routledge and Kegan Paul, 1972).

133   For an informed exposition of the Civil Rights Movement, as well as for a detailed bibliography on it, see Frances F. Piven and Richard A. Cloward, *Poor People's Movements* (New York: Pantheon Books, 1977, pp. 264–363).

134   Saul Alinsky, *Rules for Radicals* (New York: Random House, 1969).

135   Bryan T. Downes, 'A Critical Re-examination of the Social and Political Characteristics of Riot Cities', *Social Science Quarterly*, 51(1970) pp. 349–360.

136   According to Civil Disorder Clearinghouse, Brandeis University, cited by Joe Feagin and Harlan Hahn, *Ghetto Revolts. The Politics of Violence in American Cities* (New York: Macmillan, 1973, p. 105).

137   *Justice Magazine*, February 1972, p. 21.

138   Civil Disorder Clearinghouse, Brandeis University, cited by Feagin and Hahn, *Ghetto Revolts*, p. 105.

139   The importance of ethnic fragmentation in the control of protest from the working class in America has been emphasized by numerous contemporary social scientists. An informed discussion on the issue can be found in Stanley Aronowitz, *False Promises: The Shaping of American Working Class Consciousness* (New York: McGraw-Hill, 1973).

140   Quote from Feagin and Hahn, *Ghetto Revolts*, p. 197.

141   *Report of the National Advisory Commission on Civil Disorders* (New York: Bantam, 1968).

141bis Peter H. Rossi, ed., *Ghetto Revolts* (Chicago: Aldine Publishing Co., 1970) and, more significantly, Peter H. Rossi, Richard A. Berk, and Bettye K. Eidson, *The Roots of Urban Discontent: Public Policy, Municipal Institutions, and the Ghetto* (New York: John Wiley, 1976, The Wiley Series in Urban Research).

142   Seymour Spilerman, 'The Causes of Racial Disturbances: A Comparison of Alternative Explanation', *American Sociological Review* 35 (1970), pp. 627–649; and 'The Causes of Racial Disturbances: Tests of an Explanation,' *American Sociological Review*, 36 (1971), pp. 427–442.

143   Friedland, *Central City*.

144   Feagin and Hahn, *Ghetto Revolts*.

145   For an analysis of the evolution of public response to blacks after the riots, see James Button, 'The Effects of Black Violence: Federal Expenditure Responses to the Urban Race Riots', (Austin, Texas: University of Texas, January 1972), cited by Feagin and Hahn.

146   'Report from Black America', *Newsweek*, 30 June 1969, cited by Feagin and Hahn, *Ghetto Revolts*, p. 279.

147   William F. Ford and John H. Moore, 'Additional Evidence on the Social Characteristics of Riot Cities,' *Social Science Quarterly*, 51(1970), pp. 339–338.

148   Spilerman, 'Racial Disturbances', 1970.

149   Bryan T. Downes, 'Social and Political Characteristics of Riot Cities: A Comparative Study', in Norval D. Glenn and Charles M. Bonjean, eds., *Blacks in the United States* (San Francisco: Chandler, 1969, pp. 427–443).

150   Spilerman, 'Racial Disturbances', 1971.

151   Robert M. Jibou, 'City Characteristics, Differential Stratification and the Occurrence of Inter-racial Violence,' *Social Science Quarterly*, 52(1971), pp. 508–520.

152   For development on the 'space of freedom' as a material basis for social movements, see Boyte, *Backyard Revolution*, p. 37. Boyte himself relies largely on E. P. Thompson.

152bis For an empirical analysis of the influence of autonomous social norms in the black revolts, see: Peter K. Eisinger, *Protest Behavior and the Integration of Urban Political Systems* (Madison: University of Wisconsin, Institute for Research on Poverty, Discussion Paper, 1971).

153   Joel Aberbach and Jack Walker, 'The Meanings of Black Power,' *American Political Science Review*, 64 (1970).

154   T. M. Tomlinson, 'The Development of a Riot Ideology among Urban Negroes' in Allen D. Grimshaw, ed., *Racial Violence in the United States* (Chicago: Aldine, 1969).

155   Social programmes initiated by the Federal Government largely legitimized the possibility of grassroots organizing through the Community Action Programme. See Peter Marris and Martin Rein, *Social Reform*.

156   John M. Goering, 'The National Neighbourhood Movement', *Journal of the American Planning Association*, (1979), pp. 506–522; and Janice Perlman. 'Grassrooting the System' in *Social Policy*, (Sept. 1976).

157   John H. Mollenkopf, *Community Organization and City Politics* (Cambridge, Mass.: Department of Government, Harvard University, 1973 Unpublished Ph.D. thesis.

158   Mollenkopf studied the community mobilization against urban renewal in Boston, Cambridge, San Francisco and Berkeley, on a comparative basis, to formulate a series of hypotheses, grounded on in-depth case studies, to be tested by the analysis of a national sample of community organizations.

159   See, for instance, R. P. Taub, G. P. Surgeon, S. Lindholm, Ph. Betts Otti, and A. Bridges,

'Urban Voluntary Associations, Locality Based and Externally Induced', *American Journal of Sociology*, 83, 2(1977), pp. 425–442.

160 Saul Alinsky, *Reveille for Radicals* (Chicago: University of Chicago Press, 1947); and *Rules for Radicals* (New York: Random House, 1969).

161 Michael P. Connolly, *A Historical Study of Change in Saul D. Alinsky's Community Organization: Practice and Theory, 1939–1972* (Minneapolis: University of Minnesota, Ph.D. Dissertation, 1976).

162 Joan E. Lancourt, *Confront or Concede. The Alinsky Citizen-Action Organizations* (Lexington, Mass.: Lexington Books, 1979).

163 We relied, particularly in Chicago, San Francisco, and Oakland on our pesonal contacts with Alinsky-inspired community organizers, as well as on comments by Janice Perlman on the basis of her extensive experience in the analysis of community organizing in America.

164 V. I. Lenin, *What is to be Done?*, 1902 (Read in Spanish: V. I. Lenin, *Obras Escogidas*, 3 volumes, Moscow: Ediciones del Progreso, 1960).

165 Lancourt, *Alinsky's Community Organizing*, (Ph.D. Thesis Brandeis University, School of Social Work, 1977). The Ph.D. Thesis was the source for Lancourt's book *Confront or Concede*; we read the thesis before the book appeared.

166 *Op. cit.*, p. 443.

167 John Hall Fish, *Black Power, White Control: The Struggle of the Woodlawn Organization in Chicago* (Princeton: Princeton University Press, 1973).

168 *Op. cit.*, p. 76.

169 The characterization of metropolitan concentration, suburban segregation, and institutional fragmentation as the key issues in the post-war pattern of American urban development are presented and justified in Castells, *The Urban Question*, part 5.

170 See Douglas Yates, *The Ungovernable City* (Cambridge, Mass.: MIT Press, 1977).

171 Roger Alcaly and David Mermelstein, eds. *The Fiscal Crisis of American Cities* (New York: Vintage Books, 1977).

172 For a discussion of the connection between the development of collective consumption and urban mobilization, see Castells, *City, Class and Power* (London: Macmillan and New York: St. Martins Press, 1979).

173 See William Tabb, *The Political Economy of the Black Ghetto* (New York: W. W. Norton, 1970).

Part 2 Housing Policy and Urban Trade Unionism: The Grands Ensembles of Paris

1 For the urban evolution of Paris between 1945 and 1970 see Jean Lojkine, *La Politique Urbaine Dans La Région Parisienne (1945–1972)* (Paris: Mouton, 1973). Also, the special issue of the journal *Espaces et Sociétés*, 'Paris: Urbanisme, Classes, Pouvoir', (Paris: 13–14, 1974). For the process of formation of Parisian suburbs, see Jean Bastie, *La Croissance De La Banlieue Parisiennc* (Paris: Presses Universitaires de France [PUF] 1967); P. H. Chombart De Lauwe, *Paris. Essais de sociologie (1952-1964)* (Paris: Editions Ouvrières, 1965); Jacqueline Beaujeu – Garnier and Jean Bastié, *Atlas de Paris et de la Région Parisienne*, (Paris: Berger – Levrault, 1967).

2 The classical analysis on the process of production and management of the French *Grands Ensembles* is Edmond Preteceille, *La Production Des Grands Ensembles* (Paris: Mouton, 1973).

3 See, for instance, M. Castells and F. Godard; *Monopolville* (Paris: Mouton, 1974).

4 See Gilbert Mathieu, *Peut-On Loger Les Français?* (Paris: Seuil, 1965); also G. Ebrik and P. Barjac, *Le Logement, Dossier Noir de la France* (Paris: Dunod, 1970).

5 See Institut National de la Statistique et des Etudes Economiques (INSEE) Census, May 1954; also INSEE Housing Survey, October 1955.

6 See Pierre George *et. al.*, *La Région Parisienne* (Paris: PUF, 1965).

7 See François Ascher and Chantal Lucas, 'L'Industrie du Bâtiment: Des Forces Productives à Libérer', *Economie et Politique* (March 1974); also, Pierre Riboulet, 'Une Construction Primitive Pour Une Societé Développée' in *Espaces et Sociétés*, 6–7 (1973), pp. 115–125.

8 Suzanna Magri, *La Politique de l'Etat en Matière de Logement des Travailleurs* (Paris: Centre De Sociologie Urbaine (CSU), 1973).

9 Christian Topalov, *Capital et Propriété Foncière* (Paris: CSU, 1973).

10 Claude Pottier, *La Logique du Financement Public de l'Urbanisation* (Paris: Mouton, 1975).

11 Louis Houdeville, *Pour Une Civilisation de l'Habitat* (Paris: Editions Ouvrières, 1969), especially pp. 153–166.

12 Christian Topalov, 'Politique Monopoliste et Propriété du Logement', *Economie et Politique* (March 1974); also: S. Magri, *La Politique de l'Etat*.

13 The best study on the institutional and financial mechanisms of the SCIC is Christian Topalov, *La*

SCIC: Etude Monographique d'un Groupe Immobilier Para-Public (Paris: CSU, Research Report, 1969).

14 Alain Lipietz, *Le Tribut Foncier Urbain* (Paris: Maspero, 1974).

15 Bernard Lamy, *Nouveaux Ensembles d'Habitation et leur Environment,* (Paris: CSU, 1972); also, Preteceille, *Grands Ensembles.*

16 Henri Lefebvre, *Le Droit à La Ville* (Paris: Anthropos, 1968).

17 Paul Clerc, *Grands Ensembles Banlieues Nouvelles* (Paris: PUF, 1967); similar trends can be observed in the more recent data presented in Michel Pincon, *Les HLM, Structure Sociale de la Population Logée* (Paris: CSU, 1976, 2vols.).

18 See the striking results of the sociological inquiry on attitudes and social behaviour in the public housing units by Alain Touraine, Nicole Cleuziou, Françoise Lentin, *Une Société Petite-Bourgeoise: Le HLM* (Paris: Centre de Recherche d'Urbanisme, Research Report, 1966).

19 On the evolution of French housing policy and its underlying causes, see M. Castells 'Urban Crisis, State Policies and the Crisis of the State: the French Experience', in, *City, Class and Power,* pp. 37–61.

20 Eddy Cherki, Dominique Mehl, Anne-Marie Metailie, 'Urban Protest in Western Europe', in Colin Crouch and Alessandro Pizzorno, eds., *The Resurgence of Class Conflict in Western Europe Since 1968* (London: Macmillan, 1978, vol. 2, pp. 247–77).

21 Data on Sarcelles were directly gathered by our research. See the Methodological Appendix for a description of sources.

22 Survey by Compagnie d'Information et d'Amenagement (CINAM), 1962.

23 See the most accurate study of the evolution of the French economy after 1965, *Fresque Historique du Système Productif Français* (Paris: INSEE, 1974).

24 According to INSEE, Housing Survey, 1970.

25 Christian Topalov, *Les Promoteurs Inmobiliers* (Paris: Mouton, 1974).

26 Jacques Henrard, *Le Financement Public du Logement* (Paris: CETEM, Research Report, 1975).

27 Data on the Val d' Yerres were gathered by our research. See the Methodological Appendix, pp. 343–45.

28 The *prefecture,* headed by the *prefet,* was the delegation of the central government in each *departement,* the French administrative units above local governments. It was suppressed in 1982.

29 *Animation sociale:* a combination of social work and community action. For a description and analysis of the mechanism see Jean Marie Charon, 'L'Animation Sociale ou Comment Désamorcer les Mouvements Sociaux Urbains', *Espaces et Sociétés,* 12 (1974), pp. 135–77.

30 See Jean-Claude Chamboredon and Monique Lemaire, 'Proximite Spatiale et Distance Sociale: Les *Grands Ensembles* et Leur Peuplement', *Revue Française de Sociologie,* 11 (1) (1970).

31 A female clerical worker in 1974 received an average monthly salary of 900 francs for 45 hours of work per week. In addition, in the Val d' Yerres, they needed an average of two and half hours per day to commute to Paris. Thus 57 hours per week and 228 per month represented their minimum time of non-domestic work. Since they were paying an average of 400 francs for child care, their actual monthly wage was 500 francs, that is 2·20 francs per hour! (In 1974 this represented approximately 15 English pence or 30 American cents.)

32 For an analysis of this new urban policy, literally a zone of Concerted Planning, see Jacotte Bobroff and Fabia Novatin, 'Stratégie Tactique et Necessite de Classe: la Politique d'Albin Chalandon', *Espaces et Sociétés,* 2 (1971).

33 Or *Plan d' Occupation du Sol,* a land-use plan with legal status that may be enforced by law.

34 For sources on urban struggles in Paris see 'Contre-Pouvoirs dans la Ville', the special issue of the Paris-based Journal *Autrement,* 5(1975).

35 Although the electoral shift to the left in the *Grands Ensembles* of Paris is a well-known trend of French politics, it has not yet been statistically charted. An attempt is underway in the broader framework of a statistical analysis of the social determinants of left wing voting in French municipal elections (1947–77) by Michael Aiken and M. Castells (see the Methodological Appendix). It could also be argued that the trend towards left wing voting is a more general tendency of French politics during the 1970s. In fact we are assuming that, for the middle class, there is a significant difference in political behaviour according to place of residence. For instance, technicians and professionals of similar status seem to vote differently depending upon their location in the city of Paris or in the suburban *Grands Ensembles.* The reason for such a difference is not, obviously, the difference of the physical environment, but a crucial intervening variable: the level of urban mobilization triggered by the specific living conditions associated with the *Grands Ensembles.* The experience of collective protest against interests generally associated with business and a right wing government seems to lead to left wing voting. Our current research on the French municipal elections will try to explore this problematic on more rigorous grounds. (See note in Methodological Appendix, for some preliminary statistical findings presented in 1982 by Michael Aiken.)

36 See the excellent analysis of the evolution of the problematic underlying French urban movements by Dominique Mehl, 'Les voies de la Contestation

Urbaine', *Les Annales de la Recherche Urbaine*, 2 (1979).

37 The actual decision making process of the *Circulaire Guichard* was described to the author in personal conversation by a high ranking French civil servant, who received the orders from Guichard, Minister of Equipment, after a tempestuous cabinet meeting. Although the anecdote could not be accepted as scientific evidence, it considerably reinforced our personal belief in the proposed interpretation. For a broader interpretation of the sudden change in French urban policy, see the empirical study by Monique Dagnaud, *Le Mythe de la Qualité de la Vie et la Politique Urbaine en France* (Paris: Mouton, 1976).

38 See the collection of studies presented in Colloque De Recherche Urbaine, *Aménagement Urbain et Mouvements Sociaux* (Paris: CRU, 1978).

39 See the special issue, 'La Démocratie par l'Association?', of the Paris based journal *Esprit*, June 1978.

40 For a description of the evolution and objectives of the CSCV (formerly the CSF), see the book by its Secretary General, Louis Caul-Futy, *Ça Bouge Dans Les Quartiers* (Paris: Syros, 1978).

41 Jean Lojkine, *Le Marxisme, l'Etat et la Question Urbaine* (Paris: PUF 1977).

Part 3 City and Culture: The San Francisco Experience

1   From a letter from San Francisco's Planning Director, Mr: Dean Macris to Supervisor Harry Britt, chairman of the Board of Supervisor's Planning Committee, 10 May 1981.

2   Jerry Carroll, 'San Francisco Charming and Changing', *San Francisco Chronicle*, 16 May 1980.

3   Source: Economic Research Division, Security Pacific National Bank, 1971.

4   Source: 1970 US Census.

5   Source: 1950: US Census; for 1980: US Census, Preliminary Count; for 1975: California Department of Finance, Population Research Unit.

6   Charles Lockwood, *Suddenly San Francisco: The Early Years of an Instant City* (San Francisco: The San Francisco Examiner, A California Living Book, 1978).

7   Mel Scott, *The Future of the San Francisco Bay Area* (Berkeley: University of California, Institute of Governmental Studies, 1963).

8   John Mollenkopf, *Community Organization and City Politics* (Cambridge, Mass.: Department of Government, Harvard University, Unpublished Ph.D. thesis, 1973).

9   Chester Hartman, *Yerba Buena: Land Grab and Community Resistance in San Francisco* (San Francisco: Clide, 1974).

10 Melvin Webber, 'The BART Experience – What Have We Learned?' *The Public Interest*, 45 (1976), pp. 79–108.

10bis Source: Association of Bay Area Governments *Census Data Bulletin No. 1* (Berkeley: ABAG 1981).

11 For an analysis of the new forms of urbanization in America, sometimes referred to as the post-industrial city, see: John Mollenkopf, *The Politics of Urban Development in the US* (Princeton: Princeton University Press, 1983).

12 Mel Scott, *The San Francisco Bay Area. A Metropolis in Perspective* (Berkeley: University of California Press, 1959); J. Vance, *Geography and Urban Evolution in the San Francisco Bay Area* (Berkeley: Institute of Governmental Studies, University of California, 1969). For an intelligent analysis of recent data concerning the Bay Area, see James M. Simmie, *Beyond the Industrial City?* (Berkeley: Association of Bay Area Governments, 1981, mimeographed).

13 Frederick M. Wirt, *Power in the City, Decision-Making in San Francisco* (Berkeley: University of California Press, 1974, particularly chapter 10).

14 Census data on ethnic minorities in San Francisco, as everywhere in America, are rather confusing and subject to caution. First of all, since definitions of racial and ethnic categories were changed for the 1980 Census, race and ethnic totals for 1980 are not comparable to previous totals. Thus, although the decade 1970 to 1980 seems to show spectacular upward trend for Asians and for Other Races, as well as a moderate downward trend for blacks, nothing conclusive can be said on it, given the lack of comparable figures. Even more complex – and very important for our study – is the size of the Latino population. In 1980 there were in San Francisco, according to the US Census, 83,373 people of 'Spanish origin', but since their ethnic definition was considered different from their racial definition, they were included either as Whites or as Others. In any case, they represented 12.3 per cent of the total population. Since they can only be included as Whites or as Others, we have made two hypotheses: 1 All Others are Hispanic – that would maximize the proportion of non-Hispanic whites in the total population; under this hypothesis, whites are scaled down to 359,213 people or 52.9 per cent of the total population. 2 San Franciscans of Spanish origin follow the same pattern that was

observed by the US Census at the national level, i.e. 40 per cent of those counted classified themselves as Others. This second hypothesis appears to be more likely. It is worth remembering that, Hispanics have consistently claimed that they are undercounted. To be sure, illegal immigrants escape the Census. On the basis of our field work, we have estimated that in the Mission District about 20 per cent of Latino residents were workers who had not been counted. Therefore it seems plausible that Latinos account for at least 15 per cent of San Francisco's population and that ethnic minorities make up about 50 per cent of the city's residents.

15   For an analysis of the patterns of evolution of American central cities, see Roger Friedland, Crisis, *Power, and the Central City*.

16   Harvey Zorbaugh, *The Gold Coast and the Slum* (Chicago: University of Chicago Press, 1927).

17   See Citizen Housing Task Force (CHTF), *The San Francisco Housing Dilemma: What Can be Done?* (San Francisco: San Francisco Mayor's office, typewritten report, 62 pages, November 1980).

18   John Mollenkopf summarizes all existing studies on the matter in his report, *The San Francisco Housing Market in the 1980s: An Agenda for Neighbourhood Planning* (San Francisco: Report to the San Francisco Foundation, 1980, mimeographed).

19   Source: San Francisco Department of City Planning, based on the 1950–80 US Census.

20   CHTF, *Housing Dilemma*.

21   Op. cit.

22   There are no reliable comparative data of housing quality that ranks San Francisco in relationship to other central cities of large metropolitan areas. This is because existing studies combine San Francisco and Oakland as one metropolitan area, completely distorting the data. But it is almost generally-held by experts in the field, such as Professor Allan Jacobs, formerly Director of City Planning in San Francisco, that the city's housing stock is very well-maintained.

23   For an analysis of the influence of the 'pro-growth coalition' in urban politics see, John Mollenkopf, 'Neighbourhood Mobilization and Urban Development: Boston and San Francisco, 1968–1978' *International Journal of Urban and Regional Research*, 5. 1(1981).

24   For analyses of minority neighbourhoods in San Francisco see: Ralph M. Kramer, *Participation of the Poor* (Englewood Cliffs, N. J.: Prentice Hall, 1969); Arthur E. Hippler,

Hunter's Point: A Black Ghetto in America (New York: Basic Books, 1970); Marjorie Heins, *Strictly Ghetto Property: The Story of 'Los Siete de la Raza'* (Berkeley: Ramparts Press, 1972); Mollenkopf, *Community Organization*.

25   For the analysis of the emergence of a middle class as a major social basis for neighbourhood movements, see Mollenkopf, 'Neighbourhood Mobilization and Politics and Urban Development'.

26   See the very detailed analysis of San Francisco's local government presented by Wirt, *Power in the City*.

27   See Walton Bean, *Boss Rueff's San Francisco: the Story of Union Labor Party, Big Business and the Craft Prosecution* (Berkeley: University of California Press, 1972).

28   Wirt, *Power in the City*, pp. 114–122.

29   Paul Eliel, *The Waterfront and General Strikes, San Francisco, 1934* (San Francisco: San Francisco Industrial Association, 1934), cited by Stephen E. Barton, *Understanding San Francisco*, 1979.

30   We have benefited from the thorough and well-documented, unpublished analysis of the history of San Francisco's local politics by Stephen E. Barton, *Understanding San Francisco: Social Movements in Headquarters City* (Berkeley: Department of City Planning, University of California Berkeley, 1979, 87 typewritten pages).

31   For an explanation of BART see: Peter Hall, *Great Planning Disasters* (Berkeley: University of California Press, 1982, chap. 4).

32   Personal interview with Professor Jack Kent, founder of 'People for Open Space', San Francisco.

33   Harry Bridges, a communist during the 1930s who was the leader of the Longshoremen's Union, and the historical labour figure in San Francisco.

34   Mollenkopf *Community Organization*, pp. 257–320.

35   See the book fundamental to understanding San Francisco's urban policies: Allan Jacobs, *Making City Planning Work* (Chicago: American Society of Planning Officials, 1978).

36   Hartman, *Yerba Buena*.

37   See 'Highrise, Housing and Politics in San Francisco', in Jim Shoch, ed., *Where Has All the Housing Gone?* (San Francisco: New American Movement, 1979).

38   Mollenkopf, *Neighbourhood Mobilization*.

39   Jim Jones, the leader of the People's Temple, whose mystical exodus ended tragically in Guayana, put his constituency's vote behind Moscone, receiving in exchange some influ-

ence in the operation of the Housing Authority – an example of the unlimited deals afforded by coalition politics.

40 The evaluation comes from several convergent sources that estimate between 12,000 and 20,000 as the number of people who were involved in the coalition. (Source: interviews with Ben Martinez, Mike Miller, Juan Pifarre, among others; the Stanford University Study; and the local press – for instance the *San Francisco Sunday Chronicle and Examiner*, dated 19 July 1970, cites the figure of 12,000.) It has to be noted that these were people organized by all kinds of voluntary organizations, all members of the coalition, including Churches and social agencies. Active militants on the MCO committees probably numbered around 1,000 in the 1970–71 period. There is no doubt that, relative to the population of the Mission District, it was one of the most widely supported urban mobilizations in America within the last 20 years.

41 An approximate reconstruction of the resident population in 1970 of the Mission District (including Mission and Inner Mission) is provided in the Methodological Appendix (pp. 352–53).

42 For a documented summary of the urban and social history of the Mission District see, *A Plan for the Inner Mission* (San Francisco: Mission Housing Development Corporation, March 1974, pp. 6–14).

43 The total population of the Mission neighbourhood has had little variation for 30 years: 52,000 in 1940; 53,000 in 1950; 51,000 in 1960; 51,870 in 1970. But the Spanish-surname population jumped from 5,530 in 1950, to 11,625 in 1960, to 23,183 in 1970. Although there are no available figures for the 1980 census all experts expect that there will be a slight increase of Latinos and Filipinos in the context of a fairly stable population. The data have been collected by the Stanford University Research Team: Noelle Charleston, Robert Jolda, Judith Waldhorn, *Summary of Trends in Housing and Population in the Mission Model Neighbourhood, 1940-1970* (Stanford: Stanford University Community Development Study, 1972, mimeographed).

44 According to the Stanford Community Development Study, the Mission contains 10 per cent of San Francisco's 2,000 historic buildings.

45 The mean of salary distribution in the Mission in 1969 was around 8,000 dollars while in San Francisco as a whole it was 10,908 dollars. 11 per cent of the families were on welfare, against 5 per cent in San Francisco (Stanford Research

Team: Mission Model Neighbourhood).

46 The percentage of the residents over 25 years old who did not have junior high school education was 41 per cent in the Mission, compared to 23 per cent in San Francisco. The percent age that did not have a high school degree was 82 per cent compared to 67 per cent in San Francisco. College-educated adults represented only 7 per cent of the population against 17 per cent of the San Francisco residents. (Data collected from the 1970 Census by the San Francisco Department of City Planning.)

47 For data on this trend, see Methodological Appendix, pp. 000–000.

48 San Francisco Department of City Planning, *The Mission: Policies for Neighbourhood Improvement* (January 1976, mimeographed); also the extensive data provided by, *A Plan for the Inner Mission* San Francisco: Mission Housing Development Corporation, March 1974, two volumes.

49 *Mission 1970 Census: Population and Housing* (San Francisco Department of City Planning, January 1973, mimeographed); and especially Roger Herrera, *Inner Mission Housing Strategy* (Draft document for Citizen Review, San Francisco Department of City Planning, January 1980).

50 See the evaluation of overcrowding as a consequence of recent immigration flows, as established by Herrera, *Housing Strategy*.

51 For a description of the low riders phenomenon, see pp. 120–21.

52 BART has two much – used stations at the meeting of Mission and 24th Street, and Mission and 16th Street; both are favourite meeting places.

52bis *Chicano* – an American with Mexican origins.

53 See the brilliant and well-informed, although passionately partisan, account of this protest: Marjorie Heins, *Strictly Ghetto Property: The Story of 'Los Siete de la Raza'* (Berkeley: Ramparts Press 1972).

54 In the terminology of the ethnic minorities in California, the 'Anglo' are the English speaking whites. The 'Latinos' (many of whom only speak English) are considered white by the Census but are not 'Anglo'. 'Anglo' is thus a category of social experience more than a statistical boundary.

55 Founded and controlled by the Progressive Labour Party, an American Maoist group, formed by ex-members of Students for a Democratic Society (SDS).

56 A Federal agency – the executive branch of the war on poverty.

57 According to the Federally required mandate,

the formula for which became notorious because of the attacks on it by conservative critics of the programme; e.g., Daniel P. Moynihan, *Maximum Feasible Misunderstanding. Community Action in the War on Poverty* (New York: The Free Press, 1969).

58 A radical Latino youth group that tried to emulate the Black Panthers. Heins, *Ghetto Property* provides some information on them. They were a minor element in the district but acquired symbolic value by pointing out the spectrum of Latino riots . . . that never came.

59 For an analysis of the meaning of the Model Cities Program in America see Peter Marris and Martin Rein, *Dilemmas of Social Reform.*

60 Cesar Chavez is the leader of the California Farm Workers, most of them of Mexican origin. He became a nationally prominent figure by the heroic and successful struggle of his union against the agricultural employers. His role was often compared to the one played by Martin Luther King in the very early stages of the black movement.

61 One of the basic elements of the Alinsky model of community organizing is the difference between the president (elected by the grassroots) and the staff director, selected because of his capability and experience. As a consequence, the staff director must change very rapidly to avoid becoming hidebound by bureaucracy. Mike Miller followed the rule to his great regret.

62 San Francisco State College, a well-known university located in San Francisco and funded by the State of California, went on strike for several months in 1969 to support special measures to increase admission for minority students and to design new academic programmes better adapted to their needs. The movement became highly radicalized when faced by stiff opposition and many of the Mission cadres, as well as other minorities, became politicized as a result of their experience in that movement.

63 As a result of such an open representation, the board of the MCO was composed of the following positions: 1 president; 25 executive vice-presidents for: Mexican-Americans, Central Americans, Latin Americans, Puerto Ricans, Afro-Americans, Filipino Americans, Anglo-Americans; Pacific Islanders; Nicaraguans; Salvadorians, Cubans; Europeans; Americans; Mexican Nationals; American Indians; Irish Americans; Italian Americans; Colombians; business, labour, and national sectors; clergy; blacks; senior citizens; and youth.

63bis Cornbread cooked in thin slices – typically Mexican.

64 Stanford University researchers and students played a major role in advising the MCO and designing the Model Cities Proposal. The basic elements of the strategy can be deducted from the analysis of the report presented to the National Science Foundation by the Joint MCO – Stanford Research Team, *Mission Model Neighbourhood.*

65 Red-lining: the practice of most banks refusing loans for housing improvement or home ownership in poor urban areas. For a thorough analysis of red-lining in the Bay Area, see Martin Gellen, *The Dynamics of Institutional Mortgage Disinvestment in the Central City* (Berkeley: University of California, 1979, unpublished Ph.D. thesis in the Department of City and Regional Planning).

66 Significantly enough, a similar conflict developed between black militants and the leadership in another successful Alinsky-inspired organization: the Woodlawn Organization in the Chicago ghetto. At least such is the argument developed in the careful research monograph by Fish, *Black Power, White Control*, and discussed above, pp. 63–5.

67 After leaving the presidency, Ben Martinez was severely injured in a motorcycle accident and was unable to work for a long time. His sudden disappearance from the Mission's political scene aggravated the confusion. He subsequently left the Mission and went to live and work in Los Angeles.

68 A federation of charitable agencies.

69 See data in Methodological Appendix, pp. 352–53.

70 'Angel dust' is a cheap chemical drug, widely used by the Mission youngsters, prolonged use of which induces irreparable and grave brain damage.

71 For an appraisal of the interaction between neighbourhood movements and Federal policies in America see John M. Goering, 'The National Neighbourhood Movement' *Journal of the American Planning Association*, 45,4(1979), pp. 506–514.

72 Particularly the records of meetings, list of participants, and press accounts of militant actions, as kept in the archives of the MCO which we consulted, and as noted in the independent study by the Stanford University Research Team, which was, in turn, confirmed by our own interviews with a broad range of informants.

73 The difference established between *social movement* and *social mobilization* or *struggle* is important here.

74 For a description of the Alinsky model of community organization, see Michael P. Connolly, *A Historical Study of Change* in Saul D. Alinsky's *Community Organization: Practice and Theory, 1939–72* (Minneapolis: University of Minnesota, 1976, unpublished Ph.D. thesis; and Joan E. Lancourt, *Confront or Concede: the Alinsky Citizen-Action Organizations* (Lexington, Mass.: Lexington Books, 1979).

75 Charleston, Jolda, Waldhorn, *Mission Model Neighbourhood.*

76 Mission Housing Development Corporation, *A Plan for the Inner Mission*, p. 14.

77 *Op cit.* (We should point out to those who know San Francisco that Dolores Park is not included in the Inner Mission.)

78 This is a programme that provides public aid to improve the building to minimum legal standards. The programme requires a significant financial effort from the occupants, and generally results in the upgrading of the building while moving out a high proportion of the poor people.

79 In 1975, 85 per cent of Inner Mission residents were renters. The market for rental housing in San Francisco is a busy one. Yet the rents paid in the Mission in 1970 remained within the range of low and moderate rents (see Methodological Appendix, p. 000.)

80 Operation Upgrade and Mission Planning Council, *16th. Street: A Neighbourhood Study* (San Francisco: The Mission Planning Council, 1977, mimeographed); the information was confirmed by our own interviews, as reported in the Appendix, pp. 356–57).

81 Comment transmitted by a *La Raza en Accion Local* staff member during our interview.

82 San Francisco Department of City Planning, *Changes in San Francisco Housing Inventory, 1977* (San Francisco, 1979, mimeographed report, NB table 19).

83 Reliable statistical information on recent immigration flows does not exist on the Mission. Nevertheless, there is general agreement amongst experts that there was an increase of immigrants from Central America, particularly during the period from 1975–80. This is the opinion of Obeca, of a specialist in the San Francisco Planning Dept., of *La Raza*, of the Latino Unity Council, of Latinos for Affirmative Action . . . and it is also our opinion.

84 Mission Planning Council, *24th. Street Problems and Possibilities* (San Francisco: MPC, 1976, mimeographed report).

85 Such is the judgment of the Mission Housing Development Corporation, as recorded in our interview.

86 Interview with the Mission Liason Expert of the San Francisco City Planning Department. Prices went up sharply in 1981, putting the minimum ceiling at about 126,000 dollars.

87 Memo from *Operation Upgrade: Citizens for a Cleaner Mission. 'A Position Statement'* (San Francisco, 15 December 1976, typewritten document).

88 San Francisco Consortium, *Community Organizations in San Francisco* (San Francisco: SFC, 1974).

89 This does not mean electoral mobilization cannot obtain progress. It means that in the event of repeated frustrations, working class people tend to drop out of the electoral system.

90 Estimates of the San Francisco gay population (obviously unrecorded in the Census Data) vary according to different sources. Deborah Wolf, in her book, *The Lesbian Community* (Berkeley: University of California Press, 1979) affirms that, '. . . it has been estimated that by 1977 about 200,000 homosexual women and men, out of a total population of 715,000 live in San Francisco at any one time . . .' (p. 74). Besides the fact that San Francisco's population in 1977 had gone down to 672,700, the figure for the gay population seems overestimated. Claude Fischer, on the basis of several sources including his own survey, considers a more accurate estimate to be that 12 to 15 per cent of all voting-age population adults in the city are homosexual. Nevertheless the visibility and power of homosexuals far exceeds this figure, 'They probably represent 20 per cent or more of the white, Anglo population, and may comprise 25 to 30 per cent of all white Anglo *men* living in the city.' C. S. Fischer, *Dwelling Among Friends* (Chicago: University of Chicago Press, 1981, pp. 237–49 and p. 424).

Most political analysts, including Richard Schlachmann, specialist on gay-voting, believe gays represent 25 per cent of the voters in San Francisco. While gays tend to be active in the political system, a large proportion of the city's ethnic minorities (including foreigners) do not register as voters, and yet there is *some* gay presence among them, which would slightly increase the numbers. In fact, the only serious way of obtaining a reliable estimate would be to ask a representative sample of the population what their sexual preference is. We only know of one properly designed survey in 1980 which included such a question in its poll. It is the *unpublished* survey conducted by Professor Richard De Leon, of the Political Science Department at San Francisco State University, for the City Charter Commission of the City of San Francisco, on a representative sample totalling 1,377 individuals. The findings are presented in the Methodological Appendix.

According to this source the total gay population would be much higher: 24·4 per cent for men, and 17 per cent of the total. If we stay at the level of the total population, where more estimates are made, 17 per cent of the estimated 678,974 population in 1980 represents 115,675 individuals, which corresponds, very roughly, to the commonly cited figure of about 100,000 and to a somewhat higher figure of the estimated registered voters. We can therefore reasonably say that the gay population in San Francisco must be between 110,000 and 120,000 individuals, two-thirds of them being gay men and one-third lesbians. (If we extrapolate the proportions of De Leon's survey, this figure actually fits with Dr. Wolf's more informed estimate of the lesbian population of about 35,000 women.)

91   Barry D. Adam, 'A Social History of Gay Politics' in Martin Levine, ed., *Gay Men: The Sociology of Male Homosexuality* (New York: Harper and Row, 1979, pp. 285–297).

92   See Nora Gallagher, 'The San Francisco Experience' (*Playboy*, January, 1980. *Homophobic* (and *homophobia*) is used in this sentence and elsewhere in the book to mean 'gay-hating'.

93   One of the most perceptive theoretical analyses of the relationship between gay culture and social organization, particularly developing the two themes about the importance of visibility and resocialization for gay people is Jeffrey Escoffier, 'Stigmas, Work Environment, and Economic Discrimination against Homosexuals', *The Homosexual Counseling Journal*, 2, 1(1975). See also: Erving Goffman, *Stigma: Notes on the Management of Spoiled Identity* (Englewood Cliffs: Prentice Hall, 1963).

94   See Sol Licata, *Gay Power: A History of the American Gay Movement 1970-1975* (Los Angeles: University of Southern California, 1978, unpublished Ph.D. thesis).

95   Martin Levine 'The Gay Ghetto' in Levine, ed., *Gay Men*.

96   As defined by Louis Wirth, *The Ghetto* (Chicago: University of Chicago Press, 1928).

97   Laud Humphreys, 'Exodus and Identity: The Emerging Gay Culture' in Levine, ed., *Gay Men*, pp. 134–147.

98   For such an analysis we refer to books such as Levine, ed., *Gay Men*; Alan P. Bell and Martin S. Weinberg, *Homosexualities: A Study of Diversity Among Men and Women* (New York: Simon and Schuster, 1978); and Laud Humphreys, *Out of the Closets: The Sociology of Homosexual Liberation* (Englewood Cliff: Prentice Hall, 1972).

99   See the research monograph by Deborah G. Wolf, *The Lesbian Community* (Berkeley: University of California Press, 1979, p. 72 and following for this particular point).

100   Jack H. Hedblom, 'Social, Sexual and Occupational Lives of Homosexual Women' in *Sexual Behavior* 2, 10(1972).

101   Howard Becker, ed., *Culture and Civility in San Francisco* (New Brunswick, Transactions, 1971).

102   See Frederick M. Wirt, *Power in the City*, p. 122 onwards.

103   In what follows a basic source is the extraordinary work done by the Gay History Project Collective in the Bay Area. Some of this work has been summarized in an article by John d'Emilio 'Gay Politics, Gay Community: San Francisco's Experience', *Socialist Review* 11, 1(1981), pp. 77–104. Much of the information and ideas in our text are inspired by this work although we have considerably broadened the base of our information as a result of our own interviews.

104   As established by A. Kinsey et al., *Sexual Behaviour in the Human Male* (Philadelphia and London: W. B. Saunders, 1948), and *Sexual Behaviour in the Human Female* (Philadelphia and London: W. B. Saunders, 1958).

105   Barbara Weightman, 'Gay Bars as Private Places', *Landscape*, 25, 1(1980).

106   Karla Jay and Allen Young, *Lavender Culture* (New York: Harcourt, Brace, Jovanovich, 1980).

106   Allen Ginsberg, *Howl* (San Francisco: City Light Books, 1956).

107   Jack Kerouac, *On the Road* (New York: Viking 1957 and London: André Deutsch 1958; Penguin 1972).

108   See Paul Goodman, *Growing up Absurd: Problems of Youth in the Organized System* (New York: Random House, 1960).

109   Harvey Milk, aware of the possibility of being murdered (as were John and Robert Kennedy, Martin Luther King, and other political reformers in America) tape recorded his political testament, citing the names of people whom he wanted to take his place on the board of supervisors, and those whom he did not want nominated.

110   Gallagher, 'The San Francisco Experiment'.

111   See William Ketteringham, *Gay Public Space and the Urban Landscape. A Preliminary*

Assessment (A paper delivered to the Association of Pacific Coast Geographers Conference, June 1979).

112 Bureau of Census, *Urban Atlas* (Washington D.C.: Government Printing Office, 1974).

113 Meriel Burtle et al., *The District Handbook. A Coro Foundation Guide to San Francisco's Supervisorial Districts* (San Francisco: Coro Foundation, 1979).

114 The leather culture is that of sado-masochist circles, most of which are made up of heterosexuals.

115 Most of the information on the process of gay renovation in San Francisco was obtained by interviews and documentary research carried on by our former student, Don Lee, for his Master's Thesis: *The Gay Community and Improvements in the Quality of Life in San Francisco* (Berkeley: University of California, 1980, MCP Thesis, Department of City Planning). It is worth saying that we do not share the same interpretation. We did not use his original files but did study written public information. For Don Lee's version of his own findings, we refer the reader to his thesis.

116 Don Lee, *Processes of Spatial Change in the San Francisco Gay Community* (Department of Urban Planning Berkeley: University of California, 1979, Paper for CP 298E).

117 Richard Gorman, 'Casing Out Castro' *After Dark* (June 1979) pp. 38–50.

117bis See, Don Lee, *Real Estate and the Gay Community in San Francisco* (Berkeley: University of California, Paper for Business Administration 280, 1979).

118 Kathy Butler, 'Gays Who Invested in Black Areas', *San Francisco Chronicle* (1 September, 1978).

119 Don Lee, *Castro Street Commercial District: A Preliminary Survey* (Berkeley: University of California, 1978, Department of City Planning, Paper for I.D.S. 24).

120 David Taylor, *The Gay Community and Castro Village: Who's Oppressing Whom* (Berkeley: University of California, 1978, Department of City Planning, Paper for CP 229).

121 Jerry Carroll, 'San Francisco – Charming and Changing', *San Francisco Chronicle* (16 May 1980).

122 This is even recognized by the national magazines such as *Time*. See George Church, 'How Gay is Gay? *Time* (23 April 1979), pp. 72–76.

123 See S. Laska and D. Spain (eds.) *Back to the City* (New York: Pergamon Press, 1980).

124 Don Lee, *Changing Community Structure and the Gay Neighbourhood* (Berkeley: University of California, 1980, Department of City Planning, paper for CP 211).

125 Karen A. Murphy, *The Gay Community and Urban Transformations: A Case Study of San Francisco* (Berkeley: University of California, 1980, Master's Thesis, Department of City Planning).

126 Neil Smith, 'Toward a Theory of Gentrification, A Back to the City Movement by Capital, Not People', *Journal of the American Planning Association*, 45, 4(1979).

127 For detailed information on the social organization of San Francisco's gay community, and a very good report by an outsider, see the interesting book by A. E. Dreuilhe, *La Société Invertie où Les Gais de San Francisco* (Ottawa: Flammarion, 1979). However most of the analysis presented here originates from our own interviews and observations.

128 EST is an institution that organizes sessions of collective spiritual meditation and communication which hundreds of thousands of Californians have attended.

129 Joe Flower, 'Gays in Business: The Prejudice and the Power', *San Francisco Magazine* (September 1980).

130 See data reported in the Methodological Appendix, p. 360.

131 CBS: *Gay Power, Gay Politics* Special Report, (26 April 1980).

132 According to political analyst Richard Schlachman and confirmed by other specialized pollsters in San Francisco.

133 Alice B. Toklas and Gertrude Stein lived and worked together for most of their adult lives. Only Stein obtained recognition from straight society by always keeping secret her personal life.

134 In the best tradition of the political bosses that had controlled, among many others, the Castro Valley of San Francisco which was actually called the 'Capp Corner' in old Irish times. For a good, political chronicle of Harvey Milk's activity, see: Randy Shilts, *The Mayor of Castro Street: The Life and Times of Harvey Milk* (New York: St. Martins Press, 1982) published after we had written these pages.

135 A Berkeley-based, gay activist magazine.

136 According to the coronation ceremony typical of northern California's transvestites.

137 Harry Britt was easily re-elected as supervisor in the 1980 election, in spite of the fact that the election was held under the new city-wide system. The result confirmed the fact that gays had become an electoral force in the city at large, encouraging dreams of a gay mayor in San Francisco.

138 A private 'renovation' of the old harbour pier

that converted it into a complex of restaurants, shops, and tourist attractions, all in very bad taste; the last place to visit in San Francisco.

139   In August 1980, after a heavily financed media campaign, the business groups led by the Chamber of Commerce, won a referendum in San Francisco, re-establishing the city election procedures for the board of supervisors. This was a major political defeat for neighbourhood groups, blacks, and gays.

140   According to studies commissioned by the Department of Housing and Urban Development, as cited by John Mollenkopf, *The San Francisco Housing Market.*

141   See Lewis Mumford, *The Culture of Cities* (New York: Harcourt Brace Jovanovich, 1938).

142   A typical gay around the Castro area may be characterized as having short hair and a moustache, and dressing in a T-shirt, jeans, and leather jacket. This 'code' serves to increase visibility and communication amongst gays as well as helping to identify intruders and potential attackers.

Part 4 The Social Basis of Urban Populism: Squatters and the State in Latin America

1   Bernard Granotier, *La Planète des Bidonvilles: Perspectives de l'Explosion Urbaine dans le Tiers Monde.* (Paris: Seuil, 1980).

2   Elsa Chaney, 'The World Economy and Contemporary Migration', *International Migration Review*, 13 (1979), p. 204.

3   See the data presented for selected squatter settlements in Johannes F. Linn, *Policies for Efficient and Equitable Growth of Cities in Developing Countries* (Washington, DC: The World Bank, July 1979, World Bank Staff Working Paper 342).

4   See Susan Eckstein, *The Poverty of Revolution: The State and the Urban Poor in Mexico* (Princeton: Princeton University Press, 1977); Alejandro Portes and John Walton, *Urban Latin America* (Austin: University of Texas Press, 1976); and David Collier, *Squatters and Oligarchs: Authoritarian Rule and Policy Change in Peru* (Baltimore: The Johns Hopkins University Press, 1976).

5   See Bryan Roberts, *Cities of Peasants: The Political Economy of Urbanization in the Third World* (London: Edward Arnold 1978).

6   John Walton, 'Urban Political Movements and Revolutionary Change in the Third World',

Urban Affairs Quarterly, 15 (1979), pp. 3–22; Paul Lubeck and John Walton, 'Urban Class Conflict in Africa and Latin America: Comparative Analyses from a World Systems Perspective', *International Journal of Urban and Regional Research*, 3, 1(1979) pp. 3–28.

7   See the collection of studies presented in Albert Bergesen, ed., *Studies of the Modern World System* (New York: Academic Press, 1980).

8   See Jorge E. Hardoy, ed., *Urbanization in Latin America: Approaches and Issues* (New York: Anchor Books, 1975).

9   Immanuel Wallerstein, *The Modern World System* (New York: Academic Press, 1974).

10   Andre G. Frank, *Capitalism and Underdevelopment in Latin America* (New York: Monthly Review Press; 1974).

11   In the view proposed a long time ago by Fernando H. Cardoso and Enzo Faletto, *Desarrollo y Dependencia en America Latina* (Mexico DF: Siglo XXI, 1969).

12   Richard J. Barnet and Robert E. Muller, *Global Reach* (New York: Simon and Schuster, 1974); and Folder Fröbel, Jurgen Heinriche and Otto Kreye, *The New Internationalization of Labour* (Cambridge: Cambridge University Press, 1980).

13   Colin Crouch and Alessandro Pizzorno, eds., *The Resurgence of Class Conflict in Western Europe since 1968* (London: Macmillan, 1978, 2 volumes).

14   Anouar Abdel-Malek, ed., *Sociologie de l'Imperialisme* (Paris: Anthropos, 1974); Theotonio dos Santos, *Dependencia Economica y Cambio Revolucionario* (Caracas, Nueva Izquierda, 1970); David Collier, ed., *The New Authoritarianism in Latin America* (Berkeley: University of California Press, 1979); and John Meyer and Michael Hannon, eds., *National Development and the World System* (Chicago University of Chicago Press, 1979).

15   Manuel Castells, *The Economic Crisis and American Society.*

16   Fred Hirsch and John Goldthorpe, eds., *The Political Economy of Inflation* (Cambridge, Mass.: Harvard University Press, 1978).

17   For a discussion of the new political situation in Latin America, see the collection of essays published under the heading of 'Autoritarismo y Democracia' in a special issue of *Revista Mexicana de Sociologia* 42, 3, 80 (1980).

17bis   See for instance, Paul Singer and Vinicius C. Brant, eds., *Sao Paulo: O Povo en Movimento.* (Petropolis: Vozes, 1981).

17ter   See Norbert Lechner, ed., *Estado y Politica en America Latina* (Mexico DF: Siglo XXI, 1981). Also, Osvaldo Hurtado, *El Poder*

Politico en el Ecuador (Barcelona: Aricl, 1977, particularly pp. 189–323) provides an example of the crisis of the Latin American states when confronted by the new world economy.

18   Robert B. Fox, *Urban Population Growth Trends in Latin America* (Washington, DC: Inter-American Development Bank, 1975).

19   Humberto Pereira, ed., *La Vivienda Popular en America Latina* (Caracas: Fundacomun, 1979).

20   Wayne Cornelius, *Politics and the Migrant Poor in Mexico City* (Stanford: Stanford University Press, 1975); and Talton F. Ray, *The Politics of the Barrios of Venezuela* (Berkeley: University of California Press, 1969).

21   Janice Perlman, *The Myth of Marginality* (Berkeley: University of California Press, 1976).

22   Alain Touraine, *Les Sociétés Dependantes* (Brussels: Duculot, 1976).

23   Anthony Leeds, 'The Significant Variables Determining the Character of Squatter Settlements', *America Latina*, 12 (1969), pp. 44–86.

24   See Methodological Appendix to this chapter (pp. 364–65).

25   DESAL was the Christian-Democrat sponsored bureau of social research which played a decisive role in spreading the marginality theory in Latin America. Nevertheless, if we look carefully at the impressive amount of their empirical research, the data actually contradicts their assumptions of the cultural and social effects of marginality. See DESAL, *La Marginalidad Urbana: Origen, Proceso y Modo* (Santiago de Chile, 1969, 2 volumes).

26   See Franz Vanderschueren, 'Significado Politico de las Juntas de Vecinos,' *Revista Latinoamericana de Estudios Urbanos y Regionales* (EURE) (Santiago de Chile: Centro Interdisciplinario de Desarrollo Urbano (CIDU), 1971, volume 2, pp. 67–80). Alejandro Portes, *Cuatro Poblaciones: Informe Preliminar Sobre Situacion y Aspiraciones de Grupos Marginados de Santiago* (Santiago: Land Tenure Centre, 1969, mimeographed).

27   See Magaly Sanchez Ricardo Infante, and *Reproduccion de la Fuerza de Trabajo en la Estructura Urbana: La Condicion de la Clase Trabajadora en Zonas Segregadas de Caracas* (Caracas: Universidad Central de Venezuela, Instituto de Urbanismo, 1980, 4 volumes). Also, Magaly Sanchez, *La Segregation Urbaine á Caracas* (Paris: University of Paris, Unpublished Ph.D. Thesis in Sociology, 1980).

28   Perlman, *Myth of Marginality*; Adolfo Aldunate, *Participacion y Actitud de los Pobladores ante las Organizaciones Poblaci-* onales: *Una Aproximacion a la Heterogeneidad Popular* (Santiago: FLACSO, 1971); and Manuel T. Berlinck, *Marginalidade Social e Relacoes de Clases en Sao Paulo* (Petropolis: Vozes, 1975).

29   Lucio Kowarick, *A Espoliaçao Urbana* (Rio de Janeiro: Paz c Terra, 1979).

30   See Paul Bairoch, *Urban Employment in Developing Countries* (Geneva: International Labour Office, 1973); J. Tokman and E. Klein, eds., *El Subempleo en America Latina* (Buenos Aires: El Cid Editores, 1979); and Ray Bromley and Chris Gerry, eds., *Casual Work and Poverty in Third World Cities* (Chichester and New York: John Wiley, 1979).

31   Larissa Lomnitz, *Como Sobreviven los Marginados* (Mexico DF: Siglo XXI, 1976).

32   Most of the analysis in this section originates from several discussions with Alejandro Portes and the thesis exposed in his book with John Walton, A. Portes and J. Walton, *Labor, Class and the International System* (New York: Academic Press, 1981, pp. 67–107).

33   Carmelo Mesa-Lago, *Social Security in Latin America: Pressure Groups, Stratification, and Inequality* (Pittsburgh: University of Pittsburgh Press, 1978).

34   For sources of data on housing in Mexico, see the Methodological Appendix, (p. 363).

35   Esther Marcano, *Caracas: Autoroutes et Bidonvilles* (Paris: University of Paris, 1979, Ph.D. Thesis).

36   For sources on data on housing in Mexico, see the Methodological Appendix, (p. 363).

37   Gustavo Garza and Martha Schteingart, *El Problema de la Vivienda en Mexico* (Mexico DF: El Colegio de Mexico, 1977).

38   Priscilla Connolly, Enrique Ortiz, and Gustavo Romero, *La Produccion de la Vivienda en Mexico* (Mexico, DF: COPEVI, 1976).

38bis See, for instance, Maria Elena Ducci de Colchero, *La Colonia Popular. Una Manifestación del Problema de la Vivienda*, (Mexico: Universidad Nacional Autonoma, Unpublished Master Thesis in Arehitecture, 1978).

39   Jorge Montano, *Los Pobres de la Ciudad en los Asentamientos Espontaneos* (Mexico DF: Siglo XXI, 1976).

40   Manuel Castells, 'Apuntes Para un Analisis de Clase de la Politica Urbana del Estado Mexicano', *Revista Mexicana de Sociologia*, 4(1977), pp. 161–91. And Beatriz Garcia and Manuel Perlo, 'Las Politicas Habitacionales del Sexenio: Un Balance Inicial', *Habitacion* (1981), pp. 33–45.

41   See the collection of data and analyses presented in Janet Abu-Lughod and Richard

Hay, eds., *Third World Urbanization* (Chicago: Maaroufa Press and London: Methuen, 1977).

42 See Anthony and Elizabeth Leeds, 'Accounting for Behavioural Differences in Squatter Settlements in Three Political Systems: Brazil, Peru and Chile', in Louis Massotti and John Walton, eds., *The City in a Comparative Perspective* (Beverly Hills: Sage Publications, 1976).

43 Etienne Henry, *Urbanisation Dependante et Mouvements Sociaux Urbains* (Paris: Université de Paris, Ph.D. Thesis in Sociology, Unpublished, 1974, 4 volumes); and E. Henry, *La Escena Urbana* (Lima: Pontifica Universidad Catolica del Peru, 1978); David Collier, *Barriadas y Elites: De Odria á Velasco* (Lima: Instituto de Estudios Peruanos, 1976; updated 1978).

44 They always start in the periphery of the city, but with the expansion of urban space, some of the early *barriadas* are now located in the core of the metropolitan area.

45 Jacqueline Weisslitz, *Développement, Dependance, et Structure Urbaine: Analyse Comparative de Villes Peruviennes* (Paris: Université de Paris, 1978, Ph.D. Thesis).

46 Manuel Castells, 'L' Urbanisation Dependante en Amérique Latine', *Espaces et Societes* 3(1971); also Helen Safa, ed., *The Political Economy of Urbanization in Third World Countries* (New Delhi: Oxford University Press, 1982).

47 Etienne Henry, 'Los Asentamientos Urbanos Populares: Un Esquema Interpretativo', *Debates* (Lima), 1, 1(1977) pp. 109–38.

48 David Collier, *Barriadas y Elites*, 1978, p. 61.

49 Alfredo Rodriguez and Gustavo Riofrio, *Segregacion Social y Movilizacion Residencial: El caso de Lima* (Buenos Aires: SIAP, 1974).

50 Leeds and Leeds, 'Accounting for Behavioural Differences', 1976.

51 Luis Unikel, *El Desarrollo Urbano de Mexico* (Mexico, DF: El Colegio de Mexico, 1976).

52 Jorge Montano, *Los Pobres de la Ciudad en los Asentamientos Espontaneos* (Mexico, DF: Siglo XXI, 1976). And Equipo Pueblo, *Surgimiento de la Cordinadora Nacional del Movimiento Urbano Popular: Las Luchas Urbano-Populares en el Momento Actual* (Mexico DF: Conamup, 1982); B. Navarro and P. Moctezuma, 'Clase Obrera, Ejercito Industrial de Reserva y Movimientos Sociales Urbanos de las Clases Dominadas en Mexico', *Teoria y Politica* 2, (1981).

52bis See Susan Eckstein, *The Poverty of Revolution: The State and the Urban Poor in Mexico* (Princeton: Princeton University Press, 1977).

53 See Julio Labastida, 'Los Grupos Dominantes Frente a las Alternativas de Cambio', *El Perfil de Mexico en 1980* (Mexico, DF: Siglo XXI, 1972, Volume 3).

54 Diana Villarreal, *Marginalité Urbaine et Politique de l'Etat au Mexique: Enquéte sur les Zones Residentielles Illégales de la Ville de Monterrey* (Paris: Université de Paris, Ecole des Hautes Etudes en Sciences Sociales, Unpublished Ph.D. Thesis, 1979).

55 For sources on Chile, see Methodological Appendix (p. 362). For an analysis of the overall process, see Manuel Castells, *La Lucha de Clases en Chile* (Buenos Aires: Siglo XXI, 1975); and Barbara Stallings, *Class Conflict and Economic Development in Chile, 1958-1973* (Stanford: Stanford University Press, 1978).

56 See Manuel Castells, 'Movimiento de Pobladores y Lucha de Clases en Chile', *Revista Latinoamericana de Estudios Urbans y Regionales* 7 (1973) pp. 9–36; also, Ernesto Pastrana and Monica Threlfall, *Pan, Techo, y Poder: El Movimiento de Pobladores en Chile, 1970-3* (Buenos Aires: Ediciones SIAP, 1974).

57 Cecilia Urrutia, *Historia de las Poblaciones Callampas* (Santiago: Quimantu, 1972).

58 Jaime Rojas, *La Participation Urbaine dans les Sociétés Dependantes: l'Experience du Mouvement des Pobladores au Chili* (Paris: Université de Paris, 1978, Ph.D. Thesis).

59 Franz Vanderschueren, 'Significado Politico de las Juntas de Vecinos' in *Revista Latinoamericana de Estudios Urbanos y Regionales* (EURE), 1971, volume 2.

60 According to the careful research monograph by E. Santos and S. Seelenberger, *Aspectos de un Diagnostico de la Problematica Estructural del Sector Vivienda* (Santiago: Escuela de Arquitectura, Universidad Catolica de Chile, 1968).

61 Rosemond Cheetham, 'El Sector Privado de la Construccion: Patron de Dominacion', *Revista Latinoamericana de Estudios Urbanos Regionales*, 3 (1971).

62 Jaime Rojas, *La Participation Urbaine*.

63 Luis Alvarado, Rosemond Cheetham, and Gaston Rojas, 'Movilizacion Social en Torno al Problema de la Vivienda', *Revista Latinoamericana de Estudios Urbanos Regionales*, 7(1973).

64 Jose Bengoa, *Pampa Irigoin: Lucha de Clases y Conciencia de Clases* (Santiago: CESO, Universidad de Chile, 1972).

65 For quantitative data on the evolution of the squatter movement, see Pastrana and Threlfall, *Pan, Techo, y Poder*, pp. 60–6.

66 Joaquin Duque and Ernesto Pastrana, 'Le Movilizacion Reivindicativa Urbana de los Sectores Populares en Chile, 1964–72' in

Revista Latinoamericana de Ciencias Sociales, 4 (1973).

67 See Equipo de Estudios Poblacionales del CIDU, 1973, as cited in Methodological Appendix (p. 362).

68 See Equipo de Estudios Poblacionales del CIDU, 'Experiencia de Justicia Popular en Poblaciones', *Cuadernos CEREN* (Santiago), 8 (1971). The most complete analysis on the subject is the Ph.D. thesis by Franz Vanderschueren, 1979, as cited in the Methodological Appendix (p. 362).

69 See the extraordinary study by Christine Meunier, *Revendications Urbaines, Stratégie Politique et Transformation Idéologique: Le Compamento Nueva la Habana, Santiago, 1970-73* (Paris: Université de Paris, 1976, Ph.D. Thesis).

70 Duque and Pastrana, 'La Movilizacion Reivindication Urbana', 1973.

71 According to one of the officials in charge of housing policy under Allende, Miguel Lawner. See Miguel Lawner and Ana-Maria Barrenechea, 'Los Mil Dias de Allende: la Politica de Vivienda del Gobierno Popular en Chile,' (Unpublished Research Report, 1978).

72 Alejandro Villalobos actively resisted the military dictatorship in Chile; he was murdered in the street by the junta's political police in 1975, but his death was officially announced as 'a clash with guerillas'.

73 Nueva la Habana suffered a fierce repression and became an impoverished shanty town renamed Amanecer (Dawn) by the junta.

74 François Pingeot, *Populisme Urbain et Crise du Centre-Ville dans les Sociétés Dependantes: Santiago-du-Chili 1969-73* (Paris: Université de Paris, 1976, Ph.D. Thesis).

75 Luis Alvarado, Rosemond Cheetham and Gaston Rojas 'Movilizacion Social'.

76 See Cristina Cordero, Eder Sader and Monica Threlfall, *Consejo Comunal de Trabajadores y Cordon Cerillos-Maipu 1972: Balance y Perspectivas de un Embrion de Poder Popular* (Santiago: CIDU, 1973, Working paper 67).

77 See Rosemond Cheetham, Alfredo Rodriguez, Jaime Rojas, and Gaston Rojas: 'Comandos Urbanos: Alternativa de Poder Socialista', *Revista Interamericana de Planificacion* (July 1974).

78 See, for instance, the study on Nairobi by Marc H. Ross, *The Political Intergration of Urban Squatters* (Evanston, Illinois: Northwestern University Press, 1973); and the study on Manila by Morris Juppenplatz, *Cities in Developing Countries: The Squatter Problem in the Third World* (Santa Lucia, Australia: The University of Queensland Press, 1970); or Joan M. Nelson, *Access to Power: Politics and the Urban Poor in Developing Countries* (Princeton: Princeton University Press, 1979).

79 Manuel Castells, 'Immigrant Workers and Class Struggle', *Politics and Society,* 5.1 (1975), pp. 33-66.

80 Alejandro Portes and John Walton, *Labor, Class and the International System.*

Part 5 The Making of an Urban Social Movement: The Citizen Movement in Madrid towards the end of the Franquist Era

1 For information on neighbourhood mobilization in other Spanish cities during the 1970s see Jordi Borja, *Que son las Asociaciones de Vecinos* (Barcelona: La Gaya Ciencia, 1976).

2 Housing data rely on three sources: Equipo CETA, *Diagnostico Sobre la Vivienda en Madrid* (Madrid: Centro de Estudios Territoriales y Ambientales, Informe de Investigacion, 1977, mimeo.); Eduardo Leira, *Desarrollo Urbano y Crisis de la Vivienda: el Caso de Madrid* (Unpublished manuscript); and Jesus Leal, *La Vivienda Social en Espana* (Madrid: Universidad Complutense, 1976, Ph.D. Thesis).

3 For an analysis of the evolution of Madrid between 1940 and 1975, see Eduardo Leira, Jesus Gago, Ignacio Solana, 'Madrid: Cuarenta Anos de Crecimiento Urbano,' in *Ciudad y Territorio* 2(1976), Special Issue on Madrid.

4 Oficina Municipal del Plan, *Madrid: Cuarenta Años de Desarrollo Urbano, 1940-1980.* Madrid: Ayuntamiento de Madrid, Coleccion Temas Urbanos, 1981).

5 For planning in Madrid see Fernando Teran, *Planeamiento Urbano en la Espana Contemporanea* (Barcelona: Gustavo Gili, 1978).

6 A good description of the formation of shanty towns in Madrid can be found in: J. Mayoral et al., *Vallecas: Razones de una Lucha Popular* (Madrid: CIDUR, 1977).

7 Jorge de Esteban and Luis Lopez-Guerra, *La Crisis del Estado Franquista* (Barcelona: Labor, 1977).

8 For an analysis of the relationship between the economy and the political system in Spain see Charles Anderson, *The Political Economy of Modern Spain* (Madison: University of

Wisconsin Press, 1970). For an analysis of the Spanish economy, see the classic book by Ramon Tamames, *Estructura Económica de España* (Madrid: Alianza Universided, 1980, 2 volumes).

9   All urban data on Madrid have been synthesized in Comision de Planeamiento y Coordinacion del Area Metropolitana de Madrid, *Analisis de Problemas y Opportunidades* (Madrid: MOPU–COPLACO, 1978, 12 volumes).

10   Alfonso Alvarez-Mora, *La Remodelacion del Centro de Madrid* (Madrid: Ayuso, 1978).

11   Ramon Tamames, *La Oligarquia Financiera en España* (Barcelona: Planeta, 1976).

12   Javier Garcia-Fernandez, *El Regimen de Franco* (Madrid: Akal, 1976).

13   For some evidence on the nature of decision-making in the Franquist public administration, one of the few empirical studies is Richard Gunther, *Public Policy in a No-Party State: Spanish Planning and Budgeting in the Twilight of the Franquist Era* (Berkeley: University of California Press, 1980, especially chapter 9).

14   Jordi Sole-Tura, *Introduccion al Regimen Politico Español* (Barcelona: Ariel, 1969); and Sergio Vilar, *Naturaleza del Franquismo* (Madrid: Peninsula, 1977).

15   Nicos Poulantzas, *La Crise des Dictatures* (Paris: Maspero, 1975).

16   ORT was composed of Marxist-Leninist-Maoists. Other left wing parties present in the Citizen Movement were Partido Socialista Obrero Espanol (PSOE: a member of the second International); Partido del Trabajo de España (PTE: Maoist); MCE: Movimiento Comunista de España (MCE: Maoist); Liga Comunista Revolucionaria (LCR: Trotskyte).

17   Until 1981 divorce in Spain was unlawful, except in very special cases.

18   Javier Garcia-Fernandez and Maria Dolores Gonzales-Ruiz, *Pasado, Presente y Futuro de las Asociaciones de Vecinos* (Madrid: Pecosa, 1976).

19   PSOE, the largest left wing party in Spain was reborn in 1974, and has only had real influence since 1976–77 when the democratic elections became possible. So it hardly participated in the development of grassroots organizations and social protest. This was one of the main problems of the Spanish left: it was split between a strong electoral PSOE, without grassroots influence, and a militant PCE with little chance of obtaining a significant number of votes.

20   La Corrala is the name given to dwellings typical of the architecture of sixteenth and seventeenth century Madrid. It is a four-to-eight storey building, with an internal patio served by open balconies from each floor. Rooms are aligned along a corridor parallel to the balcony. They were, and still are, places of intense social life. Most of the Spanish classical theatre, (e.g. the Lope de Vega plays) was played in these patios, with people watching and cheering from the balconies; and the patios were meeting points and spaces for celebrations. Although many old buildings of the oldest section of Madrid present similar, original patterns, only a few remain in this shape, and only one fully conserves the original structure. Still inhabited by tenants and owned by private landlords, it was, in 1976, under serious threat of demolition for lack of maintenance and interest from the landlords and authorities. The defense of La Corrala symbolised for the association the need to preserve history, housing, and community.

21   Fernando Teran 'New Planning Experiences in Democratic Spain', *International Journal of Urban and Regional Research* 5, 1(1981), pp. 96–107.

22   Popular parades largely for children, where the three kings of Evangile bring gifts for the children; it is the Spanish equivalent to Santa Claus.

23   CIDUR, *Las Asociaciones de Vecinos en la Encrucijada* (Madrid: Ediciones de La Torre, 1977); and Tomas Villasante, *Los Vecinos en la Calle* (Madrid: Ediciones de La Torre, 1976).

24   Julian Rebollo, Emilio R. Rodriguez, Carlos Sotos, *El Movimiento Ciudadano ante la Democracia* (Madrid: Cenit Editorial, 1977).

25   To code $P_{1}+$, the fostering of electoral chances for left wing political parties, as a positive effect of political change does not represent an ideological bias in our research. We would have made the same coding for an opposition party in the Soviet Union or Poland in 1980. Whatever truth exists in social change as proposed by left wing parties, it remains that they channel interests and projects that oppose the established institutional logic. So, in a given moment of history, the strengthening of their positions within the political system is a valid indicator of political change, even if they often deceive the hopes they have raised.

26   While the use of these notations might appear somewhat bizarre, their meaning has been carefully established by the preceeding explanations. They are simply shorthand expressions to avoid tedious repetitions. Each substantive interpretation will use ordinary English.

27   The most important exceptions to the analytical rules are discussed in the Methodological Appendix (pp. 374–75).

Part 6 A Cross Cultural Theory of Urban Social Change

1 Charles Tilly, 'The Chaos of the Living City' in Tilly, ed., *An Urban World* (Boston: Little Brown, 1974, p. 87).

2 Kevin Lynch, *A Theory of Good City Form* (Cambridge, Mass.: MIT Press, 1981, p. 218).

3 Alain Touraine, *La Voix et le Regard* (Paris: Editions du Seuil, 1978, p. 45).

4 See the critique of technological and economistic determinism in David Harvey, *Social Justice and the City* (London: Edward Arnold, 1973); John Friedmann and Robert Wulff, *The Urban Transition* (London: Edward Arnold, 1976); Stephen Gale, ed., *The Manipulated City* (Chicago: Maaroufa Press, 1977); Peter Saunders, *Urban Politics: A Sociological Interpretation* (London: Hutchinson, 1979); Michael Harloe, ed., *Captive Cities* (Chichester: John Wiley, 1977); Ray Pahl, *Whose City?* (Harmondsworth: Penguin, 1975); Joe R. Feagin, ed., *The Urban Scene: Myth and Reality* (New York: Random House, 2nd revised edition, 1979); Norman Fainstein and Susan Fainstein, eds., *Urban Policy under Capitalism* (Beverly Hills: Sage, Urban Affairs Annual Review, 1982); Michael Harloe and Elizabeth Lebas, eds., *City, Class and Capital* (London: Edward Arnold, 1981, particularly pp. 83–113, 161–90, 215–60, and 277–300.) and Glenn Yago, *The Decline of Public Transit in the US and Germany* (Madison: University of Wisconsin, Ph.D. Thesis in Sociology, 1980, unpublished) in which he gives the striking example of how transportation policy in America and Germany has been determined by social and political, and not technological, factors.

5 The critique of the traditional theory of urban space has already been developed in Castells, *The Urban Question*, particularly chapters 5 and 8. Also see more recent criticism of the old tradition in a clear socio-political approach to the production of space, Edward W. Soja, 'The Socio-Spatial Dialectic', *Annals of the Association of American Geographers*, 70 (1980), pp. 207–25; John Friedmann and Clyde Weaver, *Territory and Function: The Evolution of Regional Planning* (London: Edward Arnold, 1979); Enzo Mingione, *Social Conflict and the City* (Oxford: Basil Blackwell, 1981); Chris Pickvance, 'Marxist Approaches to the Study of Urban Politics' in *International Journal of Urban and Regional Research*, 1, 1(1979) pp. 218–55; and Ivan Szeleny, 'Structural Changes and Alternatives to Capitalist

Development in the Contemporary Urban and Regional System' in *International Journal of Urban and Regional Research*, 5, 1(1981) pp. 1–15.

6 Manuel Castells, 'Theorie et Ideologie en Sociologie Urbaine' in *Sociologie et Societes*, 2 (1969); for more recent developments, see Michael Dear and Allen Scott, eds., *Urbanization and Urban Planning in Capitalist Society* (London: Methuen, 1981).

7 See, for instance, in classical showcases of the pluralist theory of urban politics, Edward Banfield and James R. Wilson, *City Politics* (Cambridge, Mass.: Harvard University Press, 1963); Banfield, *The Unheavenly City* (Boston: Little, Brown, 1970); Terry Clark, *Community Power and Political Theory* (New Haven: Yale University Press, 1963); and Alan Altshuler, *The City Planning Process* (Ithaca: Cornell University Press, 1965).

8 William A. Gamson, *The Strategy of Social Protest* (Homewood, Illinois: The Dorsey Press, 1975, pp. 6, 9, 133).

9 For a critique of the ideological assumptions of the pluralist theory, see Castells, *The Urban Question*, chapter 11. Also Castells, 'Towards a Political Urban Sociology' in Michael Harloe, ed., *Captive Cities*. In fact, most of the arguments had already been developed in Castells, 'Vers une Théorie Sociologique de la Planification Urbaine' in *Sociologie du Travail*, 4 (1969).

10 David O'Brien, *Neighborhood Organization and Interest Group Processes* (Princeton: Princeton University Press, 1975, p. 175).

11 For an analysis of the structural roots of the growing importance of collective consumption, see Ian Gough, *The Political Economy of the Welfare State* (London: Macmillan, 1979); for a perceptive presentation of the continuing debate on the relationship between collective consumption and urban problems see Peter Saunders, *Social Theory and the Urban Question* (London: Hutchinson, 1981, chapter 6); for a presentation of the connection between collective consumption and urban politics, see Castells, 'Collective Consumption and Urban Contradictions in Advanced Capitalism' in L. Lindberg, et al., eds., *Stress and Contradiction in Modern Capitalism* (Lexington: Heath, 1975); for an intelligent critique of our theses see Ray Pahl, 'Castells and Collective Consumption', *Sociology*, 12 (1978), pp. 309–15; see also Roger Benjamin, *The Limits of Politics: Collective Goods and Political Change in Post-Industrial Societies* (Chicago: Chicago University Press, 1980).

12 Mancur Olson, *The Logic of Collective Action:*

Public Goods and the Theory of Groups (Cambridge, Mass.: Harvard University Press, 1965).

13 Op. cit., pp. 14–16.

14 Michael Lipsky, 'Protest as a Political Resource' in *American Political Science Review* 62, 4 (1968); also see Lipsky, *Protest in City Politics: Rent Strikes, Housing and the Power of the Poor* (Chicago: Rand McNally, 1970).

15 John Mollenkopf, *The Politics of Urban Development in the United States* Princeton: Princeton University Press, 1983).

16 See for example: Theda Skocpol, *States and Social Revolutions: A Comparative Analysis of France, Russia and China* (New York: Cambridge University Press, 1979). Alain Touraine, *Production de la Societe* (Paris: Seuil, 1973); Maurice Zeitlin, ed., *Classes, Class Conflict and the State* (Englewood Cliffs: Winthrop, 1980); Seymour Martin Lipset, *Political Man* (Baltimore: The Johns Hopkins University Press, 1981, new enlarged edition); Colin Crouch and Alessandro Pizzorno, eds., *The Resurgence of Class Conflict in Europe since 1968* (London: Macmillan, 1977, 2 volumes).

17 See the arguments for the distinction in levels of analysis between social movements and the political system in Alain Touraine *La Voix et le Regard,* chapter 5.

18 Nicos Poulantzas, *L'Etat, Le Pouvoir, Le Socialisme* (Paris: PUF, 1978).

18bis Pierre Birnbaum *La Logique de l'Etat* (Paris: Fayard, 1982).

19 See the analysis of the relationship between revolutionary movements and political parties in Christine Buci-Glucksman and Göran Therborn, *Le Défi Social-Democrate* (Paris: Maspero, 1981).

20 For recognition of the necessity of autonomous social movements to open the way for transforming the political system, see the courageous book by Pietro Ingrao, *Crisi e Terza Via* (Roma: Editori Riuniti, 1978).

21 On the possibilities and limits of social reform within the capitalist state, see Ralph Miliband, *The State in Capitalist Society* (New York: Basic Books, 1969); and Norberto Bobbio 'Esiste Una Dotrina Marxista Dello Stato?' in Rome: *Mondoperaio* (May 1976); also Erik O. Wright, *Class, Crisis and the State* (London: New Left Books, 1978; and Allan Wolfe, *The Limits of Legitimacy* (New York and West Drayton: Collier Macmillan, 1981).

22 For a critique of pluralist political theory and a presentation of the contributions and shortcomings of the Marxist-inspired political theories, we refer the reader to a major forthcoming book: Martin Carnoy, *The State:*

Theories for a New Society (Princeton: Princeton University Press, 1984).

23 Seymour Martin Lipset, 'Why No Socialism in the United States' in Seweryin Bialer and Sophia Sluzar, eds., *Sources of Contemporary Radicalism* (Boulder, Col.: Westview Press, 1977, p. 121).

24 Gamson, *Social Protest* p. 138.

25 *Op. cit.* p. 142.

26 Anthony Oberschall, *Social Conflict and Social Movements* (Englewood Cliffs, NJ: Prentice Hall, 1973).

27 Roberta Ash, *Social Movements in America* (Chicago: Markham, 1972).

28 Alberto Melucci, 'L'Azione Ribelle: Formazione e Struttura dei Movimenti Sociali' in Melucci, ed., *Movimenti de Rivolta: Teorie e Forme dell'Azione Collettiva* (Milan: Etas Libri, 1976, p. 17).

29 Alberto Melucci, *Sistema Politico, Partiti e Movimenti Sociali* (Milan: Feltrinelli, 1976); also Alain Touraine, *Production de la Société.*

30 Frances F. Piven and Richard A. Cloward, *Poor People's Movements: Why They Succeed, How They Fail* (New York: Pantheon Books, 1977).

31 *Op. cit.,* p. 1.

32 *Op. cit.,* p. 36.

33 Henri Lefebvre, *La Pensée Marxiste et la Ville* (Paris: Casterman, 1972).

34 Karl Marx and Friedrich Engels, *L'Idéologie Allemande* (written in 1845–46, first published in Moscow, 1932; Paris: Les Editions Sociales, 1962). English edition, *The German Ideology* (New York: International Publishers, 1939).

35 Karl Marx, *Grundrisse* (translation in French by Dangeville), first integral edition in French, Paris: Anthropos, 1968. English edition, *Grundrisse: Foundations of the Critique of the Political Economy* (New York: Vintage Books, 1973).

36 Friedrich Engels, *La Question du Logement* (Paris: Editions Sociales, 1964 written 1872,); English edition (New York: International Publishers, Marxist Library, volume 23). For our critique of Engels' position on housing and urban problems see, Manuel Castells, 'Revisar a Engels', Madrid: *Argumentos* (July 1979), pp. 6–20

37 Friedrich Engels, *La Situation de la Classe Ouvrière en Angleterre* (first published 1845; this edition, Paris: Editions Sociales, 1960); English edition, *The Condition of the Working Class in England* (London: George Allen and Unwin, 1950).

38 Lefebvre, *La Pensée,* p. 25.

39 Henri Lefebvre, *Le Droit à la Ville* (Paris: Anthropos, 1968).

40 Manuel Castells, 'Y a-t-il une Sociologie urbaine?', *Sociologie du Travail* 1 (1968); 'Le Centre Urbain', *Cahiers Internationaux de Sociologie* (May 1969); 'Sociologie Urbaine' (1969); and 'Structures Sociales et Processus d'Urbanisation', *Annales* (September 1970).

41 See the very detailed analysis by Sharon Zukin, 'The Cutting Edge: a Decade of the New Urban Sociology' in *Theory and Society*, 9 (1980) pp. 575–601; see also John Walton, 'The New Urban Sociology' in *International Social Science Journal*, 33, 2 (1981).

42 Saunders, *Social Theory*.

43 Alain Lipietz, *Le Capital et son Espace* (Paris: Maspero, 1976).

44 See, for instance, Christian Topalov, *Les Promoteurs Immobiliers* (Paris: Mouton, 1974); Doreen Massey and Alexandro Catalano, *Capital and Land*, (London: Edward Arnold, 1978).

45 Jean Lojkine, *Le Marxisme, L'Etat et la Question Urbaine* (Paris: PUF, 1977).

46 Collective author, *Le Capitalisme Monopoliste d'Etat: Traité Marxiste d'Economie Politique* (Paris: Editions Sociales, 1971).

47 Jean Lojkine, *La Politique Urbaine Dans La Région Parisienne* (Paris: Mouton, 1973).

48 Jean Lojkine et al., *La Politique Urbaine Dans la Region Lyonnaise* (Paris: Mouton, 1975).

49 Danielle Bleitrach, Jean Lojkine, Ernest Oary, Roland Delacroix, Christian Mahieu, *Classe Ouvrière et Social-Democratie: Lille et Marseille* (Paris: Editions Sociales, 1981).

50 It would also be wrong to consider these observations as a personal reaction against past errors on our part. Not only have we never collaborated with the French Communist Party, but I have also been considered by the French communists ideologically idealistic, and politically an independent leftist. While we always kept collegial relationships with the French Communist researchers (we published most of their work in the series we edited), we were always openly critical of their economistic approach to urbanism.

51 Manuel Castells, *Luttes Urbaines* (Paris: Maspero, 1973).

52 Manuel Castells and Francis Godard, *Monopolville: L'Entreprise, l'Etat, l'Urbain* (Paris: Mouton, 1974).

53 Manuel Castells, Eddy Cherki, Francis Godard, Dominique Mehl, *Crise du Logement et Mouvements Sociaux Urbains: Enquête sur la Région Parisienne* (Paris, Mouton, 1978).

54 Karl Marx and F. Engels: *The German Ideology*, as cited by Lefebvre, *La Pensée* p. 34.

55 Rosa Luxembourg, *L'Accumulation du Capital* (first published 1912; this edition, Paris: Maspero, 1967, 2 volumes).

56 Rosa Luxembourg, *Grèves, Partis, Syndicats* (first published 1909; this edition, Paris: Maspero, 1966).

57 As shown in the brilliant book by Christine Buci-Glucksman, *Gramsci et l'Etat* (Paris: Fayard, 1975).

58 We developed most of these ideas about the crucial role of the party in Marxist theory in, 'La Teoria Marxista de las Clases Sociales' in Raul Benitez et al., *Las Clases Sociales en America Latina* (Mexico: Siglo XXI, 1973); also see the theoretical introduction to our, *La Lucha de Clases en Chile*.

59 For a perceptive exposé of the Marxist political theory, see Hal Draper, *Karl Marx's Theory of Revolution*, Volume 1: *State and Bureaucracy* (New York: Monthly Review Press, 1977).

60 Manuel Castells, Collective Consumption and 'Urban Contradictions in Advanced Capitalism' in N. L. Lindberg, ed., *Stress and Contradiction in Modern Capitalism*.

61 Henri Lefebvre, *La Révolution Urbaine* (Paris: Gallimard, 1971).

62 Richard Sennett, *The Fall of Public Man: The Social Psychology of Capitalism* (New York: Alfred A. Knopf, 1977, Vintage Books edition, 1978, particularly chapters 3, 6, and 7); also, Richard Sennett, *Families Against the City: Middle Class Homes of Industrial Chicago, 1872-1890* (Cambridge, Mass.: Harvard University Press, 1970).

62bis Jean Remy and Liliane Voye, *Ville, Ordre et Violence* (Paris: PUF, 1981).

63 Neil J. Smelser, *Theory of Collective Behavior* (New York: The Free Press of Glencoe, 1963).

63bis *Op. cit.*, chapter 10.

64 See Charles Tilly, 'Major Forms of Collective Action in Western Europe 1500-1975', *Theory and Society*, 3, 3 (1976); and particularly the book from which this article was extracted, Tilly, *From Mobilization to Revolution* (Reading, Mass.: Addison Wesley, 1977).

65 Ira Katznelson, *City Trenches, Urban Politics and the Patterning of Class in the United States* (New York: Pantheon Books, 1981).

66 Norman Fainstein and Susan Fainstein, *Urban Political Movements: The Search for Power by Minority Groups in American Cities* (Englewood Cliffs, NJ: Prentice Hall, 1974).

67 John Rex and Robert Moore, *Race, Community and Conflict: A Study of Sparkbrook* (Oxford: OUP, 1967).

68 Particularly Chris Pickvance 'On the Study of Urban Social Movements,' in Pickvance, ed., *Urban Sociology: Critical Essays* (London: Tavistock, 1976).

69 Jordi Borja, *Estructura Urbana y Movimientos*

Urbanos (Barcelona: Universidad Autonóma de Barcelona, Department de Geografia, 1974).

70 Lynch, *Good City Form*.

70bis For the importance of our dialogue with Claude Fischer see his last book, *To Dwell Among Friends*.

71 Alain Touraine, *La Voix et le Regard; La Societé Invisible* (Paris: Seuil, 1976); *Le Mouvement de Mai ou le Communisme Utopique* (Paris: Seuil, 1968); and *Sociologie de l'Action* (Paris: Seuil, 1965).

72 Touraine, *La Voix et le Regard*, p. 49.

73 Alain Touraine, *Un Désir d'Histoire* (Paris: Stock, 1977).

74 Saunders, *Social Theory*; Walton, 'The New Urban Sociology', 1981; Castells, 'Y a-t-il une sociologie urbaine?'; and 'Sociologie Urbaine'; also Claude Fischer, *The Urban Experience* (New York: Harcourt Brace Jovanovich, 1976).

75 Anthony Giddens insists on the mistaken neglect by the theories of social change of the fundamental time-space dimensions of human experience as the material basis for social activity; see Giddens, *A Contemporary Critique of Historical Materialism* (London: Macmillan and Berkeley: University of California Press, 1981, particularly pp. 129–156).

76 Maurice Godelier, *Horizons, Trajets Marxistes en Anthropologie* (Paris: Maspero, 1973).

77 See Manfredo Tafuri, *Progetto e Utopia, Architettura e Sviluppo Capitalistico* (Rome and Bari: Laterza, 1973); also Tafuri, *Teoriae e Storia Della Architettura* (Rome and Bari: Laterza, 1968).

78 Katherine Burlen, *L'Image Architecturale* (Paris: Université de Paris, 1975, Ph.D. Thesis in Sociology); also Henri Raymond et al., *Les Pavillonnaires* (Paris: Centre de Recherche d'Urbanisme, 1966); and Philippe Boudon, *Sur l'Espace Architectural: Essai d'Epistemologie de l'Architecture* (Paris: Dunod, 1971).

79 Edwin Panofsky, *Gothic Architecture and Scholasticism* (New York: Meridian Books, 1957).

80 Kevin Lynch, *The Image of the City* (Cambridge, Mass.: MIT Press, 1960); and Lynch; *What Time is This Place?* (Cambridge, Mass.: MIT Press, 1972).

81 Susan Eckstein, 'The De-Bourgeoisement of Cuban Cities', in Irving L. Horowitz, ed., *Cuban Communism* (New Brunswick, NJ: Transaction Books, 1977).

82 Joseph Melling, ed., *Housing, Social Policy and the State* (London: Croom Helm, 1980).

83 Dolores Hayden, *The Grand Domestic Revolution: A History of Feminist Designs for American Homes, Neighborhoods, and Cities* (Cambridge, Mass.: MIT Press, 1981).

84 Psycho-analytical theory (Freud) discovered the crucial role of sexual-gender relationships in the shaping of human experience and in the structure of personality. But because of its neglect of the domination by men of women, it could not establish the connection with the analysis of social change, until the feminist movement in the 1960s laid the ground for a transformed version of the original psycho-analytical framework in which gender and sex roles are asymmetrically organized and connected to the overall social structure.

85 This was the major theoretical contribution by Marx and Engels to the history of human knowledge.

86 In this case, Max Weber is the founding father of our understanding of the autonomous and crucial role of the state in the structuring of society.

87 For an informed discussion of the new mode of production emerging in the so-called socialist countries see Rudolf Bahro, *L'Alternative* (Paris: Stock, 1979).

88 Göran Therborn, *What does the Ruling Class do When it Rules?* (London: New Left Books, 1977); Claus Offe, *Lo Stato nel Capitalismo Maturo* (Milan: Etas Libri, 1977, original in German, 1975); James O'Connor, *The Fiscal Crisis of the State* (New York: St. Martin's Press, 1973); and Erik O. Wright, *Class, Crisis and the State* (London: New Left Books, 1978).

89 Giorgy Konrad and Ivan Szelenyi, *The Intellectuals on the Road to Class Power* (New York: Harcourt Brace Jovanovich, 1979).

90 Henri Lefebvre, *De l'Etat* (Paris: Editions 10/18, 1976, 4 volumes).

91 For a discussion on this subject, see Perry Anderson, *Lineages of the Absolutist State* (London: New Left Books, 1974).

92 We use here the distinction between mode of production and mode of development approximately along the lines suggested by Touraine, *La Voix et le Regard*, p. 133 and following.

93 A useful discussion of the general conditions of articulation between energy and information in the work process can be found in Jacques Attali, *La Parole et l'Outil* (Paris: PUF, 1976).

94 For some basic discussion on the evolution of sources of productivity; see, Robert Solow, 'Technical Changes and the Aggregate Production Function', *Review of Economics and Statistics* (August 1957); Edward F. Denison, *Accounting for Slower Economic Growth* (Washington DC: The Brookings Institution, 1979); Jacques Attali: *La Nouvelle*

Economie Française (Paris: Flammarion, 1978); Larry Hirschorn, *Toward a Political Economy of the Service Society* (Berkeley: Institute of Urban and Regional Development, Working Paper 229, 1974); Victor Fuchs, *The Service Economy* (New York: Columbia University Press, 1968); Richard Meier, *Science and Economic Development* (Cambridge, Mass.: MIT Press, 1956); and Lester C. Thurow, 'The Productivity Problem', *Technology Review*, 83, 2 (1980).

95   John K. Galbraith, *The New Industrial State* (Boston: Houghton Mifflin, 1967); and Alfred Chandler, *The Visible Hand: The Managerial Revolution in American Business* (Cambridge, Mass.: Harvard University Press, 1977).

96   Nicos Poulantzas, *Pouvoir Politique et Classes Sociales* (Paris: Maspero, 1968).

97   See the work by Anouar Abdel-Malek to re-establish the autonomous role of national cultures in defining the paths of historical development. See, for instance, Abdel-Malek, *Idéologie et Renaissance Nationale: L'Egypte Moderne* (Paris: Anthropos, 1969); and, *La Pensée Arabe Contemporaine* (Paris: Seuil, 1970). For an informed discussion of the literature on nations, see Jose Ramon Recalde, *La Construccion de las Naciones* (Madrid: Siglo XXI, 1982).

98   See Charles Tilly, 'Reflections on the History of European State-Making' in Tilly, ed., *The Formation of National States in Western Europe* (Princeton: Princeton University Press, 1975, pp. 3–84).

99   George Haupt et al., *Les Marxistes et la Question Nationale: Etudes et Textes 1848–1914* (Paris: Maspero, 1974).

100 In the critique of the ideological assumptions of the concept of race, we follow Claude Lévi-Strauss' tradition.

101 Ira Katznelson, *City Trenches*; and *Black Men, White Cities: Race, Politics, and Migration in the United States, 1900–30 and Britain, 1948–68* (New York: OUP, 1973).

102 Fernand Braudel, *Civilisation Matérielle*; and *La Mediterranée et le Monde Mediterranen à L'Epoque de Philippe II* (Paris: Armand Colin, 1949); English translation, *The Mediterranean and the Mediterranean World in the Age of Philip II* (London: Collins, 1972–3, 2 volumes).

103 Immanuel Wallerstein, *The Modern World System: Capitalist Agriculture and the Origins of the European World Economy in the Sixteenth Century* (New York: Academic Press, 1974); also, *The Capitalist World Economy* (New York: CUP, 1979).

104 See Albert O. Bergesen, ed., *Studies of the Modern World System* (New York: Academic Press, 1980); also Folder Fröbel, Jurgein Heinrichs, and Otto Kreye, *The New International Division of Labour* (Cambridge: CUP, 1980).

105 See Stephen H. Hymer, *The International Operation of Multinational Firms* (Cambridge, Mass.: MIT Press, 1976).

105bis In the perspective defined by Fernando Henrique Cardoso and Enzo Faletto, *Desarrollo y Dependencia en America Latina* (Mexico: Siglo XXI, 1969).

106 See Peter Hall, *The World Cities* (London: Weidenfield and Nicolson, 1966); Hall, ed., *Europe 2000* (New York: Columbia University Press, 1977); Otis D. Duncan et al. *Metropolis and Region* (Baltimore: Johns Hopkins University Press, 1964); and David Harvey, 'The Urban Process Under Capitalism' *International Journal of Urban and Regional Research*, 2, 1 (1978), pp. 101–32.

107 See Allan Pred, *City-Systems in Advanced Economies: Past Growth, Present Processes and Future Development Options* (New York: John Wiley, 1977); and Robert B. Cohen, 'The New International Division of Labor: Multinational Corporations and Urban Hierarchy' in Michael Dear and Allen Scott, eds., *Urbanization and Urban Planning*, pp. 287–315.

108 See David Harvey, 'The Political Economy of Urbanization in Advanced Capitalist Countries: The Case of the US' in *Urban Affairs Annual Review* (Beverly Hills: Sage Publication, 1975).

109 See the collection of essays edited by Larry Sawyers and William Tabb, *Marxism and the Metropolis* (New York: OUP, 1977); Barry Bluestone and Bennett Harrison, *Capital and Communities* (Washington, DC: The Progressive Alliance, 1980).

110 Manuel Castells, *Crisis Urbana y Cambio Social* (Madrid and Mexico: Siglo XXI, 1981).

111 Manuel Castells, *City, Class and Power*.

112 See John Mollenkopf, *The North-East and the South-West: Paths Toward the Post-Industrial City* in George Burchell and David Listokin, eds., *Cities Under Stress* (Piscataway, NJ: Rutgers University, Center of Urban Policy Research, 1981).

113 An evolution that was foreseen, many years ago, by Richard Meier, *A Communication Theory of Urban Growth* (Cambridge, Mass.: MIT Press, 1962).

114 Aivin Toffler, in a somewhat superficial but perceptive manner, has popularized these themes in his best seller *The Third Wave* (New York: William Morrow and Co., 1980). A good simple description of the new technologies under way can be found in Adam Osborne,

Running Wild: The Next Industrial Revolution (Berkeley: Osborne/McGraw Hill, 1979), also see James Martin, *Telematic Society* (Englewood Cliffs, NJ: Prentice Hall, 1981; earlier version first published 1978). For a preliminary assessment of the spatial impact of this development see Thomas M. Stanback, *Understanding the Service Economy: Employment, Productivity, Location* (Baltimore: The Johns Hopkins University Press, 1979). We also benefited for the analysis of the relationship between the new technologies and spatial restructuring from talks given by Ann Markusen as she progressed towards the completion of a major book on regional political economy.

115   As Roger Friedland explains in his analysis of American central cities, *Crisis, Power and the Central City*.

116   A trend made abundantly clear by the remarkable research monograph by Anna Lee Saxenian on the formation of the Silicon Valley, the largest concentration of microelectronics industry in the world, around Santa Clara (California) and Stanford University. See Saxenian, *Silicon Chips and Spatial Structure: The Industrial Basis of Urbanization in Santa Clara County; California* (Berkeley: University of California, Department of City Planning, 1980, unpublished Master's Thesis). In relationship to the more urban-orientated managerial and professional elite, this cultural pattern seems to underlie the so-called back to the city movement that, in America, sees a tendency of middle class professionals living in places of active urban life. See S. Laska and D. Spain, eds. *Back to the City* (New York: Pergamon Press, 1980).

116bis   See Ahmed Idris-Soven et al., eds., *The World as a Company Town: Multinational Corporations and Social Change* (The Hague: Mouton, 1978).

117   Charles Tilly, *From Mobilization to Revolution.*

118   *Business Week* 27 July 1981, p. 58.

118bis   See Milton Santos, *The Shared Space: The Two Circuits of Urban Economy in the Underdeveloped Countries and their Spatial Repercussions* (London: Methuen, 1975).

119   See, for instance, Alejandro Portes, *Immigracion, Etnicidad y el Caso Cubano* (Baltimore: The Johns Hopkins University, unpublished research report, May 1981).

119bis   See Manuel Castells *Multinational Capital.*

120   See Stanback, *Understanding the Service Economy.*

121   We are indebted for information and ideas on this subject to Françoise Sabbah, from the Department of Broadcasting and Communication Arts, San Francisco State University.

122   Manuel Castells, *The Economic Crisis and American Society.*

123   Roger Alcaly and David Mermelstein, eds., *The Fiscal Crisis of American Cities* (New York: Vintage Books, 1977).

124   See for instance Conference of Socialist Economists' State Group, *Struggles Over the State: Cuts and Restructuring in Contemporary Britain* (London: CSE Books, 1979).

124bis   See Michael Harloe and Chris Paris, *The Decollectivization of Consumption* (Paper delivered at the Tenth World Congress of Sociology, Mexico, 1982).

125   Manuel Castells 'Immigrant Workers and Class Struggle', *Politics and Society*, 5.1 (1975). The analysis appears, overall, to be verified for America by the statistical and historical research on immigration currently being undertaken by Alejandro Portes, Professor of Sociology at Johns Hopkins University.

126   See Stanley Aronowitz, *False Promises: The Shaping of American Working Class Consciousness* (New York: McGraw Hill, 1973).

127   See Stephen Castles and Godula Kosack, *Immigrant Workers and Class Structure in Western Europe* (Oxford: OUP, 1973).

128   See, for instance, F. Fourquet and L. Murard, *Les Equipements du Pouvoir* (Paris: Christian Bourgois, '10–18', 1977), or Murard and Patrick Zylbermann, *Ville, Habitat et Intimite* (Paris: Recherches, 1976). The main theoretical inspiration for all this work comes from Michel Foucault, as expressed, for instance, in his book, *Surveiller et Punir* (Paris: Gallimard, 1975).

129   Jürgen Habermas, *Legitimation Crisis* (Boston: Beacon Hill, 1973).

130   Michel Crozier, Samuel Huntington, J. Watanuk, *The Crisis of Democracies: Report on the Governability of Democracies* (New York: Columbia University Press, 1975).

131   Observed for instance, in the Christiania commune, located in the core of Copenhagen in the buildings that were formerly occupied by the army; or again in the powerful squatter movements in Holland. See, for instance, Gerard Anderiesen, 'Tanks in the Streets: The Growing Conflict Over Housing in Amsterdam', in *International Journal of Urban and Regional Research*, 5, 1 (1981).

132   To be sure, we are not referring to specific societies but pointing out tendencies of the new dominant class. For instance, the Reagan administration emphasizes the role of local governments, both to dismantle the welfare state and in confidence of conservative support in most segregated communities of suburban

America. But when local governments pass rent control laws, the Republican Urban Task Force threatens them with the withdrawal of Federal funds.

133 See Margit Mayer, 'Urban Squatters in Germany', *International Journal of Urban and Regional Research*, forthcoming.

134 Manuel Castells, 'Local Government, Urban Crisis and Political Change', in *Political Power and Social Theory: A Research Annual* (Greenwich, Conn.: JAI Press, 1981, volume 2).

135 Rafaella Nanetti, *Citizen Participation and Neighborhood Councils in Bologna* (Ann Arbor: University of Michigan, Department of Political Science, 1977, unpublished Ph.D. thesis).

136 The concept of goal is ambiguous because it evokes an instrumentalism that most movements do not have. But similar notions in available literature are much worse. Parsons' values refer to the dominance of the cultural sphere (an idealistic assumption). Marxist and liberal theory's interests are not necessarily formulated as conscious expressions in the praxis of the movement; Touraine's normative orientation is basically the same concept, but we find it too obscure and too dependent on Touraine's overall paradigm.

136bis 'Self-discount' – an Italian social movement that refused in 1974–5 to pay full tarriffs for public services in the large cities, discounting percentages according to their own estimation of what was fair.

137 Monique Dagnaud and Dominique Mehl, 'Des Contestataires Comme Il Faut (Paris: *Autrement*, February 1981); and, also by the same authors, 'Profil de la Nouvelle Gauche', *Revue Française de Science Politique*, 31, 2 (1981).

138 It could be said that Madrid changed because Franco died and Spanish democracy was established. We can also reverse the argument: the Citizen Movement was a decisive factor in the establishment of democracy. It also proposed a new series of urban goals without the knowledge, and sometimes in spite of the hostility, of the left wing parties. In 1979 the municipal elections were won all over Spanish cities by a unified left that one month before was openly involved in in-fighting and had lost the general election in spite of the poor performance of the centre party. The entire urban policy and ideology in Spain was reshaped by and in the terms of the Citizen Movement. And when the Movement was largely dismantled in 1980–81 by the left that came to power and some major urban reforms were paralysed, the left entered into a crisis, and a series of dismissals dramatically pointed out the end of social change.

Foremost among the reformers was Ramon Tamames, elected deputy mayor of Madrid, and a defender of the Citizen Movement, who left the Communist Party and his strategic post in city hall to make clear his disapproval of the bureaucratic manoeuvring that had, once again, blotted out social change. After him, in 1981, Eduardo Mangada, city councillor in charge of city planning in Madrid was also expelled from the PCE and lost his seat, along with 8 of the 9 elected PCE city council members. Yet some crucial changes in urban policy were still effected in Madrid thanks to the efforts of the socialist majority. Another control that accompanies our observations is the fact that, at about the same time of the Madrid experience, the dictatorships of both Portugal and Greece collapsed. But there were very few changes in urban meaning in these countries, in spite of the development of urban movements in the Portuguese shanty towns, and the victory of the left in the municipal elections of Athens. Thus the left is capable of fostering urban reform, but a change of urban meaning requires an urban social movement.

139 Katznelson, *City Trenches*.

140 John Rex, 'The City, Castells and Althusser', *International Journal of Urban and Regional Research*, 2, 3 (1978), pp. 566–69.

141 John Foster, 'How Imperial London Preserved its Slums', *International Journal of Urban and Regional Research*, 3, 1 (1979) pp. 93–114; and also his book, *Class Struggle and the Industrial Revolution: Early Capitalism in Three English Towns* (London: Weidenfeld and Nicolson, 1974).

142 Manuel Castells, 'The Wild City', in Joe R. Feagin, ed., *The Urban Scene, Myth and Reality* (New York: Random House, 1979).

143 Our information and ideas on urban movements in different areas of the world come from three different sources: 1. From the research undertaken over 10 years and presented in this book. 2. From written sources, both scholarly and documentary, some of which are included in footnotes. 3. From our contact, exchange, and debate with urban movements in many different cities over this time span. Although these contacts were not intended as a means of research given their unsystematic and political character, they have played a major role in convincing us of the reality and fast development of a phenomenon that has largely gone unpublicized until recent times. Most of the meetings took place at the request of the urban movements themselves that were interested in (although generally critical of) our early work. Since 1969 we have had meetings with leaders

and members of urban movements in Montreal
(1969), Chicago (1969), Paris (1970–1974),
Grenoble (1970), Dunkirk (1971–73), Chile
(1970–72), Mexico (1971, 1976, 1982), Milan
(1972), Barcelona (1973, 1974, 1976), Naples
(1973), Turin (1973), Rome (1974, 1977),
Geneva (1973, 1974), Lausanne (1974), Brussels (1974, 1976), Frankfurt (1974), Lisbon
(1974), New York (1975), Boston and
Cambridge (1975, 1976), San Francisco
(1975), San Francisco Bay Area (1979–82),
Santa Monica, California (1979–82), Chicago
(1975, 1977, 1980), Copenhagen (1976), Spain
(1977–1980), Amsterdam (1979), Caracas
(1979, 1982), Nicaragua (1981), Rio de Janeiro
(1981), Ecuador (1981), Cincinnati (1982), and
Brasil (1982). The information and analyses
obtained from this dialogue with urban
movements in many different contexts have
been decisive in forming our opinion and guid-
ing our research on the subject. We have
always tried to respond to this trust by providing all the information we had from other
places, and by communicating our own ideas
and experience. We also hope that this book
will refer in a more systematic way to the
concerns we have shared with community
leaders in various countries over all these years.

144   For information on the dynamics,
programmes, and effects of urban movements
in different areas of the world, see, for instance
E. Cherki, D. Mehl, A. M. Metailie 'Urban
Protest Movements in Western Europe' in C.
Crouch and A. Pizzorno, eds., *The Resurgence
of Class Struggle in Western Europe since 1968*
(London: Macmillan, 1976, volume 2); Gianni
Cretella, Antimo Farro, Maurizio Marcelloni,
Piero Della Seta, *Lotte Urbane nel Capitalismo
Svilupatto: L'Esperienza Italiana* (Milan:
Savelli, 1980); Mario Boffi et al., *Citta e
Conflitto Sociale* (Milan: Feltrinelli, 1972);
Mattei et al., *Le Lotte de la Casa a Firenze*
(Roma: Savelli, 1975); Andreina Daolio, ed.,
Le Lotte per la Casa in Italia (Milan: Feltrinelli,
1974); Giuliano Della Pergola, *Diritto alla
Citta e Lotte Urbane* (Milan: Feltrinelli, 1974);
M. Castells, E. Cherki, F. Godard, D. Mehl,
*Sociologie des Mouvements Sociaux Urbains:
Enquête sur la Région Parisienne* (Paris: Centre
d'Etudes des Mouvements Sociaux, 1974, 2
volumes); E. Cherki and D. Mehl, *Les
Nouveaux Embarras de Paris* (Paris: Maspero,
1977); Colloque de Recherche Urbaine,
Aménagement Urbain et Mouvements Sociaux
(Paris: Centre de Recherche d'Urbanisme,
1978); Nguyen Duc Nhuan, *Revendications
Urbaines: Etude sur les Luttes Menées par les
Groupes Sociaux Residentiels* (Paris: Centre de

Sociologie Urbaine, 1975); Special issues of the
journal *Espaces et Societes* (Paris) 6–7 (1973)
and 9 (1974); Margit Mayer, *Through the Eye of
the Needle: Everyday Life, Political Conflict and
the Citizens' Initiatives Movement in West
Germany* (Frankfurt: Institüt fur England-und
Amerika Studien der JWG-Universitat
Frankfurt, 1981, unpublished report); Gerard
Anderiesen, 'Tanks in the Streets: The
Growing Conflict Over Housing in Amster-
dam' in *International Journal of Urban and
Regional Research*, 5, 1(1981); Special Issue of
the Journal *Contradictions* 'Les Luttes
Urbaines à Bruxelles' (Brussels: Editions
Contradictions, 1975); Two Special issues on
urban social movements of the journal *Jano-
Arquitectura*, 'Movimientos Sociales Urba-
nos-1' (July–August 1976), and 'Movimientos
Sociales Urbanos-2 (September–October
1976; Barcelona: Ediciones Boyma); Charles
Downs, *Community Organization and Political
Change in Revolutionary Portugal, 1974-1976*
(Berkeley: University of California, Depart-
ment of City and Regional Planning,
unpublished Ph.D. thesis, 1980); Jordi Borja,
Que Son las Asociaciones de Vecinos (Barcelona:
La Gaya Ciencia, 1975); Jordi Borja,
Movimientos Sociales Urbanos (Buenos Aires:
SIAP, 1975); Ron Bailey, *The Squatters*
(Harmondsworth: Penguin, 1973); P.
Leonard, ed., *The Sociology of Community
Action* (Sociological Review Monograph, 21,
1975); R. Kraus-Haar, 'Pragmatic Radica-
lism', *International Journal of Urban and
Regional Research*, 3, 1(1979), pp. 61–80; M.
Harloe, ed., *Proceedings of the Conference on
Urban Change and Conflict, 1977* (London:
Centre for Environmental Studies, 1978); K.
Young and J. Kramer, *Strategy and Conflict in
Metropolitan Housing* (London: Heinemann,
1978); Peter Marris, *Meaning and Action*
(London: Routledge and Kegan Paul, 1982);
Brian Elliott and David McCrone, 'Power and
Protest in the City' in Michael Harloe, ed. *New
Perspectives in Urban Change and Conflict*
(London: Heinemann, 1981); Special Issue of
the journal *Social Policy* 'Special Issue on
Organizing Neighborhoods', (Social Policy
Corporation, New York: *Social Policy*, 10, 2
September–October 1979); Janice Perlman,
'Grassrooting the System' in *Social Policy*,
September–October 1976, pp. 4–20; Ted
Wusocki et al., *Neighborhoods First: From the
70's into the 80's* (Chicago: National Training
and Information Center, 1977); John M.
Goering, 'The National Neighborhood Move-
ment: A Preliminary Analysis and Critique',
Journal of the American Planning Association,

45, 4 (1979), pp. 506–515; John Mollenkopf, 'The Postwar Politics of Urban Development', *Politics and Society*, 5, 3 (1975) pp. 247–295; John Mollenkopf, 'Neighborhood Political Development and the Politics of Urban Growth: Boston and San Francisco 1958–78' *International Journal of Urban and Regional Research* 5, 1 (1981), pp. 15–45; Marilyn Gittell, *Limits to Citizen Participation: The Decline of Community Organizations* (Beverly Hills: Sage Publications, 1980); Norman Fainstein and Susan Fainstein, 'The Future of Community Control', *American Political Science Review*, (1976) pp. 905–932; Harry C. Boyte, *The Backyard Revolution: Understanding the New Citizen Movement* (Philadelphia: Temple University Press, 1980); Gilda Haas and Allan David Heskin, 'Community Struggles in Los Angeles' in *International Journal of Urban and Regional Research*, 5, 4 (1981) pp. 546–565. Allan David Heskin, 'The History of Tenants in the United States: Struggle and Ideology', *International Journal of Urban and Regional Research*, 5, 1 (1981) pp. 178–205; Mike Miller, 'Community Organization USA: The View from the Movement in *International Journal of Urban and Regional Research* 5, 4 (1981) pp. 565–573; Robert Fisher and Peter Romanofsky, eds., *Community Organization for Urban Social Change: An Historical Perspective* (Westport, Connecticut: Greenwood Press, 1981). John Walton, 'Urban Political Movements and Revolutionary Change in the Third World', *Urban Affairs Quarterly*, 5, 1(1979); Jorge Montano, *Los Pobres de la Ciudad en los Asentamientos Espontaneos* (Mexico: Siglo XXI, 1976); Paul Singer and Vinicius Caldeira Brandt, eds., *Sao Paulo: O Povo em Movimiento* (Petropolis: Vozes, 1981); Paulo Sandroni 'As 'Greves Civicas' Como Forma de Luta de Massas na Colombia: de Rojas Pinilla (1953–57) ao Pequeno 'Bogotazo' '' (1977), *Espaço e Debates* (Cortez Editora, Sao Paulo) 1, 3 (1981) pp. 91–117; Pedro Jacobi, *Movimientos Populares Urbanos e Resposta do Estadox: Autonomia e Controle Popular vs. Cooptacao e Clientelismo* (Sao Paulo: Nucleo de Estudos Regionais e Urbanos, 1981, unpublished report); Pedro Jacobi, *Desigualdade no Consumo Coletivo e Eclosao de Movimentos Populares Urbanos* (Sao Paulo: Nucleo de Estudos Regionais e Urbanos, 1981, unpublished report); CEDEC, ed., *Contradicao Urbana e Movimientos Sociais* (Rio de Janeiro: Paz e Terra, 1977); Leda Lucia dos Reis Falcao de Queiroz, *Movimiento Amigos de Bairro de Nova Iguacu: O Povo Exige Passagem*

(Rio de Janeiro: Universidade Federal do Rio de Janeiro, 1981, unpublished Master Thesis in Engineering); Carlos Larrea-Maldonado, *Movimientos Sociales Urbanos en America Latina: Integracion y Ruptura Politica* (Quito: Facultad Latinoamericana de Ciencias Sociales, Research Report, 1979).

145 Remember David Riessman, *The Lonely Crowd: A Study of the Changing American Character* (New Haven: Yale University Press, 1950).

146 Something that has been recalled by Harry C. Boyte, *The Backyard Revolution*.

147 See Herbert I. Schiller, *Mass Communications and the American Empire* (Boston: Beacon Press, 1969).

148 Fernand Braudel, *Civilisation Matérielle et Capitalisme* (Paris: Armand Colin, 1967, volume 1); the quote is from the English translation (first published London: Weidenfeld and Nicolson; 1973, volume 1, pp. 396–8), in which Braudel is quoted as using the term 'town'. In the original French he writes 'la ville' which in English could be translated as either 'town' or 'city'; in the context however of Braudel's theory 'la ville' certainly means 'the city'. Please note the new, enlarged French edition, Braudel, *Civilisation Materielle, Economie et Capitalisme, 15e–18e Siecles* (Paris: Armand Colin: 1979, 3 volumes); English translation of first two volumes London: Collins, 1981 and 1982, third volume forthcoming).

149 Kevin Lynch, *A Theory of Good City Form*, p. 235.

150 Op. cit., p. 324.

Bibliography

Abdel-Malek, Anouar, *Idéologie et Renaissance Nationale: l'Egypte moderne* (Paris: Anthropos, 1969).
——, *La Pensée Arabe Contemporaine* (Paris: Seuil, 1970).
——, ed., *Sociologie de l'Impérialisme* (Paris: Anthropos, 1974).
Aberbach, Joel and Walker, Jack, 'The Meanings of Black Power', *American Political Science Review*, 64 (1970).
Abu-Lughod, Janet and Hay, Richard, eds., *Third World Urbanization* (Chicago: Maaroufa Press; and London: Methuen, 1977).
Adam, Barry D., 'A Social History of Gay Politics', in Martin Levine, ed., *Gay Man: the Sociology of Male Homosexuality* (New York: Harper and Row, 1979).
Alcaly, Roger and Mermelstein, David, eds., *The Fiscal Crisis of American Cities* (New York: Vintage Books, 1977).
Aldunate, Adolfo, *Participacion y Actitud de los Pobladores ante las Organizaciones Poblacionales: una Aproximacion a la Heterogeneidad Popular* (Santiago: FLACSO, 1971).
Alinsky, Saúl D., *Reveille for Radicals* (Chicago: University of Chicago Press, 1947).
——, *Rules for Radicals* (New York: Random House, 1969).
Altshuler, Alan, *The City Planning Process* (Ithaca: Cornell University Press, 1965).
Alvarado, Luis *et al.*, 'Movilizacion Social en Torno al Problema de la Vivienda', *Revista Latinoamericana de Estudios Urbanos Regionales*, 7 (1973).
Alvarez-Mora, Alfonso, *La Remodelacion del Centro de Madrid* (Madrid: Ayuso, 1978).
Anderiesen, Gerard, 'Tanks in the Street: the Growing Conflict over Housing in Amsterdam', *International Journal of Urban and Regional Research*, 5, 1 (1981).
Anderson, Charles, *The Political Economy of Modern Spain* (Madison: University of Wisconsin Press, 1970).
Anderson, Perry, *Lineages of the Absolutist State* (London: New Left Books, 1974).
Aronowitz, Stanley, *False Promises: the Shaping of American Working Class Consciousness* (New York: McGraw-Hill, 1973).
Ascher, François and Lucas, Chantal, 'L'Industrie du Bâtiment: des Forces Productives à Libérer', *Economie et Politique* (March 1974).
Ash, Roberta, *Social Movements in America* (Chicago: Markham, 1972).
Attali, Jacques, *La Nouvelle Economie Française* (Paris: Flammarion, 1978).
——, *La Parole et l'Outil* (Paris: PUF, 1976).
'Autoritarismo y Democracia', *Revista Mexicana de Sociologia* (Special Issue), 42, 3, 80 (1980).
Bahro, Rudolf, *L'Alternative* (Paris: Stock, 1979).
Bailey, Ron, *The Squatters* (Harmondsworth: Penguin, 1973).
Bairoch, Paul, *Urban Employment in Developing Countries* (Geneva: International Labour Office, 1973).
Banfield, Edward, *The Unheavenly City* (Boston: Little, Brown, 1970).
Banfield, Edward and Wilson, James R., *City Politics* (Cambridge, Mass.: Harvard University Press, 1963).
Barnet, Richard J. and Muller, Robert E., *Global Reach* (New York: Simon and Schuster, 1974).
Barton, Stephen E., *Understanding San Francisco: Social Movements in Headquarters City* (Berkeley: Department of City Planning, University of California; typewritten, 1979).
Bastie, Jean, *La Croissance de la Banlieue Parisienne* (Paris: PUF, 1967).
Bean, Walton, *Boss Rueff's San Francisco: the Story of Union Labor Party, Big Business and the Craft Prosecution* (Berkeley: University of California Press, 1972).

Beaujeu-Garnier, Jacqueline and Bastié, Jean, *Atlas de Paris et de la Région Parisienne* (Paris: Berger-Levrault, 1967).

Becker, Howard, ed., *Culture and Civility in San Francisco* (New Brunswick: Transactions, 1971).

Bell, Alan P. and Weinberg, Martin S., *Homosexualities: a Study of Diversity among Men and Women* (New York: Simon and Schuster, 1978).

Bell, Daniel and Held, Virginia, 'The Community Revolution', *The Public Interest*, 16 (1969).

Bengoa, Jose, *Pampa Irigoin: Lucha de Clases y Conciencia de Clases* (Santiago: CESO, Universidad de Chile, 1972).

Benjamin, Roger, *The Limits of Politics: Collective Goods and Political Change in Post-Industrial Societies* (Chicago: Chicago University Press, 1980).

Bergesen, Albert, ed., *Studies of the Modern World System* (New York: Academic Press, 1980).

Berlinck, Manuel T., *Marginalidade Social e Relacoes de Clases en Sao Paulo* (Petropolis: Vozes, 1975).

Berra-Stoppa, Erica, 'Estoy en huelga y no pago renta', *Habitacion*, 1, 1 (1981), pp. 33–41.

Birnbaum, Pierre, *La Logique de L'Etat* (Paris: Fayard, 1972).

Bleitrach, Danielle *et al.*, *Classe Ouvrière et Social-Democratie: Lille et Marseille* (Paris: Editions Sociales, 1981).

Bluestone, Barry and Harrison, Bennett, *Capital and Communities* (Washington, DC: The Progressive Alliance, 1980).

Bobbio, Norberto, 'Esiste una Dotrina Marxista dello Stato?', *Mondoperaio* (May, 1976).

Boffi, Mario *et al.*, *Citta e Conflitto Sociale* (Milan: Feltrinelli, 1972).

Bobroff, Jacotte and Novatin, Fabia, 'Stratégie, Tactique et Nécessité de Classe: la Politique d'Albin Chalandon, *Espaces et Sociétés*, 2 (1971).

Bolio Trejo, Arturo, *Rebelion de Mujeres: Version Historica de la Revolucion Inquilinaria de Veracruz* (Veracruz: Edicion del Autor, Editorial 'Kodo', 1959).

Borja, Jordi, *Estructura Urbana y Movimientos Urbanos* (Barcelona: Universidad Autónoma, Depastament de Geografia, 1974).

——, *Movimientos Sociales Urbanos* (Buenos Aires: SIAP, 1975).

——, *Que son las Asociaciones de Vecinos* (Barcelona: La Gaya Ciencia, 1977).

Boudon, Philippe, *Sur l'Espace Architectural: Essai d'Epistemologie de l'Architecture* (Paris: Dunod, 1971).

Bourgin, G., *La Commune, 1870-71* (Paris: Les Editions Nationales, 1939).

Bowsky, William M., *A Medieval Italian Commune: Siena under the Nine, 1287-1355* (Berkeley: University of California Press, 1981).

Boyte, Harry C., *The Backyard Revolution: Understanding the New Citizen Movement* (Philadelphia: Temple University Press, 1980).

Braudel, Fernand, *Civilisation Matérielle et Capitalisme XVe–XVIIIe Siècle* (Paris: Armand Colin, 1979, 3 vols.; English translation: *Civilization and Capitalism*, vol. 1, 1981; vol. 2, 1982, London: Collins; vol. 3 forthcoming).

——, *La Mediterranée et le Monde Mediterranéen à l'Epoque de Philippe II* (Paris: Armand Colin, 1949; English translation: *The Mediterranean and the Mediterranean World in the Age of Philip II* (London: Collins, 1972-3, 2 vols.).

Bromley, Ray and Gerry, Chris, eds., *Casual Work and Poverty in Third World Cities* (Chichester and New York: John Wiley, 1979).

Broom, John, *John McLean* (Loanhead, Midlothian: McDonald, 1933).

Bruhat, J. *et al.*, *La Commune de 1871* (Paris: Les Editions Sociales, 1960).

Buci-Glucksman, Christine, *Gramsci et l'Etat* (Paris: Fayard, 1975).

Buci-Glucksman, Christine and Therborn, Göran, *Le Défi Social-Democrate* (Paris: Maspero, 1981).

Burchell, George and Listokin, David, eds., *Cities Undes Stress* (Piscataway, NJ: Rutgers University, Center for Urban Policy Research, 1981).

Bureau of Census (USA), *Urban Atlas* (Washington, DC: Government Printing Office, 1974).

Burlen, Katherine, *L'Image Architecturale* (Paris: Université de Paris; Ph.D. thesis, 1975).

Burtle, Meriel *et al.*, *The District Handbook: a Coro Foundation Guide to San Francisco's Supervisorial Districts* (San Francisco: Coro Foundation, 1979).

Butler, Kathy, 'Gays who Invested in Black Areas', *San Francisco Chronicle* (1 September, 1978).

Button, James, 'The Effects of Black Violence: Federal Expenditure Responses to the Urban Race Riots' (Austin, Texas: University of Texas; dittoed paper, January 1972).

Capitalisme (Le) Monopoliste d'Etat: Traité Marxiste d'Economie Politique [Collective author] (Paris: Editions Sociales, 1971).

Cardoso, Fernando H. and Faletto, Enzo, *Desarrollo y Dependencia en America Latina* (Mexico City: Siglo XXI, 1969; expanded French translation, Paris: PUF, 1979).

Carnoy, Martin, *The State: Theories for a New Society* (Princeton: Princeton University Press, 1984).

Carroll, Jerry, 'San Francisco – Charming and Changing', *San Francisco Chronicle* (16 May, 1978).

Castells, Manuel, 'Apuntes para un Analisis de Clase de la Politica Urbana del Estado Mexicano', *Revista Mexicana de Sociologia*, 4 (1977).

——, 'Le Centre Urbain', *Cahiers Internationaux de Sociologie* (May, 1969).

——, *City, Class and Power* (London: Macmillan; and New York: St Martin's Press, 1979).

——, 'Collective Consumption and Urban Contradictions in Advanced Capitalism', in L. Lindberg *et al.*, eds., *Stress and Contradictions in Modern Capitalism* (Lexington: D.C. Heath, 1975).

——, *Crisis Urbana y Cambio Social* (Madrid and Mexico: Siglo XXI, 1981).

——, *The Economic Crisis and American Society* (Princeton: Princeton University Press; and Oxford: Basil Blackwell, 1980).

——, 'Immigrant Workers and Class Struggle', *Politics and Society*, 5, 1 (1975).

——, 'Local Government, Urban Crisis and Political Change', in *Political Power and Social Theory: a Research Annual* (Greenwich, Conn.: JAI Press, 1981, vol. 2).

——, *La Lucha de Clases en Chile* (Buenos Aires: Siglo XXI, 1975).

——, *Luttes Urbaines* (Paris: Maspero, 1973).

——, 'Movimiento de Pobladores y Lucha de Clases en Chile', *Revista Latinoamericana de Estudios Urbanos y Regionales*, 9 (1973).

——, *Multinational Capital, National States and Local Communities*, (Berkeley: Institute of Urban and Regional Development, University of California, Working Paper, November 1980).

——, *La Question Ùrbaine* (Paris: Maspero, 1972 & 1976; English version, *The Urban Question: a Marxist Approach*, London: Edward Arnold; and Cambridge, Mass.: MIT Press, 1977).

——, 'Revisar a Engels', *Argumentos* (Madrid, July, 1979).

——, 'Structures Sociales et Processus d'Urbanisation', *Annales* (September, 1970).

——, 'La Teoria Marxista de las Clases Sociales', in Raul Benitez *et al.*, *Las Clases Sociales en America Latina* (Mexico: Siglo XXI, 1973).

——, 'Théorie et Idéologie en Sociologie Urbaine', *Sociologie et Sociétés* (Montreal), 2 (1969).

——, 'Towards a Political Urban Sociology', in Michael Harloe, ed., *Captive Cities* (Chichester: John Wiley, 1977).

——, 'Urban Crisis, State Policies and the Crisis of the State: the French Experience', in M. Castells, *City, Class and Power* (London: Macmillan, 1979).

——, 'L'Urbanisation dependante en Amérique Latine', *Espaces et Sociétés*, 3 (1971).

——, 'Vers une Théorie Sociologique de la Planification Urbaine', *Sociologie du Travail*, 4 (1969).

——, 'The Wild City', in Joe R. Feagin, ed., *The Urban Scene: Myth and Reality* (New York: Random House, 1979).

——, 'Y-a-t-il une Sociologie Urbaine?', *Sociologie du Travail*, 1 (1968).

Castells, Manuel and Godard, Francis, *Monopolville: l'Entreprise, l'Etat, l'Urbain* (Paris: Mouton, 1974).

Castells, Manuel *et al.*, *Crise du Logement et Mouvements Sociaux Urbains: Enquête sur la Région Parisienne* (Paris: Mouton, 1978).

——, *Sociologie des Mouvements Sociaux Urbains: Enquête sur la Région Parisienne* (Paris: Centre d'Etudes des Mouvements Sociaux, 1974, 2 vols.).

Castles, Stephen and Kosack, Godula, *Immigrant Workers and Class Struggle in Western Europe* (London: Oxford University Press, 1973).

Cal-Futy, Louis, *Ça Bouge dans les Quartiers* (Paris: Syros, 1978).

CEDEC ed., *Contradicao Urbane e Movimientos Sociais* (Rio de Janeiro: Paz e Terra, 1977).

Challinor, Raymond, *The Origins of British Bolshevism* (London: Croom Helm, 1977).

Chamboredon, Jean-Claude and Lemaire, Monique, 'Proximité Spatiale et Distance Sociale: les *Grands Ensembles* et leur Peuplement', *Revue Française de Sociologie*, 11, 1 (1970).

Chandler, Alfred, *The Visible Hand: the Managerial Revolution in American Business* (Cambridge, Mass.: Harvard University Press, 1977).

Chandler, T. and Fox, G., *3,000 Years of Urban Growth* (New York: Academic Press, 1974).

Chaney, Elsa, 'The World Economy and Contemporary Migration', *International Magazine Review*, 13 (1979).

Chapman, S.D., ed., *The History of Working Class Housing* (Newton Abbot: David and Charles, 1971).

Charleston, Noelle *et al.*, *Summary of Trends in Housing and Population in the Mission Model Neighbourhood, 1940-1970* (Stanford: Stanford University Community Development Study, 1972; mimeographed).

Charon, Jean Marie, 'L'Animation Sociale ou Comment Désamorcer les Mouvements Sociaux Urbains', *Espaces et Sociétés*, 12 (1974).

Cheetham, Rosemond, 'El Sector Privado de la Construccion: Patron de Dominacion', *Revista Latinoamericana de Estudios Urbanos Regionales*, 3 (1971).

Cheetham, Rosemond *et al.*, 'Comados Urbanos: Alternativa de Poder Socialista', *Revista Interamericana de Planificacion* (July, 1974).

Cherki, Eddy and Mehl, Dominique, *Les Nouveaux Embarras de Paris* (Paris: Maspero, 1977).

Cherki, Eddy *et al.*, 'Urban Protest Movements in Western Europe', in C. Crouch and A. Pizzorno, eds., *The Resurgence of Class Struggle in Western Europe since 1968* (London: Macmillan, 1976, vol. 2).

Chevalier, Louis, *La Formation de la Population Parisienne au XIXe Siècle* (Paris: INED, Cahier 10, 1950).

Chombart de Lauwe, P.H., *Paris et l'Agglomération Parisienne (1952-1964)* (Paris: Editions Ouvrières, 1965).

Church, George, 'How Gay is Gay?', *Time* (23 April, 1979).

CIDUR, *Las Asociaciones de Vecinos en la Encrucijada* (Madrid: Ediciones de La Torre, 1977).

Citizen Housing Task Force, *The San Francisco Housing Dilemma: What Can be Done?* (San Francisco: Mayor's Office; Typewritten report, November 1980).

Clark, Terry, *Community Power and Political Theory* (New Haven: Yale University Press, 1963).

Clastres, Pierre, *Society against the State* (New York: Urizen Books, 1977).

Clerc, Paul, *Grands Ensembles Banlieues Nouvelles* (Paris: PUF, 1967).

Cohen, Robert B., 'The New International Division of Labor: Multinational Corporations and Urban Hierarchy', in Michael Dear and Allen Scott, eds., *Urbanization and Urban Planning in Capitalist Society* (London: Methuen, 1981).

Colchero, Ducci de, *La Colonia Popular: una Manifestacion del Problema de la Vivienda* (Mexico: Universidad Nacional Autonoma, Unpublished Master Thesis in Architecture, 1978).

Collier, David, *Barriades y Elites: de Odria a Velasco* (Lima: Instituto de Estudios Peruanos, 1976; undated 1978).

——, *The New Authoritarianism in Latin America* (Berkeley: University of California Press, 1979).

——, *Squatters and Oligarchs: Authoritarian Rule and Policy Change in Peru* (Baltimore: Johns Hopkins University Press, 1976).

Colloque de Recherche Urbaine, *Aménagement Urbain et Mouvements Sociaux* (Paris: Centre de Recherche d'Urbanisme, 1978).

Conference of Socialist Economists' State Group, *Struggles over the State: Cuts and Restructuring in Contemporary Britain* (London: CSE Books, 1979).

Connolly, Michael P., *A Historical Study of Change in Saul D. Alinsky's Community Organization: Practice and Theory 1939–1972* (Minneapolis: University of Minnesota; Ph.D. dissertation, 1976).

Connolly, Priscilla *et al.*, *La Produccion de la Vivienda en Mexico* (Mexico, DF: COPEVI, 1976).

'Contre-Pouvoirs dans la Ville' *Autrement*, (Special Issue, 5, 1975).

Cordero, Cristina *et al.*, *Consejo Comunal de Trabajadores y Cordon Cerillos-Maipu 1972: Balance y Perspectivas de un Embrion de Poder Popular* (Santiago: CIDU, Working Paper 67, 1973).

Cornelius, Wayne, *Politics and the Migrant Poor in Mexico City* (Stanford: Stanford University Press, 1975).

Crawfurd, Helen, *Unpublished Autobiography* (Typescript; Marx Memorial Library, London).

Cretella, Gianni *et al.*, *Lotte Urbane nel Capitalismo Svilupatto: l'Esperienza Italiana* (Milan: Savelli, 1980).

Crouch, Colin and Pizzorno, Alessandro, eds., *The Resurgence of Class Conflict in Western Europe since 1968* (London: Macmillan, 1978).

Crozier, Michel *et al.*, *The Crisis of Democracies: Report on the Governability of Democracies* (New York: Columbia University Press, 1975).

Cruz, Rafael Ortega, *Las Luchas Proletarias en Veracruz: Historia y Autocritico* (Jalapa, Veracruz: Editorial Barricada, 1942).

Dagnaud, Monique, *Le Mythe de la Qualité de la Vie et la Politique Urbaine en France* (Paris: Mouton, 1976).

Dagnaud, Monique and Mehl, Dominique, 'Des Contestataires comme il faut', *Autrement* (Paris, February 1981).

——, 'Profil de la Nouvelle Gauche', *Revue Française de Science Politique*, 31, 2 (1981).

Damer, Sean, 'State, Class and Housing: Glasgow 1885–1919', in J. Melling, ed., *Housing, Social Policy and the State* (London: Croom Helm, 1980).

Daolio, Andreina, ed., *Le Lotte per la Casa in Italia* (Milan: Feltrinelli, 1974).

Dear, Michael and Scott, Allan, eds., *Urbanization and Urban Planning in Capitalist Society* (London: Methuen, 1981).

Della Pergola, Giuliano, *Diritto alla Citta e Lotte Urbane* (Milan: Feltrinelli, 1974).

'Démocratie (La) par l'Association', *l'Esprit* (Special Issue, June 1978).

Denison, Edward F., *Accounting for Slower Economic Growth* (Washington, DC: The Brookings Institution, 1979).

DESAL, *La Marginalidad Urbana: Origen, Proceso y Modo* (Santiago de Chile, 1969, 2 vols.).

Downes, Bryan T., 'A Critical Re-examination of the Social and Political Characteristics of Riot Cities', *Social Science Quarterly*, 51 (1970).

——, 'Social and Political Characteristics of Riot Cities: a Comparative Study', in Norval D. Glenn and Charles M. Bonjean, eds., *Blacks in the United States* (San Francisco: Chandler, 1969).

Downs, Charles, *Community Organization and Political Change in Revolutionary Portugal, 1974–1976* (Berkeley: University of California, Department of City and Regional Planning, unpublished Ph.D. thesis, 1980).

Draper, Hal, *Karl Marx's Theory of Revolution*. vol. 1: *State and Bureaucracy* (New York: Monthly Review Press, 1977).

Dreuilhe, A.E., *La Société Invertie ou les Gais de San Francisco* (Ottawa: Flammarion, 1979).

Duclos, J., *'A l'Assaut du Ciel': la Commune de Paris Annonciatrice d'un Monde Nouveau* (Paris: Editions Sociales, 1961).

Duncan, Otis D. *et al.*, *Metropolis and Region* (Baltimore: Johns Hopkins University Press, 1964).

Duque, Joachin and Pastrana, Ernesto, 'Le Movilizacion Reivindicativa Urbana de los Sectores Populares en Chile, 1964–1972', *Revista Latinoamericana de Ciencias Sociales*, 4 (1973).

——, *Survey of Four Campamentos* (Santiago de Chile: Facultad Latinoamericana de Ciencias Sociales, 1971).

Ebrik, G. and Barjac, P., *Le Logement, Dossier Noir de la France* (Paris: Dunod, 1970).

Eckstein, Susan, 'The De-Bourgeoisement of Cuban Cities', in Irving L. Horowitz, ed., *Cuban Communism* (New Brunswick, N.J.: Transactions Books, 1977).

——, *The Poverty of Revolution: the State and the Urban Poor in Mexico* (Princeton: Princeton University Press, 1977).

Eisinger, Peter K., *Protest Behavior and the Integration of Urban Political Systems* (Madison: University of Wisconsin, Institute for Research on Poverty, Discussion Paper, 1971).

Eliel, Paul, *The Waterfront and General Strikes, San Francsico, 1934* (San Francisco: San Francisco Industrial Association, 1934).

Elliott, Brian and McCrone, David, 'Power and Protest in the City', in M. Harloe, ed., *New Perspectives in Urban Change and Conflict* (London: Heinemann, 1981).

Emilio, John d', Gay Politics, Gay Community: San Francisco's Experience, *Socialist Review*, 11, 1 (1981), pp. 77–104.

Engels, Friedrich, *The Condition of the Working Class in England* (London: George Allen and Unwin, 1950).

——, *La Question du Logement* (Paris: Editions Sociales, 1964; English eds., *The Housing Question*, New York: International Publishers, Marxist Library vol. 23; London: Central Books, 1975).

Englander, David, *The Workmen's National Housing Council* (Warwick: University of Warwick; M.A. thesis, 1973).

Equipo CETA, *Diagnostico sobre la Vivienda en Madrid* (Madrid: Centro de Estudios Territoriales y Ambientales, Informe de Investigacion, 1977; mimeographed).

Equipo de Estudios Poblacionales del CIDU, 'Experiencia de Justicia Popular en Poblaciones', *Cuadernos CEREN*, (Santiago), 8 (1971).

Equipo Pueblo, *Surgimiento de la Coordinadora Nacional del Movimiento Urbano Popular: Las Luchas Urbano-Populares en el Momento Actual* (Mexico, DF: CONAMUP, 1982).

Escoffier, Jeffrey, 'Stigmas, Work Environment, and Economic Discrimination against Homosexuals', *The Homosexual Counseling Journal*, 2, 1 (1975).

Espaces et Sociétés (Paris; Special Issue, 6–7, 1973).

——, 'Paris: Urbanisme, Classes, Pouvoir' (Paris; Special Issue, 13–14, 1974).

Esteban, Jorge de and Lopez-Guerra, Luis, *La Crisis del Estado Francquista* (Barcelona: Labor, 1977).

Evans, Hugh, *Towards a Policy for Housing Low Income Families in Mexico, 1950–1970* (Cambridge: Department of Architecture, Cambridge University, 1974).

Fainstein, Norman and Fainstein, Susan, 'The Future of Community Control', *American Political Science Review* (1976).

——, *Urban Political Movements: the Search for Power by Minority Groups in American Cities* (Englewood Cliffs: Prentice Hall, 1974).

——, eds., *Urban Policy under Capitalism* (Beverly Hills: Sage, Urban Affairs Annual Review, 1982).

Falcon, Romana, *El Agrarismo en Veracruz: la Etapa Radical (1928-1935)* (Mexico, DF: El Colegio de Mexico, 1977).

Feagin, Joe R., ed., *The Urban Scene: Myth and Reality* (New York: Random House, 2nd rev. ed., 1979).

Feagin, Joe and Hahn, Harlan, *Ghetto Revolts: the Politics of Violence in American Cities* (New York: Macmillan, 1973).

Fischer, Claude S., *Dwelling among Friends* (Chicago: University of Chicago Press, 1981).

——, *The Urban Experience* (New York: Harcourt Brace Jovanovich, 1976).

Fish, John Hall, *Black Power, White Control: the Struggle of the Woodlawn Organization in Chicago* (Princeton: Princeton University Press, 1973).

Fisher, Robert and Romanofsky, Peter, eds., *Community Organization for Social Change: an Historical Perspective* (Westport, Conn.: Greenwood Press, 1981).

Flower, Joe, 'Gays in Business: the Prejudice and the Power', *San Francisco Magazine* (September, 1980).

Flynn, Ann and Flynn, Vincent, 'We Shall not be Removed', in Laurie Flynn, ed., *We Shall Be All* (London: Bookmarx, 1978).

Ford, William F. and Moore, John H., 'Additional Evidence on the Social Characteristics of Riot Cities', *Social Science Quarterly*, 51 (1970).

Foster, John, *Class Struggle and the Industrial Revolution: Early Capitalism in Three English Towns* (London: Weidenfeld and Nicolson, 1974).

——, 'How Imperial London Preserved its Slums', *International Journal of Urban and Regional Research*, 3, 1 (1979).

Foucault, Michel, *Surveiller et Punir* (Paris: Gallimard, 1975).

Fourquet, F. and Murard, L., *Les Equipements du Pouvoir* (Paris: Christian Bourgois, '10/18', 1977).

Fowler, Heather, *The Agrarian Revolution in the State of Veracruz, 1920–1940* (Washington DC: The American University, 1970, unpublished Ph.D. thesis).

Fox, Robert B., *Urban Population Growth Trends in Latin America* (Washington, DC: Inter-American Development Bank, 1975).

Frank, André G., *Capitalism and Underdevelopment in Latin America* (New York: Monthly Review Press, 1974).

Fresque Historique du Système Productif Français (Paris: INSEE, 1974).

Friedland, Roger, *Crisis, Power and the Central City* (London: Macmillan, 1983).

Friedmann, John and Weaver, Clyde, *Territory and Function: the Evolution of Regional Planning* (London: Edward Arnold, 1979).

Friedmann, John and Wulff, Robert, *The Urban Transition* (London: Edward Arnold, 1976).

Fröbel, Folder *et al.*, *The New International Division of Labour* (Cambridge: Cambridge University Press, 1980).

Fuchs, Victor, *The Service Economy* (New York: Columbia University Press, 1968).

Galbraith, John Kenneth, *The New Industrial State* (Boston: Houghton Mifflin, 1967).

Gale, Stephen, ed., *The Manipulated City* (Chicago: Maaroufa Press, 1977).

Gallagher, Nora, 'The San Francisco Experience', *Playboy* (January, 1980).

Gallagher, Willie, *Revolt on the Clyde* (London: Lawrence and Wishart, 4th ed., 1978).

Gamson, William A., *The Strategy of Social Protest* (Homewood, Ill.: The Dorsey Press, 1975).

Garcia, Beatriz and Perlo, Manuel, 'Las Politicas Habitacionales del Sexenio: Un balance Inicial', *Habitacion* (1981), pp. 33–45.

Garcia-Fernandez, Javier, *El Regimen de Franco* (Madrid: Akal, 1976).

Garcia-Fernandez, Javier and Gonzales-Ruiz, Maria Dolores, *Pasado, Presente y Futuro de las Asociacions de Vecinos* (Madrid: Pecosa, 1976).

Garza, Gustavo and Schteingart, Martha, *El Problema de la Vivienda en Mexico* (Mexico, DF: El Colegio de Mexico, 1977).

Gauldie, Enid, *Cruel Habitations: a History of Working Class Housing, 1780–1918* (London: George Allen and Unwin, 1974).

Gellen, Martin, *The Dynamics of Institutional Mortgage Disinvestment in the Central City* (Berkeley: University of California; unpublished Ph.D. thesis, 1979).

George, Pierre *et al.*, *Région Parisienne* (Paris: PUF, 1965).

Giddens, Anthony, *A Contemporary Critique of Historical Materialism* (London: Macmillan; and Berkeley: University of California Press, 1981).

Gill, Mario, 'Veracruz: Revolución y Extremismo', *Historia Mexicana*, 8 (1953).

Ginsberg, Allen, *Howl* (San Francisco: City Lights Books, 1956).

Gittell, Marilyn, *Limits to Citizen Participation: the Decline of Community Organizations* (Beverly Hills: Sage, 1980).

Godelier, Maurice, *Horizons, Trajets Marxistes en Anthropologie* (Paris: Maspero, 1973).

Goering, John M., 'The National Neighborhood Movement: a Preliminary Analysis and Critique', *Journal of the American Planning Association*, 45, 4 (1979).

Goffman, Erving, *Stigma: Notes on the Management of Spoiled Identity* (Englewood Cliffs: Prentice Hall, 1963).

Goodman, Paul, *Growing Up Absurd: Problems of Youth in the Organized System* (New York: Random House, 1960).

Gorman, Richard, 'Casing Out Castro', *After Dark* (June, 1979).

Gough, Ian, *The Political Economy of the Welfare State* (London: Macmillan, 1979).

Gronitier, Bernard, *La Planète des Bidonvilles: Perspectives de l'Explosion Urbaine dans le Tiers Monde* (Paris: Seuil, 1980).

Gunther, Richard, *Public Policy in a No-Party State: Spanish Planning and Budgeting in the Twilight of the Franquist Era* (Berkeley: University of California Press, 1980).

Haas, Gilda and Heskin, Allan D., 'Community Struggles in Los Angeles', *International Journal of Urban and Regional Research*, 5, 4 (1981).

Habermas, Jürgen, *Legitimation Crisis* (Boston: Beacon Hill, 1973).

Hall, Peter, *Great Planning Disasters* (Berkeley: University of California Press, 1982).

——, *The World Cities* (London: Weidenfeld and Nicolson, 1966).

——, ed., *Europe 2000* (New York: Columbia University Press; London: Duckworth, 1977).

Hardoy, Jorge E., *Pre-Columbia Cities* (New York: Walker, 1973; first published in Spanish, 1964).

——, ed., *Urbanization in Latin America: Approaches and Issues* (New York: Anchor Books, 1975).

Harloe, Michael, ed., *Captive Cities* (Chichester: John Wiley, 1977).

——, *Proceedings of the Conference on Urban Change and Conflict, 1977* (London: Centre for Environmental Studies, 1978).

Harloe, Michael and Paris, Chris, *The Decollectivization of Consumption* (Paper at 10th World Congress of Sociology, Mexico, 1982).

Harloe, Michael and Lebas, Elizabeth, eds., *City, Class and Capital* (London: Edward Arnold, 1981).

Harrison, Bennett, *Urban Economic Development: Suburbanization, Minority Opportunity and the Condition of the Central City* (Washington, DC: The Urban Institute, 1974).

Hartman, Chester, *Yerba Buena: Land Grab and Community Resistance in San Francisco* (San Francisco: Clide, 1974).

Harvey, David, 'The Political Economy of Urbanization in Advanced Capitalist Countries: the Case of the US', *Urban Affairs Annual Review* (Beverly Hills: Sage, 1975).

——, *Social Justice and the City* (London: Edward Arnold, 1973).

——, The Urban Process under Capitalism', *International Journal of Urban and Regional Research*, 2, 1 (1978).

Haupt, George *et al.*, *Les Marxistes et la Question Nationale: Etudes et Textes 1848-1914* (Paris: Maspero, 1974).

Hayden, Dolores, *The Crand Domestic Revolution: a History of Feminist Designs for American Homes, Neighborhoods and Cities* (Cambridge, Mass.: MIT Press, 1981).

Hedblom, Jack H., 'Social, Sexual and Occupational Lives of Homosexual Women, *Sexual Behaviour*, 2, 10 (1972).

Heins, Marjorie, *Strictly Ghetto Property: the Story of 'Los Siete de la Raza'* (Berkeley: Ramparts Press, 1972).

Henrard, Jacques, *Le Financement Public du Logement* (Paris: CETEM, Research Report, 1975).

Henry, Etienne, 'Los Asentamientos Urbanos Populares: una Esquema Interpretativo', *Debates* (Lima), 1, 1 (1977).

——, *La Escena urbana* (Lima: Pontifica Universidad Catolica del Peru, 1978).

——, *Urbanisation Dependante et Mouvements Sociaux Urbains* (Paris: Université de Paris; Ph.D. thesis, 4 vols., 1974).

Herrera, Roger, *Inner Mission Housing Strategy* (Draft Document for Citizen Review, San Francisco Department of City Planning, January 1980).

Heskin, Allan David, 'The History of Tenants in the United States: Struggle and Ideology', *International Journal of Urban and Regional Research*, 5, 1 (1981).

'Highrise, Housing and Politics in San Francisco', in Jim Schoch, ed., *Where Has all the Housing Gone?* (San Francisco: New American Movement, 1979).

Hinton, James, *The First Shop Stewards' Movement* (London: George Allen and Unwin, 1973).

Hippler, Arthur E., *Hunter's Point: a Black Ghetto in America* (New York: Basic Books, 1970).

Hirsch, Fred and Goldthorpe, John, eds., *The Political Economy of Inflation* (Cambridge, Mass.: Harvard University Press, 1978).

Hirschorn, Larry, *Towards a Political Economy of the Service Society* (Berkeley: Institute of Urban and

Regional Development, Working Paper 229, 1974).

'Histoire et Urbanisation', *Annales* (September, 1970).

Houdeville, Louis, *Pour une Civilisation de l'Habitat* (Paris: Editions Ouvrières, 1969).

Humphreys, Laud, 'Exodus and Identity: the Emerging Gay Culture', in M. Levine, ed., *Gay Men* (New York: Harper and Row, 1979).

——, *Out of the Closets: the Sociology of Homosexual Liberation* (Englewood Cliffs: Prentice Hall, 1972).

Hurtado, Osvaldo, *El Poder Politico en el Ecuador* (Barcelona: Ariel, 1977, pp. 189–323).

Hymer, Stephen H., *The International Operation of Multinational Firms* (Cambridge, Mass.: MIT Press, 1976).

Idris-Soven, Ahmed *et al.*, eds., *The World as a Company Town: Multinational Corporations and Social Change* (The Hague: Mouton, 1978).

Infante, Ricardo and Sanchez, Magaly, *Reproduccion de la Fuerza de Trabajo es la Estructura Urbana la Condicion de la Clase Trabajadora en Zonas Segregadas de Caracas* (Caracas: Universidad Central de Venezuela, Instituto de Urbanismo, 1980. 4 vols.).

Ingrao, Pietro, *Crisi e Terza Via* (Rome: Editori Riuniti, 1978).

——, *Masse e Potere* (Rome: Editori Riuniti, 1971).

Jacobi, Pedro, *Desigualdade no Consumo Coletivo e Eclosao de Movimentos Populares Urbanos* (Sao Paulo: Nucleo de Estudos Regionais e Urbanos; unpublished report, 1981).

——, *Movimentos Populares Urbanos e Resposta do Estadox: Autonomia e Controle Popular vs. Cooptacao e Clientelismo* (Sao Paulo: Nucleo de Estudos Regionais e Urbanos; unpublished report, 1981).

Jacobs, Allan, *Making City Planning Work* (Chicago: American Society of Planning Officials, 1978).

Janowitz, Morris, *The Last Half Century* (Chicago: University of Chicago Press, 1979).

Jay, Karla and Young, Allen, *Lavender Culture* (New York: Jove/Harcourt Brace Jovanovich, 1980).

Jibou, Robert M., 'City Characteristics, Differential Stratification and the Occurrence of Inter-racial Violence', *Social Science Quarterly*, 52 (1971).

Juppenplatz, Morris, *Cities in Developing Countries: the Squatter Problem in the Third World* (Santa Lucia, Australia: The University of Queensland Press, 1970).

Katznelson, Ira, *Black Men, White Cities: Politics and Migration in the United States, 1900–30, and Britain, 1948–68* (New York: Oxford University Press, 1973).

——, *City Trenches: Urban Politics and the Patterning of Class in the United States* (New York: Pantheon Books, 1981).

Kerouac, Jack, *On the Road* (New York: Viking, 1957; and London: André Deutsch, 1958; Penguin, 1972).

Ketteringham, William, *Gay Public Space and the Urban Landscape: a Preliminary Assessment* (Paper delivered to the Association of Pacific Coast Geographers Conference, June 1979).

Kinsey, Alfred *et al.*, *Sexual Behaviour in the Human Female* (Philadelphia and London: W.B. Saunders, 1958).

——, *Sexual Behaviour in the Human Male* (Philadelphia and London: W.B. Saunders, 1948).

Konrad, Giorgy and Szelenyi, Ivan, *The Intellectuals on the Road to Class Power* (New York: Harcourt Brace Jovanovich, 1979).

Kowarick, Lucio, *A Espoliaçao Urbana* (Rio de Janeiro: Paz e Terra, 1979).

Kramer, Ralph M., *Participation of the Poor* (Englewood Cliffs: Prentice Hall, 1969).

Kraus-Haar, R., 'Pragmatic Radicalism', *International Journal of Urban and Regional Research*, 3, 1 (1979).

Labastida, Julio, 'Los Grupos Dominantes Frente e las Alternativas de Cambio', in *El Perfil de Mexico en 1980* (Mexico, DF: Siglo XXI, 1972, vol. 3).

Lamy, Bernard, *Nouveaux Ensembles d'Habitation et leur Environnement* (Paris: CSU, 1972).

Lancourt, Joan E., *Alinsky's Community Organizing* (Brandeis: Brandeis University, School of Social Work, 1977, unpublished Ph.D. thesis).

——, *Confront or Concede: the Alinsky Citizen-Action Organizations* (Lexington, Mass.: Lexington Books, 1979).

Lapidus, I., *Muslim Cities in the Later Middle Ages* (Cambridge, Mass.: Harvard University Press, 1967).

Larrea-Maldonado, Carlos, *Movimientos Sociales Urbanos en America Latina: Integracion y Ruptura Politica* (Quito: Facultad Latinoamericana de Ciencias Sociales, Research Report, 1979).

Laska, S. and Spain, D., *Back to the City* (New York: Pergamon Press, 1980).

Lawner, Miguel and Barrenechea, Ana-Maria, 'Los Mil Dias de Allende: la Politica de Vivienda del Gobierno Popular en Chile', in Manuel Castells, ed., *Estructura Social y Politica Urbana en America Latina* (Mexico, DF: EDICOL, forthcoming).

Leal, Jesus, *La Vivienda Social en España* (Madrid: Universidad Complutense; Ph.D. thesis, 1976).

Lechner, Norbert, ed., *Estaido y Politica en America Latina* (Mexico City: Siglo XXI, 1981).

Lee, Don, *Castro Street Commercial District: a Preliminary Survey* (Berkeley: University of California Department of City Planning; Paper for IDS 24, 1978).

——, *Changing Community Structure and the Gay Neighborhood* (Berkeley: University of California Department of City Planning; Paper for CP 211, 1980).

——, *The Gay Community and Improvements in the Quality of Life in San Francisco* (Berkeley: University of California, MCP thesis, Department of Cith Planning, 1980).

——, *Processes of Spatial Change in the San Francisco Gay Community* (Berkeley: University of California Department of Urban Planning, Paper for CPE 298E, 1979).

——, *Real Estate and the Gay Community in San Francisco* (Berkeley: University of California, Paper for Business Administration B/A 280, 1979).

Leeds, Anthony, 'The Significant Variables Determining the Character of Squatter Settlements', *America Latina*, 12 (1969).

Leeds, Anthony and Leeds, Elizabeth, 'Accounting for Behavioural Differences in Squatter Settlements in Three Political Systems: Brazil, Peru and Chile', in Louis Massotti and John Walton, eds., *The City in a Comparative Perspective* (Beverly Hills: Sage, 1976).

Lefebvre, Henri, *De l'Etat* (Paris: Union Générale d'Editions (10/18), 1976, 4 vols.).

——, *Le Droit à la Ville* (Paris: Anthropos, 1972).

——, *La Pensée Marxiste et la Ville* (Paris: Casterman, 1972).

——, *La Proclamation de la Commune* (Paris: Gallimard, 1965).

——, *La Révolution Urbaine* (Paris: Gallimard, 1970).

LeGoff, Jacques, *La Civilisation de l'Occident Médiéval* (Paris: Arthaud, 1964).

Leira, Eduardo, *Desarrollo Urbano y Crisis de la Vivenda: el Caso de Madrid* (unpublished).

Leira, Eduardo *et al.*, 'Madrid: Cuarenta Años de Crecimiento Urbano', *Ciudad y Territorio* (Special Issue on Madrid, 1976).

Lenin, V.I., *The State and the Revolution* (Moscow, 1917; London: Central Books, 1972).

——, *What is to be Done?* (London: Central Books, 1979; Spanish edition in *Obras Escogidas*, Moscow: Ediciones del Progreso, 1960, 3 vols.).

Lentin, Françoise, *Une Société Petite-Bourgeoise: le HLM* (Paris: Centre de Recherche d'Urbanisme, Research Report, 1966).

Leonard, P., ed., *The Sociology of Community Action* (Sociological Review Monograph 21, 1975).

Levine, Martin, 'Gay Ghetto', in M. Levine, ed., *Gay Men* (New York: Harper and Row, 1979).

Licata, Sol, *Gay Power: a History of the American Gay Movement, 1970–1975* (Los Angeles: University of Southern California; unpublished Ph.D. thesis, 1978).

Lindberg, N.L. ed., *Stress and Contradiction in Modern Capitalism* (Lexington: D.C. Heath, 1975).

Linn, F., *Policies for Efficient and Equitable Growth of Cities in Developing Countries* (Washington, DC: The World Bank, Staff Working Papers 342, 1979).

Lipietz, Alain, *Le Capital et son Espace* (Paris: Maspero, 1976).

——, *Le Tribut Foncier Urbain* (Paris: Maspero, 1974).

Lipset, Seymour Martin, *Political Man* (Baltimore: The Johns Hopkins University Press, 1981, enlarged edition).

——, 'Why No Socialism in the United States', in Seweryin Bialer and Sophia Sluzar, eds., *Sources of Contemporary Radicalism* (Boulder, Col.: Westview Press, 1977).

Lipsky, Michael, 'Protest as a Political Resource', *American Political Science Review*, 62, 4 (1968).

——, *Protest in City Politics: Rent Strikes, Housing and the Power of the Poor* (Chicago: Rand McNally, 1970).

Lissagaray, Prosper-Olivier, *Histoire de la Commune de 1871* (Paris: Maspero, 1976; originally published 1876).

Lockwood, Charles, *Suddenly San Francisco: the Early Years of an Instant City* (San Francisco: The San Francisco Examiner, A California Living Book, 1978).

Lojkine, Jean, *Le Marxisme, l'Etat et la Question Urbaine* (Paris: PUF, 1977).

——, *La Politique Urbaine dans la Région Parisienne (1945-1972)* (Paris: Mouton, 1973).

Lojkine, Jean *et al.*, *La Politique Urbaine dans la Région Lyonnaise* (Paris: Mouton, 1975).

Lomnitz, Larissa, *Como Sobreviven los Marginados* (Mexico City: Siglo XXI, 1976).

Lubeck, Paul and Walton, John, 'Urban Class Conflict in Africa and Latin America: a comparative Analysis from a World Systems Perspective', *International Journal of Urban and Regional Research*, 3, 1 (1979).

'Luttes (Les) Urbaines à Bruxelles', *Contradictions* (Brussels: Special Issue, 1975).

Luxembourg, Rosa, *L'Accumulation de Capital* (Paris: Maspero, 1967, 2 vols.).

——, *Grèves, Partis, Syndicats* (Paris: Maspero, 1966).

Lynch, Kevin, *The Image of the City* (Cambridge, Mass.: MIT Press, 1960).

——, *A Theory of Good City Form* (Cambridge, Mass.: MIT Press, 1981).

——, *What Time is this Place?* (Cambridge, Mass.: MIT Press, 1972).

MacAdams, Robert, *The Evolution of Urban Society* (London: Weidenfeld and Nicolson, 1966).

McHugh, John, 'The Clyde Rent Strike', *The Scottish Labour History Society Journal*, 12 (1978).

McLean, Iain, 'Popular Protest and Public Order: Red Clydeside 1915-1919', in J. Stevenson and R. Quinault, eds., *Popular Protest and Public Order* (London: George Allen and Unwin, 1974).

Madrid. Comision de Planeamiento y Coordinacion del Area Metropolitana, *Analisis de Problemas y Opportunidades* (Madrid: MOPU-COPLACO, 1978, 12 vols.).

Magri, Suzanna, *La Politique de l'Etat en Matière de Logement des Travailleurs* (Paris: Centre de Sociologie Urbaine, 1973).

Maranon, Gregorio, *Los Castillos en la Comunidades de Castilla* (Madrid: Espase-Calpe, 1957).

Maravall, Jose Antonio, *Carlo V y el Pensamiento Politico del Renacimiento* (Madrid: Instituto de Estudios Politicos, 1960).

——, *Las Comunidades de Castilla* (Madrid: Alianza Universitaria, 1979).

Marcano, Esther, *Caracas: Autoroutes et Bidonvilles* (Paris: Université de Paris; Ph.D. thesis, 1979).

Marrett, S., *State Housing in Britain* (London: Routledge and Kegan Paul, 1979).

Marris, Peter, *Meaning and Action* (London: Routledge and Kegan Paul, 1982).

Marris, Peter and Rein, Martin, *Dilemmas of Social Reform* (London: Routledge and Kegan Paul, 1972).

Martin, James, *Telematic Society* (Englewood Cliffs: Prentice Hall, 1981; first published 1978).

Marx, Karl, *The Civil War in France* (London: Central Books, 1977).

——, *Grundrisse: Foundations of the Critique of the Political Economy* (New York: Vintage Books: Harmondsworth: Penguin, 1973; 1st integral French edition: *Grundrisse*, Paris: Anthropos, 1968).

—— and Engels, Friedrich, *The German Ideology* (New York: International Publishers, 1939; London: Lawrence and Wishart, 1970).

Massey, Doreen and Catalano, Alexandro, *Capital and Land* (London: Edward Arnold, 1978).

Mathieu, Gilbert, *Peut-on Loger les Français?* (Paris: Seuil, 1965).

Mattei, Marco *et al.*, *Le Lotte per la Casa a Firenze* (Rome: Savelli, 1975).

Mayer, Margit, *Through the Eye of the Needle: Everyday Life, Political Conflict and the Citizens' Initiatives Movement in West Germany* (Frankfurt: Institut für England- und Amerika Studien der JWG Universität; unpublished report, 1981).

——, 'Urban Squatters in Germany', *International Journal of Urban and Regional Research* (forthcoming).

Mayoral, J. *et al.*, *Vallecas: Razones de una Lucha Popular* (Madrid: CIDUR, 1977).

Mehl, Dominique, 'Les Voies de la Contestation Urbaine', *Les Annales de la Recherche Urbaine*, 2 (1979).

Meier, Richard, *A Communication Theory of Urban Growth* (Cambridge, Mass.: MIT Press, 1962).

——, *Science and Economic Development* (Cambridge, Mass.: MIT Press, 1956).

Melling, Joseph, 'Clydeside Housing and the Evolution of State Rent Control, 1900–1939', in J. Melling, ed., *Housing, Social Policy and the State* (London: Croom Helm, 1980).

——, *Employers, Labour and the Housing Market in Clydeside from 1880 to 1920* (Glasgow: SSRC, University of Glasgow Conference on Social Policy, May 1978; mimeographed).

——, *The Glasgow Rent Strike and Clydeside Labour 1914-1915: the Rise of a Social Movement* (Glasgow: Department of Economic History, University of Glasgow, 1978; unpublished paper).

——, 'The Glasgow Rent Strike and Clydeside Labour: some Problems of Interpretation', *Journal of the Scottish Labour History Society*, 13 (1979).

——, *Housing, Social Policy and the State* (London: Croom Helm, 1980).

——, 'Non-Commissioned Officers: British Employers and their Supervisory Workers, 1880–1920', *Social History*, 5, 2 (1980).

——, *Scottish Industrialists and the Changing Characters of Class Relations in the Clyde Region, 1880-1918*, in A. Dickson, ed., *Capital and Class in Scotland* (Edinburgh: John Donald, 1982, pp. 61–142).

——, *Rent Strikes and Working Class Politics: The Glasgow Rent Strikes and the Rise of Independent Labour in West Scotland, 1890-1916* (Cambridge: King's College Research Centre, University of Cambridge, 1982, unpublished).

Melucci, Alberto, 'L'Azione Ribelli: Formazione e Struttura dei Movimenti Sociali', in A. Melucci, ed., *Movimenti de Rivolta: Teoria e Forme dell'Azione Collettiva* (Milan: Etas Libri, 1976).

——, *Sistema Politico, Partiti e Movimenti Sociali* (Milan: Feltrinelli, 1976).

Mesa-Lago, Carmelo, *Social Security in Latin America: Pressure Groups, Stratification and Inequality* (Pittsburgh: University of Pittsburgh Press, 1978).

Meunier, Christine, *Revendications Urbaines, Stratégie Politique et Transformation Idéologique: le Compamento Nueva la Habana, Santiago, 1970-73* (Paris: Université de Paris; Ph.D. thesis, 1976).

Meyer, John and Hannon, Michael, eds., *National Development and the World System* (Chicago: Chicago University Press, 1979).

Miliband, Ralph, *The State in Capitalist Society* (New York: Basic Books, 1969).

Miller, Mike, 'Community Organization USA: the View from the Movement', *International Journal of Urban and Regional Research*, 5, 4 (1981).

Mingione, Enzo, *Social Conflict and the City* (Oxford: Basil Blackwell, 1981).

Mission Planning Council, San Francisco, *24th Street Problems and Possibilities* (San Francisco: MPC, 1976; mimeographed).

Mission Housing Development Corporation, *A Plan for the Inner Mission* (San Francisco: Mission Housing Development Corporation, March, 1972).

Mollenkopf, John H., *Community Organization and City Politics* (Cambridge, Mass.: Department of Government, Harvard University; unpublished thesis, 1973).

——, 'Neighborhood Mobilization and Urban Development: Boston and San Francisco, 1968–1978', *International Journal of Urban and Regional Research*, 5, 1 (1981).

——, *The North-East and the South-West: Paths towards the Post-Industrial City* (Stanford: Stanford University, Programme of Urban Studies; unpublished report, 1979).

——, *The Politics of Urban Development in the US* (Princeton: Princeton University Press, 1983).

——, 'The Postwar Politics of Urban Development', *Politics and Society*, 5, 3 (1975).

——, *The San Francisco Housing Market in the 1980s: an Agenda for Neighborhood Planning* (San Francisco: Report to the San Francisco Foundation, 1980; mimeographed).

Montano, Jorge, *Los Pobres de la Ciudad en los Asentamientos Espontaneos* (Mexico City: Siglo XXI, 1976).

Moore, Barrington, *Social Origins of Dictatorship: Lord and Peasant in the Making of the Modern World* (London: Peregrine Books, 1969).

'Movimientos Sociales Urbanos 1 & 2', *Jano-Arquitectura* (Barcelona, Special Issues, July-August, 1976, and September-October, 1976).

Moynihan, Daniel P., *Maximum Feasible Misunderstanding: Community Action in the War on Poverty* (New York: The Free Press, 1969).

Mumford, Lewis, *The City in History: its Origins, its Transformation and its Prospects* (New York: Harcourt Brace Jovanovich, 1961).

——, *The Culture of Cities* (New York: Harcourt Brace Jovanovich, 1938).

Mundo, Octavo Garcia, *El Movimiento Inquilinario de Veracruz* (Mexico, DF: Sepsetentos, 1976).

Murard, L. and Zylbermann, Patrick, *Ville, Habitat et Intimité* (Paris: Recherches, 1976).

Murphy, Karen A., *The Gay Community and Urban Transformations: a Case Study of San Francisco* (Berkeley: University of California Department of City Planning, Master's thesis, 1980).

Nanetti, Rafaella, *Citizen Participation and Neighborhood Councils in Bologna* (Ann Arbor: University of Michigan, Department of Political Science, unpublished Ph.D. thesis, 1977).

Navarro, B. and Moctezuma, P., 'Clase Obrera, Ejercito Industrial de Reserva y Movimientos Sociales Urbanos de las Clases Dominadas en Mexico', *Teoria y Politica*, 2 (1981).

Navarro, Moises Gonzales, *Poblacion y Sociedad en Mexico (1900-1970)* (Mexico, DF: UNAM, vol. 1, Serie Estudio, 42, 1974).

Nelson, Joan M., *Access to Power: Politics and the Urban Poor in Developing Countries* (Princeton: Princeton University Press, 1979).

Nguyen Duc Nhuan, *Revendications Urbaines: Etude sur les Luttes menées par les Groupes Sociaux Residentiels* (Paris: Centre de Sociologie Urbaine, 1975).

Oakley, Charles A., *The Second City* (Glasgow and London: Blackie and Son, 1967).

Obershall, Anthony, *Social Conflict and Social Movements* (Englewood Cliffs: Prentice Hall, 1973).

O'Brien, David, *Neighborhood Organization and Interest Group Processes* (Princeton: Princeton University Press, 1975).

O'Connor, James, *The Fiscal Crisis of the State* (New York: St. Martin's Press, 1973).

Offe, Claus, *Lo Stato nel Capitalismo Maturo* (Milan: Etas Libri, 1977; German original, 1975).

Oficina Municipal del Plan, *Madrid: Cuarenta Años de Desarrollo Urbano, 1940-1980* (Madrid: Ayuntamiento de Madrid, Coleccion Temas Urbanos, 1981).

Olson, Mancur, *The Logic of Collective Action: Public Goods and the Theory of Groups* (Cambridge, Mass.: Harvard University Press, 1965).

Operation Upgrade: Citizens for a Cleaner Mission. 'A Position Statement' (San Francisco, 15th December, 1976; typewritten).

Operation Upgrade and Mission Planning Council, *16th Street: a Neighborhood Study* (San Francisco: Mission Planning Council, 1977; mimeographed).

Osborne, Adam, *Running Wild: the Next Industrial Revolution* (Berkeley: Osborne/McGraw Hill, 1979).

Pacione, Michael, ed., *Urban Problems and Planning in the Developed World* (London: Croom Helm, 1981).

Pahl, Ray, 'Castells and Collective Consumption', *Sociology*, 12 (1978).

——, *Whose City?* (Harmondsworth: Penguin, 1975).

Panofsky, Erwin, *Gothic Architecture and Scholasticism* (New York: Meridian Books, 1957).

Pastrana, Ernesto and Threlfall, Monica, *Pan, Techo y Poder: el Movimiento de Pobladores en Chile, 1970-3* (Buenos Aires: Ediciones STAP, 1974).

Pereira, Humberto, ed., *La Vivienda Popular en America Latina* (Caracas: Fundacomun, 1979).

Perez, Joseph, *La Révolution des Comunidades de Castile (1520-1521)* (Bordeaux: Institut de l'Université de Bordeaux, 1970; Madrid: Siglo XXI, 1977).

Perlman, Janice, 'Grassrooting the System', *Social Policy* (September-October, 1976).

——, *The Myth of Marginality* (Berkeley: University of California Press, 1976).

Perlo, Manuel, 'Politica y Vivienda en Mexico 1910–1952', *Revista Mexicana de Sociologia*, 1 (1980).

Pickvance, Chris G., 'Marxist Approaches to the Study of Urban Politics', *International Journal of Urban and Regional Research*, 1, 1 (1979).

——, 'On the Study of Urban Social Movements', in C.G. Pickvance, ed., *Urban Sociology: Critical Essays* (London: Tavistock, 1976).

——, 'The State and Consumption' (Course Unit 24 for *Urban Development* (D 202); Milton Keynes: Open University, 1982).

Pincon, Michel, *Les HLM, Structure Sociale de la Population Logée* (Paris: Centre de Sociologie Urbaine, 1976, 2 vols.).

Pingeot, François, *Populisme Urbain et Crise du Centre-Ville dans les Sociétés Dependantes: Santiago-du-Chili, 1969–73* (Paris: Université de Paris; Ph.D. thesis, 1976).

Pinkney, David H., *Napoleon III and the Rebuilding of Paris* (Princeton: Princeton University Press, 1958).

Piven, Frances F. and Cloward, Richard A., *Poor People's Movements: Why they Succeed, How they Fail* (New York: Pantheon Books, 1977).

Pizzorno, Alessandro, *Développement Economique et Urbanisation* (5th World Congress of Sociology of the International Sociological Association, Washington, DC, Proceedings, 1962).

Portes, Alejandro, *Cuatro Poblaciones: Informe Preliminar sobre Situacion y Aspiraciones de Grupos Marginados de Santiago* (Santiago: Land Tenure Centre, 1969; mimeographed).

——, *Immigracion, Etnicidad y el Caso Cubano* (Baltimore: Johns Hopkins University; unpublished research report, 1981).

Portes, Alejandro and Walton, John, *Labor, Class and the International System* (New York: Academic Press, 1981).

——, *Urban Latin America* (Austin: University of Texas Press, 1976).

Pottier, Claude, *La Logique du Financement Public de l'Urbanisation* (Paris: Mouton, 1975).

Poulantzas, Nicos, *La Crise des Dictatures* (Paris: Maspero, 1975).

——, *L'Etat, le Pouvoir, le Socialisme* (Paris: PUF, 1978).

——, *Pouvoir Politique et Classes Sociales* (Paris: Maspero, 1968).

Pred, Allan, *City Systems in Advanced Economies: Past Growth, Present Processes and Future Development Options* (New York: John Wiley, 1977).

Preteceille, Edmond, *La Production des Grands Ensembles* (Paris: Mouton, 1973).

Ray, Talton F., *The Politics of the Barrios of Venezuela* (Berkeley: University of California Press, 1969).

Raymond, Henri *et al.*, *Les Pavillonnaires* (Paris: Centre de Recherche d'Urbanisme, 1966).

Rebollo, Julian *et al.*, *El Movimiento Ciudadano ante la Democracia* (Madrid: Cenit Editorial, 1977).

Recalde, Jose Ramon, *La Construccion de las Naciones* (Madrid: Siglo XXI, 1982).

Reis Falcao de Queiroz, Leda Lucia dos, *Movimento Amigos de Bairro de Nova Iguacu: o Povo Exige Passagem* (Rio de Janeiro: Universidade Federal; unpublished Master's thesis, 1981).

Remy, Jean and Voye, Liliane, *Ville, Ordre et Violence* (Paris: PUF, 1981).

Rendall, Walter, *The Revolutionary Movement in Britain, 1900–21* (London: Weidenfeld and Nicolson, 1968).

'Report from Black America', *Newsweek*, 30 (June 1969).

Report of the National Advisory Commission on Civil Disorders (Chicago. Aldine Publishing Company, 1970).

Rex, John, 'The City, Castells and Althusser', *International Journal of Urban and Regional Research*, 2, 3 (1978).

Rex, John and Moore, Robert, *Race, Community and Conflict: a Study of Sparkbrook* (London: Oxford University Press, 1967).

Riboulet, Pierre, 'Une Construction Primitive pour une Société Développé, *Espaces et Sociétés*, 6–7 (1973).

Riessman, David, *The Lonely Crowd: a Study of the Changing American Character* (New Haven: Yale University Press, 1950).

Roberts, Bryan, *Cities of Peasants: the Political Economy of Urbanization in the Third World* (London: Edward Arnold, 1978).

Rodriguez, Alfredo and Riofrio, Gustavo, *Segregacion Social y Movilizacion Residencial: el Caso de Lima* (Buenos Aires: SIAP, 1974).

Rojas, Jaime, *La Participation Urbaine dans les Sociétés Dependantes: l'Expérience du Mouvement des Pobladores au Chili* (Paris: Université de Paris; Ph.D. thesis, 1978).

Romero, Jose Luis, *Latinoamerica: las Ciudades y las Ideas* (Buenos Aires: Siglo XXI, 1976).

Rörig, Fritz, *The Medieval Town* (Berkeley: University of California Press, 1967).

Ross, Marc H., *The Political Integration of Urban Squatters* (Evanston, Ill.: Northwestern University Press, 1973).

Rossi, Peter H. *et al.*, *The Roots of Urban Discontent: Public Policy, Municipal Institutions, and the Ghetto* (New York: John Wiley, 1976. The Wiley Series in Urban Research).

Rougerie, Jacques, *Procès des Communards* (Paris: Gallimard-Archives, 1978).

Rousseau, Jean-Jacques, *The Social Contract* [And] *Discourses* (London: J.M. Dent, 1973).

Safa, Helen, ed., *The Political Economy of Urbanization in Third World Countries* (New Delhi: Oxford University Press, 1982).

San Francisco Consortium, *Community Organization in San Francisco* (San Francisco: SFC, 1974).

San Francisco. Department of City Planning, *Changes in San Francisco Housing Inventory, 1977* (San Francisco, 1979; mimeographed).

——, *The Mission: Policies for Neighborhood Improvement* (San Francisco, January, 1976; mimeographed).

——, *Mission 1970 Census: Population and Housing* (San Francisco, January 1976; mimeographed).

Sanchez, Magaly, *La Segregation Urbaine à Caracas* (Paris: Université de Paris, 1980, unpublished Ph.D. thesis in Sociology).

Sandroni, Paulo, 'As "Greves Civicas" como Forma de Luta de Massas na Colombia: de Rojas Pinilla (1953–57) ao Pequeno "Bogotazo" (1977), *Espacoe Debates* (Sao Paulo), 1, 3 (1981).

Santos, E. and Seelenberger, S., *Aspectos de un Diagnostico de la Problematica Estructural del Sector Vivienda* (Santiago: Escuela de Arquitectura, Universidad Catolica de Chile, 1968).

Santos, Milton, *The Shared Space: the Two Circuits of Urban Economy in the Underdeveloped Countries and their Spatial Repercussions* (London: Methuen, 1975).

Santos, Theotonio dos, *Dependencia Economica y Cambio Revolucionario* (Caracas: Nueva Izquierda, 1970).

Saunders, Peter, *Social Theory and the Urban Question* (London: Hutchinson, 1981).

——, *Urban Politics: a Sociological Interpretation* (London: Hutchinson, 1979).

Sawyers, Larry and Tabb, William, eds., *Marxism and the Metropolis* (New York: Oxford University Press, 1977).

Saxenian, Anna Lee, *Silicon Chips and Spatial Structure: the Industrial Basis of Urbanization in Santa Clara County, Colifornia* (Berkeley: University of California Department of City Planning; unpublished Master's thesis, 1980).

Schiller, Herbert I., *Mass Communications and the American Empire* (Boston: Beacon Press, 1969).

Scott, Mel, *The Future of the San Francisco Bay Area* (Berkeley: Institute of Governmental Studies, University of California, 1963).

——, *The San Francisco Bay Area: a Metropolis in Perspective* (Berkeley: University of California Press, 1959).

Sennett, Richard, *The Fall of Public Man: the Social Psychology of Capitalism* (New York: Knopf, 1977; Vintage Books, 1978).

——, *Families against the City: Middle Class Homes of Industrial Chicago* (Cambridge, Mass.: Harvard University Press, 1970).

Shilts, Randy, *The Mayor of Castro Street: the Life and Times of Harvey Milk* (New York: St. Martin's Press, 1982).

Simmie, James M., *Beyond the Industrial City?* (Berkeley: Association of Bay Area Governments, 1982; mimeographed).

Singer, Paul and Brandt, Vinicius Caldeira, eds., *Sao Paulo: a Povo em Movimiento* (Petropolis: Vozes, 1981).

Sjoberg, Gideon, *The Pre-Industrial City, Past and Present* (New York: The Free Press, 1960).

Skocpol, Theda, *States and Social Revolutions: a Comparative Analysis of France, Russia and China* (New York: Cambridge University Press, 1979).

Smelser, Neil J., *Theory of Collective Behavior* (New York: Free Press of Glencoe, 1963).

Smith, Neil, 'Towards a Theory of Gentrification: a Back to the City Movement by Capital, not People', *Journal of the American Planning Association*, 45, 4 (1979).

Social Policy (New York: Special Issue on Organizing Neighborhoods, 10, 2, September-October, 1979).

Soja, Edward W., 'The Socio-Spatial Dialectic', *Annals of the Association of American Geographers*, 70 (1980).

Sole-Tura, Jordi, *Introduccion al Regimen Politico Español* (Barcelona: Ariel, 1969).

Solow, Robert, 'Technical Changes and the Aggregate Production Function', *Review of Economics and Statistics* (August, 1957).

Sombart, W., *Der Moderne Kapitalismus* (Leipzig: Duncker & Humblot, 1902–27, 3 vols.).

Spilerman, Seymour, 'The Causes of Racial Disturbances: a Comparison of Alternative Explanation', *American Sociological Review*, 35 (1970).

——, The Causes of Racial Disturbances: Tests of an Explanation', *American Sociological Review*, 36 (1971).

Stallings, Barbara, *Class Conflict and Economic Development in Chile, 1958–1973* (Stanford: Stanford University Press, 1979).

Stanback, Thomas M., *Understanding the Service Economy: Employment, Productivity, Location* (Baltimore: Johns Hopkins University Press, 1978).

Szelenyi, Ivan, 'Structural Changes and Alternatives to Capitalist Development in the Contemporary Urban and Regional System', *International Journal of Urban and Regional Research*, 5, 1 (1981).

Tabb, William, *The Political Economy of the Black Ghetto* (New York: W.W. Norton, 1970).

Tafuri, Manfredo, *Progetto e Utopia, Architettura e Sviluppo Capitalistico* (Rome and Bari: Laterza, 1973).

——, *Teoria e Storia della Architettura* (Rome and Bari: Laterza, 1968).

Tamames, Ramon, *La Oligarquia Financiera en España* (Barcelona: Planeta, 1976).

——, *Estructura Economica de España* (Madrid: Alianza Universidad, 1980, 2 volumes).

Taub, R.P. *et al.*, 'Urban Voluntary Associations, Locality Based and Externally Induced', *American Journal of Sociology*, 83, 2 (1977).

Taylor, David, *The Gay Community and Castro Village: Who's Opposing Whom* (Berkeley: University of California Department of City Planning; Paper for CP 229, 1978).

Teran, Fernando, 'New Planning Experiences in Democratic Spain', *International Journal of Urban and Regional Research*, 5, 1 (1981).

——, *Planeamiento Urbano en la España Contemporanea* (Barcelona: Gustavo Gili, 1978).

Therborn, Göran, *What does the Ruling Class do when it Rules?* (London: New Left Books, 1977).

Thurow, Lester C., 'The Productivity Problem', *Technology Review*, 83, 2 (1980).

Tilly, Charles, 'The Chaos of the Living City', in C. Tilly, ed., *An Urban World* (Boston: Little Brown, 1974).

——, 'Major Forms of Collective Action in Western Europe 1500–1975', *Theory and Society*, 3, 3 (1976).

——, 'Reflections on the History of European State-Making', in C. Tilly, ed., *The Formation of National States in Western Europe* (Princeton: Princeton University Press, 1975).

Tilly, Charles, ed., *The Formation of National States in Western Europe* (Princeton: Princeton University Press, 1975).

——, *From Mobilization to Revolution* (Reading, Mass.: Addison Wesley, 1977).

Toffler, Alvin, *The Third Wave* (New York: William Morrow and Company, 1980).

Tokman, J. and Klein, E., eds., *El Subempleo en America Latina* (Buenos Aires: El Cid Editores, 1979).

Tomlinson, T.M., 'The Development of a Riot Ideology among Urban Negroes', in Allen D. Grimshaw, ed., *Racial Violence in the United States* (Chicago: Aldine, 1969).

Topalov, Christian, *Capital et Propriété Foncière* (Paris: Centre de Sociologie Urbaine, 1973).

——, *Les Promoteurs Immobiliers* (Paris: Mouton, 1974).

——, 'Politique Monopoliste et Propriété du Logement', *Economie et Politique* (March, 1974).

——, *La SCIC: Etude Monographique d'un Groupe Immobilier Para-Public* (Paris: Centre de Sociologie Urbaine, Research Report, 1969).

Touraine, Alain, *Un Désir d'Histoire* (Paris: Stock, 1977).

——, *Le Mouvement de Mai, ou le Communisme Utopique* (Paris: Seuil, 1968).

——, *Production de la Société* (Paris: Seuil, 1973).

——, *Les Sociétés Dependantes* (Brussels: Duculot, 1976).

——, *Sociologie de l'Action* (Paris: Seuil, 1965).

——, *La Voix et le Regard* (Paris: Seuil, 1978).

——, *La Société Invisible* (Paris: Seuil, 1976).

Unikel, Luis, *El Desarrollo Urbano de Mexico* (Mexico, DF, El Colegio de Mexico, 1976).

Urrutia, Cecilia, *Historia de la Poblaciones Callampas* (Santiago: Quimantu, 1972).

Vance, J., *Geography and Urban Evolution in the San Francisco Bay Area* (Berkeley: Institute of Governmental Studies, University of California, 1969).

Vanderschueren, Franz, 'Significado Politico de las Juntas de Vecinos', *Revista Latinoamericana de Estudios Urbanos y Regionales*, 2 (1971).

Vilar, Sergio, *Naturaleza del Franquismo* (Madrid: Peninsula, 1977).

Villarreal, Diana, *Marginalité Urbaine et Politique de l'Etat à Mexico: Enquête sur les Zones Residentielles Illégales de la Ville de Monterrey* (Paris: Université de Paris, Ecole des Hautes Etudes en Sciences Sociales, 1979).

Villasante, Tomas, *Los Vecinos en la Calle* (Madrid: Ediciones de La Torre, 1976).

Wallerstein, Immanuel, *The Capitalist World Economy* (New York: Cambridge University Press, 1979).

——, *The Modern World System: Capitalist Agriculture and the Origins of the European World Economy in the Sixteenth Century* (New York: Academic Press, 1974).

Walton, John, 'The New Urban Sociology', *International Social Science Journal*, 33, 2 (1981).

——, 'Urban Political Movements and Revolutionary Change in the Third World', *Urban Affairs Quarterly*, 15 (1979).

Webber, Melvin, 'The BART Experience – What have we Learned?', *The Public Interest*, 45 (1976).

Weber, Max, *The City* (Glencoe, Ill.: The Free Press, 1959).

Weightman, Barbara, 'Gay Bars as Private Places', *Landscape*, 25, 1 (1980).

Weisslitz, Jacqueline, *Développement, Dependance, et Structure Urbaines: Analyse Comparative de Villes Peruviennes* (Paris: Université de Paris; Ph.D. thesis, 1978).

Wilding, P., 'The Housing and Town Planning Act of 1919: a Study in the Making of Social Policy', *Journal of Social Policy*, 2 (1973).

Wirt, Frederick M., *Power in the City: Decision-Making in San Francisco* (Berkeley: University of California Press, 1974).

Wolf, Deborah, *The Lesbian Community* (Berkeley: University of California Press, 1979).

Wolfe, Allan, *The Limits of Legitimacy* (New York and West Drayton: Collier-Macmillan, 1981).

Wright, Erik O., *Class, Crisis and the State* (London: New Left Books, 1978).

Wusocki, Ted *et al.*, *Neighborhoods First: from the 70's into the 80's* (Chicago: National Training and Information Center, 1977).

Yago, Glenn, *The Decline of Public Transit in the US and Germany* (Madison: University of Wisconsin; Sociology Ph.D. thesis, 1980).

Yates, Douglas, *The Ungovernable City* (Cambridge, Mass.: MIT Press, 1977).

Young, K. and Kramer, J., *Strategy and Conflict in Metropolitan Housing* (London: Heinemann, 1978).

Zeitlin, Maurice, ed., *Classes, Class Conflict and the State* (Englewood Cliffs: Winthrop, 1980).

Zorbaugh, Harvey, *The Gold Coast and the Slum* (Chicago: University of Chicago Press, 1927).

Zukin, Sharon, 'The Cutting Edge: a Decade of the New Urban Sociology', *Theory and Society*, 9 (1980).

Index

Abbé Pierre, l', 75
Accion Popular (Peru), 192
Action for Accountable Government (AAG), 165
Acuna, Bishop, 7
Adriano, Cardinal, 5
Advocate, The (magazine), 141, 161
Afghanistan, 176
Alcala de Henares, Madrid, 242, 247–9, 252
Alcoholic Beverage Commission, USA, 141
Alianza Popular (Spain), 257
Alianza Popular Revolucionaria Americana (APRA), 191–2
Alice B. Toklas Democratic Club, 163–4
Alinsky, Saul D.: model of community organization, 49, 60–5, 106, 124–5, 128; career, 61–2; and Mike Miller, 112; and Mission District, 116, 127–8
Alioto, Joseph, 103–4, 111, 114, 116, 135
Allende, Salvador, 179, 200–2, 207–9
Angola, 176
Annales, cit., 12
Artola, General, 192
Ash, Roberta, cit., 295
Asociaciones de Cabezas de Familia (Spain), 226
Asociaciones de Pobladores (Peru), 192
Association Sarcelloise (AS), 80–5

Babylon, 12, 70
'back to the city' movement, 160–1
Bambaren, Bishop, 192
Banco Obrero (Caracas), 187
Banus company (Madrid), 249–50
Barbour, Mary, 29–30, 32
Barcelona, 215, 220
Barreiro, Reyes, 39
Barriada Independencia (Peru), 194
barriadas (Lima), 190–4
BART (San Francisco), 103, 110, 131–2
Basques, 218, 220, 223
Baudelaire, Charles, cit., 290
beat culture, 141
Belaúnde Terry, Fernando, 191–3
Bell, Daniel and Held, Virginia, cit., 49
Bernardo O'Higgins *campamento* (Chile), 205

Bismarck, Otto, Prince von, 22
Black Cat (San Francisco bar), 141–2, 144
Black Panthers, 54, 119
blacks (negroes): in US inner city ghettos, 49–60, 63–7, 70–1, 172, 334; as mayors of US cities, 54; in San Francisco, 100, 104, 115
Blackstone Rangers, 64
Bloch-Lainé, François, 82
Bogota, 210
Bolio Trejo, Arturo, cit., 38
Bologna, 318
Borja, Jordi, cit., 300
Borvice, Gary, 120
bourgeoisie: and Castilla *comunidades*, 7–8, 11; and Paris Commune, 15, 19, 22, 24, 26, 333; and capitalism, 306; and human diversity, 330
Boussy (France), 323
Boyte, Harry, cit., 49
Braudel, Fernand, cit., 310, 332
Bravo, 5
Brazil, 176, 328
Bridges, Harry, 103
Briggs, Senator, 144
Britt, Harry, 138, 141, 144, 151, 164–5, 170
Brown, Willie, 104, 163
Brown Berets, 111, 118–9
Bryant, Anita, 144
Buckley, Christopher, 102
Buffalo, New York, 63
BUILD, Buffalo, NY, 63
Burgos (Spain), 8
Burton, John, 163
Business Week, 315

caballeros (Spain), 6
caciquismo, 195
Cail company (Paris), 22
callampas, 180–1
Calles, Plutarco Elías, 42
campamentos (Chile), 200–5
capitalism: and housing crisis, 36–7; and corporate interests, 175–6; and urban social movements, 297; defined, 306; and profit, 307, 310–11; challenged, 308; and development, 310; and ethnic exploitation, 316; and

labour movements, 329; and industrialization, 333

Caracas, 181, 183, 185–7

Carlos V, King of Spain, 5, 11

Carrabal, Garrido, 44

Carranza, Venustrano, 42–3

Carrefour de Recherche et d'Information (CRI), 93

Carrero Blanco, Luis, 223

Carrillo, Felipe, 44

Casa de Nicaragua, La, 118–9, 135

Casa del Salvador, La, 118, 135

Castells, Manuel, cit., 182, 297–8

Castilla: *Comunidades* (1520–22), 3, 4–15, 68–9, 71, 331–2

Castro Street Fair (San Francisco), 162

Catalans, 218, 223

Central Unica de Trabajadores (CUT), Chile, 201, 205

Central Unica del Poblador (CUP), Chile, 201

Centre Party (UCD), Spain, 247

Centro de Cambio, San Francisco, 135

Centro Operacional del Politica y Estudios sobre Vivienda (COPEVI), Mexico, 187–8

Central Social Obrero (San Francisco), 110, 126, 129, 135

CERFI, 317

Charleston, Noelle *et al.*, cit., 130

Chavez, Cesar, 112

Chelsea Community Council, New York, 63

Chicago: Northwest Community Organization, 63

Chicago School (of sociology), 292

Chihuahua, Mexico, 196

Chile: incidence of squatting in, 178; squatters and politics in, 179, 183, 190, 199, 208–9, 272, 274, 328; housing programme and urban reform, 199–200; protest in, 299; bloodshed, 323

Chirac, Jacques, 26

Christian Democrats, Spain, 271

Christiani Commune, Copenhagen, 318

Christopher, George, 102, 142

Church, churches: as enemy of Paris *Communards*, 23; mobilization of American poor, 57; and Alinsky, 61–3; in San Francisco, 110, 112–3, 119, 123, 126, 136; and gay culture, 161; and Spanish neighbourhood associations, 244, 250; repressive in Spain, 324; in Castilla, 333

Cicero, Illinois, 51

CIDU, 207

Circle of Loving Companions, 142

Cisneros, Cardinal, Regent of Castilla, 9

cities: defined, 302–4, 318–9; space and production mode in, 312

citizen movements: defined, 320

Citizen Movement *see under* Madrid

Citizens Action League, California, 65

Citizens Actions Program, Chicago, 64

City Lights bookstore, San Francisco, 141

ciudades perdidas (Mexican shanty towns), 189

Clastres, Pierre, cit., 13

Clerc, Paul, cit., 76

Clydeside *see* Glasgow

Cohn-Bendit, Daniel, 322

Colegio de Mexico, El, 187–8

Collier, David, cit., 191

Colonia El Viso, Madrid, 255

Colonias de Hotelitos, Madrid, 242, 256–7, 266

colonias de lucha, 197

colonias proletarias (Mexico), 188, 194–9

Comites Sin Casa (Chile), 200–1

Communards (Paris): social composition, 16–9

Commune of Paris *see under* Paris

Communist Parties: Chile, 205; France (PCF), 80, 83–4, 297, 325; Mexico, 44; Peru, 191; Spain (PCE), 229, 235, 247–8, 250, 255, 262, 270–75

Community Action Program (USA), 54

community organization: Alinsky's model of, 49, 60–5

Community Organization Movement (COM), USA, 57–8, 60

comuneros (Castilla), 4–7, 10–11, 71

Comunidades: defined, 8–9; *see also* Castilla

community: defined, 319

Confederacion de Trabajadores Mexicanos (CTM), 196

Confederacion General de Trabajadores (CGT), Mexico, 45

Confederacion Revolucionaria de Obreros Mexicanos (CROM), 45–6

Confédération Générale du Travail (CGT), France, 325

Confédération Nationale de Logement (CNL), France, 82, 84, 91–3, 96

Confédération Syndicale du Cadre de Vie (CSCV), 96

Connally, Michael P., cit., 60

Construction Workers' Union, USA, 110, 129

consumption, 312–3; collective, 316, 319, 323

conventillos (slums), 180–1, 207

Copenhagen, 318

CORO Foundation, 134, 153

Corrala, La, Madrid, 252–5, 264, 266

Crawfurd, Helen, 29, 32
Cuba, 176, 304, 316
Cuernavaca, Mexico, 196

Dagnaud, Monique and Mehl, Dominique, cit., 320
Damer, Sean, cit., 28–30, 34–5
Damron, Bob, cit., 148
Daughters of Bilitis, 142
Del Carlo, Larry, 120
Delescluze, Charles, 22
DESAL, cit., 180–1
Detroit, 314
development, mode of: defined, 306–7, 310; and urban change, 312–4, 326
De Young, Doug, cit., 147
Dmitrieva, Elisabeth, 19
Dobbs, Harold, 103
Downes, Bryan T., cit., 52
Dunkirk, 297
Duque, Joaquin and Pastrana, Ernesto, cit., 201, 204–5

Echeverria Alvarez, Luis, 195, 197
ecologists, 317
Economic Opportunity Council, USA, 110
El Pilar (La Vaguada es Nuestra), Madrid, 242, 249–51, 259
El Salvador, 118, 135, 176
Engels, Friedrich, 36, 296, 299
Equipo de Sociologia Urbana (EQUISUR), Mexico, 187
ethnic minorities: in San Francisco, 100–1, 105–7, 109–11, 113, 123–6, 130–2, 325; hostility to gays, 167; capitalist exploitation of, 316; community grouping, 316–7
Evans, Hugh, cit., 188
experience: defined, 305–6; and historical change, 308–9, 311
Ezquerro, Luisa, 117

Fainstein, Norman and Susan, cit., 300
Fair Share, Massachusetts, 65
Feagin, Joe and Hahn, Harlan, cit., 52
Federacion de Trabajadores del Puerto de Veracruz, 45
Federal Office for Economic Opportunity, USA, 54–5, 60
Federation of Neighbourhood Associations, Provincial (FPAV), Madrid, 229–30, 244, 267, 269, 273–4
Feinstein, Diane, 104, 120, 144, 164–5

feminism, 301, 305, 309, 317, 327; *see also* women
Ferguson, Mrs (of Glasgow), 29
FIGHT, Rochester, New York, 63
Fischer, Claude S., 300
Fish, John Hall, cit., 63–4
Florence: *Commune*, 11
Flynn, Ann and Vincent, 30
Foster, Jim, 142, 163
Foster, John, cit., 31, 324
Foucault, Michel, 317
France, 297, 299, 330; *see also* Paris
Franco, Gen. Francisco, 215–6, 223, 261–3
Frankel, Leo, 21
'free-rider dilemma', 293
Frei, Eduardo, 199–200
Friedland, Roger, cit., 52–3
Fronte Popular Tierra y Libertad, Mexico, 197
Fustel de Coulanges, Numa Denis, cit., 12

Gallagher, Nora, 144
Gambetta, Léon, 22
Gamson, William A., cit., 292, 294–5
Garcia, Rafael, 39
Garcia Mundo, Octavio, cit., 38
garden cities, 256–7
Garza, Gustavo and Shteingart, Martha, cit., 188
Gay Activist Alliance, 142
Gay Democratic Club, 164
Gay Freedom Day Parade, 162
Gay Liberation Front, 142
gays: in San Francisco, 100–1, 104–5, 129, 136, 138–9, 323, 325; numbers, 136; territorial concentration, 138–41, 145–58, 168, 172, 325; organizations, 142–3, 161, 164; as local political force, 143–4, 163–6, 168, 323; way of life, 157, 160, 172, 318; housing renovation, 158–61, 166–7; and urban culture, 161–3, 318; personal values, 166–8; hostility from ethnic minorities, 167; backlash against, 170; isolation, 323
gender relationships, 306, 308–9, 311, 335; *see also* women
Genoa, 13
GERB, *see* Groupe d'Etude et de Recherche Buxacien
Germany, 299, 314, 316, 327
ghettos *see* blacks
Gil, Portes, 44
Ginsberg, Allen, 141
Giscard d'Estaing, Valéry, 95

Glasgow: 1915 rent strike, 3, 27–37, 67–71, 304, 333–4
Glasgow Labour Party Housing Committee, 29
Glasgow Women's Housing Association, 29–30, 32, 34
Godard, Francis, cit., 297
Godillot company (Paris), 22
Golden Gate Business Association (GGBA), San Francisco, 161–2
Golden Gate Performing Arts Inc., San Francisco, 161
Gonzales, Bob, 120
Gonzales Navarro, Moises, cit., 38, 44
Gramsci, Antonio, 298
Grands Ensembles, 75–96, 320, 323, 325
'Grassot, M.', 85
green revolution, 315
Gretna (Scotland), 30
Grimes, Orville T., cit., 178
Groupe d'Etude et de Recherche Buxacien (GERB), 91–3, 323
Guichard, Oliver, 76, 93, 95

Habana, La (Cuba), 304
Habitation Loyer Modère (HLM), 79, 87, 91
Hansa cities, 13
Hardoy, Jorge, cit., 12
Haussmann, Baron Georges Eugène, 17, 19, 24, 69, 333
Hayden, Dolores, cit., 305
Henry, Etienne, cit., 193
Hibernia Bank, San Francisco, 113
Hillsborough, Bob, 144
hippy culture, 142
historical action: defined, 305
Holland, 318, 327
Home Owners Association, San Francisco, 112
House Letting and Rating Act, 1911 (UK), 28
Housekeepers Associations (*Asociaciones de Amas de Casa*), Madrid, 269–70
Housing and Town Planning Act, 1919 (UK), 27, 30
Housing and Urban Development (HUD), USA, 114–5, 132
'Hudson Guild' (New York), 63
Hunter's Point, San Francisco, 103, 109, 111, 115

immigrant workers, 316
Independent Labour Party (ILP), 29, 34
Indiani Metropolitani (Italy), 318
Industrial Areas Foundation (IAF), USA, 61–2
industrialism, 307, 310, 313, 324

Infante, Ricardo and Sanchez, Magaly, cit., 181, 183, 185
inflation, 176
informationalism (as mode of development), 307, 310, 312–3, 315–6, 324
inquilianarios see Veracruz, Mexico
International, First, 299; Third, 297–8
Iran, 176
Italy, 299, 330
Ixtacalpo, Mexico, 196, 199

Jibou, Robert M., cit., 52
Juntas de Abastecinientos y Precios (Chile), 207
Juntas de Vecinos (Chile), 200

Kansas City, 63
Katznelson, Ira, cit., 300, 310, 324
Kennedy, Michael, cit., 148
Kerouac, Jack: *On the Road*, 141
Khomeini, Ayatollah, 176
King, Martin Luther, 50, 64
Korea, 176
Kronenberg, Anne, 164

Labour Party (UK), 29, 33–4
Ladder Magazine, 142
Laird, Mary, 29, 34
Lancourt, Joan, cit., 60, 63
Latin America: squatter movements, 175, 178–9, 181, 190, 209–11, 323, 325, 334; and political radicalism, 176; employment in, 182–5; housing crisis, 188; urban populism, 325; *see also* individual countries
Latino Unity Council (LUC), San Francisco, 118, 134
Latinos for Affirmative Action, San Francisco, 117, 135
Lavapies, Madrid, 242, 251–5
Law of Urban Hypothec, 32
leadership: in US city revolts, 57–60; among squatters, 195; in Orcasitas, 243–4; in Madrid Citizen Movement, 264, 270
League of United Latin American Citizens (LULAC), 110, 116–7, 127
Lee, Don, 158; cit., 160
Leeds, Anthony, cit., 181
Leeds, Anthony and Elizabeth, cit., 193
Lefebvre, Henri, 15–6, 296, 300
Lenin, V.I., 15, 62, 298
Leninism, 298–9
lesbians: in Mission District, 133, 136; non-territorial, 140; organizations, 142; in politics, 144; and gay men, 170, 172

Levine, Martin, cit., 139
Lewis, John L., 61
Liga de Comunidades Agrarias, Mexico, 42
Lim, Johannes F., cit., 178
Lima, 190–4, 210
Lipset, Seymour Martin, cit., 294–5
Lipsky, Michael, 293
Lira, Jack, 170
Lissagaray, Prosper-Olivier, 16, 18–22
Lojkine, Jean, 297
London, 31, 317
Long, Larry H., 315
Longuet, Charles, 19
Lopez Portillo, José, 197
Los Angeles, 143, 155, 317
Louis XIV, King of France, 20
'low riders' (San Francisco), 108, 120–1
Lukacs, Georg, 298
lumpenproletariat, 184
Luxembourg, Rosa, 298
Lynch, Kevin, cit., 290, 300, 303–4, 335–6
Lyon, Phyllis, 144
Lyons: *Canuts de Lyon*, 18

MacAdams, Robert, cit., 12
McBride, Andrew, 34
McGovern, George, 163
McLean, Iain, 29
McLean, John, 28, 30, 34
McLuhan, Marshall, 272, 329
Madero, Mexico, 196
Madrid: urban issues, 215, 217–9, 224–5, 245; Citizen Movement, 216–9, 224–41, 242–56, 258–63, 264–75, 276–88, 322, 324, 327; population increases, 218, 220; shanty towns, 218–9, 221–2, 228, 235, 242–7, 258, 274; building developments and demolitions, 224, 228, 245, 252, 256, 259; historical preservation, 225, 229, 254–5, 258–9; neighbourhood associations and territories, 226–57, 258, 268; 1979 municipal elections, 236, 251, 263, 273; streets re-named, 246; popular celebrations and fairs, 254, 260–63, 271; Special Master Plan (1978), 254–5, 257–9; garden cities, 256–7; improvements, 258–63; transport and traffic, 259; politics in, 262–3, 272–5, 276–8, 278, 280–81; class in, 264–9; culture in, 269–72; role of women in, 269–71, 280; youth culture in, 271; urban movement analysed, 277–88, 322–4; in Civil War, 287; role of media in, 277, 279–80, 282, 285, 287; role of professionals in, 277, 279–80, 282, 285, 287; role of political militants in, 277, 279–80,

282–5, 287; achievements, 322; *see also* Alcala de Henares; Colonias de Hotelitos; El Pilar; Lavapies; Orcasitas
Maldonado, Alonso de, 5
Manchester, 296
Mao Zhedong, 298
Maranon, Gregorio, 7
Maravall, Jose Antonio, cit., 4, 7–8, 11–12
Marcel, Etienne, 13
marginality: theory of, 175, 179–80; characteristics, 180–5; and occupation, 181–4, 187; defined, 185, 187; and types of settlement, 188–9; and official policy, 189–90
Martin, Del, 144
Martinez, Ben, 112, 114, 116
Martires de San Cosme, Mexico, 197
Marx, Karl, 19; cit., 296, 298–9
Marxism: and Paris Commune, 15–6, 25; and Glasgow, 31; and urban social movements, 296–8; as theory, 298–9, 301; and modes of production, 309; and human diversity, 330
Mattachine Society, 141
media, mass, 330–1
Melling, Joseph, cit., 28–30, 34–5
Melucci, Alberto, cit., 295
Mesa-Lago, Carmelo, 184
Mesta (Castilian organization), 5
Meunier, Christine, cit., 201, 203–4
Mexican American Political Association (MAPA), 110, 117, 127
Mexico (state): squatters in, 178, 179, 183, 188–90; occupations, 184–5; land laws, 189; labour in, 314; urban movement, 328; capitalist expansion, 334; *see also* Veracruz
Mexico City: marginal occupations, 184–5; housing crisis, 187–8; squatters, 188–9, 194–9, 210; conditions, 189
Miami, 316
Michel, Louise, 19
Milk, Harvey, 104, 143–5, 150–1, 162, 164–5, 170
Miller, Mike, 112, 114
Mission Action Team, 121
Mission Coalition Organization (MCO): development and organization, 106, 109, 111–5, 118, 121, 128–30, 132; factionalism and caucuses, 116–7, 120–2, 126–9, 135; in community context, 122–30, 132–3; goals, 126–7; and urban theory, 323; collapse, 325
Mission Council on Redevelopment (MCOR), 110, 112, 126
Mission District, San Francisco, 103, 105; neighbourhood mobilization in, 106–37,

170–2; character, 107–9, 120–1, 133–4, 171; and urban development, 109–14, 136–7; poverty, 133–4; organizations, 134–6; conflict with gays, 156

Mission Housing Development Corporation (MHDC), 132

Mission Planning Council (MPC), 117, 134

Mission Rebels, 110

Mission Tenant Union, 112

Model Cities Program (USA), 112, 114–7, 122–3, 128, 133

Model Mission Neighbourhood Corporation (MMNC), 115–6, 127, 131

Mollenkopf, John, cit., 55–9, 293

Monterrey, Mexico, 194, 196–9, 324

Morales Bermudez, Francisco, 194

Moreau, Edouard, 19

Moscone, George, 104, 109, 120, 143–4, 162, 164–5, 172

Movimiento de Izquierda Revolucionaria (MIR), Chile, 201–2, 204–8

Movimiento de Pobladores Revolucionarios (MPR), Chile, 201–2

movimiento inquilinario see Veracruz

Movimiento Nacional (Spain), 226

multinational corporations, 175, 178, 210, 213, 215

Mumford, Lewis, cit., 12

Nanterre, 322

National Advisory Commission on Civil Disorders (USA), 50, 52

neighbourhood associations *see under* Madrid

New York City: black ghetto riots, 50; gays in, 138, 142–3, 155; Puerto Ricans in, 317

Nicaragua, 118–9, 135, 176

Nixon, Richard M., 104, 116, 122, 142

Nova, Antonio, 43

Nueva La Habana (Chilean *campamento*), 201–7

Obeca-Arriba Juntos, 110, 117, 133–4

Oberschall, Anthony, cit., 295

Obregon, Alvaro, 40, 43–4

O'Brien, David, 293

occupation: among squatters, 181–5, 205

Odria, Manuel A., 191–3

Oficina Nacional de Pueblos Jovenes (Peru), 193

Okamoto Plan (San Francisco), 131

Olmos, 39, 42, 45

Olson, Mancur, cit., 293

Operacion Sitio (Chile), 199

Operation Upgrade, 134

Opus Dei (Spain), 219

Orcasitas (shanty town), Madrid, 242–7, 274

Organizacion Revolucionario de Trabajadores (ORT), Spain, 229, 235, 247–8, 273

Ortega, Rafael, cit., 38, 45

Pacheco, Dona Maria, 68

Padilla, 5

Pamplona, Peru, 192

Paris: Commune (1871), 3, 15–26, 68, 70–1, 332–3; urban revolts, 13; Haussman's restructuring, 17, 19, 24, 69, 333; property speculation in, 24–6, 75–6; municipal power, 26, 325; population distribution, 26, 75; *Grands Ensembles*, 75–96; rent control laws, 75

Parti Communiste Français *see* Communist Parties: France

Parti Socialiste Unifié (PSU), 80, 83, 325

Partido Communiste Español *see* Communist Parties: Spain

Partido Revolucionario Institucional (PRI), Mexico, 195–7

Partido Socialista Obrero Español (PSOE), Spain, 247, 249, 250, 261, 272–5

Pastrana, Ernesto and Threlfall, Monica, cit., 200

Perez, Joseph, cit., 4, 6

Perlman, Janice, cit., 179

Perlo, Manuel, cit., 38, 43

Peru: squatters in, 178–9, 183, 190–1, 324; *see also* Lima

Phalange Party, Spain, 219, 222

Pickvance, Chris G., cit., 27, 35, 300

Pinilla, Rojas, Bogota, 210

Pink Panthers, 142

Pinochet, Augusto, 328

Piven, Frances and Cloward, Richard, cit., 54, 295–6

Pizzorno, Alessandro, 13

Plan Courant (France), 75

Plan-de-Accion Immediata (PAI), Madrid, 259

pluralism, 292–5, 330–1

poblaciones, 180–1

pobladores (Santiago de Chile), 199–209, 327–8

police: as enemy of Paris *Communards*, 23, 26; in US inner city riots, 52–4; in Mission District, 121; and San Francisco moral values, 140; attitude to homosexuals, 142; and squatters in Mexico, 196–7; and Santiago squatters, 204; in Madrid, 248

populism, 310, 316–8

Portes, Alejandro and Walton, John, cit., 211

power: defined, 305–6; state and, 310–11

Prado y Ugarteche, Manuel, 191–3
Proal, Heron, 38–42, 44–8
production: defined, 305–6; modes of, 306–11, 316; channelled consumption, 312–3; and urban goals, 326
productivity, 307
protest movements, 295–6, 299
Provincial Federation of Neighbourhood Associations *see* Federation of Neighbourhood Associations
Puerto Montt, Chile, 200
Puerto Ricans, 317

Raza en Accion Local, La (San Francisco), 112, 117, 119–20, 133, 135
Reagan, Ronald, 104, 114
Real Alternative Programme (San Francisco), 118
Rebel Workers, The (San Francisco), 118
Reid, William, 30
Rents and Mortgage Interest Restrictions Act, 1915 (UK), 27, 30
Remy, Jean and Voye, Liliane, cit., 300
revolution: and class domination, 307–8
Rex, John, cit., 324
Rex, John and Moore, Robert, cit., 300
riots: in US inner cities, 49–53, 299; San Francisco, 103; gay, 142, 144; spread of, 299; *see also* violence
Robinson, Frank, 164
Rochester, New York, 63
Rogeard, A., 19
Ross, Bob, 164
Rossi, Peter H. *et al.*, cit., 50
Rougerie, Jacques, 16–7, 19, 22
Roussel, 25
Royal Commission on Housing of the Working Class, 1885 (UK), 28
Ruben-Jaramillo, 196
Ruef, Abe, 102

Sacramento, California, 142
Saint Etienne, 21
Salamanca, 12
Salinas, 39
Salvatierra, Count of, 7
San Angel Bajo, Mexico, 197
San Francisco: and Alinsky model, 60; development and renewal, 99–105, 110, 112, 114; transport system, 100–1; racial composition, 100–1, 105, 106–8, 110–11, 325; gay community, 100–1, 104–5, 129, 138–70, 323, 325; housing, 100–1, 131; local politics, 102–5;

riots (1966), 103; neighbourhood territories, 105; open space, 131; history, 140; Chinatown, 316
San Francisco Department of City Planning, 99, 131
San Francisco Redevelopment Agency (SFRA), 110, 122, 158
Santiago de Chile, 180–2, 199–209
Sarcelles (*grand ensemble*), 77, 78–86, 323
Sarria, Jose, 141–3
Saunders, Peter, cit., 297
Scottish Federation of Tenants' Associations, 29
Scottish Housing Council, 28
Seattle, 143
Segovia, 12
Sennett, Richard, cit., 300
Sérieyx Report, 1965 (France), 82
Sevilla, 13
Shelley, John, 103
Siete de la Raza, Los, 109, 119
Silver, Carol Ruth, 120, 164
Sindicato Revolucionario de Inquilinos (SRI), Mexico, 38, 40, 45, 47
Sistema Nacional de Movilizacion Social (SINAMOS), Peru, 193–4
Sjoberg, Gideon, cit., 12
slums, 180–1; *see also* squatters
Smelser, Neil, cit., 300
social security, 184
Socialist Party, France *see* Parti Socialiste Unifié
Socialist Party, Spain *see* Partido Socialista Obrero Español
Société Centrale Immobilière de la Caisse des Dépôts (SCIC), 75, 77–85, 86–95
Society for Individual Rights, San Francisco, 142, 163
Sosa, 39
Spain: and neighbourhood movements, 215, 224–88, 324–5, 327; political regime and change, 215–8, 223–4, 225, 234, 299; economic boom, 220, 223; 1977 elections, 247; 1975 economic crisis, 252; state and church domination, 287, 324; electoral choice, 330; historical expansion and wealth, 332; *see also* Barcelona; Castilla; Madrid
Spilerman, Seymour, cit., 50–1
squatters, squatting: communities, 175; incidence by country, 177–8; and political importance, 179, 187, 190–209, 209–12; types, 180–1, 188–9; social composition and occupations, 181–4, 205; Madrid, 221; as alternative social organization, 318; *see also* Caracas; Lima; Mexico; Monterrey; Santiago de Chile

Stalin, Joseph, 298

Star (US magazine), 44

state, the: formation of, 309–10; and power, 310–11, 329–30; and alternative social organization, 317–8; and city, 332

statism, 306–8, 310

Stonewall Revolt, 1969 (New York), 142, 155, 162

Switzerland, 270, 316, 318

Syracuse, New York, 63

Tavern Guild, San Francisco, 142, 161, 165

Tejeda, Adalberto, 40–1, 44, 47

Tenochtitlan, 12

Tilly, Charles, cit., 11, 290, 300, 314, 334

Toledo, 5, 8, 12, 68, 70

Tomic, Romero Radomiro, 200

Tordesillas, 5, 11

Toronto, 143

Torreon, Mexico, 196

Touraine, Alan, cit., 179, 290, 301

Toynbee, Sir Arnold, cit., 13

trade·unions: support Glasgow rent strike, 31–2; and *grands ensembles*, 84, 91–2, 325; in Madrid, 220; and collective consumption, 316, 319, 323; and outside conditions, 326; and women, 329

Trotsky, Leon, 298

TWO *see* Woodlawn Organization, The

unemployed, 268

Unidad Popular (Chile), 201, 208, 299

Union de Centro Democratico (UDO), Madrid, 257, 261, 263, 273–4

Union of Soviet Socialist Republics (USSR), 176

United Kingdom, 27–8, 30, 35

United States of America: inner city revolts, 49–67, 68–9, 71, 299, 328, 334; electoral apathy, 330

Ur (Chaldea), 13

urban meaning: defined, 302–4, 308–9, 320; and spatial form, 311–2, 314–6

Vaguada es Nuestra, La *see* El Pilar

Val d'Yerres (*grand ensemble*), 77, 86–94, 323, 325

Valladolid, 7, 10, 12

Vanderschueren, Franz, cit., 182

vecindades (slums), 189

Velasco Alvarado, Juan, 192

Venezuela, 183, 328

Venice, 13

Veracruz, Mexico: *inquilinarios* strike (1922), 3, 37–48, 69–71, 333–4; population growth, 42–4

Versailles, 20

Vietnam, 176, 299

Villa, Pancho, 42

Villa El Salvador, Lima, 192, 194

Villalar, 5

Villalobos, Alejandro (El Mike), 202

violence, 294, 306

Wallerstein, Immanuel, cit., 310

'War on Poverty' program (USA), 49, 52

Weber, Max, 12–4

West Indians, 317

Wheatley, John, 28

White, Dan, 104, 144, 165

Williams, Hannibal, 104

Wolden, Russell, 142

women: in Paris Commune, 18–9; in Glasgow rent strike, 29–30, 32–5; in Veracruz strike, 39, 46; leadership in US inner city revolts, 57; in urban movements, 68, 268, 309, 335; and life in *grands ensembles*, 80, 90; in Chilean *campamentos*, 204, 206; in Madrid neighbourhood associations, 246, 269–71, 280; social domination of, 306, 308–9, 312; working, 329

Women's Labour League (UK), 29

Wood, McKinnon, 30

Woodlawn Organization, The (TWO), Chicago, 63–4

Workmen's National Council (UK), 28

youth, 270, 317

Zapata, Emiliano, 42

Zone d'Aménagement Concerté (ZAC), 93

Zurich, 271, 318